REJOICE! REJOICE!
BRITAIN IN
THE 1980S

Alwyn W. Turner

First published in Great Britain
2010 by Aurum Press Ltd
74–77 White Lion Street
London N1 9PF
www.aurumpress.co.uk

This paperback edition first published 2013

A catalogue record for this book is available from the British Library.

ISBN 978 1 78131 072 4

10 9 8 7 6 5 4 3 2 1
2017 2016 2015 2014 2013

Typeset in Spectrum by SX Composing DTP, Rayleigh, Essex
Printed and bound by CPI Group (UK) Ltd, Croydon, CR0 4YY

So as you raise a glass to the Eighties tomorrow night, drink
with me to the awakening of Britain. If it is to be
a dynamic decade for us all, these will be difficult and
dangerous years. But we are drinking to a country
with a future.
Margaret Thatcher, New Year's message (1979)

I pointed to the thriving stock-market our wealth-creating
government had encouraged, the lads scarcely out of their
teens making six-figure salaries in futures and commodities; she
pointed to the inner-city slums, the unemployment figures, the
bolshy pinched faces of underpaid nurses and teachers.
Terence Blacker, *Fixx* (1989)

MRS MIGGINS: So who are they electing when they have these
elections?
BLACKADDER: Oh, the same old shower. Fat Tory landowners
who get made MPs when they reach a certain weight. Raving
revolutionaries who think that just because they do a day's
work that somehow gives them the right to get paid. So
basically it's a nice old mess.
Richard Curtis & Ben Elton, *Blackadder the Third* (1987)

REJOICE! REJOICE!

ALWYN W. TURNER is an acclaimed writer on post-war Britain. He is the author of *Crisis? What Crisis? Britain in the 1970s* and *A Classless Society: Britain in the 1990s*, both of which are published by Aurum. His other books include *The Biba Experience*, *Glam Rock: Dandies in the Underworld*, *Halfway to Paradise: The Birth of British Rock* and *Terry Nation: The Man Who Invented the Daleks*. www.alwynturner.com

PRAISE FOR ALWYN W. TURNER

Rejoice! Rejoice! Britain in the 1980s

'Put[s] into cold perspective what at the time we were too befuddled with emotion to understand. . . Turner has produced a masterly mix of shrewd analysis, historical detail and telling quotes. . . Indispensable'
James Delingpole, *Mail on Sunday*

'One of the pleasures of Alwyn Turner's breathless romp through the 1980s is that it overflows with unusual juxtapositions and surprising insights. . . The tone is that of a wildly enthusiastic guide leading us on a breakneck tour through politics, sport and culture'
Dominic Sandbrook, *The Sunday Times*

'This kaleidoscopic history . . . provides a vivid and enjoyable guide to these turbulent years. Ranging broadly across popular culture as well as high politics . . .Turner brings the period alive and offers insights into both sides of a polarised nation'
BBC History Magazine, Pick of the Month

'Turner's account of the 1980s is as wide-ranging as that fractured, multi-faceted decade demands . . . deft at picking out devilish details and damning quotes from history that is less recent than you think'
Victoria Segal, *MOJO*

'Turner does an excellent job in synthesising the culture and art of the day into the wider political discourse. The result is resolutely entertaining'
Metro

Crisis? What Crisis? Britain in the 1970s

'Alwyn Turner has certainly hit upon a rich and fascinating subject, and his intertwining of political and cultural history is brilliantly done. . . This is a masterful work of social history and cultural commentary, told with much wit. It almost makes you feel as if you were there'
Roger Lewis, *Mail on Sunday*

'Turner appears to have spent much of the decade watching television, and his knowledge of old soap operas, sitcoms and TV dramas is deployed to great effect throughout this vivid, brilliantly researched chronicle. . . Turner may be an anorak, but he is an acutely intelligent anorak'
Francis Wheen, *New Statesman*

'An ambitious, entertaining alternative history of the 1970s which judges the decade not just by its political turbulence but by the leg-up it gave popular culture'
Time Out

'Entertaining and splendidly researched. . . He has delved into episodes of soap operas and half-forgotten novels to produce an account that displays wit, colour and detail'
Brian Groom, *Financial Times*

'Turner combines a fan's sense of populism (weaving in references to a rapidly expanding popular culture) with a keen grasp of the political landscape, which gives his survey of an often overlooked decade its cutting edge'
Metro

'Fascinating . . . an affectionate but unflinching portrait of the era'
Nicholas Foulkes, *Independent on Sunday*

Contents

Intro
Eighties

'This is the dawning of a new era'

It was, above all, a big decade, an era in which size became ever more important, when the people, events and debates of public life seemed to be written on a grand – if not always a glorious – scale.

It was a decade shaped by Murdoch and Maxwell, Schwarzenegger and Stallone, Heysel and Hillsborough, Live Aid and Lockerbie. Industrial conflict might have become less disruptive to the economy and to everyday life, but the strikes that did happen were epic in nature, with both the miners' strike and the Wapping dispute lasting for a year apiece. Riots grew in both frequency and scale, as did demonstrations, some of which – on Greenham Common, at RAF Molesworth and outside the South African Embassy in London's Trafalgar Square – became semi-permanent institutions. Union membership declined, but unions themselves began to amalgamate into larger entities, mimicking the mergers and takeovers that proliferated in the City of London. Even the Falklands War, minor in comparison with 1940, was considerably more serious than the Cod War against Iceland had been in the 1970s, and the period ended with Saddam Hussein threatening 'the mother of all battles' if America, Britain and their allies continued in their attempt to remove Iraqi troops from Kuwait. For internationally too, it was a time of big, bold politics, a time for Ronald Reagan and Mikhail Gorbachev to seek a resolution of the Cold War; it saw the rise of political Islam, the fall of the Soviet empire and, what was for some, the biggest story of all: the realization that human activity and industry might change the very climate of the planet, with uncertain but perhaps catastrophic consequences for the species.

Meanwhile, *Dallas* and *Dynasty* inspired the inflation of women's fashions and hairstyles, tours by pop superstars became bigger and more lucrative and were individually branded to enhance their commercial potential, while London – having resisted for so long the vainglorious machismo of tall buildings – finally sacrificed its skyline to a series of massive office blocks, from the NatWest Tower to Canary Wharf. Models mutated into supermodels, supermarkets into superstores, cinemas into multiplexes. Building societies became banks and humble record shops developed delusions of grandeur, turning themselves into megastores. High streets were eclipsed by out-of-town shopping centres, and the number of television channels, newspapers and magazines simply grew and grew. If something wasn't already big, then advertising – one of the great growth industries of the time – could make it seem so, or else the overblown price tag would suffice, as with the rise of nouvelle cuisine or the trend away from drinking pints in pubs towards bottled beers in bars.

And in Britain this swollen, steroid-pumped decade was dominated by the figure of Margaret Thatcher, the unlikeliest of Conservative Party leaders, who set a twentieth-century record as the longest-serving prime minister. 'I was eighteen when she got in,' wrote comedian Mark Steel, recalling Thatcher's political demise in 1990, 'and now I was thirty. All that time. All that time she'd strutted across my and millions of other lives, the symbol of every rotten selfish vindictive side of the human condition she could rake up and cultivate, like an evil scientist nurturing a test tube of greed and releasing it across the whole planet.'

Clearly Steel's views were not universally shared, for Thatcher won three successive general elections, but the sense of his whole youth passing him by under her rule was very common indeed. Because her long period in office coincided with the coming to political maturity of the most numerous generation in British history, a demographic bulge which had peaked in 1964, the only year that the birth-rate exceeded a million. So while nine million people were born in Britain during her term, some-where around twelve-and-a-half million others found that, on the first occasion that they were entitled to vote in a general election, she emerged as the victor. For that generation, even more than for the rest of the country, she was the one figure who shaped political perceptions, whether for good or ill, in support or in opposition, well into the next century.

When *i-D* magazine came to produce a summary of the decade in 1989, at a time when Thatcher was still in power, it concluded that she was 'almost a fact of nature', and so she sometimes appeared as, like a roaring lion, she walked about seeking whom she might devour. She was more than a prime minister, for her appeal – and the antipathy she aroused – were not merely concerned with politics; she came armed also with a philosophy and a morality about the individual and the nation that resonated in a way denied to her immediate predecessors. So powerful a brand was Thatcherism that her slogan 'There is no alternative', which had come across as hubris in the early 1980s, began to look like no more than the truth by the end of the decade, and for a while was understood to suggest that there was no alternative to Thatcher herself. The resultant sense of hopelessness and helplessness engendered in some was perhaps reflected in a report published in the *British Medical Journal* that the suicide rate doubled in the month that followed each of her general election victories.

Certainly no twentieth century leader, outside wartime, exercised anything like the dominance over the country's psyche that Thatcher achieved during those eleven and a half years. And certainly the country was a very different place by the end of her premiership. But it would be a mistake to conflate those two facts, for it was by no means certain that the changes that Britain went through were in the direction she wished. Rather it was as though she had unlocked a Pandora's box and released forces into society over which she had little or no control. She called for a return to thrift and good housekeeping, and presided over a massive increase in credit card and mortgage indebtedness; she sought to encourage the entrepreneurial spirit, and saw the City of London overrun by what detractors viewed as a generation of spivs and speculators; she wished to reverse the effects of 1960s permissiveness and found herself in a country where drug-taking had become almost the norm amongst young people, where condoms were promoted by government ministers and where home video recorders and satellite television made pornography ever more available.

Britain, the first industrial nation in the world, was now being told that it could enter a new age of prosperity if it would only abandon the tired old tradition of manufacturing and instead, cast against type, take up a role as a service-based economy. And in the wake of such thinking came a whole host of new professions, addressing needs that had never previously been identified: aromatherapists, kissograms and telecom salesmen (these last weighed down with answerphones, fax machines and brick-sized mobile phones). It was a decade that promised a new wave of wealth-producing, job-creating industrialists, but which also provided opportunities for lager louts, wheelclampers and computer hackers.

Even where commerce did triumph, it often unlocked elements in society that were antithetical to other strands of Thatcherism. Richard Branson, the founder of the Virgin group, was eulogized in the media as the exemplar of the new entrepreneurs, yet his ownership of London's leading gay nightclub Heaven (it had opened in 1979 and been purchased by Virgin in 1982) was, he observed, 'always good for a "sleaze attack" from the tabloids.' The expression 'the pink pound' was yet to be coined, but it was in the 1980s that Branson and other businessmen first saw investment opportunities in meeting the requirements of the gay market, and the result, according to the pioneering gay journalist, Peter Burton, was an impact that was as important as more overtly political campaigning: 'it has been the commercial wing which has brought homosexuality a long way out of the closet,' he wrote in 1985. The conflicting interests of economic and moral liberalism within the Thatcherite coalition would remain throughout the decade.

It is doubtful too whether Thatcher truly won over the nation to her vision of the sunlit uplands of unfettered capitalism, where market forces would set the price of everything, without necessarily worrying about its value. For as she sought to free the country from its recent history of industrial strife and underperformance, it became apparent that, for the British people, ideals of enterprise were all very well, but winning at all costs, with no thought for the loser and no care for the way one played the game, still seemed somehow wrong.

Culturally the country was unconvinced. There was a television boom in the lovable, semi-villainous rogues so beloved of British culture, and although there was a brief attempt to give them a Thatcherite edge (Arthur Daley in *Minder*, we were given to understand, 'admires Sir Keith Joseph'), characters such as Del Boy in *Only Fools and Horses*, Oz in *Auf Wiedersehen, Pet* and Robbie Box in *Big Deal* – even Vincent Pinner of *Just Good Friends* – still remained defiantly beyond the pale of respectable society: they could all be found on the spectrum that contained, at one end, the undeserving poor championed by Alfred Doolittle in *Pygmalion* and, at the other, the myth of Robin Hood. Similarly, although in the mid-1980s, British pop was dominated by the shiny, unthreatening likes of Duran Duran and Wham!, it had by the end of the decade reverted to type and produced the Happy Mondays, a Manchester group who gave every appearance of being a Dickensian gang of rogues and reprobates.

And so the British continued to cheer the plucky underdog, even if he were destined never to make it to the top, and even if he were as implausible a hero as Eddie 'the Eagle' Edwards, the short-sighted plasterer who became a star after finishing so far behind everyone else in the 1988 Winter Olympics ski-jumping competition that the rules were immediately changed to prevent the likes of him from ever competing again. Likewise the family-friendly Frank Bruno became Britain's most popular boxer since Henry Cooper. Having seen his career derailed when he lost two fights with

American journeymen, Bruno re-established his credentials when he avenged Our 'Enery's final defeat by beating Joe Bugner, the man who had taken Cooper's titles back in 1971. The fact that Bugner was now thirty-seven years old and yet the bout could attract a live crowd of 30,000, with sixteen million watching on television, said a great deal about the low level of sporting prowess for which the public was prepared to settle.

Or perhaps that Bruno-Bugner fight, staged by Essex-born businessman Barry Hearn, the man who steered snooker champion Steve Davis to commercial success, was an encapsulation of the values of the era: two also-rans of heavyweight boxing generated absurd amounts of money in a bout that did little for the reputation of either, or of the sport itself. (Both men, incidentally, went on to win world championships, Bugner doing so at the age of forty-eight, so inflated had the number of available titles become.)

But while the triumph of money was hard to avoid, that was ultimately not Thatcher's stated goal. 'Economics are the method,' she insisted. 'The object is to change the soul.' It was a theme that she had outlined to her speech-writers back in 1975, as she prepared to make her first appearance as party leader at the Conservative conference. 'The economy had gone wrong because something else had gone wrong spiritually and philo-sophically,' she remembered telling them. 'The economic crisis was a crisis of the spirit of the nation.'

There were many strands that had supposedly contributed to this situation, but perhaps two were pre-eminent. First, there was said to be a tendency on the part of many to run the country down, sliding from traditional self-deprecation into outright disparagement. The loss of faith was summed up by humorist Paul Jennings in 1982 as he proposed the introduction of a new word into the language, 'Britic', the definition of which would be: 'A person of British birth who thinks that everything Britain does is wrong and talks about "the British" as though he were of some other nationality.' To counter this, a new sense of patriotism was to be encouraged, a reborn pride in the nation's history and a hope for its future. This was largely an ideological war, to be waged in the classrooms and in the columns of the tabloid press, but in the event it was a more literal battle that came closest to achieving the objective; as Thatcher put it in 1982 when announcing to the House of Commons that, with the surrender of Argentine forces, the Falklands War was now over: 'Today has put the Great back into Britain.' The somewhat trite phrasing may have been more appropriate for a late-night radio phone-in show than for a prime minister, but it undoubtedly captured the mood of much of the nation.

Second, and more immediately pressing, there was the issue of the trade unions that had been at the core of British politics for a decade and more. Twice in recent years the governments of first Harold Wilson and then Edward Heath had tried to find a way of constraining the industrial power of the union movement through legislation, and twice those governments had been defeated at a subsequent general election. The fall of the Heath administration, in particular, had left scars on the soul of the Conservative Party that would take a long time to heal. Confronted by the threat of a miners' strike at a time when the economy was already suffering the effects of huge increases in the price of oil, Heath had announced the introduction of a three-day working week at the start of 1974, and had then called an early election, seeking a mandate that would strengthen his hand in dealing with the unions. And the people responded by removing him from office, punishing him for his evident inability to provide stable government.

The question of the relationship between parliament and the unions, however, was not so easily resolved, and while some measure of industrial peace was achieved in the next few years, the underlying tensions erupted in the first months of 1979. An attempt by James Callaghan's government to impose a maximum pay rise of 5 per cent across the whole nation was contemptuously rejected by the unions, and a series of strikes in private industry was followed by similar disputes in the public sector. The result was swiftly dubbed the winter of discontent, with the effects reaching into every area of public services: schools were closed, public places (including, most famously, Leicester Square in London) were converted into makeshift refuse-dumps, and hospitals found themselves unable to provide anything but the most urgent treatment. The disruption was relatively short-lived, certainly compared to the disputes of the coming decade, but the imagery was to live on in the collective memory. And when, in May 1979, a third successive government was defeated in a general election as a consequence of clashes with the unions, there were many who felt that the time had come for firm, decisive action, that Margaret Thatcher's anti-union rhetoric should be given a chance to find concrete expression.

The society she inherited was so torn by division and conflict, so racked by crises, that when she stood at the threshold of 10 Downing Street in May 1979 and quoted what purported to be a prayer by St Francis – 'Where there is discord, may we bring harmony' – there were plenty prepared to mock, but few who would deny the desirability of such an aspiration. The problem was that it was hard to see how the policies of her government were going to live up to such a lofty, perhaps unattainable, ideal. The encouragement over the ensuing decade of what cabinet minister Kenneth

Baker was to call 'acquisitive individualism' did not, in the minds of many, bring harmony to the nation.

Instead the 1980s were characterized by increasing divisions, between rich and poor, between north and south, between those in work and those without, divisions that were manifest in civil disorder, rising crime and rioting. There was a note of snarled hostility, of suppressed violence, that insisted on making itself heard; sometimes drowned out by the loud celebration of wealth, it was never quite silenced, and echoes could be heard in the unlikeliest of places. The conduct of disputes coarsened during the decade, so that when Robert Runcie, the Archbishop of Canterbury, was preaching in a Liverpool church in 1982, he was interrupted by hard-line Protestants demonstrating against the forthcoming visit of Pope John Paul II to Britain. He was jeered and hissed, and there were cries of 'Judas' and 'traitor', to such an extent that he was unable to continue his sermon, with newspapers reporting that 'the crowd of banner-waving men and women hurled four-letter words and vile abuse at the Archbishop'. After a failed attempt to read from the Bible, he was forced to walk out of the service, amidst a storm of catcalls, and while there was also supportive applause from other members of the congregation, it was an extraordinary display both of Christian disunity and of sheer bad manners. Nor was such behaviour confined to a single group: the Liberal MP David Alton spoke at a Bristol church later in the decade, in the midst of his campaign to amend the abortion laws, and found the church surrounded by stone-throwing protesters.

The popular leftwing slogan 'Ditch the Bitch', aimed at Thatcher, was similarly unedifying, though it was eclipsed by the work of Saatchi & Saatchi, the only advertising firm to become a household name, thanks to its association with the Conservative Party. Their best known work for the party was little more than knocking copy, which made some sense in 1979 when the Tories were in opposition, but was less impressive as the decade progressed. The 1983 campaign featured an election broadcast showing scenes from the winter of discontent four years earlier with a voice-over saying 'Do you remember?' A press advert from the same campaign compared extracts from the manifestos of the Labour Party and the Communist Party of Great Britain, under the slogan 'Like your manifesto, comrade'. The negativity continued into the 1987 election and beyond, giving the impression that the government had few achievements of its own to celebrate, or perhaps that it simply preferred attack to debate.

There was a level of aggression and verbal violence that would previously have remained in private, kept away from the public sphere. The behaviour of delegates at Labour conferences in the early years of the decade, abusing and shouting down speakers with whom they disagreed, was matched by representatives at the Conservative conference in 1981, who booed a speech opposing racism and then heckled the home secretary, William Whitelaw, when he reprimanded them for their discourteous behaviour. The lack of respect implicit in all this was, some argued, part of the decline of deference, a development that Thatcher herself encouraged and that could be seen as a sign of a healthy democracy, though its negativity was often more apparent than were its benefits. Bobby Robson, who served as the manager of the England football team between 1982 and 1990, was perhaps the best-loved man ever to have held the post, but, a casualty of the circulation wars then raging between rival tabloid newspapers, he received coverage that was abusive, insulting and personal. He took the team to the quarter-finals and then the semi-finals of successive world cups, and faced press reports calling him everything from PLONKER (a characteristically direct headline in the *Sun*) to 'a liar, a cheat and a traitor', this being *Today*'s considered verdict on the man on the very eve of his most successful tournament at Italia 90.

Amongst football fans too, longstanding rivalries became ever more vicious, with the supporters of Manchester United responding to a Liverpool banner that read 'Munich '58' (in reference to the aircrash that killed eight of the United team) by displaying their own taunting banner, 'Shankly '81', the year that the greatest Liverpool manager, Bill Shankly, died of a heart attack; accompanying chants and songs were inescapable on the terraces, as was the heightened level of hooliganism. 'In my experience there was more violence in the '70s – that is to say, there was fighting more or less every week – but in the first half of the '80s,' recalled the writer and Arsenal fan Nick Hornby, 'it was less predictable and much nastier. Police confiscated knives and machetes and other weapons I did not recognize, things with spikes coming out of them.' Journalist Robert Elms, a Queen's Park Rangers supporter, noted the same tendency: 'this is a vicious era, when the mass ends of the seventies have been distilled down to a more ruthless, more organized hardcore of tightly knit, Stanley-knife-carrying cadres.'

The coarsening of British culture could also be seen in the biggest live draws on the comedy circuit of the 1980s: Bernard Manning, Jim Davidson and Roy 'Chubby' Brown. All performed acts that were considered completely unsuitable for broadcast and, from another direction, all came under fire from the new wave of alternative comedians for the racist and sexist content of some of their material. Language itself became a battleground, here as elsewhere, so that Brown's song 'He's a Cunt' – which was broadly representative of his work – offended some by its vulgarity, others by its use of what was deemed a sexist term. The struggle for a politically acceptable language raged through the decade, reflecting a deeper ideological divide, so that, for example, a Conservative Party spokesman would be answered by a Labour Party spokesperson. Similarly the *Sunday Telegraph* reported that Labour MP Clare Short refused to refer to her first speech in the House of Commons as a 'maiden' speech, 'in the pursuit of linguistic integrity and sexual equality'. (Contemporary linguistic preferences are used in the following pages.)

It was a time of dogma and doctrine, of heated conflict, of the adoption of extreme positions. Derek Hatton, the deputy leader of Liverpool City Council, reflected that it was an era in which 'views polarized, and there was no middle ground left on which to stand.' And yet the story of the 1980s is largely one of parties and movements seeking to find that elusive common ground. Everyone was agreed that the political and social consensus that had dominated Britain since the war had come to its end, but there was no certainty what would take its place in a new settlement. Despite her series of overwhelming parliamentary majorities, Thatcher only ever attracted the support of a third of the electorate at the ballot boxes, scarcely a ringing endorsement of her vision for the future.

In 1985 a young Labour MP named Tony Blair declared that 'there is virtually a consensus against this government', which was overstating the case a little, but did at least point to the fact that Thatcherite arguments had not yet managed to score a decisive victory. Nor were they ever to do so. In 1989 the journalist Eric Jacobs and the psephologist Robert Worcester of MORI conducted an in-depth poll aimed at discovering the mood of the nation. Chief amongst their findings was that, when presented with a series of opposing views on what constituted an ideal society (along the lines of 'private interests and free enterprise' versus 'public interests and a more controlled economy'), it appeared as though Thatcherite principles had failed to transform the country. Their conclusion that more than half the population were essentially socialist in their value system was perhaps a little too simplified in its reductionism, but was an instructive counter-balance to the distortions of the British electoral system.

The consensus that did emerge from the frequently traumatic upheavals of the 1980s was partially shaped by Thatcher, but in several key respects it was in defiance rather than in support of her beliefs. Because Thatcher, of course, was not the only one seeking resolutions to the crisis of self-confidence that had descended upon the nation in the 1970s. Other major politicians had their own solutions to proffer and contributions to make, whether they were veterans such as Edward Heath, Roy Jenkins and Tony Benn, or new stars like David Owen, Michael Heseltine and Ken Livingstone. So too did a wide range of campaigners, commentators, police chiefs and even comedians. All were to help mould the new Britain, and the story of the 1980s belongs to them as much as it does to Thatcher. So dominant a figure was she, however, that she often eclipsed what else was going on in the country. And much that happened during the decade was attributed to her influence, whether it were appropriate or not, so that, for example, Kenneth Branagh could be described by *Time* magazine as 'an icon of Thatcherite initiative' simply for doing what many another actor had done, long before Thatcherism was conceived: setting up a theatre company.

There was a subtle but unmistakable change in the nature of the nation's culture, as the advent of an overtly doctrinaire prime minister, matched by an equally doctrinaire Labour opposition, produced an increasingly politicized cultural expression. One of the big television successes of the 1970s had been *The Good Life*, first broadcast in 1975, a sitcom that responded to the environmental concerns of the time by depicting Tom and Barbara Good, a suburban couple who choose to abandon the rat-race in favour of self-sufficient simplicity. There was a degree of gentle social commentary to be found here, but the series only won over a real mass-audience when it allowed the Goods' next-door neighbours, the conventional Jerry and Margo Leadbetter, to share equal billing; the show rapidly became a straightforward middle-class comedy, more stylish and of a much higher quality than the likes of, say, *Bless This House* or *Terry and June*, but not entirely unrelated. With the ending of the series, however, the actors who had played Jerry and Margo – Paul Eddington and Penelope Keith – went on to star in their own shows, and the changed times were immediately apparent.

Eddington found a new role as James Hacker in *Yes, Minister*, the definitive political comedy of the 1980s. Hacker was the newly appointed minister of administrative affairs in a government whose composition was carefully unspecified but which was clearly Conservative, and found himself engaged in a running battle with his permanent secretary, Sir Humphrey Appleby (Nigel Hawthorne), as the civil service did its utmost to frustrate every initiative that was launched, every policy that was mooted, most especially when it involved changes to the civil service itself. The series was largely based on the experience of the previous Labour government, but its central truth – that the civil service saw itself as the ultimate custodian of consensus politics, determined to draw the teeth of all would-be radicals, from whichever quarter they might come – remained relevant into the 1980s.

This was a very different world to the one portrayed in the long-running radio comedy *The Men From the Ministry* (1962–77), which had seen Richard Murdoch and Wilfrid Hyde-White (later replaced by Deryck Guyler) as hapless incompetents at the general assistance department of the civil service, whose antics included nothing more controversial than ordering 20,000 left-foot boots for the army. Rejecting the cosiness of that portrayal of Whitehall, *Yes, Minister* made few bones about its underlying message, summed up by one of the co-writers, Antony Jay, as 'undermining the concept of socialism and that the state should run everything'. At its most extreme, in the 1984 Christmas special 'Party Games', Sir Humphrey conspires with the cabinet secretary and the chief whip to stage a coup, installing Hacker as prime minister in a manner which made clear where real power lay in the establishment (as well as setting up two further series in the guise of *Yes, Prime Minister*). But the satire was not restricted to senior civil servants. Hacker spends much of his time onscreen revealing the cynicism of professional politicians: 'First rule of politics: never believe anything until it's officially denied.' Perhaps not noticing this element of the show, Thatcher cited it as one of her favourite programmes, and even appeared onstage with Eddington and Hawthorne in a sketch when the series received an award from Mary Whitehouse's Viewers and Listeners Association in 1984; playing herself, she displayed little acting ability and no comic timing.

Meanwhile Penelope Keith was also enjoying her new status as a television star in *To the Manor Born*, in which, as Audrey fforbes-Hamilton, she was even more snobbish, bossy and self-centred than she had been as Margo. Recently widowed and obliged to sell off Grantleigh Manor, an estate that has been in her late husband's family for four hundred years ('We've been here through wars, plagues, floods, famines and Labour governments!'), she finds to her horror that it has been bought by a nouveau riche millionaire Richard DeVere, played by Peter Bowles, a businessman of Czech ancestry who has made his fortune with a company named Cavendish Foods. 'He's trade,' shudders Audrey; 'at bottom he's a grocer.' Over the course of the next three years, as she lived on in the old coach-house in the grounds, constantly trying to interfere in his management of the estate, the two played out a long feud that turned inevitably to courtship.

The idea for the series had been developed by writer Peter Spence many years earlier, and had even got as far as an unbroadcast radio pilot, but didn't reach television until the autumn of 1979, some four months after Thatcher's election victory. Its timing was impeccable, seeming to capture the antagonism between the twin wings of the modern Conservative Party (the estate-owners and the estate agents, as Denis Healey once described them): Audrey represented the old feudal tradition, now in decline, while DeVere stood as the embodiment of the rise of the entrepreneur. The fact that he was regularly referred to as a grocer, echoing the occupation of Thatcher's own father, was perhaps fortuitous, but resonant nonetheless. Though many episodes were little more than mild meanderings through rural affairs, the series was, Spence said, conceived as a portrayal of a time when 'the economic and social structure of England was in the process of being turned on its head'. It proved hugely popular, with the final episode attracting a record audience of twenty-four million viewers to witness the couple getting married and Audrey returning in triumph to the manor house.

If that seemed to suggest that a truce had been sealed between the warring factions, however, it was not one that found a counterpart in real life, where Thatcher's vision of modern conservatism continued to be opposed by traditionalists. Characteristic of the battles that were fought throughout the decade was the struggle over the government's attitude towards the film industry. The first half of the decade saw a revival of British movies with the international success of films such as *Chariots of Fire* (1981), *Gandhi* (1982) and *The Killing Fields* (1984), followed by a spate of comedies about attitudes towards sex in the 1950s and '60s: *Personal Services*, *Prick Up Your Ears*, *Wish You Were Here* (all 1987). But there was little enthusiasm for such enterprise within the Thatcherite ranks. Norman Tebbit arrived at the department of trade in 1979 as a junior minister and found himself responsible for policy on the industry, a fact that baffled him entirely. 'Why do we need a films policy?' he asked the permanent secretary. 'Let's get out of films as soon as possible.' In true *Yes, Minister* style, however, he was deflected from his course and the tax-breaks for film-making remained. It was, however, only a reprieve for the industry; in the mid-1980s Tebbit returned to the department in the top position, took up where he had left off and was later able to gloat in his memoirs that he had finally achieved his goal: 'as secretary of state for trade and industry, I won that battle!' The result was that by 1990 *The Times* was reporting that 'production of movies has fallen to its lowest point since the 1920s'. The hostility was amply reciprocated; when asked what the government should do to help the film industry, Hanif Kureishi, who had written *My Beautiful Laundrette* and was one of the brightest new talents in the field, was disdainful: 'I don't think the government should do anything. They're ignorant, suburban people who wouldn't know a work of art if it bit them.'

Throughout the decade the political conflicts of the time spilled over into the cultural arena far more explicitly than they had done before, often expressed in straightforward party terms. In the 1970s popular culture had helped prepare the ground for the advent of Thatcherism by expressing discontent with where the country was heading; in the 1980s it was far more overt in its opposition, particularly in the context of that massive generation reaching adulthood. Pop music, comedy, fiction: all felt moved to remark upon political developments, normally from a hostile position. Their voices were seldom acknowledged by the Thatcher governments, but even so their impact was felt and – perhaps more than the official opposition – it was often these cultural dissidents who kept alive the idea that there was indeed an alternative to Thatcherism. Certainly they provided a running commentary on the era that was hard to ignore.

Like its predecessor, *Crisis? What Crisis? Britain in the 1970s*, this book is an attempt to depict the high politics and low culture of the time. It is structured in three sections, broadly corresponding to the three Thatcher governments. Each section starts with an overview of the period, followed by a series of chapters addressing contemporary issues. These latter are not entirely chronological but are intended to explore thematically the evolution of one of the great transitional decades in British history. If the 1970s had asked social questions about the nature of Britain, then the 1980s sought to provide political answers.

PART ONE

PUTTING OUT FIRE WITH GASOLINE
1979–83

I see no chance of your bright new tomorrow.
The Beat, 'Stand Down Margaret' (1980)

BARRY: I blame Thatcherism, you know. Yeah, it's a misguided policy. It's totally misguided and misconstrued. Mind you, the Labour Party's in such disarray, I don't think the opposition offers much alternative or consolation, does it?
Dick Clement & Ian La Frenais, *Auf Wiedersehen, Pet* (1983)

MORGUS: The stews of the cities are full of such unemployed riff-raff.
PRESIDENT: Most of them unemployed, Trau Morgus, because you have closed so many plants. It's caused great unrest.
Robert Holmes, *Doctor Who* (1984)

1

The First Thatcher Government

'Just like starting over'

> It has always seemed to me that people vote in a new
> government not because they actually agree with their
> politics but just because they want a change. Somehow
> they think that things will be better under the new lot.
> Iain Banks, *The Wasp Factory* (1984)

> Margaret Thatcher once expressed to me genuine
> admiration for Shirley [Williams] but implied that
> decisiveness was not her strength.
> Lord Longford (1981)

> ANNE JAY: It's very common, Henry, to confuse
> stubbornness with strength.
> Ron Hutchinson, *Bird of Prey* (1982)

There were precedents, of course – Sirimavo Bandaranaike in Sri Lanka,
Indira Gandhi in India, Golda Meir in Israel – but the idea that staid old
Britain, shackled by tradition and nostalgia, might choose a woman as
prime minister was a major international story, covered by news outlets all
round the world. In fact just about the only major journal not to mention
the election of Margaret Thatcher in May 1979 was *The Times*, which was
then in the midst of an epic industrial dispute. It hadn't appeared since
November the previous year, and the doubts that existed about whether
the world's most famous newspaper would ever be published again seemed
somehow symbolic of the crises and chaos of the passing decade. Similarly,
the fact that two years later it was to be bought by Rupert Murdoch, the
Australian-born owner of the *Sun* and the *News of the World*, seemed symbolic
of the 1980s' triumph of meritocracy over establishment. When the
paper did eventually re-emerge after nearly twelve months of silence,
Thatcher was amongst the first to greet it: 'The absence of *The Times* has

been tragic and overlong,' she told the Lord Mayor's banquet on the night that the presses started to roll again. 'I welcome its reappearance with enthusiasm.'

It wasn't the first occasion on which *The Times* had failed to report the big news story; back in 1955 a month-long dispute had caused it to miss the resignation of Winston Churchill as prime minister, the politician, coincidentally, with whom Thatcher was most eager to seek association. That, however, was for the future; no one in 1979 was thinking of comparisons with Churchill. Indeed no one was quite sure what a suitable comparison would be, so uncertain were the commentators of the new prime minister. To start with, Thatcher herself was not noticeably popular as an individual. In personal terms, she had trailed the incumbent, Labour's James Callaghan, right through the election campaign, but had nonetheless scored an extraordinary victory: the biggest swing against a government since the war, producing Labour's worst share of the vote since 1931, when it had been smarting from the self-inflicted wounds of Ramsay MacDonald's defection. And, despite a series of effective posters from Saatchi & Saatchi, and despite a few memorable photo-opportunities (the one that saw her holding a newborn calf was particularly striking, if devoid of any discernible meaning), the media feeling at the time was that she had failed to articulate Tory policy with any degree of conviction. Certainly that was the perception on election night in the BBC studios, as the likes of Peregrine Worsthorne and Peter Jenkins pored over the results.

But there was something about Thatcher that defied traditional analysis, something more to do with tone and image than with political content. In an election populated by overweight, pasty-complexioned, middle-aged men in crumpled suits, and with political memories still dominated by media images of the public sector strikes just a few months earlier, Thatcher stood out. 'How did she get elected prime minister?' reflected Shirley Williams, the most high-profile casualty of Labour's defeat. 'Because Mrs Thatcher – bandbox neat, with Saatchi & Saatchi smoothly organizing fields and factories, cars and calves around her – was such a contrast to the winter of discontent, the chaos, the disorder and mess.' Even if the electorate weren't entirely certain about the nature or advisability of her policies, she at least looked different.

Perhaps inevitably for the first woman to lead a major party in Britain, this question of image was central to selling the new brand of Conservatism. When she had stood against Edward Heath for the leadership of the party in 1975, she had employed the television producer, Gordon Reece, to advise on her campaign, and following her success, he remained as director of communications at Conservative Central Office. Amongst other contributions attributed to Reece, not always correctly, were a simplification of line in her dress, a new approach to microphone technique, and the lowering and softening of her voice. There was a marked change in her style in the first years, when she was still opposition leader. At its most basic, there was the adoption of the diminutive 'Maggie', a name that no member of her family or close circle had ever used, but which fitted well into a tabloid headline, and which had a more homely tone; it became universal, employed by friend and foe alike. (The alternative, Mrs T, was only used by supporters, even if it did make her sound as though she were part of a witness protection programme.)

There were also attempts to suggest that there was more to Thatcher than the slightly dated suburban woman that she sometimes appeared. Following a Conservative rally and concert at the Royal Albert Hall in 1976, the press was informed that she was really very keen on music: 'She does like New Orleans jazz, especially Duke Ellington,' an aide pointed out, leaving it unclear whether it was he or she that didn't know Ellington was born in Washington, made his name in New York, and most certainly did not play New Orleans jazz. Two years later she was a guest of the Football Association at the FA Cup final; invited to select the man of the match, she chose Trevor Whymark, which caused some consternation amongst officials since Whymark wasn't playing that day – it turned out that she really meant David Geddis, who was a late replacement and who provided the cross for the single Ipswich goal that settled the match in favour of Bobby Robson's team.

To some extent these were the traditional mistakes made by politicians when trying to play to the agenda of popular culture. But there was too a sense of her being slightly more removed from the common grain of humanity than were most MPs, a feeling that was encapsulated by what appeared to be a complete absence of humour. In a 1979 episode of the sitcom *Fawlty Towers*, even before she became prime minister, a character comments on the guide-book *What's On in Torquay* that it must be 'one of the world's shortest books – like *The Wit of Margaret Thatcher*'. It was a judgement that survived her choice of a sketch by American comedian Bob Newhart as one of her *Desert Island Discs*, and one that even her closest allies were to confirm: 'One has to remember that she has little sense of humour,' noted William Whitelaw, her deputy leader, 'and therefore if *you* have a sense of humour, you are always suspect with her.' But then Britain in 1979 was not necessarily in the mood for a jokey politician, or even for one as relaxed and unflappable as Callaghan; for many people, the country had felt for years as if it were stumbling into chaos, and the British tendency to mock, its willingness to sink giggling into the sea, was looking as though it might be part of the problem, not the solution. The Labour peer Lord Longford found himself secretly agreeing when someone suggested, in the context of Thatcher's lack of humour, that 'we in Britain had been suffering from an excess of humour', and he was not alone.

If the nation was agreed on her seriousness, it was less certain about her sex appeal, though − again inevitably − it was very much a topic of conversation in a world where female politicians were few and far between. (The number of women MPs actually went down in the 1979 election from twenty-seven to just nineteen, representing 3 per cent of the House of Commons.) Not many were prepared to agree entirely with Tory MP Alan Clark's 1980 assessment − 'she is *so* beautiful,' he drooled, 'quite bewitching, as Eva Peron must have been' − but there was an appeal that, for some men at least, couldn't quite be pinned down. 'Cette femme Thatcher! Elle a les yeux de Caligule, mais elle a la bouche de Marilyn Monroe,' as French president François Mitterrand famously claimed. Or, in the words of Sue Townsend's schoolboy creation, Adrian Mole: 'She has got eyes like a psychotic killer, but a voice like a gentle person. It's a bit confusing.' Perhaps more common was the opinion of Colin Dexter's detective, Inspector Morse; encountering a 'grimly visaged, tight-lipped' Scottish ward sister, he characterizes her as 'an ideal of humourless efficiency: a sort of Calvinistic Thatcherite'. Images of matrons, as well as governesses and nannies, became commonplace.

It was possibly no coincidence that the arrival of Thatcher in Downing Street was followed swiftly by the appearance of several female authority figures on television. After several successful books on training animals, for example, Barbara Woodhouse became a national star in 1980 with the series *Training Dogs the Woodhouse Way*, intimidating dumb creatures (and their pets) with a voice once described as 'Joyce Grenfell crossed with Lady Bracknell'. She was not, however, without her critics, particularly when she endorsed the use of choke-chains that were disapproved of by the RSPCA − like Thatcher, she was sometimes seen as being too strict, and not entirely in step with more modern liberal ways. Then there was Mrs McClusky, who took over as head teacher in the children's school soap *Grange Hill*. Her advent too attracted controversy as the prices went up in the tuck shop, thanks to a new tax known as the School Surcharge, and as she responded to a spate of vandalism and arson by introducing a prefect system, despite complaints that it was a draconian measure. When two boys are caught running an unauthorized cake stall on school premises, they are given a detention with the task of writing an essay on 'the problems of private enterprise in an authoritarian society'. Even the nightmarish, over-controlling mother of Ronnie Corbett's character in the sitcom *Sorry!* (played by Barbara Lott) had a hint of Thatcher about her.

And, after years of all-male fictional police forces, two series in 1980 finally broke the mould. Jill Gascoine appeared as Detective Inspector Maggie Forbes in the ITV drama *The Gentle Touch*, followed a few months later by the BBC entry in the field, *Juliet Bravo*. Set in a small northern town decimated by the closure of its mills, *Juliet Bravo* starred Stephanie Turner as Jean Darblay, a uniformed officer whose husband has been made redundant but who finds herself promoted to Inspector. 'Yours is a very important appointment, Jean. Very few women in England are running a town like this,' her superior tells her, adding: 'There are quite a few around who'd be pleased to see you fail. In any way.'

The same warning could have been applied to Thatcher, and behind much of the conspiratorial whispering that accompanied her early years was, as so often in British politics, an issue of class. As a would-be rival for her job, Francis Pym, once pointed out, the trouble with the Tories from his perspective was that 'we've got a corporal at the top, not a cavalry officer'. Thatcher actually came from a more elevated social background than her predecessor as Conservative leader, but, unlike Edward Heath, she made little attempt as she rose through the ranks to adapt and to fit into the highest echelons of her party, dominated as they still were by the public schools and the land-owning classes. She made no pretence of being anything other than provincial middle class, displaying an assuredness and a self-confidence that was to inspire a new generation of Tories, even as it infuriated her opponents within the party.

And opponents there undoubtedly were, chief amongst them Heath himself. In the build-up to the 1979 election, there had been much speculation about whether he would be invited to join the cabinet in the event of a Conservative victory (as he had himself welcomed his predecessor Alec Douglas-Home into his cabinet in 1970), and when asked directly about the possibility by Robin Day on election night, he had chuckled, 'It depends', with a self-satisfied air. It was to be the last occasion for some time that he appeared on television in a good mood. Thatcher decided she'd be safer with him a long way outside the tent, and offered him the job of being British ambassador to the USA; he turned it down, instead lurking on the backbenches for the remainder of her premiership, 'like a sulk made flesh,' as the journalist Edward Pearce put it.

Nonetheless, Thatcher's first cabinet was largely composed of Heath's men. The only members who hadn't served under him in 1970-74 were John Biffen, Nicholas Edwards and Angus Maude, and there were even fewer who had voted for Thatcher against Heath in the first ballot of the leadership election in 1975: just her mentor Keith Joseph and, more surprisingly, Norman St John-Stevas, a delicate soul who had served as Heath's arts minister. Importantly, however, two of those who had entered that leadership contest had now come onside: home secretary William Whitelaw and chancellor of the exchequer Geoffrey Howe. Whitelaw was the very model of a patrician Tory, but also possessed 'a sort of military loyalty to the commander-in-chief' and, having lost to Thatcher, could be relied upon for absolute support. In parliament, this was invaluable, for he was credited with having a sure touch when it came to judging the mood of the party and with being an astute political analyst ('every prime minister needs a Willie,' as Thatcher once noted). In the country more widely, it counted for little; clearly a decent man, he might, in another age, have been considered a safe pair of hands, but in the turbulent times of the first Thatcher government, his bumbling delivery and his flabby, watery-eyed face, normally bearing a doleful expression, were unlikely to win over a doubting electorate. Nor was Howe any more inspiring in the eyes of the general public. There was a story that his wife had once claimed that, 'When I married Geoffrey, he was a fiery Welshman,' but no one gave the tale any credence – a less fiery politician, it was impossible to imagine. His image was that of a plodder, a man whose most intriguing feature was the gap between his evident dullness and the extremity of the economic policies he pursued. Even when, in 1982, it was reported that he had contrived to lose his trousers while travelling on a train, the details of the story turned out to be much less interesting than the headlines: he had undressed in a sleeper compartment and the trousers had been stolen (they were subsequently recovered, minus his wallet).

Even with these allies, though, the divisions in the party and the cabinet meant that Thatcher had a desperately insecure base from which to operate, and particularly to launch anything resembling a radical pro-gramme for government. Undeterred, she proceeded to do precisely that, determined that there could be no compromise. The principal enemy was inflation, and she was quite clear how it was to be fought: 'To master inflation,' the election manifesto had declared, 'proper monetary discipline is essential, with publicly stated targets for the rate of growth of the money supply.' Quite what that meant was never to be entirely clear to much of the population. Even Sir Desmond Glazebrook, a banker in the television sitcom *Yes, Minister* was confused: 'Took me thirty years to understand Keynes' economics,' he complains. 'Then, when I'd just cottoned on, everyone started getting hooked on these new monetarist ideas. You know, *I Want to Be Free* by Milton Shulman.' (The reference, of course, should have been to the American economist, Milton Friedman, not to Shulman, the celebrated theatre and film critic.) Nor was it ever certain whether monetarism was much more than a theoretical construct – the intention was to control the amount of money in circulation, but opinions differed on how that was to be measured: a succession of different versions of this elusive concept passed through the financial pages of the more weighty newspapers, meaning little or nothing to anyone without an economist in their immediate family.

Instead the policy came mostly to be seen by the public as involving lower income tax, an unfettered market, no state intervention to assist industry, and cuts in public spending. It was an interpretation that Thatcher actively encouraged, with a rhetoric designed to appeal to the housewife, using what she called 'the homilies of housekeeping, the parables of the parlour'. The Labour MP Austin Mitchell saw it in similar terms, though obviously from an opposite standpoint; it was 'essentially a counter-revolution against 1945 carried through by a small town Poujadist brought up to scrimping, saving and the politics of the *Daily Express*, the *Daily Mail* and Hayek under the bed-clothes'. A media-friendly Tory dissident, Julian Critchley, reached for the same imagery: 'an uncongenial blend of Samuel Smiles and Pierre Poujade.' (It was somehow symptomatic of how dogma-driven politics had become that references were being so casually tossed around to something as remote as Poujadism, a short-lived petit bourgeois movement in 1950s France, whose main claim to fame was giving the world Jean-Marie Le Pen, later to found the Front National.)

In fact the groundwork for monetarism had been laid by the previous Labour government, as it was hit by yet another currency crisis and was obliged to go to the International Monetary Fund for a loan to bail the country out of its difficulties. The change in policy had been spelt out by Callaghan in his speech to the 1976 Labour Party conference, explicitly turning his back on the ideas of John Maynard Keynes that had shaped the post-war consensus: 'We used to think that you could spend your way out of recession and increase employment by cutting taxes and boosting government spending,' he declared. 'I tell you in all candour that that option no longer exists.' When he came to write his memoirs a decade later, Callaghan insisted that his words had been 'misused by Conservative spokesmen to justify their malefactions in refusing to increase public expenditure at a time of recession, of low investment and low inflation, and of record levels of jobless'. His reluctance, as an old-fashioned Labour man, to be associated with the effects of what had by now become known as Thatcherism was understandable, but it was hard to see quite where his prescription was not followed. For the first Thatcher government did precisely as he proposed. And carried on doing so, despite what Callaghan himself saw as calamitous consequences.

The first budget, in June 1979, set the tone for the next few years. The basic rate of income tax was reduced from 33 to 30 per cent, and the top rate from 83 to 60 per cent. To fund this, the two rates of VAT (previously standing at 8 and 12.5 per cent) were combined and set at 15 per cent – a move that just about fulfilled Geoffrey Howe's promise in April that 'We have absolutely no intention of doubling VAT', while honouring a manifesto pledge to simplify the tax. This shift from direct to indirect taxation, one of the key planks of Thatcherism, was to prove increasingly important, with a squeeze on everything that looked squeezable, from National Health Service charges (prescriptions rose by 600 per cent in Thatcher's first term, NHS lenses by 150 per cent, dental charges by 170 per cent) through gas and electricity prices to school meals and council rents. None of which did much for public perceptions of the Tories. A parody of the budget on the comedy series *Not the Nine O'Clock News* saw Howe putting 100 per cent tax on items such as wheelchairs, white sticks and false limbs, and commenting: 'Observers will notice I have deliberately chosen to penalize those members of the community who can't hit back.' ('So, no change there,' murmurs the commentator.)

In that first budget, too, interest rates were put up by two percentage points, and were to be raised further to reach a record level of 17 per cent in November 1979, just as inflation – fuelled by the VAT rises – was hitting 18 per cent. These pressures on industry were compounded by a rise in the value of the pound, at the expense of exports, stemming from the abolition of exchange controls that autumn (AT LAST THE £ IS FREED, exulted the *Daily Mail*) and from sterling's new status as an oil currency. This latter was of particular significance in the wake of the revolution that had overthrown the Shah of Iran in February 1979, and seen his replacement a few months later by the Ayatollah Khomeini; the consequent rise in the oil price plunged the world into its worst recession since the 1930s. In the first three years of Thatcher's premiership, oil rose from $14 to $35 a barrel, and so dire did the global situation look that books like *The Downwave: Surviving the Second Great Depression* by the economic broadcaster Bob Beckman proved hugely popular, prophesying gloom on a grand scale.

The result of this combination of international recession and government policy was devastating. Inflation reached a peak of 22 per cent on the first anniversary of Thatcher's election victory, while other effects were later summarized by Ian Gilmour, a cabinet minister at the time: 'Company profits fell by 20 per cent during 1980, output fell by nearly 6 per cent, manufacturing output fell by 15 per cent and unemployment rose from 1.3 million to over two million.' As a Conservative Party political broadcast put it: 'We did not promise you instant sunshine.' By the end of the year, unemployment had risen by 836,000, the largest rise in a single year since 1930, exacerbated by the bulge in the population. With the million-plus Britons born in 1964 hitting school-leaving age, it would have required the creation of large numbers of jobs just to keep up with demand; instead jobs were being cut in vast quantities by major employers in both the private and public sectors, while many smaller companies were going out of business altogether. 'The baby boom of the '60s has turned into the youth gloom of the '80s,' noted the *Daily Mirror*.

And, while other countries were also suffering, there was an awareness that Britain was being hit disproportionately hard. That discrepancy was at the heart of the hit television series *Auf Wiedersehen, Pet* (1983), which followed a group of seven British construction workers employed as *Gastarbeiter* on a building site in Germany, reluctant to leave home but made desperate by the lack of jobs. 'Unemployment – we're very big on that in England,' Wayne (Gary Holton) tells a German woman in bitter resignation. 'It's one of our few spectacular successes. We've managed to put more people out of work than any of our European counterparts.' And, as they discuss where to go next, with the changing of German regulations, Oz (Jimmy Nail) sums up the peripatetic pursuit of work in characteristically blunt fashion: 'The English have become the Irish of Europe.'

Amongst the sectors worst hit was the fashion industry, with the symbolic collapse of several of the best known names from the heady, optimistic days of the 1960s. Bus Stop went into receivership, Biba (which had re-opened in 1978, backed by Iranian money) closed for a second time, and Jean Varon, centred on the designer John Bates, went into voluntary liquidation. 'I could have wept,' lamented the dress designer Jean Muir, on hearing about Jean Varon. 'It's such a devastating blow for the industry.' In 1983 the upmarket lingerie firm Janet Reger, as famously worn by Joan Collins in the film *The Stud*, crashed, with the name being sold off to Berlei; Reger was later to buy the company back, but in the interim her marriage had fallen apart under the stress, and her husband, Peter Reger, who had handled the financial side of the business, had committed suicide.

Meanwhile cheaper imports and changing patterns of life were also affecting employment. In 1979, after more than a century, Singer closed its sewing-machine plant in Clydebank (an area already hit by the decline in shipbuilding) with the loss of 3,000 jobs – it appeared that, recession or no recession, women simply weren't making clothes at home as they once had. And, in warning of further technological shifts, Stephen Lowe's television play that year, *Cries from a Watchtower*, depicted a watchmaker driven out of business by the arrival of cheap digital watches; the impact of the electronics revolution had yet to be fully felt, but it was already causing concern. Elsewhere pubs were suffering (a billion fewer pints of beer were sold in 1980), premiums for home contents insurance soared in response to a rise in burglaries, and mortgage interest hit an all-time high – the rate averaged 13.3 per cent during Thatcher's first term, compared to an average 10.7 per cent under Labour in the 1970s. Times were so tight that it was even reported that local authorities had been ordered to lower the temperature in public swimming baths by 2° centigrade.

By the end of 1980 Labour were 24 per cent ahead in the opinion polls and Thatcher was well on her way to becoming the most unpopular prime minister in the history of polling. Even the Tories' natural allies in the Confederation of British Industry were panicking, with the director general, Terence Beckett, threatening a 'bare-knuckle fight' with the government if interest rates weren't soon reduced. No such fight emerged, but it was symptomatic of the alarm being felt throughout the establishment, let alone amongst the population more widely.

The one truly popular policy the government possessed was the right to buy scheme, the obligation placed on local authorities to sell council houses to their tenants if this was requested. This had actually been a policy of Harold Macmillan's government as far back as 1957, and had been revived in 1970 by Edward Heath's environment secretary, Peter Walker, but sales had then still been at the discretion of local councils, to the distress of a newly elected Conservative MP named Norman Tebbit, who called for 'government action to ensure that councils did not gratuitously nor arbitrarily prevent tenants from purchasing their houses'. He had his wish granted at the election of 1979, when the Conservative manifesto was quite explicit about its intentions, even to the extent of spelling out the concession on market prices that would be available to reflect the purchasers' status as sitting tenants: 'Our discounts will range from 33 per cent after three years, rising with length of tenure to a maximum of 50 per cent after twenty years. We shall also ensure that 100 per cent mortgages are available.' Walker himself had an even more radical proposal that would have seen any tenancy of more than twenty years be automatically converted into ownership, with nothing to pay, but that suggestion was dismissed by Thatcher for fear of arousing the resentment of mortgagees – those 'whom she regarded as "our people"' – towards those who were being given properties without the burden of mortgages.

Even without this radical element, the scheme, when introduced in the 1980 Housing Act, was one of Thatcher's great successes. When she came to power, just under a third of British families lived in council accommodation, five million tenancies, a fact that she believed was evidence of the way that 'socialism was still built into the institutions and mentality of Britain'. By the time she left office, nearly one and a half million of those tenancies had been converted to mortgages, most of them to the enormous benefit of the occupants: the discounts, combined with the rises in both house prices and council rents, meant that most had got themselves a bargain. ('Money for old rope,' as David Jason's character Del Trotter explains in the sitcom *Only Fools and Horses*.) By 1984 it was being reported that 'council tenants pay more, on average, than the average mortgagee pays in repayments'.

There were, of course, opponents of the scheme, principally Labour councils, who vehemently opposed the idea both in the principle and the practice, and who angrily denounced the fact that the regulations forbade the spending of the monies received on building new properties to replace those that had been lost. But since the intention had always been to reduce the nation's stock of public housing, their pleas fell on unresponsive ears in Westminster. Even worse, those who opposed the policy found the public were little more receptive. The 1983 Labour Party manifesto promised to stop the compulsion upon councils to sell, to remove the discounts and to allow local authorities to repurchase any homes that had been sold on by their former tenants, but by 1987 this had been amended to read: 'we will maintain the right to buy'. The latter manifesto also made pledges to 'the millions who choose to remain council tenants', though it was by no means clear that such people existed: with the exception of a few ideologues, those who remained council tenants did so out of necessity rather than choice. The millions who were unemployed or who were already in arrears on their rent, for example, were never likely to be affected by the policy, and for many others the housing they occupied was a long way from desirable.

For as the best-quality accommodation was sold off, and as funds for repairs to that which remained grew ever scarcer, it became increasingly obvious which estates remained in the sole ownership of the local authority. 'There are no fences, trees, shrubs, window boxes, sheds, prams, bikes or washing lines,' wrote journalist Beatrix Campbell of one such estate in Sunderland. 'There is no evidence of human habitation, only the appearance of absence. Everything is bare, some windows are boarded up and some broken, all the signs of vacancy and abandonment.' The families who lived in such conditions were seldom inclined to apply under the right to buy scheme, even if they had been in a position so to do. The suspicion grew amongst some that a whole section of society, and that which was least able to fend for itself, was being jettisoned. It was probably the single most significant step ever taken towards the 'property-owning democracy' envisaged by Anthony Eden, but it also entrenched divisions between the haves and have-nots in a way that would have been politically and socially unacceptable just a few years earlier.

This uneasiness was felt even in the higher echelons of the Conservative Party itself. Cabinet members, most notably Peter Walker, James Prior and Norman St John-Stevas, began giving thinly coded speeches about the need for reconsideration of their government's policies, though they were perhaps handicapped by the fact that they carried little weight with the general public – an opinion poll six months after the election revealed that 40 per cent of people couldn't name a single cabinet minister apart from Thatcher. So when, for example, their most articulate champion Ian Gilmour denounced monetarism, which 'because of its starkness and its failure to create a sense of community, is not a safeguard of political freedom but a threat to it', or when he warned that Thatcherism risked 'the creation of a *Clockwork Orange* society' with a huge gulf between the employed majority and the unemployed minority, he attracted less attention than he might have wished.

Almost the only dissident Tory who could command the front pages was Heath, but his remarks tended to come smothered in such an unattractively large dollop of self-justification that his message was often lost. 'People are realizing the merits of the last Conservative government compared with the catastrophic things they see happening to them today,' he announced in November 1980, seemingly in the hope that, despite having lost three of the four general elections he had contested as leader, he might yet be invited back for a second stint in Downing Street. And so desperate did things become that even such a bizarre possibility was not entirely beyond imagination; the right-wing MP Alan Clark recorded in his diary a discussion he had with the journalist Frank Johnson, both of them 'ardent Heath-haters of old', in which they surprised each other with their 'growing admiration for Ted'.

Collectively, these Tories who had reservations about the advisability of pursuing monetarist policies at all costs were known, in a term which seemed to originate with Thatcher herself, as 'wet', a piece of schoolboy slang intended to denote a lack of resolve. By 1980 the adjective had become a noun and had been taken up by the dissenters themselves, generally being seen to identify those who harked back to the inclusive, One Nation days of Harold Macmillan and Ted Heath; it might be said that it was actually synonymous with the word 'Conservative', as opposed to the free-market liberals who sided with Thatcher. Whatever the merits or otherwise of such playground jibes infiltrating the world of politics, the impact of the wets was less than they would have hoped (the BBC political editor, John Cole, dismissed them as 'articulate, but ineffectual'), primarily because Thatcher showed, in public at least, no sign of weakness or indecisiveness whatsoever. When it came to industrial disputes, for example, strikes that would have caused serious concern to other governments – by civil servants, and by workers in the steel industry, in the NHS and on the railways – came and went without any quarter being given. The wets, as the right wing of a broad swathe of mainstream politics that stretched through David Steel and Roy Jenkins to James Callaghan, probably enjoyed greater public support than did Thatcher, with her talk of conviction over consensus, but in the face of her resolution, their search for compromise and their apparent wish to return to the failed policies of the past simply wilted.

But still there were doubts about how long the prime minister could retain her self-proclaimed convictions, in the context of a country that appeared to be falling apart. In March 1980 Kingsley Amis noted that his friend, the historian Robert Conquest, who was amongst Thatcher's advisers, was in deep despair: 'She's had it according to him,' Amis wrote. 'All the fucking wets in the cabinet will stop her being tough enough and the effort will collapse.' A sense of doubt could even be detected in the public pronouncements of the handful of monetarists in the government. John Biffen, whose credentials were impeccable (he had supported Enoch Powell's failed bid for the leadership back in 1965, and Thatcher regarded him as 'a brilliant exponent in opposition of the economic policies in which I believed'), gave a series of interviews in which he defended monetarism, but not quite as wholeheartedly as might have been expected. 'We are not so stubborn or so ideological that we are blinkered, that we do not admit the possibility that we could be wrong,' he said in the autumn of 1980, adding a couple of months later: 'Whether we are in a very much better position to take advantage of the upswing when it comes, honestly, only time will tell.'

One of the few who could be counted on to defend the policies in their entirety was Nicholas Ridley, then a minister in the foreign office. The Eton- and Balliol-educated son of a viscount, and grandson of the architect Edwin Lutyens, Ridley shared little in common with Thatcher save for his fierce espousal of the free market: he too had voted for Powell in 1965, and had gone further by becoming the only person to resign from Heath's govern- ment because of differences over economic policy. In private he was said to be 'the most delightful and gregarious of companions', a committed countryman and a gifted painter, but he was best known as a resolute opponent of the nanny state — even when diagnosed with lung cancer in the early 1990s, he refused to give up smoking cigarettes — and as an austere politician who never let himself be deflected by electoral considerations of populism or tact. 'Bringing down the rate of inflation can only be done by restricting the money supply; and doing that inevitably causes difficulties for business and rising unemployment,' he argued, before concluding: 'The high level of unemployment is evidence of the progress we are making.'

Ridley's logic didn't convince nervous Tories, let alone those in the country threatened with redundancy notices. And though there were still some staunch Thatcherite voices to be heard in Fleet Street, urging yet stronger policies ('Mrs Thatcher's government is still spending too much, still borrowing too much,' fretted the *Daily Mail* in September 1980), rather more resonant with the public was the tone adopted from the outset by the *Daily Mirror*, which had warned as early as July 1979 that the Thatcher government was on the wrong path, as it began to cut subsidies to industry: 'Mr Heath started down this road in 1970, but had the courage to retreat when faced with the awful reality of his policy. The loss of jobs. The death of firms.' The paper concluded that 'It's better to do a U-turn than to go over the edge of a cliff'.

That expression — the U-turn — so came to dominate political comment in 1980 that Thatcher felt obliged to address it head-on in her speech to the Conservative conference that autumn: 'To those waiting with bated breath for that favourite media catchphrase, the U-turn, I have only one thing to say,' she announced, in a passage written by the playwright Ronald Millar. 'You turn if you want to. The lady's not for turning.' It got a big cheer at the time — Thatcher was one of the few leading Tories to enjoy the experience of conference, and her audience tended to respond accordingly — but the steadfast refusal to change course meant that things would continue to get worse for some time. In his autumn statement, and then again in his 1981 budget, Howe tightened the screw still further, cutting interest rates, but also reducing public spending and raising taxes. The budget in particular found few friends. As Thatcher went into the House that day, she said to her economics advisor, the arch-monetarist Alan Walters: 'You know, Alan, they may get rid of me for this.' But she was still convinced that it was the only honourable option: 'At least I shall have gone knowing I did the right thing.'

They didn't get rid of her, of course, largely because no one knew how to set about such an undertaking. The wets were deeply unhappy, but lacked any game plan and lacked too the support of the most powerful Tory grandees — the likes of William Whitelaw and of Lord Carrington, the foreign secretary — who might have sympathized but were too canny to say so. An open letter to *The Times*, signed by a total of 364 economists, regretted the harshness of the budget ('Present policies will deepen the depression, erode the industrial base of our economy and threaten its social and political stability'), but their message was simply ignored. Instead, when Thatcher addressed the CBI in June 1981, she reiterated her refusal to contemplate a U-turn: 'I can do no better than repeat words spoken by US Captain Lloyd Williams when he arrived in Northern France in June 1918 at a time when victory was almost within grasp after years of struggle but a hard fight clearly lay ahead. He said in the graphic language of a soldier: "Retreat? Hell, no! We only just got here."' (Actually it was a slight misquote; Williams is normally quoted as having said 'Retreat? Hell, we just got here.' Which is at least open to a different interpretation.)

On the other side of the Commons, the parliamentary opposition had by this stage virtually gone awol, the Labour Party being now engaged in both a civil war and a life-or-death struggle with the breakaway Social Democratic Party. The political columnist Walter Terry, writing in the *Sun* on the occasion of Thatcher's second anniversary in Downing Street, had it about right: 'It is staggering that after two years of Thatcherdom the opposition should be so appalling.' And he warned, correctly, that this was probably the lowest point she would face, the perfect opportunity for the opposition to make hay: 'Her good times are to come: vote-winning tax cuts as the election nears, the prospect of economic improvement in time for polling day.' The *Daily Mirror*, Labour's most loyal friend in Fleet Street, largely agreed, its political editor, Terence Lancaster, despairing of the party's prospects for the next election: 'Labour, clear favourite in anybody's book to win without sweat, is in the process of nobbling itself. All it has to beat is a discredited government, high on hardship and low on achievement, crammed with doubters and beset by leaks.'

But Labour was now in deeper crisis than the country itself. In the early days of Thatcher's premiership, she was so unpopular that almost any opposition party would have been capable of attracting support; Labour took an opinion poll lead over the Conservatives in August 1979 and stayed there, even touching a 50 per cent share, for the next fifteen months. But 1981 was disastrous, with the elderly and media-unfriendly Michael Foot having replaced James Callaghan as leader of the party and with the SDP offering a less extreme alternative: Labour started the year at 46 per cent in the opinion polls, and ended at 23 per cent, the biggest fall ever recorded in a single year by any party. Even worse was the realization that the pace of decline seemed to be accelerating: 17 percentage points were lost in the second half of the year.

If the parliamentary wing of the labour movement was struggling in its efforts to articulate public discontent with Thatcherism, so too was the industrial wing. The Trades Unions Congress had, over a period of decades, become accustomed to meeting ministers and being consulted by government, but now found that the invitations had dried up. In an attempt to make its voice heard, the TUC designated 14 May 1980 as a 'day of action', when union members would be encouraged to demonstrate their opposition to the social and economic policies of the Thatcher government. It was not a conspicuous success. The most militant sectors of industry – the Liverpool docks, the Yorkshire coal mines, Fleet Street – saw major disruption, but much of the rest of the country continued to work normally, with the hundred or so rallies in various towns and cities attracting only small crowds. Even within the highest echelons of trade unionism, there were doubts about the tactic, with Frank Chapple, leader of the electricians' union, the EETPU, denouncing it as unacceptable politicking: 'Democracy cannot function if government policies are to be changed, not through the ballot box, but through the disruption of industry through political strikes. If that happens, a real can of worms will be opened up and the way paved for either a right- or left-wing dictatorship.' Looking somewhat diminished by the experience, Len Murray, general secretary of the TUC, declared himself 'not dissatisfied with the total result' of the day, which was as close to accepting defeat as he was likely to come.

As the opinion polls demonstrated, the lack of support for the TUC's initiative stemmed not from any sense of contentment with government policies. Rather there was a feeling of powerlessness; if the steelworkers couldn't make any impact in a thirteen-week strike, there seemed little chance of an isolated day of rallies changing anything much. And, of course, the massive rise in unemployment did much to dampen down dissent, as Alan Clark acknowledged privately: '[Tony] Benn is absolutely right, the trade union movement is disciplined by the fear of being put on the dole and this is a considerable, though brutal, achievement.'

The word 'brutal' seemed entirely apposite to the times. Thatcher's continued insistence that the medicine might taste foul, might even have unpleasant side-effects, but would ultimately cure 'the British disease' of poor industrial relations, carried less and less weight as factories closed, dole queues lengthened and rioting broke out in towns and cities across the country. It was as though the government were wilfully pursuing a Year Zero approach that would wipe the slate clean and facilitate a new start. In the process, however, the nation seemed to be in danger of losing something of itself, a sense of hope and optimism, perhaps, or even of community, however impossible that might be to measure.

And there were signs of concern at the loss. The Glasgow-born writer and director Bill Forsyth was a critical and box-office success with *Gregory's Girl* (1981) and *Local Hero* (1983), evoking memories of the social cohesion that had been standard in British cinema in the post-war years. The veteran actor Burt Lancaster starred in *Local Hero* as an American oil boss seeking to build a refinery on the site of a fishing village on the north-west coast of Scotland, before ultimately deciding to found an astronomical observatory instead, allowing the village to survive with its simple charm intact. Key to his decision is Ben, an old beachcomber played by Fulton Mackay, who, it transpires, owns the beach, it having been given to an ancestor of his by the Lord of the Isles. No matter how much money Ben is offered, he has no desire to go anywhere else, no ambition to do anything but live on his beach, and it is on his intransigent contentment that the aspirations of a Texas-based oil company founder. Lancaster appeared in the movie because, he said, it was reminiscent of 'all those lovely Ealing comedies' of the 1940s and '50s; that, of course, was precisely why Forsyth's work also appealed to audiences.

Meanwhile BBC1 was broadcasting the early episodes of the series that would become the most cherished sitcom of the decade. *Only Fools and Horses* (1981) was written by John Sullivan and centred on two brothers – Del (David Jason) and Rodney (Nicholas Lyndhurst) Trotter – living on a housing estate in Peckham, south London with their grandfather (Lennard Pearce). Working in the black economy as fly pitchers in the local street market, Del and Rodney seldom stayed on the right side of legality, and there was some initial concern that it was all a bit too raw for a family audience. 'I dare say the BBC's switchboard was hot with outraged viewers complaining about bad language in *Only Fools and Horses*, Tuesday's new low-life comedy,' wrote Hilary Kingsley, television critic of the *Daily Mirror*. 'Well, I hope no one tampers with the series, it promises to be the liveliest for ages.' What emerged, however, was a strong moral vein that excused all the roguery, for in the world of the Trotters, family loyalty is everything, the last bulwark against a disintegrating society. Del likes to see himself as a shrewd operator, always out for the big deal that will make his fortune, but, as the older brother, his actions are restrained by his need to honour their dead mother's wishes and look after his kid brother; in compensation, he regularly invokes her memory as the clincher to win any argument with Rodney. And as the cast of associated characters grew ever larger to embrace Trigger, Boycie, Mike, Denzil, Mickey Pearce and others, it became clear that this was an extended family that formed a bantering, bickering but ultimately self-supporting unit.

Similarly *Auf Wiedersehen, Pet* drew most of its strength and popularity from its portrayal of personal loyalties holding strong, even as the working-class communities from which the characters were drawn were falling apart at the seams. And in a 1980 episode of *Coronation Street*, a soap whose appeal was based largely on its depiction of traditional British values, Elsie Tanner addressed the subject directly: 'We've still got a community here, at least a bit of one. We've still got the bush telegraph, for instance. Something happens in Arkwright Street, and they know in Jubilee Terrace two minutes later.' But Ken Barlow was unconvinced: 'Yeah, but go another couple of streets further on and you're in a different country.'

Towards the end of 1980 two deaths appeared to symbolize the passing of a kindlier, more familiar Britain. In October the 62-year-old Lady Isobel Barnett, who had become an early television star on the panel show *What's My Line?*, and who had represented for many the gentle dignity and deference of the 1950s, was found guilty of shoplifting goods to the value of 87 pence. Four days later, she was found dead in her bath, having taken an overdose of painkillers.

Then, in December, John Lennon, the ultimate embodiment of the Swinging Sixties, was shot dead outside his New York home. (The playwright Alan Bennett was eating in a New York restaurant when he heard the news and recorded in his diary the characteristically stoical attitude of the locals: '"This country of ours," sighs my waiter. "May I tell you the specials for this evening?"') There had been many deaths in the short history of rock and roll, but they had generally tended to be self-inflicted or accidental – the murder of the most famous living rock star caused genuine horror and grief, and Lennon's current single '(Just Like) Starting Over', his first release for five years, which had been slipping down the charts, went back up to the top. To keep a sense of perspective, it was replaced at No. 1 the following week by St Winifred's School Choir with their song 'There's No One Quite Like Grandma' – a fact which caused shudders of embarrassment in later life to actress Sally Lindsay, one of the choirgirls: 'We knocked John Lennon's "(Just Like) Starting Over" off No. 1 a week after he was shot dead – how fucking shit is that?'

The establishment looked no more secure. The last time a British man had been stripped of a knighthood had been in 1918, but within twenty months of Thatcher's premiership two names were added to the roll of shame: the art critic and former Surveyor of the Queen's Pictures, Anthony Blunt, lost his knighthood after he was publicly revealed to have been a communist spy, and the raincoat manufacturer Joseph Kagan – raised to the peerage by Harold Wilson – lost his on being convicted of theft (though he kept the title of Baron and his seat in the House of Lords).

And for those who felt that the country was – despite all Thatcher's exhortations – continuing to lose international status, as it had been right through the 1970s, confirmation seemed to come in September 1981, when the England football team lined up against Norway in a World Cup qualifying match. Norway was subsequently to fight its way up the food-chain of European football, but at the time it undoubtedly swam with the minnows: only five of its players were professionals, and England had never before failed to score fewer than four goals against them. The 2-1 defeat in Oslo was therefore considered a national disaster, made even worse for fans by the manner of the players' capitulation: 'I cannot remember a more inept performance by an England team in thirty years of watching them,' wrote Frank McGhee of the *Daily Mirror* in disgust. The humiliation did though produce one of the most famous pieces of sports commentary, as the Norwegian journalist Bjørge Lillelien celebrated the victory in splendidly unrestrained fashion: 'We are the best in the world! We have beaten England! England, birthplace of giants! Lord Nelson, Lord Beaverbrook, Sir Winston Churchill, Sir Anthony Eden, Clement Attlee, Henry Cooper, Lady Diana – we have beaten them all!' The somewhat eccentric list of English icons culminated in a phrase, delivered in English, that was to enter the language: 'Maggie Thatcher, your boys took a hell of a beating!'

But the underachieving performance of the national team gave a distorted view of English football, and of British sport more generally. For this was something of a brief golden age, sporting achievement being the one area of public life that offered relief from the gloom that had settled elsewhere. This was the period when English club teams were almost unassailable in Europe, winning the European Cup for six years in succession from 1977 to 1982, with three clubs (Liverpool, Nottingham Forest and Aston Villa) sharing the honours. This was too the era when Sebastian Coe and Steve Ovett were similarly dominant in middle-distance running, casually swapping world records with each other in the 800 metres, 1500 metres and mile, though even here there were signs of a divided country, with the two men popularly perceived in quasi-political terms: Coe as a smart young Tory, Ovett as a more anti-authoritarian rebel. Both won gold medals at the 1980 Moscow Olympics, alongside decathlete Daley Thompson, sprinter Allan Wells and swimmer Duncan Goodhew. In a break with tradition, however, none were recognized in the next honours list, punished for not heeding Thatcher's demand that British athletes boycott the Games, as a protest at the Soviet Union's invasion of Afghanistan.

And in terms of sporting inspiration, little could rival the performance of the England cricket team in the 1981 Ashes series. After two matches of the six-Test series, England were 1-0 down and Ian Botham was ignominiously removed as captain, having seen a catastrophic collapse in his form (he had failed to score a run in the second Test). Mike Brearley returned to the captaincy and, freed from responsibility, Botham took six for 95 in Australia's first innings in the third Test at Headingley, scored 50 and 149, and then saw Bob Willis take eight for 43 to complete one of the greatest of all Test victories. It was only the second time ever that a match had been won by a team forced to follow-on – the first had been as far back as 1894 – and at one point Ladbrokes had been offering odds of 500-1 against England winning. Similar, if not quite such extraordinary, heroics followed, and two weeks later the Ashes had been retained by a score of 3-1, the series becoming universally known as Botham's Ashes. In the absence of any comparable contribution by the country's footballers, those matches made Botham England's most popular sporting hero, an unpredictable individualist whose career seemed entirely appropriate for Thatcher's Britain: a comprehensive school boy triumphing in the most establishment of sports. The fact that later in the decade he was suspended after admitting that he'd smoked cannabis ensured that his anti-establishment credentials remained intact for a while longer, as well as prompting one of the better T-shirt slogans of the time: 'From Ashes to Hashish'.

Botham was also, alongside the Radio One disc jockey Jimmy Savile, to popularize endurance charity events in the 1980s, a trend that made a popular institution of the London Marathon. ('What a wonderful change from all the protest marches we have seen in the past few years,' enthused a *Daily Mail* reader from Weymouth, after the first race in 1981. 'Perhaps this may help to restore a bit of the old selfless spirit that made this country great.') That victory at Headingley, meanwhile, coming after a change in team leadership, even provoked the Tory backbencher Charles Morrison to speculate in the Commons: 'Was this not a good example of a change of tactics which we might emulate?'

There was another contemporary example of the desirability or otherwise of decapitating the leadership, this time in the world of soap matriarchs. ATV caused outrage in June 1981 by announcing that they wouldn't be renewing the contract of Noele Gordon, who had played Meg Richardson in *Crossroads* in over three thousand episodes since the show's inception in 1964, and around whom the entire series revolved: Meg's word in the Crossroads Motel was as final as was Maggie's in the cabinet. The coup appeared to come, symbolically enough, on Guy Fawkes night, when a firework set the motel ablaze, with the assumption that Meg had been killed; happily, it turned out that she had survived the blaze, and she lived to sail off into the distance on the *QE2* as she made a tearful farewell from the series. Fourteen million viewers watched the pivotal episode, suggesting that – despite the relentless carping of critics and despite a lack of support from within the industry for a show that was seen as having no aesthetic value – the series remained hugely popular, as did its central star. (A second body blow to loyal fans came the following year when Ronald Allen, who played David Hunter in the soap, turned up in Channel 4's comedy *Five Go Mad in Dorset*, a parody of Enid Blyton's Famous Five, as the somewhat different Uncle Quentin: 'Your Aunt Fanny is an unrelenting nymphomaniac, and I'm a screaming homosexual.')

But even if an institution as established as Meg Richardson had proved to be ultimately disposable, there remained for disillusioned Tories the problem of who could plausibly replace Thatcher if she were to be removed from office. Acknowledging the speculation that was in the air, the *Sun* ran down the list of possible contenders in a leader column in October 1981 and found them all wanting: 'Willie Whitelaw, noted for agreeing with the last person he talked to. Peter Walker, who thinks and speaks like Ted Heath. Jim Prior, who even looks like him – if people spurn the organ grinder, they certainly do NOT want the monkey! Francis Pym, the original faceless man, who has all the inspirational qualities of a glass of warm water.' It was a harsh judgement but, as an assessment of public opinion, probably not too inaccurate. So few options presented themselves that out in the country, and particularly out in the Black Country, there were even some still holding out for a hero from the past: 'He'd make a great prime minister, would Enoch,' a Wolverhampton woman told *New Society* magazine in

December 1981, but the idea that Enoch Powell, now an Ulster Unionist MP, might take over really was a pipe-dream by this stage. Nor was there anyone, it seemed, who could force a change in approach; Whitelaw acknowledged that he'd like to be able to 'influence Margaret to change some of her policies, but frankly I don't see how this can be done. It's very difficult for me to see a way round that.'

Thatcher's determination to get her own way, despite the reservations of so many of her senior colleagues, became ever more apparent as 1981 wore on. She started the year by sacking Norman St John-Stevas as leader of the House of Commons, much to the horror of the liberal establishment and at the risk of fuelling his own sense of martyrdom. 'I argued in the cabinet for a human and compassionate Conservatism,' he pleaded, though in truth her motivation was rooted not so much in ideology as in a desire to reduce the authority of Francis Pym, the most plausible leader of the wets; Thatcher removed Pym from the ministry of defence and, while keeping him in the cabinet, isolated him as leader of the House, with St John-Stevas simply discarded to make room. As the novelist Michael Dobbs, who worked closely with her, noted: 'She was ruthless when she had to be – and often when she didn't have to be as well.' In a way that was to become characteristic of dismissed wets, St John-Stevas was a couple of months later to be found presenting *Dizzy: A Man for All Seasons*, a BBC2 programme about Benjamin Disraeli, the man who originated the concept of One Nation Conservatism, in what was presumably intended to be a coded signal about where Thatcher was going wrong. And, as was to become equally characteristic, Thatcher ignored him entirely.

In autumn 1981 she engaged on an even more serious reshuffle of her cabinet that damaged the standing of the wets irretrievably. Pym held on, but Ian Gilmour was dismissed, much to his displeasure (he was 'huffy', according to Thatcher's account), and James Prior was sent in disgrace from the department of employment to the Northern Ireland office; having made it clear that he wouldn't accept such a posting, his subsequent acceptance of it did nothing to enhance his stature. And though the whispering against Thatcher continued, her merciless handling of her internal opponents was an unmistakable statement of intent.

Into the cabinet instead came a trio of politicians who would become absolutely identified with the Thatcherite era: Cecil Parkinson, Nigel Lawson and Norman Tebbit. Of these, the most significant, in terms of public profile, was undoubtedly Tebbit. Already described by Michael Foot as 'a semi house-trained polecat' while still on the opposition backbenches, he had acquired a reputation as an uncompromising right-winger who dispensed with the niceties of political discourse in favour of full-frontal attack. He was particularly effective in articulating the aspirations of the southern working class, whence he had originated, and never more so than when it was at the expense of those in the Labour Party who hadn't shared his experiences: 'It was a childhood of living in bits of other people's houses in fairly uncomfortable circumstances, and being very hard up,' he reflected of his upbringing, soon after his promotion. 'Certainly not the kind of childhood enjoyed by Mr Foot, Mr Benn and a great many others of their party.' The rather more patrician socialist, John Mortimer, was later to echo this judgement and to draw his own conclusions about the modern Tories: 'There was a time when gents used to be in the Conservative Party, but that is no longer the case. Foot, a gent; Benn, yes; Tebbit, not a gent.'

Even more than Thatcher herself, Tebbit represented skilled and semi-skilled workers in parts of the country like Essex (his constituency was Chingford), and his elevation to the cabinet, where he took over from Prior as employment secretary, set the tone for the next period of domestic politics. Though, in the event, domestic politics weren't where the survival or otherwise of Thatcherism was to be determined.

2
Comrades
'Dog eat dog'

Our type of Labourism ain't popular any more. The young
'uns and some of the punters find us too wishy-washy.
We're not fashionable. Whereas Trotskyism, Marxism,
Leninism and every other revolutionary 'ism' are the 'in'
things. At least amongst local activists.
David Pinner, *There'll Always Be an England* (1984)

My father said, 'I have worked and slaved and fought to
join the middle classes, Adrian, and now I'm here I don't
want my son admiring proles and revolutionaries.'
Sue Townsend, *The Growing Pains of Adrian Mole* (1984)

I have forgotten precisely what brand of MP old Guthrie
was; he was either right-wing Labour or left-wing
Conservative until, in the end, he gave up politics and
joined the SDP. He was dedicated to the middle of the
road.
John Mortimer, *Rumpole's Last Case* (1987)

'It was not a happy period.' James Callaghan's assessment of the aftermath of Labour's comprehensive defeat in the 1979 election was one of
the great understatements of modern political history. In fact for the
entirety of Thatcher's first term, the main opposition party seemed more
interested in fighting within itself than in challenging the government's
policies, and the self-inflicted wounds that resulted were to take years to
heal.

The problems dated back more than a decade and were rooted in a lack
of trust between the parliamentary party and a large swathe of the
membership. The 1974–79 government, led first by Harold Wilson and then
by Callaghan, had failed, in the eyes of many activists, to implement the
more radical proposals adopted by the annual conference and, worse yet,
had been obliged to make cuts in public spending in exchange for that loan

facility from the International Monetary Fund. All Labour governments, it was argued, had drifted to the right when in power, jettisoning socialism wherever possible, and now the time had come to ensure that it never happened again. The attitude was summed up in the words of Harry Perkins, the left-wing hero of Chris Mullin's novel *A Very British Coup*: 'Serves us bloody right,' he reflects. 'We offer the electorate a choice between two Tory parties and they choose the real one. Now we find ourselves back in the wilderness for five years and the country's going down the plughole.'

Accordingly, a series of reforms were proposed that would bind the parliamentary party and a future Labour government, should such an entity ever materialize. First, the leader should no longer be selected by MPs alone, but by the membership of the entire movement. Second, every MP should face a reselection procedure in between each general election, to ensure that they remained answerable and acceptable to their local party. And third, the manifesto should be drawn up by the party's governing body, the national executive committee (NEC), rather than by the somewhat haphazard process previously used, in which the leader exercised the ultimate authority. There were other suggestions, including that all personal aides and researchers used by members of the shadow cabinet should be employed directly by the party, and that there should be no more Labour peers created, but it was the three primary demands that formed the centrepiece of the internal reforms and that were to dominate the party in the immediate wake of election defeat. This was, its supporters insisted, a move to a more democratic party, liberated from the vacillations of the parliamentary leadership, who had always sought the easiest option.

It also represented a profound reinterpretation of the party structure as it had emerged in mainstream British politics. Erstwhile Conservative cabinet minister Ian Gilmour pointed out that by convention in Britain 'consensus politicians have recognized that, under our unusual system which normally gives the whole of the executive and the control of the legislature to one party even if it has won only a minority of the votes, the winning party does not have carte blanche to do whatever its extremists may happen to want.' His criticism was primarily directed at Margaret Thatcher's espousal of 'conviction' politics, but it applied equally to the restless left of the Labour Party. For the intention of the reformers was to shift the balance of power away from the leader and the MPs, towards the annual conference and the NEC. And as such, it naturally attracted the suspicions of MPs, who jealously guarded their independence and their status as representatives of their constituents, subscribing (when the whips allowed them) to the argument that Edmund Burke had famously put in 1774 to his electorate: 'Your representative owes you not his industry alone, but his judgement; and he betrays, instead of serving, you if he sacrifices it to your opinion.' The moves now afoot challenged that presumption at its core, seeking instead to make MPs in effect delegates of their local parties, a demand that had been rejected as far back as 1902 by Keir Hardie, in the dawn of the Labour Party.

Perhaps just as importantly, since even MPs have human hopes and fears, the reselection proposal threatened a large number of them with the prospect of being made unemployed, a fact which Tony Benn, while campaigning for the changes, sometimes appreciated: 'I suppose like everyone else in Britain today they are worried about their jobs and I must take that very seriously.' And the idea of stopping any future Labour peerages was hardly welcome news to those who sought a secure and comfortable retirement from the Commons.

Benn was now in a unique position, exempted from the left's attacks on the previous government, despite having been a leading member of it, because he spoke more clearly than anyone of the need for reforms. He had emerged during the 1970s as the most persuasive and charismatic leader of the left for two decades, charming, funny and impassioned, as adept in the television studio as he was at mass rallies, and his growing popularity was the source of some concern. 'The big event in the Labour Party in the early '80s was the prospect that Mr Benn would become leader, which caused mild hysteria not only amongst the right-wing media but also amongst the establishment of the Labour Party,' reflected Chris Mullin, some years later. 'It wasn't the worry that we would become unelectable, it was the worry that we would indeed be electable.' Having served as industry secretary under Wilson and having found his proposals for industrial reform blocked, Benn's dissatisfaction – together with his ability to tell the story from the inside – chimed with those thousands of activists who felt cheated by the leadership, so that although he had not originated the demands for change, they became identified almost entirely with him.

The principles behind the reform proposals were agreed at an NEC meeting in July 1979, to be put to the conference that autumn. The Labour establishment was not slow to recognize the danger, even if it was not entirely sure how to respond. 'Having lost the last general election, the Labour Party is now hard at work preparing to lose the next,' wrote Terence Lancaster in the *Daily Mirror*, warning that if the choice of leader was to be left to conference, 'Tony Benn would ride to an easy victory.' In an editorial headlined LABOUR: THE ROAD TO OBLIVION, the same paper spelt out the ultimate fear that the left's proposals on internal democracy could produce a situation where the party 'will split in two. And a split could keep the Tories in power for a generation.' Less friendly commentators came to the same conclusion at the autumn conference; Benn, wrote the *Daily Mail*, had 'planted a time-bomb which could still explode and split Labour's left wing from a new social democratic and liberal party'.

That conference was a public relations disaster for the Labour Party, setting a pattern that was to become very familiar over the next few years. The surviving MPs, fewer in number than they had been for twenty years, sat in a single ramped block, under continual attack from the rostrum and even from the platform. 'I feel like a defendant in a People's Court,' commented one, and there was little that week to dispel the impression. 'I come not to praise Callaghan but to bury him,' announced Ron Hayward, the party's general secretary, to enthusiastic cheers. He proceeded to analyse what had gone wrong: 'Why was there a winter of discontent? The reason was that, for good or ill, the cabinet supported by the MPs ignored congress and conference decisions. It was as simple as that.' A succession of speakers followed the same direction, blaming the parliamentary party for all that had gone wrong and insisting that, if only the wisdom of the conference had been heeded, things would have been well. The sustained fury that was unleashed that week upon the hapless MPs was unprecedented in mainstream British politics and did more damage to the party's image than anything since Callaghan had returned from Guadeloupe in the midst of the winter of discontent to enquire — in the words put in his mouth by the *Sun* — 'Crisis? What crisis?'

'There is no guarantee of even the politest and mildest form of applause for those who oppose the left,' noted one contemporary account. 'It is not only deference but some of the ordinary conventions of public debate that have gone.' In vain did Michael Foot try to explain that 'It is easy to say that all you have to do is to obey conference's decisions. Sometimes conference asks for contradictory things.' No one was listening. Nor did they pay much attention to Denis Healey as, recognizing that now was not the time for his brand of pragmatic politics, he shrugged off the entire experience: 'I hope next year when you have got the bad blood of the election disappointment out of your system, we will concentrate on building a party which will get back for our movement the millions of voters we have lost not to the Communist Party, not to the militant groups, but to the Tories and Liberals.'

Despite all the heat and fervour, the conference failed to provide the necessary majorities on the issues of the leadership elections and the manifesto ('We'll come back next year and put it right,' Benn promised his diary), but did accept the call for mandatory reselection of MPs, the consequence of which, as he rightly noted, was that there were now '635 vacancies for candidates in the next parliament'.

While the argument over party reforms continued, the left was simultaneously opening a second front, aimed at winning the party to a much more radical raft of policies. A special conference at Wembley in May 1980 approved a document, *Peace, Jobs, Freedom*, that spelt out a new direction for the party: in favour of unilateral nuclear disarmament and withdrawal from the European Economic Community, and advocating an alternative economic policy that was based on extending nationalization of industry and on import controls (there was, for example, to be a complete ban on the importation of cars). This new set of socialist shibboleths became known on the left simply as 'the policies', a phrase so common that it was spoken as though capitalized: The Policies. Again the tone of the conference was far from fraternal. When Healey went up to speak, he was accompanied by chants of 'Out! Out! Out!' while Terry Fields, a delegate from Liverpool and a member of the Trotskyist group Militant, spelt out the divisions that were opening up: 'To the weak-hearted, the traitors and the cowards I say: "Get out of our movement. There is no place in it for you."'

He was not alone in reaching such a conclusion. It was in the aftermath of the Wembley conference, and particularly in response to its anti-Europeanism, that the first real stirrings were heard publicly of the split that the newspapers had warned about the previous year. Former cabinet ministers David Owen (who had been booed and hissed when he spoke on defence), Shirley Williams and Bill Rodgers issued a joint statement insisting 'There are some of us who will not accept a choice between socialism and Europe.' The gang of three, as they swiftly became known, followed up with an open letter identifying the key areas of difference between them and emerging party policy: membership of the EEC, membership of NATO, parliamentary democracy and the mixed economy.

Of the gang of three, the leading figure turned out to be Owen, a politician who sometimes gave the impression of having been designed by a computer program. A handsome, articulate hospital registrar who turned to politics, he became foreign secretary at an unusually young age and appeared destined for even higher glories, but somehow he didn't quite seem right in some indefinable way. His attempts at sound bites, for example – forever urging the need to be 'tough but tender' while avoiding 'fudge and mudge' – never resonated and weren't adopted by anyone else.

He seldom made an appearance in which he didn't have to raise his hand to brush back hair that had casually tumbled across his concerned, slightly frowning forehead; it was so familiar a gesture that one would be forgiven for thinking it was deliberate. And his reputation for arrogance, for not being a team-player, would haunt him through his whole career. 'He is always trying to look the part of a future PM and not succeeding and is totally humourless,' was the conclusion of museum director Roy Strong, while Denis Healey was more forthright: 'The good fairies gave the young doctor almost everything: thick dark locks, matinee idol features, a lightning intelligence – unfortunately the bad fairy also made him a shit.'

Shirley Williams, on the other hand, was dishevelled, honest and human, as well as being that rarest of creatures, a genuinely popular politician. And Rodgers, despite having been transport secretary under Callaghan, was virtually unknown to the electorate: renowned and respected as a great organizer by his colleagues, but little seen in public. Together these three represented the next generation of social democrats, a wing of the party that had provided leadership for many years but now found itself fighting rearguard actions against the advance of the left.

Despite this emergence of an opposition to Benn, the moves towards reform continued apace; the month after Wembley, an internal commission of inquiry accepted the principle of the leader being chosen by an electoral college, comprising the parliamentary party, the trade unions, the constituency parties and the affiliated socialist societies. The battle-lines were by now very clearly drawn. The gang of three were the most visible opponents of Benn, but they were by no means without support in the parliamentary ranks, as he noted in July 1980: 'I am fed up with the right-wing leaders of the PLP: they don't agree with the party on defence, on economic policy, on the Common Market, on cruise missiles, on wages, and it can't go on for much longer.'

The problem for those who wanted to see a fight back on behalf of the parliamentarians was that the older leaders of the party's right wing were conspicuous by their inactivity. Callaghan was looking exhausted by his time in government ('a shadow of his former self,' said a *Daily Mail* editorial in 1980), and should have resigned as leader after the election defeat to allow his heir presumptive, Denis Healey, to take over, but he remained 'in the vain hope that some of the bitterness would have drained away'. He also offered a cricketing metaphor, saying that he was staying 'to take the shine off the ball' for Healey, to which the latter was later to respond that he 'not only took the shine off the ball, but ripped away the leather as well'.

Healey was, for the wider electorate, the obvious man to take Labour into the new decade. A member of the Communist Party in his student days, and a veteran of the Second World War (serving with particular distinction in the Anzio landings of 1944), he was now firmly on the social democratic wing of the party. He had been chancellor right through the last govern-ment and was known for his commitment to the redistribution of wealth, as seen in his tax-raising budgets, as well as for his forthright views on national defence. His colleagues saw him as a bruiser who only just stopped short of physical assault when disputes got heated, but for the public the perception was shaped by the portrayal of him by the television impressionist Mike Yarwood: all bristly eyebrows and a tendency to dismiss opponents with the putdown 'Silly Billy'. He never actually said any such thing (except in jokey imitation of Yarwood), but he did have a remarkable ability to produce colourfully original phrases that resonated in the popular imagination; when, for example, he wished to reply to critics of his spending cuts in 1976, denouncing them for failing to face up to reality, it was not enough to say that they were out of their minds, rather: 'They must be out of their tiny Chinese minds.' Quite what that meant, except for its hint of Maoism, was uncertain, but it was striking enough that it stuck.

But after five difficult years at the exchequer, Healey too was evidently in need of a period of recovery after the 1979 election. 'I was glad to take things a little more easily,' he wrote of the period, though he did find time to publish a well received book of photography. Meanwhile the trade union leaders, who traditionally supported the leadership, had been so alienated by Callaghan's attempt in 1978–79 to impose a pay restraint policy against their wishes that, for now at least, they found themselves more inclined to side with the left, who had opposed that policy from the outset; they too were seduced by the idea of having greater control over the parliamentary party.

In the absence of the senior right-wing figures, it was Benn who was making all the running. 'In those exhilarating years Tony seemed to be everywhere,' remembered Ken Livingstone, then the Labour leader of the Greater London Council. 'Audiences of hundreds and often thousands listened as he analyzed, examined, predicted and gave confidence that we could achieve socialism.' Like so many others, he found Benn's energy electrifying: 'Not only did every speech seem to produce a new idea or policy but each one was crafted with a care and a beauty the movement had not heard since the death of Nye Bevan.'

It wasn't a view universally shared. At the annual conference in 1980 Benn delivered one of his best-known speeches ('a competent, "prime ministerial"-type speech,' he thought), calling for an incoming Labour government to push through immediate legislation on the extension of industrial democracy and public ownership, the return of all powers from Europe and – to facilitate these moves – the abolition of the House of Lords, the latter to be achieved by the creation of a thousand new peers, who would then commit mass political suicide. 'This was cloud cuckoo land,' snorted Owen, but the reception in the hall was rapturous. 'He tells them in effect that given the faith and the will-power it will all be quite easy,' reflected Lord Longford, unhappily. 'Those who have served with him in two governments know all too well that things are not remotely like that. They cannot believe he is unaware of his own gross over-simplification. Hence the antagonism amongst the MPs is directed not only against the policies but against the man.' Longford himself had briefly been one of those colleagues, serving with Benn in Harold Wilson's first government, though he was by now a long way out of touch with what had become of the Labour Party.

This question of the personal animosity that Benn sometimes inspired was a major factor in how he was perceived. From his position, it was an irrelevancy – personality counted for much less than The Policies or the issues ('the ishoos' as they were sometimes mockingly known, in a nod to his slightly impeded delivery) – and his view became orthodoxy on the left: 'Personality clashes and the conflict of competing ambitions are a thin mask over the developing economic and social forces to which individual politicians respond,' wrote Livingstone. But there were many supporters who couldn't separate Benn's personal charm and appeal, his ever-enthusiastic optimism, from the message he was conveying. And, on the other side, there were opponents who simply wouldn't accept this reductionist position: 'Politics is about personalities and how we behave as personalities, and whether our actions point to comradeship,' argued the future foreign secretary Jack Straw, who had been elected as a Labour MP in 1979. For the press, which was almost universally hostile, it was Benn's calm, unflustered discussion of the issues that caused ever greater irritation: 'Though his tongue speaks with sweet reason, he has the mind of a ranter and the eyes of a fanatic,' fretted the *Daily Express*.

Some of the same distaste and fear was directed at the ranks of activists (as opposed to those who were simply party members) that could be glimpsed over Benn's shoulder. Long ago Sidney Webb, who had co-written the party's constitution, had claimed that constituency parties 'were frequently unrepresentative groups of nonentities dominated by fanatics, cranks and extremists', and that assessment was primarily why they had never been given power within the movement. Now they were determined to rectify the situation.

'We must not be afraid to challenge openly authoritarianism, dogma or the threat posed by the elitism of the activists,' declared Owen in a speech in January 1980, but for many the problem was simply staying awake long enough to do any such challenging. The new breed of activist tended to be young, without family commitments, often without work commitments, and with an almost insatiable desire to attend political meetings, the longer the better: 'Some of us go to meetings every night of the week,' boasted a delegate to the Labour conference, with a hint of hostility towards those who couldn't keep up. 'We used to have a lot of old people come to meetings,' explained Jim Evans, a Labour councillor in Islington, north London. 'The middle-class student types just laughed at them and mocked them, and so they stopped coming. In the old days we had meetings and then went off to the pub afterwards. These new people started coming in with sandwiches and flasks and the meetings went on until two or three in the morning.' The issue of class was a recurring theme in the complaints of the older Labour figures: 'It almost seemed as if this Seventies generation were bitter that they too had not had the opportunity of suffering real poverty and hardship like we did, but had only been able to study it at university,' scoffed Nottinghamshire MP, Joe Ashton. His colleague Austin Mitchell was similarly scornful, talking about 'power without responsibility, now the prerogative of activists as well as harlots'.

This, the Labour right complained, was the truth of the 'active not passive democracy' that Benn and his supporters wished to introduce into the party: handing over power not to the people, nor even to the mass membership, but to the ultra-committed activists who, like the labourers in the vineyard toiling all day, resented any suggestion that humble members of the electorate, arriving late in the afternoon, should be given equal consideration. To make things worse, the annual subscription to become a member of the Labour Party rose sharply, from £1.20 in 1979 to £5.00 two years later, though of course discounts were available for the unemployed. It was perhaps not entirely surprising that the membership figures fell, though this was also part of a longer trend: having reached a peak of 700,000 in 1972, individual membership had fallen below 300,000 fifteen years later. And as the party machine shrank, so too did its claim to be representative.

That 1980 conference, with his 'thousand peers' speech, was a triumph for Benn, the highest point in his attempt to transform the party. In particular, the conference finally agreed that in future the leader would be chosen not by the MPs, but by an electoral college, though it failed to agree the composition of that body. Instead another special conference at Wembley was to be held, this time in January 1981 (making four national conferences in twenty-one months – a dream come true for activists). But before that could happen, and a new system could be adopted, Callaghan pre-empted the entire process by announcing that he was, eventually, going to resign as leader, allowing one last election to be staged under the old rules.

As far as the general public was concerned, there was just one serious candidature, that of Denis Healey who, according to the opinion polls, enjoyed the support of around 70 per cent of the nation. Tony Benn, the only man with sufficient support inside the party to mount a real challenge on behalf of the activists (a survey of constituency chairmen showed him leading Healey), was effectively precluded from standing, since the left felt that holding the election was inappropriate in the circumstances, and that it would be more legitimate to wait till the new system were in place. There was also the problem that Benn didn't stand a chance of winning over sufficient numbers of MPs to avoid humiliation. Instead Michael Foot, the deputy leader and the veteran hero of the left, even if his reputation had been somewhat tarnished by his enthusiastic support for Callaghan's government, threw his hat in the ring. Two other challengers, John Silkin and Peter Shore, were rapidly disposed of, and in November 1980, Foot beat Healey in the final ballot by a margin of 139 votes to 129. So unexpected was the result that the *Guardian* journalists Simon Hoggart and David Leigh, who were busily writing a biography of Healey in the sure and certain hope of his election, suddenly had to shift to writing one of Foot instead.

The surprise was occasioned partly because Foot was self-evidently not the real choice of the MPs (it was assumed they had voted for the left option in the hope of a quiet life), partly because he was the least popular candidate amongst the wider public, and partly because he had been such a deter-mined backbencher for so long – he had only accepted a frontbench job after nearly thirty years in the Commons. But mostly Foot's elevation was unexpected because he simply didn't look like a leader for the modern world; he was, in the words of novelist Mark Lawson, 'an elderly Byron enthusiast whose barber and tailor apparently cared little for the new religion of media beauty'. In his day he had been a fine journalist and an accomplished orator, but that day was a long way distant by now, and apart from romantic nostalgia, it wasn't entirely clear what his appeal to the electorate was supposed to be. He was a year younger than Callaghan, but looked considerably older, and his image was hardly helped when, two days after his election, he fell down some stairs in the Commons and broke his ankle, ensuring that his first week as leader ended with him appearing on crutches at prime minister's questions. Nor was his authority enhanced by a poll that month demonstrating the public's belief that Benn was as powerful a figure in the country as was Geoffrey Howe, the chancellor of the exchequer: Foot might have been the leader, but people suspected the presence of a back-seat driver.

And if the danger from the left were not sufficient, there was also to the right of him the lurking threat of Roy Jenkins. A distinguished former home secretary and chancellor, and hero of the liberal left for his social reforms in the 1960s, Jenkins had left parliament in 1977 to become president of the European Commission, a job he was scheduled to leave in January 1981. In anticipation of his return to Britain, he began to make his considerable presence felt, calling in two key speeches for the introduction of proportional representation and for the creation of a radical centre party, even while admitting that such a venture might be a disaster. 'The experimental plane may well finish up a few fields from the end of the runway,' he explained, using an image aimed at capturing the imagination of cartoonists. 'But the reverse could occur and the experimental plane could soar in the sky.' It was a courageous and risky strategy, but it was perhaps his only real way back from Europe, as Jim Hacker jokingly pointed out in the sitcom *Yes, Minister* when rejecting the idea of becoming an EEC commissioner: 'It's curtains as far as British politics is concerned. It's worse than a peerage. Absolute failure, total failure. You're reduced to forming a new party if you ever want to get back.'

Hacker wasn't the only one to mock. Jenkins's inability to pronounce the letter 'r' led to him being almost universally known as Woy, while his fondness for good wine and his grand manner, seemingly so far removed from his origins in a South Wales mining family, made him an easy target for ridicule. Fleet Street's finest duly obliged ('a much loved gracious figure who is to the liberal classes what the Queen Mother is to the rest of us,' wrote Frank Johnson), while he was known in European circles as Le Roi Jean Quinze, but perhaps the most authoritative summary came from Harold Wilson: 'He was born old.' Jenkins had long been a figure of real weight and experience, and the idea that the prince over the water might join forces with the gang of three brought a new dimension to the threat they presented. Or, from another perspective, it would simply add the March Hare to complete the cast of the Mad Hatter's Tea Party that had been assembled by Owen.

Even with Benn and Jenkins loitering in the wings, Foot's unlikely promotion from understudy to leading player was not immediately seen as being a completely hopeless cause. He had inherited a party that felt like it might split at any moment, but he had at least done so when the prime minister was so unpopular that many were prepared willingly to suspend their disbelief. 'There has always been something rather engaging about this character with his shabby clothes and his unkempt (though recently trimmed) hair. Foot is a kindly, friendly man.' That was the perhaps surprising verdict of the *Sun*, which went on to promise: 'If he demonstrates his firm resolve to keep the Labour Party on the path of parliamentary democracy; if he makes clear his intention to turn it once more into a respectable and responsible force in politics; then he will find the *Sun* in his corner.' (It was a considerably more enthusiastic greeting than Ronald Reagan had received in the paper on being elected US president the previous week: 'He is not an inspiring figure.')

When therefore the Labour tribes gathered at Wembley in January 1981, the last time that many would meet in allegedly fraternal circumstances, it was under a new leader, albeit one who followed Callaghan's recent example and made no attempt to exert any leadership. The atmosphere was described by Lord Longford: 'The flavour of the conference was more assertively proletarian even than usual. Many, perhaps half, of the delegates could not have passed as working class at any time in their adult lives. Yet whenever the proletarian note was struck, it was the winner.' There was an element of 'he would say that, wouldn't he?' about his observations, but there was too more than a hint of truth.

The debate was essentially over the composition of the electoral college, though first the delegates had to dismiss the right's call for a simple one-member, one-vote ballot of the party. David Owen pointed out that no other socialist party in Europe was dominated by the block vote of trades unions in the same way that Labour was, and argued that 'to allow the block vote to choose the future prime minister is an outrage. It is a disgrace and this conference ought not to accept it.' The system of the block vote, in which a union delegation cast the agglomerated votes of all their members who had paid the political levy to the Labour Party (or rather an approximation of that number of members, since the accounting system was far from perfect), had been attracting considerable hostility ever since union leaders had begun to side on a regular basis with the left against the parliamentary leadership. It was clearly an undemocratic nonsense, with the millions of union votes cast easily outweighing those of the constituency membership, let alone those of the MPs, who existed in this context only as individual members, and its sheer inefficiency was amply on display at Wembley.

The proposal that finally won the day called for the votes in the electoral college to be split between unions, MPs and constituency parties in the proportion of 40-30-30. This was the favoured formula of the left, but its success was the result not of conspiracy or lobbying but of pure cock-up, winning through only because the delegation from the engineering union, the AUEW, failed to vote for the option that they – and the leadership – favoured, giving 50 per cent to the MPs, with the remainder split between unions and constituencies. The fact that the unions ended up with the largest proportion of the votes, but only because they themselves had made such a pig's ear of the process, did little to inspire confidence in the future operation of the much-vaunted college.

The conference had been held on a Saturday. On the Sunday the gang of four (as Owen, Williams and Rodgers, now joined by Jenkins, had become known) stole the media headlines by issuing what was instantly nicknamed the Limehouse Declaration, since it was first proclaimed at Owen's house in London's Docklands. 'The calamitous outcome of the Labour Party Wembley conference demands a new start in British politics,' it opened, and it concluded: 'We recognize that for those people who have given much of their lives to the Labour Party, the choice that lies ahead will be deeply painful. But we believe that the need for a realignment of British politics must now be faced.' In between came a statement of broad principles – a mixed economy, membership of the EEC and of NATO, decentralized decision-making, egalitarianism and the elimination of poverty – none of which was particularly new.

But then novelty was not really a requirement. The call for a new party (albeit in the thinly disguised, and obviously temporary, form of a body called the Council for Social Democracy) was intended to appeal first and foremost to disaffected Labour members, seeking an honourable way out of a party they feared had been taken over by extremists. What was needed was not new policies, but an unashamed reclaiming of the past, the promise of, as academic Ralf Dahrendorf put it, 'a better yesterday'. The claim was that the social democrats had not changed, it was the Labour Party. When Owen was urged to replicate Hugh Gaitskell's 1960 determination to 'fight and fight and fight again to save the party we love', he shrugged: 'It also needs to be said that you can compromise and compromise and compromise again and destroy the party you love.'

The Limehouse Declaration was subsequently published as an advert in the *Guardian*, accompanied by a list of a hundred supporters, including academics, ex-cabinet ministers, figures from the arts and – the sole trade union leader – Frank Chapple of the electricians. That the *Guardian* was the chosen vehicle for the advert was no accident; it was the one paper that was most easily identified with the initiative, though there were discussions at a senior level at the *Daily Mirror* about whether to back the venture, and Rupert Murdoch was later to tell Andrew Neil, his newly appointed editor of the *Sunday Times*, that 'I could tolerate it supporting the SDP' if Neil so wished (he didn't). Even *The Times* in an unexpected leader, written by departing editor William Rees-Mogg, offered some endorsement, with the suggestion that Shirley Williams would make a fine prime minister. The praise here was tempered by the paper's view of her as a 'somewhat indecisive woman, of middling intellectual attainments and mistaken views', but it did celebrate her innate courtesy and her ability to communicate: 'Mrs Williams talks to the British people in their own accents, sometimes muddled, often courageous, always human and always kind.' Other parts of the media were also encouraging, particularly since it was Labour that was likely to suffer from the birth of a new centre-left party.

Finally, two months after Wembley, the party itself was launched with thirteen MPs, though neither Jenkins nor Williams was at that stage in the Commons. It was christened the Social Democratic Party, the other founder-members having rejected Jenkins's suggestions that it be called the Democrats or the Radicals (the latter would surely have been a mistake, given his speech impediment). The launch itself was a triumph of marketing, as indeed it needed to be since there were as yet no policies to trumpet. Adverts appeared under the slogan 'The SDP – the country's waited long enough', and asked would-be members to phone in with their credit cards, a novelty at the time. (Unlike Labour, there wasn't a fixed subscription, but there was a suggested donation of nine pounds.) Thousands of applicants responded instantly, bearing out the confident predictions made the previous year by psephologists Ivor Crewe and Anthony King – for the gang of three had done their homework – about the party's prospects. Alongside ex-Labour members, there were large numbers of people who had previously not been a member of any political party, but who were now filled with enthusiasm and were, in a strange way, passionate about a party that seemed almost designed not to arouse passion. Repelled in equal part by what was perceived to be the sheer violence of the rival Thatcherite and Bennite remedies for the nation's woes, the early adherents of the SDP sensed that this was a new dawn for decency, a crusade for common sense. 'I refuse to acknowledge class barriers,' proclaimed Barry (Timothy Spall) in *Auf Wiedersehen, Pet*. 'That's the tragedy of this country, you know, the bloody polarization of the classes. That's why I joined the SDP, you know, mate – it's the party of the future, that is.'

For the more cynical, the impression was that it was all a bit too nice, the political equivalent of comfort food, albeit washed down with an agreeable Burgundy. The Peter Simple column in the *Daily Telegraph*, never very enthusiastic about anything that bore the taint of liberalism, suggested a *Make Your Own Centre Party* book: 'It lists the basic essentials: a good supply of cardboard in various thicknesses, glue, cold rice pudding (see your local cold rice pudding stockist), moderation and, most important of all, meaningless verbiage.' On television *Not the Nine O'Clock News* was soon featuring a parody of an SDP party political broadcast with Rowan Atkinson reading a fairytale as though on *Jackanory*, while in reality one of *Jackanory*'s favourite presenters wasn't much impressed, Kenneth Williams deciding that 'they're all *worthy* one feels, but terribly *dull*.' (In his memoirs Owen was to echo that verdict: 'Our policy development in those early days can best be described as worthy.') At a time when politics was becoming increasingly polarized, the SDP's progress down the middle of the road did run the risk of being a little boring; its publication on nuclear arms policy was titled *Negotiate and Survive* and may well have contained perfectly sensible proposals, but it lacked both the make-do-and-mend optimism of the official pamphlet, *Protect and Survive*, from which it took its title, and the campaigning spirit of E.P. Thompson's anti-nuclear riposte, *Protest and Survive*.

On a personal level, as the Limehouse Declaration had said, the emergence of the SDP from within Labour was for many a 'deeply painful' experience, though much more so for those who left than for those who remained. 'The sadness was mainly manufactured,' wrote Austin Mitchell, who might have been, but wasn't, tempted to jump ship. 'The break was not a great party split like 1931 but a public relations event. Real feelings were deader. The mood was one of inevitability, as if a formal decision long taken was merely being ratified.' Even so, he experienced the bitterness that comes with civil war as members of his own constituency party defected. The situation was covered in Sue Townsend's fictional chronicle of the era, *The Secret Diary of Adrian Mole, Aged 13¾*, as the diarist finds trouble at his girlfriend's house: 'Pandora's parents have had a massive row. They are sleeping in separate bedrooms. Pandora's mother has joined the SDP and Pandora's father is staying loyal to the Labour Party.' The following day he reveals in awe: 'Pandora's father has come out of the closet and admitted that he is a Bennite.' As Mole reflects, 'It is a sad day when families are split asunder by politics.'

The fact that it was Pandora's and not Adrian's family who were thus divided indicated perhaps the greatest of the SDP's problems. As *Sun* columnist Jon Akass, pointed out: 'the SDP remains a party that is visibly middle class. They are a posh lot. They can argue that they are not posh at all, that they have impeccable working-class origins, but they are betrayed by the clothes they stand in and by their accents.' Party politics in Britain had always had their roots in cohesive class-blocks, and the omens were not good for parties that bucked the trend.

Even so, the initial success of the venture was extraordinary. Opinion polls gave the SDP, at first alone and then in combination with the Liberal Party (the two parties became known as the SDP-Liberal Alliance or, more commonly, the Alliance), consistently strong leads right through 1981. Indeed the problem became one of managing expectations at a time of astonishing performances in a string of parliamentary by-elections. The first came in July in the rock-solid Labour seat of Warrington (even in the disastrous year of 1979 the party had scored over 60 per cent of the vote) and was tailor-made for Williams, but her inexplicable decision not to enter the contest left an opening for Jenkins, who came a narrow second and hugely enhanced his reputation – now not merely a thinker, but a fighter. If the result were repeated across the country, predicted an overheated BBC computer, there would be a Liberal/SDP government with 501 seats in the House of Commons, while Labour would be reduced to 113 MPs and there would be just one Tory remaining. In November Williams made her move, taking nearly half the vote in a by-election in Crosby, a safe Tory seat, and returning to the Commons in triumph. In between Warrington and Crosby came Croydon North-West, where the local Liberals insisted on fielding their own candidate, and still saw the unknown Bill Pitt win on a swing of 29.5 per cent. And then, finally, in March 1982 Jenkins won at the second attempt, becoming MP for Glasgow Hillhead.

So febrile and heated had the times become that at the Liberal assembly in Llandudno in the autumn of 1981, the party's leader David Steel ended his speech with a peroration that he never quite lived down: 'I have the good fortune to be the first Liberal leader for over half a century who is able to say to you at the end of our annual assembly: go back to your constituencies and prepare for government!' As Owen noted drily in his memoirs: 'The Llandudno air was so intoxicating that not even the hardened pressmen at the conference laughed.' Unfortunately for the Liberals, Not the Nine O'Clock News did laugh, replaying the speech but cutting from Steel, as the applause and cheering mounted, to a shot of massed ranks of gurgling toddlers, as though they were his audience.

Owen's sarcasm hints at the tensions that lay behind the scenes as the SDP built ever-closer links with the Liberals, but at the time, little of this was in the public domain, remaining backstage as the poll triumphs continued. By June 1982 the SDP in the Commons had risen to an all-time high of thirty MPs, with a steady stream of defectors having swollen the ranks, some of them those threatened with deselection by their constituency parties. David Pinner's novel *There'll Always Be an England* caught something of the pressures of the period, with a Labour MP under attack from a Trotskyist activist in his local party and toying with the idea of leaving, even though he claimed to understand the motivations of his opponents: 'communism only gains control over the minds of the young if the society they live in is diseased – as our society is. For wherever there is inequality, people will search for extreme solutions. So all these budding Trots and Marxist-Leninists are only the symptom of the disease.'

There were, though, nagging worries about the SDP's prospects, primarily the fact that few of the Labour converts were frontline politicians – Bryan Magee and George Cunningham were well respected figures, but in terms of public standing they could hardly claim to rank alongside, say, Roy Hattersley or Merlyn Rees, let alone Callaghan and Healey. There was too the failure to make inroads into the government benches: Christopher Brocklebank-Fowler was a founder member of the new party, becoming the first Conservative MP to cross the floor in 75 years, but not one of his colleagues followed him, despite his own predictions that 'up to six' Tory MPs would do so. Had the SDP been able to attract both Hattersley and perhaps Peter Walker, the longer-term outlook would have been much more positive.

As the Alliance bandwagon moved smoothly up through the gears, Labour renewed its squabbling in the slow lane, this time over who should occupy the seat next to the driver. After the Wembley conference, the *Daily Mirror* had told its readers: 'Another loser was Denis Healey. He will surely be challenged for his post as deputy leader. And under the new formula he will probably be defeated.' On 1 April 1981 (the detail of it being April Fool's Day didn't go unnoticed by the media) Tony Benn duly announced that he would indeed be standing against Healey for the deputy leadership. 'The timing could not be more unhappy from Labour's point of view,' noted the *Daily* Mail, trying hard to keep itself from chortling, as it pointed out that the first opinion poll since the launch of SDP showed the new party in the lead.

The deputy leadership of the Labour Party had never been much of a job. It gave the incumbent a seat on the NEC, but little else, even in terms of status, and although Clement Attlee and Michael Foot went on to become leader, there had been many more who had never made the transition: Nye Bevan, George Brown and Roy Jenkins amongst them. Healey had become the deputy pretty much by default (he quoted an American vice-president saying the job was worth nothing more than 'a pitcherfull of warm spit'), but now found himself engaged in a struggle for the soul and future of the party, so symbolic were the stakes being played for. Healey himself predicted that a victory for Benn would cause half the shadow cabinet to resign and several unions to disaffiliate from the party, a not implausible scenario. It was hard to dispute Benn's argument that there was little point in having created the electoral college if it was never to be used, but the timing and manner of the election did little for the party's standing amongst the public.

The campaign was, to start with, ridiculously long – nearly six months – and its conduct was hardly an advertisement for a democratic party aspiring to be the government of the country. The reception accorded to Healey at mass meetings, in particular a rally against unemployment in Birmingham towards the end of the campaign, was shameful, with him being so heavily barracked that he was unable to speak. 'The orgy of intolerance must have cost Labour a million votes,' wrote Roy Hattersley, adding that the behaviour of Benn supporters who had drifted in from outside the party 'would not have been out of place at a Nuremburg rally'. Foot was similarly scathing, saying it was 'a piece of planned hooliganism, a disgrace to the traditions of free speech for which the Labour movement has always stood.' The presence of television news cameras to capture the event only exacerbated the issue.

Hattersley's point about Benn's campaign attracting support from beyond the party was perfectly correct. The myriad far left groups, now overwhelmingly Trotskyist, had become ever more visible during the leftward drift of Labour, and for the most part they came together to throw what weight they had behind Benn, despite a long tradition of reserving their greatest venom for each other (as caricatured in the Monty Python film *Life of Brian*, where the leader of the People's Front of Judea explains that 'the only people we hate more than the Romans are the fucking Judean People's Front'). Even those who stood outside the Labour Party saw a victory for Benn as a victory for the left more generally and thus a step towards a socialist Britain.

Those six months also saw a severe ratcheting up of the media rhetoric against Benn, and nowhere more so than in the pages of the country's most popular newspaper, the *Sun*. 'If he wins, then it's goodbye to the Labour Party we have known for more than 80 years,' ran one report. 'A cross on the ballot for a party which has Benn waiting in the wings for its top job is a cross for the bleak and cold regimes of Eastern Europe and for a government on their model,' claimed another. And all of it was encapsulated in the headline: MR BENN — IS HE MAD OR A KILLER? When the paper's political editor, Walter Terry, was challenged by the journalist Mark Hollingsworth on whether he really believed Benn was mad, he was less equivocal: 'Yes, I think Benn is mad and a lot of Labour people agree with me.' He was correct in at least the second half of his statement, for it was not just the press that was making the running; Denis Healey too was happy to join in, suggesting that Benn was in favour of the 'sort of People's Democracy the Russians set up in Eastern Europe after the war'. None of it was very edifying.

Two left-wing comedy writers were later to record their impressions of the campaign. From inside the party, John O'Farrell saw it as an adolescent disorder: 'The Labour Party rank and file regarded its leadership in the same way that I regarded my parents, and would not miss an opportunity to embarrass them.' From outside, Mark Steel, a member of the Socialist Workers Party, was even more sceptical, commenting on the union block votes cast in favour of Benn: 'If those figures had represented the real level of support for Benn's ideas, what an exciting time it would have been. But whenever there was a ballot amongst all union members, it went overwhelmingly to Healey. In opinion polls, Healey led Benn by 72 per cent to 20 per cent.'

Steel was right to point to the lack of any widespread support for Benn. For while he had the overwhelming endorsement of the activists, these were by definition a small and self-appointed group, not dissimilar to the Elect in Calvinism. It would have been more impressive if Benn could similarly attract the support of rank-and-file trade unionists, but here the evidence was less convincing: ballots in unions representing public sector (NUPE), print (NATSOPA) and post office (POEU) workers all went in favour of Healey. So too did a poll of the Transport and General Workers Union, the largest of the block votes, with one executive officer suggesting that perhaps personalities did matter after all: 'The fact is that many of our members simply don't like the way Mr Benn has campaigned. He has turned the Labour Party upside down in order to get himself elected deputy leader. Many of our members have reacted to that, not because they don't like his policies.' A significant feature in those unions who did ballot their members (there was no requirement so to do) was that women were less likely to support Benn than were men.

When the election was held at the conference in September 1981, the TGWU actually backed John Silkin, the doomed third candidate, in the initial ballot, before then switching its vote to Benn. It wasn't quite enough, and Healey won the second and final ballot by a margin of just under 1 per cent ('by an eyebrow,' he said, in reference to the bushy growths that had formed the basis of Mike Yarwood's impression of him for so many years). The crucial factor, it was quickly agreed, was the behaviour of a handful of left MPs who had voted for Silkin and then abstained on the second ballot. And chief amongst them was Neil Kinnock, the coming man in the next generation who had, some felt, a vested interest in marginalizing Benn to ensure his own advance. The actions of those MPs were bitterly denounced by others on the left ('traitors' snapped Margaret Beckett, who would herself one day become deputy leader), and Kinnock was allegedly assaulted by one of Benn's supporters, though he managed to find a suitable quip for the whole experience: 'It's been a hell of a year, this past week.'

Benn was, as ever, full of positive thinking: 'It was a victory because from the very beginning right through to the end — and we are nowhere near the end — we have won the argument,' he told a meeting that evening. He even presented an optimistic face to his diary, but deep down he must have known that he was deluding himself. And, as the tide began to turn against him in the party, he was to suffer a rare loss of composure. When nine MPs who had voted for Healey subsequently defected to the SDP, he had a moment of madness and announced to the press that he was now the de facto deputy leader of the party. He had to be reminded of his own dictum by a left-wing colleague, Dennis Skinner: 'we are concerned with policy on behalf of the people we represent, and it is not about individuals.' In any event, it wasn't much of an argument; by the same token, Healey could now claim to be leader, since several future defectors had allegedly voted for Foot the previous year in an attempt to scupper the party's fortunes. (So expected was this tactic, even at the time, that David Owen and Bill Rodgers had taken care to show their completed ballot papers to others to prove that they'd voted honourably for Healey.)

Although the deputy leadership election caught all the coverage, the 1981 conference also saw some other straws in the wind. The left won a vote in support of unilateral nuclear disarmament, but was defeated on a motion to withdraw from NATO, and lost several key seats on the NEC to right-wingers. It was even reported that moves were afoot to remove Benn from his powerful position as chair of the NEC home policy committee, though in the event he was to remain for another year. Most significantly, the party enjoyed an immediate poll boost as a reward for making the right decision about the deputy leader; a survey for Thames TV showed Labour on 36 per cent, the Tories on 30 per cent, and the Alliance starting to fade on 29 per cent. The possibility of a serious recovery was now on the cards, if only Labour could avoid any further self-inflicted wounds. Unfortunately, it couldn't.

Part of the problem was Foot's inability to handle public relations. At a trivial, but sadly memorable, level this was manifest in his appearance at the Cenotaph on Remembrance Sunday in November 1981, where the leaders of the main political parties were to lay wreaths. As they left for the ceremony, David Steel said to Foot, 'You're not going to wear that coat, are you?' and Foot replied, 'What's wrong with it? My wife just bought it last week.' Indeed, there was nothing inherently wrong with the garment ('That's a smart sensible coat for a day like this,' the Queen Mother told him), but it was incongruous in the context of the state's most solemn occasion, and particularly so when the media decided to say he was wearing a donkey jacket. Actually it was a dark blue-green overcoat, more akin to a duffle-coat than to a donkey jacket, but the terminology stuck, as did the alleged slight to the nation's war dead. In an outbreak of mockery from which Foot never recovered, Fleet Street nicknamed him Worzel Gummidge, after the scarecrow played by Jon Pertwee in a popular children's television series, and the *Daily Mail* ran a feature titled DRESS YOUR OWN MICHAEL FOOT, which included a cut-out paper doll of the Labour leader, complete with scruffy clothes, CND badge and flat cap. Of such things were politics now made, though Foot was unable to see why anyone cared. Even when his wife, Jill Craigie, persuaded him to have a haircut and buy a new suit, he was still capable of inadvertently under-mining her efforts; 'I sat next to him on the front bench,' recalled Austin Mitchell, 'and looked down to see odd socks.'

Shortly after the donkey jacket episode, the BBC screened an adaptation of John le Carré's spy novel *Smiley's People*, in which George Smiley (played by Alec Guinness) comes out of retirement to deal with one last case of an agent who has been found shot dead. And as Smiley stumbled frailly round Hampstead Heath, where the killing occurred, trying to find clues that will make sense of what has happened to his world, many viewers couldn't help but be reminded of Foot, the most famous real-life denizen of the Heath. When one of the young turks who have replaced Smiley at the Circus suggests that the dead man was 'potty', George snaps back: 'He was loyal and honourable. In a shifting world, he held fast. So, yes, maybe he was potty.' Like Smiley, Foot looked like a leftover from another age, a time when presentation meant nothing and integrity everything. In itself, that was an admirable attribute, and one of the key reasons why he was so cherished within the party, even if it didn't play very well in the media. Much worse tended to result when he decided to assert his authority, almost invariably picking the wrong issue and the wrong approach.

In December 1981 James Wellbeloved, a former Labour MP who had defected to the SDP, asked Margaret Thatcher during prime minister's questions about the adoption by Bermondsey Labour Party of the hitherto unknown Peter Tatchell as its parliamentary candidate. To the surprise of both sides of the House, Foot seized the opportunity to make his own statement: 'The individual concerned is not an endorsed member of the Labour Party and, so far as I am concerned, never will be endorsed.' The phrasing was puzzling – Tatchell clearly *was* a member of the party – and led some to speculate that Foot had got confused with either Peter Taaffe or Tariq Ali, two veteran figures of the revolutionary left, but he later clarified that he had meant to say 'candidate' not 'member'. It also emerged later that he had been given notice the day before of Wellbeloved's intended question, thus removing the possibility that it was all off-the-cuff and of no great significance.

Tatchell's offence had been an article in the left journal *London Labour Briefing*, in which he had argued: 'We must look to new, more militant forms of extra-parliamentary opposition which involve mass popular participation and challenge the government's right to rule.' When asked to elaborate, he commented, 'I am referring to mass peaceful protest, such as the People's March for Jobs,' but that reassurance was evidently insufficient for Foot: 'Parliamentary democracy is at stake,' he warned Labour MPs, in a characteristically wild exaggeration. 'There can be no wavering on that.'

It was hard to see quite what all the fuss was about. Foot had himself addressed the March for Jobs (an unsuccessful attempt to reignite the fire of the 1930s hunger marches), the TUC's day of action had been overtly political, and in April 1981 a hundred Labour MPs had abandoned the Commons chamber to stage a demonstration outside the department of employment. Extra-parliamentary activity had always been a strong feature of the Labour Party, and Tatchell was not noticeably upping the ante. Nor, however, was he the kind of candidate with whom much of the old Labour Party felt instinctive sympathy; a young sociology graduate who had left Australia to avoid conscription, he had been active in campaigning for gay rights, on women's issues and against the Vietnamese War. Simply having written his article in *London Labour Briefing*, a journal associated with Ken Livingstone's trendy new left that now controlled the Greater London Council, was sufficient to damn him in many people's eyes, including those of Bob Mellish, the sitting MP for Bermondsey.

The Bermondsey party was typical of many constituency branches in places where Labour had been in power for decades. At its peak it could claim over 3,000 members, but that had been in the 1930s; by the time Tatchell joined, membership had fallen to under 400, and there was growing impatience with Mellish, who had served as an MP since 1946 and was due to retire. The fact that he had accepted a job on the London Docklands Development Corporation, a body whose very existence the Labour Party opposed, did him no favours, and the split locally was between Mellish and the activists, a microcosm of the wider struggles in the party, with Tatchell a popular and well supported figure. But Foot's intervention – effectively turning the issue into a vote of confidence in his leadership – was sufficient to persuade the NEC to overturn Tatchell's candidature: it would be 'an electoral disaster', Foot said, in what could only be described as a self-fulfilling prophecy. When Mellish subsequently left the party, threatening to resign as an MP and force a by-election if Tatchell was re-selected in a new vote, and then when Tatchell was indeed duly re-selected as the candidate, Foot was obliged to climb down, having damaged his already fragile authority still further by his wavering, and having done everything he could to ensure that the coming by-election would be as difficult as possible for Labour.

Or perhaps not quite everything yet. The day before the by-election, in March 1983, the NEC spent the whole day expelling from the party five members of the editorial board of the Trotskyist newspaper *Militant*. Nobody who knew anything about the British left could possibly have mistaken Tatchell for a Trotskyist, but that hadn't stopped Fleet Street from bracketing him with Militant, and the foolishness of giving hostile newspapers an opportunity to run stories about Labour extremism on the day of a by-election was a token of the sheer incompetence being displayed by the party's leadership.

And the papers were indeed hostile, to an unprecedented degree. The attacks that Benn had endured in 1981 were now visited upon 'Red Pete', though this time with a virulently anti-gay angle. Since Tatchell was not at this stage publicly out as a homosexual, and no concrete evidence of his sexuality could be found, the stories were delivered with sufficient innuendo to avoid libel actions, while leaving readers in no doubt about their subtext: he was 'a rather exotic Australian canary who sings some odd songs,' said the *Daily Express*, knowingly. At its most innocuous this was manifested in the regular press descriptions of his clothing, with the implication that only a homosexual would be so fastidious about his wardrobe: he had 'a male model's flair with clothes,' nudged the *Daily Mail*, while the *Daily Telegraph* pointed to his 'wide leather belt atop trendy cord jeans and two-tone wine and beige laced shoes.' Coming from the same sources that had made an issue of Foot's scruffiness, this focus on Tatchell's neat attire suggested that those on the left were in something of a no-win situation.

Following fifteen months of abject coverage, much of it to the discredit of Fleet Street and all of it stemming from Foot's original outburst in parliament, the by-election result was worse even than could have been expected. The Liberal candidate, Simon Hughes, representing the Alliance, won on a 50 per cent swing, though even he was later to apologize for the sheer nastiness of the campaign against Tatchell.

Coming so soon before an expected general election, the result gave a boost at a crucial moment to the Alliance parties, whose fortunes had been in decline. And taking a working-class London seat from Labour went some way towards countering the mocking claims that the Alliance was a middle-class hobbyhorse. Other indications, however, simply reinforced that prejudice. For the 1983 general election, the twinned parties ran a series of open meetings under the title Ask the Alliance, demonstrating little save that they had the support of the cream of up-market quiz-show hosts: the meetings were chaired by Bamber Gascoigne from *University Challenge*, Magnus Magnusson from *Mastermind* and Steve Race from *My Music*, together with Ludovic Kennedy of the highbrow review show *Did You See?* It seemed something approaching parody when the prominent SDP member Richard Attenborough, having just directed the 1982 film *Gandhi*, made the outlandish claim that, had the opportunity only been available to him, the Mahatma would surely have voted SDP. (In the 1987 election the *Sun* picked up on this concept and employed a medium to reveal the voting intentions of other historical figures: Henry VIII and Boadicea went Tory, Stalin was a Labour supporter, while Keir Hardie had defected in death to the SDP. Genghis Khan, though, was a 'don't know'.)

Bermondsey was just about the last chance for Michael Foot's Labour to indulge the addiction to political self-harm that had characterized the party since the 1979 election. With a second national defeat now inevitable, rival factions began to seek out who might be held to account for the coming catastrophe. The left blamed a pusillanimous leadership, while the right blamed the left, and, though both sides were agreed that the SDP were largely responsible for keeping Thatcher in power, there was no agreement over who was responsible for their emergence. ('He's created the SDP single-handed,' said Kinnock of Benn.)

But if blame were to be apportioned, it should surely have been laid at the door of the party's MPs. Given one last opportunity in November 1980 to choose a leader, they threw it away in panic, turning their collective back on Denis Healey, the one man who could have led them to victory, and opting instead for the candidate who they thought their constituency activists would prefer, Michael Foot. Their fear was that if Healey won, he would be challenged under the new rules by Benn, and a bloody civil war would ensue. That, of course, is precisely what happened, except that it was the deputy leadership that was at stake; the conflict that haunted the MPs' dreams could scarcely have been more unpleasant. And with Healey at the helm, it is unlikely that the SDP would have come into existence. That fact, together with the likelihood that Healey would have fought harder to get a larger share of the electoral college reserved for MPs, would almost certainly have ensured a defeat for Benn, the continuing dominance of the polls by Labour, and a probable victory for a Healey-led party at the next general election. (Norman Tebbit admitted that private polling for the Conservatives showed that the situation could have been retrieved as late as 1983: 'If Healey had been the leader or if he were to replace Foot before a 1984 election it would be touch and go'.) Even many on the left were to later recognize the mistake they'd made; Eric Heffer, the self-proclaimed proletarian MP for Liverpool Walton, who voted for Foot 'on an interim basis until the new leadership electoral college was in being when Tony Benn could stand', was later to exclaim: 'What fools we were not to vote for Denis!'

But the Parliamentary Labour Party had a crisis of self-confidence that led to political paralysis. Seeking to drift with the tide, it simply sank. It didn't believe in the party, it didn't believe in its leader, it didn't even believe in itself. Ken Livingstone recorded a member of the shadow cabinet telling him, 'If I woke up tomorrow and found we had won the election, I'd leave the country.' This state of funk wasn't simply attributable to the fear of being deselected, for it applied equally to Labour members in the Lords: 'Collectively we are so terrified of raising our heads above the parapet, for fear of unspecified retribution,' lamented Lord Longford in 1981. Normally, when threatened with losing their seats, MPs tend to look at changing their leader, but the disaster of 1979 had been so bad, and the subsequent events so horrible, that few believed it could get any worse. It could, and it did.

3
Alternatives

RICK: Finally, after years of stagnation, the TV people have
woken up to the need for locally based minority
programmes, made by amateurs, of interest to about two
or three people.
Rik Mayall, Lise Mayer and Ben Elton, *The Young Ones* (1982)

Make the most of every day,
don't let hard times stand in your way.
Give a wham, give a bam, but don't give a damn,
'cos the benefit gang are gonna pay.
Wham!, 'Wham Rap!' (1982)

Even our protests were hopeless – neat little marches
down Blind Alley.
Derek Jarman, *The Last of England* (1987)

In April 1979 the *Radio Times* listed the first appearance of a new satirical
comedy show on BBC2 entitled *Not the Nine O'Clock News*, starring seven
virtually unknown performers. Anyone tuning in, however, would have
been disappointed, for the previous week the House of Commons had
recorded a vote of no confidence in the government, a general election had
been called, and the BBC had pulled the programme in the interests of
avoiding political controversy. It was to take another seven months before
the show finally made it to the screen. When it did, the cast had been
slimmed down and now featured Rowan Atkinson, Pamela Stephenson,
Mel Smith and Chris Langham (for the second and subsequent series,
Langham was replaced by Griff Rhys Jones). The result was the most
celebrated and popular cult comedy show since *Monty Python's Flying
Circus*, indeed considerably more popular than that, for a compilation
screened on BBC1 at Christmas 1980 attracted eighteen million viewers,
while three records of highlights from the series spent a year between them
in the album charts.

It had been five years since the last series of *Monty Python* and, with the exception of the solo projects by the members of the team, the show had left little trace on the television schedules. Furthermore the wave of Oxbridge graduates who had made that programme – in addition to the slapstick of *The Goodies* and the satire of *That Was the Week That Was*, creating a distinctive strand of comedy in the 1960s and early 1970s – seemed to have come to an end with the emergence from Cambridge of Graeme Garden in 1964. The next generation of students chose more orthodox career paths and didn't follow them into comedy, and it began to look as though the supply of new talent from the universities had dried up.

In the absence of such graduates, the comedy on television towards the end of the 1970s had reverted to type and looked little changed from a decade earlier. The few sketch shows that existed, such as *The Two Ronnies*, which ran for fifteen years right up to 1986, were – like the variety shows of Tommy Cooper and Morecambe and Wise – essentially part of the light entertainment tradition, with song-and-dance routines, musical guests and nothing more offensive than saucy postcard innuendo. The other comedy staple was the family-flavoured sitcom, including most typically *Happy Ever After* (1974), with Terry Scott and June Whitfield as suburban couple Terry and June Fletcher. This was perfectly agreeable fare but so limited that its chief writer John Chapman eventually walked out, complaining that there were no new permutations to be wrung out of the format; the BBC, reluctant to lose such a fine property, rebranded the show as *Terry and June* (1979), gave the couple a new surname – Medford – and ran it for another nine series, maintaining a consistent audience of over ten million viewers.

There was, however, a clear public appetite for an alternative, demonstrated by the enthusiasm with which a small group of new comedians were received in certain quarters. Jasper Carrott, Mike Harding, Max Boyce and Billy Connolly all came from the unlikely background of folk-clubs, broke through to a national audience through hit records rather than television – though all but Connolly were rewarded with their own television series in the late 1970s – and were of a similar age (Harding, Carrott and Boyce were born within twelve months of each other). More importantly, they departed from the traditional stand-up format of simply telling jokes. Instead, drawing on their working-class origins outside London, there was a new emphasis on story-telling, on observational humour, on a much more individualist style of delivery that prefigured some of what was to come. Popular though these comedians were, however, there was little sense of their emergence being anything more than a one-off event; and there was no indication of future stars to come from the same source.

If the arrival of the folk comedians was one hint of the future, another came in the form of the Radio 4 series *The Hitchhiker's Guide to the Galaxy*, first broadcast in 1978. It was written by Cambridge graduate, Douglas Adams, who had contributed a sketch to the last-ever episode of *Monty Python*, despite being ten or more years younger than the regular cast. Characteristically that had been a piece satirizing bureaucracy, which became one of the central themes of *Hitchhiker's*, in which a human, Arthur Dent (Simon Jones), is saved just before the Earth is destroyed to make way for a hyperspace bypass; he spends the remainder of the series wandering the universe, including a visit in the second series to a planet, Brontitall, where he is monumentalized in a vast statue, commemorating the moment when he staged a quiet rebellion against the tyranny of machines (especially those that failed to understand how to make a cup of tea).

Here was a clear return to the Oxbridge tradition, using the Python blueprint to construct a rambling but coherent narrative that would become a long-running cult, spreading into novels, records, television and ultimately the cinema. And the following year came *Not the Nine O'Clock News* to relaunch the Oxbridge sketch show (Mel Smith and Rowan Atkinson had studied at Oxford, Griff Rhys Jones at Cambridge). The series did not seek to copy *Monty Python* – it opted for a slick professionalism, making no attempt to emulate the earlier show's surreal juxtapositions, its excursions into history and cross-dressing, its refusal to end sketches with a punchline – but there was a discernible influence, particularly in the fascination with other television formats. Indeed the parody of the high-brow talk-show, a standard Python target, reached new heights with the sketch about a professor who has made a breakthrough in communicating with a gorilla; the primate in question, Gerald, turns out to be highly articulate, capable of quoting Aristotle in the original Greek and a fan of the music of Johnny Mathis.

The debt was made explicit in a sketch mocking the reaction accorded to the film *Monty Python's Life of Brian* (1979). In a debate hosted by Tim Rice on the BBC2 chat show *Friday Night, Saturday Morning*, the Python stars John Cleese and Michael Palin had tried patiently, but with growing exasperation, to explain to the journalist Malcolm Muggeridge that the movie wasn't actually blasphemous at all, while the always preposterous Mervyn Stockwood, Bishop of Southwark, smugly fingered the ostenta-tiously large cross around his neck and made the occasional snide comment. *Not the Nine O'Clock News* countered with a studio discussion of a film by the General Synod of the Church of England, *Life of Christ*, described as 'a thinly disguised and blasphemous attack on the life of Monty Python'. Rowan Atkinson appeared as the bishop who had directed the film, toying with a camera lens on a chain around his neck and simpering his way through a mock apologia: 'The Christ figure is not Cleese, he's just an ordinary person who happens to have been born in Weston-super-Mare at the same *time* as Mr Cleese . . .'

The series also featured songs which were, as ever with such things, of a hit or miss nature, but did include at least one bullseye in 'Nice Video – Shame About the Song', ridiculing the pop industry's obsession with promotional films. Again the influence of an earlier generation could be seen: Bill Oddie, first in the radio series *I'm Sorry I'll Read that Again* and then with the Goodies, had been working for years on songs that sounded like perfect recreations of current pop styles, while being undermined by the lyrics.

John Lloyd, the co-creator of *Not the Nine O'Clock News*, saw the show as following in the Oxbridge tradition, though he argued that where *That Was the Week That Was* had been characterized by its optimism about the power of satire to change society, and *Monty Python* had mostly opted out in favour of whimsy, now there was a 'sad and cynical conclusion that the world cannot be changed so we might as well go down laughing'. There was, however, a strong vein of protest in the show, with a relentless line of attack on the government, on nuclear weapons and on the monarchy, and an edge that hadn't been seen on television for many years. In particular the 1980 sketch 'Constable Savage' was deliberately contentious with its depiction of Rhys Jones as the eponymous police officer being given a dressing down by his superior (Atkinson) for bringing a string of ridiculous charges: 'loitering with intent to use a pedestrian crossing', 'looking at me in a funny way', 'coughing without due care and attention'. The list of nonsense culminates in the incredulous comment: 'In the space of one month you have brought 117 ridiculous, trumped-up and ludicrous charges. Against the same man.' It then transpires that the victim of Savage's attentions is black, and what had seemed like an absurd joke turns out to be an attack on racism in the police force.

This was very definitely a return to the humour that had made *That Was the Week That Was* such a controversial programme. A brief sketch in that series, written by a young John Cleese, had seen a man saying 'Good evening' to a policeman and promptly getting beaten up, with the officer remarking, 'Just a routine enquiry, sir'. But that had been in 1962, and in the years since, British comedy had mostly returned to a more traditional image of the police on the suburban beat (Deryck Guyler's portrayal of Corky in the *Sykes* series being the most memorable). In the wake of *Not the Nine O'Clock News*, others followed the lead. The following year, for example, the Radio 4 comedy series *Injury Time* included Rory McGrath in a parody of Shaw Taylor's *Police 5* programme, appealing to the public for help in solving a crime: 'Otherwise, they say, they'll go out and arrest the first black person they see – it's never let them down in the past.'

Like the folk comedians, the success of *Not the Nine O'Clock News* helped prepare the way for what was to become known as alternative comedy ('It was the first show at that time which was capable of being watched by a seventeen-year-old,' as Rhys Jones later pointed out), but there was no immediate sign that it was anything more than an isolated exception to the norm. A couple of months earlier *The Comedians*, the show that had made household names of Charlie Williams, Frank Carson and Jim Bowen in the early 1970s, had enjoyed a return to ITV, with producer Johnny Hamp predicting big things for his new stars Charlie Daze, Ivor Davies, Mick Miller, Harry Scott, Roy Walker and Lee Wilson. To celebrate the occasion, the *Daily Mirror* ran a full-page spread on these comedians, inviting them each to contribute a joke; of the six gags, three were standard Irish stories: 'Heard about the Irish fellow who had his arm amputated so he could sail around the world single-handed?' Even here, however, the concern over racist humour that had become an issue over the last couple of years was making its presence felt, and Hamp insisted that Irish jokes would be banned from the show unless they were told by Irish comedians.

But the old tradition of comedy was still very much in evidence. It was in 1979 that Benny Hill, who had been named TV Personality of the Year as far back as 1955, began his conquest of America, with syndicated highlights of his Thames TV sketch show proving so popular, according to one report, 'that a 1988 survey of Florida schoolchildren revealed that although many of them did not know London was our capital, they all associated one person with Britain: Benny Hill. A riot broke out in a California gaol when prisoners were prevented from watching his show.' In his own country Hill was to become a controversial figure as the Thatcher years wore on. Never much liked by critics ('what a strange survivor his humour is,' marvelled Joan Bakewell), he was to be reviled by many of the new comedians for what was perceived of as a reactionary style of humour, though at this stage he was under attack from another quarter altogether: in 1981 the moral campaigner Mary Whitehouse wrote to the heads of all the companies that advertised during his show, asking if they knew that they were supporting the broadcasting of pornography during family viewing time.

The same alliance of liberal critics, right-wing moralists and right-on comedians was also to be found ranged against Bernard Manning, the Manchester-based stand-up whose humour, wrote Michael Ginley, had 'its roots in the savage conditions endured by the working-class poor in the nineteenth century'. Technically Manning was the most accomplished of the comics to break out from the northern club circuit in the 1970s, and he was also the most transgressive, capable of subverting expectations like few others. 'We'll have no more Jewish stories tonight, I've just discovered that I lost my grandfather at Auschwitz,' ran one gag. 'He fell out of the machine gun tower.' Only Barry Humphries' character Dame Edna Everage could rival him for cruelty and obscenity, though that wasn't what made him the most notorious figure in 1980s comedy. 'I don't want to sound like a preacher,' said Ben Elton, the man who came to personify alternative comedy for the public, 'but we can make people laugh without being racist or sexist. Bernard Manning's mother-in-law jokes and jokes implying that all Irish are stupid are out.' So personalized had this dislike become that at the opening of the Jongleurs comedy club in Camden Lock, north London, a burning effigy of Manning was thrown into the adjacent canal. His humour wasn't much better received when he appeared in 1982 at the opening night of Factory Records' Hacienda club in Manchester.

The way that comedy became such a contentious issue was indicative of the polarization of culture in the period. The alternative comedy that followed in the wake of *Not the Nine O'Clock News* saw a rebirth of the crusading spirit of *That Was the Week That Was*, mixed with the absurdism of *Monty Python* and the bellicose personal commitment of Lenny Bruce (whose work was revived in the West End in 1979) and of Richard Pryor (whose groundbreaking *Live in Concert* film was released in Britain in 1980), but there was also, and perhaps most importantly, a large dose of post-punk anger. And, just as punk had directed much of its fury against other strands of rock and roll, so did alternative comedy come with an ad hoc agenda that challenged the established order in television humour, hence the attacks on Benny Hill and Bernard Manning.

The catalyst was the opening in 1979 of the Comedy Store, the first comedy club in London since the Establishment, founded by Peter Cook, had closed its doors fifteen years earlier. Followed shortly by its offspring, the Comic Strip, and by the muscling in on the Oxbridge-dominated Edinburgh Fringe Festival, the Comedy Store provided a platform for the coming generation, the likes of Rik Mayall, Keith Allen, Ben Elton and the double act of Dawn French and Jennifer Saunders. Their success saw the sprouting up of other comedy clubs, first in the capital and then in major towns and cities across the country, establishing a network of live venues that seemed never to stop growing; by the mid-1980s there were an estimated fifty clubs in London alone. The confrontational, chaotic atmosphere in the early days of this circuit was again reminiscent of the excitement of punk rock in 1976–77: 'It was crowd control, really,' commented Alexei Sayle, the first compere of the Comedy Store. 'You never knew whether some lunatic with a machete would leap on to the stage.' Punk may have shifted far fewer units than the record industry had hoped, but its influence and inspiration were to be felt for many years.

The rise of alternative comedy was chronicled in fictional form in Martyn Harris's 1992 novel *The Mother-in-Law Joke*, told from the point of view of Phil First, a comedian who works the clubs as part of a double act, makes it to television and finds himself gradually assimilated into the mainstream he had once hated. Early on in the story he offers a definition of the new approach, emphasizing that although there was a political agenda, it was often more implicit than explicit: 'Alternative comedy. It's just a matter of trying to get away from stuff like Jimmy Tarbuck and Bernard Manning. You try not to do nig-nog jokes or Jewish jokes or sexist jokes. Don't do jokes at all really.' The old style of interchangeable gags that could be told by anyone from Bob Monkhouse to Des O'Connor was replaced by what Frank Skinner identified as a more individual approach: 'What was said on stage roughly represented that comic's view of the world.' Or, as seen by Les Dawson, a disapproving older comic: 'To these performers, the lavatory, sexual organs, tampons, body smells were all acceptable subjects for humour.' He wasn't the only one to worry about the nature of some of the material. In 1983 Channel 4 screened a series titled *The Entertainers* that featured most of the big names from the circuit including Paul Merton, Helen Lederer and Hale and Pace, but felt itself obliged to put one episode out at 11.25pm rather than in its usual 8.30pm slot because it included, in a routine by French and Saunders, the word 'clitoris'. The word 'penis', on the other hand, had been deemed permissible for broadcast before the 9pm watershed that divided family viewing from adult programmes.

Just as significant as the content was the age of the audience. Previous comedy had emerged primarily from the music halls or from the variety and seaside theatres, where it played to multi-generational audiences, making it eminently suitable for transfer to the limited number of British television channels, with both BBC1 and ITV chasing the family audience. Even the northern clubs, despite the blue humour that was permitted, catered for a wide age-range. The alternative comedy clubs, on the other hand, attracted an overwhelmingly young and mostly middle-class audience; this was essentially a monocultural market, populated primarily by students and by readers of the music press. And there was no reason to assume that it would necessarily attract a larger audience than punk had managed: 'For now their appeal looks like being narrower than previous comedy waves,' wrote Bryan Appleyard in *The Times* in 1981, while also noting that the new comedians 'are the standard "creative" types who emerged from the art and drama schools in the sixties to form groups and have done so again to become comics.' (He was not entirely correct about their backgrounds: although the stars of alternative comedy were not from Oxbridge, they were largely the beneficiaries of university education, with Manchester and Sussex universities being particularly influential.)

Nonetheless, alternative comedy became a regular presence on television, in part at least as a consequence of Thatcherite principles, despite a hatred of her regime being one of the unifying threads in the movement. 'In her hunger for the free market,' noted the producer Harry Thompson, 'the lady ruled that 25 per cent of BBC TV programmes (not to mention 100 per cent of Channel 4 shows) should come from the independent sector. A rash of hurriedly created independent companies suddenly needed to find wholesale new talent, new ideas and a whole new outlook.' One of the easiest ways to fill the airtime turned out to be recruiting stand-ups from the alternative circuit and giving them a national platform to articulate what were often anti-Thatcher opinions.

Even so, the viewing figures for the flagship programme of the new wave, *The Young Ones*, an exuberantly ill-disciplined show about four students sharing a house (first broadcast on BBC2 in November 1982), did not suggest that the nation was entirely ready to embrace this development. By the end of its six-week run, the series was registering in the top ten most-watched programmes on the channel with an audience of 3.3 million, but it was being outperformed by other comedies, including *Yes, Minister* and *The Further Adventures of Lucky Jim* (which proved to be no funnier than his original adventures in the 1954 Kingsley Amis novel), while the most popular show was *Des O'Connor Tonight*. None of these, however, got anywhere near the really big comedies broadcast that week over on BBC1: *Hi-De-Hi!* (with 11.2 million viewers), *The Morecambe and Wise Show* (11.1 million), *Are You Being Served?* (10 million), *Three of a Kind* (9.45 million) and *The Likely Lads* (9 million). The second, and final, series of *The Young Ones* did slightly better, topping the 4 million mark.

Regardless of viewing figures, the impact made by the programme was considerable. Structurally it remained a sitcom, depicting a closed environment in which neither escape nor progress was possible, but in almost every other respect it subverted the genre. There was always a musical item performed by a group appearing in the living room of the house (thus ensuring that the programme fell within the purview of the variety rather than the comedy department at the BBC and therefore worked on a higher budget), the live action was frequently interrupted by puppets, and there was a casual disregard for such conventions as continuity. The characters were unstable – actors would often break out of character to address the camera directly, while Alexei Sayle appeared every week in a variety of roles, though he made no attempt to vary his performance – and the location was equally uncertain: excursions were made into other television shows and even, on one occasion, into Narnia. And running through it all was a vein of exaggerated slapstick, even a violent stupidity, that owed something to *The Goodies* and a great deal to Tex Avery's animated films of the 1940s.

Up against the light entertainment that still dominated the British media, and at a time when Thatcherism had begun to recover from its depths of unpopularity and looked as though it might well emerge triumphant from its travails, the very existence of the programme seemed to its devotees like a beacon of hope, providing an alternative voice, an attitude seen nowhere else on television. It swiftly became a cult favourite, effortlessly being voted best television programme in the music weekly, the *NME* (following on from *Not the Nine O'Clock News* two years earlier), and winning over the more perceptive humorists of an older generation: 'this is the best, brightest, most inspired TV comedy since *Monty Python*,' wrote Miles Kington, the inventor of Franglais. 'Also the funniest.' He went on to compare it to the formula used in the radio version of *Hancock's Half-Hour* in the 1950s: 'put four or five egocentric monsters in the same house and let them get on with their fantasies.'

What was unusual about this particular combination of characters was the way they exemplified, even exaggerated, the diversity of contemporary youth style. Neil (Nigel Planer) was a nouveau hippie, forever depressed and forever making lentil dinners; Vyvyan (Adrian Edmonson) was a punk, though confusingly his studded jacket spelt out the words 'heavy metal', engaging in random acts of violence and destruction; Rick (Rik Mayall) was a caricature student, dressed in badge-ridden charity-shop clothes and spouting puerile politics, often in poetic form; and Mike (Christopher Ryan) was the self-proclaimed cool one, almost a parody of the Fonz in the American series *Happy Days*: always on the make, but ultimately as sexually inadequate as the others. At the time the media were busy trailing the splintering of youth culture, and the disparate characters seemed to echo and parody this. 'Today youngsters divide very clearly into cults – punk, skinhead, heavy metallers, mod or Ted,' the *Birmingham Post* told its readers in 1981, and the *Sun* provided much the same service with a feature headlined SEVEN TRIBES OF BRITAIN, which identified a slightly different roster: rockabillies, heavy metal, new psychedelics, punks, new romantics, skins and mods. Part of the appeal of *The Young Ones* was the way it played with these reductive concepts, blurring the boundaries and then throwing the mutated results together in a pressure-cooker of mutual loathing and dependency.

The series was also, ironically, a unifying force, bringing together those self-same tribes. For despite the clumsiness of the newspapers' analysis, there was some truth in the idea that youth culture had fragmented by the start of the decade, much of it feeding on previous post-war cults. First out of the blocks had been a rockabilly revival, with a donkey-jacketed look that was distinct from the traditional Ted image, while sharing much of the same music. That had been followed by a mod revival, complete with disturbances in seaside resorts, and by a considerably more violent skinhead revival (in 1980 Lord Home and Lord Chalfont were separately reported to have been assaulted by skins). There was even a punk revival in the lumpen shape of Oi! Music, and an attempted psychedelic revival, though this never got much beyond London, with the Regal clothes stall in Kensington Market and the Groovy Cellar club in Soho. The fallout from punk also saw a loose alliance of more sombre fans who gathered at the Futurama festival, first staged in Leeds in September 1979 when it featured performances by Public Image Ltd, Cabaret Voltaire and Joy Division; the associated image tended to come with heavy overcoats, suitable for both the depressed economy and the climate of northern cities. From the north too came the first stirrings of what would become goths, complete with back-combed hair and clothes in such intense shades of black that they seemed to have sucked the health out of the pallid faces they surrounded. Meanwhile London contributed a vein of exhibitionist clubbing in a scene that produced such luminaries as Steve Strange, Boy George and Spandau Ballet; misleadingly named new romanticism, and associated in the public's mind with frills, flounces and eyeliner, there was actually little sartorial continuity here from week to week, just a love of dressing up in as outlandish a fashion as possible.

Much of the approach of these latter groupings was rooted in the various styles pioneered by David Bowie at various stages of the 1970s, and, unlike the various cult revivalists, many adopted elements of his literary and artistic aspirations in a way that made them perfect for analysis by the increasingly theory-driven weekly music press, particularly the *NME*, then the market leader. For punk had transformed the parameters of modern rock music, adding, for a short while at least, a requirement that any new movement wishing to be taken seriously should come with at least a token nod towards some form of ideology about the nature of art and preferably its place in society.

No such claims could be made for the contemporaneous New Wave of British Heavy Metal (NWOBHM as it was catchily known to its adherents), though it did produce some of the biggest British exports of the era with bands like Iron Maiden, Def Leppard and Saxon. More to the taste of theorists in this field proved to be Venom, who inaugurated a new development in heavy metal with their early-1980s albums *Welcome to Hell*, *Black Metal* and *At War with Satan*. Combining the technical incompetence of punk with the Satanic lyricism of 1970s band Black Sabbath, they created an alternative, underground style of the music: faster, less flamboyant and more nihilistic than before, perhaps reflective of their recession-hit native city, Newcastle-upon-Tyne. Venom made little commercial impact at the time, but their initiative went on to influence a bewildering number of sub-genres (black metal, thrash metal, death metal, speed metal) that were, to the outsider, mostly indistinguishable from each other. Although the most successful acts that followed were American groups – Metallica, Slayer, Megadeth – a new benchmark was set by the Ipswich band Napalm Death (launching yet another sub-genre known as grindcore), whose commitment to speed and economy of style meant that their 1987 debut album *Scum* included twelve tracks that were under a minute long, one of them, 'You Suffer', barely topping the one-second mark. The guttural vocals, distorted guitars and flailing drums identified this music as being ultimately derived from heavy metal, but only in the sense that, say, saxophonist Anthony Braxton was derived from New Orleans jazz: it had reached a level of abstraction that was closer to the avant-garde. What remained, however, was the audience, still predominantly drawn from the ranks of teenage boys, forming a separate sub-species that shuffled along within the massed ranks of youth culture.

The fragmentation of these cults suggested that the onward march of youth, so dominant since the advent of rock and roll, was now suffering a crisis of identity. There was no confidence on display here, no obvious unifying thread. And the decade went on to witness the sightings of a wide variety of other alleged sociological groups – Yuppies, Sloane Rangers, Young Fogeys – as though the cultural confusion were not merely related to music but to the future of the nation itself.

Or perhaps it was that the new rock tribalism simply reflected the triumph of style over music. Certainly the industry was changing. Although the weekly music press was passing out star journalists who could break into the mainstream media in a way that their predecessors had never managed – Julie Burchill, Tony Parsons, Danny Baker, Paul Morley, Garry Bushell amongst them – its position as the arbiter of pop fashion was slipping. The first four years of the decade saw the sales of the four surviving weekly newspapers (*NME, Melody Maker, Sounds, Record Mirror*) fall by 50 per cent, while sales of music publications generally increased by 35 per cent, the difference being the result of a new generation of magazines, both self-conscious style sheets like *The Face* and *i-D* and pure pop titles such as *Smash Hits* and *No. 1*. These glossy magazines, more interested in celebrating image than analyzing the music itself, were also the product of punk, which had continued the British rock tradition of an art school interest in the look of pop. They were augmented by the tabloid newspapers, displaying a new-found interest in youth culture, in the hope of increasing circulation. John Blake, who had created a pop gossip column titled Ad Lib in London's *Evening News* to cover the capital's clubbing scene, was enticed to do the same at the *Sun* in 1982, and launched BIZARRE. 'Simply the first column ever published in a national newspaper which encompasses every aspect of being young in Britain today,' boasted the paper. 'BIZARRE is about Pigbag and hang-gliding, Space Invaders and pacey paperbacks, the Rolling Stones and zoot suits. BIZARRE will be a must every day for everyone with a zest for life.' It was followed by similar ventures in other papers. Together with the magazines, these columns chronicled the British pop movement that was, for the first time in two decades, to sweep to international success.

Because out of the patchwork that was alternative youth culture at the start of the decade was to emerge a generation of globally successful pop bands, whose obsession with style led to an eager embrace of the new medium of video, just in time for the launch of the MTV channel in America in 1981 with its insatiable appetite for such promotional films. Acts such as Culture Club, Duran Duran, Wham!, Eurythmics and the Police were to score No. 1 hits in America over the next couple of years. Behind them came Soft Cell, Dexys Midnight Runners, Madness, A Flock of Seagulls and Kajagoogoo, and by July 1983 eighteen of the top 40 US singles were by British acts, breaking a record that had stood since the glory days of the British invasion in the mid-1960s. The brand of highly polished pop that was mostly purveyed by these bands seemed a long way removed from their roots in the recession years of the first Thatcher government, a fact that was not accidental; when drummer Jon Moss persuaded Boy George to change the name of their band, Sex Gang Children (they became Culture Club), he argued that audiences had had enough of the decadence that had been celebrated in the new romantic clubs of London: 'They want a reason. They want to believe in something. They want faith. They want to work.'

This phase of pop had originated with Gary Numan, who reached No. 1 in the summer of 1979 with both 'Are "Friends" Electric' and 'Cars' (the former under the group name Tubeway Army, the latter as himself). His low-budget, unglamorous take on Bowie's Berlin albums initiated a wave of electronic pop that came to characterize much of the soundtrack to the first half of the decade, but just as influential was his hands-on involvement in the music business itself. 'A year ago Gary Numan spent his days queuing at Slough Job Centre or collecting his £19.75 dole,' enthused the *Daily Mail* in October 1979, but now 'he has already formed a merchandising company to market his own T-shirts, posters, badges and programmes, cutting out the middle man.' This too was part of the legacy of punk: the discovery that it was possible to augment gig income by selling badges and seven-inch singles at the venue; Numan simply turned this sense of garage-band enterprise into a major merchandizing operation. He showed an equally astute grasp of potential new markets with the 1980 release of *The Touring Principle*, the first rock video sold for home consumption. Perhaps unsurprisingly, he was one of the few rock stars openly to support Margaret Thatcher.

Others were learning the same lessons. Adam and the Ants had formed their own fan club in 1978, when they were still an unfashionable band, dismissed by the London elite, and Adam continued to keep a tight control of merchandizing when he became the nation's biggest pop star in 1980–81; he even went (unsuccessfully) to court to try to establish copyright on his distinctive make-up. And taking the punk ideal of releasing records on an independent label to a new level, Jerry Dammers, leader of the Coventry ska band the Specials, launched 2 Tone Records, which operated as a fully autonomous company under the umbrella and distribution of Chrysalis. Its first twelve singles all reached the charts, an unprecedented achievement in British pop music, and included not only releases by the Specials themselves, but also the debut records by other bands who blended the rhythms of ska with the attitude of punk: Madness, the Beat and the Selecter.

Gary Numan was an exception; for the most part these examples of entrepreneurship espoused a more leftist brand of politics, much of it centred on race. The breakthrough of 2 Tone came at the tail-end of Rock Against Racism, a movement that had been launched in 1976 and had brought punk, new wave and reggae bands together on shared bills around the country in a successful attempt to combat the racism of the National Front. The 2 Tone bands, many featuring line-ups that were as racially mixed as their sound, added their weight to the cause, playing at the gigs and creating a style that had an immediate political impact as well as a longer-term musical influence. Their era, however, was brief. The Specials broke up in 1981, following a radical second album, *More Specials*, on which Dammers took unexpected departures into lounge music, John Barry soundtracks and spaghetti westerns and, in the process, alienated some of his own band (guitarist Roddy Radiation said it made him feel 'physically sick'). Others continued, but with the withdrawal of the presiding genius of Dammers, and despite the continuing success of the increasingly pop-orientated Madness, the bands of the ska revival were soon eclipsed by a more durable generation of groups, employing synthesizers to create a white version of soul pop.

'The music scene was healthier than it had been in a long time,' noted Boy George, reflecting on this shiny new wave of groups, after the downbeat imagery of punk and post-punk. 'Suddenly it was okay to be rich, famous and feel no shame. Some saw it as a natural consequence of Thatcherism.' And yet, in the unlikeliest of places, there were traces of political resistance to be found. Depeche Mode's second album, *A Broken Frame*, came in a sleeve that resembled a communist propaganda poster; Spandau Ballet wore clothes inspired by Soviet constructivism; the Human League offshoot Heaven 17 launched themselves with the single '(We Don't Need This) Fascist Groove Thang'; 'Wham Rap', the first single by Wham!, was a witty and defiant celebration of life on the dole; and Sade's debut album, *Diamond Life*, included 'When Am I Going to Make a Living?', a song whose message of resilience in the face of unemployment was set to a light quasi-jazz backing. The chorus of 'Dance Stance', the 1980 debut single by Dexys Midnight Runners, comprised a list of great Irish writers from Oscar Wilde to Laurence Sterne in a rebuttal of jokes about stupid Irishmen. Even 'Land of Make Believe', a No. 1 hit for Eurovision Song Contest winners Bucks Fizz, was said by its lyricist, Pete Sinfield, to be an attack on Thatcher:

> Something nasty in your garden's waiting
> patiently till it can have your heart.

The early years of Thatcherism were a golden age for political pop, a time when it was possible for the Beat to have a hit with the self-explanatory

'Stand Down Margaret', for UB40 to do likewise with 'One in Ten' about the unemployment statistics, and for the Jam to reach the top three with the class-conscious 'Eton Rifles'. (In 2008 the then leader of the Conservative Party, David Cameron, revealed that when he was an Eton schoolboy, this last single was particularly popular with him and his chums. 'Which part of it didn't he get?' snapped songwriter Paul Weller. 'It wasn't intended as a fucking jolly drinking song for the cadet corps.') This level of engagement was to fade somewhat in the face of the riches available to those who could crack the American market, but for a while pop music – like the new comedy – seemed to provide a forum for alternative points of view to be expressed.

Beyond the charts, the Notsensibles won over some fans with their ironic single 'I'm in Love with Margaret Thatcher', while the Exploited sounded a more aggressive note with 'Maggie' on their *Horror Epics* album: 'Maggie, Maggie, Maggie, Maggie, you fucking cunt!' And beyond even them were the more fiercely committed bands, led by the most successful under-ground group of the decade, Crass, an anarchist collective who were based in a commune and whose every song was a political statement. The music may have been conventionally primitive punk, on little more than nodding terms with melody, but their self-produced, self-released records always retailed at a low price-point and tended to come in fold-out poster-sleeves, featuring collages that were as uncompromising as was the music. All of this was received with great enthusiasm by those who were devotees and, while there was never any question of the band making an impact on the charts or on television, they could by the time they split up in 1984 claim sales of two million records. They had also become perhaps the best-known anarchists in the country though, as *Sounds* magazine pointed out, this status brought its own contradictions: 'Their complete control over their records and their unbridled assaults on all things authoritarian made them the reluctant leaders of an anarcho-punk movement that was about anything but leaders.'

Crass were the most visible band in terms of their commitment. Typical of many others, now mostly lost to rock history, were To The Finland Station, who took their name from Edmund Wilson's book about the birth of socialism, and whose 1981 single, 'Domino Theory', was issued on the cooperative label Melodia (not to be confused with the Soviet state record company); over a scratchy guitar and drum-machine backing, a simple pop tune carried lyrics that addressed cold war tensions:

> Russian troops on the Polish border;
> the western world is grieving.
> But where are the headlines for
> American arms in El Salvador?

Such outward-looking sentiments were unusual, though such was the tenor of the times that even the charts did feature the occasional excursion into foreign affairs, albeit in the less radical shape of Kim Wilde's 'Cambodia' (1981) or the Human League's 'The Lebanon' (1984).

If the swathes of songs inspired by Thatcher and Thatcherism – others were later contributed by Elvis Costello, Morrissey, Kirsty MacColl and many, many more – reflected a newly politicized aspect to pop lyrics, just as important was the increase in the numbers of young people in the dole queues, which in turn provoked a rapid expansion in the number of groups being formed. Many of the bands who made it, and most of those who didn't, started their careers while unemployed, using supplementary benefit to subsidize their early years within a tolerant DHSS structure that was, at least partially, responsible for the great explosion of British pop; when so many were on the dole, pressure from the benefit office to seek work was greatly reduced and time for artistic pursuits increased. As with the arrival of alternative comedians on television, the musicians railed against Thatcher, and helped create a cultural resistance to her politics, but their careers were often indebted to her.

Music and comedy were not the only beneficiaries of the new culture of unemployment. There was too a boom in performance poetry, inspired by the popularity of John Cooper Clarke in the late 1970s. Recognizing a cheap option when they saw one, rock promoters began to put on poets as support acts at gigs: John Hegley, Attila the Stockbroker, Seething Wells, Anne Clark, Mark Miwurdz, Little Brother all benefited, as did a couple of the future stars of alternative comedy, Porky the Poet (Phill Jupitus) and Mark Jones (Mark Lamarr), teenage author of 'Too Fast to Live, Too Young to Work':

> I'm the James Dean of the dole queue
> You've got to admire my cheek –
> Trying to work out how to live fast and die young
> On seventeen-fifty a week.

In more orthodox literary fields, Clive Barker, the horror writer and filmmaker, made his name with his short story collections, *The Books of Blood* (1984), after nine years of being unemployed, during which time he regularly had to justify his status to the DHSS: 'In the end, they even called me in for one of those heavy interviews where they locked the door. I told them I wrote plays and produced a whole file of them out of a bag. I might not have been paid for them in those days, but I believed in what I was doing.'

Similarly, Jon Gaunt, who was later to become a Sony Award-winning broadcaster, was then trying to establish himself as a playwright, with the help of the Enterprise Allowance Scheme: 'The basic principle was that you had to invest at least a grand in your new business and then the government would allow you to pick up a payment of forty quid a week for a year while you got the company off the ground.' Having just been awarded a thousand pound grant from West Midlands Arts, he used the money to sign up for the scheme: 'We then re-circulated the grand to other mates so that they could do the same thing and hey presto we were all off the dole and in business.' Alan McGee was another who enrolled: 'The Tories — I hate giving them credit for anything — had this thing called the Enterprise Allowance Scheme, and I was part of that.' Securing a bank-loan for his thousand pound contribution, McGee set up Creation Records, which in 1984 released 'Upside Down' by the Jesus and Mary Chain, acclaimed at the time as the best debut single by a British band since the Sex Pistols, and was later home to acts like Primal Scream, My Bloody Valentine and Oasis.

And, perhaps the unlikeliest beneficiary of all, there was *Viz* comic. Initially produced as a fanzine by Chris Donald, a DHSS clerk in Newcastle-upon-Tyne, together with his brother and a friend, it was launched in 1979 as a joyously crude parody of *The Beano* and sold by hand around local pubs and record shops. The Enterprise Allowance Scheme enabled Donald to spread its reach until, in 1985, its distribution was taken up by Virgin; it ended the decade as one of the most successful magazines in the country, with a circulation of more than a million. Proudly refusing to grow up, it specialized in behind-the-bike-sheds humour and sheer silliness, and successfully appealed to schoolboys of all ages, with a huge cast of characters that included the Fat Slags, Finbarr Saunders ('and his double entendres') and Johnny Fartpants. Despite its declared intention never to be educational or political, many of the comic's satirical thrusts, aimed at the mass media (in its parodies of tabloid newspapers) and at a host of other targets including militant feminists (the Andrea Dworkin-inspired Millie Tant), provided a running commentary on the decade that was more effective than many of its contemporaries. 'If the future generations look back on the literature of the age,' wrote the era's greatest humorist Auberon Waugh, 'they'll more usefully look to *Viz* than they would, for instance, the novels of Peter Ackroyd or Julian Barnes, because *Viz* has a genuine vitality of its own which comes from the society which it represents.'

These recipients of government funding, however, were not noticeably grateful to their patron: 'We weren't children of Thatcher; we hated her,' insisted Alan McGee. Interviewed in 2009, Norman Tebbit, who had launched the scheme (under the slogan 'Inside every unemployed person, there's a self-employed one'), professed himself unfazed by the hostility towards the government displayed by so many of the artists involved: 'It is slightly ironic. But of course, in some cases, they found themselves as entrepreneurs in a nice, free-market, liberal capitalist system, where they weren't paying tax but they were able to earn money and build themselves a business.' He added, a little ruefully: 'In many cases they built themselves a lot more capital than I've managed to build myself.'

Quite apart from the way that alternative viewpoints were thus being encouraged, there was a further irony in this informal and unofficial system of supporting artistic endeavour. For the Thatcher government had firmly set its face against the subsidizing of the arts, both because of its belief in the virtues of the free market economy, and because, as Jim Hacker put it in *Yes, Minister*: 'Why should the rest of the country subsidize the pleasures of the middle-class few? Theatre, opera, ballet — subsidizing art in this country is nothing more than a middle-class rip-off.' Confronted by such Thatcherite logic, his establishment-minded permanent secretary, Sir Humphrey Appleby, is scandalized: 'Subsidy is for art, for culture. It is not to be given to what the people want, it is for what the people don't want but ought to have. If they want something, they'll pay for it themselves.'

Sadly, one of those organizations that did expect people to pay for it themselves — the D'Oyly Carte Opera Company that had been bringing Gilbert and Sullivan's work to audiences for over a century — found itself unable to survive in the absence of subsidy, and closed in 1982. Elsewhere, however, much of the arts establishment did not noticeably suffer during the Thatcher years, at least for those administrators who knew their way round the corridors of power. 'In the long run the Conservative government was to work in the Museum's favour,' recalled Roy Strong, director of the Victoria and Albert Museum in London. 'At no other time in my career had I known so many people in power.' It compared favourably, he found, with the last years of Labour, when the V&A had had to close on Fridays because of cuts. In the great institutions there was a change of emphasis away from education and towards entertainment, as they pursued private sponsorship, but the high arts remained mostly the preserve of Hacker's 'middle-class few'; when the Arts Council conducted a survey in 1989, seeking to discover how the subsidized arts were being consumed, it found that, in a three-month period, 6 per cent of the population went to the theatre, 4 per cent to a gallery, 2 per cent to a classical concert and 1 per cent to the ballet.

The subsidies had continued despite the horrified cries that accompanied the sacking of Norman St John-Stevas as arts minister in 1981. (To be strictly accurate, he was sacked from his position as leader of the House, and then took umbrage, refusing to stay on as arts minister without a seat in cabinet.) It was 'bad news for anyone who cares for the arts,' noted Lord Longford in his diary, adding that the man was 'an aesthete amongst philistines'. The outcry that accompanied the departure of St John-Stevas was such that one might justifiably have feared that henceforth all writers would lay down their pens, musicians cast aside their instruments and painters turn despondently away from unfinished canvases. For where now was the point in self-expression if the cabinet were to be open only to barbarians and, more importantly, if there was to be no champion fighting to ensure that government money be made freely available to the creative industries? It could, however, have been much worse for the artistic establishment. Nicholas Ridley was at different times offered the job of arts minister by both Edward Heath and Margaret Thatcher, but turned it down on both occasions; given that his opposition to state involvement in industry was such that he made other Thatcherites look positively interventionist, perhaps the arts got off lightly.

Nonetheless the sense of betrayal in artistic circles was real enough, and the opposition to Thatcherism was, if not quite total, then certainly the majority position. It was strengthened year after year as waves of students left further education to find that unemployment was no respecter of academic qualifications. 'I had an English degree certificate,' remembered Giles Smith, 'which, in the shrivelled job market of the 1980s, was about as useful as a brass-rubbing.' He pursued instead a rock and roll fantasy, playing with unsuccessful band the Cleaners From Venus, before ultimately finding his calling as a sports journalist. There had, of course, long been those who had turned their backs on the career paths mapped out for them, but now it seemed almost as though it were becoming the norm, the result of a society that, having relentlessly expanded university provision over three decades, had now abruptly turned about-face and decided not to put a premium on education for its own sake after all. As Leslie Titmuss, the Tory MP created by John Mortimer, put it: 'I can't see how reading English is going to be the slightest help to the economy. It's not going to produce jobs. It's going to do damn all for the prosperity of the country.'

This was to become a recurrent theme in the fiction of the decade. Gulliver Ashe in Iris Murdoch's novel *The Book and the Brotherhood* (1987) is similarly affected, despite an Oxford education: 'Gulliver had gone through the routines of pitying the unemployed and blaming the government. Now he was experiencing the thing itself. Often did he think resentfully, it's not fair, I'm not the *kind of person* who is unemployed!' And, being an Iris Murdoch character, he was overwhelmed by it all: 'It was just absurd to feel so ashamed, so bedraggled, so useless. He just knew that he was being destroyed by an alien force, sinking into an abyss out of which he would never climb.' Less elevated was Elvis Simcock in David Nobbs's television comedy *A Bit of a Do* (1989), who had studied philosophy at university: 'I'm registered as a philosopher at the job centre,' he says hopefully. 'No luck yet!' And less elevated still was Eric Catchpole in the comedy-drama *Lovejoy* (1986), who was unimpressed by getting a job working for the eponymous antique-dealer. 'I don't reckon I'm going to fancy this antiques lark,' he complains, and his father puts him straight: 'Given the state of Mrs Thatcher's Britain, polytechnic dropouts like you don't have much choice.' Others would have been grateful for the opportunity: 'These days you gotta go to Cambridge just to get a job sweeping the streets,' despairs a schoolgirl in the series *Big Deal* (1984).

The feeling of futility was expressed in a letter published in the *Guardian* in 1981: 'As a young, unemployed, first-class honours graduate contemplating the amount of "freedom" provided by my weekly £18.50 Giro cheque, I would be very happy to have Mr Benn as prime minister, or even to become part of the Eastern bloc, if this meant I could get a job.' An editorial in *The Times* was later to wince at a similar cinematic plotline: 'the implication in *A Letter to Brezhnev* is that the teenage heroine would be better off in the Soviet Union than unemployed in Liverpool.'

Related to these was a slew of fictional characters in direct descent from Gordon Comstock in George Orwell's *Keep the Aspidistra Flying* and Jimmy Porter in John Osborne's *Look Back in Anger*, staging their own personal rebellions against society's values, with an awareness of inevitable defeat: not drop-outs as might have been recognized in the 1960s, but rather opt-outs. The pattern had been set in Guy Bellamy's comic novel *The Secret Lemonade Drinker* (1977) with its central figure of a teacher who had abandoned his job and found himself instead running a launderette. 'I am one of life's misfits, neither square nor round,' he declares. 'There is no hole I fit in.' Within a couple of years he would have found the field heavily populated, with even characters in period sitcoms joining him. Simon Cadell was cast in *Hi-de-Hi!* as Jeffrey Fairbrother, an Oxbridge lecturer in the late 1950s who 'thought that he was being stifled by the academic world and that life was passing him by', and so goes to work as the entertainments manager in a holiday camp. 'I'm in a rut,' he worries. 'My wife's left me because she says I'm boring, my students fall asleep in lectures because I bore them. And worst of all, I'm boring myself.'

Rodney Trotter in *Only Fools and Horses* was almost a parody of the type. Forever being teased because he has two 'O' Levels and was briefly enrolled in an art college (he got thrown out for smoking cannabis), he knows he ought to aim higher than being 'an apprentice fly-pitcher', but never quite gets round to doing anything about it until his wife pushes him. But the ultimate example was Hywel Bennett's portrayal of the eponymous hero in the ITV sitcom *Shelley* (1979), which was created by Peter Tilbury 'after experiencing life on the dole and finding that his education counted for little'. Shelley has a PhD but no inclination to put it to any use, and is unashamed by his lack of drive: 'If you are one of those people who think that our Welfare State is a disgrace, that people who sponge off the state are criminal,' he says by way of introduction, 'I am one of those scroungers.' When asked at the dole office, 'What sort of work would you like to do?', he replies with absolute honesty, 'None. I don't like work.'

To some extent this vein of opting out was an attempt to laugh off the harsh social climate of a country that found little room for those who didn't quite fit, a trend that didn't apply solely to the newly graduated. In 1982 Britain's best radio disc jockey, Johnnie Walker, returned from a self-imposed five-year exile in America to take up a job on a proposed re-launch of the old pirate station, Radio Caroline, where he had defied the law in the 1960s. When that opportunity fell through, he found himself unemployed and becoming so demoralized that even applying for jobs began to seem beyond his reach: 'Being on the dole, turning up to sign on – it was all such a dispiriting experience and my confidence was at a very low ebb. It seemed an absolute age since I'd done a live radio show. Maybe I just couldn't do it anymore.'

But there was too a growing weariness amongst the more politically motivated of Walker's generation, the radicals of the 1960s generation, a sense that their dreams of progress towards a new Jerusalem had been cruelly crushed. The theme of disillusion was to become almost a commonplace in the decade. 'You start asking yourself: all this activism and commitment – where does it get you, what good does it ever do?' asks a 52-year-old university lecturer in Robert Barnard's novel *A City of Strangers* towards the end of the 1980s. 'Remember when we used to laugh at Feiffer and Peanuts, and sing "Little Boxes"? And where did it all get us? A decade of Thatcher and the market as God.' The despondency passed on to a younger generation of characters, including Charles in David Lodge's *Nice Work* (1988), who explains to his partner why he's giving up an academic career to become a merchant banker: 'You and I, Robyn, grew up in a period when the state was smart: state schools, state universities, state-subsidized arts, state welfare, state medicine – these were things progressive, energetic people believed in. It isn't like that anymore. The left pays lip-service to those things, but without convincing anybody, including themselves. The people who work in state institutions are depressed, demoralized, fatalistic.' As Loretta Lawson, the central figure in Joan Smith's crime novels, says: 'I've got no money – I work in the public sector.'

Mostly, though, it was the middle-aged who were experiencing a loss of faith. 'I don't believe in anything,' despairs Alix in Margaret Drabble's *The Radiant Way* (1987). 'I believe it's all hopeless. Hopeless. It's all over. There's no way back, and no way forward that we can go. We're washed up.' Even those who didn't quite give in to such levels of misery were often just going through the motions. 'He had been too publicly committed and for too long to renege now,' wrote P.D. James of her left-wing character Maurice Palfrey in *Innocent Blood* (1980). 'He felt like an old campaigner who no longer believes in his cause but finds it enough that there is a battle and he knows his own side.' It was not just the triumph of the right that was giving concern, for the new, more aggressively proletarian left was equally threatening. Palfrey feels an instinctive antagonism towards those in the next generation with whom he might once have sided: 'He had become increasingly petty, irritated by details, by the diminishing, for example, of their forenames, Bill, Bert, Mike, Geoff, Steve. He wanted to enquire peevishly if a commitment to Marxism was incompatible with a disyllabic forename.' In John Mortimer's novel *Summer's Lease* (1988) the elderly Haverford Downs, played in the television adaptation by John Gielgud, although still writing a column for a leftist magazine, notes 'with a sense of humiliation and disgust that the pages of the *Informer* were now given over to articles on gay rights, the "politics of feminism" and peer pressure towards glue-sniffing in the inner cities'.

This feeling that the young left – whether they were attracted to Trotskyism, Bennism or identity politics – no longer respected their elders and betters was not confined to fiction. In a 1979 essay in *Encounter* magazine titled 'Inquest on a Movement', David Marquand, a former Labour MP and a leading disciple of Roy Jenkins, had complained that the party had become dominated by a proletarianism that allowed little room now for the middle-class intellectual strand that had been part of the left from the outset. In the words of Jenkin Riderhood in Murdoch's *The Book and the Brotherhood*: 'Learned people, intellectuals, have lost their confidence, their kind of protest is being esoteric. And at the other end it's smashing things. There's a gap where the theories ought to be, where the *thinking* ought to be.'

Perhaps the inevitable conclusion came with the 1981 television version of Malcolm Bradbury's 1975 novel *The History Man* about Howard Kirk, a self-regarding sociology lecturer whose radicalism had made him a big fish in the small pond of his redbrick university, but who is starting to feel the pinch. The last episode ended with a caption explaining that Howard voted for the Conservatives in 1979. Similarly, when Henry Simcox, in John Mortimer's *Paradise Postponed* (1985), had published his first novel 'his name had been connected with a group of angry young men; now he was a grumpy, late-middle-aged man. Once his political ideas had been thought as red as his hair; now he gave many warnings on the menace of the left and wrote articles for the Sunday papers on the moral disintegration of life in Britain today.' In real life too there had been a drift to the right on the part of former radicals like Hugh Thomas, Paul Johnson and Kingsley Amis. ('Bloody good, eh?' wrote the last to Philip Larkin on the occasion of Thatcher's election victory.)

Many such figures tended to insist that they had not abandoned their radicalism, nor discarded their youthful idealism. As the former Labour MP Woodrow Wyatt was keen to point out: 'I would not like posterity to believe I ever joined the Tory party which has been anathema to me all my life.' Rather, his intense devotion to Thatcher was 'because she is not a conservative either. She's nothing like those wets like Ian Gilmour, Jim Prior and [Francis] Pym. She is a radical making a revolution which horrifies many conservatives.' There was an element of self-delusion here, but also a kernel of truth, confirming the position adopted by the newspaper that would become most closely associated with Thatcher's period in office. 'The *Sun* is not a Tory newspaper,' declared a front-page editorial on the day of the 1979 election. 'The *Sun* is above all a RADICAL newspaper. And we believe that this time the only radical proposals being put to you are being put by Maggie Thatcher and her Tory team.'

This proclaimed radicalism was a key element in the appeal of Thatcher. She effectively annexed much of the language of the 1960s left and claimed for herself the role of challenging the monolithic, centralized state. 'The balance of our society has been increasingly tilted in favour of the state at the expense of individual freedom,' she argued in the introduction to the 1979 manifesto. 'This election may be the last chance we have to reverse that process, to restore the balance of power in favour of the people.' Her ministers continued to stress the theme. 'Less government is good government,' declared John Moore, echoing Henry David Thoreau's hallowed anarchist dictum: 'That government is best which governs least'. Her opponents on the left fiercely rejected such claims, of course, citing as evidence of her contempt for democracy such developments as the centralization of the police force, the transfer of power from local councils to Whitehall, the withdrawal of trade union rights from workers at the intelligence agency GCHQ, the abolition of elections to the Greater London Council. But then, as she herself pointed out, in a manner reminiscent of Lewis Carroll's Humpty Dumpty: 'Sometimes when you use the same words, they may not have the same meaning.'

It was a battle that Thatcher largely won, the rhetoric of rights and choices and freedoms appealing to a large section of the public. Thatcher's identification of the unions with the state, and her portrayal of herself as the radical outsider, intent on challenging institutionalized authority, was a vote-winner. It threw the left on the defensive, so that the Labour Party seemed constantly to be fighting rearguard actions, seeking to protect a status quo from which support was fast draining away. This remained an issue throughout the decade, with change after change being opposed until it had been implemented and had been seen to win popular approval, at which stage Labour accepted it. The impression given was that the party was hidebound and dogmatic, and yet paradoxically lacking in principle.

Even more worrying for the left was the fact that it was losing the argument in places that it should have been able to take for granted. Despite the hostility of alternative comedy and of rock and roll, Thatcher was proving popular amongst a substantial number of those who would shortly enter the voting booths for the first time. In November 1982 Tony Benn met a group of sixth-form students and was depressed by the experience. 'I notice now that there are Thatcherites in every audience. She has armed a lot of bright young people with powerful right-wing arguments,' he wrote in his diary. 'I am no longer dealing with the old consensus but with a new breed of right-wing concepts.' At the other end of the spectrum, there was a mirror image of the right's victory. Mark Steel was later to reflect on the south London squat culture that he inhabited at the time, the very epitome of alternative society, and to conclude that those who professed themselves to be anti-establishment were simply self-delusional: 'There was little interest in trade unions and still less in the values of socialism, because "they're just more institutions telling us what to do". It occurred to me that the aspirations of the armchair anarchists amounted to a belief that everyone should get on with their own thing, or to put it another way, alternative Thatcherism.'

Mike Leigh's 1988 film *High Hopes* showed the inevitable outcome as the central character Cyril (Philip Davis), a motorcycle courier living on a north London council estate, rails against the dying of the socialist light, worries about the personal effects of disillusion ('I'm scared of getting bitter'), and admits the futility of his life: 'I'm a dead loss. Don't do nothing, just sit here moaning.' That feeling of futility was captured too in Edward Fenton's novel *Scorched Earth* (1985), which told the story of ten days in the lives of a group of unemployed youth in London, united by a fondness for cannabis, a hatred of the media, a need to fill up time and a feeling of being excluded from the new Britain. When one of the characters is told that there's no point banging your head against the wall when you could knock on the door and ask to be let in, he replies despondently, 'There's not too many doors being opened at the moment. And there's a hell of a lot of people banging on the walls.'

And as the left continued to fight amongst itself, both within the Labour Party and between Labour and the SDP, large numbers simply walked away from the squabble, so that half of all those between the ages of eighteen and twenty-six simply didn't vote in the 1983 general election. Worse still, a MORI survey revealed, amongst those who did vote, 27 per cent of the young unemployed – those assumed to have the greatest reason of all to dislike Thatcherism and all its works – gave their support to the Conservative Party.

4
Resistance

'We're living in violent times'

Soon the red blood will be boiling,
And blue blood will be dead.
UB40, 'Little by Little' (1980)

STEVE RAMSEY: I come from a place where, unless you're
suffering from severe brain damage, you don't talk to the
Old Bill.
Ray Jenkins, *Juliet Bravo* (1981)

Thatcher has been stimulating attitudes which lead
logically to fascism. City democracy – which is as relevant
today as in Greece 2,500 years ago – and a healthy
community politics are a bulwark against it.
David Blunkett (1983)

As the recession of the early 1980s dragged on, there was little enough to bring cheer to the nation. Perhaps the one big exception was the wedding on 29 July 1981 of Prince Charles to Lady Diana Spencer, closing the book – as it seemed at the time – on who would marry the man claimed by gossip columnists to be the world's most eligible bachelor. In the years since 1976, when Charles had left the Royal Navy, the media had been obsessed with his alleged love-life, and a succession of young women from the British aristocracy and from the diminished ranks of Europe's royal families were paraded through the pages of the popular press as prospective, or sometimes actual, fiancées. The front-runner was for a long while assumed to be Princess Marie Astrid of Luxembourg, though the most significant proved to be Lady Sarah Spencer, whose younger sister would ultimately achieve the honour of providing the House of Windsor with a future heir.

It was the first wedding of a Prince of Wales in over a century, and it was a hugely popular event. He was thirty-three years old and the heir to the throne of the United Kingdom, she was twenty and the daughter of the 8th Earl Spencer; as the Archbishop of Canterbury said in his address, 'Here is the stuff of which fairy tales are made'. The media leapt gleefully at his image, though they might have done well to note his qualifying statement that this was an inadequate approach to life 'because fairy stories regard marriage as an anti-climax after the romance of courtship'. So, of course, it was to prove, and Runcie, who knew the couple, was later to admit that 'it was an arranged marriage'.

At the time, however, few were expressing such doubts and even fewer were permitted to make them public. The media was overjoyed to welcome such a photogenic and glamorous addition to the royal family, so clearly a step up from Princess Anne's choice of Captain Mark Phillips, while workers in memorabilia firms were amongst the few who were putting in extra shifts that summer. It seemed as though the entire world was temporarily infatuated with the new princess, none more so than the American heavy metal star, Ted Nugent: 'I'd drag my dick through a mile of broken glass just to wank off in her shadow,' he declared. In a more conventional tribute, the country's leading pop group, Adam and the Ants, celebrated by releasing a single titled 'Prince Charming' and, capitalizing on the huge television audience for the wedding, the BBC issued an album of their coverage; both records went to No. 1 in their respective charts.

Even so, there were a few discordant elements to be heard beneath the carefully arranged mood music. Anne's wedding in November 1973 had coincided with the declaration of a state of emergency, amidst a fuel crisis that would soon bring down the government of Edward Heath; this time Charles's wedding came in the same month as major riots in many towns and cities. Neither nuptial was thus entirely sprinkled with fairy dust, but the key difference was that where the power cuts and the emergency restrictions of the Heath government had been endured by the entire country, duke and dustman alike, the uprisings of the summer of 1981 provided no such sense of unity; rather they revealed that this was a divided nation, despite the enthusiastic embrace of the fantasy wedding by most of the population.

Amongst the dissident voices was that of King Juan Carlos of Spain, who objected to the fact that the couple's honeymoon on the royal yacht *Britannia* was scheduled to include a high-profile stopover in the disputed territory of Gibraltar. Despite the Queen's annoyance at his attitude ('After all, it's my son, my yacht and my dockyard,' she insisted), he turned down an invitation to attend the wedding. So too did Barbara Cartland, the romantic novelist and step-grandmother of the bride, on the grounds that it was 'common to cry in public', and the Reverend Ian Paisley, because 'I'm a plain man and I don't particularly enjoy pomp and ceremony'. None of these attracted a great deal of coverage, nor even did the London Borough of Lambeth's message of congratulations, which expressed the hope 'that the common problems of newlyweds – unemployment, housing waiting lists, high mortgage rates and soaring inflation – do not detract from their future happiness'. Instead the media focused for its spoilsport stories on Ken Livingstone, the recently elected leader of the Greater London Council (GLC), who refused to take up his allocated seat in St Paul's Cathedral, and instead spent the day greeting supporters of republican prisoners in Northern Ireland: a thousand black balloons were released by demonstrators at County Hall to mark the moment.

The attacks directed at Livingstone, as a minor theme within the media excitement over the occasion, were not without precedent. He had been exciting suspicion in some quarters ever since the Labour Party had won the GLC elections in May 1981, and had immediately followed their victory by deposing the current leader of the Labour group, Andrew McIntosh, in favour of the more left-wing Livingstone. The event was presented as a political coup – 'His victory means full-steam-ahead red-blooded socialism for London,' warned the *Sun* – but it was hardly unexpected; the *Daily Telegraph* had pointed out the week before: 'If Labour is put in control of County Hall next week, it will almost certainly be led by Mr Ken Livingstone.' For precisely that reason, the BBC had sent its cameras along to Livingstone's own count on election night, while back in the studio Robert Mckenzie concluded: 'my analysis of the people elected tonight shows that if the left-wing want to, they have got the votes to get rid of Mr McIntosh and put in Mr Livingstone.'

It was an exciting moment for the left, coming in the midst of Tony Benn's bid to become deputy leader of the Labour Party, and at a time when Margaret Thatcher was at her lowest ebb in terms of popularity. On closer examination, however, the voting figures for that round of local elections were less encouraging than they might have seemed at first glance. Despite successes in Manchester, Liverpool, the West Midlands, Derbyshire, Staffordshire and Cheshire (the latter taken by Labour for the first time), the psephologist Ivor Crewe warned that the swing simply wasn't strong enough: 'If London again proves to represent the nation,' he wrote, 'Labour is in serious trouble.' The turnout for the GLC election was 44.5 per cent, with Labour taking 42 per cent of the vote, a couple of points ahead of the Conservatives; it had therefore won the support of just 18.5 per cent of the electorate, and even then, of the fifty Labour councillors that were elected, Livingstone reckoned only twenty-two were on the left of the party. Had the newly launched SDP been sufficiently organized to contest the election, the result would have been very different indeed, and would probably have produced an Alliance administration. In their absence, the left, despite being in a minority, proved themselves ferociously well organized and ended up not only with the leadership but with every one of the major offices in the new administration. On this somewhat slender base, Livingstone was determined to build a new style of local government, overtly political in its desire to change society, rather than merely to provide services, putting an end to what he contemptuously dismissed as 'old white men coming along to general management committees and talking about rubbish collection'.

By the time Livingstone came to power in London, the pattern had already been set in terms of press coverage of left-wing council leaders. In 1980 the *Daily Mail* had thundered against the Walsall council led by former print worker Brian Powell ('This little Kremlin in the heart of England'), inaugurating a period when local authorities were regularly denounced for daring to challenge the establishment. By 1981 the conflict between local and national governments was sufficiently high on the public agenda to warrant the commissioning of *United Kingdom* in the BBC's Play for Today strand in 1981. Written by Jim Allen and starring Colin Welland and Ricky Tomlinson, it told the story of a council refusing to implement Whitehall-directed cuts and coming under attack from the police. 'Who would say that it could not happen here?' wondered the reviewer for *The Times*, while Allen was even more bullish in interviews than in the play itself. 'You can predict with absolute certainty there's going to be more riots,' he was reported as saying. 'But I don't like the way the riots have been going – just wild and indiscriminate. There's got to be direction. The councils should be organizing the people.'

What distinguished the GLC from the likes of Walsall was, first, the fact that it was in power in London, in full view of the media, and, second, that Livingstone was a gifted communicator and self-publicist, possessing a mischievous sense of humour that continually wrong-footed his opponents. He was also the recipient, willing or otherwise, of increased press attention when Tony Benn was hospitalized in June 1981 with what was diagnosed as Guillain-Barré Syndrome. Although Benn was discharged after two weeks, there was a temporary reluctance in Fleet Street to resume the more vicious level of attacks and, as Livingstone recognized, 'I was the next best thing to run as a sort of end-of-civilization-as-we-know-it.' The two men had already been linked by press and public alike: Paul Johnson called Livingstone 'the poor man's Benn', while a graffito in London proclaimed: 'Ken Livingstone is John the Baptist to Tony Benn's Jesus'. Now they became virtually synonymous as leftist bogeymen, though still with the GLC leader seen as the junior member of the team – few recognized at the time that his influence was to be more profound than that of Benn.

As the press campaign against him gathered force, Livingstone claimed that Conservative Central Office was touting stories around Fleet Street about his allegedly deviant sexual practices, even if there was little consistency to the stories: they included both his supposed predilection for schoolgirls and his presence at an orgy where 'he was buggered by six men in succession'. Kelvin MacKenzie, editor of the *Sun*, sent reporters to dig out some dirt on the man and was furious with the lack of results: 'Fucking newts!' he exploded. 'All you can find is newts?' In fact, Livingstone kept not newts but salamanders, as he had already made clear in an interview with *The Times*: 'I feed them on slugs and woodlice. They just live under a stone, come out at night and are highly poisonous,' he explained disarmingly. 'People say I identify with my pets.' The reality was that the worst crime that could have been laid at his door, on a personal level, was a lamentable dress sense that stooped so low as to include safari suits, but for some reason this evaded Fleet Street's normal fascination with left-wing fashion.

In terms of his policies, too, the charge sheet was not quite as long as was claimed, since much of what Livingstone represented, however controversial at the time, came to be seen as conventional political wisdom. He argued that the domestic rates should be abolished and replaced by a local income tax, a policy adopted a decade later by the Liberal Democrats; he suggested that loitering in public lavatories in the hope of entrapping homosexual men was no job for a police officer; and he ensured that the first item from the manifesto to be implemented was free travel on public transport for pensioners.

This last was a curtain-raiser to the central policy on which Labour had been elected in London: a pledge to reduce fares on public transport by 25 per cent, following similar initiatives in Sheffield and elsewhere in the country. (An initial proposal to abolish fares altogether had been popular in some sections of the party, but had foundered on opposition from the trade unions, unwilling to lose the jobs of ticket collectors and bus conductors.) In the event, the policy, known as Fares Fair, was implemented alongside a complete restructuring of the fares structure, introducing the concept of a simplified zonal system – previously each journey had been individually priced – and the result was even stronger than the manifesto pledge, with a 32 per cent cut in fares. The funding for this was to be raised by a supplementary rate demand right across London, a development that aroused considerable indignation in Bromley, a borough in south-east London that was not served by London Underground. Why, the Conservative council in Bromley, wondered – with some justification – should their residents be expected to subsidize cheap transport for tourists and for those living in the central London boroughs? Advised that there was a possibility of the supplementary rate being illegal, the council took the GLC to court, and promptly lost. On appeal, however, the verdict of the lower court was overturned, and the GLC then appealed to the House of Lords where, to their and most commentators' surprise, five Law Lords ruled unanimously in December 1981 that the policy was indeed illegal. The fact that it had been a key commitment in the manifesto – where the supplementary rate had also been trailed – was ruled to have no legal significance. Nor did the song 'Give Us Back Our Cheap Fares' by the country's leading girl group Bananarama, released as the b-side of their hit 'Really Saying Something' (1982), manage to get the decision reversed.

There were many who felt that the Law Lords' verdict was politically motivated, inspired by a wish on the part of the establishment to teach Livingstone a lesson. For he was by then attracting the most hostile coverage he was ever to receive, though the central cause for complaint was not his fares policy but his call for negotiations with the IRA and Sinn Fein as the only way to achieve a peaceful settlement in Northern Ireland. And that remained the greatest of all political taboos in Westminster and Fleet Street.

Terrorist attacks on mainland Britain were much reduced from their peak years, while in Northern Ireland the level of republican violence was also decreasing: 1980 saw fifty people killed by the IRA, around a fifth of the numbers killed in 1972, the worst year of the conflict. But the explosion in October 1981 of a nail bomb near the Chelsea barracks of the Irish Guards, killing two civilians, brought the nightmare back into public conscious-ness. It was in these circumstances that a speech by Livingstone to the Tory Reform Group at Cambridge University came to dominate the headlines. His comments that the IRA were not 'just criminals or psychopaths' failed to win over the leader-writers: 'The conscience of the whole country is affronted by his remarks,' said the *Daily Express*; 'he is certainly not fit to run Britain's capital city,' decided the *Daily Mail*; while the *Sun* gave up half its front page to a photograph of Livingstone, accompanied by the headline THIS DAMN FOOL SAYS THE BOMBERS AREN'T CRIMINALS, and a description of him as 'the most odious man in Britain'. (In the interests of balance, the other half of the front page was a story headed TORIES ON THE ROCKS, with a poll showing that only 44 per cent of Conservative voters still backed Thatcher.) Even other Labour members of the GLC were by now becoming impatient with Livingstone's ability to generate negative publicity; apart from anything else, there was no obvious reason why he should have been addressing Tory undergraduates at Cambridge in the first place.

Livingstone wrote to *The Times* to clarify his position in purely practical terms: 'The point I was trying to make is that to seek to crush the IRA as if they were simply criminals or lunatics will not work. It is the policy that has been tried for generations and still the killing persists.' The terrorists were politically motivated, so that 'if one is caught others come forward to take his place'. He also insisted that 'I abhor all violence'. The protestations of pragmatism and pacifism, however, were a little disingenuous, for Livingstone also had a more straightforward political motive: 'I have been consistently in favour of withdrawal from Ireland,' he declared elsewhere. 'It is in fact the last colonial war.' Support for British withdrawal from Northern Ireland was far from uncommon amongst the public, but it was seldom expressed by leading politicians, and certainly not with an anti-imperialist argument. He had gone further in a radio interview on the British Forces Broadcasting Service, coming close to an incitement to mutiny: 'What I would say to everyone who's got arms in Northern Ireland, whether they are in the British Army or the IRA, is to put those arms down and go back to your home.' It was this political position, as much as his comments about criminals, that was largely at the root of the press attacks. Nonetheless the use of the word 'criminals' was carefully chosen and very heavily loaded in 1981, for it alluded to the issue that had provoked the hunger strike by prisoners in the H-blocks of the Maze jail near Lisburn, a campaign whose first fatality had come just two days before the GLC elections.

The IRA had used the tactic of the hunger strike before, most notably with the sisters Marian and Dolours Price, convicted in 1973 of planting car bombs in London, who had demanded the right to be transferred to a prison in Northern Ireland. After a 200-day campaign (the length reflecting the fact that they were force-fed), they had won their demand. Their success, although it came with personal consequences for Dolours Price, who was to develop anorexia, established that it was a weapon that could again be deployed.

More recently the hunger strike had, somewhat unexpectedly, been adopted by the Plaid Cymru politician, Gwynfor Evans, who announced in

May 1980 that he would be fasting to death, starting in the autumn, unless the government honoured its pre-election promise to set up a Welsh-language television channel. Along with more than two thousand others, he was already refusing to pay his TV licence in protest, and there had also been attacks on television transmitters, but it was the threat of a former MP killing himself that brought home the passions aroused by the cause, even if some were unsympathetic: 'Gwynfor Evans can only die once,' argued Delwyn Williams, Conservative MP for Montgomery. 'If this government or any other government gives in to a threat of suicide by this foolish old man, what will be the next cause he threatens to die for?' The government didn't agree, and in September approved the introduction of the channel, to Evans' delight: 'This is the biggest victory we have ever won for the Welsh language. It will go far to secure the future for the language.' And, despite initial reservations, William Whitelaw, the home secretary who made the decision to go ahead with Sianel Pedwar Cymru (S4C), himself came round to approving: 'This channel has been a great success and for once I have reason to be glad that I bowed to pressure, not a usual experience.' S4C became best known for its children's series, including *SuperTed*, the first British animation to be screened on the Disney Channel in America, and *Sam Tân* (*Fireman Sam*); they were unlikely products of a hunger strike.

The month after the government's capitulation on S4C, six IRA prisoners and one from the INLA splinter group launched their own hunger strike, demanding to be treated as political prisoners and not as ordinary criminals: given the rights of free association, of exemption from work and of wearing civilian clothing, rather than prison uniforms. This status had in fact been granted in 1972 (again after a hunger strike) but rescinded in 1976, since when there had been a campaign to have it restored. Initially this had taken the form of refusing to wear uniforms, instead going naked or using blankets for covering. It escalated into what became known as the dirty protest – a refusal to wash and the smearing of excrement on cell walls – and then into the hunger strike. The fast ended 53 days later amidst some confusion, the republicans claiming that the government had promised concessions, while Thatcher was insistent that 'this was wholly false'. In any event, no concessions were forthcoming and, at the beginning of March 1981, the most famous hunger strike of all began, when Bobby Sands, an IRA man serving fourteen years for possession of firearms, refused food. He was to be joined at periodic intervals over the next months by others, one at a time, to maximize the potential publicity.

Thatcher's approach remained resolutely uncompromising through-out: 'What the terrorist prisoners wanted was political status,' she wrote later, 'and they were not going to get it.' The republicans were equally uncompromising and over the next two months it became ever more likely that deaths would result. The stakes were raised still further when the parliamentary seat of Fermanagh and West Tyrone became vacant and Sands was nominated as the republican candidate, standing on an Anti H-Block/Armagh Political Prisoner ticket. He was duly elected to the House of Commons on 9 April, though obviously unable to take his seat, an event that attracted worldwide attention to the campaign (and prompted the swift passage of the Representation of the People Act 1981, banning any prisoner from standing for election). Thatcher was unmoved: 'Crime is crime is crime,' she insisted. 'It is not political, it is crime.' From the outset, the decision had been taken not to force-feed, and with no movement on either side, Sands died on 5 May after sixty-six days of refusing food. He was twenty-seven years old.

Sands' funeral was attended by upwards of one hundred thousand people, and there was an escalation of terrorist attacks, but the sense of outrage was not confined to republicans in Northern Ireland. There were demonstrations across Europe, Lech Walesa, leader of the Polish free trade union Solidarity, expressed his sympathy, and various French towns renamed streets in Sands' name. Not to be outdone, the Iranian government renamed Winston Churchill Street in Tehran, where the British Embassy stood, as Bobby Sands Street. More significantly, there was an upsurge in republican feeling in America, which helped to fund IRA activities for the remainder of the civil war. And, although Thatcher showed no regret at his death ('He chose to take his own life; it was a choice that his organization did not allow to many of its victims'), there were signs that there might be movement elsewhere in the British political establishment: James Callaghan spoke in the Commons in favour of an independent Ulster, despite being asked not to do so by Michael Foot, while Roy Jenkins was reported to have 'now made up his mind after much reflection that Britain should "withdraw" from Northern Ireland'.

Other prisoners followed on from Sands and, by the time the strike was called off in November 1981, a total of ten men had starved themselves to death. It was, wrote Thatcher, 'a significant defeat for the IRA', but it was also a significant victory for Sinn Fein, the republican movement's political wing. Its profile was now raised internationally, and it had established the principle of contesting Westminster elections; henceforth the republicans were to pursue a twin-track strategy of armed struggle and political engagement, as encapsulated in the slogan 'a ballot paper in one hand and an Armalite in the other'. The path from here to the peace process launched during John Major's premiership was to be a tortuous one, but a step had been taken. At the time, however, no one could plausibly have predicted any such outcome. Amongst the most depressing aspects of the whole eight-month campaign was the way in which the sacrifice of human life came to seem less and less important. Sands had attracted massive coverage and support, but there was a law of diminishing returns, as even sympathizers with the cause acknowledged. 'For the media and supporters alike, the gruesome truth was similar to the later moon landings,' wrote Mark Steel. 'It was impossible to get as emotional about the fifth as the first.'

The same sense of exhaustion applied to the media's treatment of the entire conflict, which largely comprised routine outbreaks of fury sweetened with suitably sentimental stories, as emerged from the 1982 London park bombings. One IRA device exploded in Hyde Park as mounted soldiers of the Blues and Royals were passing; minutes later, a second destroyed the bandstand in Regent's Park, where the band of the 1st Battalion, the Royal Green Jackets was performing. Seven musicians and four soldiers were killed that day, but the press attention focused on a horse named Sefton that was seriously injured in the attack. A fortnight later Sefton was considered well enough to meet the media at a photo-call, though according to a rumour recorded at the time by Alan Bennett: 'Sefton has so far recovered that his wounds no longer register on camera so make-up is applied.'

The prevailing attitude was summed up by a cynical television reporter in Douglas Livingstone's 1985 television drama *We'll Support You Evermore*: 'The trouble with Northern Ireland is the built-in boredom factor.' The play starred John Thaw as Geoff Hollins, the father of a British officer found murdered by the IRA. 'Your son was a hero,' he's told by the authorities. 'You can be proud of him.' But Hollins suspects they're hiding something, and travels to Belfast in an attempt to uncover the truth of the death. What he actually finds is 'the only Third World country in Europe', a decaying alien environment in which every word and deed is swathed in cultural subtleties he can scarcely begin to comprehend. 'It's supposed to be the same bloody country,' he says in bewilderment, shortly before he returns home, and an army liaison officer puts him straight: 'I can't imagine you really believe that.' Hollins' sheer bewilderment, as he stumbles into an army patrol in the Falls Road and is directed back through the wall of the Peace Line to the Shankill Road, reflected the feelings of much of mainland Britain.

This was the context in which Ken Livingstone, 'the IRA-loving, poof-loving, Marxist leader of the GLC' (to use the words of the *Sunday Express*), made his comments about the need for communication with republican leaders, since they were clearly not ordinary criminals. Unsurprisingly, his words fell on deaf ears in both Westminster and Fleet Street, and periodic explosions of violence continued to punctuate the decade.

Less inflammatory, though cheekily provocative nonetheless, was the GLC's decision to exploit the prime location of County Hall, just across the Thames from Parliament, to display a huge banner announcing the number of unemployed people in London. Not that there was any agreement on what the figures actually were. By 1983 the official statistics showed that there were three million unemployed in the country (12 per cent of the workforce), but there had been substantial changes to the way the numbers were compiled, and the 'real' figure – or rather the one that bore direct comparison with the methodology used in 1979 – was closer to four million. Or, as *New Socialist* magazine, saw it: 'When those on special government schemes and those not claiming benefits are counted, five million people who want a job have not got one.' From the other side of the political divide, Norman Tebbit was later to say that there was so much systematic fraud in claiming, 'such widespread abuse, that I think it is now quite reasonable to doubt if unemployment ever reached three million at all.' He was, for once, on the losing side of the argument and, despite all the disputes, the expression 'three million' became the accepted shorthand for mass unemployment, and the best-known statistic of the decade.

Behind the figures lay very considerable discrepancies, in terms of race, age and location. According to the 1971 census, unemployment amongst men of Asian and Afro-Caribbean descent was 138 per cent of the level experienced by white men. Ten years later, with unemployment having more than tripled, that differential alone would have produced many more black unemployed, but in fact the recession impacted disproportionately in terms of colour, to such an extent that even the *Sun* recognized there was an issue here: 'Unemployment in Britain rose by 37 per cent in the year up to last August,' it reported in late 1980. 'Amongst black people it rose by 47.5 per cent.' Even in the relative prosperity of London and the south-east there were places where unemployment, more especially youth unemployment, became an habitual way of life, as described by a character in Martin Millar's Brixton novel *Milk, Sulphate & Alby Starvation*: 'Everyone I know is broke, no one ever has any money apart from a brief flurry on giro day, sitting celebrating this fortnight's pittance in the pub and maybe even lashing out and buying something to eat.' Rural areas too often suffered disproportionately, though seldom attracted much attention: in 1983 the unemployment rate stood at

17.5 per cent in Cornwall and at 25.5 per cent in the Western Isles, way above the national average.

But it was the north of England, where the decline in manufacturing industry was most concentrated, that tended to be the primary focus of political concern. In Hartlepool, it was reported, it was more likely that a school-leaver would get a place at university than a job. The resultant desperation was encapsulated in the story of Graeme Rathbone and Sean Grant, two unemployed 19-year-olds in the Merseyside town of Widnes, who committed suicide together in the summer of 1981. 'What have we got left to live for now there is no work for anyone?' they wrote, before killing themselves with the exhaust fumes of a stolen car. 'All teenagers have to do is hang around street corners getting moved on by police who think you are up to something.' Interviewed afterwards, the mother of one said that her son had become increasingly withdrawn in the last months of his life and, when she had asked him why he was sitting around at home and not going out, he had replied: 'Well, there's nowhere to go, Mum. There's no jobs, no money, there's nothing to do. You just walk up and down the street. It's the same every day.' The story sparked the creation of one of Mike Leigh's more depressing films, *Meantime*, which centred on the relationship between two unemployed brothers (played by Phil Daniels and Tim Roth), set in the East End of London.

The dispiriting tedium of youth unemployment was caught in the Specials' single 'Do Nothing' (1980), written by guitarist Lynval Golding: 'I'm just living in a life without meaning, I walk and walk, do nothing.' As the decade developed and began to become obsessed with ascribing a financial value to everything, it was discovered that even inactivity had a price: in 1985 a Kent farmer named Eddie Waltham was reported to be employing youths at a wage of £50 a week to walk around his cherry orchard banging bits of wood together to scare off starlings. So desperate were the times that five unemployed school-leavers moved from Birmingham to take up these roles as human scarecrows.

It wasn't just the young. Amongst the most famous fictional creations of the first Thatcher term, was Yosser Hughes, who became a symbol of the wastelands of the north. First seen in Alan Bleasdale's 1980 television play *The Black Stuff*, which followed a gang of six Liverpool labourers laying tarmac on a job in Middlesbrough, Yosser (played by Bernard Hill) was a nightmare character fuelled by violence, greed and hatred. When the gang stop to give a lift to a female student who's hitch-hiking to Leeds, Yosser greets her with a leer: 'Been raped recently, love?' The original drama was followed two years later by a series of five plays, *Boys from the Blackstuff*, that included 'Yosser's Story', where he struck a much more pathetic figure. Increasingly gaunt, dressed in shabby black clothes, and with scars across his forehead from his tendency to headbutt anyone and anything that stood in his way, he now looked like a Scouse incarnation of Frankenstein's monster, the unwitting creation of a society that can find no place for his lack of talents. 'He wasn't very good at anything,' notes his ex-wife, Maureen, a condition exacerbated by his own frank admission that 'Nobody likes me'. His plea to everyone he encounters: 'Gis a job', became something of a national catchphrase, a plea to the government, and was used on a Labour Party document, 'Working Together for Britain', about youth unemployment. As he sinks into mental illness, however, even that desperate cry subsides in favour of a simple declaration, 'I'm Yosser Hughes', as though – with his job, his children and his house all taken from him by a system over which he has no control – the only thing he has left to hold onto is a memory of his identity. 'I thought I knew where I was going once,' he says simply, in a rare lucid moment. 'There's nowhere left to go.'

The fear amongst many was that the persistence of unemployment would pass onto the next generation, in effect to Yosser's children. In 1981 Jack Chambers, the president of the National Union of Teachers, warned that school discipline was being adversely affected as children witnessed unemployment in their families and concluded that this was destined to be their future too. There was also, he said, an increasing number resorting to alcohol, drug and solvent abuse.

Drugs, of course, had been a central part of youth culture since at least the 1960s, but over recent years there had been a shift in the market position of the substances involved, with amphetamines and LSD used to heighten sensory perceptions, being overtaken by glue and heroin, the function of which was mostly deadening. The pursuit of oblivion through solvent abuse had seemed exotically alien when New York band the Ramones included the song 'Now I Wanna Sniff Some Glue' on their 1976 debut album; by 1981 the numbing effects were turning up in the home counties' world of Ruth Rendell's detective Inspector Wexford, called out to Sewingbury Comprehensive 'where there was an alarming incidence of glue-sniffing amongst 14-year-olds'. Nationally, the number of deaths attributed to solvents rose from thirteen in 1980 to sixty-one, two years later, with one estimate suggesting that 10 per cent of teenagers were regular users of glue and other inhalants, and that one in three 14-year-olds had tried it.

Parallel to this was the rise of heroin, a trend linked to the overthrow of the Shah of Iran and the subsequent Islamic revolution. 'Desperate businessmen are using heroin as a compact way of getting their frozen capital out of the country,' reported the *Daily Mirror* in the summer of 1979. 'Farmers in the opium-growing north of the country have doubled their acreage this year.' The result, the paper said, was a spectacular collapse in the price of the drug on the British market, from £200 a gram to just £50 in the space of six months. Soon it was possible to buy a wrap for five pounds, and by 1984 there were an estimated 50,000 regular users in the country. In response, the government launched an awareness campaign, under the slogan 'Heroin screws you up', though it wasn't an unmitigated success: 'We were warned,' remembered health minister Edwina Currie, 'that the horribly pimply youth who was the main focus of some of the 1986 advertisements was in danger of becoming a cult hero, with requests for his poster coming in, so we put a stop to that and his face disappeared from our campaigns.' Meanwhile the children's television soap *Grange Hill* was running a storyline about the addiction to heroin of schoolboy Sammy 'Zammo' McGuire (Lee Macdonald), out of which emerged the 1986 hit single 'Just Say No'.

As ever in a recession, one route out of the ranks of youth unemployment was through recruitment into the police and the armed forces. In Reginald Hill's 1984 crime novel *Exit Lines*, he wrote of 'a trio of young constables whom Detective-Superintendent Dalziel had unkindly nicknamed on their arrival two months earlier Maggie's Morons, suggesting that their recruitment into the force was more the result of Mrs Thatcher's economic policies than a natural vocation'. Charley Frostick, another character in the same novel, talks about why he took the other route and chose to join the army: 'It's better than being out of work. I was pig-sick of that. In the end it was either the police or the army and I didn't fancy running into bother with my old mates.'

The idea that there would be 'bother' seemed almost taken for granted, as increasingly it was being. Fay Sampson's novel for teenagers, *Sus*, told the story of a group of provincial youth who find themselves harassed by the police at every turn. 'What did I do wrong?' asks one after an encounter with yet another officer, and his black friend replies: 'You don't have to *do* anything. You just got to be sixteen, that's all. You're young. You're male. To the fuzz, that scores two out of three. You want to try being black as well?' The central scene in the book sees the main character going on a CND march and being beaten up by the police, after which he's tricked into signing a confession that sees him prosecuted for assaulting a police officer in the course of his duty. (The title of the novel referred to the so-called sus law that gave police officers the right to stop and search anyone on suspicion of wrong-doing without having to account for that suspicion – it was widely believed that it was used to target black youth in particular.) So commonplace did the idea of conflict between police and youth become that eventually even alternative comedy began to send it up; in the sitcom *Filthy, Rich and Catflap*, written by Ben Elton, Rik Mayall's character turns to the camera after a scene of police violence and sneers: 'If you don't like the police, next time you get beaten up try calling an alternative comedian.'

The relationship of the police with the public was to come under ever greater strain during the decade. In North Wales in 1980, there was considerable concern over the tactic of mass arrests in the wake of nationalist-inspired arson attacks on English-owned holiday homes. 'People were taken from their beds during the night or snatched from the street and then held for several days,' wrote criminologist Phil Scraton. 'With no access granted to lawyers and no information given to friends and relatives concerning their whereabouts, those arrested virtually disappeared for several days. Eventually they were returned to their homes without being charged.' There were many who saw such actions as being a deliberate form of intimidation, a view articulated by Ken Livingstone: 'The police are one of the most worrying aspects of society and have become a very political organization indeed.' A similarly heavy-handed approach was most notoriously directed towards areas with a substantial black population, where it was alleged that the policing was compounded by an overt racism. 'When you canvas police flats at election time,' claimed Livingstone, 'you find they are either Conservatives who think of Thatcher as a bit of a pinko or they are National Front.'

The 1980 film *Babylon*, directed by Franco Rosso and set in south London, made these themes explicit, showing a black character being violently assaulted and framed by police officers, for no reason other than to alleviate their boredom. It ended with a police raid on a club, where a sound system battle was being staged; as the picture faded and the credits rolled, the soundtrack carried a defiant chant of 'We can't take no more of that!' It was to prove a prophetic slogan.

The late-1970s had seen sporadic conflict between the police and black youths, particularly at the annual Notting Hill Carnival, but it was not until the Thatcher years that the underlying hostilities really exploded. When they did, in April 1980, it was unexpectedly not in London, Liverpool or Birmingham – their time would come – but in Bristol. Unnoticed by the rest of the country, tensions had been building in the city for some time: black unemployment had doubled over the last four years, at a time when it was in decline locally amongst white workers, and there had been a steady stream of complaints about a campaign of police harassment that had, amongst other things, closed down all but one of the black-owned cafés in the St Paul's area, where prostitution, cannabis-smoking and unlicensed drinking were said to be rife. It was a mass raid by uniformed policemen and drug squad officers on that last remaining café that provoked a spontaneous fight back by some 2,000 youths, forcing the police off the streets for several hours. Buildings and police cars were burned, causing an estimated half-a-million pounds' worth of damage, before order was restored.

This was not, despite the inevitable tone of much of the coverage, a race riot as such, a conflict between white and black; rather, in the words of one St Paul's resident: 'This is the start of a war between the police and the black community.' Twelve people were later charged with riotous assembly, a serious offence that brought a potential sentence of life imprisonment, but none was convicted. From the state's perspective, the most worrying aspect of the events was the withdrawal of the police at the height of the disturbances; it was 'unacceptable', insisted William Whitelaw, and he set up an inquiry into the police response to the riot, though not into their prior behaviour, nor into what might lie at the root of the problem. Perhaps he felt there was little need, since the answer was relatively obvious and required government action that was unlikely to be forthcoming. 'The causes, then, lie in the squalor and deprivation of decayed urban centres, in empty lives, and lack of work and opportunity,' noted an editorial in the *Sun*. 'These same conditions exist on a far greater scale in other cities: Liverpool, Manchester, Newcastle and London itself.'

Indeed they did, as did heavy-handed policing, and a year later a police operation in Brixton, south London sparked an explosive two days of rioting, more serious than any comparable disorder thus far in the century. The estimated damage this time amounted to £6.5 million, while hundreds were injured, with police casualties outnumbering civilians by around three to one. Petrol bombs were used on a widespread scale for the first time on the British mainland, and several buildings were burnt down, though the arson was not indiscriminate: the local Law Centre and the branch of Marks & Spencer remained untouched, while a pub with a reputation 'of having in the past discriminated against black people' was attacked. So too was a newsagent that 'was alleged to have refused to serve homosexuals'. It was, said Whitelaw, 'a shameful episode in our nation's life.' Amongst those arrested was the future comedian Mark Steel ('Sorry about the colour, sarge,' said the arresting officer apologetically), who recorded his observations at the station: ' "Black bastards," said a copper as he smashed a truncheon into the face of a lad stood about ten yards from me. A line of black youth descended the stairs at the back of the station, each of them with their face covered in blood.' Others provided similar stories of police action; John Clare, the BBC's community affairs correspondent, witnessed three officers attack a photographer who was taking a picture of a man being arrested: 'his camera was wrenched away, thrown into the gutter and stamped on,' it was reported, and the photographer 'was severely beaten up with the police aiming at his groin: the motorcycle he had been riding when he took the picture was dragged along the road and its petrol tank ripped open'.

Again this was not a race riot, but an attack on a seemingly indifferent society and on policing practices. 'Fuck monetarism, fuck the free market, and more specifically fuck the police,' as one sympathetic writer put it. 'There is police violence,' a retired detective, John Scott, told the Labour Party conference later that year, 'and while there are many people in the police force who are not racially or politically prejudiced, the vast majority are.' Other commentators were keen to explore a wider dimension; journalist John Cole, soon to become the BBC's political editor, drew parallels with the American riots of the mid-1960s and concluded: 'The *casus belli* of a youth war therefore lies in unemployment, bad housing, the breakdown of morality and of family/school discipline, a more rebellious attitude to authority in this generation, over-reaction by the police, the violence of youth culture, of some rock music . . . The list trails on to infinity.'

Political reaction was divided, even within the Labour group on Lambeth Council, within whose environs Brixton lay. The council leader, Ted Knight, complained about saturation policing not merely before but after the event: 'Lambeth is now under an army of occupation,' he said, claiming that the police were using the 'same apparatus of surveillance that one sees in concentration camps.' More publicly, an editorial in the magazine *London Labour Briefing*, a journal particularly associated with both Knight and Livingstone, caused some controversy with an editorial that argued: 'An alternative view would be that the street fighting was excellent, but could have been (and hopefully, in future, will be) better organized.' Such attitudes were never going to be condoned by the party's national leadership, but they did presage future events, identifying the left as apologists for riotous behaviour in a way that would become particularly associated with Bernie Grant in Haringey. And there was a further hint of the future when another Lambeth councillor, the then unknown Peter

Mandelson, broke ranks to denounce Knight, claiming that he was 'screaming and raging and saying the most bizarre things'.

The official government response again fell to Whitelaw as home secretary. Less than a week before the Brixton riot, he had rejected Enoch Powell's latest call for the repatriation of black Britons to their countries of racial origin, with an unequivocal endorsement of a multi-racial society that wasn't shared by all members of his party: 'Black people are part of this country and part of our future.' Now, he managed to resist the press calls for immediate and draconian action and instead appointed Lord Scarman – said to be one of the more liberal members of the judiciary, though he had been one of the Law Lords who ruled against the GLC's Fares Fair policy – to chair an inquiry into the riots. Whitelaw's statement to the Commons concluded that 'we must develop policies designed to promote the mutual tolerance and understanding upon which the whole future of a free democratic society depends', and he was later to claim, with some justification, that: 'The thing I am proudest of is that I managed to handle the riots in 1981 without being forced to take more repressive measures.'

Even as Scarman was installing himself in Lambeth Town Hall to collect evidence for his inquiry, the first week of July 1981 saw another outbreak of rioting, first in Toxteth, Liverpool, followed swiftly by Southall in West London, Moss Side in Manchester and Handsworth in Birmingham. There were smaller disturbances too in a dozen other places, including Leeds, Preston, Wolverhampton, Hull and again in Brixton. The worst of these were in Toxteth, where the police used CS gas for the first time on the mainland and where the first fatality was recorded – a disabled man named David Moore was killed after being hit by a police van driving on a footpath. Gradually the wave of disorder subsided, just in time for the nation to celebrate the royal wedding, but a pattern had been set that was to recur throughout Margaret Thatcher's premiership.

When Scarman did deliver his report, it was critical of the police, even if some felt that it pulled its punches: 'racial prejudice does manifest itself occasionally in the behaviour of a few officers on the street,' he conceded, but 'the direction and policies of the Metropolitan Police are not racist.' He recommended that greater efforts be made to recruit black officers, and that racist behaviour be made a disciplinary offence, with dismissal as the normal penalty. What was most striking was the placing on official record for the first time of extremely hostile attitudes towards the police and of so many anecdotal accounts that they could hardly be ignored – even amongst many black people of an older generation, the Scarman Report came as a revelation.

The balanced and carefully weighted liberalism of Scarman's words, however, was enough to infuriate some senior officers. James Anderton, the chief constable of Greater Manchester, claimed that, if the report's recommendations were implemented, 'the character of the British police would never be the same again.' More subtly, the Metropolitan Police staged a propaganda counter-offensive by releasing crime figures that showed for the first time the race of the offender, but only in the categories of robbery and violent theft, as though wishing to imply that it was black criminality that caused all their problems. They were rewarded by front-page headlines such as the *Sun*'s THE YARD BLAMES BLACK MUGGERS — HUGE RISE IN STREET CRIME. When asked why there was no similar racial breakdown for other, perhaps more serious, crimes such as rape or murder, Assistant Commissioner Gilbert Kelland explained that the figures for robbery were a response to 'public opinion and pressure': 'There is a demand for this information from the public and from the media on behalf of the public.' Sections of the media were indeed satisfied, but many others remained unconvinced; Lord Lane, the Lord Chief Justice and not a man noted for his radical tendencies, dismissed the statistics as being 'mostly misleading and very largely unintelligible.'

The emphasis on race in the Scarman report and in the media coverage was to some extent a criticism that the government was content to accept. Much more concerning would have been if the blame had been directed at its economic policies. Yet, despite Whitelaw's insistence that of those arrested in Brixton 'the majority, far from being unemployed, held steady jobs', there were some in the Conservative Party with a sneaking suspicion that mass unemployment had a part to play in the wave of civil unrest. One party member at the 1981 conference had the temerity to raise it as a possibility, provoking Norman Tebbit's most famous comment: 'I grew up in the '30s with an unemployed father. He didn't riot. He got on his bike and looked for work, and he kept looking till he found it.' In an unfairly distorted form ('on your bike'), that response came to symbolize for millions what was perceived to be the Tories' callous indifference to the unemployed, and Tebbit came to rival Thatcher herself as a hate figure for the left. It was a position that for the most part he appeared to enjoy greatly, though there were times when even he could be riled. In early 1983 he suggested that those on the dole weren't really trying hard enough: 'despite the three million unemployed I had been unable to find someone to paint the gates of my home in Berkhamstead'. He wasn't amused when he subsequently found the gates daubed with red paint, with demonstrations being staged outside.

Although the ravages of unemployment were to continue, festering into the next century, the images of those few weeks in July 1981, when the streets of so many British cities seemed to have been taken over by rioting mobs, juxtaposed with the pomp and celebrations of the royal wedding, were perhaps the most emblematic of how divided society had become. And just as the wedding produced a No. 1 single in 'Prince Charming', so too did the riots. 'Ghost Town' by the Specials was the high point of the politicized pop of the early-1980s, a record that captured the claustrophobic desolation of boarded-up high streets and urban decay, and it reached the top of the charts as Toxteth was in flames. The lyrics were sparse and effective ('No job to be found in this country, can't go on no more, people getting angry'), but it was the perfection of the production, the bleakly beautiful sound, that made it such a triumph. For many the single became a touchstone: 'the most effective opposition to Her Majesty's Government', in the words of John O'Farrell. Others weren't so certain. It so happened that the record was a hit at the time of the 900th edition of *Top of the Pops* and, to celebrate this historic event, the veteran disc jockey David Jacobs was invited back to present the show on which he had worked so often back in the 1960s. And as 'Ghost Town' came to an end, his comment inadvertently summed up the mood of the nation: 'Oh dear, that wasn't very cheery, was it?'

5
War

'People are stupid'

> The definition of a human being is one who hates and
> fears and wants to be rid of nuclear weapons. Because
> they're the evil, they're the modern equivalent of the
> devil, of Antichrist – they are all we'll ever know of hell.
> Ruth Rendell, *The Veiled One* (1988)

> Calling generals and majors:
> Your World War III is drawing near.
> XTC, 'Generals and Majors' (1980)

> When British territory is invaded, it is not just an invasion
> of our land, but of our whole spirit. We are all Falklanders
> now.
> *The Times* (1982)

The Eurovision Song Contest did not enjoy a particularly vintage year in 1982. Staged in Harrogate, following Bucks Fizz's triumph with 'Making Your Mind Up' the previous year, the competition included a high proportion of off-the-peg Eurovision songs ('Bem-Bom', 'Halo Halo', 'Video Video') and was dominated by Germany's Nicole singing the rather insipid 'A Little Peace', which became an international hit after it won the tournament by a record margin. More interesting was the appearance by Finnish rock star Timo Kojo, performing 'Nuku Pommiin', whose chorus was translated as 'Don't drop, don't drop, don't drop that neutron bomb on me'. Regrettably it finished in last place, having failed to score a single point.

Despite the lack of recognition by the international juries, the fact that an anti-nuclear song had reached Eurovision at all was entirely typical of the times. For the political pop of the early 1980s concerned itself not merely with unemployment and deprivation, but with the impending fear of nuclear war; hit songs that addressed the subject ranged from

Orchestral Manoeuvres in the Dark's jaunty electronica on 'Enola Gay' (the name of the airplane that dropped the first atomic bomb), through Haysi Fantayzee's playground pop of 'Shiny Shiny' and Nena's bubblegum protest '99 Luftballons', to Iron Maiden's hard-rocking 'Two Minutes to Midnight'.

The root cause of this spate of records was ultimately the election to the American presidency in 1980 of Ronald Reagan, a man who aroused more hatred internationally than perhaps any previous incumbent had achieved. From an American perspective, he was the obvious choice for a country that had suffered unexpected economic and military defeats in the 1970s, had seen the presidency besmirched by Watergate and had ended the decade with foreign relations disasters in Iran and Afghanistan. In the midst of this national identity crisis, Reagan appeared as a populist figure who evoked simpler times and the uncomplicated values of mom, apple pie and overwhelming military force. Which, of course, was precisely the same combination that worried much of the rest of the world. His denunciations of communism echoed those of Margaret Thatcher, who had made her international name with an anti-Soviet speech while in opposition that earned her the sobriquet the Iron Lady, and the two made for a formidable partnership, leading the West into a ratcheting up of the Cold War into what amounted virtually to a crusade.

Their work was not confined to rhetoric. In the autumn of 1979 the government confirmed that Britain's ageing nuclear weapons system, Polaris, would be replaced by a new system, Trident, as planned by the previous Labour administration. And that December the defence secretary, Francis Pym, announced that Britain would shortly be hosting 160 American nuclear-armed cruise missiles at bases in Greenham Common and Molesworth, and sparked what was to become perhaps the biggest single-issue struggle of the 1980s.

The Campaign for Nuclear Disarmament had been founded in Britain in 1957 and had enjoyed some considerable popularity until the signing of the 1963 Test Ban Treaty began to erode its support. By 1979 the membership had fallen to little more than two thousand, and the group appeared moribund. But the decision on cruise missiles reignited the popular passion and gave the left a standard around which to rally. In 1980 the Labour Party adopted CND's proposals – the dismantling of Britain's nuclear weapons system, and a refusal to accommodate American missiles – as official policy, membership of the organization began to climb rapidly towards one hundred thousand, and a wave of mass demonstrations followed, with quarter of a million congregating in October 1981. 'I should think it was the biggest political meeting ever held in the history of British politics,' wrote Tony Benn, one of the leading advocates of nuclear disarmament, 'unless you include the Peasants' Revolt, and even then I'm not sure as many came out at any one time.' That total was exceeded eighteen months later when four hundred thousand congregated in Hyde Park to witness, amongst the usual speeches, the debut live performance in the capital by the Style Council, the band formed by Paul Weller after he split up the Jam.

Aside from pop music, popular television series were also doing their bit to promote the issue of nuclear war, often reflecting the serious and widespread concerns that existed at the time. In 'Coins', a 1980 episode of *Juliet Bravo*, George A. Cooper played Major Adams, a retired man building up a huge stash of tinned food in his shed. 'I was in the war. The next one won't be fought with guns,' he warns. 'When Russia does come, I'll have everything down here necessary – I won't be caught.' The three heroes of the sitcom *Only Fools and Horses* went a step further and built their own fallout shelter in the 1981 episode 'The Russians Are Coming', a show that also revealed that Rodney Trotter had staged a hunger strike in protest at the arrival of cruise missiles, even if it did last only a day and a half. And the *Doctor Who* series 'Warriors of the Deep', although set a hundred years in the future, was based on the premise that nothing had changed in the intervening century: 'There are still two power blocs, fingers poised to annihilate each other,' sighs the Doctor.

This level of commentary went largely without adverse criticism, but a string of more heavily promoted screen dramas attracted serious controversy. They were prefaced by a 1981 BBC revival of John Wyndham's science-fiction classic *The Day of the Triffids*, written thirty years earlier. Largely faithful to the original novel, still it articulated contemporary fears, particularly when speculating that the meteor shower that has blinded most of the human population was caused by malfunctioning weapons. 'We were walking on a tightrope for a hell of a long time,' comments one character. 'Sooner or later, a foot had to slip.' Another expresses the fear of surviving the apocalypse: 'It's going to be a pretty strange sort of world that's left to survive in. I don't think we're going to like it a lot.'

These two themes – of the inevitability of disaster and of the horrors that will follow – were the staples of the nuclear blockbusters that appeared in the mid-1980s. *The Day After* (1983) was an American television film considered so important by ABC, the network responsible, that on its first broadcast it was screened without any commercial breaks (though this was perhaps due in part to the difficulty of getting anyone to sponsor such a depressing message), attracting a claimed 100 million viewers. Set in and around Kansas City in the build-up to and aftermath of a nuclear war with the Soviet Union, it followed a traditional disaster movie structure: Act I introduces us to a disparate cast of characters, whose personal fortunes we then follow in Act II as catastrophe strikes – the full extent of the horror is revealed, the fragility of civilization ripped apart, and then the struggle begins to bring order to a world turned upside-down. All that was missing was the final act of redemption, when normality should be restored. Instead the movie ended with a wish-fuelled and slightly pompous caption: 'It is hoped that the images of this film will inspire the nations of this earth, their peoples and leaders, to find the means to avert the fateful day.' They didn't. But the film did provoke a lively debate between those on the right, who denounced it as pro-Soviet propaganda, and those on the left, who insisted that it was far too cheery: in particular, complained disarmers, the concept of nuclear winter was not even mentioned. 'It wasn't a very good movie,' admitted its director Nicholas Meyer, saying that the chief feature of the script was its 'seductive banality', but he also insisted that that was the point: he didn't want viewers to be distracted from the central message by their appreciation of its aesthetic qualities.

A month later the film arrived on ITV in Britain, to a similarly mixed reaction and to confusion in the government ranks. Weeks before its screening, Michael Heseltine, the defence secretary, was quite clear that it was a valuable contribution: 'I hope people watch that film, because it is the single strongest argument for nuclear deterrence that I know, because the Soviets must never be in a position to believe they could inflict that on us.' A week later, however, having now seen the film, he made a formal complaint to the Independent Broadcasting Authority (the IBA was then the regulatory body for the ITV network), insisting 'that it provided an unbalanced portrayal of the role of nuclear weapons in deterrence' and 'that there was quite obviously a political message in the film.' He demanded that there should be balance, leaving ITV executives bewildered: '*The Day After* is basically a dramatized story about the nasty after-effects of a nuclear bomb. What do you do to balance it? Show the nice after-effects?'

The self-appointed guardian of broadcasting morality, Mary Whitehouse, also objected to the screening of the film, on the grounds that it might upset 'immature minds', a concern that might have seemed borne out by a *TV Times* poll revealing that half of those aged between fifteen and eighteen expected to see a nuclear war in their lifetime. Except that it wasn't just the 'immature': a 1980 poll for the BBC showed that 40 per cent of the adult population believed nuclear war to be likely in the next ten years.

Whitehouse also objected to the BBC's *Threads* (1984), made by Mick Jackson. It too covered the effects of a nuclear strike on a provincial city, in this instance Sheffield, but if *The Day After* was a disaster movie writ large, *Threads* took as its model the tradition of *The Wednesday Play*, a much smaller canvas. Indeed it opened almost as a parody of the problem plays of the 1960s with a working-class lad getting his girlfriend pregnant and the couple deciding to get married rather than have an abortion. Thereafter, despite some entertaining observations about modern British values (artworks are stashed away safely before the attack, a union leader calls for a strike to protest against the imminent holocaust), it became a much bleaker proposition. Where the American version had given us Jason Robards, playing an everyman role as a decent doctor retaining standards in the face of adversity, *Threads* offered no hope for humanity: it showed a world reverting to a brutal hunter-gatherer life, with language and society disintegrating, and with radiation sickness damaging the next generation and then the one after.

In the wake of *Threads*, the BBC finally abandoned its twenty-year ban on Peter Watkins' anti-nuclear film *The War Game*, an early target of Whitehouse's campaigning. Commissioned but never broadcast in 1965 (though it did win a BAFTA and an Oscar), the play, delivered in the form of a documentary, had claimed that nuclear war was 'more than possible' before 1980. Officially it had been proscribed because it was considered 'too horrifying for the medium of broadcasting', but government pressure – and, more significantly, fear of government pressure – also had a part to play. Now it was finally screened as yet another horrific vision of the consequences of nuclear war. The government was still hostile to such work, but it seemed to have less sway now over a BBC that was clearly determined to explore such issues, and also prepared to look beyond the weaponry to the related industry of nuclear power.

The BBC series *Edge of Darkness* (1985) started with Detective Inspector Craven (Bob Peck) seeing his only daughter, Emma, gunned down in front of him. Initially believing that the killer was after him, possibly in retaliation for his involvement with IRA informers in Northern Ireland, he subsequently discovers that Emma's work as a scientist had involved her in conflict with the nuclear power industry, and the trail gets complicated. As he's drip-fed information and misinformation by the British and American secret services, by a Trotskyist group called Socialist Advance, by a corrupt trade unionist, and even by the ghost of his dead daughter, Craven uncovers a massive conspiracy to take over the world by the nuclear industry. 'This future nuclear state,' warns one of the characters, 'will be an absolute state, whose authority will derive not from the people, but from the possession of plutonium.' If all this seemed a bit paranoid, commented the series' writer Troy Kennedy Martin in 1989, that's because 'it was written in paranoid times' when 'born-again Christians and Cold-War warriors seemed to be running the United States.' And, with privatization firmly on the political agenda, 'it was only a matter of time before Mrs Thatcher's entrepreneurs would get their hands on the nuclear waste business.' Chris Mullin, looking back on the television adaptation of his novel, *A Very British Coup*, could only agree with Kennedy Martin's assessment of the era: 'There was a lot of paranoid talk going on.'

Similar conspiracy themes turned up in Martin Spellman's screenplay for the film *Defence of the Realm* (1985). A Labour MP, former chairman of the Commons defence committee, is revealed to have been seeing a woman who is also seeing a KGB agent, in what appears to be a re-run of the Profumo affair, but the reporter sent to cover the story discovers that this is merely an establishment smear campaign, intended to cover up the crash in East Anglia of an American plane carrying nuclear weapons.

Despite all protestations at objectivity and balance, there was a clear anti-nuclear theme running through these works, as the Thatcher government bitterly complained to anyone who would listen. Previously the thesis underlying most popular fiction on nuclear conspiracies had been that the Soviet threat was all too real and was being aided by collaborators, fellow travellers and foolish dupes in Britain. Typical was Fred and Geoffrey Hoyle's 1978 novel *The Westminster Disaster*, in which a small group of terrorists assemble a nuclear bomb in London on orders from Moscow, with the assistance of a Marxist academic at Imperial College, London, a former Labour MP and a trade union activist. Britain was widely portrayed as being betrayed by the spinelessness, at best, of its ruling elite; in Gavin Lyall's thriller *The Secret Servant* (1980), a retired wing commander is described as 'one of the few MPs who still think this country's worth defending'. This tendency was also to be found in the 1982 film *Who Dares Wins*, celebrating the work of the SAS, whose role in successfully ending a terrorist siege at the Iranian embassy in London in 1980 had brought the regiment to widespread public attention for the first time. Here the state was pitted against a CND-type grouping called the People's Lobby: 'We must remember that the vast majority of the People's Lobby are sincere pacifists,' explains a senior police officer. 'We are dealing with the hard-core revolutionaries who are using the peace movement as a cover.'

But *Who Dares Wins* was something of an exception to the tenor of the times, and it couldn't be denied that most of the screen fiction dealing with issues of war and peace had a very different message, one summed up by Harry Perkins in *A Very British Coup*, as he makes a televized prime ministerial broadcast to announce the realization of Labour's and CND's hopes that Britain could again set an example for the world. 'In two weeks' time,' he says, 'experts will dismantle and destroy a one-megaton Polaris warhead. With this action, we will also be dismantling the idea that our freedom somehow depends on the fear of annihilation. It is an absurd, an obscene idea. We want no part of it.'

The assumption was that all reasonable, humane people must surely agree that nuclear weapons were inherently evil; the only real issue was whether one supported unilateral disarmament by the British, reaching for some kind of moral high-ground, or whether Britain's weapons should be negotiated away in a bilateral or multilateral deal that would see the Soviet Union remove an equivalent number of theirs. It was an assumption that came close to orthodoxy in artistic circles. 'Poets must be allowed to feel the full horror of nuclear warfare even more than ordinary mortals,' observed Lord Longford, thinking of his dramatist son-in-law, Harold Pinter, though he might also have looked to the likes of Edward Bond, whose six-hour trilogy *The War Plays* was staged at the Barbican Centre in 1985, or Martin Amis, whose *Einstein's Monsters* (1987) was a collection of short stories all concerned with nuclear weapons.

But the government was evidently not run by writers or artists. And the government was very firmly in favour of nuclear weapons, arguing that they were the only reliable defence against Russian aggression; for those believed in a potentially imminent invasion of Britain by the Soviet Union, the nuclear option was the sole guarantor of peace. After watching *The Day After* and similar films, Heseltine concluded: 'Whatever the horrors portrayed, the essential fact remained: Soviet nuclear weapons were targeted on Western cities.' And his job was clear: 'We had to win the argument and turn the tide.'

It was not a simple task, for by now even the language of the debate was against him, the word 'peace' having effectively been claimed by anti-nuclear campaigners as their own, much as the expression 'pro-life' was subsequently annexed by anti-abortionists. But Heseltine was one of the more adaptable politicians of the time and, when government research showed that the framing of terms was crucial to winning the propaganda battle, he adopted a new linguistic policy: CND were henceforth referred to as 'one-sided disarmers', the names of specific weapons systems were avoided, and the phrase 'Britain's independent deterrent' became standard.

While it remained on this general level, with its undertones of patriotism, the government proved effective in arguing its case. It was less impressive when the discussion moved back to the realities of nuclear war, finding itself out of tune with the times. The 1980 pamphlet, *Protect and Survive*, explained 'how to make your home and your family as safe as possible under nuclear attack', and was roundly derided as soon as it became public, since few really believed in the possibility, let alone the desirability, of surviving a nuclear strike, even if one did whitewash one's windows. When a nuclear missile is found in the kitchen belonging to *The Young Ones*, Neil follows what he understands to be official guidance and paints himself white, while the animated film of Raymond Briggs' 1982 book, *When the Wind Blows*, mocked the absurdities and inconsistencies of government advice; its central character, James Bloggs' displays levels of optimism and faith in central authority that Candide would have admired: 'Ours not to reason why,' he says, as he constructs his safe haven, 'ours but to, er, something or other.'

Meanwhile, the home office minister, Douglas Hurd, attempted to reassure MPs that they shouldn't rely on American studies of the effects of nuclear attack, because 'British houses tend to be somewhat more solid than American houses', and then had to break off to deal with the laughter that ensued. 'Why the giggles?' he demanded, puzzled that his faith in the construction industry to save humanity wasn't universally shared. And behind the scenes a script was being drafted for the first broadcast in the aftermath of an attack on Britain. 'This is the Wartime Broadcasting Service,' it was to begin. 'This country has been attacked with nuclear weapons.' It went on to give advice on how we should deal with these new circumstances, recommending that we stay at home, close the windows, turn off the gas and conserve our water stocks: 'Water must not be used for flushing lavatories; until you are told that lavatories may be used again, other toilet arrangements must be made.' Just as helpfully, some thought, *Viz* comic offered IMPROVE YOUR GOLF AFTER THE BOMB, a handy guide to how a nuclear holocaust may impact on your game: 'After a nuclear explosion you may find that some of your fingers have dropped off. This will almost certainly affect your grip.'

If the government couldn't count on film-makers, playwrights or musicians to support the fight back against the rise of CND, it did at least have the vast majority of newspaper circulation on its side. In the immediate face of overwhelming cultural hostility, however, this wasn't always enough. Few developments, for example, were as roundly ridiculed by the mainstream press as the concept of the nuclear-free zone, intended to demarcate areas through which nuclear weapons and waste would not be allowed to pass, and where there would be no participation in civil defence exercises based around nuclear war. First propounded by Manchester council in 1980 and subsequently adopted by dozens of other local authorities, the nuclear-free zones were depicted with tiresome regularity by their opponents as Canute-like attempts to halt the progress of radiation at city borders; yet a 1983 opinion poll in London showed majority support for the idea, with even Conservative voters splitting narrowly in favour. But, as the general secretary of CND, Bruce Kent, was later to acknowledge, 'the steady drip of the main-line media' did eventually make an impact.

And the battle lines were by now stretched so wide that the conflict favoured those with greater resources at their disposal. A new government offensive came with the rise of peace studies as a subject in secondary schools. Peace studies had been a part of university life for some time, but they hit the headlines in 1982 when a number of local educational authorities were discovered to have authorized their introduction into the school curriculum. The education minister Rhodes Boyson, himself a former headmaster, led the charge against the proposal: 'It is the teaching of unilateral disarmament, which is an open invitation to the Soviets to take control of the world by threatening nuclear war,' he thundered, 'an encouragement to lay down our arms and let anyone walk over us and destroy our society.' Political propaganda, insisted the government, had no place in the classroom, though the Ministry of Defence somewhat under-cut that line of attack by issuing its own leaflet aimed at the classroom; titled *How to Deal with a Bully*, it put the case for Nato and for a strong defence policy to counter the Soviet threat.

Despite the controversy, when a 1983 study polled half the education authorities in the country, it found that peace studies had rapidly secured a foothold in school life: 12 per cent of Conservative and 31 per cent of Labour authorities offered the subject. Whether it should be taken seriously as a cause for alarm, however, remained doubtful. In 1986 Dr Armando Galfo, a former colonel in the US Air Force but now a professor of education, conducted a survey of thirty thousand British schoolchildren and concluded: 'Pupils in the schools where peace studies have been introduced did not display signs of the indoctrination feared by the government.' In fact it tended to work in reverse, with CND support strong in independent schools where the curriculum was considered right-wing, and anti-CND opinions most vociferous in schools that taught peace studies. As ever, children were proving remarkably resilient when confronted with the wisdom of their elders. Nor were teachers quite so extreme as their critics maintained: a poll for the *Times Educational Supplement* shortly before the 1983 general election showed that 44 per cent intended to vote Conservative, a long way ahead of support for the Alliance and for Labour. ('Like mice voting for cats', snapped Labour's education spokesperson, Neil Kinnock.)

Perhaps more worrying was the concern expressed by a delegation of teachers who met Douglas Hurd in 1982: that children were becoming so frightened by the threat of nuclear war that it was, apparently, disrupting their ability to learn and causing nightmares. A report in the mental health magazine *Inside Out* supported such claims, with Dr James Thomson of Middlesex Hospital insisting that 'Children's worries, anxieties, nuclear nightmares and terrors are getting worse.' It was far from clear whether the existence of peace studies ameliorated or aggravated this trend, but even the nation's most famous schoolboy was affected. 'I keep having nightmares about the bomb,' Adrian Mole wrote in his diary. 'I hope it isn't dropped before I get my GCE results in August 1982. I wouldn't like to die an unqualified virgin.'

As in so many other areas of British life in the early 1980s, the issues raised by nuclear weapons, the questions of war and peace, revealed a divided country, increasingly split between two diametrically opposed positions, squeezing out the compromise for which – if the Alliance poll results were to be believed – a substantial section of the people yearned. There was no unifying thread that brought the nation together, no single narrative that could be shared by a clear majority. This was a development that had been apparent since the divisive days of the 1970s, and was now growing more evident month by month. 'Britain needs another war,' wrote the political journalist Tom Nairn, more in irony than anger. 'This alone would recreate the peculiar spirit of her nationalism, rally her renegade intelligentsia (as in the 1930s), and reconcile the workers to their lot.' He added: 'Unfortunately, war of that sort – like her empire – is a lost cause.' What he hadn't calculated was that in these desperate times, a full life-or-death struggle in which the country's existence was threatened was not needed; a mere approximation would suffice. So it would prove with the conflict over the Falklands Islands in 1982.

Situated three hundred miles off the southern tip of Argentina in the South Atlantic, the Falkland Islands had long been the subject of rival claims to sovereignty. Britain had been in unbroken possession since 1833, and the couple of thousand inhabitants in the early 1980s unanimously wished to remain British, but Argentina had inherited a claim on the territory when gaining independence from Spain and was growing increasingly vocal in its demands. Recognizing the difficulty of defending the place militarily, given the huge distance from Britain, Whitehall sought a diplomatic solution that involved the handing over of ownership of the Islands to Argentina in exchange for being allowed to lease them back. Nicholas Ridley, as a minister in the foreign office, twice visited the South Atlantic, produced a plan along these lines and proposed it in parliament in December 1980, only to be met with the fury of the Tory backbenches. Having recently seen the former colony of Rhodesia transformed into Zimbabwe in a deal sponsored by Britain, they saw the voluntary relinquishing of one of the last remaining trophies of empire as being a step too far, and the Ridley plan fell. Argentina began to express impatience at the collapse of the talks.

Six months later, a review of the defence forces – by which was meant an attempt to find cuts in public spending – saw the announcement of the withdrawal of HMS *Endurance*, the Royal Navy vessel that had been stationed in the South Atlantic as a token symbol of Britain's obligations to the Falklands. The scale of the economy was so small as to be trivial – *Endurance* cost £3 million a year, set in the context of a defence budget that allowed £8 billion for the Trident nuclear programme – and several elder statesmen, including Lord Carrington, the foreign secretary, and James Callaghan, cautioned against the withdrawal of the ship ('I beg you, prime minister, not to scrap the *Endurance*,' urged Callaghan), but to no avail. If the move was considered to be without significance by the British government, Argentina read it as a lack of commitment.

None of this registered with the general public, very few of whom had then heard of the Islands. When the Central American state of Belize finally got full independence from Britain in September 1981, for example, the *Daily Mirror* helpfully provided its readers with a list of what was left of the British empire: Hong Kong, Gibraltar, Diego Garcia, Virgin Islands, Cayman Islands, Montserrat, Pitcairn, St Helena and the Turks & Caicos Islands. It forgot even to mention the Falklands. Even many of those who regarded themselves as being reasonably well-informed about the world would have struggled to identify the location of the Islands, though some might have recalled that when a dissident in Aldous Huxley's dystopian novel *Brave New World* is being sent into exile, so that he might write poetry without disturbing the stability of society, he asks for the most remote, forlorn and uncomfortable conditions, the better to inspire his work, and is promptly despatched to the Falklands.

The attention given in government to the issue was scarcely more substantial; there were so many more pressing domestic matters to be addressed. Margaret Thatcher herself had no particular interest in the Falklands (she didn't like the Ridley plan, but did nothing to stop him proceeding, and it was her insistence on cuts that had caused the *Endurance* decision — 'a military irrelevance,' she declared in her memoirs), and she subsequently faced considerable and reasonable criticism for allowing the crisis to develop. But ultimately none of that really mattered. When things began to go wrong, the British people were hardly surprised to find that their government had been incompetent and had taken their eye off the ball — such was only to be expected; what was entirely unforeseen was the ruthless determination to put the matter right, once the mistake had been discovered.

In December 1981 General Leopoldo Galtieri became president of Argentina at the head of a junta in a coup against the existing military president, Roberto Viola. Faced with an economic recession that put Britain's in the shade, he saw the unresolved dispute as a way of deflecting public hostility towards the government. The first move came in March 1982 with the raising of the Argentine flag by civilians on South Georgia, part of an island group east of the Falklands. Again it provoked little interest in Britain: 'The news was all rubbish,' wrote comedian Kenneth Williams in his diary, 'apart from a scurry in the Falkland Islands where some impertinent Argentineans are pinching scrap metal or something.' On 2 April Argentine troops landed on the Falklands themselves to seize control of the Islands, and suddenly it became impossible to ignore what was happening. The foreign office, however, did its best; lacking up-to-date information, one of its ministers, Humphrey Atkins, issued a flat denial in the Commons, and when the press desk was contacted by the BBC for confirmation of the news, the night duty officer laughed off the suggestion of an invasion: 'Believe me, if anything was happening, we would know about it.'

The response in Westminster was to reinforce the differing perceptions of where Britain now stood in the world, as seen in the entries made that day by the two principal political diarists of the time. 'It's all over. We're a Third World country, no good for anything,' despaired Alan Clark, the right-wing Conservative MP for Plymouth Sutton, who had once looked like he might become a serious military historian. 'I have a terrible feeling that this is a step change, down, for England. Humiliation for sure and, not impossible, military defeat.' From the other end of the political spectrum, Tony Benn was unconvinced that any of it really mattered: 'Some 1,800 British settlers do not constitute a domestic population whose views can be taken seriously, or rather whose views can be allowed to lead us into war.'

There was some uncertainty quite what the mood would be when the House of Commons convened the next day for an unscheduled Saturday sitting to debate the situation. Thatcher spoke first, aware that she had a great deal of ground to make up, that having British territory invaded on her watch did not enhance her status as prime minister. 'The people of the Falkland Islands, like the people of the United Kingdom, are an island race,' she said, sounding a Churchillian note that would become very familiar. 'They are few in number, but they have the right to live in peace, to choose their own way of life and to determine their allegiance.' She announced that a military and naval task force was already being assembled that would shortly depart for the South Atlantic, though there was no indication whether or not it was expected to see action. It was Michael Foot's response, however, that won the greatest praise from the government benches; in the absence of his foreign spokesman, Denis Healey (away on a trip to Greece), Foot was notably bellicose: 'There is the longer-term interest to ensure that foul and brutal aggression does not succeed in our world. If it does, there will be a danger not merely to the Falkland Islands but to people all over this dangerous planet.' Edward du Cann, chairman of the Tory backbenchers, promptly congratulated him: 'The leader of the opposition spoke for us all.'

Support from his own side was less forthcoming for Foot. From the right, Callaghan thought that 'it was important to find a way out, short of a full-scale amphibious assault with all the casualties that might accompany it.' From the left, Benn made a political calculation: 'We should not tie the Labour Party to Thatcher's collapse. Public opinion would shift very quickly if there was a humiliation.' And the Old Etonian maverick Tam Dalyell, who predicted that 'the Falklands could become a British Vietnam in the South Atlantic', challenged his leader soon after the debate, only to be slapped down: 'I know a fascist when I see one,' snapped Foot, for whom memories of Franco and Hitler were still fresh.

The Conservative Party too was split, though, as was its fashion, it didn't parade its divisions in public in quite the same way as Labour. As the task force spent the next few weeks sailing towards the Falklands, and as American-led negotiations ground away into futility, there were many who saw an opportunity finally to be rid of Thatcher, the leader who had aroused such hostility within her own party. 'They are within an ace, they think, of bringing her government down,' seethed Alan Clark. 'If by some miracle the expedition succeeds they know, and dread, that she will be established for ever as a national hero. So, regardless of the country's interest, they are determined that the expedition will not succeed.' The journalist John Cole also noted a reluctance to follow through the military option: 'I estimated towards the end of April that up to one-fifth of Conservative MPs wanted a diplomatic settlement on the best terms Francis Pym could negotiate.' Pym, Thatcher's greatest rival, was now foreign secretary, replacing Lord Carrington who had resigned in the immediate aftermath of the Argentine invasion, and was thus in pole position for the race to succeed, should the venture end in disaster.

In the event, these doubts in the darker corners of Westminster counted for little, for the nation took to the prospect of conflict with much greater alacrity than many predicted. 'In a strange way the British people had decided that they were not going to be pushed around by Argentina,' remembered William Whitelaw, and he was perfectly correct. Partly the public response was determined by the nature of the enemy. The military dictatorships that were then so characteristic of South America had long been perceived with a vague but nonetheless real suspicion, as summed up in 'Blood Sports', a 1980 episode of the television drama series *The Professionals*: 'The haves have it all; the peasants have what they stand up in,' says George Cowley (Gordon Jackson), describing an unnamed Latin American country, and Bodie (Lewis Collins) snorts, 'Maybe they should try democracy.' But there was also the feeling that Britain had had about as much as it could take of decline, and that it was time to assert its historical power.

There were, of course, many who opposed what seemed increasingly likely to be a military conflict — an anti-war demonstration organized by CND attracted quarter of a million people — but their voices were scarcely heard as a kind of war fever gripped the country from top to bottom. Conservative MP Matthew Parris missed the Saturday debate, being in his constituency: 'When I did return to Westminster on Monday, something seemed to have come over the whole place. All other concerns were forgotten, all other business relegated. It was as though we were fighting for our national life.' Similarly Roy Greenslade, features editor at the *Sun*, was away on holiday at the time of the invasion. When he suggested on his return that the whole enterprise was stupid, he was sharply rebuked by Wendy Henry, one of his journalists: 'You'll have to watch that. That's a very unpopular view to hold round here.' And, despite some assumptions, it wasn't just older generations who were affected; an opinion poll at the time showed that 'young people were more in favour of military action than were their elders'. Even so, there was not quite the hysteria that critics claimed, for there were plenty capable of keeping a sense of perspective. Jim Davidson, a working-class London comedian who was the alternative to alternative comedy and whose enthusiasm for the Falklanders' cause was greater even than that of Thatcher herself, was then a director of Bournemouth football club. He remembered being in the boardroom at half-time during a match against Wigan when news came through that HMS *Sheffield* had been hit, the first British loss: 'After the newsflash, everyone just started quietly talking again, and carried on nattering about football,' he wrote in horror. 'I couldn't believe that they had just pushed the news to one side.' The headlines might be dominated by a nation at war, but everyday life continued as normal.

Of these various responses, it was the one represented by Wendy Henry that was to prove most controversial in the long-term. Indeed it was Henry's reaction to the news that the first Argentine ship had been hit that was to provide the most famous headline of the decade, the one word GOTCHA. Unfortunately, by the time the paper reached the newsstands, it had become clear that the cruiser *General Belgrano* had been not merely hit, but sunk with a loss of over three hundred lives. Subsequent editions changed the headline, but it remained long in the memory to symbolize what some saw as the over-jingoist, blood-lustful attitude of the right-wing press, and particularly of the *Sun*, 'the lunatic nationalistic pride' that was later condemned by Admiral Sandy Woodward, the commander of the task force. Much of the rest of the *Sun*'s coverage, however, was no more than crudely humorous – including offers of T-shirts bearing slogans like STICK IT UP YOUR JUNTA and BUENOS AIRES IS FULL OF FAIRIES – and, though some doubted the taste of such jokes in the face of a real war, there was truth in David Owen's analysis that it should be seen 'more as an amusing morale booster than a sign that jingoism was running rife in the UK'. In this light, it was perhaps not much different to Flanagan and Allen singing 'We're Going to Hang out the Washing on the Siegfried Line' or Spike Jones and His City Slickers laughing at 'Der Fuehrer's Face' during an earlier conflict.

It was also noticeable that, despite its gung-ho fervour, the *Sun* actually lost sales during the course of the Falklands War, while the *Guardian*, which remained steadfastly sceptical about the whole episode, increased its readership. But with only sporadic and partial information being received from the South Atlantic, the media coverage became a major part of the story. In particular the BBC came under fierce attack for refusing to refer to 'our ships' rather than 'British ships', and was condemned by the right for aspiring to impartiality: 'The elaborate even-handedness jarred cruelly with those whose lives were at risk, with those of us who took ultimate responsibility for committing our forces, and with the general public,' wrote Norman Tebbit. But he was wrong, on the last count at least; a survey revealed that 81 per cent of the country approved of the BBC coverage. And Prince Charles, delivering a speech to the Open University, made it clear that so too did he. Nor was it only liberal-inclined commentators who were prepared to utter uncomfortable truths even during the conflict: 'If the Falkland Islanders were British citizens with black or brown skins, spoke with strange accents or worshipped different gods,' wrote Peregrine Worsthorne in the *Sunday Telegraph*, 'it is doubtful whether the Royal Navy and Marines would today be fighting for their liberation.'

In military terms, it was a far from straightforward operation. To begin with, there was the sheer distance involved. The Falklands were some eight thousand miles away and although there was a British territory, Ascension Island, around the halfway point that could be used as a staging post, the base there was on lease to America. Even when permission for its use had been given, the facility still required a major refit to cope with the traffic it would have to handle, and it remained sufficiently distant to mean that any planes flying to the South Atlantic would require mid-air refuelling: to launch a raid against the airfields in southern Argentina that were supplying the invading forces, it was calculated that seventy-six refuelling tankers would need to take to the skies to service a flight of four bombers. Establishing air superiority was always going to be a problem. Control of the seas was less so, though even here there were serious dangers: the task force included not only vessels of the Royal Navy, but also the cruise liners *Queen Elizabeth II* and *Canberra*, pressed into service as troop ships – they had hurriedly been fitted with some defences, but remained desperately vulnerable. Beyond that there was the ultimate issue of staging a landing on the Falklands. The only real objective was Stanley, the capital of the Islands (now renamed Puerto Argentina by the occupiers); if that could be captured then it was assumed the war would be won. But Stanley had been heavily fortified, there were still many civilians living there, and the British assault force was vastly outnumbered by Argentine troops.

There were also political considerations. World opinion was overwhelmingly on Britain's side – a United Nations resolution had unequivocally condemned the Argentine invasion, and support was also forthcoming from NATO and from the European Community – but that could change in the event of protracted hostilities. So too could support at home, where there was nervousness in the highest quarters. 'A lot of my job,' recalled Sir Terence Lewin, the chief of the defence staff, 'was trying to give the cabinet confidence that the services would deliver what they said they could deliver, because we hadn't had a war for a long time.' Even those with military experience themselves – William Whitelaw and Francis Pym had fought in the Second World War, and John Nott, the defence secretary, had served as a Gurkha officer in Borneo – expressed doubts at various points of the campaign. It was mainly to address these concerns that the first operation was the retaking of South Georgia, a militarily insignificant target but one where victory might produce a morale-boosting propaganda victory. So it was to prove: a naval bombardment was followed by the Argentine troops surrendering even as British troops were landing. Asked to comment, Thatcher was visibly relieved that the operation had gone so well. 'Rejoice!' she replied. 'Just rejoice at that news and congratulate our forces.' The papers duly obliged, with the headlines reading: REJOICE! REJOICE!

A week later the hostilities commenced in earnest. A series of long-range bombing raids from Ascension Island, further than any comparable mission that had ever been undertaken, saw the airport at Stanley hit, though not put decisively out of action. The *General Belgrano* was sunk by a British submarine – causing some controversy amongst those who were opposed to the war, since the ship was, despite initial government claims, not within the exclusion zone that had been declared around the Islands – and then, two days later, the *Sheffield* was hit by an Exocet missile. The fact that this latter was an aerial attack was a sobering revelation: it was known that Argentina possessed Exocets, not that it had the capability of firing them from its Etendard aircraft.

Back in Britain, news of these initial engagements was sporadic. The journalists who had sailed with the task force were severely limited in the reports they were able to send, since communications were dependent entirely on the military, whose priorities seldom coincided with those of the press. There was no live television coverage and footage – even photographs in many instances – could only be sent back by boat; unlike Vietnam, and certainly unlike the conflict in Kuwait at the end of the decade, this was not a media war. Instead the country was reliant on the press conferences given daily by the ministry of defence, whose official spokesman, Ian McDonald, became a familiar figure, slowly and carefully intoning the limited information that the government deemed appropriate to share with the public; he was frequently compared to a speak-your-weight machine in tribute to the dryness of his delivery.

Finally (as it seemed to those at home) on 21 May, seven weeks after the Argentine invasion, and following ten days of heavy bombardment from air and sea, British troops landed on the Falklands, establishing a bridgehead at San Carlos on the west coast of East Falkland, some sixty-five miles away from Stanley. Over the next couple of days, with the fleet now in close proximity, four more British ships were lost to Argentine attack. Where the Argentine air force was proving highly effective, however, the troops on the ground were much less so. In the most celebrated battle of the war, four hundred and fifty men of the 2nd Battalion of the Parachute Regiment recaptured the settlement at Goose Green in the face of an Argentine force that out-numbered them by nearly four to one. Amongst the sixty-four British troops who lost their lives in the engagement was the battalion's commanding officer, Lieutenant-Colonel Herbert 'H' Jones, who was posthumously awarded the Victoria Cross. Again the target was not of great military relevance – it lay some way south of the route from San Carlos to Stanley – but again it was a major propaganda victory, establishing the overwhelming superiority of the British troops over their Argentine counterparts.

There was one major reverse to come: an Argentine air attack on the landing craft *Sir Galahad* and *Sir Tristram* in Bluff Cove cost nearly a hundred dead and injured in Britain's worst day of casualties. It was not sufficient to halt the advance on Stanley, however. On 13 June British forces took the key defensive positions around the capital, most famously Tumbledown Mountain, and on the following day white flags were raised in the town to signify the final Argentine surrender.

All through the protracted build-up to hostilities, there had been considerable doubt about the possibilities for success of the mission, and the *Sunday Times* was not alone in warning that to try to regain the Falklands by force would be 'a short cut to bloody disaster'. In the aftermath, however, following what had been a remarkably swift and efficient operation, there were some on the left quick to downplay the significance of the achieve-ment. 'After thirty-seven years of post-war decline, Britain had finally been able to beat the hell out of a country smaller, weaker and even worse governed than we were,' wrote Ken Livingstone, while Labour MP Joe Ashton belittled the endeavour with a football metaphor: 'the equivalent of Arsenal beating Brentford'. These judgements were less than fair. Britain was certainly a stronger country militarily, but this was primarily because it was a nuclear power, possessing weapons that were of no use in this conflict at all, and in the name of which the conventional forces had been starved of funds. (The fact that a non-nuclear nation was prepared to invade British territory, some felt, somewhat undermined the argument for a nuclear-based defence policy.) The Argentine forces occupying the islands were far from negligible, the enemy air force was formidable, and the proximity of the mainland gave them support that the British troops lacked; even if they had been the equivalent of Brentford, they were at least playing at home.

The political risk too was considerable. Had British losses been much higher than the 258 fatalities that were sustained, if, say, all the Argentine shells that hit British ships had exploded, it would have become increasingly difficult to retain support in the country. And anything less than military victory would surely have ended Thatcher's premiership, so totally had she identified herself with the war. While some in her cabinet had wavered, displayed signs of hesitancy as military action became ever more probable, she had remained firm, insisting that this was a defining moment in British history. Her attitude was summed up in an exchange with Alexander Haig, the American secretary of state, when she pointed out that the desk at which she sat was the same one used by a predecessor when abandoning Czechoslovakia to its fate in 1938: it was a mistake she was determined not to repeat, for her model was very definitely Winston Churchill, not Neville Chamberlain.

The fact that the conflict could not be mentioned without evoking her image was, of course, one of the reasons why the left was so damaged by the Falklands. At the time, few Western nations had much experience of war since 1945, and those that did had hardly covered themselves in glory as they pursued colonial, post-colonial and neo-colonial adventures, whether it was France in Algeria, Britain in Suez or the USA in Vietnam. The Falklands was different: a rapid, decisive response to invasion by a foreign power. And it had Thatcher's name all over it. She ensured that this remained the situation, taking the salute at the victory parade in London, making an early visit to the Islands, and referring to it in seemingly every speech for years to come. 'We fought to show that aggression does not pay and that the robber cannot be allowed to get away with his swag,' she told a rally that summer, and this was essentially the interpretation of the war that most of the nation shared. 'We fought with the support of so many throughout the world,' she added, though she was unable to resist the Churchillian echoes of 1940: 'Yet we also fought alone.'

And perhaps it really was her finest hour. What had previously been seen as terrible political faults − her stubbornness in following her own course, her refusal to listen to other points of view − were now magically transformed into the greatest of her virtues: rigidity had become resolution, pig-headedness had become perseverance. The Falklands defined Thatcher, in the eyes of her supporters and detractors alike, both for the three hundred thousand people who turned out for the victory parade and for the band Crass, whose single asked: 'How Does It Feel to Be the Mother of a Thousand Dead?' Just as the Falklands without Thatcher came to be unthinkable, so too did Thatcher without the Falklands.

The other reason why the successful outcome of the war so demoralized the left was that the campaign had exposed an uncomfortable truth. In the Labour Party, wrote John O'Farrell, the war 'split activists directly along class lines: working-class members in favour and middle-class members against. On reflection the same split happened in my family: Dad who put HP sauce on his chops was in favour, Mum who put mint sauce on hers was against.' Or, as Julie Burchill pointed out rather more provocatively in *The Face* at the time: 'the left will have to learn that craven pacifism does not appeal at all to the proletariat.' The internal problems of Labour – its arguments over party democracy, the departure of the SDP, the deputy leadership contest – had already served to alienate many of the party's natural voters; now Thatcher's unashamed populism seemed likely to draw off yet more support. Despite Foot's enthusiastic support for the government's actions, Labour benefited not at all, for Foot was still seen as the man from CND, leading a party that was openly split on the correct response to the Argentine actions. Even after the surrender, the continuing controversy over the way the government had lied about the position and course of the *General Belgrano* when it was sunk (which Tam Dalyell, in particular, turned into a long-running crusade) did more to harm Labour than the Conservatives, since any mention merely gave the Tories the opportunity to talk yet again about the Falklands victory. And anyway, as Alan Clark pointed out: 'What does it matter where it was when it was hit? We could have sunk it if it'd been tied up on the quayside in a neutral port and everyone would still have been delighted.' His assessment was undoubtedly correct: for most people, the facts that the country was at war and that an enemy cruiser had been torpedoed were sufficient.

In the more rarefied circles of the left, the explosion of public patriotism and flag-waving was considered to be so vulgar as to be unacceptable in polite society. 'Now they are singing "Britannia Rules the Waves" outside Downing Street,' shuddered Alan Bennett in his diary on the day of the Argentine surrender. 'It's the Last Night of the Proms erected into a policy.' The novelist Salman Rushdie, meanwhile, could not help returning to the imagery of the governess: 'Hers are the politics of the Victorian nursery: if somebody pinches you, you take their trousers down and thrash them.' But elsewhere the Falklands entered British mythology with little difficulty. In a 1986 episode of *Only Fools and Horses* an expatriate south Londoner arrives in the Nag's Head and begins running down the country: 'The stench of defeat's everywhere,' he says. 'The old place has got no guts anymore.' And finally Del Boy loses his patience and his temper:

'Somebody else said that a little while ago. A little jumped-up general from Buenos Aires, and if you're not careful, you'll get what the Argies got.'

One other consequence of the war was, inevitably, a legacy of suspicion between the two nations involved. In popular terms, this was symbolized by the meeting of England and Argentina in the quarter-final of the football World Cup in 1986. Footballing relations had been poor for twenty years, since a controversial encounter in the 1966 tournament, but the Falklands had given an added edge, as seen in the *Sun*'s front-page headline on the day of the match: IT'S WAR SENOR!, an angle that was mirrored in the Argentine media. The fact that Argentina went on to win with two contrasting goals by Diego Maradona in the space of five minutes – the first a blatant and deliberate handball, the second a sublime piece of dribbling that was later to be voted the Goal of the Century – did nothing to restore harmony between the rival supporters, though the *Sun* did have the wit to echo its earlier headline: OUTCHA! Maradona became the great pantomime villain for England supporters (and something of a hero for Scotland fans), particularly since he offered no apology for cheating on the first goal, explaining that it was scored 'a little with the hand of Maradona and a little with the hand of God', but his attitude was not unprecedented. As a player with Barcelona, he had faced Manchester United in the 1984 Cup-Winners' Cup and made it perfectly clear where he stood: 'I would want to beat the English, even if we were playing marbles,' he declared. 'I am very much Argentinean.' (His relationship with English fans might have been different had Sheffield United been successful in their attempt to lure him to Bramall Lane in 1978.)

The tense relationship also surfaced, more unexpectedly, in Alan Hollinghurst's novel *The Swimming Pool Library*, in which the central character, William Beckwith, cruises a young Latin-American in a bar and only discovers back in the man's hotel room that he's Argentinean. 'But what about the war?' he asks, and his pick-up, Gabriel, hastens to reassure him. 'That's all right,' he says. 'You can suck my big cock.' Even so the subject can't be entirely avoided, and later on Gabriel suggests, 'I could whip you for what you did to my country in the war.' But Beckwith demurs: 'I think that might be to take the sex and politics metaphor a bit too seriously, old chap,' he replies.

In the real political world, it was clearly the Tories who emerged victorious from the war. On the eve of the Argentine invasion, the polls had showed all three parties running neck-and-neck, but a by-election in Beaconsfield, Buckinghamshire, conducted during the fighting, showed which way the wind was blowing. It produced the only by-election swing to the Tories of the entire decade as they retained a safe seat; the Alliance did increase their share of the vote, but only at the expense of the Labour candidate, who, despite being a personable young moderate named Tony Blair, managed to lose 10 percentage points and his deposit. Thatcher, having recorded the lowest-ever satisfaction rating for a prime minister – just 25 per cent of the population – now saw that figure climb above 50 per cent; she was still a long way short of the 79 per cent once achieved by Harold Macmillan, but it was a major improvement.

When, in the aftermath of victory, Thatcher called an early general election for June 1983, she was condemned in some quarters for riding on the army's coat-tails but no one was greatly surprised. There were, after all, few other concrete achievements on which the Conservatives could call. Certainly the worst of the recession was over – indeed, in technical terms the economy was no longer in recession at all, since gross domestic product was now on the rise, though it had not yet returned to the levels of 1979 – and inflation had been falling for over a year, reaching a fifteen-year-low by the election. But the recovery was hardly built on the most secure foundations. Immediately following the Falklands, the government had stimulated a consumer boom by abolishing hire-purchase restrictions and other credit regulations, encouraging the public to spend its way out of recession, and there were some who argued that the resultant feelgood factor was not sustainable, since the collapse of manufacturing meant that this demand was soaked up in imports. (Interest rates went up immediately after the election.) Others were keen to point out that the economic improvement came as a result of the abandonment of monetarism – the money supply grew well beyond the stated targets as billions of pounds were pumped into the economy – and from an unplanned devaluation of the pound, both of which had long been policies advocated by Peter Shore, the Labour Party's shadow chancellor. It was not entirely clear, some reflected, what the monetarist experiment had achieved: despite the benefits of North Sea oil, the recession in Britain had been longer and deeper than in comparable countries that imported their fuel.

Even so, for most of the population the twelve-month period leading up to the election was a welcome relief from the dark days of 1981, and the government could reasonably claim that the corner had been turned. 'National recovery has begun,' claimed the Conservative manifesto, and set out what it called the stark choice for the country: 'either to continue our present steadfast progress towards recovery, or to follow polices more extreme and more damaging than those ever put forward by any previous opposition.' The Thatcherite project was presented as a work in progress, with the good times soon to come. 'The rewards are beginning to appear,' urged the manifesto. 'If we continue on our present course with courage and commonsense, those rewards should multiply in the next five years.'

Thatcher's boldest political move during the campaign was to skate over the fact that the numbers of the unemployed had officially reached three million. Unemployment had been such a huge factor in British politics since the 1930s, and particularly as the dole queues had so relentlessly lengthened in the last few years, that it seemed heretical to pay it so little attention. Yet Thatcher's calculation proved to be entirely correct; a Gallup poll in 1983 showed that only 13 per cent of the electorate were themselves hit by unemployment, and by the time of the election, as Labour MP Austin Mitchell pointed out: 'The standard of living of those in employment had risen since 1979. The national decline in living standards was wholly concentrated on the unemployed. An issue Labour was counting on to turn the people against the government had also turned them against each other.'

The election campaign was marked by an overwhelming vote of confidence in the government from Fleet Street. The Mirror Group papers were the only ones to endorse Labour (if not its policies) throughout the campaign, though the *Guardian*, *Observer* and *Daily Star* at least remained neutral until the last few days. All the others enthusiastically backed the Tories, who could thus count on the support of daily newspaper sales of 11.4 million, somewhere around 75 per cent of circulation, massively out of proportion to the share of the vote they would win. And the coverage in those papers was personal in a way that it had never previously been, much of it targeted directly at Michael Foot. Clive James in the *Observer* called him 'a floppy toy on Benzedrine,' while the *Sunday Telegraph* referred to him as 'an elderly, ranting pamphleteer waving a stick in Hampstead'. The *Sun* settled for 'an amiable old buffer, his jacket buttoned too tight, his collar askew, his grey hair falling lankly,' while its headline summed up the general Fleet Street attitude: DO YOU SERIOUSLY WANT THIS OLD MAN TO RUN BRITAIN?

Apart from personal abuse, the other line of attack was the accusation that Foot was just the front man. 'The party's leftwing wanted Michael Foot as a figurehead, a ventriloquist's dummy who would repeat whatever message was fed into his head,' insisted the *Sun*. 'In him they found a willing dupe.' In a subsequent attack they identified THE LEFTIES WHO WOULD RUN BRITAIN IF LABOUR WON POWER THIS WEEK naming all the usual suspects — Tony Benn, Ken Livingstone, Arthur Scargill — as well as trying out a few new names, including Michael Meacher and Paul Boateng, neither of whom ever graduated to become serious bogeyman figures.

In any event, the Labour campaign was disastrous: thoroughly disorganized, focused on preaching to the faithful in public meetings rather than to the unconverted through the media, and with a spectacular level of disunity that allowed a hostile press to focus on disarmament and Europe to the exclusion of more core themes: unemployment, health and education. When Labour did try to concentrate on these issues, Thatcher effortlessly turned the spotlight back on their weak points, so that when Denis Healey accused the Tories of trying to dismantle the NHS, Thatcher's response was that she had 'no more intention of dismantling the National Health Service than I have of dismantling Britain's defences'. Even worse was James Callaghan's contribution: he considered an election campaign the ideal time to air again his view that his party's defence policy was dangerous nonsense.

Nor was the campaign helped when two front-bench spokespeople, Healey and Neil Kinnock, broke ranks and made off-the-cuff comments about the Falklands that were seized upon by the newspapers; Healey suggested that Thatcher 'glories in slaughter', while Kinnock replied to a comment that 'Mrs Thatcher's got guts' with a quip that didn't really work: 'It's a pity that other people had to leave theirs on the ground at Goose Green in order to prove it.' Back on safer, if less specific, ground, Kinnock redeemed himself a little with a magnificent speech at the end of the campaign, denouncing what he saw as Thatcher's abuse of power, 'toughened by Tebbitry and flattered and fawned upon by spineless sycophants, the boot-licking tabloid knights of Fleet Street and placemen in the quangos.' He went on: 'If Mrs Thatcher wins on Thursday, I warn you not to be ordinary. I warn you not to be young. I warn you not to fall ill. I warn you not to get old.'

Elsewhere, the Alliance campaign suffered from having two leaders, Roy Jenkins and David Steel, with the former nominated as prime minister designate in the highly unlikely event that they won power. He was undoubtedly the senior figure, but did little to enthuse the electorate outside north London; Steel, despite having no ministerial experience at all, was by far the more popular, offering the kind of clean start that many sought from the centre alternative. The combination of the two men was attractive to some, but confusing to many more.

And Thatcher, secure in the knowledge that the opposition was fatally split, proceeded serenely around the country, giving a masterclass in how to stage-manage an election campaign. Her progress culminated in a rally for youth staged at Wembley that attracted a 2,500-strong audience, consumed by wild enthusiasm. 'It will be seen as a remarkably adept piece of political salesmanship,' judged *The Times*, though the 'youth' theme was perhaps overstretching things a little: the comperes were Bob Monkhouse and Jimmy Tarbuck, with a combined age of ninety-eight, while the only pop star they could attract was Lynsey de Paul, who hadn't troubled the top ten in nearly a decade; she debuted a new number entitled 'Tory, Tory, Tory'. Also attending was a motley collection of sports figures including swimmer Sharron Davies, judo champion Brian Jacks, Arsenal manager Terry Neill, boxer Alan Minter and world snooker champion Steve Davis. 'That was probably my biggest mistake, getting involved in that,' reflected the last, five years on. 'It was bad for my image.' The most famous contribution came from disc jockey and comedian Kenny Everett, whose jocular suggestions ('Let's kick Michael Foot's stick away', 'Let's bomb Russia') attracted much adverse criticism. 'Mr Everett may be the foolish face of Toryism. But his audience was the ugly one,' reflected the *Daily Mirror*. 'The kind of mind which enjoys rightwing extremist support is the kind of mind that laughs at Mr Everett.' The criticisms were met head-on by Thatcher. 'They were just cheering because they were having tremendous fun,' she retorted. 'I really just begin to wonder what has happened to a British sense of humour.' It was an interesting reversal of what was perceived to be her own humourless nature.

(It wasn't noted at the time, but little of this was new, even in the choice of venue. Back in September 1964 Harold Wilson had launched Labour's election campaign with a rally at what was then called the Empire Pool, Wembley, with contributions by a Welsh male-voice choir, Vanessa Redgrave, Harry H. Corbett – in his sitcom incarnation as Harold Steptoe – and Humphrey Lyttelton's Jazz Band.)

When the returns came in, they showed a low turnout – always a sign that the result is a foregone conclusion – and a landslide victory for the Conservatives in terms of parliamentary seats, with a majority of 144 over all other parties, though its share of the vote actually went down slightly from 1979, and was even lower than Alec Douglas-Home had achieved when losing in 1964 to Wilson. The Alliance, cheated as third parties tend to be by the electoral system, got 25.4 per cent of the vote and just 3.5 per cent of the seats, the main losers in the partnership being the SDP who returned only six MPs, a far cry from the twenty-nine with which it had gone into the election. But the real story was the humiliating disaster that befell the Labour Party; for a moment during the campaign it looked as though it might even slip behind the Alliance in terms of the popular vote and, though it avoided that calamity, it ended up just two percentage points in front.

The scale of the débâcle was frightening. Under the electoral rules of the time, a candidate needed to secure 12.5 per cent of the constituency vote in order to retain his or her deposit: Labour lost its deposit in 119 seats, more than one in six of those contested, most of them in the south, where the party had virtually disappeared. By way of comparison, it had lost a total of eighty-four deposits in the previous eleven general elections, and in 1983 the Alliance lost just twelve deposits and the Tories only five. Looked at another way, Labour got a lower average vote per candidate than at any election since 1900. Even amongst its core support, little was certain: Labour won the support of only 39 per cent of trade unionists, with the Tories hard on their heels on 32 per cent, while in Wales the party won just 38 per cent of the votes, where in 1960 it had topped 60 per cent. Bryan Gould, who had lost his Southampton seat in 1979, was one of the lucky ones, returning to the Commons for the Dagenham constituency, where a previous candidate 'had in one post-war election campaigned on the slogan "Give him a 40,000 majority"'; Gould got a majority of under three thousand.

Unless one were a hardcore Thatcherite, the election was a catastrophe, not merely for the Labour Party, but for the country that was clearly going to be deprived of an effective opposition for another four or five years. But given the behaviour of the previous period, and given the appallingly inept campaign, only the most absurdly optimistic Labour supporter could have expected anything different. There was at least one. 'The Alliance is beginning to grow at the expense of the Tories,' wrote Tony Benn, a week before polling day, 'and it is possible that enough Tories will vote for the Alliance to allow Labour to slip in.' He was wrong, and in the wipe-out he himself lost the seat which he had held – with a brief interruption while he fought to renounce his peerage – since 1950. Re-entering a world outside parliament was fraught with small difficulties, as the former postmaster general discovered to his horror that 'the cost of stamps is astronomical'. There was a brief consolation when he indulged his love of gadgets to buy an answerphone – 'an absolutely amazing invention' – before he realized it was 'also a bit of a curse because you have to ring people back, and that increases the phone bill.' The following month he found that his telephones had been cut off; in the disruption to his routine, he had forgotten to pay the bill.

Benn's defeat was the highest-profile loss of the election, and seemed entirely appropriate to the occasion. The party had fought on a platform of his devizing – had he been the leader, the manifesto would have remained the same – and it had been comprehensively routed. But still, Benn's optimism remained undimmed: 'for the first time since 1945 a political party with an openly socialist policy had received the support of over 8½ million people,' he wrote triumphantly in the *Guardian*. But it wasn't the best image to evoke, for in 1945, with a much smaller electorate, the Labour vote stood at just under twelve million; in the intervening years, the party had fallen 22 percentage points in the share of the vote. A more accurate appraisal came from Austin Mitchell, who wrote of Labour 'rescuing disaster from the jaws of defeat'. And there could be little argument with Alan Clark's gleeful summary: 'a government majority of 140 and no opposition of any kind in sight.'

PART TWO

WHEN THE WIND BLOWS
1983–87

It was a quiet Friday morning in Downing Street. The prime minister was stewing over a draft bill to privatize the armed forces.
Robert Barnard, *Political Suicide* (1986)

LAMBERT LE ROUX: What I do is a natural thing. There is nothing unnatural about making money.
Howard Brenton & David Hare, *Pravda* (1985)

JACK BOSWELL: We don't have jobs, we just have optimism.
Carla Lane, *Bread* (1986)

6

The Second Thatcher Government

'The edge of heaven'

> Authoritative, Mr Kinnock is not. But nobody should
> underestimate his appeal – especially to women and to
> young voters. The freckle-faced scamp with a heart of
> gold is a cliché of the silver screen.
> *Daily Mail* (1984)

> Who will be watching football in ten years' time?
> Terry Cooper, player-manager of Bristol City (1984)

> British industry looks more and more like a museum, with
> old, rusty equipment and men in overalls looking like
> creatures from a past industrial era.
> Tony Benn (1984)

Its official title was *The New Hope for Britain*, but the Labour Party's manifesto for the 1983 election is best remembered by the phrase used by Gerald Kaufman to describe it: 'The longest suicide note in history.' In fact, it wasn't quite as lengthy as that suggests – around 20,000 words, compared to the 25,000 words in the manifesto prepared by the Sheffield Labour Party for the local government elections in the same year – but it was remarkably wide-ranging, covering policies on everything from forestry to the Falkland Islands, from a minimum wage to water-based sports. Or, as Roy Hattersley put it, 'it only seemed interminable'. The accusation at the time was that the manifesto was of such an extreme left-wing nature that it was bound to alienate voters, particularly on withdrawal from Europe without a new referendum, on further nationalization of industry, and on defence (though the actual wording on the latter showed signs of a fudge that was never destined to hold: 'Unilateralism and multilateralism must go hand in hand if either is to succeed'). It was, in short, a rounding up of every last detail of The Policies, with little regard for coherence or priority.

And yet by this stage the left had already suffered key setbacks: the 1981 defeat for Tony Benn in the deputy leadership contest had been followed at the 1982 conference by a clutch of right-wing victories in the elections to the National Executive Committee. Benn himself had lost the chairmanship of the NEC's home policy committee, which he had held for eight years and which had been the base of his power within the party; he had been replaced by John Golding, an MP who was also a senior trade unionist and very much on the right of the party – he was said to regard political theory as being 'in the same league as crossword puzzles'. Which left a query about why the manifesto, this 'list of meaningless promises', as Peter Shore called it, was so readily adopted by the new regime. And the answer appeared to be that, along with most of the country, Golding realized that the election was lost even before the polling date was announced, and had concluded that the strategic interests of the Labour Party were best served by blaming the defeat on the left: 'Why not lose it on Benn's terms and teach him a lesson?' as he said to Hattersley.

If that wildly risky slash-and-burn tactic suggested that the right had regained control of the party, the public were hardly aware of the development. Indeed the immediate aftermath of the election suggested that normal business was being resumed. Michael Foot was obviously expected to step down as leader, given his age and the humiliating nature of the defeat, but he was not accorded the courtesy of announcing the move himself; instead Clive Jenkins, leader of the ASTMS union, informed the media that Foot was resigning and that his union would support Neil Kinnock as the successor. Other unions swiftly joined in, declaring for Kinnock, frequently without balloting their members, and the race was as good as won almost before the starting-pistol had been fired. Other candidates did enter – Hattersley, Shore and, in the absence from parliament of Benn, Eric Heffer for the left – though none of them had a hope of winning, and the impression given was that Labour remained firmly under the control of the trades unions, as Heffer pointed out: 'Prominent trade union leaders had decided who would get the job in advance of the election being declared.' Nor did the fact that Kinnock's major backers were Jenkins and Moss Evans, leader of the TGWU, both of them Welsh, as was Kinnock, offer much point of contact with the southern English seats that Labour needed to win. (Kinnock was the third leader in a row to represent a Welsh constituency.)

In the SDP there was also a backstage coup to remove the incumbent leader. Shirley Williams and Bill Rodgers had failed to keep their seats – in the case of Williams, it was for the second general election in a row – and

David Owen simply informed Roy Jenkins that it was time for a change. Rather than engage in a divisive contest, and probably lose, Jenkins stood aside and Owen finally became the leader of a party, even if he did only have five MPs sitting alongside him. David Steel too decided to stand down as leader of the Liberals, but was talked out of it by his colleagues, and instead took a short sabbatical from politics.

So comprehensive was Margaret Thatcher's victory, then, that she came close to an extraordinary triple-crown performance that would have seen the departure of the leaders of all three opposition parties. Instead she had to comfort herself with finally seeing off the man once considered her principal rival. Francis Pym had taken a step too far during the campaign when he asked the voters not to give the Conservatives too big a majority ('Landslides, on the whole, do not produce successful governments,' he pointed out on the BBC programme *Question Time*), and after the inevitable landslide he was removed from the front-bench. Thatcher's own position now seemed virtually unchallengeable. The successes in the Falklands and then at the ballot-box, combined with an opposition that was still divided, left her stronger than any prime minister for decades, at least within the political classes in Westminster, Whitehall and Fleet Street. In the country, it was a more mixed picture. She was still more admired than loved, and still as hated as she was admired, but she sailed on regardless, untouched by those who refused to agree with her.

She was untouched too by the caricatures that became more savage, and more personal, as her authority grew. Most famously there was *Spitting Image* (1984), an ITV series created by Peter Fluck, Roger Law and Martin Lambie-Nairn which featured grotesque puppets caricaturing public figures and appearing in short, satirical sketches. Much of the early media outrage was reserved for the very fact of the programme's existence, and for its irreverent treatment of the royal family — TV'S CRUELLEST SHOW TAKES A SWIPE AT THE QUEEN MOTHER, revealed a horrified *Daily Mirror* — but over the next few years it became the main purveyor of satire to the nation, popular enough to provide the cast with a No. 1 single in the shape of 'The Chicken Song' in 1986 (the second No. 1 to rhyme 'Eskimo' with 'Arapahoe', to the delight of those who wrote trivia questions). It was, however, somewhat hit or miss: the puppets, everyone was agreed, were magnificent, but it took some time for the quality of the jokes to catch up. And it was never quite certain that the attacks were very well directed: Thatcher was initially depicted as a ranting bully dressed in a man's suit, but the portrayal did her no harm, since it merely emphasized her strength, an attribute that was much vaunted by her supporters.

Nor did the parody in the film *Whoops Apocalypse* (1986) hurt her, though possibly this was because it failed to attract much of an audience. The film starred Peter Cook as a fictional prime minister Sir Mortimer Chris, who wins a minor conflict in Latin America and then goes mad, denying that unemployment is caused by his government's policies, and arguing instead that it's the work of 'pixies, sprites, elfin folk, all manner of goblinery'. But he has a solution: if ten thousand workers jump off a cliff every week, it will create ten thousand new jobs. And so popular has he become that the proposal is greeted with enthusiasm. 'Well, I think he's bloody marvellous. He brought us through the war, and I think he can do the same for the economy,' says one of those just about to be sacrificed. 'I'm proud to leap to my certain death for Britain.' As Sir Mortimer puts it: 'A prime minister has to be resolute. But you can't be resolute without showing you're strong. And you can't show you're strong without blowing people up.'

This was, despite the attacks, the economic highpoint of Thatcher's period as prime minister. The repeated claims that she wanted to build a land fit for entrepreneurs finally appeared to be bearing fruit and, if some worried that the success stories seemed to be based in the retail, services and financial sectors while manufacturing was still struggling, their opinions were mostly lost in the media babble of voices belonging to those who were making more money, and paying less tax, than for a very long time. And it wasn't simply the rich who were celebrating; for the most part, the middle classes and the upper sections of the working classes also benefited in financial terms, even if this was largely based on the way that credit, in terms of both cards and mortgages, had become easier to obtain than ever before.

Of the personnel changes in parliament, the most significant was the arrival of Kinnock since, despite the continuing threat of the Alliance, Labour was still the only plausible alternative government in the short term. Despite his alleged apostasy in the deputy leadership contest, when he had abstained rather than vote for Benn, Kinnock was considered to be on the left, and an enormous amount of faith was vested in him as the man who could reverse the party's declining fortunes. He won the leadership by a huge margin in the electoral college, but closer analysis revealed a worrying inconsistency: he secured large majorities amongst the trades union and constituency sections, but fewer than half the MPs voted for him, and conspicuous amongst those who looked elsewhere were not only the rival candidates but other senior figures in the parliamentary party, including James Callaghan, Denis Healey, Gerald Kaufman, Merlyn Rees and John Smith. He did enjoy the support of two newly elected MPs of whom big things were expected – Gordon Brown and Tony Blair – but his shadow cabinet was necessarily formed of people who not only had a good deal more experience than he had of government (for he had none), but had also in the main voted against him, leaving him a sometimes isolated figure: 'He was widely regarded by his senior colleagues as a lightweight,' remembered his former trade and industry spokesperson, Bryan Gould. 'He had few friends he could trust.'

The press picked up on this insecurity and exploited Kinnock's perceived immaturity to great effect. FUNNYMAN KINNOCK IS JESTER A BORN LOSER, said the *Sun*, insisting that he was out of his depth, however likeable he appeared, however good his jokes were. The attacks were seen to hurt, for he seemed remarkably thin-skinned for a senior politician, and were therefore redoubled. Gould met him one evening in 1984, after he 'had had a few drinks' and 'was dismayed at what I saw of his state of mind. It was clear that media criticism was getting to him. He talked of throwing it all in.' As Healey remarked to Hattersley: 'It's all right for us. We've been up to our eyes in shit for years. He's not used to it.' Nor was his cause helped by his first photo-opportunity as leader; walking along Brighton beach hand-in-hand with his wife, Glenys, he fell over and was almost drenched by an incoming wave.

Nonetheless, Kinnock brought to the job some important attributes for Labour. During the general election campaign, Foot had expressed his regret that there were too many intellectuals in the senior ranks of the party at the expense of the working class, and had added in this context that Kinnock would be a good leader; as the party's press officer, Andy McSmith, later pointed out, he 'had a working-class background which, in that particular phase of Labour Party history, was an immense advantage'. Furthermore, in an era that was increasingly dominated by 20-second soundbites designed for television consumption, he was by far the best platform speaker of his generation, and one of the few genuine orators left in the country. In the eyes of the Labour Party, nurtured on Aneurin Bevan, Michael Foot and Tony Benn, a facility with, and love of, words didn't make Kinnock the 'Welsh windbag' so often portrayed in the media, but rather a man who connected with a great tradition. And the fact that he was a man steeped in Labour history undoubtedly helped him in his mission to re-orient the party. It was an aspiration he spelt out early on; during the leadership campaign, he had not only defended the policies of the manifesto, but also hinted that he had done the electoral arithmetic and was prepared to appeal beyond the Labour heartlands: 'We can only defend the have-nots of our country and the world, if we secure the support of the "haven't-got-enoughs", yes, and in addition, those who "have enough". That is not retreat, that is realism. It is not caution, it is calculation.'

Over the course of the parliament, he began slowly to steer a new course that would ultimately see Labour turn its back on virtually every major proposal of that 1983 manifesto. It was a process that, ironically, was greatly helped by the internal reforms for which the left had fought so hard. For Kinnock was the first leader to be elected under the new rules of the electoral college, and within the movement in the country, he thereby enjoyed a degree of authority and legitimacy that had been denied to his immediate predecessors. Furthermore, the power that had been given to the leadership of the unions, at a time when they were flirting with the left, was now thrown firmly behind him. A series of policy documents in the middle of the decade began to reposition the party and to unveil the language that would in the next decade become associated with Tony Blair's rebranding of 'New Labour'; they included 'A New Partnership, A New Britain', 'People at Work: New Rights, New Responsibilities' and 'Modern Britain in a Modern World: The Power to Defend our Country'.

Much of this was subsequently attributed to the work of Peter Mandelson, a grandson of Labour legend Herbert Morrison, who was appointed the party's director of communications in September 1985. His role was often exaggerated (by him as much as by anyone) to the detriment of, say, Charles Clarke and Patricia Hewitt, Kinnock's chief of staff and press secretary respectively, who arguably made equally significant contributions to reforming Labour, and he became, for better or worse, the personification of what was happening to the party; for the right, he was seen as a necessary evil; for the left, who disapproved both of his politics and of what was seen as his self-regarding pomposity, he was simply evil.

The term 'spin doctor' had yet to make its way across the Atlantic – as late as 1989 the *Sunday Times* felt obliged to provide a definition for readers ('a person who gives a slant or "spin" to a proposal, policy etc') – but when it did, Mandelson was ready to be acclaimed as such a figure, appearing to revel in his role as the one Labour man who knew how to manipulate the media, who valued public relations and stage management while all around were obsessing over detailed policies. He himself had worked in the media, as part of the team that produced LWT's current affairs show *Weekend World*, and undoubtedly his efforts did a great deal to sharpen the party's image at a time when it had never been worse, but claims that he was interested only in presentation were wide of the mark; there was also a strong political agenda. Despite being a former member of the Young Communist League, he was firmly on the right of the party – early on he had a 'political crush on Shirley Williams', according to his biographer Donald Macintyre – and few would have been surprised had he been amongst those defecting to the SDP. But a familial loyalty to the Labour Party ran deep within him, and he remained. And now that he was in a position of influence, he did all that he could to frustrate the left.

But the changes were already happening before Mandelson's arrival. Tony Benn re-entered parliament as MP for Chesterfield in March 1984, following a by-election when Eric Varley resigned his seat (Varley had earlier stepped down from the shadow cabinet, becoming the first British politician to utter the phrase 'I want to spend more time with my family'). On his return, he found the parliamentary leadership very different; in June he noted in his diary that he had received a letter from Kinnock 'suggesting that we should use certain "buzz" words to emphasize the Tory link with waste and incompetence and Labour's compassionate approach. It was just written by advertising agents, no hard political content.' Even as Mandelson was settling into his new job, Benn was already losing some of the optimism that had sustained him over the years: 'what a misery it is to be in the Labour Party,' he lamented.

The most commented-upon aspect of the new-look party was the ditching of the traditional logo of the red flag and the substitution of a red rose, launched at the 1986 conference, a gathering that ended with Kinnock and his wife throwing armfuls of red roses into the audience in what was hoped would be a voter-friendly photo-opportunity. (A 'triumph of image over substance' was Mandelson's honest appraisal of the adoption of the red rose.) Journalist Robin Oakley of *The Times* suggested that a new version of 'The Red Flag' should be adopted in keeping with the new logo:

> The people's flag is deepest pink,
> We're really nicer than you think.

Benn, suitably inspired, produced his own version, with a promise that the struggle was not yet over:

> The people's rose in shades of pink
> Gets up my nostrils and it stinks,
> But ere our limbs grow stiff and cold
> Our old Red Flag we shall unfold.

As Kinnock began to abandon the imagery and positions that had come to characterize Labour, it was not just Benn who felt himself cheated. Here, it seemed to many on the left, was yet another case of a supposedly socialist leader selling out his principles, the only difference being that he was doing it without even waiting to move into Downing Street. He insisted that he was trying to restore a sense of realism to replace the impotent protest that had previously prevailed – 'Better to light a candle, than curse the darkness,' as he wrote – but his approach was not always appreciated. Comparisons were instead sought with previous leaders, Ramsay MacDonald being evoked in a version of the Redskins' 1985 single 'Kick Over the Statues' that was titled 'The Ramsey McKinnock Mix', while comedian Alexei Sayle combined personal abuse with more recent memories: 'I haven't got much faith in Neil Kinnock,' he observed. 'If I'd wanted a bald Harold Wilson, I would have asked for one.' (A particularly cruel comparison, this, since Kinnock had, as recently as 1983, denounced Wilson as 'a petty bourgeois', adding 'he will remain so in spirit even if made a viscount'.) Of more substantial concern was the way that opinion polls, despite an early boost following Kinnock's election as leader, and despite the way that he was clearly taking much of the movement with him, showed he wasn't yet touching the population beyond. He was, as Robert Barnard put it in his novel *Political Suicide*, 'a red-haired, smiling man, whom everybody seemed to like, but nobody much wanted to vote for'.

The arguments for modernizing the party were rooted in the perceived decline of the industrial working class that had traditionally formed the bedrock of Labour support. The recession officially over, there were now jobs being created, even some manufacturing jobs, but they weren't necessarily in the places where the losses of the early 1980s had hit hardest – by 1986 it was estimated that there were as many people employed making pleasure-boats in the south as there were building ships in the yards of the north – and it seemed as though whole cites, indeed whole regions, were being written off, as though the boom years that were being promised would bypass large parts of the country, perhaps permanently. Thirty per cent of the jobs lost in the course of the first Thatcher government had been in the south-east; in the recovery of the second administration, three-quarters of the new jobs that were created were in the same region.

In 1984 the *Daily Mirror* journalist Anne Robinson returned to her hometown of Liverpool for a report on the state of the city as the slump continued: more businesses were still closing than were opening, and a quarter of the workforce had no job, with youth unemployment in some areas reaching 90 per cent. The world she found was already far removed from the rebellious days of 1981: 'There isn't any anger left in Toxteth. The spirit of revolution has vanished,' she wrote. 'Talking to ordinary people in Liverpool is like interviewing the recently bereaved.' Instead there was simply a grim resignation, a belief that things were unlikely ever to get better, an attitude epitomized by an unemployed 21-year-old, who spoke wistfully about losing her childhood dreams of travelling, though her ambitions even then had not stretched far: 'I wouldn't have minded going to Manchester for the day,' she said. 'I'll probably never go now.' She was living with the father of her 3-year-old child, and he too was unemployed. It was a far from unusual position, and some women were prepared to see the positive side, that at least their men were at home to help with the childcare: 'No question of my husband going drinking or gambling,' one woman told Robinson.

A year or so earlier, the writer Beatrix Campbell had recreated George Orwell's odyssey through the Depression-hit north of the 1930s that had produced his book *The Road to Wigan Pier*. In her own account, *Wigan Pier Revisited*, she observed the same phenomenon: 'one of the first things you notice in northern cities hit by unemployment is babies, lots of babies, with very young parents. Unemployed men in denims and trainers pushing buggies. The sight of teenage fathers is striking because it is in such stark contrast with the role of their own fathers.' As Robinson wryly pointed out: 'They've discovered equality in a way feminism never intended.' (It wasn't simply the young who were affected as Michael Elphick's unemployed character, Sam, explained in the sitcom *Three Up, Two Down* when he volunteered to look after his new-born grandson: 'Mrs Thatcher has given me plenty of free time for babysitting.')

And the reason for there being so many babies, an older woman in Sunderland told Campbell, was that having a baby was the only alternative to the exhausting futility of trying to look for work: 'You don't need to get a job when you're a mam. When you're a mam, somebody *needs* you.' The economic consequences of such a decision were harsh. The benefits system had been devised as a stop-gap measure to tide people over periods of hardship; it was not intended provide long-term care, and made little provision for one-off costs such as, say, a pair of shoes, but there were many who could see no prospect of any other source of income ever materializing.

The most memorable illustration of the limitations of the welfare state was provided by a 1984 *World in Action* programme, designed to see if a Conservative MP – in this instance Matthew Parris – could live for a week in Newcastle-upon-Tyne at the level of benefit deemed sufficient for an unemployed man by his government. Parris lasted for just five days before the money ran out. 'Perhaps the sharpest lesson I drew from that experience,' he wrote, 'was that unemployment is not only a problem of the pocket but of the spirit; and that once the spirit is broken neither money nor training can easily help.' The same year Alan Clark, not widely known for his bleeding heart, was greeted on a visit to Leicester by a group of unemployed demonstrators and got out of his ministerial car to hear their complaints: 'Gravely I listened. At intervals I asked *them* questions. I told them that if there was no "demand" no one could afford to pay them to make things. They quietened down. But that's a glib point, really. It's foul, such a waste.'

The riots earlier in the decade had produced one notable result: the direct involvement of Michael Heseltine, the environment secretary, in what he hoped would be the regeneration of Liverpool. A self-consciously energetic politician, and one of the very few businessmen to reach cabinet rank under Margaret Thatcher, he attempted to secure the involvement of major companies and private sector finance, knowing that public funds were not readily available; and he concluded that the city's decline might be reversed by planting thousands of trees and staging a garden festival to reclaim derelict areas in the docks. The festival, staged in the summer of 1984, was a success in terms of tourism – it attracted more than three million visitors – but Anne Robinson found little enthusiasm for it in the period leading up to the opening; the work was going to outside contractors, she was told, and there were few jobs for local people. The only ones who seemed to be benefiting were those who made their own opportunities: 'In broad daylight I watch three teenagers cart away a hefty cement mixer.' A woman passing by saw the same sight and simply laughed, 'God helps those who help themselves.' When asked what she thought of the regeneration work, the woman shrugged: 'The dogs are made up with the trees. That's all that happened.' Even Heseltine himself recorded that, '"Give us jobs, not trees" was the word on the streets of Toxteth,' though his own perception of the people of Liverpool didn't seem to incline him in that direction: 'Their instant sense of humour at least in part explains a certain ill-discipline that makes them difficult to organize in manufacturing industries.'

As the hard times continued outside the south-east and the midlands, as union membership continued to decline, so too it appeared that a whole way of life was dying, a self-sufficient culture that had had Labour running through its veins. And Labour's long tradition of being the party of the industrial working class meant that it too was looking in danger, representing an ever-shrinking base, linked in the public perception with the past, not the future.

Symbolic of the changes being wrought in society was the state of the national sport, which was already showing signs of drifting away from its working-class heartlands. In the 1982–83 season, as the Football League announced that it would in future be known as the Canon League, having embraced sponsorship, Tottenham Hotspur became the first British football club to be floated on the stock market – both developments were early indications of the serious money that would soon come into the game. The following season, the distribution of gate money in League matches was changed: previously a share of receipts had gone to the visiting club, so that a smaller club, say Swansea City or Brighton and Hove Albion, benefited from the much larger attendances possible at Anfield or Old Trafford; now that was amended to allow the home club to keep the entire proceeds, helping to institutionalize wealth inequality in the sport.

At the end of that season Keith Burkinshaw resigned as the manager of Spurs, partially in protest at the new business culture at the club; as he walked away, he nodded back at the ground where he had spent eight years and was quoted as saying mournfully, 'There used to be a football club over there.' Around the same time Terry Neill, manager of north London rivals Arsenal, was reacting badly to the attitude of his overpaid players in a 3-0 loss at Leicester City: 'What use is a £250 win bonus when they're on £1,500 a week,' he snapped. 'They don't know what it is to hunger for goals and glory. On days like today I think they just want to pick up their money and go home.'

If a new-found cupidity was afflicting football, it couldn't entirely obscure more established failings, including lack of investment and self-inflicted violence, symbolized by the twin catastrophes of May 1985. First came the death of fifty-six fans in a fire at Valley Parade, the Bradford City ground, followed less than three weeks later by the death of thirty-nine fans, mostly Italian, at Heysel Stadium in Belgium, during the European Cup Final between Liverpool and Juventus. In both instances, the poorly maintained and outdated structures of the stadiums were implicated in the high death tolls, but there was no avoiding the fact that in the latter case the trigger for the disaster was the violent behaviour of some Liverpool fans. The hooliganism that had blighted the game for twenty years had finally reached its inevitable tragic outcome. All English clubs were promptly banned from European competitions – seventeen clubs were to be affected before the ban was lifted five years later – and there were suggestions that the national team might also be excluded from competitions. 'Heysel was a horrible, horrible shock,' said the England manager, Bobby Robson. 'You felt ashamed.'

That shame, combined with the nightmare of Bradford, proved disastrous to the state of English football, with plummeting attendances in the 1985–86 season: a fall of 9 per cent in the opening months, ending with a total of just eighteen million passing through the turnstiles, a far cry from the post-war peak of forty-one million in the days of Clement Attlee's government. This was despite the absence from the television of highlight programmes for the first half of the season, as the League bickered with the broadcasters, the latter increasingly dissatisfied with the return on their investment. *Match of the Day* had once attracted up to thirteen million viewers, but that had fallen in the mid 1980s to just six million. As a television spectacle football was a fading attraction, and not just because of the unflatteringly short shorts that were then fashionable, nor because of Jimmy Hill's increasingly self-parodic and sanctimonious presentation; rather it was the fact that, despite the excitement of watching players like Glenn Hoddle, Ian Rush or Gary Lineker, the crowd shots of fans penned in like cattle behind security fences were hardly the stuff of which entertainment is made. Meanwhile Canon announced that they were ending their sponsorship of the league as soon as contractually possible. 'The season following Heysel was the worst I can remember,' wrote Nick Hornby; 'everything seemed poisoned by what had gone on in May.'

In the place of football came a new-found television interest in other sports. A public appetite had already been detected by schedulers for ice-skating and bowls, while darts was proving the most unlikely of ratings-winners, largely thanks to the cult appeal of commentator Sid Waddell, who delivered pithy summaries in a Northumberland accent: 'There's only one word for that – quintessential!' So familiar did darts-players become that when Dexys Midnight Runners appeared on *Top of the Pops* to mime to their hit 'Jackie Wilson Says', a song about the American soul singer, they did so in front of a huge photograph of the chubby face of Scottish darts champion Jocky Wilson. The incident entered pop mythology as one of the programme's most preposterous mistakes, though the truth was some-what different. 'For a laugh, we told the producer to put a picture of Jocky Wilson behind us,' remembered the band's singer, Kevin Rowland. 'He said, "But Kevin, people will think we've made a mistake." I told him only an idiot would think that.'

But if there was one sport that really benefited from the abrupt decline in football's standing, it was snooker. The game had been steadily growing in popularity since the explosive arrival of Alex 'Hurricane' Higgins, who had won the world championship at his first attempt in 1972, but the 1980s were to prove its golden age, coinciding with the rise of Higgins' arch-enemy, Steve Davis. The two men represented polar opposites in the sport – Higgins the self-destructive, emotionally charged, temperamental genius, Davis the poker-faced automaton who also happened to be the best player the game had ever seen – and their rivalry was pure box-office.

They were supported by a cast of characters so diverse that for a while they made snooker look like the new wrestling: Cliff 'the Grinder' Thorburn, David 'the Silver Fox' Taylor, Willie 'Mr Maximum' Thorne, Ray 'Dracula' Reardon, 'Steady' Eddie Charlton and the enormous 'Big' Bill Werbeniuk, a Canadian man-mountain suffering from a neurological disorder that apparently required him to drink vast quantities of lager: a pint a frame, to top up the six pints he consumed before each match. Then there was Jimmy 'Whirlwind' White, a south London street-waif so pale and emaciated he looked as if he hadn't seen daylight since he gave up formal education at the age of eleven; he had both form and style, having been arrested during the Brixton riots, and having got into trouble with snooker's governing body for his unauthorized wearing of the logo of Savile Row tailor Tommy Nutter during a televized match. Indeed so redolent was snooker of professional wrestling that G.F. Newman's script for the film *Number One* suggested that everyone thought the game was similarly rigged, that matches were fixed in advance: 'This isn't a sport, son,' says manager Mel Smith to his talented young star, Bob Geldof, 'any more than horse racing or boxing.'

There was initially some uncertainty about how television should package snooker. For several years the most popular incarnation had been *Pot Black*, launched by the BBC in 1969 in the dawn of colour television, though it was hampered by being a one-frame knockout event, which did scant justice to the game. A doubles tournament was staged for several years, as was a national team-based competition (though the fact that England entered two teams suggested the appeal wasn't quite international enough to make this worthwhile), and there was even an attempt at pro-celebrity snooker, with Higgins being partnered by rock and roll guitarist Joe Brown, and Davis teaming up with Radio One disc jockey Dave Lee Travis. But once it became clear that the principal appeal stemmed from seeing individuals being put under unrelenting pressure for hours on end – nearly fifteen million viewers watched Thorburn grind down Higgins in the 1980 world final – the gimmicky formats fell by the wayside, and the focus was placed solely on the mano-a-mano mental combat at which snooker excelled. The precision required to perform at the highest level was such that every note of tension was amplified by the cameras, so that the viewers could watch a player crumble under the pressure. It was the perfect television sport, with a restricted playing area that fitted neatly on the screen and with unbearable reaction shots of players slumped disconsolately in their chairs, waiting for an opportunity to return to the table, as they tried to forget the missed shot that had let their opponents in.

The huge television audiences drew from right across the social and age spectrum, with a particular appeal to female viewers (more than 70 per cent of the fan mail received by snooker stars was said to be from women). The sport benefited from the way a tournament could fill hour upon hour of daytime broadcasting, thereby attracted the unemployed, housewife and pensioner constituencies, and from the scheduling of the world championships, timed to climax on a bank-holiday weekend in spring to maximize its potential market. There was something here for the whole family to watch together, in a way that football simply couldn't match any more.

The key moment was Davis' first world title in 1981, the prelude to his subsequent domination of the game; he went on to win five more titles in the decade and to spend seven years as the world's number one. Unlike his competitors and predecessors, he was an advertiser's dream: a clean-cut, responsible and reliable young man, incapable of causing offence. More than that, he was managed by the Essex-born accountant Barry Hearn, who might almost be seen as the embodiment of the decade: a hustler on the make in relentless pursuit of success, status and publicity. Hearn was perhaps the first man in Britain to see where the real money was to be made in sport: not simply in winning tournaments, or even appearing in the occasional advert for Brylcreem or Brut aftershave, but in the corporate world that was largely invisible to the mainstream public: 'Davis's work is endorsements, company days, promotion back-up,' he explained. This was a very different beast to the old concept of snooker being the product of a misspent youth; this was the very embodiment of Thatcherite values: the cult of the entrepreneur and the celebration of big money deals.

Other players, who didn't speak the same language of enterprise, found it hard to keep up with the new commercialism, particularly Terry Griffiths, a former postman from West Wales who joined the Matchroom management stable fronted by Hearn and Davis. 'Being with them a lot has changed me as a person,' he reflected, as he struggled to fulfil the promotional duties required of him, and to get back to anywhere near the form that had made him world champion in 1979. 'We've got different views on so many things. Our *lives* are so different. I tried to mix the two lives up together as best I could, and I found it very difficult.' He added: 'I think a lot about it and I've changed a great deal over the last few years. And really, being truthful, I don't really like the kind of person I've turned into.'

Griffiths' problems encapsulated the confusion that reigned within snooker in the first half of the 1980s. This was a traditional working-class pastime that was now becoming a lucrative cross between light entertainment and hard-nosed business. On the one hand, it was virtually the only sport where smoking was banned in the audience but was permissible (almost compulsory) for the participants, a game that was historically fuelled by alcohol and gambling; on the other, it was being celebrated by the *Daily Mail* for the 'charm, politeness and unpatronising talk' of the players, for the way that 'they dress beautifully', and for the fact that 'they do not cheat: therein, in an era when the public is tired of the tawdry, the ugly, the sly and the banal, is the secret of their astronomical success'. By the middle of the decade, it seemed as though family-friendly finance had triumphed over the game's seedy roots, with Davis said to be the highest-paid sportsman in Britain, and to be appearing on television more than anyone else save for newsreaders. So big had the game grown that even its peripheral figures were in demand for adverts: commentator 'Whispering' Ted Lowe provided the voice-over for a Davis-fronted baked beans commercial, and match referee Len Ganley pushed Carling Black Label lager. Meanwhile Hearn's stable were collectively promoting Matchroom, a range of men's toiletries from Goya ('for men who play to win').

The sport's appeal was such that even Ken Livingstone said he relaxed from politics by playing snooker on the quarter-sized table he had installed in his bedsit, while Pete Davies in his dystopian novel of the near-future, *The Last Election* (1986) could only see further growth; in a country run by the Money Party, the green baize has become the opiate of the people, as a cable television channel called 147 entertains the unemployed mass-millions 'with a twenty-four hour a day diet of non-stop snooker, snooker, snooker'.

The onward march was not entirely without problems. Davis was world champion, but the outlaw Higgins branded himself 'the people's champion', with some justification, for he remained hugely popular, largely because of his unpredictability: one could never be sure whether he would leave a tournament in disgrace, having headbutted a referee, or in glory, having swept all before him in a breathtaking display of implausible potting. He stood valiantly against the gentrification of his sport, gloriously winning the world title again in 1982 and, after beating Davis in a 1985 match, turned to the television cameras to announce: 'We are fucking back!' In case anyone should misunderstand his enmity with Davis, he spelt it out on TV-AM the next day: 'I hate him.' He became a tabloid fixture, with colourful tales of his personal and professional lives – he was 'a walking time bomb who could literally explode without warning, causing serious injury to anyone nearby,' according to *Viz*. And there were further scandals involving the amorous pursuits of 'Randy' Tony Knowles ('the snooker player who pots more birds than balls') and the addiction to cocaine of the young Canadian star Kirk Stevens, who tended to wear a black shirt with white waistcoat and flares, as favoured the previous decade by John Travolta in *Saturday Night Fever*. But all of this was forgotten in the excitement of the 1985 world championship final, when Dennis Taylor, long considered a journeyman on the circuit, overcame an 8-0 deficit in frames to beat Steve Davis on the final ball of the final frame to win 18-17. Eighteen and a half million viewers stayed up past midnight to watch the victory of the slightly podgy, bespectacled David over a gaunt and ashen Goliath, shredding television viewing records with every frame.

That match was snooker's finest fifteen hours, and it came just weeks before the disasters at Bradford and Heysel. Soon after, the brewer John Courage – who had a one million pound endorsement deal with Davis – announced that they were discontinuing their sponsorship of the England football team. The following year, Davis lost again in the final, this time to the 150-1 outsider, Joe Johnson, whose victory, as an unglamorous, mixed-race northerner from Bradford (his father was Asian), gladdened the hearts of anti-Thatcherites everywhere. Neither Taylor nor Johnson, however, was in the same bracket as the cheerfully disreputable devil-may-care likes of Higgins, White, Knowles or Stevens; rather they epitomized the triumph of hard work, honesty and perseverance in the face of seemingly insurmountable odds. They were more akin to Dire Straits, a pub rock band who had survived the punk explosion by keeping their heads down and producing competent, tasteful, if uninspiring, music and were rewarded with a sequence of four albums in the first half of the decade that spent an average of 200 weeks each in the charts, one of them – *Brothers in Arms* – becoming the biggest album of the 1980s in Britain.

There was, perhaps, a lesson in here for the Labour Party, in terms of the reinvention of working-class culture for a new era: 'traditional values in a modern setting,' as Tony Blair would put it the following decade. But there was too a lesson for the Conservative Party. In later years, particularly after the advent of the even duller, even more talented Stephen Hendry, Davis began to win the popularity and affection that he undoubtedly deserved, but at his peak he was not much loved by fans. The former Labour MP now turned broadcaster, Brian Walden, saw in the lukewarm reception he was accorded a symbol of where the country was going wrong. 'Order, method, discipline, plus a stern control of eccentricity, is the passport to triumph in the modern world,' he wrote, but 'the marvellously proficient Davis is clapped with some reluctance. Does this not prove what an essentially frivolous people we are?' Instead the public warmed to the perpetual underdog Jimmy White, six times a world championship finalist, never a winner, perpetually undone by his addiction to the glamour of the flamboyant shot at the expense of craftsmanship and safety-play. If there was truth in Walden's analysis, it should have worried Margaret Thatcher, suggesting that despite her apparent political triumph at the polls, the nation remained unconvinced by the values she held so dear. Where she had once been seen as the rebel, kicking against the dominant orthodoxies, she now looked like she was the establishment, and if the new order she was ushering in really did require the 'stern control of eccentricity', then it was by no means clear that the British people were eager to embrace it.

At the same time that Steve Davis was being beaten by Joe Johnson in the biggest upset that snooker had witnessed, the government too was experiencing for the first time defeat in the House of Commons. As home secretary, William Whitelaw had had his own version of the old actors' adage about not working with children and animals: 'I was well known for my reluctance to become involved in legislation over Sundays, alcohol, animals and sex – subjects which tended to arouse fierce passions and cause immense parliamentary difficulties, usually without solving the problems.' But the much less astute Douglas Hurd was now in the home office, and in 1986 he brought the Shops Bill to Parliament, intending to relax the restrictions on Sunday trading in England and Wales that had been imposed by the 1950 Shops Act. The existing law was, as Hurd pointed out, 'confused and widely ignored': fish and chip shops, for example, were prevented from opening on the Sabbath, but Chinese takeaways were not, since no one in 1950 had foreseen their rise, and though it was legal to sell newspapers and periodicals, the sale of books was banned, so one was prohibited from buying a copy of the Bible, but could happily stock up on pornographic magazines. Meanwhile many shops – DIY stores and garden centres prominent amongst them – were simply ignoring the law, and local councils, who were responsible for enforcing it, lacked the resources and the will to stop them. To make the situation yet more absurd, these regulations did not apply north of the border, for Scotland was not covered by the legislation.

The Bill proposed sweeping away all the restrictions, and it met with substantial opposition both from church groups led by Robert Runcie, the

Archbishop of Canterbury, who were determined to protect Sunday as a day of worship, and from the shop workers union, USDAW, who were equally determined to stop their members' hours being extended. The former won over large numbers of Conservative backbenchers, the latter convinced the Labour Party, and the Bill was rejected at its second reading, a highly unusual fate for a piece of government legislation; sixty-eight Tory MPs defied a three-line whip to vote against the measure. 'The trade unions, churches, small shopkeepers and the women's movement have all been campaigning against Sunday opening,' exulted Tony Benn in his diary. 'It was the first time that the supremacy of market forces had been thwarted, and it sort of indicated that the Tories can't be certain of getting away with the rest of their policies.' He was a little premature – if it was the first Commons defeat for the Thatcher government, it was also the last – but there was a feeling abroad that the government was losing touch with a crucial section of its support, not merely the regular churchgoers, but also the traditionally minded people who may have grumbled about restrictions on Sunday shopping, yet still had an instinctive attraction to the rhythms of life that had been accepted for centuries. And Benn was right to identify that the focus on market forces was the key to why the Thatcherite coalition was showing signs of strain: the veneration of profit did not sit easily with many of those who were natural Tories.

Elsewhere the crusade to establish a moral hegemony, to inspire the nation with the traditional virtues of thrift, decency and sound defence, was not helped by a series of scandals that punctuated Thatcher's second term in office. The first sign of trouble came on election day itself in 1983, when Cecil Parkinson, the chairman of the party, told Thatcher that he had had an affair with his secretary, Sarah Keays, and that she was pregnant with his child; he had been pencilled in as the next foreign secretary, but was now shuffled off instead to the department of trade and industry. In due course the story broke in the media and, unable to hold on to even that less sensitive post, he was obliged to resign. When Thatcher was challenged on how Parkinson's decision not to seek a divorce in order to marry Keays chimed with her much-vaunted Victorian values, she responded: 'What is more Victorian than keeping the family together?'

It wasn't much of a scandal, in truth, for the talk of family values was always more a question of convenience than commitment. All of Thatcher's cabinets contained a number of divorcees (she was married to one herself) and even, in the case of Nigel Lawson, the new chancellor of the exchequer, a man who had indeed left his wife for his mistress, with whom he had already had a child. But Parkinson was implausibly being talked about as Thatcher's political son and heir – 'He is big already, but he is going to be very big,' wrote journalist Edward Pearce, shortly before the election – despite his chief attribute appearing to be that he looked like a matinee idol manqué in a British B-movie about airline pilots (unlike Norman Tebbit, who actually had been a pilot, but didn't have the requisite image). Consequently his departure was seen to cause Thatcher some collateral damage.

So too was the behaviour of Jeffrey Archer, who, having already upset some by claiming that many unemployed young people were 'quite unwilling to put in a day's work', went on to add to the gaiety of the nation with a hugely entertaining libel case. In 1986 the *News of the World* published a story alleging that the best-selling novelist, who doubled as deputy chairman of the Conservative Party, had paid money to a prostitute named Monica Coughlan, though it stopped short of saying that the two had ever had sex. The *Daily Star* followed up the story, but took less care with its wording, and made it clear that, in their view, there had been a sexual relationship. Thatcher was reportedly worried by the signals that were being sent out to the public: 'We can take one or two people running off the normal track but when everybody starts doing it, it's far more difficult to sustain the position,' she told her friend, Woodrow Wyatt. 'When behaviour like this becomes the norm then the public don't like it.' Archer issued writs against both papers, but while the *News of the World* swiftly settled out of court, the owner of the *Star* was reported to have been less willing to cede to demands for a front-page apology: 'Why should we give in to that little shit?' And so it proceeded to the courts.

The trial was chiefly celebrated for the summing up by Justice Caulfield, who gave every sign of having been smitten by the charms of Mary Archer, appearing as a character witness for her husband: 'Your vision of her will probably never disappear,' he told the jury. 'Has she elegance? Has she fragrance? Has she been able to enjoy, rather than endure, her husband, Jeffrey?' And, he wondered, would Archer, a man married to such a goddess, really be 'in need of cold, unloving, rubber-insulated sex in a seedy hotel, round about a quarter to one on a Tuesday morning, after an evening at the Caprice with his editor?' (The implication that a writer who had spent several hours with his editor might have little left in the way of libido was one of his few genuine insights.) Despite the widespread mockery that greeted the summing up, the jury at least were convinced, and found for Archer, awarding him record damages of half a million pounds; the final bill, including costs, for Express Newspapers, owners of the *Star*, amounted to more than double that. Fourteen years later, Archer was himself in the dock, being sentenced to four years in gaol for perjury during the libel trial, though it was too late to be of any comfort to Lloyd Turner, the editor of the *Daily Star*, who had lost his job as a result of the earlier verdict and had died in 1996 from a heart attack brought on, his widow believed, by the stress of the libel trial.

There were other shorter-lived scandals, including comments by ministers Alan Clark, who claimed that black British people were worried about being 'sent back to Bongo Bongo Land', and John Butcher, who suggested that northerners 'tended to be workshy'. There was the 2nd Earl of Gowrie, who resigned as arts minister in 1985 because it was, he insisted, impossible to live in London on a salary of just £33,000 per annum (the average wage when Thatcher fell from power was still nearly £20,000 short of that figure). There were Conservative MPs Keith Best and Eric Cockeram, obliged to announce they wouldn't seek re-election after being discovered to have improperly made more than one application for British Telecom shares. And then there was Harvey Proctor, forced to step down not because of the extremity of his views, but because of his predilection for acquiring the services of male prostitutes and spanking them if they got the answers wrong when playing the board-game Trivial Pursuit. There was even a spate of leaks of supposedly classified material by civil servants (Clive Ponting, Sarah Tisdall) and security officers (Cathy Massiter). And, most destructive of all for the government, was the Westland affair, though few were sure whether this was truly a scandal at all, or indeed quite what it was supposed to be about.

Westland Helicopters was a company hitherto mostly unknown to the general public, save for those who kept an eye out for product placement in the television action series *The Professionals*. But in late 1985 it hit the front pages when it transpired that the firm was struggling and that a dispute over its future had arisen between Michael Heseltine, the defence secretary, and Leon Brittan, the trade and industry secretary: the former wished to see a European-based consortium salvage the firm, while the latter, backed by Thatcher, favoured a merger with the American company Sikorsky. The details were lost on many, who responded in the same way as a character in David Lodge's novel *Nice Work*; seeing a headline that reads LAWSON DRAWN INTO FRAY OVER WESTLAND, she doesn't bother to read the story because: 'It is enough for her to know that things are going badly for Mrs Thatcher and the Tory party; the details of the Westland affair do not engage her interest'. Instead the whole case was seen – probably correctly – in terms of Heseltine jostling for political position, and of Thatcher being determined to put him in his place.

For, with the departure of Pym, Heseltine had emerged as the most convincing rival to Thatcher. Just about the only senior Conservative who could appeal both to the faithful and to wavering Alliance voters, he had achieved a strong standing in the party by siding with neither the Thatcherites nor the wets; his involvement in Liverpool appealed to the One Nation Tories, while his resolute performance on defence in the face of CND had won over those that Alan Clark called 'the Union Jack buffs'. He had also been for some years the most popular speaker at the annual conference, for reasons outlined by Jon Akass in the *Sun*: 'He can tell a good joke, for a start. He also represents the kind of golden lad that every Tory mother sees, or hopes to see, in her son. Very few Tory mothers want their sons to grow up like Ted Heath.'

Part of his appeal was that he was a self-made millionaire, a fact that also provoked many of the patronizing attacks on him by the more patrician elements in the party, from agriculture minister Michael Jopling's comment that he was a man who 'bought his own furniture', to William Whitelaw's horror-struck realization that he was 'the sort of man who combs his hair in public'. The hair was a particular source of amazement in a profession not noted for tonsorial extravagance; journalist Frank Johnson wrote that 'He's about seven foot tall and he's got blond hair that looks a wig', Simon Hoggart defined the verb 'to heseltine' as meaning 'to build up a monumental pile of blonde hair, fix it in place with a complicated system of scaffolding and webs, and then spray it with lacquer', while television presenter Robin Day refused to believe that he could ever be appointed defence secretary: 'His hair is too long.'

Nonetheless, he did become defence secretary and was one of the major successes in Thatcher's government until the Westland crisis blew up. At a cabinet meeting in January 1986, after months of negative press coverage, Thatcher announced that, in order to calm the situation, all future statements about Westland should be approved in advance by the cabinet office, and Heseltine replied that, if that were the case, 'Then I must leave this cabinet.' He stalked out of Number Ten and told a journalist outside that he had resigned, a development that was not yet apparent to his erstwhile colleagues in the cabinet room, who had shrugged at his departure and moved on to a discussion about Nigeria. At a subsequent press conference, Heseltine explained that the way the affair had been conducted was 'not a proper way to carry on government and ultimately not an approach for which I can share responsibility.'

Two weeks later, Leon Britten also resigned, though somewhat less willingly than Heseltine, and Thatcher's ability to hold her government together was being called into question, giving an impression that events were slipping out of her control. When Labour then choose Westland as the subject of a Commons debate, there was a genuine belief, including in her own mind, that she herself might not survive. Fortunately for her, Neil Kinnock, seldom one of the great parliamentary performers, delivered an opening speech that was unanimously considered to be amongst his worst ('long-winded and ill-considered,' reckoned Thatcher; 'unbelievably incompetent and windy,' agreed David Steel) and let her off the hook. 'For a few seconds Kinnock had her cornered, and you could see fear in those blue eyes,' wrote Alan Clark in his diary. 'But then he had an attack of wind, gave her time to recover.' When Heseltine made his own contribution to the debate, and didn't strike directly at Thatcher, it was evident that the crisis had passed.

By any normal political standards, Heseltine's career should then have been at an end, but he refused to slink away from the fray. Instead he went into a form of internal exile, waiting for the chance to strike a more decisive blow, while protesting his loyalty to the party and the leadership in speech after speech as he became a fixture on the constituency circuit. And he did retain a high level of support in the country. His 1987 book *Where There's a Will* was a No. 1 best-seller, despite being some way short of gripping, and opinion polls consistently found that he was the public's choice of next Conservative leader (though amongst Tory voters, he was regularly outpolled by Norman Tebbit). All this despite the fact that no one quite understood why he had actually resigned, save that there had been a clash of egos and style: there was no clearly delineated policy difference or point of principle that could be discerned. It was later pointed out, however, that after Heseltine walked out of the cabinet that morning, the meeting continued and ultimately turned to the vexed question of the proposal to replace the rates, as a means of funding local government, with a new system that would become known as the poll tax; as Heseltine's confidant Michael Mates was to observe ruefully: 'Perhaps that would have been a better issue.'

Meanwhile few tears were being shed over Brittan's departure from government, mostly because, in Thatcher's words, 'so many people think he comes over extremely badly on television and he is not a good communicator. They find him awful to look at. He's very clever but he is really not an alert politician.' Or, as Alf Garnett put it in the sitcom *In Sickness and In Health*: 'Looks like Morrie the fishmonger, that one does.'

Those comments, alongside the snide attacks on Heseltine, suggested that snobbishness was still rife in the party, despite Thatcher's own beliefs.

'As Mrs Thatcher had gone up in the world, so the Conservative Party had come down in it,' wrote Tory MP Julian Critchley in his novel *Hung Parliament*, and Alf Garnett agreed: 'The leader of a spiv government,' he ranted. 'She's ruined the Tory Party, she has. Her and people like her.' Somewhat more unpleasantly, the former prime minister, Harold Macmillan, sniffed that the cabinet seemed to have 'more Estonians than Etonians'. Leon Brittan and Lord Young did indeed have family origins in the Baltic states, but really this was crude and barely-disguised anti-Semitism, aimed also at other Jews in government, including Nigel Lawson, Malcolm Rifkind and Michael Howard. Nor did Macmillan's implication that Thatcher had dispensed with the old school tie entirely stand up to examination: of the five men she chose during her premiership to serve as her parliamentary private secretary, four came from Eton, with the exception being the Winchester-educated Ian Gow, while her most committed ideological supporters in cabinet were Etonian Nicholas Ridley and Harrovian Keith Joseph.

More damaging was Macmillan's remark that the government comprised 'a brilliant tyrant, surrounded by mediocrities', for this chimed far too clearly with an increasingly voiced opinion. Denis Healey put it in more robust terms, alleging that she presided over 'a cabinet of neutered zombies', while a character in Robert Barnard's *Political Suicide* concluded: 'People always talk about the prime minister as tough, but I don't think it's tough to surround yourself with pipsqueaks.' Chris Emmett, one of those providing the voices for the puppets on *Spitting Image*, saw it from a professional angle: 'Look at the present cabinet. From an impressionist's point of view there couldn't be a more boring faceless lot in the universe. They all have perfect, plummy, Tory, middle-class voices.'

These judgements were a touch unfair on a cabinet that included in the mid-1980s such heavyweight figures as Geoffrey Howe, Nigel Lawson, William Whitelaw, Norman Tebbit and Douglas Hurd, but as the decade wore on, and as the big names began to drop out for one reason or another, they were seldom replaced by people of equal stature, and the criticisms came to seem ever more valid. The 1985 arrival in cabinet of Kenneth Baker, for example, scarcely filled his opponents with fear or his colleagues with admiration – 'I have seen the future and it smirks,' commented one of the latter – and yet he would in due course come to look like a major player, so poor did the competition become. (*Spitting Image* portrayed him as a slug with a human head, which did little to endear him to the programme: 'It lacked subtlety, wit and all those things that maintained satire over the ages,' he complained in later years.)

The cabinet as it stood in 1983, however, was strong enough to resist the temptations proffered by the Central Policy Review Staff when they set out a radical agenda for the next term, including the abolition of the National Health Service, the ending of index-linked benefits and the removal of state funding from further education. Though she was talked out of them, Thatcher was in sympathy with the ideas, an indication perhaps that her claims to represent the silent majority were not always matched by reality; certainly any party that went to the country in the 1980s proposing to charge for visits to a GP – let alone for dismantling the NHS entirely – would have got short shrift at the polls. In the absence of such radical policies, however, there was a certain lack of direction to the second term. Despite the economic successes that were loudly trumpeted, the middle years of the decade were dominated not by new initiatives, but by conflicts with a series of old enemies: the miners, the IRA, local councils. And what seemed like a period of political drift was accompanied by the inescapable sound of grumbling over cuts in public services.

This latter was considered particularly unfair by those in government. Having come to power pledged to curb public expenditure, the Tories were now caught in a trap of their own making, finding it almost impossible to make the overall savings they had promised, but nonetheless being judged by their rhetoric. 'Our opponents had convinced the great majority of the electors that we had "cut" the National Health Service, and most other things beside, when in fact never had so much been spent on the social services,' complained Norman Tebbit in his memoirs. 'We were getting neither the bun nor the halfpenny in this controversy.' Nicholas Ridley was similarly keen in his memoirs to emphasize that, while GDP rose by 25 per cent during the decade, spending on health rose by 37 per cent (even allowing for inflation) and on social security by 35 per cent, though he skipped over the fact that much of the latter was the result of increased unemployment.

However much they protested, the reality was that ministers simply weren't believed, and the imagery of cuts entered deep into the public psyche and into popular culture. In Ruth Rendell's novel *The Veiled One*, the action springs from a blackmailer who is trying to raise money so that her husband can have a hip replacement. As Inspector Wexford explains: 'If he was to have this operation on the National Health Service, it was possible he would have had to wait up to three years, by which time she feared he might be totally crippled. Three or four thousand pounds would pay for the replacement to be done privately and for hospitalization.' More powerful still was the BBC television series *Casualty*, set in the accident and emergency department of a general hospital in the fictional city of Holby. Its very first episode set out the agenda unequivocally, with complaints voiced about lack of resources, low pay and a shortage of hospital beds. Meanwhile some unemployed men are seen moonlighting at the docks, where they get injured in a gas leak from a broken canister containing materials that are intended for use in chemical weapons; these are being exported illegally to the Middle East by a woman who boasts that she's 'one of the new entrepreneurs'. As the series progressed, the government became so exercised by what it saw as anti-Tory propaganda that Edwina Currie, then a health minister, was dispatched to see Bill Cotton, the managing director of television at the BBC, to explain that the NHS wasn't really facing cuts at all. 'It is a rather inaccurate representation of what happens in an accident and emergency department,' she told the press, displaying little sign of understanding the nature of drama, though to her credit she had distinguished herself from many other politicians by refraining from comment until she had watched the series: 'I do not believe in criticizing something I have not seen.'

There was truth in the government's claims that public spending was increasing faster than inflation, and truth too in the insistence that the economy was in a rude state of health – as long, that is, as one lived in the south of England or in the midlands, where many were enjoying the good times. But even in those regions, there remained areas of great deprivation, and nationally the unemployed figures remained stubbornly above three million, with the rate being 60 per cent higher in the north than in the south. And for all the prosperity that was being celebrated by the media, it was hardly an era of calm and comfort, for the country remained dangerously divided. This was a time of a renewed spate of riots, and of two of the longest-running and most bitter industrial disputes of the century, in the miners' strike and the Wapping dispute, none of which suggested that a new, stable Britain was being built by the Thatcherite revolution. And then, in the words of Penny Rimbaud, the drummer with Crass, 'having struck a decisive blow to the heart of the British working classes by crushing the miners and their union, Thatcher and her cronies turned their interests towards their next "enemy within": alternative Britain'.

For several years a free festival had been staged at Stonehenge to celebrate the summer solstice, attracting tens of thousands to one of the last surviving remnants of the underground culture of the 1960s. By the early 1980s the original hippies had been augmented by a new generation, collectively referred to as new age travellers, since many lived in converted vans, buses and caravans, moving around the country as ad hoc mobile communities. In July 1985 the quango English Heritage, which was the official custodian of Stonehenge, and had more interest in tourists than in travellers, obtained a court order banning the staging of a festival that year, and the police set up a four-mile exclusion zone around the stones, complete with roadblocks, to prevent travellers reaching the site. When a convoy of a hundred or so travellers was intercepted by the police, while heading towards the exclusion zone, it was cornered in a bean-field and attacked with considerable force. Kim Sabido of ITN was one of the few reporters who covered the incident, recording a piece in which he described 'some of the most brutal police treatment of people that I have witnessed in my entire career as a journalist'. (He had previously reported on the miners' strike and on riots in Northern Ireland.) He concluded: 'There must be an inquiry.' There was no such inquiry, and Sabido's report on what became known as the Battle of the Beanfield was not even carried on television that evening. Further clashes followed over the next couple of years as the police continued to harry travellers, displaying an antagonism that was summed up by the reported comment of the chief constable of Hampshire in 1986: 'If only they would return to a conventional way of living, there would be no problem.'

Indeed that sometimes appeared to be the prevailing attitude. There was an intolerance of dissident opinion and, particularly, of dissident behaviour and lifestyles. Or perhaps it was simply that there was now more dissident behaviour around to concern the authorities. Back in 1978 William Whitelaw, then in opposition, had warned against the social effects of youth unemployment: 'If boys and girls do not obtain jobs when they leave school, they feel that society has no need of them. If they feel that, they do not see any reason why they should take part in that society and comply with its rules. That is what is happening.' Of the millions who had left school since then, many had, of course, moved on to further education or into employment, but many others had not done so, and were finding themselves pushed to the peripheries of society, whether through choice or necessity. The new age travellers were perhaps amongst the more extreme examples of those who turned their backs on 'a conventional way of living', but they were far from alone. In 1985, despite the economic recovery in the south-east, unemployment in London boroughs like Hackney, Islington and Lambeth still stood at 20 per cent.

That unemployment rate was even higher amongst young black people, and unsurprisingly the tensions in society remained greatest in those urban areas with a large black population. In 1985 a new wave of riots broke out, fewer in number but more costly in terms of fatalities and injuries than those of 1981. In September two Asian men died of smoke inhalation during a riot in Handsworth, Birmingham, and a report sponsored by the local council concluded: 'The police are viewed by a substantial proportion of Handsworth residents as an ill-disciplined and brutal force which has manipulated and abused its powers in dealings with the black community over a long period of time.' Later that month, in a police raid on a Brixton house, Cherry Groce, the mother of the man the officers were seeking, was shot and paralyzed from the waist down; the outrage caused by the shooting provoked a riot that lasted for forty-eight hours. Then, in October, came the most notorious of all the riots, on the Broadwater Farm estate in Tottenham, north London.

Again it was a police raid that sparked the disturbances. Officers illegally entered the house of Cynthia Jarrett without a warrant, having arrested her son and taken his keys. While they were searching the house, Jarrett collapsed and, with no help being offered, died of a heart attack. A protracted and violent confrontation ensued between the youths on the estate and the police, during the course of which one officer, Keith Blakelock, was stabbed to death. He was, perhaps surprisingly, the first police officer to be killed in a riot on the British mainland since Robert Culley in 1833. The inquest jury on that occasion had returned a verdict of justifiable homicide, 'indicating that the violent charge of the police deserved to be met with violence'; the verdict was later overturned. This time, six residents of the estate were charged with murder, amidst hysterical media coverage. Three had the charges dismissed by the trial judge, largely because of their treatment by the police; the remaining three were found guilty and sentenced to life imprisonment, though the sentences were quashed in 2001 after the court of appeal accepted evidence that the alleged confessions, the centrepiece of the prosecution case, had been tampered with. Meanwhile an inquiry into the disturbances, conducted by Lord Gifford, had suggested that, despite the Scarman Report, little had changed and that there was a 'factor of racialism in the response of the rank and file of police'.

The day after the riot, Sir Kenneth Newman, chief commissioner of the Metropolitan Police, blamed the violence on 'leftwing infiltrators', and the press eagerly ran with his suggestion. The *Daily Telegraph* noted the presence of 'white, bearded men in sandals, many accompanied by girls,' which suggested they weren't fully up to speed with developments in the look of the revolutionary left. The *Daily Express* had an even more extraordinary story: 'Street-fighting experts trained in Moscow and Libya were behind Britain's worst violence,' it claimed, working itself up into a frenzied fantasy about 'a hand-picked death squad hell-bent on bloodshed'. It turned out, happily for the nation's peace of mind, that the story was entirely untrue, being the work of the notorious Fleet Street hoaxer Michael 'Rocky' Ryan, a man responsible for planting dozens of fictitious stories in British newspapers; the secret of his success, he used to claim, was 'Always tell them what they want to hear', and it's hard not to see the *Express* story fitting precisely into that category.

Meanwhile, as Newman was busy speculating about leftist rabble-rousers, Bernie Grant, the leader of Haringey council (the first black politician to become a council leader in Britain), made it clear that in his view the police were responsible for damaging community harmony and for provoking the riot: 'I condemn the police action and do blame them for the death of Mrs Jarrett.' The following day, he spoke at a rally and uttered the comment that would make him into a hate figure for the media: 'The police were to blame for what happened on Sunday night and what they got was a bloody good hiding.' In fact, although he did use those words, they were prefaced by 'The youths around here believe . . .', which gave an entirely different context to his words, and articulated an indisputable truth. He was also to point out the uncomfortable reality that, for those excluded by society and denied a public voice, sometimes violence was an effective shortcut to attracting the attention of national politicians: 'Had it not been for the disturbances, they would never have heard of the estate and never have visited Tottenham.'

None of this, of course, was what the national leadership of the Labour Party wanted to hear, busy as it was distancing itself from the past. As Peter Mandelson complained, it 'is very hard when it comes to law and order and Bernie Grant in one sentence eclipses everything we have to say'. Grant was no Marxist, nor was he even particularly left-wing by the standards of the day, but simply by generating hostile press coverage, he clearly represented the kind of person that Neil Kinnock had no wish to see representing the new model party. 'Kinnock today distanced himself from Bernie Grant over his attack on the police for the death of Mrs Jarrett,' wrote Tony Benn in his diary. 'He distances himself from everyone.'

7
Identities
'Standing on their own two feet'

There may be minorities we have not yet discovered.
Delegate at SDP conference (1982)

LADY MARY EVANS: The penis these days attracts no envy whatsoever.
Malcolm Bradbury, *Porterhouse Blue* (1987)

MATTHEW FAIRCHILD: My life is going to be earnest, joyless, sexless and humourless. I reckon I'm definitely ready for the Young Socialists.
John Stevenson & Julian Roach, *Brass* (1983)

There was a joke that became very familiar over the course of the Thatcher years. An early sighting came in a 1979 episode of *Not the Nine O'Clock News* in a sketch where Chris Langham plays a businessman seeking a new appointee to his board: 'We're looking for a pregnant woman who is black, blind, deaf, tall, epileptic, in her late-50s and an ex-convict.' In 1980 it turned up in *Yes, Minister*, with Sir Humphrey Appleby explaining that 'The ideal quango appointee is a black, Welsh, disabled, female trade unionist. We're all looking around for one of them.' The joke proved remarkably resilient, so that in 1986 the *Sun* was parodying the policies of Labour councils: 'Sack all council workers who are white, able-bodied hetero-sexuals'. And the following year John Mortimer's character Horace Rumpole was talking about 'the leader of the South-East London Council widely known as Red Ron Probert', and saying that 'His ideal voter was apparently an immigrant Eskimo lesbian, who strongly supported the IRA'.

By this stage, with every permutation seemingly wrung from it, the gag had become rather tiresome, but more importantly there had been a notable shift in the target. Where the early versions had ridiculed big business and the civil service, seeking to tick boxes for the purposes of public relations, the obsession with minorities was now seen exclusively in terms of Labour local councils; what had been a mockery of the right-wing establishment had been turned on the left. Or rather on the 'loony left', this being the tabloid shorthand for Labour councils that had become universally adopted by the mid-1980s.

The phrase 'loony left' was even more venerable than the diversity joke with which it was so frequently linked, though its frame of reference also underwent a change. In 1974 Simon Jenkins had written in the *Guardian* that 'popular worries about Mr Anthony Wedgwood Benn appear to be less that he is a leftie than he may be a loony,' and the following year the phrase itself was in use, as left-wing MP Les Huckfield warned fellow members of the Tribune group that if they continued to criticize Harold Wilson, they ran the risk of looking like 'the loony left'. There were a few other references in the next few years, mostly within the Labour Party, but the real start of its popularity came when it was picked up by outsiders; a 1980 guide issued by the Conservative Party to their candidates in the forthcoming GLC elections warned: 'Political interference in the police could ultimately lead to a totalitarian state. Included in the proposals of the "loony left" are the disbandment of the Special Branch, the Special Patrol Group and the illegal immigration unit.'

Thus the 1970s uses of the expression had concentrated on those who opposed Wilson's watering down of Benn's attempted industrial legis-lation; to this, the Conservatives had added the allegedly undemocratic proposal that oversight of the Metropolitan Police might be transferred from the home secretary to the local authority (as elsewhere in the country). However radical some might think these ideas, they were at least within the mainstream of political activity. What transformed the phrase was the arrival of Ken Livingstone as the leader of the GLC and a new focus on what were known as 'minority interests'. Arguing that politics had long been the near-exclusive preserve of white middle-aged men, the GLC began an attempt to open itself to representations from other groups, principally from women, the working-class, ethnic minorities and homosexuals but also from children and the elderly. This was a real break from traditional politics as practised centrally by both major parties (though some local councils had already introduced positive discrimination policies), and it attracted hostility from all sides.

Much of the ensuing barrage of criticism, which continued for most of the decade, was concentrated on two targets: first, on the awarding of grants, however small, to community groups that contained in their names dangerous trigger-words such as black, Asian, peace, women or lesbian and gay; and second, on a new awareness of the political power of language. It was the latter that seemed particularly to offend opponents, though a sensitivity to language was not exactly unprecedented: it had its roots in the American civil rights movement of the 1960s that had gradually supplanted the word 'negro' with 'black' (which was itself now giving way to 'African-American'), and it had been developed by the women's movement the following decade. As early as 1977 *Daily Mail* journalist Anne Batt had been arguing the case for the use of non-sexist language by the media, though that newspaper was not noticeably at the forefront of the struggle for diversity, as Livingstone pointed out: 'In addition to distorting our policies, papers such as the *Daily Mail* invented new ones. A typical example was the story that we had forbidden staff to ask for black coffee, as this was racist. However many denials we issued, one paper after another ran the story without checking the facts.'

A spate of media myths did indeed emerge, and became self-perpetuating. 'Most of the stories about councils banning black dustbin bags and making children sing "Baa Baa Green Sheep" were actually made up by the tabloids,' wrote John O'Farrell, 'but I witnessed people taking their cue from these fictitious examples and starting to condemn people for asking for black or white coffee.' During the 1987 Greenwich by-election, a child was sent home from a nursery in Islington, north London, for singing the nursery rhyme 'Baa Baa Black Sheep', apparently because there had been so many stories about it being banned that a nursery worker had believed this to be official policy. It wasn't, and the next morning Glenys Kinnock went along to a Greenwich nursery to be filmed singing the rhyme. Nonetheless the story persisted and, at the subsequent general election, the SDP filmed the comedian John Cleese telling the tale all over again for a party political broadcast. The fact that it was Islington attracting attention was again no surprise; conveniently situated for Fleet Street, it had long had a reputation for being the looniest of boroughs, and former Labour MP George Cunningham had campaigned, unsuccessfully, as an SDP candidate in 1983 under the nudging slogan: 'You'd have to be mad to vote Labour in Islington now.'

There was also media censure of such lunatic concepts as anti-racist history and non-sexist maths being taught in London schools, though little coverage of what they might actually mean to the children involved. 'We were set a question that asked: "If a student is cycling from X to Y, and covers a distance of three miles, travelling at fourteen miles an hour, how long does it take her to arrive?",' remembered sometime Labour MP, Oona King, a north London pupil in the early 1980s. 'I remember bursting with wonder and amazement. It was the first time in my life that an unidentified active person was a *girl*. It could have been a boy, but for no particular reason it was a girl. A girl who *did* something.'

Beyond the myths and misrepresentations, there was a serious issue about the composition of Labour's constituency. 'We recognized that the narrow definition of the working-class as white skilled workers was no longer appropriate to describe the diversity we saw around us,' wrote Livingstone. 'We saw that the black youth who has never had a job, the mother working in the home harder than most men work outside it, and the gay couple whose lives are circumscribed by the ignorant fears of others, are all part of the working class as it exists in our city.'

There were those on the liberal left who worried that this agenda was encouraging people to be seen as first and foremost members of a specific group, rather than as individuals, and there were those on the more old-fashioned left who also had problems with both the language and practice of what were becoming known as identity politics, seeing it as diluting the traditional focus on class. 'I would no more expect phrases such as "blind as a bat" to be eliminated from usage, than "blackboard",' insisted David Blunkett, then the left-wing leader of Sheffield Council. (The 'blackboard' story was a frequently cited example of lunacy; one of the characters in P.D. James' novel *Devices and Desires* is an ex-teacher, sacked for refusing to use the new terminology of 'chalkboard'.) Blunkett himself was frequently lumped in with the loony left, for no better reason than the fact that he was blind and could therefore be counted as a member of a minority, though in reality he had little truck with what he considered to be London faddism. Livingstone remembered a 1982 meeting in Sheffield when Valerie Wise announced the creation of the GLC women's committee; Blunkett whispered to Livingstone: 'You're not really setting up a women's committee, are you?' and then 'chuckled so much that he almost fell off his chair when I confirmed that this was the case'. Four years later Sheffield did create a women's unit, but it was buried in the personnel department and had neither the autonomy or authority of its equivalent in the GLC.

Even more distant was the attitude of Liverpool City Council, then in the control of members of the Trotskyist group Militant, who were always happy to sneer at, in the words of their most media-friendly figure Derek Hatton, 'the London boroughs with their obsessions about anti-racist and anti-sexist issues', though such deviationist indulgence was apparently not confined to Islington, Lambeth and Camden: 'even Manchester, Sheffield and other Labour councils across the country could sometimes display the same attributes.' Indeed in this analysis, even Neil Kinnock exemplified the same tendency. These 'middle-class intellectuals' were 'the true "loony left",' Hatton insisted, 'more concerned that we called the chairman the chairperson or a manhole cover a personhole cover, than they ever were about the real issues.' ('Manhole' was another popular story, though such structures had always been known officially as inspection chambers.) Mark Steel, a member then of the SWP, saw the whole endeavour as a product of powerlessness: 'It was as if the councillors worked out they couldn't change the world, or even the borough, so the one thing they could change was the language, or whether the person carrying out the cuts was a man or a woman.'

From the right of the Labour movement, Joe Ashton was furious at a world in which 'Any loony cause could get a grant', while Eric Hammond, who replaced Frank Chapple as general secretary of the electricians' union, denounced the GLC for supporting 'terrorist groupies, lesbians and other queer people'. Kinnock himself tended to avoid the phrase 'loony left' in favour of his own, more homely formulations, as when commenting on a school students' strike in 1985: 'The kids are being exploited by a bunch of dafties.'

The emergence of a new left, that drew in groups from outside the Labour Party with no political allegiance, and that was most powerfully articulated by Ken Livingstone, was thus distrusted right across the political spectrum. Amongst the few exceptions was Tony Benn, who had spotted that the nature of politics was changing as far back as 1971, when he had called on pressure groups, single-issue campaigners, churches and others to enter a debate about Labour's future. ('Why not add Women's Lib and the "gay" groups?' sniped a party official, whose ideological descendants were still very much in evidence a decade and a half later.) Benn's endorsement of a politics of diversity did much to legitimize the new approach, particularly amongst activists in trade unions, though he sometimes struggled to engage with the emergent groups: 'They had no socialist analysis,' he wrote after meeting a group of women peace campaigners; 'they were just deeply morally committed, and they felt that everyone had a duty to contribute directly and that all representative government and even CND itself tended to diminish people's sense of personal responsibility.'

Despite the initially hostile reception that they received, it appeared over the following years that the London left had not been as misguided as was commonly assumed at the time, but merely ahead of the game. But perhaps the most radical aspect of the loony left, the one that really threatened the established concept of politics, proved less durable; the desire for direct personal involvement, as espoused by the peace women that Benn met, slowly withered in the wake of repeated

Conservative election victories, and did not outlast the decade in any major way.

At the time, however, there was a genuine excitement about the idea of participation. At its simplest, this was manifested in the huge CND demonstrations and the massive rise in the membership of that organization, mirrored by other groups, including the likes of Greenpeace and Amnesty International. It produced a new militancy on the issue of animal rights, from the growing cultural unacceptability of wearing fur, through the rise of politically motivated vegetarianism, and up to the actions of hunt saboteurs, of whom it was estimated in 1981 there were more than four thousand, with numbers growing. It could be seen too in the consumer campaigns against apartheid, particularly in the boycott of South African goods and of Barclays Bank because of its involvement in that country; the fact that this latter tended to be primarily the concern of student unions attracted some scorn, but probably made it more rather than less effective, since it held out the threat that the next generation of high-earners would be taking their custom elsewhere.

The same issue provoked one of the more extraordinary demonstrations of the era, when the City of London Anti-Apartheid Group announced in 1986 that they would be demonstrating outside the South African Embassy in London's Trafalgar Square twenty-four hours a day, every day, until Nelson Mandela was released, a seemingly absurd proposition at the time. Despite repeated police attempts to close the protest down, however, and despite the group being expelled from the mainstream Anti-Apartheid Movement, they were still there when Mandela finally walked free in February 1990, having maintained an unbroken presence throughout and having, in the words of a chargé d'affaires, regularly caused 'disturbance to the normal functioning of the Embassy'.

More impressive still was the demonstration on Greenham Common in response to the announcement that American cruise missiles were to be situated at the RAF base there. Some forty demonstrators marched from Cardiff in 1981 and established a women-only peace camp that was to remain even longer than the missiles themselves. The group initially met with some sympathetic coverage in the media, and a 1982 demonstration that involved thirty thousand women encircling the base, and hanging photographs and personal mementoes on the fence, proved to be one of the most moving protests of the era. 'It really gives you a lump in the throat,' commented a Press Association journalist, while Alison Whyte from CND described a 'hard-bitten *Sun* reporter staring at mile after mile of baby clothes, toys and family photographs, with tears streaming down his bearded face. He said he had never seen anything like it in his life.'

The sympathy was short-lived, however, and by 1983 the press was awash with stories of lesbianism, squalor and degradation: 'Whatever idealism first inspired the anti-nuclear sit-in at Greenham Common, it is fast being overwhelmed by rancour, intolerance and, sadly, sheer bitchiness,' claimed the *Sun*, while the *Daily Express* summed up the Greenham women as 'this ragtag and bobtail of politically motivated harpies'. One of the few to offer any support on Fleet Street was the future television presenter Anne Robinson, then of the *Daily Mirror*, when she visited the camp: 'Most of the women I could just as easily have bumped into in a bus queue,' she wrote. 'What Greenham Common women suffer from more than anything else is a distorted public image and they are too proud and weary to improve it.' The public perception was indeed poor, attracting hostility not only from the right but also – because of its refusal to allow male participation – from many on the left. Nonetheless, the political effect of the demonstration was impressive; more than any other campaign, it put the issue of cruise missiles on the public agenda, while the experience changed the lives of its participants, especially in regard to perceptions of the police. 'At first, women who were predominantly white and middle-class and unused to political activity were horrified at how quickly the police could be turned into an attacking force, fuelling rather than defusing potential conflict,' wrote Rebecca Johnson. 'I remember the real shock of hearing them lie under oath during trials. Childhood conditioning to respect and trust the police had gone deep, and acknowledging the reality caused some painful readjustment.'

The sheer longevity of the peace camp burned it into the public consciousness, and into fiction. Adrian Mole's mother went to Greenham, while Inspector Wexford's daughter, Sheila, in Ruth Rendell's detective series was arrested for cutting the perimeter fence at a military base. 'When peace is so beautiful,' she asks her father, 'and what everyone wants, why do they treat workers for peace like criminals?' And, by providing a visible example of women's self-organization, Greenham also brought public awareness to feminist separatism and even to lesbianism, hitherto seen in the mass media – when acknowledged at all – either in terms of Eton-cropped androgyny or of pornographic fantasy, but now reborn as a political force. There was some gentle satire in the 1980s (Robyn Penrose in David Lodge's novel *Nice Work* joins a women's group at Cambridge University, where 'Several members of the group were lesbians, or tried to be'), but mostly there was furious denunciation by the press, which suggested that some real boundaries were being challenged.

By the end of the decade, snapped a character in Denise Danks' crime novel *Better Off Dead*, lesbianism had come to represent a new set of clichés: 'slogans, sisterhood, feminism, the struggle against sexual stereotypes and male dominance, dungarees, militant socialism, the loony left, the campaign against nuclear disarmament, Greenham Common, green issues, save the whale, and maybe, right at the end of the list, porn movies.' And, she adds bitterly, the new perception is that: 'Passion, romance and sex between two women don't really come into it because lesbianism's fundamentally a political statement against a heterosexual society's conditioning of the sexes.' The world of Danks' series of novels, depicting an alternative London of hard-to-let council flats, computer hackers and market stalls selling bootleg cassettes, was offset by the explicit references to Enid Blyton, with the heroine Georgina Power based on George from the Famous Five books: 'I wondered what sort of character George would be, having had that father and that insufferable cousin Julian,' explained Danks. The answer appears to be that times have changed and she's now a hard-drinking, cannabis-smoking journalist with a hyperactive and varied sex life, though she is – perhaps surprisingly – heterosexual. Her 'insufferable cousin', the respectable and responsible Julian Kirren, however, has fared less well in adult life and doesn't survive the first chapter of the first novel: he's found hanging from the ceiling in women's underwear and a rubber mask, after a bout of autoerotic asphyxiation goes wrong.

The growing awareness of lesbianism was reinforced by the BBC2 television adaption in 1990 of Jeanette Winterson's novel *Oranges Are Not the Only Fruit* (1985). Stripping away most of the allegorical matter and narrative discursions that were present in the novel, the television version – also written by Winterson – was a much more direct tale, focused exclusively on the central story of a young girl being brought up in the 1970s by a strictly religious mother and discovering that she is homosexual. There was here no ambiguity, no question of which side the viewers were expected to take as a teenage girl's early sexual experiences were counterposed with the rigid, fundamentalist faith of her mother: in one particularly distressing scene of exorcism, the girl is tied down and gagged while a Pentecostal pastor straddles her body and prays for her deliverance from the demons that are said to be possessing her.

The series attracted not only enormous critical praise (it won a BAFTA for best drama series), but also a substantial audience, with around six million viewers. An even more powerful image was to come later in the year, however, as the Czech-born tennis star Martina Navratilova won a record-breaking ninth singles title at Wimbledon and celebrated by climbing through the crowd to embrace her team of supporters, including her lover, Judy Nelson. Diane Hamer, who had worked on the Channel 4 series *Out*, was amongst those who saw a major breakthrough in the visibility of lesbian relationships: 'I thrilled to the knowledge,' she wrote, 'that tens of millions of viewers around the world were at that moment watching two lesbians publicly display their love for each other.'

Also present for the occasion was Billie Jean King, whose outing in 1981 had started a scare about lesbianism on the tennis circuit: 'Many of today's top women players are homosexual,' declared the little-known British player Linda Geeves, 'and a good percentage of them are actively recruiting new talent.' Much press attention was directed towards the precocious American star Tracy Austin, who had in 1979 become the youngest-ever winner of the US Open at the age of sixteen; she 'had to have a bodyguard to protect her from lesbian advances in locker rooms,' reported the *Daily Telegraph*, and though her agent dismissed such claims ('That's ridiculous!'), the spate of stories in 1981 illustrated two ideas that were then fixed firmly in the minds of public, press and politicians alike: that homosexuals preyed on the young, and that if a young person were to be exposed to homosexuality, he or she would almost inevitably renounce the attractions of heterosexuality. Much of the political fire that would be directed during the decade at lesbians and gay men was rooted in such assumptions, and the response to Navratilova's embrace of Nelson suggested that they were firmly in place as the new decade dawned: MARTINA TURNS GIRLS INTO GAYS read the *Sun* headline, over an article in which Australian tennis legend Margaret Court expressed her concerns.

For despite Denise Danks' checklist of new left clichés, in the wider culture more traditional depictions of lesbianism still persisted. In 1988 Cissy Meldrum, played by Catherine Rabett in *You Rang M'Lord*, became Britain's first lesbian in a mainstream sitcom (Sarah B'Stard in *The New Statesman* had previously been seen in bed with another woman, but she was definitely bisexual). Cissy was 'a member of the Communist Party and a bit of a tomboy,' remarked writer David Croft. 'This character gave us a chance to touch gently on lesbianism.' But, gradually eclipsing Cissy, the dungaree-clad feminist who was assumed to be lesbian even if she wasn't became a stock image of the 1980s. The stereotype that was portrayed came with a strait-laced attitude to sex of which Mary Whitehouse might almost have approved, a caricature that some found wasn't entirely divorced from reality. John O'Farrell tells the story of a woman sleeping on his sofa after a party. When she then got into bed with him, he assumed that his luck was in, only to be told off for his sexist attitudes to women. 'When a man is looking for signals that a woman might be interested in him, her climbing into his bed in her underwear might reasonably be interpreted as minor encouragement,' he mourned. 'But not in the world of the new puritans. Eve tempted me with the apple and then told me it was South African.' Others were less respectful. 'Dungarees are quite sexy in their own way,' mused journalist Andrew Collins, looking back on his student days in the 1980s. 'Something in the knowledge that if you unhooked the straps the trousers would fall to the floor in a heap.'

The essential worthiness of much of the new left was summed up for some by the case of the novel *Down the Road, Worlds Apart* by Rahila Khan, which explored the experience of Asian schoolgirls in Britain. Listed for publication in 1987 by the feminist firm Virago, eight thousand copies of the book had been printed before it was discovered that the author's name was a pseudonym, concealing the identity of the Reverend Tony Forward, a 37-year-old white Anglican vicar. Virago were unamused by the revelation and, rather than celebrating Forward's creative leap of imagination, withdrew the novel.

There was much that could be mocked, but there was too an alternative concept of participatory democracy being built by those working outside the established system, such that, as Bruce Kent put it, campaigners 'took the discussion out into the market-place and made it possible for ordinary people to join in'. Such a development was largely due to frustration at the slow movement of mainstream politics, for the feminist wave that had been building in Britain throughout the previous decade showed little sign of making an impact on Westminster, even if a woman were now prime minister. 'She's an honorary man,' says a character in Edward Fenton's *Scorched Earth*. 'Probably when she dies they'll discover she was really a man.' It was scarcely an original remark, for jokes about Margaret Thatcher's alleged lack of femininity were as common on the left as those about one-legged aboriginal lesbians were on the right; actor Steve Nallon even made a career playing her on comedy shows like *KYTV* and *The New Statesman* and providing her voice on *Spitting Image*. But repetition did not make it any more accurate.

A lot of such comments were often rooted more in class and geography than in gender. 'I'm a plain straightforward provincial,' Thatcher insisted, and she showed absolutely no interest in a feminism that was still essentially metropolitan, and that was largely populated by those much younger than herself. The age difference was crucial in how Thatcher was perceived by the products of the demographic bulge of the 1950s and 1960s, particularly those who were the beneficiaries of the expansion of tertiary education: it wasn't simply her policies that failed to register with so many; culturally too, there was no point of contact. She was born in 1925, thirteen years before David Steel and David Owen, seventeen years before Neil Kinnock, and twenty years before Ken Livingstone. She was thus a student at university during the Second World War, and was already thirty years old, a mother of two and twice an election candidate, by the time rock and roll and independent television appeared. So when she appeared on *Desert Island Discs*, the closest she got to a pop song was Irene Dunne's 'Smoke Gets in Your Eyes' from the 1935 movie *Roberta*. Kinnock, on the other hand, a former member of the Gene Vincent Fan Club, went for the much more obvious choice of John Lennon's 'Imagine' when he was invited on the programme. Thatcher herself recognized that there was an age factor that needed addressing, telling Norman Tebbit that the party needed as chairman 'someone young, to counter the Steel-Owen image,' though her choice was perhaps a little wide of the mark: John Selwyn Gummer was always going to look more at home in the pages of the *Church Times* than in those of *The Face*. (Michael White in the *Guardian* put it best: 'Mr Gummer is 43, but sounds about 17 and what comes out suggests that he has been 52 since he was about eight.')

Perhaps some of the same misguided thinking lay behind Thatcher's appearance on the children's BBC1 show *Saturday Superstore* in 1987, where she reviewed the new single releases. (She worried that Pepsi & Shirley's 'Heartache' didn't have a strong enough melody, while the Style Council's 'It Didn't Matter' also failed to impress.) It was a surreal episode, in which she descended on kids' TV like the goddaughter of Lord Reith, completely out of context in this new, slightly chaotic world, but refusing to compromise her style at all. Subsequent party leaders – Neil Kinnock, John Major, Tony Blair, David Cameron – worked hard to make a virtue of their supposed normality when appearing on television; they were the kind of people, one was supposed to believe, whom one might meet in the pub, or at least at a dinner party. Thatcher, on the other hand, was never natural on screen; she addressed the nation not as an equal, but as if it were a child or a slightly confused elderly relative. Or, in Keith Waterhouse's magnificent phrase: 'She talks to me as if my dog had just died.'

Simply on a personal level, then, she appeared to the new left as something akin to an antediluvian alien. The fact that she also had no allegiance to the women's movement, probably wasn't even aware of the ideological split between radical feminism and socialist feminism over the issues of patriarchy and class, came as no great surprise. Perhaps this was part of the reason why the gender gap that had traditionally favoured the

Conservatives – in the 1950s they had scored eight percentage points higher amongst women than amongst men – disappeared entirely in her election victories. She was certainly reluctant to include women in her cabinet, though Baroness Janet Young did have a brief spell as leader of the House of Lords, but then the opposition was little better: in the annual elections to the shadow cabinet in 1985, Labour MPs found no room at all for even a token woman to be included alongside the fifteen men, and the rules were subsequently changed so that all ballot papers had to include votes for at least three women.

The shortage of women MPs in senior posts was partly a structural issue in the way the Commons organized itself, as future cabinet minister Tessa Jowell pointed out in 1980: 'There are lots of practical difficulties facing women. There is no crèche at the Commons and the hours are designed for out-of-town MPs who wouldn't know what to do with their long and lonely nights if the House sat all day.' Teresa Gorman, who replaced Harvey Proctor as the Conservative MP for Billericay in 1987, recalled that the problems began with the constituency meeting to select a parliamentary candidate – at one of which, she records, a woman candidate was asked 'What will your husband do for sex when you get to Westminster?' – and continued onto overtly sexist comments and sexual harassment in the House of Commons, 'a workplace full of hostile, elderly gentlemen who still believed in their heart of hearts that Parliament was no place for a woman.' There remained a perception, in many quarters, that women in the main shouldn't concern themselves overmuch with politics. 'It is doubtful if Neil Kinnock has made a major pivotal decision all his married life which has not had the approval, and frequently the lead, of his wife Glenys,' opined the *Daily Mail* in 1986. And in case anyone should misunderstand and conclude that this described a desirable and proper marital relationship, the language of the *Mail* made it clear that it thought otherwise: 'Her influence on him, and on the shape of the Labour Party and therefore the very history of the nation, is unrelenting.'

There was even greater distrust in political and press circles of overt homosexuality. Maureen Colquhoun, the first out lesbian MP, had lost her seat in 1979 and, although in 1984 the newly elected member for Islington South, Chris Smith, became the first male MP to come out, there was no sign of a rush to follow him. The Conservative Matthew Parris had earlier made a speech in the House leaving little doubt that he was gay, but it had gone entirely without notice. And that was it. There were plenty of other gay MPs, of course – even Thatcher's parliamentary private secretary, Sir Peter Morrison, was, remarked Edwina Currie, 'what they call "a noted pederast" with a liking for young boys' – but the subject of homosexuality was considered too politically sensitive to discuss openly. Attempts to get Labour's national executive committee to commit itself to equalizing the ages of consent for heterosexual and homosexual acts were voted down, and the best that the famously all-embracing 1983 manifesto could offer was: 'We are concerned that homosexuals are unfairly treated. We will take steps to ensure that they are not unfairly discriminated against.' (Which seemed to leave open the possibility of fair discrimination.) In 1985 the Labour conference debated lesbian and gay rights for the first time, and called for a full policy to be developed, but when at the end of the decade, Ken Livingstone again raised the question of the age of consent at the NEC, it was again defeated.

If Westminster politics was reluctant to take up the issue of gay rights, it was still far ahead of many other areas of public life. It wasn't until 1990, for example, that a professional footballer was to come out. Justin Fashanu had emerged as a precocious talent at Norwich City, for whom he scored *Match of the Day*'s Goal of the Season in 1980, and had become the first black player to command a million pound transfer fee, but his career largely lost direction during the decade and he never realized his early promise. The revelation of his homosexuality did nothing to make his life any easier and in 1998, shortly after his retirement from the game, he committed suicide. At the time of his death, he was still the only out footballer.

As with so much else in the 1980s, the subject of how far one could combine a public role with being out as a lesbian or gay man was addressed in crime fiction. In Peter Robinson's *A Dedicated Man* Inspector Banks 'had known a sergeant on the Metropolitan force for six years – a married man with two children – before finding out at the inquest into his suicide that he had been homosexual'. In the next generation, however, Sergeant Wield, in Reginald Hill's Dalziel and Pascoe novels, has a happier experience. 'When he first joined the Force, there had been no debate about concealment. But time and times had changed things, and now, though he did not delude himself that coming out would not still harm his own career, he felt a growing dissatisfaction with the path of secrecy he had chosen.' He does finally come out to his colleagues and is met with a variety of responses from his colleagues and superiors; significantly, the most important figure, Dalziel, is sympathetic and even gives him advice on manners, warning him not to out a councillor who's also gay: 'Just because you've come up on deck, don't rock the boat for them as prefer to remain down in the hold.'

Little of this translated into the screen adaptations of detective fiction, but television did offer the most deliberately provocative gay imagery of the era in Stephen Frears' Channel 4 film *My Beautiful Laundrette*, which showed Omar (Gordon Warnecke), a young man of Pakistani heritage living in south London, and his childhood friend Johnny (Daniel Day Lewis), now a recovering racist, with whom he has an affair. The centre of the film lies in Omar's attempt to resolve where he stands between the rival positions of his despairing father Ali (Roshan Seth), who wants nothing to do with his adopted country – 'They hate us in England' – and his uncle Nasser (Saeed Jaffrey), who can see nothing but opportunity: 'In this damned country, which we hate and love, you can get anything you want,' he explains. 'That's why I believe in England. Only you have to know how to squeeze the tits of the system.' Nasser is a Thatcherite entrepreneur, revelling in the ascendancy of money – 'There's no question of race in the new enterprise culture,' he insists – and as he exults, so does Ali despair of seeing his intellectual socialism ever make progress: 'Oh dear,' he laments, 'the working class are such a great disappointment to me.' But it was the interracial gay scenes, rather than the political observations, that attracted most attention at the time, a fact that was probably not unanticipated by writer Hanif Kureishi: 'I like sex in the movies,' he said, 'and I wanted this film to be entertaining. Most British films are as slow as watching Geoff Boycott batting.'

In real life it was still largely left to entertainers to make the running. Two of the biggest pop stars of the early 1980s, Boy George and Marc Almond, made little attempt to conceal their sexuality in their stage personae – though they were both much more cagey in interviews – while pop's willingness to play with issues of gender and sexuality caused a steady stream of both outrage and confusion: the cross-dressing imagery adopted by Annie Lennox of the Eurythmics was so convincing that MTV in America demanded to see a copy of her birth certificate before screening the band's videos, so they could be assured she was genuinely a woman. And in 1983–84 debut hit singles for Frankie Goes To Hollywood ('Relax') and for Bronski Beat ('Smalltown Boy') were not only created by gay men, but addressed gay subjects in their lyrics. Even more influential was the arrival on television of comedian Julian Clary, who took the camp tradition of comics like Frankie Howerd and Larry Grayson and made it explicitly homosexual; when he delivered a double entendre, there was no possibility of mistaking his thrust, and there was little point left in the limp-wristed caricature of gay men by the time he had parodied it out of existence. When the ex-footballer Jimmy Greaves said on TV-AM that he thought Clary was 'a prancing poofter' who shouldn't be allowed on family television, Clary responded with mock indignation that he didn't prance, he minced; and Greaves gracefully backed down, sending a dozen red roses in apology.

Clary was sufficiently established on the comedy circuit to appear on the Channel 4 series *Saturday Live*, which took over from *The Young Ones* to become the cult television comedy of Thatcher's second term. Primarily associated with Ben Elton (though the first series had a succession of hosts, including Michael Barrymore, who was definitely not out at the time), the series attracted an audience of little more than two million, but in certain circles it was required viewing. Apart from anything else, the message of the new comedy was still largely being carried around the country by television, and *Saturday Live* 'was more or less the only place people from outside London could see alternative comedy,' as Frank Skinner from the West Midlands remembered. As such it was eagerly seized upon by its devotees. 'Ben Elton speaks directly to me, he speaks directly to all of us from his pulpit on *Saturday Live*,' wrote Andrew Collins, reliving his student days. 'I've never seen the hall's coffee bar as packed as it is now.' Sometimes, he added, 'we've all found ourselves clapping the TV.'

Elton made an unlikely hero — with his single-buttoned, spangly suit jacket, narrow tie, mullet haircut and large glasses, he looked like nothing so much as a bassist in an American new wave pop band from 1980 — but his impassioned, breakneck monologues berating the state of modern society ('basically fast food is rubbish, I don't know why they don't just flush it down the toilets, cut out the middleman, eh?') , and his attacks on Thatch, as he referred to the prime minister, were a unifying element for anyone under the age of thirty who had any sympathy with the new left. As Mark Steel was to point out, these rants 'became hugely popular, though few people said they enjoyed them because they were funny, more because "at least someone's having a go at the Tories".' Or, in Boy George's words, 'Watching Ben Elton was like, yeah, good, I'm glad there's someone out there who's having a go about it.' Steel similarly recalled a gig he played at a Labour club in Watford in 1985, where he was told: 'We're so looking forward to your show; we could do with a really good laugh about how terrible the Tories are.' The fictional Phil First, in Martyn Harris's novel *The Mother-in-Law Joke*, has much the same analysis of why alternative comedy enjoyed its boom years in the middle of Thatcher's era: 'There is so little in the way of effective political opposition. A loss of faith in seventies radicalism; the lack of any new agenda for the left. So people express their distaste for the government by laughing at it.' It didn't sound much like the basis for comedy with any lasting appeal, and for the most part it wasn't.

Others were unconvinced at the time by the Ben Elton school of comedy. 'He lacks a sense of humour, taking himself very seriously indeed,' wrote Anthony Thorncroft in the *Financial Times*: 'He is also a bigot. You can attack men, not women; whites, not blacks; the middle class, not the workers.' The review opened with probably the most offensive insult that the critic could have delivered: 'Ben Elton is the Bernard Manning of alternative comedy.' Bryan Appleyard in the *Sunday Times* was no more impressed: 'You can reduce some young audiences to hysterical applause just, in effect, by saying you don't like Margaret Thatcher. If satire is that easy, why work harder?'

Attacks from such quarters, of course, did nothing to dampen the enthusiasm of the 'young audiences', though the charge that, despite alternative comedy, the left had little sense of humour was not entirely inaccurate. And it was a charge that was frequently levelled. In the novel *Exterminating Angels* (1986), written by Peter Busby and Sarah Dunant, a revolutionary group adopt an imaginative approach to terrorism: blowing up the house of a property speculator, filling the swimming-pool at an oil tycoon's house with oil, and kidnapping a racist Tory MP for the purpose of injecting him with a pigment that turns his skin black. As a result, they attract the support of the public, who see them as Robin Hood figures. 'They are entertaining,' admits one character, somewhat reluctantly. 'Rather surprising, isn't it? You don't expect the extreme left to have a sense of humour. They're usually relentlessly fierce and dull, like feminists.' But by amusing the middle-classes, the terrorists find themselves up against the ultimate power of the British state to absorb threats: 'We've been integrated into the structure,' worries the group's leader. 'Either we deromanticize our image and make the establishment take us seriously, or we'll be castrated by it.'

The imagery was exactly the same as that used by Jonathan Miller back in 1961, when warning about the dangers of assimilation faced by the satire boom of that era: 'It is the threat of castration by adoption; of destruction by patronage.' And, inevitably, such was ultimately the fate of alternative comedy. 'The Tories had won two elections and were going to win a third,' says Phil First in *The Mother-in-Law Joke*, 'while all the left had to offer was an Unpopular Front of ill-assorted "isms". Reg and I were getting rich on a Tory-engineered consumer boom, and to pretend otherwise was the self-indulgent posturing of a superannuated student Trot.' By the end of the decade, Ben Elton was filling in for Terry Wogan as host of his primetime BBC1 chat-show, and starring in his own series on the same channel, cosily entitled *The Man From Auntie*, now part of the light entertainment establishment against which he had railed.

If many on the left were indeed somewhat humourless by nature – the 'new puritans' described by John O'Farrell – then perhaps they were no more than a reflection of the period. For the 1980s in Britain were not years characterized by great outpourings of joy and warmth. Both left and right had drawn their own conclusions about the crises that racked the nation in the previous decade, and both were grimly determined that radical changes needed to be wrought. Consequently the campaigns by peace women, anti-apartheid protesters, anti-racist activists, hunt saboteurs and others, were more noted for stridency than for lightness of tone; this was serious business and, in common with the Thatcherite revolution, it was pursued with an earnestness and fervour that frequently failed to connect with a wider public, the people Peter Mandelson referred to as the 'average, unpolitical, non-aligned voters'.

As that comment suggests, the perception of the Labour leadership under Neil Kinnock was that the new left posed a threat to its attempt to re-position itself. It wasn't that Kinnock necessarily disagreed with, say, the idea of women playing a greater role in society, more that the media's relentless hostility, leavened only by its mockery of activists, made certain issues look too hot to handle. And so, although more people might turn out for a CND demonstration than could be motivated to join the Labour Party, there was little attempt to build on the campaigns developing outside parliament to expand the party's base.

The conflict between the new identity politics and the Labour leadership was evident in the issue of black sections that arose in the middle of the decade. Black activists, particularly in London, began to call in 1983 for separate sections to be organized within constituency Labour parties, based on the model of the existing women's sections, but they met with immediate opposition, both from the left – Eric Heffer and *Militant* were opposed in their own ways – and from above: 'It would create significant problems of racial definition which could lead only too easily to endless unproductive acrimony,' pronounced Kinnock in 1984. The following year, two of the of the leading campaigners, Sharon Atkin and Diane Abbott, met him to press their case, but again found themselves rebuffed. He asked who would be eligible to join, and was told that the sections would be open to anyone who considered themselves black. 'Can I consider myself black?' he asked, and they replied: 'Patently not, because you're so obviously white.' He later told the press: 'I consider, and so do most other people, the idea of a segregated section on the basis of colour or racial origin to be repellent.'

Despite the opposition, several local parties did set up unofficial black sections, starting with Vauxhall and Lewisham East in London, though their contribution didn't always seem to be characterized by compromise and comradeship. 'The Labour Party itself perpetuates racism,' claimed a booklet produced by the Vauxhall branch for the 1984 conference. 'It is an institution rooted in a racist society and its own routine practices, customs and forms of organization exclude black people from the structures of power as effectively as if they were barred from membership.' A conference resolution that year to set up official black sections was rejected by the union block votes.

It was a contentious issue and one that produced a series of anomalies. The Enfield and Barnet branch of the far-right National Front passed a resolution welcoming the idea 'as the first stage in the realignment of British politics on racial lines,' adding that: 'These sections clearly indicate both the inability and unwillingness of blacks to integrate into British society.' Meanwhile a selection meeting in the Brent South constituency chose Paul Boateng as its parliamentary candidate, but was faced by a demonstration led by Sharon Atkin because the local party didn't have a black section, even though all those on the shortlist were themselves black. The gradual adoption of leading black figures as parliamentary candidates – Diane Abbott, Bernie Grant, Keith Vaz, Russell Profitt (who had been the party's only black candidate in 1979) – took much of the steam out of the campaign, leading some to conclude that all along it had been, in Roy Hattersley's words, 'really a vehicle for promoting the parliamentary ambitions of metropolitan, middle-class professionals'. *Militant* came to much the same conclusion. The one major casualty amongst the leading lights of the movement was Atkin; chosen as the candidate for Nottingham East, she was removed by the national executive following a public meeting in early 1987, at which she angrily replied to criticism that she'd become part of the system: 'I don't give a damn about Neil Kinnock and the racist Labour Party.' The presence of television cameras at the meeting ensured that her message was widely disseminated.

By now a general election was imminent, and nerves were getting strained. In February 1987 all the issues about the new left resurfaced in a by-election for the Greenwich constituency in south London, held until his death by Labour's Guy Barnett. 'Our candidate would ordinarily have handled the campaign quite adequately,' wrote Bryan Gould, now one of the key Labour strategists. 'The media spotlight, however, focused on her political past, as an extreme left-winger, and exploited her uncertainty in handling the press.' Actually the candidate, Deirdre Wood, wasn't particularly extreme at all, just a local politician, a former GLC councillor, who was in the wrong place at the wrong time. The media had evidently decided it was time to re-run the

Bermondsey campaign and she was cast as this month's whipping boy. Lacking evidence of any serious charges of extremism, the *Daily Mail* instead got excited by discovering that she was living with a man who wasn't the father of her children and who had been a shop steward during the winter of discontent. She had also said she was 'forty-ish', and the *News of the World* took great delight in revealing that actually she was forty-four; this was run under the somewhat misleading headline DEIRDRE'S BIG FAT LIE, which hinted at where much of the media coverage was heading: she simply wasn't svelte enough. Certainly she was no match for the much more cheerful-looking figure of the Alliance's Rosie Barnes, who won the seat with a 28 per cent swing, though virtually all of this came from the Conservatives rather than from Labour. It was the SDP's first by-election gain in nearly three years and, followed shortly by the Liberals retaining their Truro seat after the untimely death of David Penhaligon, it gave the Alliance a major boost at Labour's expense as the general election approached.

Amidst the dismay that ensued, a memo written by Patricia Hewitt, Kinnock's press secretary, was leaked to the *Sun*: 'The gays and lesbians issue is costing us dear amongst the pensioners, and fear of extremism and higher taxes is particularly prominent in the GLC area.' It was an unexpected charge from a former general secretary of the National Council for Civil Liberties, let alone from someone who had voted for Tony Benn in the 1981 deputy leadership contest, and it was an argument that Ken Livingstone was keen to refute, pointing out that, although there had indeed been a swing to the Conservatives in London in the 1983 general election, it had been considerably lower than the national average.

And that general election had been held at a time when the GLC was plumbing its lowest depths of bad press and unpopularity; since then the Conservative Party had done everything in its power to change the public's perception of the council. The Tories' 1983 manifesto had been quite explicit about its intentions: 'The metropolitan councils and the Greater London Council have been shown to be a wasteful and unnecessary tier of government. We shall abolish them.' And so the government duly introduced a bill to close down the offending authorities, though Norman Tebbit perhaps gave a truer picture of the reasoning behind the move, when he denounced the GLC as being 'Labour-dominated, high-spending and at odds with the government's view of the world'. Livingstone similarly pointed out that there was 'a huge gulf between the cultural values of the GLC Labour group and everything that Mrs Thatcher considered right and proper'. This was a conflict of political values, much more than it was a question of penny-pinching.

The GLC immediately launched a campaign to promote itself, to draw attention to the services it provided and to campaign against the abolition proposal. Brilliantly conducted, the strategy focused on the simple question of democracy, under the slogan: 'Say No to No Say'. It was one of the great advertising success stories in a decade that was itself increasingly dominated by advertising. By March 1984 a poll in London's evening newspaper, the *Standard*, was showing a massive turnaround, with 52 per cent now saying they were satisfied with the GLC and with Labour enjoying a 10 per cent lead over the Conservatives in the capital, at a time when the party was trailing by 2 per cent nationally. To compound the issue, the government realized that abolition could not be completed before the next GLC elections were due in May 1985, and that the Tories were likely to take a pasting. 'The 1985 elections cannot be allowed to go ahead,' wrote environment secretary, Patrick Jenkin, to Thatcher in a state of high panic. (The letter was leaked to the GLC by a transsexual dominatrix, who had found it in a client's briefcase while he was tied to a bed.) And the elections were indeed cancelled, allowing Livingstone the opportunity to ramp up the message that the whole abolition programme was an abuse of democratic process; newspaper adverts showed a picture of him with the message: 'If you want me out, you should have the right to vote me out.' In the face of huge public support for the campaign, most of the hostile coverage in the papers began to tail off, with even the *Daily Mail*, under the headline THE MAN RUNNING RINGS ROUND MAGGIE, admitting that 'When it comes to the propaganda war, Livingstone is much too fast for her'.

The reinvention of Livingstone, now no longer the bogeyman figure lurking stage-left, but instead a cheeky chappie standing up for the democratic rights of Londoners, played to his strengths in bucking the trend: here was a leading left-wing figure who self-evidently did have a sense of humour and who, having settled into his public role, enjoyed teasing the media. 'Marxism? I'm not sure what it means,' he said. 'I've never even read Karl Marx: I prefer science fiction.' He promoted his 'belief that the personal was political and politics affected every aspect of our daily lives' and made it popular, setting out an alternative social agenda for a future Britain. The public relations operation that facilitated the transformation in image, however, didn't come cheap. Livingstone admitted as much when pointing out that the GLC's campaign helped prepare the way for the Kinnock-led Labour Party to take advertising seriously: 'The Party could not spend on anything like the scale of the GLC between elections.' The Tories railed against 'propaganda on the rates' and the 1986 Local

Government Act prohibited local authorities from spending money on political advertising, but by then the damage had been done.

With the huge Conservative majority in the Commons, all the legislation easily passed through parliament (though a handful of senior Tories, including Patrick Cormack, Ian Gilmour, Edward Heath, Francis Pym, Geoffrey Ripon and Peter Tapsell, voted against) and the GLC was duly abolished in March 1986. The final concert at the Royal Festival Hall under the GLC's administration ended with a candlelit performance of Joseph Haydn's 'Farewell' Symphony, a piece in which, as each musician finishes their part, they snuff out their candle and leave the stage, until the hall descends into silence and darkness.

It was, for the government, a largely pyrrhic victory, denting the image and reputation of the Conservative Party much more than it harmed the political platform promulgated by the council, or the career of its chief protagonist. The following year Livingstone was elected as MP for Brent East, and had become sufficiently acceptable that his services were being sought out by advertising agencies: most famously he appeared in a television promotion for British cheeses, espousing the virtues of Red Leicester. By the end of the decade he had succeeded Tony Benn as the leading figure on the left, as Benn himself recognized in 1989: 'There is no doubt that Ken will be the left candidate against Neil if we lose the next election.' In case there was any confusion about how deeply he had penetrated the national psyche, confirmation of his status came the same year in the sitcom *Birds of a Feather*, in a scene set in a job centre. 'Everyone here looks so downtrodden,' says Tracey (Linda Robson) and Sharon (Pauline Quirke) replies, 'That's 'cause they are, Tracey. Welcome to the backside of Thatcher's economic miracle.' To which Tracey retorts: 'Oh, don't start getting all Ken Livingstone with me.'

8
Enemies

'When two tribes go to war'

> We agreed that the miners' strike was the key battle
> ground on which a spectacular victory could turn the tide
> of public opinion in favour of the government. The Lady
> must *not* give in on this. Unpopular though she is at the
> moment, she could not be loathed as much as
> Arthur Scargill.
> Alan Clark (1981)

> Both the right and the left share the same awe at the
> thought of the miners on the move – they bring down
> governments, they are the labour movement's
> prizefighters, our local heroes.
> Beatrix Campbell, *Wigan Pier Revisited* (1984)

> We refuse to abandon the weapon of chaos.
> Derek Hatton (1985)

The fact that both Thatcherism and the new left were largely seen by outsiders as having a southern bias was indicative of the division between north and south in Britain that had long existed, but was now becoming ever more exaggerated and ever more remarked upon. 'Mrs Thatcher has special compasses made with the north taken off,' joked Alexei Sayle, while Susie Blake's caricature of a television continuity announcer, in the sketch series *Victoria Wood – As Seen on TV*, put the other point of view: 'We'd like to apologize to viewers in the north,' she said in a cut-glass accent. 'It must be awful for them.'

Inevitably this was a somewhat crude division that didn't acknowledge the substantial variations within regions, but the concept of a newly prosperous south drifting further away from the ravaged industries of the north was a powerful image that took firm root in the culture of the times. And, it was alleged, it was not simply neglect that was leading to a two-speed Britain; there was also a government prejudice against the Labour heartlands, exemplified by the way that the defence procurement programme – one of the most valuable parts of government spending, accounting for half of the aerospace industry – was directed, with 56 per cent of the budget spent in the south-east. It was an impression not helped by Margaret Thatcher's 1985 visit to Wallsend in Tyne and Wear, when a local journalist suggested to her that, in some people's opinion, 'you don't care about us, indeed you have forgotten about us.' She replied that what was needed was to accentuate the positive, to celebrate the fact that there was 80 per cent employment and good work being done: 'Don't you think that's the way to persuade more companies to come to this region and get more jobs for the people who are unemployed – not always standing there as Moaning Minnies?' The unexpected use of the Second World War slang expression for an air-raid siren, Moaning Minnie, ensured that the comments received wide, and not very favourable, coverage.

If there was one issue that symbolized the split between the new Thatcherite vision of where the country should be heading and the neglected north, it was the role of trades unions. Thatcher had been elected at the end of a decade when union power was generally felt, including by many union members themselves, to have become too great, and a large part of her appeal was her insistence that steps would be taken to curtail it. Progress, however, was initially slow, partly because Jim Prior as employment secretary didn't share Thatcher's instinctive dislike of unions, and partly because of a determination not to repeat the mistakes of Edward Heath's government, which had created a block of legislation restricting the activities of unions and then found it useless in the face of concerted resistance. This time, there was to be a gradual approach, spread over several years and several Employment Acts, whittling away the rights that had been gained by unions.

By the middle of the 1980s, with further contributions having been made by Prior's successor, Norman Tebbit, most of the legislation associated with the Thatcher government was in place: unions no longer enjoyed legal immunity from being sued for damages, secondary picketing of businesses beyond the strikers' employers had been outlawed, the practice of the closed shop had been phased out, and secret ballots had been made compulsory for strike action to have any legal standing, for the election of union leaders and for the authorization of a political fund (on which the Labour Party largely depended for its finance). Crucially, there was to be no room for martyrs, since the penalty for infringement of the new laws was not imprisonment, as under the Heath legislation, but court-imposed fines, non-payment of which would lead to the seizing of union funds, a process known as sequestration. 'If necessary I will surround every prison in this country with police – and if needs be the army,' Tebbit told his civil servants. 'Under no circumstance will I allow any trades union activist, however hard he tries, to get himself *into* prison under my legislation.'

It wasn't simply employment law that was deployed to attack unions. Clause 6 of the 1980 Social Security Act changed the rules so that benefits payable to the dependants of someone who was on strike would have a deduction made to allow for strike pay, whether this was actually paid or not. Patrick Jenkin, secretary of state for social services, explained that this measure 'will save public money to a modest extent, but that is not its main concern. The government was elected, amongst other things, to restore a fairer bargaining balance between employers and trade unions. Clause 6 represents one of the steps taken to that end.' The intention, Jenkin added, was 'to fix responsibility for the support of strikers' families where it rightly belongs, namely, upon the unions.'

Little of this legislation was new, but was rather a return to the programme outlined by Stanley Baldwin's government in the aftermath of the 1926 general strike, and summarized by *The Times*: '(1) No strike shall be legal unless it is authorized by a majority of the members of the trade union concerned voting by secret ballot. (2) Peaceful picketing to be restricted and controlled, and forbidden altogether at a man's private residence. (3) Benefit funds to be separated from the fighting funds of a union, and the latter to be liable to an action for damages arising out of an illegal strike. (4) Members of a trade union to intimate in writing their desire to subscribe to the political fund of the union.' Much of that was enacted (though not the secret ballots) and was subsequently repealed by Clement Attlee's government in the late-1940s. Now it was all back on the agenda and, in due course, on the statute books. It began to seem as though trade unions were considered as being on a par with prostitutes: in the same way that prostitution was officially legal, but virtually every activity that might promote or facilitate its practice was outlawed, so the right to strike remained, but the right to strike successfully had become almost impossible. And, just as Thatcher would never have countenanced meeting the women who flooded into London from the midlands and north on British Rail awayday tickets to ply their trade, so too did the trade union leaders wait in vain for an invite to Number Ten.

Behind the legislation was the reality that the union movement was in rapid decline. Having grown steadily since the war, membership reached a peak of twelve million in 1979, and then began to fall more quickly than it had risen, so that by the 1983 election a tenth of that number had gone. Unemployment was largely responsible for the fall, and fear of unemployment largely responsible for a simultaneous decline in levels of militancy. 'What has happened in shop floor behaviour through fear and anxiety,' noted Douglass Wass, permanent secretary to the treasury, 'is much greater than I think could have been achieved by more cooperative methods.'

There was one other legacy from the Heath years that haunted the Conservative Party: the sense that there was unfinished business with the National Union of Mineworkers (NUM), whose two strikes in the early 1970s had ended in total victory, the second largely credited with bringing down the government in the general election of February 1974. Two members of Heath's cabinet had argued against his decision to call that election: Margaret Thatcher and Keith Joseph; now they were the leading lights in a new administration and conflict with the miners was widely expected. While still in opposition, Thatcher had asked her fellow ideologue Nicholas Ridley to prepare a strategic analysis of how a Conservative government might respond to politically motivated trade unionism. His paper, which was leaked to *The Economist*, suggested that 'the eventual battle' should not be with gas or electricity workers, and that the miners would be the most likely opposition. It therefore recommended 'a Thatcher government to: a) build up maximum coal-stocks, particularly in the power stations; b) make contingency plans for the import of coal; c) encourage the recruitment of non-union lorry drivers by haulage companies to help move coal where necessary; d) introduce dual coal/oil-firing in all power stations as quickly as possible'. It went on to suggest that it would be advisable 'to cut off the money supply to the strikers, and make the union finance them', and to provide 'a large, mobile squad of police equipped and prepared to uphold the law against violent picketing'. This, Ridley later insisted, was merely 'a list of sensible precautions', showing that Thatcher 'knew, even as far back as 1978, that she would face a pitched battle mounted by Arthur Scargill', and that she further knew 'it would be a political assault designed to overthrow her government'.

Scargill, the anticipated enemy, was second only to Thatcher herself as the most divisive figure of the decade. Like Peter Mandelson, he was a former member of the Young Communist League, but while neither man had progressed to become adult members of the Communist Party of Great Britain, choosing instead to join the Labour Party, Scargill never moved to the right as did Mandelson. Indeed some suspected that the CPGB was too gradualist in its approach for him, too content to build its strength slowly in the upper echelons of the trade unions, not sufficiently committed to the grand public gesture. Rather there was in Scargill's approach something akin to syndicalism – the belief that trade unions themselves were sufficient to overthrow capitalism without recourse to political parties – combined with a love of the limelight. He was by a long way the most articulate union leader of his generation, an electrifying platform speaker, with a voice loud enough to ride any wave of cheering, while also being capable of disconcertingly calm, reasonable, unflustered performances in television studios.

He had been elected leader of the Yorkshire miners in 1973 and, during those earlier strikes against the Heath government, had been the man widely credited with developing the tactic of the flying picket that had done so much to ensure their success. Disinclined to follow any path that might smack of compromise, he had built a strong following as a leader prepared to fight at all times for the interests of his members, and in December 1981 he was elected president of the NUM. By that stage, one confrontation with the government had already appeared and receded. In early 1981 the National Coal Board (NCB) had produced proposals to close 23 pits and make 13,000 miners redundant, to which the NUM, under the leadership of Joe Gormley, had responded with a threat of a national strike. Aware that the preparations outlined by Ridley had not yet been completed, and that the miners would attract widespread support from other sectors, the government backed down. 'I do not deny for one moment the acute embarrassment this means for the government,' admitted cabinet minister John Biffen, before pointing out that he didn't 'come into politics to be a kamikaze pilot'.

As those preparations were put in place, however, a conflict looked increasingly inevitable, and the rhetoric was gradually ramped up, as Alan Bennett noted in the wake of the Falklands War: 'There has been a noticeable increase in the use of the military metaphor in public debate. Tebbit, the employment secretary, yesterday talked of campaigns, charges and wars of attrition. And the flag figures. The danger of such talk, of course, is that it presupposes an enemy.' Thatcher herself was subsequently to make explicit the link she saw between the Argentine military dictatorship and the unions: 'We had to fight an enemy without in the Falklands. We always have to be aware of the enemy within, which is more difficult to fight and more dangerous to liberty.' That phrase, 'the enemy within', was to cause outrage to many, but Thatcher wasn't the only one using such language. In his first conference speech as leader, Neil Kinnock had adopted similar terminology from an opposite standpoint: 'Those who prate about

Blimpish patriotism in the mode of Margaret Thatcher are also the ones who will take millions off the caring services of this country. I wonder they don't choke on the very word patriotism. They are the enemy, they must be defeated.' And the NUM in particular was regularly described by both sides in militaristic terms: 'the party's traditional enemy,' as Conservative Alan Clark called them, or 'Labour's brigade of guards,' as seen from the left by Eric Heffer.

In March 1984 the NCB announced a programme of pit closures that would see 20,000 men lose their jobs, and miners at Cortonwood colliery in Yorkshire, one of those pits threatened with being shut down, walked out on strike. Others joined them and within a week Scargill had announced that this was now deemed to be a national strike, as he called on all NUM members to withdraw their labour. Thus began perhaps the most famous dispute in Britain's industrial history, a year-long struggle that changed the lives of hundreds of thousands and that became symbolic of a major shift in modern British history, ending with the death of the Labour movement as it had been known for decades. It was epic in scale, often heroic in its conduct, and seemingly destined for defeat from the outset.

It was not, however, a strike that was universally observed. The Nottinghamshire pits, in particular, continued to work, with very few miners heeding the call to withdraw their labour, a pattern repeated in the Midlands, South Derbyshire and Leicestershire, and much attention centred on the refusal of the union to hold a national ballot on strike action. This was not yet a legal requirement and, although the NUM had in the past normally balloted its members, the action taken this time was perfectly constitutional; it just wasn't very astute politically. Peter Heathfield, the union's general secretary, argued that 'it cannot be right for one man to vote another man out of a job', and that, since the proposed job losses were not spread across the country (Nottinghamshire, for example, was not going to be affected), a national ballot would have been inappropriate. Tony Benn was later to add that it would also have been pointless. In the 1970s a national ballot had rejected a proposed incentive scheme, but the Nottinghamshire miners had gone to court and secured a ruling that they could have their own separate vote; when they did, they decided to accept the scheme. In these circumstances, Benn said, 'The issue of a national ballot was really irrelevant because had it occurred – and the NUM nationally had come out in favour of a strike – Nottinghamshire area would have won permission for its own ballot and remained at work; and if it had gone the other way the Yorkshire area would have come out and other areas would have had to decide whether to give support.' Whatever the logic of these claims, the failure to ballot the members handed the NUM's opponents a potent propaganda weapon, and even within the Labour movement there were many who agreed with Roy Hattersley's argument that 'it was Arthur Scargill's duty to either convert or outvote those of his members who thought only of themselves'.

The drifting away of Nottinghamshire from the mainstream of the mining industry had been apparent in the 1983 general election, when the Conservative candidate Andy Stewart had won the newly created constituency of Sherwood, despite the fact that it included twelve pits and an unusually high concentration of mineworkers. Now, in the face of the county's non-participation, Scargill returned to the tactic of the mass picket, sending large numbers of striking miners into the Nottinghamshire coalfields to dissuade those still working from continuing so to do. And in response the police, having learnt from the 1970s, adopted similar tactics; the area was flooded with thousands of officers from around the country to ensure that those who wished to go to work might do so, an approach that some feared was the start of a de facto national police force. More controversial still was the setting up of roadblocks to prevent the passage of anyone suspected of being a picket: in the first six months of the dispute, estimated the chief constable of Nottinghamshire, there were nearly 165,000 cases of people stopped from entering the county.

Striking miners naturally saw this as an infringement of their right to free movement about the country. Their opponents saw it as a reasonable attempt to prevent the mass physical intimidation of individuals seeking to go about their lawful business and attend their place of employment. Appropriating one of the most venerated slogans of the left, the government now proclaimed the importance of the 'right to work', infuriating all those who regarded Thatcherism as being synonymous with unemployment. This right, it was argued, was now being threatened by the mass pickets, 'the bully boys of Arthur's army' as they were called by Ian MacGregor, the man appointed chairman of the NCB in 1983.

While the media and the government focused on the lack of a ballot and on incidents of violence by pickets, the NUM and its supporters saw the policing of the strike as a key issue. Stories abounded of police aggression, of unprovoked violence and of deliberate intimidation in areas where the strike was solid. 'They were animals,' said a woman in a mining village in South Yorkshire, after seeing police break up a picket. 'They were hitting anyone they could find. I was once in favour of the police but there's no way they will get any help from me now.' This breakdown in trust was amongst the most notable effects of the strike, much of it stemming from the behaviour of officers from outside forces in what was seen as virtually an army of occupation. George Moores, the chairman of the South Yorkshire police committee talked about seeing 'rosy-cheeked nice lads turned into Nazi storm-troopers,' and added that it would be 'twenty years before some policemen in South Yorkshire are forgiven for what they've done in the pit villages and on the picket lines.' There were stories too of the police lines being augmented by soldiers, and of deliberate taunting by officers, waving wads of banknotes at pickets in celebration of the overtime pay they were receiving.

Little of this was aired in the news media at the time. The majority of journalists, photographers and television cameras situated themselves behind police lines, a position that suggested both the sympathies of their employers and the relative safety that was to be found there – better to face a ragged shower of sticks and stones than a cavalry charge of baton-wielding police. The consequence was that most of the media coverage depicted the hostility and violence of pickets, not of police. Nonetheless, the imagery that later passed into the collective memory of the dispute tended to show the conflict from the other side. The role of the force could be seen, most famously, in the film *Billy Elliot* (2000), set in a mining town in Durham during the strike, with the silent, menacing presence of the police an inextricable part of the urban setting. The issue was addressed too in Reginald Hill's novel *Under World* (1988), set in a Yorkshire mining village after the strike, where Dalziel ruminates on the legacy of the strike and its implications for policing by consent in the future: 'They brought a lot of cockneys up from the Stink, but, bloody Cossacks, them lot. All they know is rape and pillage.' Another fictional detective working in the county, Peter Robinson's DCI Banks, sees the effect on members of the force, as he's told about the character of an officer murdered while policing an anti-nuclear demonstration: 'He was handy with his truncheon, Gill was. And he enjoyed it. Every time we got requests for manpower at demos, pickets and the like, he'd be the first to sign up. Got a real taste for it during the miners' strike, when they bussed people in from all over the place. He was the kind of bloke who'd wave a roll of fivers at the striking miners to taunt them before he clobbered them.' The issue of overtime pay even turned up in a 1986 episode of *Casualty*: 'It's alright for you boys, innit? Every time there's a strike, another hundred coppers start taking out mortgages,' says an ambulance worker bitterly to a policeman. 'If I was on your wages, maybe I could join the property-owning democracy as well.'

Amongst the few journalists trying to keep an even-handed approach was Paul Routledge, the labour editor of *The Times*, who wrote of picket-line violence: 'Without equivocation it ought to be stopped. All of it, the stone throwing by miners *and* the baton charging by policemen who actually seem to enjoy a week away from home for a pityard punch-up. And don't tell me they don't because I've seen them at it.' There was also Paul Foot, whose sympathies lay more squarely with the strikers; he reported in his *Daily Mirror* column about the excitement on Fleet Street when word arrived of a Derbyshire miner, Pete Neelan, having his car and garage set on fire and his house spray-painted with the word 'Revenge'. Sadly, when the journalists arrived to get the full story, they discovered that he wasn't one of the heroic working miners but merely a striker, and they all disappeared again without filing their copy.

These were isolated voices. Most of the media comment saw the strike as being a personal political crusade by Scargill and, with impressive consistency, used the imagery of the Second World War against him. SCARGILL AND THE FASCISTS OF THE LEFT ran a headline in the *Daily Express*, while John Junor, editor of the *Sunday Express*, continued the analogy: 'Hitler used his thugs to terrorize into submission people who disagreed with him. Isn't that precisely what is happening now at night in Nottinghamshire mining villages?' Most notoriously, the *Sun* obtained a photograph of Scargill with his right arm outstretched in a gesture that coincidentally resembled a Nazi salute, and proposed to run it with the headline MINE FUHRER. The paper's print workers refused to print the article and instead the paper appeared with a virtually blank front page, containing just a brief statement from the management: 'Members of all the *Sun* production chapels refused to handle the Arthur Scargill picture and major headline on our lead story. The *Sun* has decided, reluctantly, to print the paper without either.' The picture ran elsewhere, the *Daily Express* captioning it with a little more subtlety: 'Napoleon of Barnsley'.

The personalized focus on Scargill was a deliberate tactic by the government and its supporters, who knew how controversial a figure he was, though their task was undoubtedly made easier by his own self-publicizing inclinations. It was a successful ploy, and not simply amongst the more obvious readers of tabloid papers; Routledge revealed that the Queen had suggested to him the strike was all down to one man: 'she felt that the dispute was essentially promoted by Mr Scargill.' But the personalization was resented by many in the rank and file of the union. 'We're not Scargill's cannon fodder,' insisted Terry Harrison, an NUM branch secretary in Kent. 'He is responding to decisions we have taken in our branches. We have got a leader who does what we tell him to.' Morris Bryan, another Kent miner, agreed: 'Arthur Scargill is pursuing the policy of the union. It's not his policy, it's been formulated by the union.' Such support was not universal, even on the left of the Labour Party: 'Personally, I didn't like Scargill. I thought his ego had taken over,' wrote John Prescott later. 'In my view it was "me me me" in so much of what he was doing and saying.'

Many of the themes that had developed in the early weeks of the strike came sharply into focus with the confrontation at the Orgreave coking plant in South Yorkshire in June 1984. A mass picket, seeking to close down the plant, was met by large numbers of police – estimates varied between five thousand and ten thousand on each side – and in the violence that ensued, mounted police made repeated charges. Amongst the injured was Scargill himself, briefly admitted into hospital. The television images of the battle horrified much of the nation (with the BBC accused of misleading the public about the order of events, so that the use of horses was seen to be reactive rather than unprovoked), and Tony Benn was not alone in concluding that 'A kind of civil war is developing; there is no parallel that I remember in my lifetime'. That was indeed how it looked: armies of strikers and sympathizers trying to impose their will by force and being prevented only by even greater force. Even the government's natural supporters were disturbed; the strike had been 'bungled by both sides in the most pig-headed fashion,' despaired actor Kenneth Williams in his diary. 'Thatcher deserves to lose popularity over it: I'm not surprised she's down in the polls. Governments are supposed to be competent not obdurately stupid.'

There was no consensus either in the police establishment. South Yorkshire's assistant chief constable Tony Clement made it clear that Orgreave was not simply part of an industrial dispute: 'If the pickets here win by force, the whole structure of industrial relations and policing and law and order and civil liberties is all gone.' And although his view was certainly the majority position within the force, John Alderson, the former chief constable of Devon and Cornwall, was prepared to sound a discordant note: 'For the first time we have seen the police having to resort to some kind of paramilitary style of policing which we have always associated with continental police forces and always prided ourselves in having avoided having to introduce.'

While the headlines were thus occupied, the everyday reality behind the dispute was the hardship endured by those on strike and their families. The cuts in benefits that had earlier been introduced bit deep, for there was no strike pay, just a daily allowance provided to those who did a stint on the picket-line. The DHSS also deducted from benefit payments any loans made to families by social work departments in local councils, while for single men, there was no income at all. In the resulting desperation, Labour

MP Joe Ashton noted that 'in Barnsley market local stalls were soon selling wedding rings for £5 each,' and Benn described the scene at the Labour Club in his Chesterfield constituency: 'it was like a field hospital, with people crowding in to collect food parcels. There are miners' wives who are expecting babies, and the DHSS refuse to help with money for prams or cots or nappies, and this is causing great anxiety.' The use of the benefit system as an adjunct to the government's industrial policy, pointed out Peter Hain, was a new and powerful weapon, turning the achievements of previous Labour administrations against the people they were intended to help: 'Because the poor are now more dependent on state benefits than in pre-welfare days when they had to rely on community self-help, they are more vulnerable to attacks on these benefits.'

What emerged in response was an alternative welfare system, with the establishment of kitchens serving meals and distributing food parcels. A large network of support across the country, involved upwards of a million people – 'the biggest and most continuous civilian mobilization to confront the government since the Second World War,' according to the *Financial Times* – and raised an estimated £60 million and made huge donations in kind. An endless round of benefit events was staged, featuring acts as diverse as Wham! and Napalm Death, as well as Crass's last ever gig, and making folk-punk singer Billy Bragg a national figure ('it energized the entire music industry,' commented *NME* editor Neil Spencer). Every Saturday for months there were bucket-wielding groups in high streets across the country, urging shoppers to 'dig deep for the miners', and offering in return for their contributions a sticker calling for 'Coal, Not Dole'.

Most noticeable about this support campaign was the fact that it was so enthusiastically embraced by the new left. It effectively took over from CND as the single unifying issue around which a disparate movement could rally, even though the cause seemed so firmly fixed in an old Labour world of a male-only manual industry. This was, it felt to many, not simply a strike, but a crusade against everything that Margaret Thatcher stood for, a civil war between two different philosophies who didn't even seem to share a common language: the government and Ian MacGregor talked of 'uneconomic pits', the NUM's supporters spoke of 'mining communities'. The gulf in values, in the visions of society, that lay behind those two phrases motivated hundreds of thousands who opposed Thatcherism.

Journalist Julie Burchill was one of many to ridicule the incongruity of a group such as Lesbians and Gays Support the Miners – 'as though a single gay or lesbian from the mining community could *ever* have come out and *been themselves*, and continued to live in a pit village' – but the interaction of such organizations with striking miners did much to spread the new left's agenda beyond its London base. Interviewed by Robin Denselow, Red Stripe from the a cappella group the Flying Pickets, remembered putting striking miners up in a house in London: 'Miners from the Welsh valleys found themselves living alongside women who wore pink hair or Mohican haircuts, swore, accused them of being sexist, and insisted on being treated as equals. The miners were "shocked" by their supporters, and their attitudes changed too.' It was far from one-way traffic: the leading role taken in the dispute by the Miners' Wives Support Groups changed miners' opinions, but it also reinvigorated a women's movement that had been in danger of retreating into theoretical abstraction. And if there were one symbol of the transformations effected during the course of the strike, it was the presence of a contingent of miners, complete with brass bands, at the head of the 1985 Gay Pride march. Nor was it simply a political exchange. Mark Steel, in Derbyshire for a benefit gig, stayed with a striking miner and was greeted with: 'I hope thee's got some of that wacky baccy. That's bloody marvellous stuff, that is.' When Steel explained that he didn't have any cannabis, the miner was confused: he'd never encountered it before the strike, but had recently come to the conclusion that every Londoner who was supportive of the strike was bound to be carrying a stash.

While the spirit was undoubtedly willing, however, the power of the new left was simply not up to the task of ensuring victory for the miners. The strike had faced an uphill struggle from the outset, with the government not only being better prepared, but also choosing the timing of the dispute, at the start of spring, just as the demand for energy was coming to the end of its seasonal peak. Unlike the 1970s, there were to be no power cuts, no significant disruptions to other industries as a result of the miners' actions – the only people who went without heating the following winter were striking miners and their families. 'Mrs Thatcher has been beaten once too often by the miners,' noted the *Daily Mirror* as early as March 1984. 'This time she holds most of the cards and she intends to win.' The NUM's sole chance of success lay in the hope that other groups of workers would join. It rapidly became apparent that no such development was going to happen.

At the time and in the years to come, much anger was directed by the left at the leadership of the Labour Party and the TUC for failing to provide full support for the strike or for the miners themselves. In fact, Neil Kinnock, scion of a South Wales mining family, had addressed the issue of policing the pickets: 'What would be the instinct of any red-blooded man in this House, having put his family to all that inconvenience and near-misery, if he saw someone riding roughshod over his picket line?' he had asked rhetorically in the Commons. 'I know what my attitude would be. In fact, I should be worried if it were not the case.' But that had been in February 1972; his position had changed over the intervening twelve years and now he mostly sat frustrated on the sidelines, infuriated by the way that the strike was postponing his attempts to re-orientate the party, reluctant even to push the issue of civil liberties. The situation wasn't aided by a personal animosity between him and Scargill. For more than two months of the strike, the two men didn't even meet. 'What's the strategy, Arthur?' Kinnock asked, when finally they did. 'What's the game plan? Tell me and I'll see what we can do.' But Scargill didn't answer, and the suspicion grew that there wasn't really any strategy at all, just the tactic of mass-picketing that had worked back in 1972, but was now being contained by the police.

Frank Chapple, whose union included the power-station workers, acknowledged that his members had the ability to cause real disruption to society, which might well have swung the dispute in favour of the miners, but he insisted: 'They had not used that strength on their own behalf and would not be compelled or manipulated to do so for some other group with the muscle to throw up a blockade.' Bill Sirs, general secretary of the steel-workers union, was similarly reluctant to become involved: 'I am not here to see the steel industry crucified on someone else's altar.' But the truth was that even if other union leaders had thrown their weight behind the miners, there was no guarantee that a call for action would have been heeded. The union movement was already in full retreat, having lost every conflict with the government over the last four years (save for when, as with the miners in 1981, the government had refused to give battle); the leadership was weak, demoralized and unable to rely on the support of their members, a large proportion of whom had voted Tory in 1979 and again in 1983. And still the lack of an NUM ballot rankled: if Scargill couldn't persuade a fifth of his own members to come out, why should others risk their livelihoods?

Amongst the wider public, polling evidence showed a steady loss of support for the action, and certainly nothing comparable to the position enjoyed by the NUM in the strikes of the previous decade: in February 1974 a Gallup poll had found that 52 per cent said their sympathies were with the miners, with only 24 per cent siding with the employers; in December 1984, these figures were reversed. 'It was as if we were the same crowd each time,'

Mark Steel wrote of the massive anti-Thatcher demonstrations of the early 1980s. 'The protest movement wasn't reaching beyond its own ranks of around 150,000 people and it was dawning on those of us that despised her that she was getting away with it.' The numbers might be greater now, but the essential problem remained: the strike alienated rather than attracted potential support. The longer it continued, with the chance of victory slipping ever further from the grasp of the NUM, the uglier the conflict became. A new depth was reached in November 1984 with the killing of a South Wales taxi driver named David Wilkie, who had been driving a working miner to work when two strikers dropped a concrete block from an overhead bridge onto his car. The two men were convicted of murder, though this was later reduced on appeal to manslaughter.

The odds were clearly against the miners, and though the sheer length of the dispute meant that there were moments when it seemed that the tide was turning for them, outright victory never seemed to be a real possibility. Just four weeks into the strike the *Daily Mail* ran a headline MINERS START 'SLOW DRIFT BACK TO WORK', which was absurdly premature, but did set the tone for much of the media coverage as autumn arrived and a drift back did occur. Although the numbers of those returning to work were distorted for propaganda purposes, the trend was clear and reality could not be ignored indefinitely. In March 1985, nearly a year after the strike had begun, the 63 per cent of miners who were still out staged simultaneous marches back to their pits, having suffered the biggest defeat the trade unions had faced in over half a century.

The closure programme that had triggered the strike was now put into full force, and over the next year some thirty-six mines were closed, with massive job losses that were as disruptive and damaging as everyone had always been known they would be. 'Take away the coal and their lives were finished,' lamented Joe Ashton. 'In other towns redundant men could move down the road a couple of miles and take their skills to another factory. When a pit shut, there was no other factory. Coal-mining skills, unlike engineering, are not transferable or of any use in any other industry.' The financial costs to the nation were also heavy; somewhere between three and five billion pounds were spent beating the strike, in addition to the cost of the closures and redundancies that followed, though the chancellor, Nigel Lawson, professed himself unconcerned: 'It was essential that the government spent whatever was necessary to defeat Arthur Scargill.' As with the Falklands, it had been an expensive victory, but like that war, it was seen in Conservative circles as a defence of basic principles. 'Margaret Thatcher's government had broken not just a strike but a spell,' wrote Norman Tebbit in his memoirs. 'Parliament had regained its sovereignty.'

By this stage, however, Tebbit's own life had been horribly turned upside down. For while the miners' strike was still continuing, amidst all the inflated talk of enemies within, a more clear-cut enemy came close to scoring its greatest ever propaganda success. In the early hours of 12 October 1984, with the Conservative Party gathered in Brighton for its annual conference, the IRA detonated a bomb in the Grand Hotel, where Thatcher and most of the party's leadership were staying. Five people – including the MP Sir Anthony Berry – were killed, and many others injured, amongst them both Tebbit and his wife, Margaret, the latter left permanently disabled. Rescuers continued to work through the rubble until, seven hours after the explosion, the chief whip, John Wakeham, became the last person to be pulled out alive from the wreckage. Thatcher herself escaped unharmed, though the windows to her suite were blown in and the bathroom destroyed, and she went on to deliver her speech that afternoon to the conference, displaying a calm and resolve that merely enhanced her status: 'The fact that we are gathered here now, shocked but composed and determined, is a sign not only that this attack has failed, but that all attempts to destroy democracy by terrorism will fail.'

The scale of the atrocity, the attempt to murder the prime minister, was unprecedented in the Northern Ireland war – indeed one had to look back to the Gunpowder Plot or the Cato Street Conspiracy for a parallel – but it could, as Alan Clark noted in his diary, have been much worse: 'If they had just had the wit to press their advantage, a couple of chaps with guns in the crowd, they could have got the whole government as they blearily emerged – and the assassins could in all probability have made their getaway unpunished.' The same thought occurred to another diarist, Alan Bennett: 'If the IRA had really wanted to succeed they should have left a sniper behind and he would have had an easy task.'

The attack was greeted as a tremendous propaganda coup by the IRA. 'Today we were unlucky,' read the group's message, admitting that it had been responsible, 'but remember we only have to be lucky once.' In the longer term, however, it did nothing to improve their chances of victory; Thatcher had already lost one of her closest colleagues, Airey Neave, to a terrorist bomb shortly before the election in 1979, and the Brighton bomb simply reinforced her implacable opposition to any thought of com-promise. The failed attempt to kill her and her cabinet ensured that the IRA and its political wing, Sinn Fein, would be locked out of talks for the remainder of the decade. The following year, the IRA claimed to have detonated more explosives than in any other year since the conflict had resumed in 1969, but they were peripheral to the main political event: the talks between the London and Dublin governments that led to the signing of the Anglo-Irish Agreement in 1985. The Agreement was hailed at the time as a major breakthrough, allowing the Republic a symbolic involvement in the North's affairs in exchange for recognizing that there could be no unification of Ireland without the consent of the people. In truth there was little concrete on which to build, save for the contribution the negotiations made towards breaking down barriers of mistrust and suspicion between the two governments. That was in itself a not inconsiderable achievement, but the absence of the major parties from the North meant that both the Unionists and the Republicans were infuriated, and without their participation no real progress was possible. In her memoirs, even Thatcher professed herself disappointed with what had been gained: 'Our concessions alienated the Unionists without gaining the level of security co-operation we had a right to expect.'

The Brighton bombing took over the media for a brief while, but then, as ever with the issues of Northern Ireland, it faded from the headlines, too intractable to hold the interest of either journalists or public. Meanwhile the government, in conflict with its traditional enemies in the NUM and the IRA, was also being threatened with a final showdown in the long-running conflict with local councils.

Central government had, from the mid-1970s onwards, been steadily reducing the level of its funding for local authorities, with the result that councils were obliged either to cut back the services they provided or to increase the rates, the local property tax that then existed. From a Conservative perspective, too many authorities – particularly those under Labour control – chose the latter option, burdening residents and businesses with ever higher taxes in order to fund overtly political programmes. Consequently a Rates Act was passed in 1984 that would enable Whitehall to determine the maximum budget for any council that it believed was performing poorly; should councillors choose to defy this by setting a tax-rate that was higher than that permitted, they would face disqualification from holding public office and be personally fined. A list of eighteen councils who were thus to be rate-capped (as the process was known) was issued, all of them Labour-controlled, with the exception of Portsmouth, which many assumed had been included solely as a nod towards being even-handed. The other seventeen authorities, together with a further nine who were also in dispute with the government, came together and agreed on a common tactic: not to set a rate at all, in the hope of forcing confrontation. The government would then be obliged to remove more than a thousand councillors from office, and install administrators, a procedure so complicated as to seem almost impossible to achieve.

The best-known figure in the proposed defiance was Ken Livingstone, but with his recent rehabilitation, his position as the media's favourite hate figure had been usurped by Derek Hatton, the deputy leader of Liverpool Council. A member of the Trotskyist group Militant, who had spent decades building their numbers within the Labour Party, Hatton was widely seen as the major player in Liverpool, with the actual leader of the council, John Hamilton, kept in office to act as something between a figurehead and a fig leaf. When interviewed by David Selbourne of *New Society* magazine, Hamilton conceded the point: 'I am the leader but I don't have power,' he said, somewhat pitifully. Hatton, on the other hand, did have power and appeared to enjoy his new-found fame immensely, sporting a sharper line in clothes than other politicians and driving a Jaguar with a personalized number-plate DEG5Y ('Degsy' being his favoured diminutive). He and other Militant leaders were also alleged to behave like town-hall thugs, using the council's security force as a private army. 'Yes, they were loyal to us, and yes, some of them were heavy-looking lads,' admitted Hatton. 'There were occasions, I will concede, when some of them got out of hand, and went over the top.' And, he added: 'Certainly they acted as my minders on some occasions.'

But while Hatton was taking the headlines, behind the scenes it was David Blunkett, leader of Sheffield Council, who emerged as the most weighty figure in the fight to defend what was seen as the cause of local democracy. In 1983 he had been elected to the national executive committee at his first attempt, the first person elected by the constituencies section for 35 years who wasn't then and never had been an MP. His own record in Sheffield seemed to some to vindicate the need for rate-capping (rates virtually doubled within his first two years in office), but he was an attractive personality, much less combative than the likes of Hatton, and conveying a sense of honesty and decency. The fact that he was accompanied at all times not by heavy-duty minders but by his guide-dog, Offa, did his image no harm either. Clearly he had a bright future in the party, and being barred from office for non-compliance with the new law was not a particularly attractive career option. Nonetheless he tried to hold the line of not setting a rate: 'Being martyrs is not what we seek,' he insisted. 'Martyrs fail. We intend to succeed.' But with no indication that the government might back down, and with little sign of support from the public – or even from councillors, who were beginning to worry about those fines and the prospect of being disqualified – it became clear that martyrdom was the most likely outcome.

The united front crumbled rapidly. The GLC, deeply split and in a state of confusion, ended up setting a rate that was actually lower than the level permitted by government, while Blunkett was unable to hold the Labour group in Sheffield together, and again a legal rate was set. Others too abandoned the struggle, with only Liverpool and Lambeth holding out until the summer, by which stage their councillors had become liable for the penalties specified under the Act. The collapse of the campaign produced much bitterness on the left, with many blaming Livingstone and Blunkett in particular. As Hatton bragged: 'Councils like Islington and Sheffield saw themselves as rebels cast in the same mould as Liverpool. But when it came to the crunch they just didn't have our bottle.'

When Liverpool finally did set a rate, it was fixed at a level well below that needed to meet the council's spending, a new tactic designed to ensure that bankruptcy would become a real possibility within months. This would then, it was hoped, provoke a crisis, though what was then supposed to happen was unclear, save for providing a propaganda victory; it would, claimed Hatton, 'hammer home the sharp reality of our arguments: that unless more money was available to Liverpool from the central funds, then jobs were really on the line.' The inevitable crash came in September 1985 when the council announced that by the end of the year it would have run out of money and wouldn't be able to pay the council's thirty-one thousand employees. Consequently redundancy notices, giving the statutory three months' notice, were sent round to the employees' homes, some of them in a fleet of taxis that had been requisitioned to ensure delivery, a move that brought the wrath of the unions down upon the council. As even Hatton was to admit: 'We had badly miscalculated.'

This should have been, and was intended to be, a battle with government, and in some quarters there was excitable talk of opening a 'second front' to augment the struggle of the miners. But the anticipated confrontation with Thatcher never came and, rather than the government, it was the Labour leadership that placed itself in the front line.

In October 1985, at the Labour Party conference in Bournemouth, Neil Kinnock, who had opposed the tactic of defying rate-capping and who shared no common ground with Hatton at all, save for them being in the same party, used the example of Liverpool as the climax of what became his most famous speech. 'I'll tell you what happens with impossible promises,' he said, turning his attention to the left after an hour spent attacking the Conservatives. 'You start with far-fetched resolutions. They are then pickled into a rigid dogma, a code, and you go through the years sticking to that. Outdated, misplaced, irrelevant to the real needs, and you end up with the grotesque chaos of a Labour council – a *Labour* council! – hiring taxis to scuttle round a city handing out redundancy notices to its own workers.'

As it became clear just how explicit this assault on Militant in Liverpool was to be, the hall erupted. Initially the noise was dominated by howls of protest, with the television pictures showing Derek Hatton on his feet and shouting 'Liar!' The Liverpool MP Eric Heffer, sitting alongside Kinnock as a member of the NEC, stood up and climbed down from the stage, walking out of the hall ('It was too much to bear,' he wrote later). He was followed by the Young Socialist representative on the NEC, the Militant-supporting Frances Curran. When Kinnock resumed, the audience was still far from settled and his next statement reignited the clamour: 'You can't play politics with people's jobs.' By now, though, the noise was mostly coming from supporters, recovering from the shock of a Labour leader – a *Labour* leader – publicly laying into the left. At the end of the speech, he was given a standing ovation, amidst prolonged cheers.

Tony Benn, who also left the hall early, came across a delegate in tears: 'I can't understand what they've done to our party,' she wept. But elsewhere there was jubilation. Benn's old enemy, Denis Healey, was exultant: 'Neil's speech was of historic importance. He has shifted the centre of gravity of the Labour movement.' Roy Hattersley stressed the other crucial dimension of what Kinnock had been aiming for: 'It was historic because it will change the country's perception of the Labour Party.' The actress Glenda Jackson, later to become a Labour MP, sent Kinnock a note: 'At last, at last – thank you, thank you.' And the party's newly appointed director of communications, Peter Mandelson, declared it 'the most moving, most exciting speech I've ever heard.'

After years of conferences that had more often damaged than boosted the party, Kinnock's dramatic denunciation of the left also played well with the public. Ten days before the conference started, a Gallup poll had the Alliance on 35 per cent, and the Tories and Labour level on 29 per cent; a Harris poll immediately afterwards showed Labour on 39 per cent, the Tories on 32 per cent and the Alliance on 27 per cent. Kinnock's success brought him a new status, sufficiently worrying to the Conservatives to prompt Norman Tebbit towards the end of the year to ask him outside in an encounter in the Commons lobby. 'I'm not too old to take you on, sonny boy,' the Tory hard man was alleged to have snarled, though – to the disappointment of many – the altercation never reached the stage of fisticuffs.

The primary political consequence of the collapse of the rate-capping campaign, together with the loss of the miners' strike, was the growing dominance of the centre-right on Labour's national executive committee. NEC members like Blunkett and Michael Meacher, who had previously voted solidly with the left, began to transfer allegiance to the reforming leadership. Seven months after the conference, in May 1986, the first of a succession of Militant supporters from Liverpool were brought before the NEC, charged with membership of a proscribed organization and bringing the Labour Party into disrepute, a process that saw sixteen members expelled from the party. It was at the NEC hearing that Tony Mulhearn, perhaps an even more powerful figure than Hatton in Liverpool and in Militant, if not as celebrated by the media, finally admitted how foolish it had been to give ammunition to Militant's enemies: 'We did make a tactical error in handing out the redundancy notices.' Combined with the legal moves against councillors, the expulsions ended the dominance of Militant in Liverpool, one of the few successes that world Trotskyism had been able to claim in the second half of the twentieth century. Looking back on the era, Hatton was keen to stress the achievements: 'we created 6,000 new jobs, we built 5,000 new houses, we changed the education system, and raised the whole level of political awareness within the city.' And, with some justification, he cited as evidence of their success the fact that, despite all the attacks from almost every quarter, the May 1986 council elections saw the Labour group in the city increase their strength.

For Kinnock, that speech and the reception it received was about as good as his tenure as leader was ever going to get. It announced his real arrival on the centre-stage of British politics after two years of struggling to establish his authority, and it was one of the most significant moments in the post-war history of the Labour Party, marking the effective end of the left's power within the party. One didn't have to be a member of Militant, however, to experience a sense of regret that while Thatcher had spent her second term fighting external enemies in the shape of the NUM, the IRA and the GLC, Kinnock's finest moment came with an attack on a faction within his own party.

It was the Labour conference of the following year that saw the dawn of the red rose as the party's new symbol. And, after Neil and Glenys Kinnock had flung roses out into the audience, the hall broke into a spontaneous rendition of the chant from the football terraces that had been adopted by the striking miners: 'Here we go, here we go, here we go', sung to the tune of John Philip Sousa's 'Stars and Stripes Forever'. It was evidently intended as a rallying cry, in anticipation of the election that was widely expected the following year, but it was hard not to see it as being also an elegy for a Labour movement that, with the twin defeats of the miners and Militant, would never be the same again.

9
Moralities

'I don't want to change the world'

> She had the appearance, dress and voice of a Victorian
> governess, an intimidating woman who was accustomed to
> getting her own way. Perhaps because of some atavistic
> fear of female authority, few people stood up to her and
> when Winifred asked a question she expected to get an
> answer.
>
> P.D. James, *A Taste for Death* (1986)

> It is increasingly apparent that this renewed call for
> censorship is a figleaf concealing the desire to suppress
> work which is morally or politically challenging.
>
> Hanif Kureishi (1985)

> He wasn't suitable to be a police officer. He was much too
> partial to a battle with 'enemies' of whom he took far too
> sharp a view. He wasn't the kind of man you could depend
> on to ensure a democracy. He wasn't a quick thinker,
> either. The Met was too full of people like him, and it
> was no good the bosses upstairs saying they had to take
> what they could get. With three million unemployed,
> they could get whatever police force they wanted.
>
> Derek Raymond, *He Died with His Eyes Open* (1984)

In January 1983 the host of ITV's current affairs programme *Weekend World*, the former Labour MP Brian Walden, suggested to Margaret Thatcher that she was trying to build 'a more self-reliant Britain, a thriftier Britain, a Britain where people are freer to act, where they get less assistance from the state, where they're less burdened by the state', adding that these are 'what I would call Victorian values. The sort of values, if you like, that helped to build the country throughout the nineteenth century'. She agreed whole-heartedly (how could she not?). 'Those were the values when our country became great,' she concurred, and thereafter she was associated with a desire to return to 'Victorian values', though she hadn't actually used the phrase herself.

Given the prevailing perception of the Victorian era – a vague concept of a rigid sexual code, complete with myths about piano legs being covered for the sake of decency – it was inevitable that the public response to this imagery would focus not so much upon the relationship between state and individual as upon personal, sexual morality. When Thatcher's fellow traveller, Nicholas Ridley, attempted to summarize the concept, even he was drawn into the thorny undergrowth where politicians attempt to preach morals: 'hard work, good housekeeping, thrift – "neither a borrower nor a lender be" – private charity, birth in wedlock, condemnation of violence and rioting and the mob, and freedom under the law.' Clearly the message about the desirability of 'birth in wedlock' was not one that all members of the cabinet felt able to heed (Cecil Parkinson, who spent most of Thatcher's second term on the backbenches, was to return in 1987 as trade and industry secretary), but the message that registered with the public was that this was a government setting its face against the permissive society supposedly ushered in during the 1960s.

This had been an important strand in Thatcher's early electoral success; here at last, it was believed, was a political leader with whom Mary Whitehouse might find common cause. Whitehouse had founded a seemingly doomed campaign against the erosion of traditional family virtues – particularly as depicted on television and in the cinema – in the early 1960s, before the permissive society had even been named, but she had to wait until Thatcher's election in 1979 before finally being accorded an extended interview on the BBC, her greatest bête noire. There was a suspicion that the tide was turning in her favour, and for much of the ensuing decade she was even more visible than she had been previously. She was also becoming more overtly political, denouncing not only the various nuclear dramas, but also the BBC's coverage of the Falklands, using terms indistinguishable from those of Norman Tebbit: 'To spread alarm and despondency was a treasonable offence in the last war. One wonders what succour this sort of broadcasting gives the people in Argentina.' Sometimes it appeared as though she were still fighting the battles of a previous era – she attacked a 1981 edition of the sitcom *Till Death Us Do Part* for mocking the Queen while, as a *Daily Mirror* reader pointed out, 'she ignores the fact the show was peppered with racialist insults' – but she was always happy to weigh in against new developments as well, so that the BBC soap opera *EastEnders* was seen by her as 'thirty minutes of undiluted anger, hatred, bitterness, all linked with sexual infidelity'.

In most of this, she was perfectly in accord with the instincts of the prime minister, and yet, despite Thatcher's sympathy for Whitehouse's work, there was a fundamental division between them. Whitehouse's philosophy was rooted essentially in social deference; she was instinctively anti-democratic, concerned that the self-indulgence previously restricted to the elite, and therefore of limited impact, was now being adopted by the masses, with potentially calamitous consequences for social stability. This trend could only be reversed by a wholesale return on the part of the middle and working classes to the virtues and values of the past.

Thatcher, on the other hand, had no time for deference. Indeed she arguably did more to destroy existing social structures than perhaps any other prime minister in British history; her time in office was punctuated by attacks on the establishment of the church, academia and the professions, assaulting the very institutions on which had been built the public morality of the previous century. So while her call for a restoration of Victorian values might have some success on an economic front, freeing capital and binding the hands of the unions, when it came to morality, she was whistling in the wind; there was no chance of such a return on her watch. Despite her regular excoriation of the 1960s, Thatcher was actually the politician who most facilitated the social mobility promised by that decade, and with social mobility also came moral mobility, little of it to the taste of the political right. Seeking to create a new Eden, she was confronted with the truth that free will can lead to disobedience. The inherent contradiction in Thatcher's position, seeking to be both economically libertarian and morally strict, was manifest in the 1988 foundation of the Broadcasting Standards Council, intended to extend censorship of television just as the range of channels was increasing. Her greatest media supporter Rupert Murdoch objected strongly: 'as she is urging everybody to be individual and be responsible, surely they can be entrusted to see what they like on television.'

That contradiction ran through the right, splitting those who evoked a traditional morality from those who emphasized a social revolution against all entrenched vested interests. There was common ground on certain issues – support for capital punishment, a distaste for homosexuality, a suspicion of foreigners, a hatred of anything that smacked of socialist collectivism – but there was too a deep divide in cultural terms: the middle-aged, middle-class, suburban verities of the moral right, associated with Whitehouse, never sat easily with the more youthful, cash-fixated, urban aggression of Murdoch's *Sun*. Thatcher had built a coalition of seemingly disparate forces in society during her rise to power, but it was defined more by what it opposed than what it espoused, and despite all attempts to frame a new moral consensus to accompany a new political settlement, it never quite gelled and she largely failed to win over the country. Meanwhile the left, despite starting the decade in complete disarray amidst a welter of splits — between union fixers and parliamentary compromisers, social democrats and Marxist theoreticians — found itself increasingly coalescing around the new identity politics; as the Labour Party shed its shibboleths, it turned instead towards a liberal morality that centred simply on allowing individuals to pursue different lives without excluding themselves from society, so long as they didn't pose a direct threat to capitalism.

But in the meantime there was a series of running battles, with victories and defeats on both sides, as the right attempted to roll back the waves of liberalism and lowered standards that were supposedly threatening to sweep away proper British standards of decency. The campaign to claw back ground on the medical termination of pregnancies, for example, continued, as it had ever since the Abortion Act, introduced by David Steel back in 1967, had legalized the practice in the United Kingdom (except in Northern Ireland). Parliamentary attempts by James White and William Benyon in the 1970s to make it more difficult for women to gain access to abortion had failed, and in the Thatcher years there were further such moves by James Corrie and David Alton (this latter was actually the fourteenth challenge in parliament to the 1967 Act), but none succeeded until the Human Fertilization and Embryology Act of 1990 reduced the upper limit from twenty-eight to twenty-four weeks. Amidst the clamour that surrounded every such Bill, it was not always clear where the public stood. Two opinion polls were published in February 1980, at a time when the Corrie Bill was seeking to reduce the upper limit to twenty weeks, and were in direct contradiction to each other: one, for *Women's Own* magazine, revealed that 80 per cent of women wanted to retain the status quo, the other — on behalf of the British section of the World Federation of Doctors Who Respect Human Life — found that 80 per cent of women favoured the twenty-week option. The former position was probably a more accurate depiction of what society was prepared to accept: so many people had by now been affected by the Act (the number of abortions averaged around 150,000 per year in the 1970s) that it was exceedingly unlikely an abolitionist consensus could ever be established.

There was less doubt about the public attitude to the death penalty, which had effectively been ended in 1965, though it remained theoretically on the statute books for a handful of offences until absolute abolition in

2004. Again there were periodic attempts in parliament to restore capital punishment for certain classes of murder, led by a small band of Conservative MPs, including most of the anti-abortionists, who argued for the death penalty on a pro-life basis: 'We believed that restoring capital punishment would save lives,' explained Tory MP David Amess. Despite majority support in the country – and indeed in Downing Street – for such a policy, however, all the efforts were defeated comfortably.

More successful were the efforts by the right to curb pornography or at least its visibility. In 1981 the Conservative MP Tim Sainsbury introduced a private member's bill (a particularly apt phrase) aimed at regulating the contents of sex-shop windows: the Indecent Displays (Control) Act was duly passed, as was the Local Government (Miscellaneous Provisions) Act of 1982 that gave local councils the power to license sex shops and cinemas. The result was seen in an episode of *Only Fools and Horses* in which a character known as Dirty Barry finds his sex shop being closed by the council: 'Margaret Thatcher's ruined this business,' he moans. The intention of shielding those who had no desire to encounter pornography was generally seen as reasonable, and neither Act attracted much controversy, though nor, ultimately, did they do much to halt the growing availability of pornography – space allocated to pornographic magazines on the top shelves of newsagents continued to grow, while the rise of home video recorders made films much more accessible than they had been in the days of Super-8 movies imported from Amsterdam. There was another side to the issue, however, that was revealed in 1981 when the Trading Standards Department of Westminster Council announced that they were thinking of bringing a prosecution under the Trades Descriptions Act against the movie *Emmanuelle in Space* because it didn't live up to the promise of its magazine adverts. An inspector for the council commented: 'The film itself is very tame. The advertisements show photographs of steamy sex scenes with actors and actresses who are not in the film.' Apparently it didn't even deserve an X certificate.

The over-enthusiastic selling of pornography had long been one of the pitfalls faced by prospective consumers, but it was certainly true that the material then widely available was very mild by the standards of a later age. Those who didn't live within striking distance of Soho were essentially dependent on the two major magazine distributors, W.H. Smith and John Menzies, neither of whom were prepared to take any risks on the few titles they handled. Nicholas Whittaker, who worked on both *Fiesta* and *Razzle* magazines in the 1980s, was later to write about the control exercised by the distributors, demanding the right to vet each issue for content that went too far for a top-shelf reader, in the same manner as the Lord Chamberlain had once acted as custodian of the London stage: 'Recently, one picture with a white blotch on the model's leg had been ordered to be replaced: it could have been misconstrued as "male semen". Even four-letter words could get us into trouble if they were used too often or printed in too large a type size (10pt maximum, no usage in headlines or titles).' The result was a self-censorship that produced, in the words of Martyn Harris' character Phil First: 'Girls on horseback, girls in bubble baths, girls in the innocent athletic sweat-sheen of the squash court. And even when they are all togged up in the tart's gear of stockings and suspenders and basques it's all so stunningly innocent: such anodyne anaphrodisiac *fun*.'

If there was an alternative, it came not in the selection of shots, but in the choice of the models who appeared. In 1979 Kenneth Bound, editor of *Mayfair*, the only British pornographic magazine stocked by W.H. Smith's own shops, explained that the British man liked to see real women: 'He likes to feel she is approachable. *Playboy* and *Penthouse* girls have a plastic perfection which puts them out of his reach. He doesn't want fantasy – he wants flesh and blood.' It was a tendency that led at the end of the 1980s to the launch of the very British *Splosh!* magazine, whose proprietor had discovered a hitherto uncatered-for sexual fetish; messy sex had escaped the attention of even such dedicated researchers as Magnus Hirschfeld and Richard von Krafft-Ebing, but now those with a penchant for seeing women in a state of undress, while covered with tinned custard or with baked beans, could find their needs met.

In that same 1979 interview Bound also identified what he thought was the coming trend. 'Boobs went out of fashion once we began to show pubic hair,' he said. 'Recently I have detected signs that boobs could be making a comeback – more and more readers are asking for them. Not just any boobs, but big boobs. I call them cannonballs – and they're tomorrow's turn-on.' He wasn't far wrong. In 1983 the *Sun* featured for the first time as its Page Three pin-up the sixteen-year-old Samantha Fox, the youngest topless model thus far to be featured in a national newspaper. She had earlier entered the Miss *Sunday People* competition, but had come only second when the female journalists on the paper decided that, with a bra size of 36D, her breasts were too large. Or as *Viz* comic put it, parodying the stilted pun-laden phraseology of Page Three captions: 'Modelling has become *big* business for sexy pin-up girl Samantha Fox. For saucy Sam, 20, has got big tits.' Others followed, including Maria Whittaker and Debee Ashby, with Fox having set trends both for extreme youth and for large-breasted models, the latter culminating in the surgically enhanced likes of

Melinda Messenger and Jordan in the 1990s. Public tastes and the practice of the trade were, it seemed, subtly changing.

The process was noted in Dan Kavanagh's 1987 novel *Going to the Dogs*, which featured a retired Page Three model, named Belinda Blessing, whose chief attribute – apart from her particularly spectacular breasts – is her sheer ordinariness: 'She looked really friendly, you know, the sort of girl who might have poured that pint for you, who you might have grown up with, who you could show off to your mum without worrying.' But she has become disillusioned with those who have followed in her wake: 'Girls of sixteen off the train from Leeds and Bradford, all squidgy with puppy-fat, dropping their blouses as soon as their foot touches the platform.' Even Larry Lamb, who as editor of the *Sun* in the 1970s had introduced the Page Three feature, was beginning to worry about the direction, as the women got 'younger and younger, and more and more top-heavy'. There was no agreement on what this development might mean, though there were those who suspected that the daily celebration of compliant teenage girls might constitute part of a rearguard action against the rise of assertive feminism.

In the eyes of the *Sun*, the *Daily Mirror* and the *Daily Star*, the papers that printed these photographs, they were a long way removed from pornography, but not everyone shared their perspective. In 1986 the Labour MP Clare Short, emerging as a serious voice on the new left, introduced a Bill seeking to ban the 'display of pictures of naked or partially naked women in sexually provocative poses in newspapers'. Under parliamentary procedure, it was never going to make any progress, but it did make Short a nationally known figure as the *Sun* began to ridicule 'killjoy Clare', and it did reveal a groundswell of support for her view that such imagery was degrading to women: when *Women's Own* again turned to its readers for guidance on the issue, it discovered that 93 per cent were in support of Short's objectives if not necessarily her broader beliefs. She returned to the theme in 1988 with a similar Bill, this time attracting support from some right-wing Tory MPs, including the newly elected Ann Widdecombe, who was making her own reputation as a tireless campaigner against abortion. Lord Denning, the most famous ex-judge in the country, weighed in with his backing, and added – as the battle lines became a little blurred – that he also believed in tougher gun laws, the return of hanging and the introduction of castration for convicted rapists. As he said, in words with which Short was unlikely to have agreed: 'Men must learn to respect, be courteous and chivalrous to women, they are the weaker vessel. We need to recover traditional values.'

The feminist critique of popular culture did not stop at pornography and Page Three pin-ups. Fay Weldon's 1983 novel *The Life and Loves of a She-Devil* was adapted as a BBC serial in 1986, starring Julie T. Wallace as Ruth Patchett, a meek, put-upon housewife whose husband (Dennis Waterman) leaves her for a best-selling romantic novelist, Mary Fisher (Patricia Hodge). Reinventing her life, Patchett sets up an employment agency for women, intended to help them empower themselves ('I am the Second Coming, and shall do for women what Jesus did for men,' she proclaims) while also furthering her personal vendetta against the couple who have betrayed her. Amongst her targets as she seeks to change the world is the romantic fiction industry. 'Look at this!' she winces, holding up one of Mary Fisher's books. 'This is the sort of romantic trash that women devour, women in their millions. Well, how can they develop any moral sense or ever hope to reach emotional maturity if they read such rubbish?'

But the disparagement of romantic fiction was no more successful than the campaign against Page Three. A study in 1985 showed that a third of women were regular readers and that the industry's leading publisher, Mills and Boon, was busily producing twenty new titles a month, with an average print run of one hundred thousand, despite each being available for only a few weeks. The most celebrated of their writers, Sheila Holland, who worked under various pseudonyms but was best known as Charlotte Lamb, was earning such sums from her work that she moved to the Isle of Man to escape the clutches of the Inland Revenue. Meanwhile romance proved, as ever, to be the genre most likely to be borrowed from public libraries, with the likes of Victoria Holt, Dorothy Eden and Jean Plaidy leading the pack. There were developments within the genre during the decade – Lamb herself even attracted some critical attention for *A Violation* (1983), which dealt with the aftermath of a rape – but the consistent level of public enthusiasm for what remained at heart a staunchly traditional art form suggested that perhaps the country wasn't changing as rapidly as some would have liked.

The union of the moralist right and the new left to attack pornography was not an isolated incident. For there emerged during the decade what journalists Larry Elliott and Dan Atkinson were later to term 'the nagocracy – those forever going on at their fellow citizens to take more exercise, eat more fruit, drink "sensibly" and reduce their salt intake', and its membership was drawn from right across the political spectrum. As far back as 1978 smoking had been banned at the Labour Party conference, and the example was followed elsewhere, so that although the Tobacco Workers Union was kind enough to leave a complimentary pack of

The 1982 Falklands War provoked a wave of patriotism, as seen in the crowds welcoming the SS *Canberra*'s safe return to Southampton (right). Some of the media coverage of the war was criticised for taking this patriotism too far, particularly the *Sun*'s first edition when the Argentine ship the *Belgrano* was hit (below).
Rex Features & News International

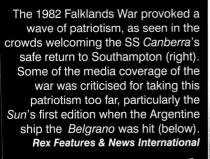

The first generation of mobile phones were status symbols whose size made them hard to ignore.
Homer Sykes Archive/Alamy

Even more unavoidable in the late 1980s was the government's campaign to raise awareness of the threat posed by AIDS.
Sally and Richard Greenhill/Alamy

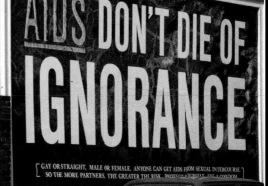

The riots that hit Britain in 1980-81 were the most visible manifestation of a deeply divided country. *PA Photos*

The miners' strike of 1984-85 revealed these divisions even more sharply, with the police being used – some claimed – as a political force to suppress the trade union movement. *PA Photos*

Editor Kelvin MacKenzie and proprietor Rupert Murdoch with the first edition of the *Sun* produced at Wapping. *PA Photos*

There was further industrial conflict in the Wapping dispute of 1986, though it failed to stop production of News International's papers. *Mirrorpix*

Street demonstrations returned at the end of the decade, with Salman Rushdie's novel *The Satanic Verses* being burned by Muslims, outraged at its alleged blasphemy. ***Sipa Press/Rex Features***

Tony Benn speaking at the Trafalgar Square demonstration against the introduction of the poll tax in 1990. The anti-poll tax campaign did much to bring down Margaret Thatcher as prime minister. ***PA Photos (both)***

Snooker player Steve Davis represented the new face of sport in the 1980s – family-friendly, uncontroversial and much sought-after for sponsorship deals. *PA Photos*

The competition between Sebastian Coe, seen here winning the 1500 metres at the 1980 Moscow Olympics, and Steve Ovett (no. 279) wa a sporting rivalry widely seer in political terms. *PA Photos*

England had already checked out of their hotel at the Headingley Test in 19 anticipating another heavy defeat, wh Ian Botham came in to bat. By the en of the day his century had turned the game, and by the end of the series, when England had improbably regain the Ashes, his pugnacious batting an bowling had made him a national he *Getty Images*

Innovative businessman Clive Sinclair, after a string of successes with calculators and computers, found only failure when he tried to launch Britain's first electric car, the C5. *Getty Images*

Anita Roddick, founder of The Body Shop chain of stores, was amongst the new breed of entrepreneurs whose achievements were celebrated in the 1980s. *Getty Images*

The most popular of these entrepreneurs was Richard Branson, who branched out from the music business into publishing, ̄n production and air travel. *Getty Images*

Derek Fowlds, Paul Eddington and Nigel Hawthorne in *Yes Minister,* the definitive political comedy of the 1980s. ***NILS JORGENSEN/ Rex Features***

The cast of *Auf Wiedersehen, Pet*, a comedy drama rooted in the unemployment of the early 1980s as British workers found jobs abroad. ***ITV/Rex Features***

The most controversial comedian of the decade Bernard Manning, who offended the moral righ with his language, and the left with material tha was often rooted in race. ***Rex Features***

The new wave of alternative comedy was the antithesis to Manning, and made its first television breakthrough with the cult success of *The Young Ones*. ***Mirrorpix***

Pop music was at its most political in the early 1980s, with bands like The Specials articulating the frustrations and anger of those who felt themselves marginalised in society. *Getty Images*

Boy George (below) and Culture Club led the movement that turned the post-punk era into a worldwide success story for British bands. *Andre Csillag/Rex Features*

Frankie Goes to Hollywood (above) were seen by many critics as embodying the triumph of packaging in pop, using political imagery and slogans to sell records. *Ian Dickson/Rex Features*

Live Aid in 1985, initiated by Bob Geldof, was the biggest music event of the decade and launched a new era in pop music. *Getty Images*

Michael Heseltine on the day in 1986 that he resigned from the cabinet over the Westland affair. Few followed the details of the story, but many saw him as the natural rival to Margaret Thatcher
Getty Images

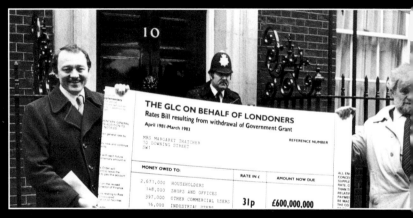

Ken Livingstone (above left) was the leader of the Greater London Council 1981-86, and emerged as the most influential leader of the left during the decade
Getty Images

A tearful Margaret Thatcher, accompanied by her husband Denis, leaves Downing Street in November 1990, having been forced out of office by her own party.
Trinity Mirror/ Mirrorpix/Alamy

cigarettes on everyone's seat at the 1980 TUC women's conference, smoking was still forbidden in the hall. In 1982 British Rail attempted to stop smoking in the buffet cars of its Southern Region trains, but found itself overwhelmed by complaints and was forced to rescind the order. It was a rare victory for smokers. BR's more normal attitude was summed up in the reply given by an official to a commuter who complained about the absence of ashtrays on a smoking carriage: 'We have removed them all to make it easier for our cleaners to do their jobs. Smokers should stop smoking and then there would be no mess in the carriages.'

Two years later the practice was outlawed on London Underground trains, despite a survey of passengers showing just 18 per cent in favour ('a gross intrusion into the liberty of the individual,' stormed the non-smoking Conservative MP for Dulwich, Gerry Bowden), though it remained for a while legal on tube platforms and in the rear seats upstairs on double-decker buses. The Underground ban was announced as being for a trial period of one year, but no one really expected to see again the familiar, fog-ridden smoking carriages. Similar prohibitions were introduced on buses in Belfast, Plymouth, Cardiff and Darlington, amongst other towns and cities, while the Newcastle-upon-Tyne Metro, which opened in 1984, was non-smoking from the outset. In 1984 too a new question was added to the forms for those wishing to adopt children, asking whether the prospective parents were smokers; the habit would not in itself be enough to invalidate their application, but it would count against them.

'I think the crucial argument is that we're living in a free country and we must be free to make our own decisions,' argues Sir Humphrey Appleby in *Yes, Prime Minister*, when confronted with proposals to stop people smoking. 'After all, government shouldn't be a nursemaid. We don't want the nanny state.' That same phrase had turned up in Bernard Levin's denunciation of the smoking ban at the 1978 Labour conference: 'The nanny state has been with us for a long time, but it is now shoving its long, bony nose into more and more areas once thought reserved for individual decision.' The concept of the nanny state was to become increasingly common, often mixed up with the conventional portrayal of Thatcher herself as a nanny figure, and there were those prepared to point out the peculiarity of a laissez-faire government meddling in people's lives. 'Interference from the nanny state,' wrote Christopher Dunkley in the *Financial Times*, 'does after all look rather odd in this Thatcherite age when we are all supposed to be taking more responsibility for ourselves and our families.' Perhaps in an attempt to circumvent this argument, there was an attempt to change the meaning of the expression, to politicize it and apply it instead to larger areas of policy, specifically those of the left, so that an editorial in *The Times* called on the government to reduce its spending on 'the basic structure of the nanny state in the five major areas of public subsidy — health, welfare, education, defence and agriculture.'

But the idea that the nanny state was manifested in public spending on education never took hold, and it continued to be seen in the terms outlined by Nicholas Ridley: 'The strange thing about this new Puritanism is that it is not directed at upholding the interests of society as a whole; rather, it is a crusade to stop others doing what they want or taking risks with their own lives.' He, like others, was convinced that the anti-smoking initiatives were just the first step on the road. 'After the triumphs of the campaign against smoking,' wrote Michael Wharton in his 'Peter Simple' column in 1981, 'the next campaign on the dirigiste medical list — the campaign against drinking — is getting under way. The "problem of alcohol" is becoming a familiar phrase.' He was quite correct. A report to the British Medical Association in 1986 claimed there were serious health dangers associated with drinking, even to those consuming less than 'the established safe maximum of fifty-six units of alcohol a week'. This guideline had been set in 1970 by the Royal College of Psychiatrists, and while not quite so lenient as a French slogan of the 1960s — 'Santé sobriété: jamais plus qu'un litre de vin par jour' (which added up to seventy units a week) — it was now deemed to be too lax. After some confusion about where a safe limit could be set, the figures of twenty-one units per week for men and fourteen for women were adopted as official government advice. The suspicion that these might be slightly arbitrary levels, plucked from thin air, was strengthened in 1995 when they were adjusted upwards by the government to twenty-eight and twenty-one units respectively, following a report that said the earlier guidelines were 'unrealistic'.

At the same time a government committee headed by John Wakeham was producing proposals that would 'improve understanding of how alcohol works [and] encourage sensible drinking'. As part of this initiative he 'met both the BBC and IBA and it was pointed out to them that it was not helpful to have endless soap operas based in pubs'. Elsewhere a new code of practice for the advertising of alcohol was issued, in an attempt to make the products of the drinks industry less appealing to their customers, but still this was not enough for some. The *Daily Mirror* wanted yet tougher action, with the banning of all television advertising, of drinking in public and of sales of alcohol through supermarkets and corner shops. 'Drunken violence is a spreading disease,' it trembled. 'The yobs are everywhere. They infest football, the cities and the shires. They come from the slums and the yuppie belt. They can be unemployed or earning a fortune.'

Meanwhile, the advertising of cigarettes was still just about legal in the print media, though so heavily restricted that it required considerable creativity to convey any message at all. Amongst the best-known adverts of the time was a picture of a sheet of purple silk ripped through with a single slash, revealing a white background; it was intended to promote Silk Cut and was denounced by feminists as encouraging violence towards women – it expressed 'the desire to mutilate as well as penetrate the female body,' as an English lecturer explains in David Lodge's *Nice Work*. There was also a creative series for the Winston brand that had a tagline drawing attention to the restrictions, together with a visual pun: 'We're not allowed to tell you anything about Winston cigarettes,' ran a typical example, 'so here's a wok in the Black Forest', accompanied by an image of a Chinese cooking-pot nestling in a gâteau.

Politicians from all sides could participate happily in arguments on such subjects. As social services secretary in James Callaghan's government, David Ennals had suggested a ban on smoking in public places back in 1979, while the future Conservative cabinet minister Brian Mawhinney called for an end to free medical treatment for those who fell ill as a result of smoking or drinking. But the tendency was primarily identified in the public's mind with Edwina Currie, who was appointed health minister in 1986 and issued herself with a private mission statement: 'My interest is the health of the nation. Not just its health care, and not just the NHS part of health care, and certainly not just the hospital part. The whole hog: are we a fit and well country?' This was, she came to realize, 'all part of the Thatcher revolution', with the state handing back responsibility for health to the people.

'She has something of a reputation in the House for having an opinion on everything,' Conservative MP Ann Winterton had sniffed of her colleague some two years earlier, and Currie went on to extend that reputation nationally with a series of high-profile speeches and interviews. She soon became a prominent media figure, portrayed as that bossy woman who was always telling old people to wear woolly hats, northerners to eat fewer chips and women that cervical cancer can be transmitted through sex, so 'don't screw around'. She was 'renowned as a bit of a nag,' reflected Teresa Gorman, a simplified and unfair distortion, but one with which Currie sometimes appeared to collude and she became, for many, the public face of the nagocracy. It was a time when the newspapers were growing fond of picking up reports from scientific journals that seemed to suggest yet another everyday activity carried risks (Richard Ingrams, the former editor of *Private Eye*, compiled a book of such health scares, *You Might As Well Be Dead*, demonstrating the dangers of everything from bracken and celery to aerobics and giving up smoking), and there was some concern that the government were increasingly keen on enforcing such messages. From here, some felt, it was but a short step to images of snooping, of bureaucracy creeping into the lives of ordinary people, a fear parodied in *Viz* with the strip 'The Bottom Inspectors', in which uniformed officers, acting on the orders of the feared Ober-Bottom-Führer, invade people's homes to ensure their bottoms are clean, dry and of an approved size.

But although Currie received the media attention, the new puritans of the left were seldom far behind. For just as Thatcher's endorsement of individual choice clashed with her instinct to control what she saw as anti-social behaviour, so too did the left's agenda of tolerance come into conflict with its own desire to protect the sensibilities of its favoured groups.

In 1975 a previous Labour administration at the GLC had attempted to end entirely the practice of censoring films shown in London that were aimed at adults, a move initiated by Enid Wistrich, as chairman of the council's Film Viewing Board, with the support of her vice-chairman, Ken Livingstone. They had met fierce opposition from Mary Whitehouse, and had ultimately been defeated when rebel Labour councillors had joined the Conservatives in voting against the proposal. For anyone who hoped that the issue might return under the new Labour administration led by Livingstone, there was only disappointment to come. 'I believe I was wrong on censorship in 1975,' he explained, 'and when in 1985 the Women's Committee complained to the BBFC that they were not being tough enough in cutting the violence against women from the films they were certificating, I supported them.' In this climate, it was perhaps not entirely surprising that the suppression of what became known as video nasties passed through parliament with little resistance.

The rise of the video cassette recorder had first been noted in 1981, when the wedding of Charles and Diana had seen a doubling in the number of such machines in Britain. By the following year one in five households owned a VCR and, with the restricted amount of television channels available in Britain, the numbers continued to grow rapidly, so that by 1986 there were more homes with a video than with a car, and penetration of the market rose above 50 per cent shortly afterwards. With the machines came a new class of films, movies that had flopped at the cinema but were able to become posthumous hits on video (they were briefly known as V-movies), so that, for example, the 1982 British horror film *Xtro*, which had hardly set the nation's box-offices alight, was by autumn 1983 riding high in the top five video rental charts, nestling amongst more conventional fare like *Sophie's Choice* and *Star Trek II – The Wrath of Khan*. There was at this early pioneering stage no system for classifying video releases, and no consensus on where they fitted into the practice of censorship: they were consumed at home rather than in the cinema, but they were clearly not the same as television programmes, which were beamed in without invitation and which remained highly regulated. And the cause of greatest concern was the way that video might change the experience of viewing a film, allowing repeated replays, screen stills and the use of slow-motion; no longer was the viewer a passive receiver of a story, he or she could now – to a limited extent – reshape it and thereby, it was feared, emphasize the goriest moments.

The absence of regulation was never likely to remain for very long, particularly when newspapers discovered that hitherto obscure horror movies were becoming quite popular, and might be viewed by children, whether inadvertently or otherwise. The term 'video nasty' was coined and applied to a range of films, including *The Driller Killer*, *SS Experiment Camp*, *Cannibal Holocaust* and indeed *Xtro*. Most notorious of all was *I Spit on Your Grave*, directed by Meir Zarchi, which had been released in 1978 under the less controversial title of *Day of the Woman*, to something less than universal critical acclaim, though it won a Best Actress award for its star, Camille Keaton, at the Catalonian International Film Festival. It was a stark film, devoid of incidental music, and resembling nothing so much as a Jacobean revenge drama in its depiction of a rape victim meting out justice to her assailants, accompanied by the kind of visual shock that a dramatist like John Webster would have recognized and applauded. Like some of the other nasties, though not all by any means, it merited a solid artistic defence of the horrors depicted, but there were few prepared to make such a case. The title alone, together with a detailed description of selected incidents from the narrative, was enough to damn the film in the minds of all fair-minded people.

And anyone who didn't damn it was by definition beyond the pale. 'I bitterly regret,' lamented Conservative MP Jerry Hayes, 'that those middle-class people who sit on beanbags wearing Gucci accessories in the Hampstead flats which are bedecked with Laura Ashley decorations and talk about world affairs should allow their children to see the type of video films with which we are dealing.' Others were prepared to widen the scope of the argument, so that the right-wing philosopher Roger Scruton wished to add anti-nuclear films like *The Day After* to the charge sheet: 'There is no more excuse for displaying a realistic picture of nuclear catastrophe than for displaying a realistic picture of a pregnant woman being cut up with a chain saw, or a live child being slowly disembowelled by hungry cannibals.' Leading the attack was the *Daily Mail* which, in a famous editorial, RAPE OF OUR CHILDREN'S MINDS, listed some of the scenes available for viewing in the films, and then made its traditional argument that we were betraying the country's finest hour: 'Britain fought the last World War against Hitler to defeat a creed so perverted that it spawned such horrors in awful truth. Now the nation allows our own children to be nurtured on these perverted horrors and on any permutation of them under the guise of "entertainment".' And it concluded, with at least a show of reluctance: 'The whole instinct of this newspaper is against regulation and restriction. But on the issue of video nasties we have no doubt whatsoever that regulation and restriction is the only answer.'

The proposed response was twofold: first, to broaden the powers of the British Board of Film Censors to include the classification of video cassettes, comparable to that used for the cinema, and second, to produce a list of films that the director of public prosecutions said were illegal under the Obscene Publications Act. There was certainly public support for at least the first of these moves; a Gallup poll in autumn 1983 showed that a majority favoured censorship of videos, though only 8 per cent said that they had themselves been offended by watching a film on video. When this minority was asked which films had caused offence, the resulting list included not only nasties like *I Spit on Your Grave*, but also mainstream Hollywood horrors including *The Exorcist* and *An American Werewolf in London* and even Oscar-winning classics *The Deer Hunter* and *One Flew Over the Cuckoo's Nest*.

If that seemed to muddy the waters even more than Scruton was managing, then the situation wasn't clarified by studies showing that children were regular viewers of this material, since one of these was conducted by Dr Guy Cumberbatch of Aston University and included a number of titles that he'd made up himself – the non-existent films were identified as being amongst those his respondents claimed to have seen. His debunking work, however, was eclipsed by the research initiated by the Parliamentary Group Video Enquiry and conducted by Dr Clifford Hill, which claimed at one point that the popularity of *The Best Little Whorehouse in Texas* was 'an indication of how freely pornographic films are available for viewing on VCRs in Britain'. It was hard to take seriously anyone who thought that a lightweight comedy starring Burt Reynolds and Dolly Parton, a piece that went on to be the biggest box-office musical of the decade, was a work of pornography. There was also the irony that the musical – the original stage version had played to great acclaim at London's Drury Lane theatre – derived much of its humour from a hypocritical alliance between politicians and television moralists. And yet Hill's research was widely, and for the most part uncritically, reported as proving the nation faced imminent moral collapse if steps weren't taken. And, if there were any doubt about the dangers faced, Professor Ivor Mills of Addenbrookes Hospital in Cambridge was on hand to point out that watching onscreen violence was potentially lethal: 'It is theoretically possible that a child could reach such a state of excitement that the heart begins to beat irregularly, blood stops circulating to the brain and the result is death.'

That was further than most were prepared to go, and the majority of campaigners were content with the argument that the depiction of violence would inevitably cause viewers to wish to enact similar violence of their own. Speaking for the government in the ensuing parliamentary debate, David Mellor, then a home office minister, seemed to have precisely this problem of distinguishing fiction from reality: 'No one has the right to be upset at a brutal sex crime or a sadistic attack on a child or mindless thuggery on a pensioner if he is not prepared to drive sadistic videos out of our high streets,' he declared. By the same token, presumably, no one had the right to complain about being burgled unless they had first called for the banning of E.W. Hornung's *Raffles* books. It was left to the Conservative backbencher, Matthew Parris, to try to establish a distinction between the glorification and the condemnation of brutality, suggesting that, for example, it would be hard for the League Against Cruel Sports to show a kill in a fox hunt without upsetting some people. 'Many British people have seen bull fighting, and that is the main reason why it is so greatly disliked,' he pointed out. 'Showing people things can make them change their minds about them, not make them want to copy them.'

His voice went unheeded and the 1984 Video Recordings Act was passed onto the statute book. The list of prohibited films was also published, with some seventy-four movies being included at one point or another. Their absence from the shelves of video rental stores was mourned by few, though the banning of Sam Raimi's *The Evil Dead*, one of the major horror works of the decade and the single most rented video of 1983, did raise some eyebrows. For those with long memories, it was all too reminiscent of the index of banned publications circulated by the home office in the 1950s to chief constables, a list that numbered more than a thousand books (including works by Guy de Maupassant and Daniel Defoe) and four hundred magazines, including *Jiggle*, *Titter* and *Oomph*.

There had been a time when left-wing intellectuals would have opposed such moves, at least on the grounds that censorship of art by the state is always to be regretted, and might even perhaps have adopted a positive attitude to the nasties, in the manner of Iris Murdoch's character David Crimond: 'He praises horror films because they show that behind cosy bourgeois society there's something violent and disgusting and terrible which is *more real!*' But by the mid-1980s, such figures were thin on the ground – with the honourable exception of the academic Martin Barker, who edited a collection of essays on the genre for Pluto Press – and instead the left largely followed the right's lead, albeit with a feminist angle, as Labour MP Margaret Beckett tried to explain in the Commons: 'Pornography represents the violent abuse of submissive women as normal sexual behaviour.'

Despite such supportive voices from the left, there was no doubt that the passing of the Video Recordings Act was seen as a major victory for the right in its struggle to reverse the 'anything goes ideas of the 1960s', which the president of the Association of Chief Police Officers blamed for a 'decline in public and private morality'. The position of the police was critical, for the war against liberalism was fought not merely in legislation but in the intensification of policing practices. This was especially notable in the case of James Anderton, who became chief constable of Greater Manchester in 1976, and had by the 1980s established himself as one of the leading figures on the moral right. 'I sense and see in our midst an enemy more dangerous, insidious and ruthless than any faced since the Second World War,' he declared. 'I firmly believe that there is a long-term political strategy to destroy the proven structure of the police and turn them into an exclusive agency of a one-party state.' The target of his criticism was, of course, not the Thatcher government – which, some thought, was following precisely that strategy – but the left, with its desire to use police committees as a check on the force's power.

Like Whitehouse, Anderton appeared to see criticism of traditional morality as being part of a political plot to undermine society, thereby necessitating the firmest possible action. So while, on the one hand, he was announcing that 'armed police officers, travelling in signed police vehicles, are patrolling Greater Manchester round the clock' (seemingly in contravention of Home Office guidelines that guns should be used only as a 'last resort'), his force was also 'carrying out a vigorous anti-pornography campaign', using powers under the Obscene Publications Act. 'Police used intimidation techniques to scare retailers, and used sledge hammers to break down walls to find stock,' remembered Michael Butterworth, co-founder of the city's Savoy Books, a progressive literary publisher that was regularly hit. 'They drove about the city Eliot Ness-style on the tailgates of police vans.' It was Anderton too who was amongst the first to recognize the new threat posed by video cassettes; when Peter Cook found that the BBFC wouldn't allow the film he had made with Dudley Moore, *Derek and Clive Get the Horn*, to be shown in cinemas, on grounds of blasphemy and extreme obscenity, he had it released instead on video in 1980, and Anderton promptly seized eight hundred copies, sending the distribution company into bankruptcy. And it was a police raid on a record shop in Manchester that brought the members of Crass into court to receive the ultimate validation of having their music denounced by the police as 'audio nasties' and condemned by a bench of magistrates: 'It is our opinion that these records breach the Obscene Publications Act in that they might have a tendency to deprave and corrupt people likely to come into contact with them.'

Anderton's obsession with moral degeneracy was parodied in the television comedy *The New Statesman* in the form of a police chief named Sir Malachi Jellicoe. 'He has recently organized public book burnings of volumes he deems blasphemous, obscene or both,' claims a Labour MP. 'So wide are his criteria that there are now only sixty-seven books left in the East Yorkshire public library system!' And Anderton's other concern is also seen, as Jellicoe blackmails Rik Mayall's character Alan B'Stard into passing a law that arms the whole force – 'You've struck a blow for justice and Jesus,' Jellicoe says approvingly.

The fears that were raised by an armed police units were seen too in Eric Saward's 1984 *Doctor Who* story 'Resurrection of the Daleks', which opened with one of the most startling images of the series, as two seemingly normal British bobbies on the beat suddenly pull out machine pistols and shoot down unarmed civilians. Filmed in Butler's Wharf just as London's Docklands was being redeveloped, and set in the present, the story shows the Daleks as having created a cohort of duplicate human beings. Placed in positions of authority on Earth, these replicants survive the Doctor's latest battle with the Daleks, and the two police officers, together with their alien commander, are last seen still at large on the streets of London. There were others, however, who believed that the availability of firearms to the police was still too restricted. The film director Michael Winner set up the Police Memorial Trust in 1984 in response to the shooting dead of PC Yvonne Fletcher while policing a demonstration outside the Libyan

Embassy; the aim of the Trust was to erect memorials to police officers killed in the course of their duties, though Winner was always happy to broaden the agenda: 'So many would have been saved if they'd been armed. Think what the English police force have to face. They're the only disarmed police force in Europe.'

The role of the police was an issue that continued to divide society and commentators through the decade. Peter Burden, the *Daily Mail*'s chief crime correspondent, claimed that there was 'a conspiracy to destroy the public acceptance of the British police and the morale of the force and thus remove one of the major obstacles from the left's plans to disestablish our society and reshape it in a new and authoritarian form'. But even in the tabloid press, there was some concern at developments: 'Their job is to uphold the law, not make it,' insisted a *Daily Mirror* editorial. 'That isn't what has been happening recently – particularly in the miners' dispute. There has been a change in the police's role. A change not authorized by parliament or discussed by it.'

No one else went so far as the anarchist paper *Class War*, which regularly printed pin-up photos of policemen injured in riots or on picket lines under the strapline HOSPITALIZED COPPERS, but public unease was not restricted to the extremist left or to striking miners and the youth of Brixton. There was a growing mood of disillusion and even the most celebrated officers were touched by a new lack of respect; PC Trevor Lock, who had been held hostage during the 1980 Iranian Embassy siege and had won the George Medal for gallantry, was forced to move from his house in Dagenham because, as Scotland Yard explained, 'the pressures on the family have led to several incidents at school and in the local vicinity, including harassment of the younger members of the family and deface-ment of the family car.' (The word 'pig' was scratched on the vehicle.) By the end of the decade, even those who should have been considered the natural allies of the police were losing faith: 'I fear that the police have abandoned their old class allegiances,' complained Alan Clark. 'Indeed many of them seem to carry monstrous chips, and actually to enjoy harassing soft targets. And where has it got them? Simply widened the circle of those who resent and mistrust the police.'

The image of the force was not helped by a nine-part fly-on-the-wall documentary series, *Police*, broadcast by the BBC in 1982, showing the work of the Thames Valley police. The most influential episode was 'A Complaint of Rape', in which a woman with a history of mental illness reported being raped by three strangers and was subjected to extremely sceptical, even hostile, questioning by male detectives; her story was 'the biggest bollocks I have ever heard', she was told by one. The woman commented to the film crew, in the absence of the police, that she now understood why so many rapes went unreported, and she went on to sign a statement withdrawing her allegations. The response to the programme was immediate: the media were outraged and the chief constable, Peter Imbert, professed himself 'absolutely horrified', insisting: 'This is not the way in which a rape case is normally investigated in the Thames Valley police.' It was a reassurance that didn't quite sit with the announcement that special units would now be set up to handle all future complaints of rape, though the development was nonetheless widely welcomed.

A month earlier there had been similar criticisms of Judge Bertrand Richards who handed down a £2,000 fine, with no custodial sentence, to a man convicted of raping a 17-year-old woman, explaining that, since the victim had been hitch-hiking alone at night, she 'was guilty of a great deal of contributory negligence'. The outcry that greeted this sentence, and then the episode of *Police*, did much to change the justice system's attitude towards rape – one subject on which the moral right and the new left could unequivocally agree – though there were still controversies to come. In 1984 a London minicab driver named Christopher Meah, who had been convicted of the violent rape of two women, was awarded £45,750 in compensation for the brain damage that he had earlier suffered in a car crash, these injuries being, it was said, the cause of him committing his crimes. His victims, having been awarded between them just a tenth of that sum by the Criminal Injuries Compensation Board, brought a civil action to seek redress from Meah himself and in 1985 were awarded a total of £17,560. Again there was a justified sense of outrage at the disparity between the two awards – particularly since both were made by the same judge – and again the public response helped the judicial system take a step forward.

In 1986 a rape committed when three men broke into a vicarage in Ealing, with the intention of burglary, caused even greater concern. Several newspapers, led by the *Sun*, were censured by the Press Council for articles – published in the days before charges were brought – that did all but name the victim, Jill Saward, breaching the spirit though not the letter of the law requiring that complainants in rape cases remain anonymous. The law was subsequently amended to extend anonymity from the time of allegation rather than charge, and at the same time removed the anonymity previously accorded to defendants in rape trials. When the three men were convicted, many were horrified by the judge's comments that 'the trauma suffered by the girl was not so great,' and Saward herself, who went on to campaign on sexual violence issues, condemned the sentences accorded to the criminals; she was 'shocked at the way the judge seems to have treated rape and burglary as roughly comparable crimes'.

A key contribution to the change in attitudes towards rape and in other fields was made by the unexpected resurgence of crime fiction, commenting directly on the legal process and on society more generally. It had long been accepted that the golden age of detective fiction had been the 1920s and '30s, a period dominated by Agatha Christie, Dorothy L. Sayers, Ngaio Marsh and Margery Allingham, and that its time had been and gone. But as the 1980s wore on, it became clear that we were in the midst of a new, perhaps even more golden age. It started, in terms of television, with revivals of the established classics, most notably the ITV production of Agatha Christie's *Why Didn't They Ask Evans?* in 1980. Christie herself had had no fondness for television and for several years prior to her death in 1976 refused to sell the rights to her work, but the success of *Evans* led to a spate of successful transferrals to the small screen, including LWT's *The Seven Dials Mystery* (featuring Lady 'Bundle' Brent) and *Partners in Crime* (featuring Tommy and Tuppence Beresford), as well as the better-known series of *Miss Marple* and *Poirot*, starring Joan Hickson and David Suchet respectively. By the end of the decade, they had been joined by the most famous creations of her contemporaries: Sayers' Lord Peter Wimsey (played by Edward Petherbridge), Marsh's Inspector Alleyn (Simon Williams, followed by Patrick Malahide) and Allingham's Albert Campion (Peter Davison), as well as Jeremy Brett's definitive portrayal of Sherlock Holmes.

If it had remained with these familiar figures, the boom in detective shows might have amounted to little more than the mystery wing of the heritage television at which Britain excelled, manifest in such series as *Brideshead Revisited* and *The Jewel in the Crown*. But to these revivals was added a new generation of sleuths, many of them long-established in literature, even if they had taken some time to be noticed. When Julian Symons wrote his history of detective and crime fiction, *Bloody Murder*, in 1972, he concluded gloomily that the detective story was: 'A declining market. Some detective stories will continue to be written, but as the old masters and mistresses fade away, fewer and fewer of them will be pleasing to lovers of the Golden Age.' It is notable he made no mention of either P.D. James or Ruth Rendell, who had launched their most famous creations, Adam Dalgliesh and Inspector Wexford, in *Cover Her Face* (1962) and *From Doon with Death* (1964) respectively. Colin Watson's history of the genre, *Snobbery with Violence*, published in 1971, was similarly silent on the two acknowledged queens of the modern detective novel, not recognizing in them the harbingers of a crime renaissance. However, Symons went on to admit, that his expectations could yet be confounded: 'Another Depression on the scale of the '30s would also be likely to falsify most of the predictions above.'

Perhaps it was indeed the recession of the early 1980s that reawakened a taste for the classical detective story, or perhaps a growing realization that the style of series like *The Sweeney* and *The Professionals*, with their 'bully-worship' (as George Orwell once described Edgar Wallace's novels), didn't sit easily in the modern Britain of the Scarman report and the miners' strike. Whatever the cause, as the public reputation of the police fell, so did the stock of the fictional detective rise. British television in the 1980s was awash with sleuths, the new generation including television originals such as *Shoestring*, *Bergerac* and *Taggart*, in addition to adaptations of Dalgliesh and Wexford. The era also saw the writings of Robert Barnard, Reginald Hill, Sheila Radley, Ian Rankin, Derek Raymond, Peter Robinson and Margaret Yorke and many others, some of which were also to be televized. Most popular of all was *Inspector Morse*, created by Colin Dexter. From 1987 he was portrayed on television by John Thaw, who neatly symbolized the changing of the fictional guard, as he moved from the aggressive vigilantism of Inspector Jack Regan, patrolling London's mean streets in *The Sweeney*, to the Wagner-loving, crossword-solving Morse in middle-class Oxford. He was still unorthodox, of course, still a bit of a maverick, but he had lost his taste for neat Scotch in favour of real ale, while his new sidekick was Sergeant Lewis (Kevin Whately), a sensible family man who bore no resemblance to the rough and tough George Carter (Dennis Waterman) in the earlier series. The Ford Granada had become a Mark 2 Jaguar.

With a few exceptions – the anonymous narrator of Raymond's Factory novels, Rankin's John Rebus exploring the seedier side of Edinburgh with 'its crooks and bandits, its whore and gamblers, its perpetual losers and winners' – these characters primarily inhabited the small towns and middle-class world that had characterized the golden age. Even in *Taggart*, firmly located in Glasgow, the murderers whose stories were told in the first three series included a couple of small businessmen, a guest-house owner, a doctor, a philosophy student, a dentist and an ex-probation worker, as well as a group of bereaved parents meting out justice to the drug dealer responsible for their children's deaths. Despite the urban setting, this is a world away from *The Sweeney*; there are no car chases, just Sgt Livingston running after teenagers and getting bitten by the occasional dog, and there is little suggestion of a criminal class separate from society: these are just ordinary, respectable people caught up in their own lives. And, at the other extreme of television detection, there was Jim Bergerac, investigating much smaller problems on Jersey and learning 'to take the smooth with the smooth'.

Though the backdrop might have suggested a retreat from the city to the closed communities of Agatha Christie (encapsulated by Colin Watson as Mayhem Parva), there was an edge, to the literature at least, that was far removed from the cosiness of Miss Marple, an engagement with society, a desire to comment on contemporary mores. And although the likes of Morse and Dalgliesh spent much of their time behaving as though they were still autonomous detectives in the tradition of Holmes and Poirot, capable of solving any case through the exercise of their intellect, the central characters were still police officers, and couldn't fail to notice the changing role of the force in the modern world. In one of Rendell's novels, Inspector Burden initiates the putting of coloured lights in the tree outside the police station 'in the interest of promoting jollier relations with the public'. His boss, Wexford, disapproves of the gesture, but it's revealing that there was a perceived need for such a move: 'surely you couldn't go on feeling antagonistic towards or afraid of or suspicious about a friendly body that hung fairy-lights in a tree in its front garden?' Elsewhere Peter Robinson's character Inspector Banks was becoming increasingly dis-illusioned with the new role of the force: 'he had many objections to the way the government seemed to look upon the police as a private army of paid bully boys to pit against people with genuine grievances and a constitutional right to air them.' He consoles himself with the thought that he's a detective 'and he didn't have to go on crowd control, bashing the bonces of the proletariat.' But even detectives are affected by the rise of what Reginald Hill's Andy Dalziel refers to as 'porkism', as his own sergeant concludes: 'A man's got to be mad to stay in a job where the public hates you and Maggie Thatcher loves you.'

Most political of all was Derek Raymond's detective sergeant, who reflects on the police powers promised in a new piece of legislation (presumably inspired by the controversial Police and Criminal Evidence Act of 1984): 'It was what I thought of as banana laws – the law of a society in the process of breaking down. Once properly tightened up, it would have meant that I could stop and arrest a man in the street simply because I didn't like the look on his face, or the way his pockets bulged. It would have synchronized nicely with the plastic ID cards that every citizen would be required to carry by then, and before long we would have turned the country into a birdcage.'

Many of these novels also began to depict the increasing role of women in the police force: Adam Dalgliesh was joined by DI Kate Miskin, and Sheila

Radley's character DCI Doug Quantrill by DS Hilary Lloyd, while John Rebus was seen from the outset as junior to DI Gill Templer. What disappeared, perhaps surprisingly, was television's attempt early in the decade to create series about officers from ethnic minorities. In 1981 George Harris had become the first black star of a British detective series, appearing in the title role of *Wolcott*, of which the executive producer, Barry Hanson, remarked: 'There is a racial problem involving criminals and police and ignoring it won't make it go away.' And the same year had seen David Yip star as DS John Ho in *The Chinese Detective*, a man who joins the police force in an attempt to revenge himself on a bent copper, now retired, who framed his father. Running through the series was the overt racism of his immediate boss DCI Jim Berwick (Derek Martin), outraged at Ho's appointment: 'It's one of those attempts at lip-service to our multi-racial society.' But he's warned by a personnel officer at Scotland Yard that Ho is safe from his attacks: 'Sack a coloured policeman? That's Race Relations Act. Questions in the House.' Ho, on the other hand, rides out this resentment, contenting himself with the usual assortment of gimmicks that come with television detectives (he wears a parka, drives a Morris Minor and idolizes the Japanese writer Yukio Mishima) and with making sardonic observations on his world: 'I've plumbed all depths of depravity,' he says, 'but so far, not conservatism.'

Both those series were set in London, a location that also formed the backdrop to the one major series of the decade centred on uniformed police officers, as opposed to detectives: *The Bill*. Although it came to be seen as simply another soap, the series initially caused almost as much controversy as *The Sweeney* had in the previous decade: serving police officers were shown previews but were so hostile that they declined an invitation to the launch party, while Leslie Curtis, chairman of the Police Federation, criticized the series for depicting racial prejudice within the force. As the spokesman for the rank-and-file officers, Curtis became a familiar figure in the media; he also objected to proposals to make racial discrimination a disciplinary offence in the force, but attracted most publicity when he responded to a debate at the 1984 Labour Party conference about the miners' strike with an accusation that the party had 'indulged in an orgy of police bashing, vilification and downright dishonesty.' He went on to hint darkly of non-cooperation if Labour got elected: 'We wonder how it will be possible to serve the people of this country in some future crisis of this nature if the party in power adopts a policy of blaming the police.'

Disquiet over what was seen by many on the left as the increasing politicization of the police was not confined to such high-profile comments. There was a suspicion that James Anderton was not alone in wishing to patrol public morality, and that the force was at times helping to set the legislative agenda. In 1983 there were three times as many prosecutions brought for prostitution in England and Wales as there had been in 1979, and the following year the Sexual Offences Bill was first debated; it introduced the offence of kerb-crawling, the first time that the clients of prostitutes faced criminalization.

More contentiously, 1988 saw a greater number of convictions and cautions for indecency and soliciting by gay men than there had been since the mid-1950s, when male homosexuality was illegal, and it came in the same year that Section 28 of the Local Government Act enshrined in law the principle that local authorities 'shall not intentionally promote homosexuality', nor 'promote the teaching in any maintained school of the acceptability of homosexuality as a pretended family relationship'. It was the first anti-gay law to be passed in twentieth-century Britain and came as a result of growing pressure from Conservative backbenchers who regarded homosexuality as being unnatural and immoral, and who wanted decisive action: 'I think Clause 28 will help outlaw it and the rest will be done by AIDS, with a substantial number of homosexuals dying of AIDS,' said the Leicester MP Peter Bruinvels. 'I think that's the best way.'

The immediate cause around which public opinion was rallied was a report that a London primary school had in its library a copy of Susanne Bösche's picture book *Jenny Lives with Eric and Martin*, a work for children that told the story of a 5-year-old girl being brought up by her father and his male lover; the ensuing media storm prompted the education secretary, Kenneth Baker, to call for the book's withdrawal from schools and the arts minister, Richard Luce, to thunder against public libraries that stocked such material while banning Biggles novels and books by Enid Blyton. Arguing that, in the words of Roger Scruton, local authorities were seeking 'to disabuse children of their innocence, and to enlist them in the cause of sexual liberation,' the right made the controversial volume a centrepiece of its attempt to stop councils 'promoting homosexuality'. From the other side, the campaign against Section 28 became one of the great liberal causes of the time, with its passage marked by an invasion of the BBC's news studio just before transmission – muffled cries could be heard from a lesbian who, out of shot, was being sat upon by newsreader Nicholas Witchell – and by demonstrators abseiling down from the gallery of the House of Lords; Rachel Cox, one of those involved in the latter demonstration, explained: 'We did it because we are very angry lesbians'.

This was perhaps the high-tide mark in the resurgence of the moralist right, the moment when it seemed that the rise of liberalism might yet be decisively reversed. The British Social Attitudes survey conducted in 1988 revealed that public opinion was drifting strongly in favour of the right's agenda, so that where, in 1983, 50 per cent of people had disapproved of doctors giving contraceptive advice to the under-16s, that had now risen to 60 per cent, following a prolonged campaign by Victoria Gillick, a mother of ten who had unsuccessfully fought a case all the way up to the law lords to prevent doctors from providing such advice without parental consent. A similar shift in opinion was seen in terms of pornography, of sex outside marriage and, most noticeably, of homosexuality: the proportion saying that homosexual relationships were always or mostly wrong had risen in five years from 62 per cent to 74 per cent. But there was a marked discrepancy between the capital and the rest of the country; half of Londoners said there was nothing wrong with homosexuality and that gay men should be allowed to teach in schools – only 10 per cent in Scotland agreed with the former proposition, only 28 per cent in Wales with the latter. The pendulum was swinging back in favour of conservative, traditional morality.

This stumble in the growing liberalization of the nation had already been noted. In 1987 *EastEnders* had become the first British soap opera to depict two out gay men in a stable relationship – Colin Russell (played by the future Labour MEP, Michael Cashman) and Barry Clark (Gary Hailes) – and had even shown them kissing. The ensuing media outrage demonstrated how far homosexuality still had to go towards acceptability: 'The tabloids were screaming,' remembered Cashman; 'they outed my partner, we had bricks through the window, and there were questions in parliament about whether it was appropriate to have a gay man in a family show when AIDS was sweeping the country.' In the same year Kenneth Williams and Hugh Paddick were invited to appear on television to revive one of their outrageously camp sketches from the 1960s radio comedy series *Round the Horne*, and Williams was full of trepidation: 'the subject of homosexuality is now in great disfavour. When we were performing the Jule & Sand stuff in the '60s the atmosphere was utterly different, and of course, nobody knew about AIDS.' It was an opinion supported by the British Social Attitudes survey of 1988: two-thirds of the population said that government warnings about AIDS should tell people that some sexual practices were morally reprehensible, and just under a third said that the condition was 'a punishment to the world for its decline in moral standards'.

The sexually transmitted condition known as Acquired Immune Deficiency Syndrome, in which the immune system is progressively weakened, leaving the sufferer vulnerable to infections, had first been noted in Los Angeles in 1981, with a cluster of deaths – mostly amongst gay men – from PCP, an otherwise rare form of pneumonia. That, it soon transpired, was just one of many conditions that could result from being infected with HIV, the virus established as the cause of AIDS; the consequences were invariably fatal. The syndrome received early coverage in specialist publications ('we must endure the publicity which sensationalizes another "gay disease",' noted *Gay News* in November 1981), but first attracted mainstream attention in Britain in 1983 with a BBC *Horizon* programme 'Killer in the Village', primarily set in Greenwich Village, New York. By that stage there had been around 450 deaths in America from AIDS-related illnesses and Terrence Higgins, in whose name the leading British campaigning group was to be established, had already died in London. The *Horizon* documentary also drew attention to the possibility of Factor VIII blood products having been contaminated, with the consequent risk that haemophiliacs, who depended on Factor VIII, might become infected. Some seven months later, however, the government was still in denial about this possibility, health minister Kenneth Clarke announcing that, 'There is no conclusive evidence that Acquired Immune Deficiency Syndrome is transmitted by blood products.' By the end of the decade there were 1,200 haemophiliacs known to have been infected with HIV, with forty-nine having already died.

The first couple of years of the syndrome's progress in Britain were characterized by some hysterical reporting, with a particular emphasis on the fact that it was primarily gay men who were showing up as being infected. The expression 'gay plague' became accepted media shorthand, with the *Daily Telegraph* one of many to indulge in Biblical language: 'California and New York, the happy stamping grounds of homosexuals in America, are the original homes of these "wages of sin".' And indeed the imagery of Old Testament plagues was not entirely inappropriate, for the spread of the condition did at times resemble the arbitrary and remorseless taking of the first born: if this was a 'gay plague', there was little logic to the way that the attrition rate was greatest amongst haemophiliacs. As ever, the *Sun*'s coverage tended towards the extreme, most notoriously when it reported an anonymous psychologist as saying in 1985: 'All homosexuals should be exterminated to stop the spread of AIDS. It's time we stopped pussyfooting around.' As late as November 1989 the paper published a headline claiming that STRAIGHT SEX CANNOT GIVE YOU AIDS – OFFICIAL, although it was later forced to back down and admit: 'The *Sun* was wrong to state that it was impossible to catch AIDS from heterosexual sex. We apologize.' The same year, columnist George Gale in the *Daily Mail* was making his own position clear: 'active homosexuals are potentially murderers,' he wrote; 'the act of buggery kills.' The condition even crept into entirely unrelated stories, as when Martin Stevens, the Conservative MP for Fulham, died in 1986 shortly after a holiday in West Africa: TORIES' GAY MP 'DIDN'T DIE OF AIDS' read one headline.

In an attempt to combat the media-induced mix of complacency and ignorance, to concentrate minds on how serious and widespread the epidemic might become if it spread into the wider heterosexual population, medical bodies repeatedly warned of its potential severity, though they sometimes tended to add to the hysteria, most notably when the Royal College of Nursing suggested there might be up to a million cases of AIDS in Britain by 1991. That proved to be a huge overestimation; the figures for 1989 showed 2,296 cases of full-blown AIDS in the country, of which 95 per cent fell into the three highest risk groups of gay men, heroin users and haemophiliacs, though the numbers infected with HIV were unknown. There was at the time no treatment for the condition and no expectation of survival.

A disproportionate number of these sufferers was to be found in London, not merely because the capital had the largest gay community in the country, but because – as the British Social Attitudes showed – it was less judgemental than other parts of the country, and therefore provided the promise of refuge for the infected. Even in London there were stories of, for example, ambulance workers refusing to deal with AIDS patients, but these were as nothing to the paranoid treatment reported by the *Independent* to have been accorded to the corpse of an AIDS victim in a Yorkshire hospital: 'His parents are not allowed to see his body. He is put into two sealed bags, one inside the other. He is taken away to be buried in a special steel coffin. Over the place where he is buried, heavy flagstones are laid.' Such were the fears of the time.

And those fears were being stoked up by the moral crusaders, seizing on AIDS as a weapon to be deployed against society's growing tolerance since the 1960s towards homosexuality. Mary Whitehouse called for the Channel 4 gay series *Six of Hearts* to be banned 'in view of the rising incidence of AIDS', but it was James Anderton who made the issue his own with a speech in December 1986. 'As the years go by I see ever-increasing numbers of them swirling around in a human cesspit of their own making,' he said of homosexuals. 'Why do these people freely engage in sodomy and other obnoxious practices, knowing the dangers involved? These are the questions we should ask instead of publicizing the wearing of condoms.' The *Sun* greeted his contribution with enthusiasm, and though the official government position was the studied neutrality expressed by health minister Tony Newton — 'It is for people to make their own moral judgements' — Margaret Thatcher was more ambivalent: 'Some people have made their position very clear. Thank goodness they have.' And once Anderton had given establishment legitimacy to an anti-gay argument, others soon joined in. Typical of many was Lady Saltoun of Abernethy, an obscure member of the royal family by marriage and a hereditary member of the House of Lords: 'I think it is fairly safe to assume that homosexuality, and very often promiscuity, are against the natural order of things,' she opined. 'I do not think it is possible to get away from the wrath of God altogether.' Thatcher's favourite religious leader, the Chief Rabbi Immanuel Jakobovits, was also clear on his message: 'Say plainly: AIDS is the consequence of marital infidelity, premarital adventures, sexual deviation and social irresponsibility — putting pleasure before duty and discipline.' More perceptive perhaps was the conclusion of Edwina Currie two decades later: 'Anderton was a prize ass, but his antics were no joke. He was a cruel and wicked man.'

Anderton's intervention came at a time when the government, somewhat belatedly, was embarking upon a massive information campaign. Television adverts featuring the portentous voice of actor John Hurt were broadcast with the slogan 'Don't Die of Ignorance', in preparation for the delivery of leaflets to the 23 million households in the country. Immediately after that, Aids Week in February 1987 saw a coordinated season of programmes on both BBC and ITV, including *First Aids* which featured pop stars, *Spitting Image* puppets and comedians such as Rik Mayall, Stephen Fry and Hugh Laurie. For months it became difficult to turn on a television set without seeing a demonstration of how to put a condom onto a banana, while Durex became the first such product to advertise at a football ground, with signs appearing at Cardiff City's stadium. 1987 also saw The Party, the first all-star AIDS benefit in Britain, staged at Wembley Arena with appearances by, amongst others, George Michael and Elton John, the latter finding new layers of poignancy in the Shirelles song 'Will You Still Love Me Tomorrow'. There was, however, a slight downside to all this publicity, as the manufacturers of a board game titled Orgy found: the IBA banned it from advertising on television because 'people would associate the word orgy with sex and it would counteract the campaign on AIDS'. And there was also over-reaction in some quarters: a Welsh

Community Health Council complained when a doctor in the soap *Casualty* revealed that she had two lovers before her current partner – this, it was claimed, sent out dangerous messages about the acceptability of promiscuity.

With the publicity offensive came a shift in media emphasis. Talk of a 'gay plague' gradually receded, though it was for a while replaced by the equally inappropriate imagery of the disaster movie, as though AIDS were a real-life remake of Terry Nation's 1970s television series *Survivors*, in which a disease is accidentally released that kills most of humanity. (Nation himself saw plans for an American re-make of *Survivors* abandoned because of television sensitivities over AIDS.) Panics were reported about the dangers of becoming infected by everything from a mosquito-bite to communion wine to the communal baths in football changing-rooms. But the fact that a Conservative government was prepared to see the problem as being medical rather than moral – issuing guidelines that recommended the use of condoms, refusing to condemn sexual practices in the way demanded by Anderton – was in itself a remarkable development. It required a rapid education for some: 'Oral sex?' the social services secretary, Norman Fowler, was reported to have commented. 'I had no idea you could get it from talking dirty.' And it was far from the instincts of many in the party, including, according to Currie, the prime minister: 'I remember her telling the Smoking Room loudly in June [1986] that she disapproved of advertising condoms on TV.'

Thatcher's objections were overcome, but many retained reservations about the tastefulness of the subsequent campaigns: the novelist A.N. Wilson described the advert for Mates condoms as plumbing 'a new depth for vulgarity'. And the correct tone to adopt for government literature was the subject of much debate, with Lord Hailsham, the Lord Chancellor, pedantically furious at the language used in the leaflet: '"Sex" means you are either male or female,' he complained. 'It does not mean the same as sexual practices. Nor does "having sex" mean anything at all.' Meanwhile Frank Dobson, Labour health spokesperson, came to a more common-sense conclusion that 'You won't stop people shagging', and that therefore the only option was to promote safe sex, rather than worry about morality. His main concern was that the word 'condom', seldom used up to that point, was too clinical and that 'rubber johnny' would be better. He also proposed a slogan for the campaign – 'If you must have it off, put it on' – that the government chose not to employ.

Other adverts in the campaign, however, were just as direct as his suggestion, including one that showed a blood-covered needle with the message: 'It only takes one prick to give you AIDS'. That, of course, was aimed at intravenous drug users, pointing out the dangers of sharing syringes with others. This was a particular problem in Edinburgh, where a police crackdown on drugs had seen the confiscation of all equipment from users; combined with a change in policy by the Pharmacist Society to stop the sale of needles, it was a move that proved disastrous. Needle exchange schemes were eventually set up, but by then hundreds had been infected.

Some of the advice seemed to be given more in hope than expectation, such as the recommendation that a condom be worn during fellatio and that a thin sheet of rubber be employed during cunnilingus. As the hero of Mark Lawson's novella 'The Nice Man Cometh' reflected: 'Once you went as far as the use of dental dams, hadn't sex become like a holiday for which so many inoculations were required that it was hardly worth going?' Nonetheless, the essential message – use a condom, don't share needles – was communicated with an efficiency that undoubtedly helped reduce the figures for future infection. Surveys showed an immediate change in behaviour, and gradually the worst excesses of reporting were curbed. Writing in 1989, Currie expressed her pride in what had been achieved: 'The problems were not hushed up or ignored or denied. They were, and are, tackled with vigour and vision in this country. The leap in the dark was taken with a sure-footedness which augurs well for the future.' Twenty years on, she held to the same view: 'We nipped it in the bud.'

For those affected, however, it was a terrible time, when a simple blood test could turn into what was effectively a death sentence. The filmmaker Derek Jarman learnt that he was HIV-positive in 1986 and commented: 'No metropolitan gay man can be sure he will be alive in six years' time.' He died in 1994.

10
Boom
'Let's make lots of money'

> oz: You know the reason I left this country in the first
> place, don't you? I'll tell you in a word – Margaret bloody
> Thatcher, that's why. I'd had it, I was up to there with
> what she created. Bloody wasteland. Desolate. Nae joy,
> nae hope, nae nowt.
> Dick Clement & Ian La Frenais, *Auf Wiedersehen, Pet* (1986)

> It is no longer true that only very very stupid, vulgar
> people who went to public school can make money.
> Now, very very stupid, vulgar people who left state
> school at sixteen can do too.
> Mark Lawson, 'The Nice Man Cometh' (1991)

> Oi you, shut your mouth and look at my wad!
> Harry Enfield as Loadsamoney (1987)

Margaret Thatcher's first term in office had been characterized by an increasingly divided society and by a major economic recession. Her second term saw little change in terms of bringing unity to the country, but it could at least claim that the economy was recovering and that individuals were benefiting. Inflation remained below 5 per cent during the period, and average wages rose by 14 per cent in real terms. The basic rate of tax had been cut from the 33 per cent inherited by the Conservatives in 1979 to 27 per cent, and in the 1987 budget, not even the duty on cigarettes and alcohol was raised. As the obsession with monetarism gradually faded from the agenda, there were substantial increases in public spending, and the value of the *Financial Times* index of shares rose rapidly through the period.

On the other hand, unemployment remained – even on official figures – over three million throughout, but this was now being regarded, at least in Westminster, as a fact of modern life. Once there had been a commonly-held belief that high levels of unemployment were politically unacceptable, so that the Conservatives could attack the Callaghan government with the 'Labour Isn't Working' poster campaign; that era now felt like a long time ago. The consensus that had dominated politics since the Second World War was based not merely on specific policies but also on a shared set of assumptions about how one could judge the success of those policies. It was this that the Thatcherite revolution had swept away, so that, for example, the rate of unemployment was less significant than the rate of inflation. Labour did not yet agree on such values, but it would do so in time and in the interim, the Conservatives simply insisted on their own criteria to the exclusion of all others: many of the areas where Labour criticized the government (increasing inequality in society, the running down of public services, a reduction in social housing) were seen as positive virtues in Thatcherite terms and were proudly proclaimed. This was a government that not only turned its back on egalitarianism, but refused even to pay lip service to the concept of equality.

'I am sure that Margaret Thatcher does not believe it is possible to provide free public services of a quality that will satisfy everyone – so that even the rich prefer to use them,' argued Nicholas Ridley. 'If council housing were made so good that nobody wanted to own their own home, how much would that cost? Nor would it be desirable, because it would remove choice from people in deciding in which house and where they want to live.' The same was true of education and of health, with Thatcher refusing to cede any ground when challenged on her own use of private medical cover rather than the National Health Service: 'I exercise my right as a free citizen to spend my own money in my own way, so that I can go on the day, at the time, to the doctor I choose and get out fast.' Taking care of oneself and one's family was seen as the ideal to which all should aspire, leaving the welfare state to survive simply as a basic safety-net, providing essential services to those unable to afford to look after themselves. There were some limits to this philosophy – although the wealthy could also presumably pay a security firm for protection, the role of the police was never called into question – but the essential argument remained. In the words of Mark Lawson's character Garry McKenzie: 'It's like teeth, isn't it? If you can pay for gold fillings, then you get them. If you can't, then, no question, a man-made substance should be available to the work-shy, who are in genuinely life-threatening pain.'

The extent to which this perspective was accepted by the general public was hard to gauge. Certainly in terms of housing, it was broadly recognized that council housing was not the preferred option for the majority – the success of the right to buy scheme was evidence of that – and by the end of the decade two-thirds of households were owner-occupied, with over half of manual workers owning their homes (the phrase 'property ladder' entered the language in the 1980s). But the requirement for publicly provided health care and education remained high on most people's agendas. During the course of the decade, the number of Britons with private health insurance doubled, but this still meant that only 5.4 million were covered, just below a tenth of the population and around the same proportion as there were children in private education. For everyone else, the state system was not simply a safety-net, but a fundamental part of life. In 1983, at the height of the debate over nuclear weapons and with the Falklands War fresh in the memory, Thatcher had elided over this stubborn refusal by the public to accept her position by arguing the case for a strong defence policy: 'If we were to sacrifice defence to the needs of the welfare state, the day might come when we should have neither peace nor freedom.' But in her second term, a new angle was needed, and Thatcher found it in the appropriation of yet another leftist slogan from the past, adopted from either John Lennon or Robert Lindsay's portrayal of Wolfie, leader of the Tooting Popular Front in the television sitcom *Citizen Smith*, depending on one's generation: 'We Conservatives,' she told the 1986 conference, 'are returning power to the people.'

The successes she was trumpeting in that speech were council house sales and the privatization of many industries that had formerly been under state control. This latter programme had begun tentatively in the first years, with the sale of shares in BP and British Aerospace – leaving the government with minority holdings – and some peripheral parts of British Steel and British Rail. But it was after the second election victory in 1983 that it really began to take off: British Telecom, Jaguar Cars, British Gas, the National Bus Company, the British Airports Authority and British Airways were all floated on the stock market during the second term, to be followed by Rover Group (as the former British Leyland was now known), British Steel and the electricity industry. Some of this was actively welcomed by the public, either because, as with British Leyland, the company had become seen as a bottomless pit into which tax revenue was poured and second-rate products emerged, or because a lack of any competition at all was seen to allow a poor service; in 1976 Shirley Williams had commissioned a survey into customer satisfaction with the nationalized GPO and found that 40 per cent of people condemned the standards of postal services and telecommunications. Tom Jackson, leader of the post office workers, had warned in the early days of Thatcher, as the Post Office was split into separate post and telecom sections, that if the telecom monopoly was ended, there would be a flood of imports of 'Mickey Mouse phones', but few really believed they would be any worse than the current state-approved equipment.

While there was public approval in specific instances, however, the concept of privatization was regarded with some suspicion when it was turned into a general article of faith. 'How much more of our infra-structure is to be turned over to state-licensed spivs?' lamented the journalist Philip Norman, as rumours spread about the possible privatization of the London Underground. The former Conservative prime minister, Harold Macmillan, now ennobled as the Earl of Stockton, was amongst those outraged by the process, drawing an analogy with a family in financial difficulties that finds itself obliged to sell its assets: 'First of all the Georgian silver goes. And then all that nice furniture that used to be in the salon. Then the Canalettos go.' His son, Maurice Macmillan, made the same point in less exalted terms: 'selling the furniture to pay for the food'. Thatcher responded by taking the image literally, snorting that, unlike the Macmillans, her family had never had any silver to sell, while Ridley was later to stretch the metaphor to breaking point: 'the "family silver" was costing a great deal in anti-burglar precautions, insurance, cleaning and maintenance. The sale proceeds were not what counted – it was avoiding the running costs.'

To many of those without Canalettos, or even a salon in which to put their nice furniture, the share issues were frequently seen as a fine opportunity to make a little money. The offer price tended to be below the market value, so it was possible to apply as a small shareholder and then sell swiftly at a profit; more than a fifth of adults in the country bought into at least one of the privatizations. For those who lacked the disposable cash to do this, however, there seemed very little gain in the entire process, save for the promise of better services and the certainty of higher prices. A more democratic option had been proposed by the economist Samuel Brittan, whereby the shares would be divided equally between all British adults and simply given to them to do as they wished, but David Owen was one of the few senior politicians to embrace the proposal and he failed to convince his own party of its appeal.

The effects of the privatization programme, and of the measures taken to ensure that the companies were attractive to private enterprise, were widespread. For employees, there was a loss of jobs and of job security. 'He has this future in British Steel; Nigel's whole future is as good as sealed,' sang XTC on their 1979 hit single 'Making Plans for Nigel'. But by the time of the sell-off in 1988, some 70 per cent of jobs in British Steel had been lost, and Nigel, if he were still there, would have been distinctly nervous about his prospects. The process of 'rationalization', of reducing the workforce in anticipation of selling the company off, was satirized in an Alexei Sayle sketch that showed a publishing firm, Prucock & Limpet, cutting down on over-manning in the novels of Charles Dickens: 'We simply don't need 127 characters in *Martin Chuzzlewit* anymore, doing the job that Jeffrey Archer can do with a couple of MPs and a prostitute.'

Then there was a massive increase in the numbers of people owning shares, trebling in the first ten years of Thatcher's time in office, so that by the end of the decade there were more shareholders than trade unionists in the country. In 1987 Rupert Murdoch discovered that around 20 per cent of *Sun* readers had bought shares for the first time in the previous months, and told the editor, Kelvin MacKenzie, to introduce a *Sun* Money page. The *Daily Mirror* also had a financial section every week, and even the *Daily Star* made a token effort in the same direction. Talk of bear and bull markets, of options and futures, was briefly heard in the tabloid world. Other changes feeding into what was sold as a new era of popular capitalism included the Building Societies Act of 1986, which allowed societies such as the Abbey National to convert themselves into banks, and a 1988 change in regulations that permitted employees to opt out of the state earnings-related pension scheme (SERPS), prompting a huge growth in the number of those seeking help from financial advisers.

Privatization also injected a flood of new money into advertising, since many of the share issues came with massive publicity campaigns ('If you see Sid, tell him' was the slogan for the most famous of these, a British Gas campaign that came with a budget of £22 million). The result was the further bloating of an already excessive industry, for advertising in Britain was enjoying its most spectacular era, feeling confident enough to call in big-name film directors to make television commercials: Ridley Scott for Barclays Bank, Hugh Hudson for the Fiat Strada and, most bizarrely, Ken Russell for Shredded Wheat. Much of this looks in retrospect to have been simply big-budget posturing, for none were as naggingly memorable as the contemporary low-tech campaigns for the likes of Shake 'n' Vac (applied to one's carpets, it 'put the freshness back') or Kellogg's Bran Flakes (which were 'tasty, tasty, very very tasty'). Nor were they as well received, let alone remembered, as the Hovis advert, complete with brass band playing Dvorak's *New World Symphony*, which had been made by Ridley Scott in 1974 before he went to Hollywood. (It was parodied in 1981 by comedian Tony Capstick on his hit single 'Capstick Comes Home', seeking to put the record straight on the nostalgic mythology being purveyed: 'We had lots of things in them days they haven't got today – rickets, diphtheria, Hitler . . .') But the advertising boom, the instant shininess of a typical commercial break on prime-time ITV, together with the genuine affluence being enjoyed by a substantial proportion of the population, did help change the country's image of itself.

There was a new feeling that almost anything and everything was for sale, from state-owned industries downwards. Conspicuous consumption was embraced by the media and a whole range of designer brand names became household names, at least in those households where mere consumption failed to bring satisfaction in itself; for in some circles it was no longer sufficient to buy expensive things, now one was obliged to flaunt the labels upon them, as if one feared that others wouldn't recognize good taste when they saw it and required some form of subtitling. From Lacoste and Fila to Giorgio Armani and Dolce and Gabbana, clothing firms began to proclaim their names on the outside. The most exclusive brands responded by making their name more easily available to those prepared to pay to be used as an advertising hoarding: 'A pair of faux pearl earrings, a quilted handbag, a bottle of Coco; for a fraction of the price of the Chanel suit, a "wannabe" could access the Chanel aura,' noted Bevis Hillier in his survey of the era. (The word 'wannabe' was characteristic of the times, first spotted as a description of those young female fans of the American pop singer Madonna, who copied her look and sought to emulate her behaviour.)

It wasn't merely luxuries that began to be marketed in earnest. Things that had previously been thought of as free – or at least free at the point of delivery – were now being packaged for sale: water came not from taps but in bottles, exercise was no longer confined to a jog around the park but involved membership fees at a club or gym, and soon television services were to become available for a monthly subscription. Those who had spent years building a record collection were persuaded to buy it all over again, this time on compact disc, and time itself was available at a price: British Telecom's speaking clock service now announced that 'The time sponsored by Accurist will be . . .', while reproduction furniture was marketed as being pre-distressed, to provide instant patina for those wishing to buy the illusion of history. And in one of the most controversial stories of the era, a woman named Kim Cotton reluctantly became a household name when it was revealed that she had acted as a surrogate mother for another couple, and had been paid £6,500 for her work in carrying their child; the widespread coverage she received ensured that such payments were made illegal.

Nor were the few traces left of the Corinthian sporting ideal immune to the new world of the market-place. Athletics had effectively abandoned its tradition of amateurism in 1981, with Sebastian Coe going on to become the first 'amateur' track and field athlete to advertise a product on television (he was selling Horlicks); by 1987 Steve Cram, his successor as Britain's best middle-distance runner, was reported to be charging £15,000 a time to appear on a British track. That same year an unedifying dispute soiled the image of the Oxford and Cambridge Boat Race: five American rowers mutinied against the coach and club president of Oxford, thus drawing slightly shocked public attention to the practice of bringing in established foreign athletes on short post-graduate courses to strengthen the teams. And yet there was a glimmer of hope to be found here, for a reserve Oxford team, without the ringers, went on to win the event.

Similarly the world of publishing began to experience a revolution that would be completed the following decade with the abandonment of the Net Book Agreement, the practice that prevented books from being sold below their cover price. This time-honoured agreement was still precariously clinging on to existence in the 1980s, but elsewhere there were signs that the industry was about to be transformed out of all recognition. Indeed it might almost be claimed that it was finally becoming an industry, leaving behind the image of committed amateurism that it had purveyed for so long. A wave of mergers and takeovers saw a succession of smaller publishing houses swallowed up by conglomerates with the reputation of being run by faceless financiers rather than by the kindly, author-friendly old gentlefolk of the fabled past. In 1986 the company Bloomsbury Publishing was founded, claiming that it would cherish the publisher-author relationship as the heart of its business practice, and yet it too represented a major break with the past; boasting what *The Times* described as 'an acceptable management mix of smooth marketing men and sympathetic editorial types', it was launched with a barrage of publicity, backed by a £2 million investment from the City – publishing was now seen as an area of interest to venture capitalists.

As the industry changed, so marketing and promotion, once regarded as being a trifle vulgar, became desirable attributes when publishing a book. Scale was now all-important, so that when Clive Barker was launched as a first-time author with the simultaneous publication of three volumes of short stories, *The Books of Blood*, it was the biggest event in horror fiction since the emergence of Stephen King the previous decade, and made Barker an instant star. Even in the world of literary fiction, things were not as they had been. The Booker Prize for the best novel by a writer from the

Commonwealth or from Ireland, which had been pottering quietly along since 1969, suddenly became a news story in 1980 when two of the biggest names in British literature were seen as slugging it out for the award: Anthony Burgess with *Earthly Powers* and William Golding with *Rites of Passage*. The coverage was aided by the fact that the two men each had a book in his back-catalogue that was instantly recognizable to the public through cinematic adaptation (*A Clockwork Orange* and *Lord of the Flies*) and both benefited from the resultant publicity, but the real winner was the Booker itself. The following year Salman Rushdie became a major figure in literature when his second novel, *Midnight's Children*, won the award, and from that point on the phrase 'Booker-shortlisted' was not merely a boast on a paperback jacket, but a guarantee of sales. The annual rigmarole of the long list and the short list and the squabbles between the five-strong judging panel became a regular fixture for the press and the reading public, provoking in equal measure bafflement, as when Keri Hulme's impenetrable *The Bone People* won, and outrage, as when Robertson Davies' *What's Bred in the Bone* lost out to Kingsley Amis' *The Old Devils*. Like the Oscars, the Booker had become primarily a marketing exercise. And the selling of books was also changing. In 1982 Tim Waterstone, a former manager at W.H. Smith's, opened the first Waterstone's bookstore, initiating the move away from the small independent shop towards the American model of supersized retailing. It would take some time for this to become the norm, but the template had been created.

It would be an oversimplification to see the mid-1980s as witnessing the loss of traditional British business virtues of decency and courtesy, where a gentleman's word was his bond, in the face of a voracious American ethos, with the pursuit of profits at all costs, but there was undoubtedly a sense that an honourable code of values was being left behind. And yet even in those places where American culture was at its most obvious, such as the public's embrace of television series such as *Dallas*, *Dynasty* and *Fame*, money did not always win the day. The enthusiasm for these shows reached fever pitch in 1980 with 24 million watching on BBC1 the season's cliff-hanger episode of *Dallas* in which J.R. Ewing (Larry Hagman) was shot; the next episode, which revealed who had done the shooting, was screened some months later, following a summer of fevered speculation in the media, and added another 3.5 million to that total. So big had *Dallas* become that in 1985 Thames TV put in a secret bid to buy the forthcoming series, offering nearly half as much again as the BBC were then paying. The resultant outcry came not merely from the BBC, but from the other ITV companies, worried that once the informal agreement not to poach shows from another channel was broken, a price war for successful series would result. The IBA threw its weight against Thames, sparking rumours that the company might be stripped of its franchise, and insisted the series be returned to the BBC. The era of the gentlemen's agreement, it appeared, was not quite over, even if the decision was primarily motivated by self-interest: in the face of the coming threat from multi-channel satellite broadcasting, the established duopoly had chosen to resist the lure of quick money and to close ranks, defending their established practices.

Alasdair Milne, director general of the BBC, called it 'one of the most bizarre episodes in the history of television', but it was also one of the more unusual episodes of the mid-1980s generally, for it was seldom that such an outcome was reached. 'We're living in a land where sex and horror are the new gods,' proclaimed Frankie Goes to Hollywood on their 1984 hit 'Two Tribes', but they were, as ever, getting a little over-excited; in fact, the moral campaigners had done their best to sweep sex and horror out of sight, and now money ruled virtually unchallenged, as the massive marketing and merchandising campaign for Frankie themselves demonstrated. The new gods were actually the recently discovered tribe known as yuppies, a term born in America to describe the supporters of Gary Hart's presidential campaign in 1984, and standing for young urban (or upwardly-mobile) professionals.

The concept of the yuppie was initially intended to be positive, to reflect the aspirations of those who had grown up in the shadow of Vietnam and Watergate and now wanted what Hart called 'a new generation of leadership with new ideas'. By the time it caught on in Britain, however, it had transferred meaning and was instead used in the context of the newly-rich traders in the City of London, following the deregulation of the financial markets in the so-called Big Bang of October 1986, which saw traditional trading floors replaced by computer screens and fusty old business practices driven out by international investment banks. Yuppies too were to be found in the worlds of advertising, public relations and the media, identifiable, it was said, by their fondness for the cumbersome early mobile phones and for massive Filofaxes — a small looseleaf binder intended for the storage of personal information that had been around since the 1920s but suddenly and inexplicably became essential. Frequenting wine bars and bistros, and talking loudly of money in multiples of thousands (now known as Ks), yuppies were noted more for their ostentatious flaunting of newly-made wealth than for their idealism, taste or culture. 'In the beginning Victoria had been amazed at the depths of his ignorance,' notes a character in Justin Cartwright's novel, *Look at It this Way*, of a successful art director working in advertising: 'history, literature and science were to him simply sources for visual ideas. They had no standing of their own. He had once asked Victoria who Einstein was "in real life". He had seen images of him with his electric-shock hair, but had no idea what his day job had been.'

In the second half of the decade, the term came to be self-applied by yuppie wannabes, including most famously Del Trotter in *Only Fools and Horses*, cheerfully adopting the trappings believed to be essential for the role: 'Del thinks all you need is a Filofax and red braces,' mocks his brother, Rodney. Another such was Lynn Packard in Robert Barnard's novel *A City of Strangers*: 'Lynn had many of the characteristics of a yuppie: he dressed like one, he spoke like one (his voice high, somewhere between the hectoring and the hysterical, the vowels twisted by some invisible vocal screw), he played squash and computer games, and got boisterous or objectionable in night-clubs and casinos. But when it came down to it he was not quite young enough, or, crucially, quite upwardly mobile enough to be a yuppie. He was manager of the Foodwise supermarket in town.' It was hard for the term 'yuppie' to survive such bathos, and it largely faded from the vocabulary of all but the laziest of journalists and the activists of the left, for whom it became a cherished insult.

Nevertheless it was possible to discern a definite cultural shift; in the 1960s the Conservative MP Gerald Nabarro had bemoaned the way that in post-war Britain 'it has been considered in many circles to be slightly "off" to be eager, slightly improper to be thrusting, not done to be ambitious'. Now, such qualities were increasingly looked upon as being acceptable, desirable and celebrated in the highest circles in the land. Of those who graduated from Oxford in 1971, just 59 per cent had found employment in the private sector; a quarter-century later, the proportion had risen to 81 per cent, with the call of public service proving considerably less attractive than that of the City.

The idea that a new tribe, perhaps even a sub-class, was emerging took root and the thrusting young Thatcherite became a staple of 1980s fiction. The purest example was probably Alan B'Stard in the television sitcom *The New Statesman*, a Conservative MP, blue in tooth and claw ('nouveau riche little parvenu,' snaps his father-in-law), whose entry in *Who's Who* lists his recreations as: 'Making money, drinking, driving, dining out on other people's expenses, boogying, bonking, droit de signeur, grinding the faces of the poor.' Under criticism from his own leader after being caught out in yet another political outrage, he whines, 'I was just trying to be true to the spirit of Thatcherism,' and she snaps back: 'All you care about is number one.' At which he's genuinely baffled: 'I thought that's what Thatcherism's all about.' Inevitably a platoon of real Conservative MPs was soon drummed up by the newspapers to condemn the series, with Geoffrey Dickens explaining that, although he hadn't actually seen the series, it was 'destructive to the fabric of society'.

Synthetic fury also greeted the television drama, *Paradise Postponed*, written by John Mortimer, of whom MP John Butcher thundered: 'This oily member of the TV establishment has made money for fifteen years by eroding the self-confidence of the British. Now this up-market punk is making another pile complaining about the loss of self-belief. Inevitably, he pokes elegant fun at loss of socialist conviction but the true venom is reserved for the portrayal of the Tory as an out-and-out twit.' The twit in question, Leslie Titmuss, was a grammar-school boy whose inexorable rise made him a rich man in the property boom of the early 1970s, then a Conservative MP and ultimately a cabinet minister under Thatcher. The son of a clerk in a brewery, he appeals to a constituency selection meeting on purely Thatcherite terms: 'You know what my parents are? They're the true Conservatives! And I can tell you this: they're tired of being represented by people from the City or folks from up at the Manor. They want one of themselves! You can forget the county families and the city gents and the riverside commuters. They'll vote for you anyway. What you need to win is my people. The people who know the value of money because they've never had it.' His success is built on his absolute self-confidence, as another character recognizes, wondering 'what it must be like to have been born without a sense of doubt. Would that be a blessing or a curse or a mere physical deprivation, like being born without a sense of smell?' Titmuss was believed to have been inspired by Peter Walker, with just a pinch of Norman Tebbit.

A similar, if less public, career path is followed by Jonty Fixx, the hero of Terence Blacker's novel *Fixx*. He graduates from working with the Kray twins to make his money in property (alongside 'that deeply mis-understood man, Peter Rachman') and as an asset-stripper in the early 1970s, but he finds his real home in 'a sort of unconventional, free-ranging task-force' during the Thatcherite years. Entirely amoral, motivated simply by a desire to defend capitalism, he's the man to call on when dirty tricks are needed: 'This strike, says Downing Street, sort it out, will you. Encourage the moderates, organize the opposition within the workforce, arrange a few stunts to convince the world the strikers are vicious commie hooligans, killers even.' And he revels in the anonymous power he wields: 'I see our little band of low-profile public servant entrepreneurs as vigilantes, stalking the land under cover of night, working boldly on behalf of the greatest cause known to man, that of freedom and enterprise.'

The idea that such characters derived personal pleasure from their heartless pursuit of profit seemed to haunt the imagination of their chroniclers. 'Charles had always enjoyed dismissing people,' wrote Margaret Drabble of Charles Headleand in her novel *The Radiant Way*. 'He had cleared the stables not of filth and corruption but of nice woolly ageing men in their fifties, polite, gentlemanly, incompetent men. He had done it in the name of progress once, in the name of productivity now, but his own impulse had remained the same: the prospect of confrontation or a dismissal, be it of a fellow-director or of a hundred or two employees had stiffened his sinews and made his spirits rise.' Just to be clear that we should know where to stand, Headleand continues to fight the good fight at home, where he enjoys a sado-masochistic relationship with his wife, Liz. Likewise Robert Barnard's risible character Lynn Packard, the yuppie manager of Foodwise, also had a new spring in his step as the sun shone brightly in the high noon of Thatcherism: 'Previously he had been aggressively out for himself. Now that had widened, had become an article of faith: self-interest was the guiding principle of life, the market was supreme, and people who disregarded that fact were heretics, or just plain ignorant. He had become a born-again free marketer.' Sadly, in this instance, his wife is less taken with this development than he might have hoped: 'The thrusting young man she had found exciting; the strident evangelist, she had to admit, was something of a bore.'

In truth, of course, the character type was far from new. Edward Fox-Ingleby, the Conservative MP who narrates A.G. Macdonell's 1938 satirical novel *Autobiography of a Cad*, is almost indistinguishable from Alan B'Stard: 'I am, and have always been, a friend of the people, and a democrat of democrats, but that has never prevented me from detesting and execrating the people at the same time with all my heart.' Like his counterparts in the 1980s he too was in thrall to financiers, as he showed when he became responsible for planning the future shape of the City of London: 'The redundant churches in the City were to be pulled down, with all the reverence due to Wren's reputation and, of course, to the sacredness of the sites; the sites were to be reverently deconsecrated and sold to the banks and insurance companies, the financial stability of which is the cause of the eminence of London as the money centre of the world.' All that had changed was that what had once been the exception now seemed more like the rule.

As if to ensure that parallels were drawn with the bad old days, the television comedy series *Brass* revived all the old clichés of callous 1930s industrialists in a spirit of gleeful caricature, with Timothy West's portrayal of arms manufacturer Bradley Hardacre a particular joy. 'If it's a crime to have initiative and enterprise, and take pleasure in the exhilarating cut and thrust of the marketplace, where this country sinks or swims – very well, I plead guilty,' he declares piously, before looking at his watch and adding: 'I can't stand here talking all day; I've got men to lay off.' Little excites him more than 'the thrill of stripping underused assets away from the body of some moribund company to reveal the vital, throbbing, profitable form within.'

A similar, if more high-minded, attempt to satirize the present by use of the past came in Caryl Churchill's play *Serious Money* (1987), which emerged from the Royal Court Theatre to enjoy success in the commercial world of the West End. Written in rhyming couplets, with deliberate reference to the seventeenth-century genre of the city comedy, it even incorporated some of Thomas Shadwell's 1692 drama *The Volunteers* as a prologue, as though suggesting that, despite Thatcher's claim to Victorian values, the modern world was reverting to an even earlier stage of naked money-worship. Certainly the greed depicted here had little in common with any nineteenth-century version of conservatism that, say, the 7th Earl of Shaftesbury might have recognized.

But the most successful marriage of present standards to past situations came in the unlikely form of the historical sitcom *Blackadder*. The first series, *The Black Adder*, created and written by Rowan Atkinson and Richard Curtis, was set in an alternative history, in which Henry Tudor lost the battle of Bosworth in 1485, with Atkinson in the title role as an ineffectual and vain member of the Yorkist royal family. As the first major piece by one of the stars of *Not the Nine O'Clock News*, it had great hopes vested in it, but although it attracted an audience (a larger one, indeed, than any other comedy show during its run, with the exception of the venerable *Candid Camera*), there was a sense of disappointment when it was discovered that it wasn't really very funny. But the BBC kept faith and commissioned a new series. Atkinson moved to focus exclusively on acting, allowing the recruitment of Ben Elton to become Curtis' co-writer, a dream-team combination of the Oxbridge and alternative currents in comedy, and the subsequent series – *Blackadder II*, set in Elizabethan times, *Blackadder the Third*, in Regency Britain, and *Blackadder Goes Forth*, in the trenches of the First World War – established it as one of the great television sitcoms.

Where the first Blackadder had been notable for his stupidity, his descendants (all played by Atkinson) were cut from a very different cloth. Edmund Blackadder, in the Curtis/Elton incarnation, was a Thatcherite parody stranded out of his time: a 'lower-middle-class yobbo', as Pitt the Younger calls him. Clever, casually callous and desperate for social and financial advancement, he would have enjoyed the company of Leslie Titmuss and Alan B'Stard, but has the misfortune to be born (and re-born) in a world where he's surrounded instead by entrenched interests, facing alone an establishment that always beats him back into place. His constant attempts to improve his situation are repeatedly thwarted by the whims and stupidity of those with authority over him, so that his only recourse is to outdo them with the wit of his repartee, score snide points where possible and vent his rage on his even more stupid servant, Baldrick ('the Creature from the Black Latrine'), played by Tony Robinson, a future member of Labour's national executive committee. His powerlessness in the face of his superiors became the central theme in particular of *Blackadder Goes Forth*, the last episode of which, 'Goodbyeee', ended with him and Baldrick, together with Lieutenant the Honourable George St Barleigh (Hugh Laurie) and Captain Darling (Tim McInnerny), advancing into No Man's Land to their certain death. That episode was also one of the most powerful anti-war statements to emerge from a generation that had been partially shaped by the revival of CND.

The fictional Thatcherites were matched in real life by concerns that the next generation of Conservatives was drifting ever further from One Nation traditions. The Federation of Conservative Students was closed down in 1986 by Norman Tebbit, himself no moderate but nonetheless horrified by a libertarian tendency that ventured beyond such straight-forward issues as the support for apartheid and the repatriation of immigrants into much more charged areas: the legalization of drugs and the abolition of the age of consent. Such arguments never quite came in from the fringes, but even in the parliamentary party, there was a new kind of Tory receiving the leader's patronage who wasn't to everyone's tastes. Thatcher, wrote Edwina Currie in her diary, was 'wide open to the ideas of people like John Redwood and David Willets (blond prat), all young, fit, wealthy and ignorant, and, when they're not wealthy yet, at least trying to forget their poor past'. A few days later she added Peter Lilley to the list, with an almost audible shudder, as she looked on the future of Toryism: 'Those staring eyes, those faces inappropriately young (Lilley is older than me) without smile lines or wrinkles, those unlived-in bodies. Not my kind of people.'

The fictional images of Thatcherite characters were, of course, largely created by those who opposed everything the modern Conservative Party represented, and as such were most revealing of the prejudices and concerns of their makers. Thatcher's endorsement of materialism was regularly attacked – though seeking to improve living standards for the majority is not an entirely dishonourable aim for a government – while there was also a horrified but irresistible fascination with the alchemical ability of financiers and bankers to conjure up money where none had previously existed. And that fascination itself was satirized in David Lodge's novel *Nice Work*, where an academic specializing in post-structuralist theory finds himself getting interested in the processes of the City: 'This isn't business,' he explains to his partner. 'It's not about buying and selling real commodities. It's all on paper, or computer screens. It's abstract. It has its own rather seductive jargon – arbitrageur, deferred futures, floating rate. It's like literary theory.' So seduced does he become that he ultimately abandons his career to become a merchant banker instead: 'I regard myself as simply exchanging one semiotic system for another.'

Even if the caricatures were inevitably simplistic, they should none-theless have caused some concern to the right, for by sheer weight of numbers, if nothing else, they suggested the aim of establishing a new social consensus was not being achieved. The slogan 'greed is good' had, it seemed, limited cultural resonance; it might motivate behaviour but was seldom to be acknowledged even to oneself. That slogan came from Michael Douglas' character Gordon Gecko in *Wall Street* (1987), one of a string of major American films that ran through the decade – *Trading Places* (1983) and *Pretty Woman* (1990) were others – and that explicitly rejected the new orthodoxy, offering romantic images of solid old business values in opposition to the modern world of corporate raiding and insider trading. The moral coming out of Hollywood was, in the words of Gecko's antithesis Carl Fox in *Wall Street*, that one should 'create instead of living off the buying and selling of others'. Even in the land of the free market, it seemed, the message of Reaganomics and Thatcherism was struggling to combat older myths. And as the decade wore on, and stories of corruption and insider dealing began to circulate, so it began to seem to some of the more astute commentators that the Conservatives were storing up trouble for themselves by associating too closely with 'that stinking, sweating, heaving mess of the square mile of the City' (as a character in the television series *Bird of Prey* described it).

'Here are a group of their chums earning enormous sums,' warned Peter Kellner in the *Independent* in December 1986, 'and the impression is gaining ground that many of them are spivs.' The following month the story broke of dubious practices in the attempted takeover of Distillers by Guinness, which ultimately led to several prominent businessmen being jailed for false accounting and theft. Such stories – if not court cases – proliferated as the decade progressed. Most famously, in 1990 inspectors from the Department of Trade concluded Mohamed and Ali Fayed had 'dishonestly misrepresented their origins, wealth and business interests' when buying the company House of Fraser, including Harrods department store, in 1985. There were calls for the Fayeds to be banned from holding company directorships, but no action was taken.

Kellner's description caught the mood of the times: the yuppies and the City traders never endeared themselves to the general public, being widely seen as barrow-boys who had simply switched from selling women's tights to dealing in oil futures. But those on the other side of the Thatcherite revolution in business, where old-fashioned entrepreneurial activity was being encouraged, enjoyed a much higher status, regardless of their personal political persuasions. Figures such as Anita Roddick of the Body Shop, Andrew Lloyd-Webber of the Really Useful Group and Alan Sugar of hi-fi and electronics firm Amstrad were celebrated as the creators of their own companies and therefore deserving of their wealth. Recreating the great capitalist icon of the self-made businessman, they were, unlike the yuppies, perceived as being on the side of Carl Fox, not that of Gordon Gecko.

The occasional impression of misguided amateurish enthusiasm only enhanced the appeal, as when Clive Sinclair, the man who had brought the pocket calculator and the home computer to the mass market, launched the C5, billed as the first electric car. Actually it was a battery-powered tricycle that seated a single person, was open to the elements and, though marketed for use on the streets, resembled nothing so much as the wooden crates on wheels made by Wellington in the *Daily Mirror*'s comic strip *The Perishers*; it was of comparable power as well, with a top speed of just 15 miles per hour. A commercial disaster, it attracted barely more than 15,000 purchasers, despite retailers like Comet slashing the price from £400 to £250, and within ten months of the launch in 1985 the company, Sinclair Vehicles, had gone into receivership. The Sinclair C5 immediately became the butt of comedians' jokes, and the image wasn't improved when a Bristol man named Anthony Thompson became the first person convicted of taking and driving away one of the vehicles, having not perhaps fully thought through the problems of fleeing from the scene of the crime; the owner 'reported it missing and police caught Thompson nearby with the machine'.

Biggest of all these entrepreneurs was Richard Branson, founder of the Virgin company at the tail-end of 1960s idealism. Through the following decade Virgin had built a substantial brand, retailing and then releasing records, and Branson had become a major figure within the music industry, particularly when he signed the Sex Pistols, then on the rebound after being sacked by EMI and A&M. There had been further ventures into book publishing and film production, but to the wider world he was largely unknown, to the extent that when, in 1984, he announced he was launching a new transatlantic airline, he was invariably described in the press as a 'pop tycoon' or a 'pop millionaire', identified principally as the label-boss of Boy George (Culture Club had accounted for 40 per cent of Virgin's profits the previous year). The enhanced status that the airline gave him was seized with great gusto, as he discovered an appetite and aptitude for publicity, and thereafter he missed no opportunity for self-promotion; aided by such stunts as breaking the record for the fastest crossing of the Atlantic by boat, and making the first Atlantic crossing by hot-air balloon, he ended the decade as the best-known businessman in the country. He was also one of the few with genuine popular appeal; his boy-scout enthusiasm was irresistible to the media, and his informal, jumper-clad image, complete with shaggy blond hair and beard, fed into the veneration of amateurism, giving him the appearance of being the capitalist equivalent of a trendy Church of England vicar. In fact, he fitted perfectly the original Gary Hart definition of a yuppie, but benefited from sharing little in common with yuppies as commonly understood in Britain.

So rapidly did his profile rise that when, in 1986, he decided to follow the example of the likes of the Body Shop by floating Virgin on the stock market, there were more applicants than for any other share issue that decade, apart from the de-nationalized companies. It did not, however, prove to be a happy experience. Branson had previously operated on instinct, approaching business ventures with the same approach that prompted him into ballooning: he enjoyed, he said, 'setting myself huge, apparently unachievable, challenges and trying to rise above them.' That, he discovered, was not how the City worked, and he rapidly found himself stifled by the short-term caution of his new directors. 'I began to lose faith in myself. I felt uneasy about making the rapid decisions I have always made,' he wrote. 'In many ways 1987, our year of being a public company, was Virgin's least creative.' By 1988 he had had enough, and a management buyout brought the company back into private ownership. His evident sense of relief at being free again to pursue his own ventures reinforced public suspicion of the City.

The popularity of such figures, the acceptance of wealth as long as it was judged to have been honestly acquired, perhaps suggested that the reservations expressed in the novels, films and television programmes of the period were little more than niggling doubts, a slightly shamed admission that what might be good for the individual was not necessarily good for society. Because it was inescapably true that when individuals were confronted with the idea of making what Dire Straits identified on their 1985 hit single as 'Money for Nothing' (a staple on Alan B'Stard's car stereo), they wished to participate if at all possible. If it wasn't in the shares of privatized companies, then it was in property, for while the headline rate of inflation might now be under control, house prices were soaring: between 1984 and 1987 the amount of money lent for the purpose of buying domestic properties increased from £17 billion to nearly £30 billion, as people rushed to exploit what seemed like a guaranteed return on their investment in bricks and mortar, aided by the financial deregulation that allowed high street banks to enter the mortgage market and by the rush for business by the newly demutualized building societies. Geographical variations, however, revealed the deep divisions in the country's fortunes: in the mid 1980s annual house price increases averaged 20 per cent in London, 6 per cent in the Midlands and less than 2 per cent in the north of England. There was a simultaneous collapse in the number of new homes being built in the social housing sector – down from 100,000 in 1979 (scarcely a peak year in itself) to just a quarter of that figure by 1990 – but that attracted far less attention. Anyway it was beyond the control of individuals, the consequence of government policy and, while few might overtly subscribe to the devil-take-the-hindmost philosophy espoused by B'Stard, there was a certain averting of eyes, a sense of a greed that dare not speak its name.

With the reduction of council housing, and with changing social attitudes, the concrete tower blocks that had typified the 1960s and early 1970s also receded from view, many of them demolished to be replaced by low-rise blocks constructed in traditional, uncontroversial bricks and tiles. Supplanting the tower block as the most familiar architectural image of the period was arguably the out-of-town Tesco superstore, normally built in a vernacular style that might have made sense in a market town but which looked decidedly odd as a single-storey building sprawling over 70,000 square feet and adrift in the midst of a vast car park.

Or perhaps the icon of the times was the 'themed' shopping mall, as seen in historic cities like Bath, York and Winchester, and from which not even Ruth Rendell's fictional Kingsmarkham could escape, with the construction of 'the Barringdean Centre, the new shopping centre built to look like a castle. That was the style modern planners thought suitable on the outskirts of an ancient Sussex town where nothing genuinely medieval remained'. Despite the intentions, it 'looked less like a real castle than a toy one, the kind you have to assemble from a hundred plastic bits and pieces'. The largest of the new malls — the largest in Europe — was the Metro Centre in Gateshead, a vast temple to consumerism. There was a time, reflects a character in David Pinner's novel *There'll Always Be an England*, when 'we built cathedrals to the greater glory of God and as monuments to our own artistic genius. Today we build glittering shopping centres that sell things that we don't really need to buy, in order to convince ourselves we're living life to the full'. Others were also worried by what these developments revealed about modern Britain. 'With their sanitized environments, crowd control systems, air-conditioning and surveillance cameras,' noted *i-D* magazine, the malls 'have become a vision of a free market future, where there's nowhere to go but the shops, and all you have to do is spend.' In 1976 Johnny Rotten of the Sex Pistols had sneered, 'Your future dream is a shopping scheme'; in 1989 the Design Museum, funded by private money, was opened by Margaret Thatcher and proclaimed, as part of its ethos, that shopping was 'one of the legitimate cultural pursuits of the eighties'.

What was officially intended as the architectural embodiment of the age was the regenerated area of east London that had once been known as the docks but was now rebranded Docklands, almost as though, in the absence of any working docks, they were to become a theme park. A new quango, the London Docklands Development Corporation, was set up, charged with encouraging private enterprise to relocate to the area and thereby to restore its fortunes. To this end, virtually all planning restrictions were removed, though huge amounts of public money were required to sugar the pill and to provide the necessary transport infrastructure. Even so, it was hard to claim that the results were particularly impressive in architectural terms: One Canary Wharf — for which Thatcher laid the foundation stone in 1987 — may have been Europe's tallest office block, but it was also a profoundly boring building. More emblematic still, some thought, was the News International print works in Wapping, which even the official history of *The Times* admitted 'could lay a reasonable claim to being one of the most ugly superstructures in London'.

Other projects to regenerate former docks were undertaken in Bristol, Cardiff, Glasgow and Liverpool. Combined with the retail parks and superstores, and with the inexorable spread of McDonald's and subsequently Burger King restaurants, the result was a built environment that looked very different to that which had gone before. The 1984 Virgin Films' production of George Orwell's novel *1984* starring John Hurt and Richard Burton made the point in reverse. Slightly dull and uninspired though the movie was, it remained true to the look and culture of the novel: the weaponry is old-fashioned, television screens are black and white, the clothing is drab, and middle-class housing is based on modernist blocks while the proles still live in back-to-backs. Writing in an era of austerity, and with the imagery of war and Stalinism uppermost in his mind, Orwell had conjured up an England that was a clear extension of the 1940s: a monocultural society crippled by rationing, emasculated by an institutionalized fear of sex and stifled by enforced conformity. Even as recently as the end of the 1970s, this was still recognizable as a potential vision of a future Britain, but by 1984 itself, the year that had stalked the British cultural imagination for so long, it was starting to look hopelessly dated, rendered obsolete by the shiny new consumerism of rampant Thatcherism.

Part of the new Britain that was being built was a desire to take centre-stage in the sporting world, reflecting the growing financial muscle of what was now known as the leisure industry. Given the country's history and reputation for hooliganism, football tournaments were clearly not an option, and attention turned instead to the Olympic Games. In 1979 Horace Cutler, then leader of the GLC, suggested that London might try to stage the Olympics in 1988, not having hosted them since the Austerity Games of 1948, and a proposal was costed out, with a new stadium in Docklands, though the projected loss of £221 million (expected to double if inflation continued on current trends) seemed somewhat less than attractive, and the bid was ultimately not submitted. Then it was Birmingham's turn, bidding for the 1992 Games; when the votes were cast, the city came fifth in a field of six, narrowly beating Amsterdam but easily losing out to Barcelona, a result matched next time round by Manchester, which lost out to Atlanta, though it did manage to attract more support than Belgrade.

The fact that it was Birmingham and Manchester rather than London making the bids probably doomed the attempts, but was revealing of the ambitions of cities beyond the capital to reinvent themselves. Birmingham in particular, having recently built the National Exhibition Centre, was keen to promote itself internationally, a project that came with some successes as well as some humiliating failures. The appointment of Simon Rattle as the principal conductor of the City of Birmingham Symphony Orchestra was a major coup, as was the subsequent relocation of Sadler's Wells Royal Ballet to become the Birmingham Royal Ballet, but the

Birmingham Superprix, a short-lived experiment to stage a Formula 3000 road-race in the city, could hardly claim the same.

More consistently impressive was the marketing campaign launched in 1983 under the slogan 'Glasgow's Miles Better', which came with an image of Mr Happy from Roger Hargreaves' 'Mr Men' books, and was intended to give Scotland's biggest city a more friendly image for business and tourism. (A car sticker for its nearest rival proclaimed 'Edinburgh's Slightly Superior'.) The success of the campaign was partially responsible for Glasgow being named Cultural Capital of Europe for 1990, a decision that initially attracted much media derision – previous recipients of the honour had been somewhat more obvious choices, including Florence, Athens, Berlin and Paris – but which proved to be highly successful. In the build-up to that event, the city was chosen as the venue for a national garden festival in 1988, following on from Liverpool in 1984 (in the interim there had been a similar festival in Stoke-on-Trent). Again, it was not received with whole-hearted enthusiasm by everyone: 'City of Culture,' moans a character in Iain Banks' novel *Espedair Street* (1987): 'bloody garden exhibitions; just mair excuses fur the businessmen tae make a killin. Fresh paint on the double yellow lines an a bigger subsidy fur the opera.'

The rise of other cities was primarily at the expense of Liverpool, which had once been unquestionably the second cultural capital of the country, or possibly the first, if American poet Allen Ginsberg was to be believed: 'Liverpool is at the present moment the centre of the consciousness of the human universe,' he had declared. But that had been in the mid-1960s, and even then, at the height of the Merseybeat boom that made the city internationally fashionable, there had been problems; while the rest of the country was largely prospering, Liverpool's unemployment stood at 30,000 and decline was setting in. The two decades to 1985 saw the population of the city fall by a third, with the downturn becoming particularly sharp in the Thatcher years, resulting in the loss of 65,000 jobs, most of them in manufacturing and in the docks, as Britain's trade turned away from the Atlantic and towards Europe. Little of this was unique to Liverpool – Birmingham, for example, lost 40 per cent of its manufacturing jobs and 20 per cent of its population between 1973 and 1983 – but it was Merseyside that became symbolic of the depressed north, perhaps because it had further to fall. For here the economic slump was matched by a cultural waning, as film critic Alexander Walker noted when writing of the 1985 movie *Letter to Brezhnev*, set in the city: 'Liverpool, once the pride and a great part of the profit of 1960s Beatlemania, is now a city ousted from its place in pop mythology by the depression of the 1980s.'

The popular images of Liverpool now came from the likes of *The Boys from the Blackstuff* and from *Brookside*, a television soap opera created by Phil Redmond – best known for *Grange Hill* – that debuted on the opening night of Channel 4 in 1982. Unlike its Mancunian rival *Coronation Street*, ground-breaking in its time but now considered to be somewhat cosy in its depiction of working-class life, *Brookside* strove for realism from the outset, both in its production – it was filmed on a purpose-built cul-de-sac in Liverpool – and its subject matter: it covered life on the dole, picket lines and the resort to the black economy, all in language that was soon deemed inappropriate for broadcast before the 9pm watershed. In later years it descended into absurd sensationalism with armed sieges and bodies buried under patios, but in its early days it was an impressive series, and in Sue Johnston's portrayal of Sheila Grant, it created a truly great soap character ('one of the really remarkable television performances of our day,' enthused the channel's chief executive, Jeremy Isaacs, with some justification). In particular, the 1986 storyline that showed Sheila's response to being raped, and the effect it had on her relationship with her husband, Bobby (Ricky Tomlinson), was genuinely harrowing.

Whatever the show's merits, however, its relentless depiction of hard times did little to enhance the national image of Liverpool. Nor did *Bread*, a hugely popular sitcom created by Carla Lane and first broadcast in 1986. Centred on Nellie Boswell (Jean Boht) and her five grown-up children, its principal contribution can be seen in retrospect to have been the blending of sitcom and soap conventions. *To the Manor Born* had earlier made popular the concept of a story arc, with the courtship and ultimate marriage of Audrey fforbes-Hamilton and Richard DeVere offering a way out of the traditional sitcom impasse, but *Bread* took this considerably further, giving all the major characters continuing storylines. Significantly the highest viewing figures came with a 1988 episode that saw the wedding of Nellie's sole daughter Aveline (Gilly Coman) to Oswald, the climax to the fourth series but not an ending, for this was only halfway through the show's run. Such developments had previously been seen in American series – the appeal of shows like *Taxi* and *Cheers*, for example, lay almost as much in their plotlines as in their jokes – but were still new to British television.

At the time, however, attention was more focused on the family's resilience in the face of adversity. 'We run a business, a survival business,' insists Nellie. 'Everyone pulls their weight. We don't want any weak links in the chain.' And the need for survival tactics is evident in a society that is looking decidedly shaky, so much so that even the Catholic church is seen in decline: 'Oh Lord, where has the fear gone?' laments a priest. Some critics praised the series for showing that 'the famous Liverpool sense of humour and the famous Liverpool capacity for family loyalty are proof against all the vicissitudes of inner-city decay'. Others were less impressed, and denounced it either for celebrating welfare fraud, or for perpetuating the image of the city as being full of scroungers. Its most striking character was the leather-trousered Joey (Peter Howitt), who drove a Jaguar but was seldom seen earning money except by exploiting the benefits system, a theme that dominated much of the family's existence: 'We got a booklet from the Social Security office, and we read it from cover to cover,' says Aveline. 'It's amazing, the things you can claim for.' It was, as it happens, an overly rosy picture of the system, which was primarily based on discretionary grants. More common in real life was the experience of a Coventry man, reported by Beatrix Campbell, who applied to the DHSS for a clothing grant to replace his one pair of trousers which had acquired holes: 'They told me that the trousers would need to be stolen from me to qualify. But they couldn't be because I never take them off.' (Those grants that did exist would later be replaced by loans from the Social Fund.)

It all amounted to a very negative portrayal of Liverpool, and the popular image of the city was adversely affected during the 1980s. 'People in other parts of the country are actually frightened of us,' said Bobby Shack, a locally popular nightclub comedian. 'If you meet Londoners, they don't want to know you.' Yorkshire-born Alan Bennett referred to it as 'that sentimental, self-dramatizing place', an impression that was hardly corrected by Beryl Bainbridge's book *English Journey* (inspired by J.B. Priestley's 1934 classic), which said that the question of who was responsible for the city's decline wasn't important: 'It hardly matters now. It's too late. Someone murdered Liverpool and got away with it.' The city's depressed state inspired a series of terrace chants from fans of other football clubs: 'You've got one job between you', sung to the tune of 'Guantanamera', and a rewriting of Liverpool FC's anthem 'You'll Never Walk Alone':

> Sign on, sign on
> With no hope in your heart
> And you'll never work again,
> You'll never work again.

Such taunts were, in part at least, a tribute to the continuing success of Liverpool and Everton football clubs, who, between them, won the league championship every year from 1982 to 1988. For much of that period too, a generation of Liverpool bands inspired by punk continued to innovate:

Teardrop Explodes, Echo and the Bunnymen, Dead or Alive, Frankie Goes to Hollywood. But in both football and rock and roll, the baton was ultimately to be passed to north-eastern rivals in Manchester, even if the change wasn't immediately apparent in either instance. No one suspected in 1986 that the arrival of manager Alex Ferguson at Manchester United was to herald an unprecedented period of domination by a single club in English football, even if he did make it clear early on that his ambition was 'to knock Liverpool off their fucking perch'.

Nor was it obvious in November 1983 when Frankie Goes to Hollywood broke into the charts with their debut single 'Relax' that, although it would go on to reach No. 1 and sell a million copies in Britain, it would be eclipsed in cultural terms by the achievement of a Manchester band also enjoying their first hit that same month: the Smiths with their second release, 'This Charming Man'. That record never got higher than No. 25 and during their lifetime the group only managed two singles that reached the top ten, but even in 1980s pop music, sales figures were occasionally deceptive, and it was the Smiths, not Frankie, who were to go down in rock history as the Beatles of their generation. That status was not entirely justified, for the Smiths never had the same cross-class appeal enjoyed by the biggest rock acts, as the Style Council's Mick Talbot pointed out when it was put to him that the band's singer Morrissey was a spokesman for youth: 'He's only a spokesman if you go to college or university.' Nonetheless, Manchester did, for a while at least, take on the mantle of being the country's most important rock city – not least because of the promotional abilities of Tony Wilson, the head of Factory Records – while Liverpool never regained its pre-eminence.

Neither Frankie Goes To Hollywood nor the Smiths, as it happened, were present for the defining musical event of the mid-1980s, Live Aid, the concert set up to raise money for famine relief in Ethiopia. Frankie didn't appear because they turned down the invitation, though vocalist Holly Johnson had sung on the preceding Band Aid record 'Do They Know It's Christmas?', and the Smiths didn't appear because they weren't big enough to be invited in the first place; if they had been considered, Morrissey's condemnation of that single might possibly have scuppered their chances: 'One can have great concern for the people of Ethiopia,' he explained, 'but it's another thing to inflict daily torture on the people of England. It was an awful record considering the mass of talent involved.'

He was perfectly correct about the quality of 'Do They Know It's Christmas?'. Co-written by Bob Geldof of the Boomtown Rats and Midge Ure of Ultravox, it featured the cream of the current chart stars, and judged on musical merit was very poor indeed. But, as Geldof repeatedly pointed out, 'This is not just any record. It is a way of helping to stop people from dying.' The record went on to sell three and a half million copies and did undoubtedly did save lives, while Live Aid, the subsequent all-star concert, raised an estimated £150 million for the cause. Staged in July 1985, Live Aid started at Wembley with the Band of the Coldstream Guards, ended some seventeen hours later in Philadelphia with a performance by a mixed crowd of stars singing the American charity single 'We Are the World', and was punctuated by Geldof appealing for donations (though, despite popular memory, he never actually called on people to 'Give us your fucking money'). It was televised in its entirety on BBC, and so successful was the broadcast that it was reported that shops experienced the worst day of Saturday trading ever recorded.

It was an extraordinary occasion, and one that most of the population embraced with enormous enthusiasm, though inevitably there were some doubters. 'In a period where the very ethos of a planned, socialized and welfarized society is running down,' wrote *New Socialist*, 'a happy story where an individual can be seen to put the world to rights is of tremendous ideological value. Value, that is, to an interest group which depends on fostering Victorian charity and free-market fantasies.' More entertainingly, it aroused the ire of playwright John Osborne: 'A generation of self-besotted yoof that can be gulled by such dismal stuff deserves the fine mess they've gotten us into,' he ranted, though his charge seemed a little unfair; the state of British society, let alone of the catastrophe afflicting Ethiopia, could hardly be blamed entirely on the youth of the nation. There were also those who pointedly drew attention to the fabulous career boost that the concert gave to the acts that appeared, though Geldof, whose inspiration the entire project had been and whose motives were impossible to impugn, was one of the very few who benefited not at all in terms of sales. And as a musical spectacle, some critics argued, it was not all that one might wished. 'A shambles,' wrote Terry Coleman in the *Guardian*. 'One of the worst shows I've ever seen,' added Jonathan King in the *Sun*, denouncing the 'self-interested motives of the bands involved'.

The effect on the industry, however, was profound, bestowing upon it legitimacy and respectability, qualities that have seldom been productive of great rock and roll. Joan Baez, who opened the Philadelphia show, wrote of looking out at a much more homogenous audience than she was used to; she dubbed them yumarfs, 'young upwardly mobile American rock fans', and their taste was to dominate the next generation of rock, with its ever bigger tours of the world's sports stadia. Music was already beginning to turn away from the political engagement that had characterized the early years of the 1980s, but Live Aid hastened that process, replacing politics with charity, abandoning commitment for the more nebulous concept of caring. And while receipts had always a key part of pop – it is the only field of artistic endeavour that has always defined itself by weekly charts of comparative sales – there now seemed to dawn an era where a veneration of sheer size was the only measure of success. Even during Live Aid itself, Midge Ure found himself worrying that industry egos were destroying the purity of the project: 'All of us had built this organization to fight against huge, big conglomerates, to cut through the red tape. Now we were doing the exact same thing, becoming what we vowed never to be.' The following year, Norman Tebbit turned up at the British Phonographic Institute award ceremony (later known as the Brits) to present a BPI outstanding contribution award to Elton John and to Wham!, congratulating them on breaking open new markets with their concerts in the Soviet Union and China respectively. It was a far cry from the Specials denouncing the ghost towns of the Thatcherite recession.

By the end of the decade the Glastonbury festival, one of the last great survivors of the idealistic hippie era, had also been transformed. It had long ceased to be a free event, but had retained its radical credentials by donating profits to CND from 1981 onwards. But in 1987, remembered the organizer, Michael Eavis, 'We had an invasion of drug dealers. They arrived in their new BMWs, and we knew we had to do something about them.' The festival was not staged the following year and when it resumed in 1989, at a time when the music scene was dominated by illegal free raves, it had become a far more respectable event: for the first time, the police were involved in the planning and monitoring of the event, with the result that there were 356 arrests for possession of drugs. 'It made the world of difference,' reflected Eavis.

Where rock music led, comedy was not far behind; indeed each exerted a reciprocal influence on the other. There had been a series of high-profile benefit gigs for Amnesty International dating back to the Secret Policeman's Ball in 1976, primarily comedic in their casts but with musical contributions that had included Bob Geldof in 1981, while Bono, singer with Irish band U2, was later to cite the events as a key inspiration on his own campaigning: 'I saw the Secret Policeman's Ball and it became a part of me. It sowed a seed.' The first Comic Relief, in 1986, followed the same course: live shows at the Shaftesbury Theatre in London that were then edited down for television, raising funds for famine relief. But two years later Comic Relief turned itself into a conventional telethon, taking up seven and a half hours of primetime television on BBC1, in imitation of the already established Children in Need, though with a plastic red nose replacing Pudsey Bear as a logo; some six million people were estimated to have taken part in fund-raising around the event. Dominated by the likes of Lenny Henry, Griff Rhys Jones and Rowan Atkinson, the television coverage also featured some of the more traditional acts from the older variety tradition, leading to some unlikely encounters backstage as, for example, when Ben Elton found himself chatting with Jim Davidson and asked if he was going to stay all evening. 'No,' Davidson replied deadpan, playing up to his stereotype on the alternative circuit. 'I've got a National Front meeting at nine.'

As with Live Aid, there were critics: 'every programme had idiots wearing plastic noses and behaving stupidly,' wrote Kenneth Williams in 1988. 'I have never been more sick of all this charity crap than in the last few years! It has become a mundane gimmick now and lost all the novelty value it once possessed: just an excuse for a lot of people to indulge themselves.' And again there was the danger of charity and commerce combining to draw the teeth of a dissident art form. In a parallel development, the former chaos of the Edinburgh Fringe Festival was fast being turned into a corporate event, serving as annual auditions for alternative comedians seeking to break into television: 'Agents and directors of production companies with Filofaxes would sit frowning through shows,' recalled Mark Steel, 'occasionally consulting each other to ask, "Could we use this?"'

There was, however, one major exception to youth culture's turn away from politics. Red Wedge, launched in 1985, was an initiative led primarily by Paul Weller and Billy Bragg that was intended to encourage political participation by young people. Closely associated with the Labour Party, though never officially a part of it, Red Wedge staged a series of concerts through the country that featured a range of acts including the Communards, Aswad, Madness, Lloyd Cole and even the Smiths, before going on to work at a grassroots level, setting up local youth projects. Comedians like Dawn French and Lenny Henry, as well as the inevitable Ben Elton, also showed up at various events, as did David Yip of *The Chinese Detective*. Bragg saw it as essentially a one-way street ('we're doing the party a mega fucking favour'), and Weller was later to express scepticism about the Labour politicians who were supposed to be behind the project: 'They were all in for themselves,' he said. 'It was all firm handshakes and distant eyes.' But Neil Kinnock at least was an enthusiastic supporter, perhaps seeing it as a chance to redeem his musical credibility after appearing in a video for comic actress Tracey Ullman's version of 'My Guy' the previous year, a collaboration that did neither any favours — coming off the back of three consecutive top ten hits, the record failed to make the top twenty, and Ullman's recording career was never to attain the same heights again.

Red Wedge was at least more successful than that, though it was to produce its own disappointments. On the night of the subsequent general election in 1987 (Kinnock was on the cover of the *NME* that week), a party was held at the Mean Fiddler in London, which sank slowly into gloom as the results came in. 'The way I felt,' said Billy Bragg, 'was that somebody who I had great faith in – the British public – had betrayed me. It wasn't a personal betrayal but I had to accept that 42 per cent of the people who I sit with on the tube or the bus would actually vote for Thatcher.' But if the initiative didn't succeed in swinging the electoral arithmetic to Labour, it did have an impact on the party itself, according to Annajoy David, a former vice-chair of CND who ran the campaign: 'Red Wedge gave the Labour Party its confidence back,' she insisted, adding that 'the big cultural message did get through.' That was certainly true in the longer term, for just as Rock Against Racism had made the National Front a deeply unattractive option for youth in the late-1970s, so the campaigning of various leftist musicians in the mid-1980s helped shift public opinion back towards liberalism and away from the moral right. LABOUR USES GAY JIMMY TO WIN OVER THE VOTERS screamed a *Sun* headline and, though it was hardly a shock revelation – for surely there were few pop fans who didn't know that Jimmy Somerville, formerly of Bronski Beat and now of the Communards, was homosexual – the paper had the makings of a point: the fact that no comparable rock star would have dreamt of campaigning for the Tories did ultimately make a difference to cultural sensibilities. (In 1986 the *Sun* also revealed that two members of the Hull band, the Housemartins, were gay, which was news to the group, who all happened to be heterosexual.)

As it turned out, Red Wedge was the last great flourish for politically committed rock music, eclipsed in the election year of 1987 by the success of the songwriting and production team of Mike Stock, Matt Aitken and Pete Waterman. Having already established themselves as makers of hi-NRG hits for the likes of Hazell Dean and Divine, and scoring a No. 1 hit with Dead or Alive's 'You Spin Me Round (Like a Record)', Stock Aitken and Waterman re-emerged in 1987 as purveyors of lightweight dance-pop, with a succession of new acts – Mel and Kim, Sinitta, Sonia – as well as the already established Bananarama and Samantha Fox, the latter having graduated from Page Three, and two Australian soap stars, Jason Donovan and Kylie Minogue. There was also Rick Astley, who joined the company on the Youth Opportunity Programme, one of the government's schemes for the young unemployed, and ended up with a short-lived but incredibly successful career, reaching No. 1 around the world with 'Never Gonna Give You Up' and 'Together Forever'.

Little here was new – there were strong echoes of Nicky Chinn and Mike Chapman, who had been similarly ubiquitous in the days of glitter pop the previous decade – but the sheer inanity and production-line quality of the records aroused the ire of many critics. This was, many claimed, nothing more than cynical exploitation of artists and audiences alike – again hardly a novel development in pop music – but the instantly identifiable sound was undeniably popular and it even exported successfully to America, to the distress of critics everywhere. 'I think all that is coming to an end,' reflected Mark Ellen, the editor of *Q* magazine in August 1988, 'and we are seeing the rise of singer-songwriters like Tracy Chapman with songs that are actually about something.' He was wrong; the following year Stock Aitken and Waterman scored seven No. 1 hits in Britain, ending the decade with their inferior remake of 'Do They Know It's Christmas?' at the top of the charts.

Even as those records were providing the soundtrack for the latter years of Thatcherism, there emerged on *Friday Night Live* in the spring of 1987 the comedy character who seemed to capture the mood of the times. Created by Harry Enfield and known only by his catchphrase of 'Loadsamoney', the character was intended to satirize the greed of the boom, a loutish London plasterer who shouted with a kind of infantile aggression about his restricted areas of interest – cars, women and money – while waving a huge wad of banknotes in the faces of the audience. (The fistful of cash was inspired by the behaviour Enfield had seen on the terraces of Tottenham Hotspur, as London fans taunted supporters of visiting clubs from the impoverished north in the same manner as police officers had goaded striking miners.) 'All you need to know about politics,' he leered, 'is that Mrs Thatcher's done a lot of good for the country, but you wouldn't want to shag it.'

Like Johnny Speight's creation Alf Garnett, however, Loadsamoney was picked up by those he was supposed to be satirizing, much to Enfield's displeasure. 'I think he's a complete bastard,' he insisted, outlining his distaste for rampant capitalism: 'You go to Canterbury and the whole town stinks of American fast food. You know: flash cars and everyone living in Barratt homes.' Nonetheless the character did become seen as in the words of the lexicographer Jonathon Green, 'Thatcherism's shameless golem'. When a picture of Loadsamoney was used without permission on the front page of the *Sun* to advertise a bingo promotion, Enfield instructed solicitors to seek a published clarification that he did not endorse the paper, but found the *Sun* unwilling to let go of such a potent symbol: 'We believe you ought to buy yourself a sense of humour,' a leader column advised, and Enfield backed off, recognizing that this was a battle he was unlikely to win.

The character didn't survive the decade, being killed off in a 1989 evening of *Comic Relief*, and had actually enjoyed very little television exposure during his lifetime – no more than a handful of five-minute spots within other programmes. But despite his brief existence, Loadsamoney made more of an impact than almost any other comic character of the 1980s. And he came as close as anyone to encapsulating what was for many the vulgarity of the naked, self-promoting, essentially unBritish greed of Thatcherism in its boom years; even if some did find it regrettable that he should be a plasterer and not, say, a banker or a futures trader.

PART THREE
UNDER THE GOD
1987–90

This is the late eighties, Harry. People don't have expectations any more. They're grateful for anything they can get.
Andrew Davies, *A Very Peculiar Practice: The New Frontier* (1988)

THE MASTER: Survival of the fittest. The weak must be eliminated so that the healthy can flourish.
Rona Munro, *Doctor Who* (1989)

'The question is this. Either you believe in market forces or you don't.'
    'Well, actually, I'm afraid to say I don't.'
    'You don't?'
    'No. I used to, of course, when I was a child, but like everyone else, I discovered as I grew older that it was all made up.'
Stephen Fry & Hugh Laurie, 'Bank Loan' (1990)

11
The Third Thatcher Government

'The only way is up'

How Thatcherite must Labour become in order to appeal
to the new working class?
Peter Mandelson (1987)

You don't have to be a member of the Militant Tendency
to feel that there is something wrong when a hospital
doctor makes less in a week than an inexperienced
stockbroker can pick up before lunch on Monday.
David Thomas, *Daily Mail* (1987)

That's what makes the Phelans frightening. They have
nothing. Jack Phelan was the new underclass: riotous,
savage, with nothing to lose. It frees you from an awful
lot of restraints and inhibitions.
Robert Barnard, *A City of Strangers* (1990)

'This is the most successful campaign in the history of the party,' Neil
Kinnock told the parliamentary Labour Party, at its first meeting after
the general election of 1987. 'It has been recognized as such by our
opponents and the pundits.' He continued to list the achievements for
some time, before turning to the negative side of the balance sheet: 'I must
mention some failures. One is that we failed to win the election.' That was
certainly true, but it wasn't quite the whole truth. The result was appalling
for Labour, the second worst general election defeat since the Second
World War, as the party recorded just 31 per cent of the national vote
(compared to the 37 per cent managed in 1979) and again failed to make any
serious impression in the south-west and south-east of England and in East
Anglia, in all of which the Conservatives gained an outright majority of
votes cast. And it still managed to attract just 3.5 million votes from trades
unionists, a long way from the block vote at conference, which stood at six

million. The Conservative majority in the Commons was reduced, but still stood at a huge 102 seats. By any normal historical standards, this was failure on a grand scale.

But then this wasn't an election that was judged by normal historical standards. Evaluations were instead conducted in the shadow of the catastrophe of 1983, and seen in that half-light, Kinnock could indeed claim some successes – primarily that Labour had come a clear second, beating the SDP-Liberal Alliance by eight percentage points. The threat that Labour's slide might see them eclipsed as the major opposition party had been defeated, and while asserting the right to be runner-up in a three-horse race wasn't much to brag about, it did at least keep alive hopes for the next contest. Meanwhile the immediate future for politics was summed up in an election night *Spitting Image* special, broadcast as polls closed, which ended with assorted Conservative MPs singing the Nazi song 'Tomorrow Belongs to Me' from the film *Cabaret*. It was presumably intended as a chilling warning from history, though it was hard to be satirical when Alan Clark had already identified the original as one of his favourite movie sequences ('that wonderful, uplifting scene in the beer garden when the young SA boy leads the singing').

The election campaign itself had been centred almost entirely on Kinnock himself, with the opening party political broadcast, directed by Hugh Hudson of *Chariots of Fire* fame, devoted exclusively to him. The film, known as *Kinnock – The Movie*, hinged on two major speeches: the attack on Liverpool council in 1985 (complete with reaction shots of Derek Hatton, an unusual appearance by Militant in a Labour broadcast), and a performance in Llandudno, when he abandoned his prepared text for an impromptu and impassioned defence of equality and fairness. 'Why am I the first Kinnock for a thousand generations to go to university?' he demanded and, though it was easy to find faults in his logic – universities had only existed for around thirty generations – it was inspiring at the time. Footage was also included of Neil and Glenys walking along cliffs by the sea, perhaps in an attempt to erase the earlier coastal imagery of the couple, when he fell over on Brighton beach.

It was a slickly-made piece of work which got a mixed reception from his opponents. 'Packaging which owed a lot to Andrex,' David Owen declared loftily, but his SDP colleague Bill Rodgers was more impressed. 'It was a film worthy of Leni Riefenstahl at her most dangerously persuasive,' he reckoned, saving his criticisms for an Alliance broadcast which featured Rosie Barnes, the heroine of Greenwich, alongside a pet rabbit: 'Her well-meaning chatter about the family could have been a commercial for shampoo or sliced bread.' More importantly the broadcast gave Kinnock a personal boost in the polls, and became the first election film to get a repeat screening, due – it was claimed – to public demand; it replaced a planned broadcast on the NHS scheduled for the end of the campaign. This, believed Norman Tebbit, now chairman of the Conservative Party, was a major error: 'to repeat the film, as they did, drew attention to its lack of substance.' He was right, of course, but then it wasn't clear that Labour wanted to see much emphasis placed on substance, for Kinnock didn't always look comfortable with some of the policies he was articulating. 'You don't think I believe in this shit?' he asked Peter Mandelson privately. 'Peter, it's crap, it's crap.'

Subsequent analysis of the election showed that Kinnock's personal standing rose by six percentage points during the campaign, but that both Labour and the Conservatives ended with almost exactly the same share of the vote with which they had started. A Fabian Society pamphlet also pointed out that 'The increase in the Labour vote in 1987 came from a higher turn-out amongst Labour supporters rather than from any growth in identification with Labour'. For all of Labour's much-heralded professionalism in presentation, nothing had really changed: Kinnock could appeal to and sometimes inspire Labour traditionalists, but was still unable to broaden the brand appeal. And the Conservatives, despite a somewhat lacklustre campaign, could still count on the affluent south and midlands to return them to government. There was no headline-grabbing youth rally at Wembley this time round, though Andrew Lloyd-Webber did write a theme tune for the campaign, and a family-orientated event did bring out some old favourites including Adam Faith and Frank Ifield; also present was Errol Brown, formerly the singer with the band Hot Chocolate, who performed John Lennon's 'Imagine', in what might well have been an act of subversive irony. The most effective single element in the campaign, which ran under the slogan 'Britain's booming – don't let Labour wreck it', was a typically negative Saatchi & Saatchi poster showing a soldier with hands raised in surrender and the strap-line: 'Labour's Policy on Arms'.

But if Labour could take hope from the election, and the Conservatives could take control of the country, the Alliance could take nothing positive at all. Its share of the popular vote was down by less than three percentage points, but there was a fine line between respectability and disappointment, and they had stepped backwards over it. Some seats were lost, including that of Roy Jenkins, beaten by Labour's George Galloway in Glasgow Hillhead, and of the twenty-two MPs remaining, just five belonged to the SDP, with David Owen the sole parliamentary survivor of the valiant gang of four who had set out to break the mould of British politics. They had come remarkably close to achieving their objective, but it had been a tall order at the best of times, and in the increasingly bitter class warfare of the mid-1980s, it seemed that the middle-class Alliance had simply been squeezed out of contention.

Immediately the demand was raised from David Steel and others that the six-year betrothal should now be solemnized, and a formal marriage of the two parties be conducted. Owen was vehemently opposed to any such union, believing that the radical left-of-centre SDP he was trying to build would be sacrificed on the nuptial altar, but there was an inescapable logic to the process that was hard to escape. Under Britain's first-past-the-post electoral system, it was tough enough for a third party to keep its head above water, but it merely made things harder if it confused the issue by choosing to have two heads, particularly when they belonged to men as uncooperative as Owen and Steel appeared to be. The popular perception of the pair was largely set by their *Spitting Image* portrayal, where Steel was represented by a puppet small enough to be slipped into the pocket of the dominant and bullying Owen, but the reality was almost exactly the opposite. Steel, despite his youthful appearance and his taste in junior-executive striped shirts with white collars, was a competent and experienced politician, who had led his party for eleven eventful years, from the spectacular downfall of Jeremy Thorpe, through the Lib-Lab pact in the latter days of James Callaghan's government, to the building of the Alliance. Owen, on the other hand, was constantly being outmanoeuvred by those he appeared to consider unworthy of being his equals. And so he was again.

The call for a merger of the two parties was put to a vote of the members, with Owen leading the 'no' campaign, along with most of his parliamentary colleagues. Indeed Charles Kennedy was the only SDP MP to support the merger; he begged the party not to lose itself 'in a welter of self-indulgence and self-destructive recrimination', but it did so anyway and, though the result saw the proposal approved by 57 per cent of SDP members, the bitterness of the debate led some to reminisce unhappily about the behaviour of the Labour Party in 1981. 'I feel ashamed,' one member wrote to Rodgers. 'If those at the centre are incapable of demon-strating that consensus can be a reality, we deserve the scourge of extremism. Internal warfare, fratricide – where is the party of partnership?' The Liberals meanwhile, who had never before been in the position of abandoning their party to form a new one, were considerably more enthusiastic, an attitude helped by the suspicion that this was less a genuine merger than a takeover. Owen decided not to go along with the majority, and together with two other MPs – John Cartwright and Rosie Barnes – withdrew from the process, leaving Robert Maclennan to lead the party into merger talks. (This was something of a turnaround for Maclennan, since he had been firmly in the Owenite camp and had earlier been reported, in his days as a Labour MP, to have believed 'that the Liberals were poison and should be avoided'.)

Following extensive and exhaustive negotiations, the new party came into existence in March 1988, though it wasn't as clean a break as might have been hoped; the Owenite rump remained behind, clinging on to the identity of the SDP, while a handful of Liberals also split to keep the name of their party similarly alive in a much-reduced fashion. The new entity adopted the name of the Social and Liberal Democrats (the label Liberal and Social Democrats would have been more accurate, but the initials more loaded) and chose Paddy Ashdown as its leader. This latter was probably the wisest decision it took in its first years. Ashdown had only been elected to the Commons in 1983, but he had a more interesting background than most of his colleagues – he had served with the Royal Marines and the secret services – and his lack of political baggage was, in the circumstances, an advantage: the arguments over the future of the Alliance had done substantial damage to an endeavour whose chief selling-point had been its lack of dogmatic in-fighting; a clean break was more than welcome.

While Ashdown was finding his feet, however, there was the very real possibility that the SLD might find themselves outflanked by the SDP, for Owen remained a major public figure, with a standing far in excess of the forces he now commanded. His future role became one of the great political conundrums of the time. In a system akin to the American model, he would have been a credible presidential candidate, but in the tribal world of Westminster, he was seen to be a bit adrift, and rumours abounded that he was keen either to join the Conservatives or to rejoin Labour. Of these, the second option was highly unlikely: Labour had strayed too far from its chapel roots for there to be much rejoicing over this particular sinner, even if he were to profess himself repentant, which he showed no signs of doing. And there wasn't much love lost between him and Kinnock, with the Labour leader accusing him of possessing 'an ego fat with arrogance and drunk with ambition'. The idea of pursuing his career amongst the Tories was more plausible; Rupert Murdoch had suggested in 1986 that Margaret Thatcher make him deputy prime minister, with the idea that he might one day inherit the top job, and in 1988 Thatcher herself took his wife, Debbie, to one side after a Downing Street dinner and confided: 'Your husband has a big choice to make and it can no longer be avoided. There are only two serious parties in British politics and we women understand these things; it is time he made up his mind.'

But long before these kites were flown, Owen had explicitly ruled out the possibility of joining forces with the Tories, and to renege on that would have been a difficult political step to take. And so he kept his ever-decreasing party going, contesting by-elections against the SLD to the detriment of both, in what he described as a 'battle of the mice'. In the 1989 contest in Richmond, North Yorkshire, caused by the departure of Leon Brittan to become a European commissioner, the SDP and SLD candidates scored more than half of the vote between them, but split their support sufficiently to allow the Conservative candidate, William Hague, to emerge as the victor, despite recording a 24 per cent drop in support, the worst performance by a Tory candidate since Thatcher had come to power. The coup de grâce came the following year at a by-election in Bootle, where the SDP candidate polled a derisory 155 votes, beaten not merely by the Liberal Democrats (as the SLD had now renamed themselves) and by the Green Party, but also by the candidate from the leftover Liberal Party. Even worse, the rock and roll singer Screaming Lord Sutch, who had long been contesting seats under the banner of the Monster Raving Loony Party, attracted two and a half times as many votes. Faced with such public humiliation, Owen announced that the party was to dissolve itself, though even now he was not quite prepared to throw in the towel. 'He said that while his party might now be dismissed as a joke, he believes that he personally still has credibility,' recorded future Conservative MP Gyles Brandreth in his diary, after encountering Owen in the studios of TV-AM. His hopes appeared to depend on the weight that his backing would add to Labour's cause in the next general election: 'in the event of a narrow Labour victory he can see himself as a possible foreign secretary.' Few others shared his vision.

While David Owen, the gang of one, was thus providing a stark demonstration of Enoch Powell's dictum that all political careers end in failure, the Labour Party was taking the next steps down the road of reinvention. Following the third consecutive election defeat, Denis Healey — the man who really should have been foreign secretary, if not prime minister — finally retired from the frontbench after more than two decades, and other established figures, including Peter Shore, also stepped aside. In the subsequent vote by MPs for the shadow cabinet, Bryan Gould, a leading modernizer, came top with John Prescott second, while Gordon Brown and Jack Straw made their debuts in the list, and Tony Blair only narrowly missed out. There was a sense of a changing of the guard, of a new generation taking charge. And its first task was to ditch as much as possible from the legacy of The Policies.

Accordingly, a series of policy review groups were set up, which in due course reported back with the findings expected of them. Published in 1989 as *Meet the Challenge, Make the Change* – a document whose title seemed aimed more at the party than at the electorate – the reviews revealed that Labour no longer saw state ownership of industry as a key ambition, that its taxation aspirations were now a Thatcherite 20 per cent basic rate and a modest higher rate of 50 per cent, and that most of the trade union legislation introduced by the Tories was to be accepted, including secret ballots for strike action and leadership elections. (Blair, as employment spokesperson, threw in a rejection of the closed shop as an afterthought later in the year.) On the other key issues, withdrawal from Europe had already been dropped in the 1987 manifesto, while defence was held over for the moment, since it was such an explosive subject, though Kinnock made no secret of having abandoned his belief in unilateral nuclear disarmament. Frontbench spokespeople now made sure that all pledges and proposals were now followed by the cautious phrase 'as resources allow' or, more long-windedly that everything depended on 'the situation we inherit in each case and on the constraints of finance and legislative time.'

None of this was achieved painlessly. Everything the party had stood for just six years earlier had been cast aside, and its place taken by everything that the hated SDP had stood for. 'The distance between the leadership and the rest of the movement is, at best, rather sad,' wrote David Warburton, a far-from-extreme union official. 'At worst it is demoralizing.' Bryan Gould expressed the same opinion when he came to write of the period: 'there was a growing disillusionment and apathy as regards the direction in which the policy review and other changes were taking the party.' Ron Todd, who had succeeded Moss Evans as general secretary of the Transport and General Workers Union, put it rather more directly at the 1988 conference: 'Nye Bevan is spinning in his grave as the last vestige of controversy, of political opinion, of socialist content, is ground out of the election literature, in favour of glossy pink roses, a sharp suit and a winning smile.'

Similar comments were being made in private by senior figures in the party. Paddy Ashdown recorded in early 1989 the comments of Michael Meacher, formerly regarded as Benn's lieutenant but now considered a Kinnock supporter, talking about 'how demoralized they are in the highest reaches of the Labour Party.' He admitted that 'they could not win the next election, that Kinnock was considered useless and that they were all in the depths of despair.' A year later, Ashdown was noting in his diary another conversation, this time with Austin Mitchell: 'He believes that Kinnock is becoming a crypto-Tory and there is every possibility of a hung parliament. He said Kinnock wouldn't pull it off and it was time the Labour Party realized that.' Bryan Gould and Robin Cook were also reported to have expressed doubts about whether Labour could win a majority at the next time of asking, and there were persistent rumours that John Smith, the new shadow chancellor, might be tempted to stage a coup against Kinnock, though nothing ever materialized.

And from the left, there was simple despondency, as expressed by Benn: 'I think the Labour Party may be in a state of terminal decline.' Such apocalyptic fears were not as exaggerated as they might appear. Membership of the party was continuing to decline (though Richard Attenborough did rejoin in 1990, presumably having received fresh instructions from Gandhi), while the activist base was shrinking, and even in electoral terms there was no obvious benefit being gained: in the first two years of the new parliament, Labour failed to take any new seats at by-elections (in fact, they lost one to the Scottish Nationalist Party), while opinion polls continued to show the Conservatives in a strong lead, at one stage touching a 50 per cent share. What was the point of all the reforms if they weren't matched by public acceptability? What, indeed, was the point of the Labour Party, if not even its leadership knew what they believed in any more? Kinnock was fast coming to be seen as a man who, having sold his soul to the devil for electoral preferment, was likely to be cheated on the deal. Or, as Jim Sillars of the SNP put it: 'To get into Downing Street, Neil Kinnock would boil his granny down for glue.'

On the other hand, there was an equally valid question: What was the alternative? Certainly there seemed no appetite within the party for a return to the old days. In 1988 Tony Benn finally challenged Kinnock in a leadership contest, the first time he had stood for the leadership since Harold Wilson's resignation twelve years earlier, but as an event it generated none of the excitement of the 1981 campaign for the deputy's position – it was more a question of history repeating itself, the first time as tragedy, the second time as nothing very much at all. Kinnock won 89 per cent of the vote, and though Roy Hattersley did less well in a simultaneous election for the deputy leadership, he still secured two-thirds of the vote as he saw off both Eric Heffer, Benn's running-mate, and the more substantial challenge of John Prescott. In the process, Labour's standing in the polls took another knock, such was the lingering public suspicion of Benn, but he was by now a largely peripheral figure. The second stage of the Kinnock project was failing to win the affection of the party, let alone the country, but there was clearly no great desire to join battle for the cause of socialism, just an atmosphere of cowed submission: the left's agenda had been rejected in 1983, now the right's alternative was facing the same fate and no one knew quite what to do next, save to trudge gloomily onwards in the Micawber-like hope that something would turn up.

The signs were not good. The economic boom continued through after the election, fuelled further by Nigel Lawson's budget in 1988, which cut the basic rate of income tax from 27 to 25 per cent and the top rate from 60 to 40 per cent. Amongst the public justifications offered for this renewed assault on higher tax rates was that paradoxically it increased revenue, since the wealthy would then make less effort to avoid paying, but in private Lawson was prepared to admit: 'I like that argument but it isn't true. More tax would have come from the top one to five per cent in any case because the salaries of the top earners have been put up so enormously. But still, let's go on using the argument.' Indirect taxes were still on the rise, of course, with eye-tests and dental examinations now attracting charges for the first time (though neither raised quite the same furore as had the imposition in 1984 of VAT on fish and chips and other takeaway food). But interest rates were low, unemployment fell below 10 per cent in November 1987 for the first time in six years, and house-prices were booming – up 40 per cent in some areas in the eighteen months following the election (YUP! IT'S JUST LIKE A WIN ON THE POOLS, enthused the *Sun*), so that the average house-price now equalled four-and-a-half times average earnings. 'Mr Lawson has a lot to be complacent, smug and arrogant about,' wrote the veteran political journalist Colin Welch.

During the same period, however, came the first warnings that not all was as secure as it seemed. The stock market was also booming in the summer of 1987, and there were those who were getting suspicious. 'Stock market is up again,' wrote Kenneth Williams in his diary in July 1987. 'I don't trust these endless rises! It has got to fall quite drastically soon. The world's economic state is parlous in view of the enormous budget deficit of the USA and the endless debts of South America and East Europe.' Three months later came Black Monday, when the Dow Jones recorded its biggest-ever percentage fall for a single day, and the rest of the world, including London, responded in similar fashion. It was, despaired *The Times*, 'the unthinkable – the roaring Eighties, the years of easy prosperity, could be over'. *Class War* was more succinct, capturing the moment when reality seemed to catch up with the City yuppies in the headline FILO-FUCKED!

Coming so soon after the celebrated Big Bang of financial deregulation, the speed and scale of the crash was blamed by some on the new era of international, 24-hour-a-day markets and on program trading, in which computer systems took the place of human judgement. Indeed one of the best crime novels of the decade, Denise Danks's *The Pizza House Crash*, centred on the idea of computer hackers trying to tweak the market by sending subliminal messages to the screens of traders, brainwashing them with the single word 'SELL', thus provoking a wave of panic that got out of control. It was a surprisingly plausible hypothesis.

The timing of the crash was particularly poor for the government, which was in the process of selling off the remainder of its stake in British Petroleum. The offer price for the shares had been pitched at what was considered a bargain level, in pursuance of the privatization ideal, but in the aftermath of Black Monday the shares fell below that price, leaving the investment banks that had underwritten the offer in serious danger of being out of pocket. This was, one might have assumed, precisely the kind of unforeseen circumstance for which underwriters were employed, but the prospect of losing money proved sufficiently intolerable that they demanded the state take action to protect their position – and the Bank of England duly obliged. Free market enterprise, it appeared, was not actually in the business of taking risks at all; at least not when it had a government that, despite its aversion to subsidizing industry, could be relied upon to bail out private finance. Indeed, the government's main concern at the time appeared to be that the Bank was trying to take all the credit for the decision: 'there has been an attempt to knock the gilt off the chancellor's gingerbread,' as a Downing Street statement put it.

Lawson's inflationary 1988 budget was all the more extraordinary for coming not only early in a parliament – politically an unusual time for giveaways – but also in the wake of Black Monday, just at a time when it looked as though the self-congratulatory office blocks sprouting up in the City might actually be castles built on sand. In the short term his injection of further cash and credit into the system worked, but there was bound to be a comedown and, in the second half of 1988, it duly came; interest rates, having been cut three times following the budget, began to rise steadily again, and in October 1989, two years on from the stock market crash, they reached 15 per cent. Inflation too was rising, so that by November 1988 Labour frontbencher Gordon Brown could mock Lawson's earlier claims that his target was zero inflation: 'Does he think that that promise is still credible when, after five budgets and six autumn statements, inflation is now higher than when he became chancellor?' And so the tide began to turn against the government. A parody of 'Hark! The Herald Angels Sing' that circulated around the City of London at Christmas 1988 captured the prevailing mood that the boom years were slipping away:

> Dazed from many a drinking-bout,
> Your yuppie's now a lager lout.
> See him, failed, tired and boozy,
> Shedding tears in his Jacuzzi;
> Life's no longer full of glee –
> He's on the shelf at twenty-three.

It wasn't simply the economy. There was a wider sense that things weren't quite right in the country, symbolized by a spate of disasters. In March 1987, 193 people lost their lives when the *Herald of Free Enterprise* cross-channel ferry capsized as it left Zeebrugge. Many of the passengers were *Sun* readers on a trip sponsored by the newspaper, which was offering a £1 return fare for a day of buying cheap alcohol and cigarettes. Allegedly the event was subsequently known in the *Sun* offices as 'drowned for a pound', but the paper's public response was slightly less callous: it organized a benefit event at the London Palladium, starring Bernard Manning and Jim Davidson, while a version of 'Let It Be', produced by Stock Aitken and Waterman and performed by 'the usual hotch-potch of clashing celebrity vocals' (as one of the participants, Boy George, put it) was released on the *Sun*'s own record label, and went to No. 1 under the name Ferry Aid.

In August that year an unemployed man named Michael Ryan shot dead sixteen people before killing himself in Hungerford, Berkshire in an act of mass-murder hitherto unknown in Britain. Then in October the southeast of England was hit by the worst storm for nearly three centuries, killing eighteen people and destroying more than fifteen million trees. The following month, eleven were killed when the IRA detonated a bomb at a Remembrance Day ceremony in Enniskillen, an act so extreme that even the official Soviet news agency, Tass, condemned it as 'barbaric', while Sinn Fein itself was moved to apologize. In November, a fire at King's Cross underground station in London cost thirty-one lives, and Paul Johnson described 1987 in the *Daily Mail* as THE YEAR OF DISASTER. It was unfortunately not the end, for the following year proved even more costly with an explosion on the Piper Alpha oil-rig in the North Sea in July claiming 167 lives, and in December, a terrorist bomb exploded onboard a jumbo jet, Pan Am flight 103 from London to New York, killing 270 in the air over Lockerbie and on the ground. January 1989 saw a further 47 deaths near Kegworth in Leicestershire, when a passenger plane suffered an engine failure and crashed into the embankment of the M1 motorway.

The media struggled to make sense of many of these incidents, since they appeared to be isolated, disconnected from the established narratives of news. But then, in April 1989, came a disaster that fed directly into a set of time-honoured prejudices. Liverpool were playing Nottingham Forest in an FA Cup semi-final at Sheffield Wednesday's ground, Hillsborough, when an overcrowded section of Liverpool supporters, overwhelmed by an influx of further fans, resulted in a deadly crush that killed ninety-six people. Tapping into the long-running story of football hooliganism, the *Sun* in particular caused great offence with a front-page editorial headlined THE TRUTH. 'Drunken Liverpool fans viciously attacked rescue workers,' it asserted. 'Police officers, foremen and ambulance crew were punched, kicked and urinated upon by a hooligan element in the crowd. Some thugs rifled the pockets of injured fans as they were stretched out unconscious.' None of this was true – hooliganism had no part to play in the events that day – and, in the ensuing outcry, sales of the paper on Merseyside collapsed by nearly 40 per cent, staying low for months and years to come. The broadcaster Brian Hayes captured the mood of many when he directed a diatribe against the paper's editor Kelvin MacKenzie on live television, challenging him to phone in to justify his coverage: 'Mr MacKenzie, you're living in a cartoon land where no one ever gets hurt and nothing lasts for longer than a moment. But the pain you and your paper cause to many people lasts much longer than the moment it takes to read the page. Titillation for a few column inches destroys lives, Mr MacKenzie.'

Some other reporting was more accurate, with the *Economist* magazine directing its fire at the football authorities: 'For complacency and incompetence, there's nothing like a cartel; and of Britain's surviving cartels, the Football League is one of the smuggest and slackest.' The subsequent report by Lord Justice Taylor was clear that the immediate blame for the disaster lay with the police's failure to handle the situation, but went on to recommend that the terraces on which generations of fans had stood should now be removed, in favour of all-seater stadiums, and that the fences erected at the front of stands (introduced as an anti-hooligan measure to stop pitch invasions) should now be removed. The resultant changes to the grounds of clubs in the top divisions changed the face of football for ever, beginning a long process of social rehabilitation for the sport.

Thatcher's third term in office was marked too by a series of health scares around the farming of food. In 1986 the government admitted that Bovine Spongiform Encephalitis (BSE) had entered the British beef industry, and early jokey stories about 'mad cow disease' soon turned to alarm with the realization that it might cause an outbreak of variant Creutzfeldt-Jakob disease (vCJD) in humans. In 1989 the sale of cows' brains for human consumption was banned, but by then the disease had spread into the breeding stock and the following year France became the first country to ban the import of British beef. Soon afterwards, the agriculture secretary, John Selwyn Gummer, staged a photo-opportunity in which his daughter Cordelia supposedly bit into a burger to demonstrate the safety of British beef and, though it later transpired this was a set-up and she hadn't herself eaten the burger, Gummer's public standing – which had never been particularly high – took a knock from which it never quite recovered. BSE remained an issue for over a decade, and provoked a massive cull of infected cattle, though scores of human deaths from vCJD did occur.

Meanwhile, an entirely separate story had broken in relation to the dangers posed to humans by modern farming. In 1988, Edwina Currie had her attention drawn to a massive rise in the incidence of food poisoning caused by *Salmonella enteritidis*, which was now being found not merely in chickens but in their eggs. There was even an outbreak of the infection in the House of Lords that year, while the bacterium had also hit the headlines when the meat snack Peperami had a nationwide recall in response to the discovery of contamination. A series of warnings, advising people about the safest ways of cooking eggs, was issued by the department of health, but was little heeded until Currie in a television interview commented that 'most of the egg production in this country, sadly, is now infected with salmonella.' In fact, most production was not infected, though there had already been more than twenty deaths that year, but the phrase scarcely seemed a catastrophic error, except for the egg industry, whose sales had already been falling and now collapsed overnight. Caught in a massive media storm, Currie resigned and her career in government came to an abrupt end.

Bernard Ingham, the prime minister's press secretary, was later to write that 1988 saw the end of the good times for the government: 'At the time, it could scarcely go wrong. All this ended in December that year when Edwina Currie, a junior minister at the department of health, scrambled her eggs with excessive amounts of salmonella. After that nothing went right for the government.' It was an unfair charge to lay, however implicitly, at Currie's door – and seemed to skate over the impact of, say, rising interest rates – but it was certainly the case that there was a perceptible shift in public opinion as the year drew to a close. There had been an economic boom that was supposed to have heralded a rebirth of the nation and yet, as the signs appeared of an incipient new recession, it seemed that much had been left undone during the good years.

For some, this feeling was encapsulated in the increased numbers of visibly homeless people on the streets, 'the sort of people you step on when you come out of the opera,' as Conservative minister Sir George Young ill-advisedly put it. 'At the beginning of the war,' wrote Ian Gilmour, 'beggars vanished and were not seen for forty years. Then in the 1980s they reappeared on the streets of London.' Justin Cartwright's novel, *Look at It this Way* (1990), shared the same perception: 'They were everywhere. They begged at stations, outside supermarkets and in the streets. There were tens of thousands of them loose on the streets. Most of them were mental or alcoholic. A few seemed simply to be suffering from a complete loss of self-esteem. Some muttered and swore, some gathered in convivial groups drinking. Some busied themselves obsessively collecting scraps.' Stories began to appear in the media about those for whom begging had become a lucrative career option, replacing the tales that had once been prevalent of benefit scroungers, and echoing the Sherlock Holmes story 'The Man with the Twisted Lip' from a century earlier.

Undoubtedly there were such cases, but they amounted to a drop in a rising ocean. By 1989, according to the Salvation Army, there were 75,000 homeless people in the capital, most of them in hostels, bed-and-breakfast hotels and squats, and other cities were proportionately suffering even steeper rises in the numbers involved. The expression 'cardboard city' came into use in the middle of the decade to describe the congregations of rough sleepers sheltering in cardboard boxes in parts of London such as Lincoln's Inn Fields, the South Bank Centre and the Embankment, while doorways in many of the chief shopping streets of the city were also occupied after dark by those with nowhere else to go. When Mother Teresa of Calcutta visited London in 1988 and toured the sites, she was horrified at what she saw: 'I didn't know what to say. There were tears in my eyes.'

It was scarcely a new issue – a deputation of homeless people had marched to see Sir Keith Joseph when he was housing minister back in 1962 – but it was exacerbated in the late 1980s by the house-price bubble, by the discrepancy in wealth between the capital and other parts of the country, and by the policy of care in the community, which had seen thousands of long-stay patients discharged from mental health institutions without sufficient funds being provided for their rehabilitation. The problem of homelessness hadn't been so visible in living memory, and it added to a feeling that the fabric of the nation was fraying.

So too did the spread of the term 'the underclass' from America. The idea that a self-perpetuating stratum might emerge with no stake whatsoever in society, save for the claiming of benefits, had been touted by Joseph himself in 1974: 'A high and rising proportion of children are being born to mothers least fitted to bring children into the world and bring them up,' he had said in a speech at Edgbaston. 'Some are of low intelligence, most of low educational attainment. They are unlikely to be able to give children the stable emotional background, the consistent combination of love and firmness, which are more important than riches.' Identifying a potential problem and resolving it, however, were entirely separate questions, and there had been little in the way of government policy to address the emergence of an underclass.

If, indeed, there was such a thing, and there were many on the left who regarded such talk as a dangerous irrelevance in the analysis of class. 'What the Labour Party has done,' wrote Tony Benn in late 1987, 'is to accept the Tory description of class – that there are the employed affluent workers on the one hand and the unemployed no-goods on the other – and to say the latter are an "underclass" which just has to be catered for in some way.' But by the end of the decade, a Gallup poll revealed that 85 per cent of the population believed that there truly was an underclass, and there were some commentators prepared to broaden the assault into a more general- ized critique of modern Britain. 'The working class has come a long way in recent years, all of it downhill,' wrote Tony Parsons in 1989. 'Something has died in them – a sense of grace, all feelings of community, their intelligence, decency and wit.' Amongst the symptoms he identified were the drinking on the streets of cans of high-strength lager, tattoos on women and the ownership of large dogs given names such as Rambo, Rocky and Napalm. The trend towards big dog breeds – German shepherds, rottweilers, dobermans – would lead in later years to a media panic and the passing of the Dangerous Dogs Act, but as early as 1985 they were being recognized by some as a worrying development. 'It's a guide to the changing mood of the country,' reflected Ferelith Hamilton, editor of *Dog World* magazine. 'I think the rise of the guard dog is very much a reflection that we are a more violent, more fearful society.' By the end of the decade there were stories of illegal dog-fighting in various parts of the country, featuring pit bull terriers and similar breeds, and even of man-versus-rottweiler bouts.

Others were expressing similar fears over the impact of arcade video games, which had rapidly been gaining in popularity since the launch of Space Invaders in 1978. Initially this new form of recreation was seen as being probably neutral, perhaps even beneficial, so that an early press portrait of snooker player Steve Davis could claim: 'he has brought to the game a boyish freshness and enjoyment, the kind which he himself finds in playing the electronic games of Space Invaders. This could be the root of his calmness.' Even at that stage, however, there were warning signs, for it wasn't just the clean-living Davis but also the more disreputable Alex Higgins who was attracted to the game; predictably enough, Higgins went too far and was docked world ranking points when he arrived late for a tournament, having spent too long shooting screen aliens out of an electronic sky. In 1981 there were press reports of a 13-year-old in Dudley who was put in local authority care after he stole £300 to feed his Space Invaders habit, while the 1983 pilot episode of *Taggart* saw the eponymous detective challenged about wasting his time playing Pac-Man in a pub, and shrugging: 'Sherlock Holmes had his violin . . .' Increasingly the perception was that of the characteristically apocalyptic Martin Amis in his novel *Money* (1984): 'In the arcade the proletarian ghosts of the New York night, these darkness-worshippers, their terrified faces reflected in the screens, stand hunched over their controls. They look like human forms of mutant moles and bats, hooked on the radar, rumble and wow of these stocky new robots who play with you if you give them money.'

The change in attitude was partly the result of a shift in the nature of the games themselves in the middle of the decade. In the early titles the player was cast in the role of defending Earth from alien hordes (Space Invaders), of being in a spaceship shooting down flying saucers and asteroids (Asteroids, 1979), or of flying through an alien environment under attack (Defender, 1980). Variations came with being chased through a maze by malevolent ghosts (Pac-Man, 1980) and saving a woman who had been kidnapped by a giant ape (Donkey Kong, 1981). This latter title introduced the character of Mario, an unimposing Italian plumber who lacked any of the normal attributes of the superhero, save his ability to jump enormous heights and distances; his everyman image proved popular and he went on to appear in more than two hundred video games, becoming the mascot of the Nintendo corporation. What was common to all of these early games was that the player was essentially on the side of good in a conflict against evil, however loosely defined these concepts were. But in the mid-1980s a new genre emerged that was based on close combat: Karate Champ (1984), Way of the Exploding Fist (1985), Street Fighter (1987). Inherently amoral and seen as more violent – or, at least, more immediately physical in their violence and thus more easily mimicked in real life – these attracted wider criticism; there was as yet no outcry comparable to that which had greeted the video nasties, but there were concerns that these games had nothing constructive to add to society. There was also the worry, implied by Amis, that this was yet another depressing aspect of American culture destined to come to Britain.

Margaret Thatcher had arrived in Downing Street with a clear mandate for change, even if her ability to deliver hadn't always been trusted. But implicit in that mandate, and central to her appeal for many voters, was a belief that she was at root old-fashioned, a throwback to an earlier image of Britain. And yet, as the smoke from the battles of the mid-1980s cleared, and as the feeling of affluence began to be threatened even in the midlands and the south, it became clear that this wasn't entirely the case. Rather the country seemed to have imported from America not merely a reverence for wealth, but an untidy collection of social problems that were likely to last much longer than the economic recovery, as well as a pursuit of the advertising chimera of a new, improved world. Britain had changed, and it was not entirely convinced that it liked what had happened. Many of the changes were incremental and almost imperceptible, but together they amounted to a radical transformation of society and culture, away from the solid, if imperfect certainties of the post-war era to something akin to a state of permanent revolution, in which traditional values of respect, loyalty and consideration for others appeared to hold little sway.

On a perhaps peripheral level, this could be seen in the discarding by television of an entire era of British comedy. Some of the biggest stars in the field – Dick Emery, Tommy Cooper, Eric Morecambe, Kenneth Williams – died during the decade, but for those established figures who remained, the going was about to get difficult. In 1985 Eric Sykes was given a special award at the Festival Rose d'Or in Montreux for his outstanding contribution to television comedy, and after the ceremony approached BBC executive Bill Cotton with some ideas for programmes, only to be told: 'Your day's gone, Eric. We're now into alternative comedy.' It was a first blast of the chill wind about to blow through the industry, and others too were noticing its effects. 'I was still contracted to the BBC, but I had an uneasy feeling that such was the change taking place in light entertainment generally that it wasn't an alliance destined to last,' wrote Les Dawson of the period, and sure enough in 1990 he was informed (by a journalist, not by the BBC) that both the series he hosted – *Blankety Blank* and *Opportunity Knocks* – had been scrapped. The following year Russ Abbott was dropped from the BBC schedules, after six series with the corporation, as were Little and Large, after eleven series. Things were little better on the commercial channels: Thames TV terminated the contracts of Benny Hill in 1989 and of Jim

Davidson in 1990. 'Political correctness was taking over,' remembered the latter; 'I actually thought that that was the end of the line for my type of comedy.' Ian Tough of the Krankies, also cast aside by the BBC, was more philosophical: 'It was just the end of that style of variety entertainment.' As time went on, it seemed ever more appropriate that Tommy Cooper had collapsed with a fatal heart attack while appearing onstage on a live broadcast of the variety show *Live From Her Majesty's* in 1984.

For there was little discernible future in the strand of comedy that had emerged from the variety tradition, with the very notable exception of Victoria Wood, who had first appeared on television in 1974 (and subsequently turned down the offer to join *Not the Nine O'Clock News*), but who had to wait until the 1980s to achieve real success. The roots were now withering, and there had been a noticeable drop in quality over recent years: Little and Large had their place, but few believed they were the new Morecambe and Wise, while Jim Davidson's sitcoms (*Up the Elephant and Round the Castle* and *Home James!*) are rarely remembered with any great fondness. By the same token, of course, Hale and Pace, of whom London Weekend Television held such great hopes, didn't turn out to be the new Morecambe and Wise either, and Rowland Rivron's series (*Set of Six* and *The Groovy Fellers*) seldom make the lists of great television comedies. Few critics shed any tears at the passing of the light entertainment tradition, but many of the acts who found themselves unceremoniously cleared from the listings pages were still attracting substantial audiences, and – in the case of Sykes and Dawson – were highly revered. Nor could it be said that those making the decisions were entirely sure of their ground in this new world of classless anti-racism and anti-sexism. In the late 1970s Bill Cotton ordered the removal of the dance troupe Ruby Flipper from *Top of the Pops* on the grounds, remembered choreographer Flick Colby, that 'the British public didn't want to see black men dancing with white women'. And when in 1981 the Krankies, hired to host the children's series *Crackerjack*, asked why the audience seemed only to consist of 'upper-class, plummy kids,' they were told by another executive, Robin Nash, that they were recruited from a public school because: 'You need to have discipline in the studio.' Nash went on to become head of comedy at BBC television.

In the circumstances, it is less than surprising that television, though fascinated by alternative comedy, didn't know quite what to do with it. In terms of stand-up, the personal, quasi-confessional nature of the comedy club circuit struggled to find a sustainable television format, while the sitcom genre demanded a level of writing that – with the outstanding exception of *Blackadder* – was seldom in evidence, and it was not clear how mainstream television was going to accommodate the new generation of performers.

The most obvious talent to emerge from the early days of the Comedy Store, for example, was Alexei Sayle, a ferocious, fast-talking comedian who specialized in abusing the audience, but when he relocated to television in *Alexei Sayle's Stuff* (1988), he emerged as a far more traditional performer. His monologues to camera continued to sneer at middle-class lifestyles, but in the absence of a live audience lacked some of their bite, while the sketches were strongly reminiscent of *Monty Python's Flying Circus* with their surreal juxtapositions of high and low culture (Einstein writing scripts for George Formby, Giorgio de Chirico and William Shatner sharing screen space) and their parodies of television discussion shows. At its best, *Stuff* was amongst the funniest sketch shows ever, and did contain some of the most memorable gags of the decade: 'In the old days, people used to be named after what they made – like Carter if they made carts, Cooper if they made barrels, Thatcher if they made people sick'. But it felt as though it were falling between two stools: more conventional than Sayle's early fans would have wanted, without ever seeming likely to breakthrough to a mainstream audience as *Not the Nine O'Clock News* had.

In fact the format that would provide employment for stand-up comedians was being quietly established elsewhere, with the improvizational game show *Whose Line Is It Anyway?* (1988), hosted by Clive Anderson on Radio 4. When it transferred to television on Channel 4, it made stars of Paul Merton, Tony Slattery and others, and established that panel games were the ideal environment for new comedians to make their mark. A deluge of such series followed over the next couple of decades.

The other option was, ironically, a re-embrace of the comedy traditions that were proving so unfashionable amongst commissioning editors in television companies. Armed with the success of Loadsamoney, and his other character from *Saturday Live*, a Greek kebab-shop owner named Stavros, Harry Enfield and his co-writer Paul Whitehouse created in *Harry Enfield's Television Programme* (1990) and then *The Fast Show* (1994) a revival of the format purveyed in their childhood by Dick Emery: sketches featuring a recurring cast of characters, most of whom amounted to little more than a single catchphrase. In essence it was not unlike a less rude television version of *Viz* and indeed when Channel 4 screened an animated version of that comic's *Roger Mellie – The Man on the Telly* in 1991, it was Enfield who provided all the voices save for that of Mellie himself, who was voiced by Peter Cook.

Meanwhile Channel 4 was screening a version of *Vic Reeves Big Night Out* (1990), starring the double act of Vic Reeves and Bob Mortimer, which had been building a fanatical live following for some time. An anarchic parody of a variety show, complete with silly catchphrases, slapstick violence and terrible speciality acts, it looked like alternative comedy, but was equally indebted to the music hall tradition and even to the great humorist J.B. Morton (particularly in 'the twisted court of Judge Nutmeg'). It also showed the influence of Morecambe and Wise in the bickering relationship between the two stars, and of Les Dawson in its love of high sounding but meaningless language: 'A small eighteenth-century Shropshire village,' Reeves would begin portentously, bathed in a sinister green light as thunder crackled and leaves blew across the studio. 'The gables creak uneasily, spitting forth the venom of the judicial system, right bent on bias and dogmatic prejudice. Rickets, illegitimacy and scurvy is the peasants' lot, while the rich grow fat on sexual gratification, veal and arbitrary decisions. Reason leads to death, truth holds no sway. Magnets, currants and junket are held sacred.' The series was a magnificent folly that restored much of the subversive, amateurish chaos that British comedy had lost with the move to television in the 1950s.

In this new world, there were established comedians who were more than capable of holding their own. The *Sunday Times* television critic, Patrick Stoddart, was not alone in appreciating series by both Alexei Sayle and Les Dawson, while concluding: 'if you care for fat comics doing slightly off-centre stuff, I prefer Dawson's to Sayle's any day, if only because he has such immaculate timing.' The programme he was reviewing, however, *The Les Dawson Show*, was the last comedy series the star was to make. 'Everything must change,' shrugged Ian Tough, but there was something deeply regrettable about a system that left a great talent like Dawson sunk in misery. 'I began to feel that nobody wanted me any more,' he remembered. 'When the television was on, I'd moodily watch the new wave comedians and that would plunge me into a deeper hole of depression.' But he was resilient enough to survive such setbacks, and he returned to stand-up glory at the 1990 Royal Variety Show, where he found his old form, and even some of his old jokes from the early years of Thatcherism. This was Dawson at the Variety Club Awards in 1982: 'The recession hasn't affected me: I was a flop when there was a boom.' And this was him at the 1990 Royal Variety Show: 'It's been a disappointing year for many people. As we all know, this great nation of ours is going through a severe economic depression. Not that depression bothers me: I was a failure during the boom.' There was a sense that things were coming round full circle.

12
Media

British newspapers, by and large, are now more prejudiced
than they have ever been, more irresponsible in their use
of facts than they have ever been, and in some instances
more dishonest than they have ever been.
Roy Hattersley (1986)

What shall we do with Rupert Murdoch?
What shall we do with Rupert Murdoch?
What shall we do with Rupert Murdoch early in the
morning?
Burn, burn, burn the bastard . . .
Picket-line song (1986)

There is a new channel on television. It is called Channel
Four and it is for minorities, like intellectuals and people
that belong to jigsaw clubs. At last I have found my
spiritual viewing home.
Sue Townsend, *The Growing Pains of Adrian Mole* (1984)

'We are accustomed to suffering,' wrote the *Daily Mail*'s television
critic, Peter Paterson, in 1988, 'as television grabs more hours of
airtime without the talent to fill it.' It was a comment that might have been
seen as applying across the whole range of broadcast and print media in the
1980s, for there was an explosion of new outlets, facilitated by advances in
technology, changes in government policy and the breaking of union
practices, without there always being any readily discernible increase in
quality. When Margaret Thatcher came to power, there were just three
television channels available, broadcasting for around fourteen hours a day
each — by the time she left Downing Street, there were four terrestrial
channels, many more available via satellite, and the schedules had expanded
in both directions, backwards to take in breakfast, and forwards past the
traditional closedown around midnight. During the same period, dozens of

new magazine titles were launched, and a slew of national newspapers, both dailies and Sundays, appeared for the first time, some of which (the *Mail on Sunday*, the *Independent*, the *Sunday Sport*) were to find a market, while others (the *Post*, *Sunday Correspondent*, *News on Sunday*) fell by the wayside. It was, in short, an era of almost unprecedented expansion in the media.

In terms of newspapers, at least, the first mutterings of revolution were heard in 1978, just prior to Thatcher's election, when the *Daily* and *Sunday Express* were bought by Trafalgar House, with Victor Matthews becoming chairman of a group that was renamed Express Newspapers. Arguing that 'Fleet Street is not overmanned, it is underworked', Matthews identified spare capacity at the group's plant in Manchester, previously used only for printing the *Sunday Express*, and decided to utilize the machinery to produce the *Daily Star*, a tabloid that became the first national daily to be launched since the *Daily Mirror* back in 1903. It was seen from the outset as a plunge downmarket for Lord Beaverbrook's old company. 'No newspaper in history lost sales by projecting beautiful birds,' insisted founding editor, Derek Jameson. 'Sex sells – that goes for pictures and words. So the *Star* will have its daily quota. Bigger and better than anyone else.' The paper was so enthusiastic about salacious stories and topless pin-ups (they were known as Starbirds) that it rapidly acquired a reputation for making the *Sun* look classy; a sketch on *Not the Nine O'Clock News* saw a customer buying a copy and then hiding it inside an edition of *Men Only* to avoid embarrassment. It was controversial from the outset. The communist daily, the *Morning Star*, attempted to get a court injunction against the paper's use of the title, but the judge refused, commenting that 'only a moron in a hurry' would mistake the two products, while feminist campaigners in Manchester targeted the launch posters so that instead of reading A STAR IS BORN, they read A STAR IS PORN.

That reputation survived, though for a brief period in the early 1980s, under the editorship of Lloyd Turner, the paper made a bold effort to outflank the *Daily Mirror* on the left. Aiming itself at the young 'factory-gate reader', it provided not only serious coverage of unemployment and the plight of pensioners, but also wholehearted support for the Labour Party; in fact it was the only national paper to back Michael Foot in his bid for the party's leadership. The experiment wasn't to last, and management pressure brought about a volte-face in time for the 1983 election, when Turner wrote a front-page leader headlined SORRY MICHAEL, WE CAN'T VOTE FOR YOU, blaming the change of position on: 'The militants with hard eyes and closed minds who want to put a stranglehold on the party and shackle its leaders to a manifesto which owes more to Marx than the facts of modern life.' Thereafter the *Star* reverted to type.

Indeed in 1987, following its humiliation in the law courts at the hands of Jeffrey Archer, it went considerably further downmarket than any daily had yet managed, when it merged with the *Sunday Sport*. This latter had recently been launched by the pornography entrepreneur, David Sullivan, on a skeleton staff (there were reportedly just nine journalists employed) and blended a high nipple-count with the implausible sensationalism pioneered in America by the *National Enquirer* and the *Weekly World News*. The sport element of its title initially included the presence of a column by World Cup-winning captain, Bobby Moore, but it was the 'news' stories that gained the paper a cult following, with its love of UFOs, dead celebrities (from Elvis Presley to Adolf Hitler) and bizarre juxtapositions; headlines included MUM GIVES BIRTH TO AN 8lb TROUT, VIRGIN MARY BUILT OUR SHED and the inevitable LUCAN SPOTTED ON MISSING SHERGAR.

The marriage of the *Daily Star* and the *Sunday Sport* brought together the two crudest and least subtle national papers to create what veteran journalist Charles Wintour called 'the most vulgar and unpleasant daily tabloid in the country'. It should have been a perfect match but, as Derek Jameson pointed out: 'Tabloid readers are all for spicy pictures and stories, but they don't want tits leaping out at them from every page.' The new version of the *Star* provided precisely that, achieving a higher nipple-count than some top-shelf magazines and hitting an historic low with the debut of topless model Natalie Banus. Born Natalie Jay, she had studied at the Royal Ballet School until her breasts grew too large for a career in ballet to be a serious option, and she moved instead to the Italia Conte stage school. It was while she was a pupil there, at the age of 15 years and 11 months, that she first appeared in the paper, wearing just bikini bottoms, with her arms crossed her chest, accompanied by the salivating slogan: 'Just 30 days till Natalie goes topless'. And a topless photo was duly published on her sixteenth birthday, which meant, of course, that it was taken while she was still underage and was therefore in breach of the 1978 Protection of Children Act, though no prosecution was ever mounted. (Banus later starred in a short-lived West End play titled *Page 3*.) It was all too much for the delicate sensibilities of *Star* readers and the paper lost half a million daily sales, nearly half its circulation, in the space of six weeks. Journalists also made their excuses and left and, most worryingly of all, Tesco led a movement of big name advertisers withdrawing their business. The association with the *Sport* was promptly ended, but by then the damage had been done, and the *Star* never quite recovered from the shock.

Apart from the short-lived attempt to provide a populist voice for the left, and the even shorter-lived search to find a lowest common denominator, the *Star*'s major contribution to the culture of newspapers was the introduction early in the decade of bingo; millions of cards were distributed, numbers were published daily in the pages of the paper, and huge sums in prize money were offered in an effort to lure readers away from rival publications. There were two obvious stumbling-blocks to the concept: first, the danger that it would prove prohibitively expensive, which could be dealt with by ensuring that hardly any winning cards were ever printed, and second, that it fell foul of the Gaming and Lotteries Act, since it was purely a game of chance with no skill involved and was therefore illegal. Officially the defence against this was that checking numbers and crossing them off represented a basic skill, though in reality, as Jameson predicted to his legal advisers, it wouldn't ever prove to be an issue: 'Who the hell do you think is going to sue us for giving away money?' Sales of the *Star*, which had stabilized below a million, briefly rose to 1.9 million, mostly at the expense of the *Sun*, which responded by hitting back with its own game. And so were born the bingo wars, one of the defining features of Fleet Street in the 1980s, with other papers launching variations on the same basic theme, reaching something of a nadir when *The Times* created its own version, Portfolio, based on the stock market. 'Bloody hell, it was a knockout,' remembered Jameson. 'And it's worked wonders for every other paper that's applied it.'

The initial wave of competitions gradually died out, but there was a resurgence in 1984 when Robert Maxwell bought the *Daily Mirror* and offered a million-pound prize in a bid to reclaim circulation that had been lost to the *Star* and the *Sun*. The latter again retaliated with the same offer and won the race to produce a winner, with a Bristol man named David Parsons becoming the first person to win £1 million in a British competition. Amongst others who tried out the same strategy was the *Star*'s elder sibling, the *Daily Express*, which launched the Millionaires Club, discovering in the process a new flaw, as the then-managing director of Express Newspapers was later to admit: 'The odds were heavily stacked against there ever being a "reader millionaire", although eventually we did have a winner – a man of such a doubtful past and reputation that we had to whisk him quickly out of the public eye, and our pages, so we never gained the hoped-for publicity.'

The arrival of Maxwell in Fleet Street, buying Mirror Group Newspapers – as well as the *Daily* and *Sunday Mirror* it published the *People* and the Scottish titles, the *Daily Record* and the *Sunday Mail* – realized a long-held personal dream of owning his own national newspaper. It was confirmed in the early hours of Friday, 13 July, and the consequences were enough to make the most rational of his employees become superstitious; Geoffrey Goodman, industrial editor of the *Daily Mirror*, was to remark in retrospect: 'I was in the company of someone who was evil, possibly clinically insane.'

The full extent of Maxwell's megalomania was not immediately apparent, and – thanks to his fondness for litigation – much of his immorality was not to become known until after his death in 1991, but the self-obsession of the man was unmistakable. He announced that there were just two requirements for his editors: 'One: the papers must retain their broadly sympathetic approach to the labour movement. Two: the papers must and will have a Britain-first policy.' He omitted to mention a third requirement: that they should promote him and his works at all times, a development that came as no great surprise to those who had encountered him in previous incarnations. Back in 1965, when he was a newly elected Labour MP, Tony Benn had concluded: 'He really is rather a thrusting man who regards the House of Commons as a place where he can push himself.' Little had changed since. As a Jewish refugee from Czechoslovakia who had escaped the Nazis, and had built a publishing empire on the back of his own endeavours, Maxwell saw himself in the mould of the swashbuckling populist entrepreneur. His newly acquired papers dutifully purveyed this image. At his instigation, the *Daily Mirror* adopted the masthead slogan FORWARD WITH BRITAIN, but it might more honestly have said FORWARD WITH MAXWELL: it was Maxwell's face that was used to launch the *Mirror*'s bingo campaign, Maxwell who was seen to be seeking a resolution to the miners' strike, Maxwell who initiated what Bob Geldof called 'rather melodramatic "mercy flights" to Ethiopia' during the famine in that country. The relentless coverage made him a nationally recognized figure, but not someone who was ever embraced by the public in the way that, say, Richard Branson was; rather he came across as a rather bluff bully. Nor did the personalization of his papers do much for sales, which fell markedly while his hand was on the tiller.

While Maxwell was courting and creating publicity, his chief Fleet Street rival, Rupert Murdoch, was notably more reticent, seldom appearing in public or giving interviews, while contriving to remain considerably more influential in shaping British culture. He entered the 1980s as the proprietor of the *Sun* and the *News of the World*, respectively the biggest selling daily and Sunday papers. Of these, the *Sun* was probably the single most significant publication of the decade, not simply because of its sales, but because it reached such a vital section of the electorate – members of the working class who generally read no other papers and weren't compulsive viewers of current affairs television – and because it pushed such a strong political agenda, entirely supportive of Thatcherism and often a step or two ahead of what she was able to do at any given time; it was frequently the *Sun* that took arguments to the people, securing public support even before many members of the cabinet and the parliamentary party had been convinced.

It hadn't always been like this. The *Sun* had started as a Labour paper, chasing the readership of the *Daily Mirror*, but had switched horses in the late 1970s, around the same time that its circulation overtook that of its rival, and became unshakeably Conservative with the arrival of Kelvin MacKenzie as editor in 1981. MacKenzie, as a former grammar-school boy from south London, evidently regarded himself as Thatcherism made flesh and, despite the prime minister's popularity then being at a record low, never lost faith. The paper he produced was technically the best tabloid Britain had ever seen, funny, irreverent and capable of creating a real sense of community: if you were part of the *Sun*'s happy family of readers, there was a security in belonging to a world where common sense and prejudice merged into a single attribute, and where the enemy was clearly defined. The paper was also capable of taking a position on complex issues so succinctly that it was scarcely necessary to read beyond the headline; when the General Synod of the Church of England debated the church's attitude to homosexuality in the priesthood, the *Sun* summed up the conclusion with the headline PULPIT POOFS CAN STAY and there could be no mistaking the meaning, whether one agreed with it or not.

In a purely negative sense, as well, MacKenzie's *Sun* was one of the more creative newspapers in British press history, most notoriously when it published, under the banner of 'World Exclusive', an interview with Marcia McKay, widow of Sergeant Ian McKay VC, a hero of the Falklands War. It was in fact a complete fabrication, cobbled together from existing quotes and from the imagination of journalists in response to what was seen as an external threat: the *Daily Mirror* had secured a genuinely exclusive interview and the *Sun* had no intention of being left behind. The *Mirror* responded with an editorial headlined LIES, DAMNED LIES AND *SUN* EXCLUSIVES but it made little difference; the *Sun* went on to repeat the trick with a similarly stitched-together article when it failed to get an interview with Simon Weston, who had received terrible injuries as a Welsh Guardsman when the *Sir Galahad* was hit during the Falklands: 'He is so hideously scarred people turn their heads from him in horror in the street,' wrote the *Sun*, the paper that boasted of its support for 'our boys' during the war in the South Atlantic.

There was some doubt about the extent to which the *Sun*'s political positions made any impact on its readership; a survey after the 1983 general election found that only 63 per cent of readers thought the paper was pro-Tory, and many, when asked, insisted that they bought it for the sports pages alone. But even there, an impact was made, as a shop steward told Tony Benn in 1982: 'the men read the *Sun* from back to front, starting with the sports news, then page 3, then the front page, past eight pages of Tory propaganda,' he said. 'This is the real problem. The workforce is conservative, the *Sun* both shapes and reflects it.' The paper's pre-eminence meant that it attracted a great deal of criticism, perhaps the most insidiously effective of which came from the comedian Jasper Carrott who, in his Saturday night BBC1 show *Carrott's Lib* (1982), began to mine a new vein of jokes, mocking *Sun* readers for their stupidity (as in a *Sun Readers' Trivial Pursuit* with such questions as 'Did Britain's prime minister win the last election?' and 'Who wrote Joan Collins' autobiography?'), but the cultural tide remained with MacKenzie, and the sales and power of the paper remained high for most of the decade: it could almost lay claim to being the theoretical journal of Thatcherism.

To augment this mighty organ, in 1981 Murdoch's company, News International, added *The Times* and the *Sunday Times* to its stable. With the new titles, it could claim around 27 per cent of daily newspaper circulation in Britain (putting it second behind Mirror Group) and 31 per cent of the Sunday circulation. The size of this market share meant that once Murdoch's interest in the papers became known, there were calls for the takeover bid to be referred to the Monopolies Commission – Harold Wilson was amongst many Labour MPs signing a Commons motion demanding that the bid be 'stringently examined' – but the reality was that the most likely alternative to a Murdoch purchase was the closure of *The Times*, and the leaders of all the main print unions wrote to Michael Foot, asking him not to press for an enquiry since jobs were at stake. Even if he had, it was unlikely that a Conservative administration, so actively supported by the *Sun*, would have put obstacles in Murdoch's way, but the support of the unions – whose power in Fleet Street was unequalled anywhere in the private sector – undoubtedly made easier the government's decision to allow the takeover to proceed. Such support was less forthcoming in later years.

It was not, however, Murdoch who was to strike the first blow against the print unions. Instead it was the hitherto unknown Eddie Shah, a former floor manager on *Coronation Street* and now the owner of the Stockport-based *Messenger* group, a collection of six local newspapers.

The problems faced by the newspaper industry in the early 1980s were twofold: on the one hand, battles with unions were endemic (as witnessed most spectacularly by the dispute that had prevented *The Times* from publishing for nearly a year); and on the other, the technology that was used, compared with that available in other industrial countries, was primitive in the extreme, largely unchanged in nature since the nineteenth century. The two issues were, of course, interrelated; the hot metal process common to all newspapers was not only costly and cumbersome, but required a large number of men to operate it, and union leaders had no intention of allowing any changes that would reduce the workforce. Back in the 1950s, it was said, the *Daily Telegraph* had bought printing presses that, due to a failure to reach agreement with the unions, were still sitting at the paper, having never been used, when they were sold as scrap metal more than thirty years later. Similarly, when *The Times* returned to the news-stands in 1980, the unions had conceded the introduction of computers, but only if everything that journalists typed – still using manual type-writers – was then retyped by members of the National Graphical Association (NGA) in a practice known as 'double key stroking'; no journalist was allowed to touch a computer keyboard. There was an old joke asking how many people worked in Fleet Street producing the national newspapers, to which the answer was, 'About one in four'. In the face of this refusal to modernize, proprietors seemed powerless, largely because they were unwilling to cooperate with each other, as the sometime *Daily Telegraph* editor Bill Deedes admitted when discussing the Fleet Street unions: 'Over and again, they made ridiculous demands of one newspaper or another, witnessed the failure of the industry to close ranks, and scored. They had never lost. They believed they could never lose.'

Eddie Shah was the man who showed they could be beaten. In 1983, he introduced new technology at his Warrington print works and announced that he was unilaterally ending the closed shop that had hitherto been run by the NGA. The subsequent dispute lasted for seven months and became increasingly bitter, with Shah invoking the new union legislation and with thousands of demonstrators descending on Warrington to support the union. Prefiguring the miners' strike that was to come, a series of battles between pickets and police dominated the news agenda, reaching a climax in November with what was claimed to be an attack on a mass picket by equally large numbers of police, using riot-control equipment and tactics that had previously been seen as an instrument of last resort, but that were now seemingly used as the first option. Or, as seen from the other side of the fortified stockade, it was a life-threatening outbreak of mass violence.

'The mob's on the rampage,' Shah told Andrew Neil, editor of the *Sunday Times*, in a panicked telephone call. 'My men have their backs against the corrugated gates trying to keep the pickets from smashing them down. If they get in here we're going to be killed.'

Neil Kinnock, who had only just been elected Labour leader, was keen to distance himself from such scenes – 'I condemn without reservation the violence at Warrington whoever uses it,' he told the Commons – but the battle-lines were clearly drawn: the TUC in support of the NGA, and the government standing four-square with Shah. At its peak the dispute caused a complete shut-down of all national papers for four days, but union muscle proved unequal to the task of fighting on two fronts, both against the police and in the courts (the NGA lost an estimated two million pounds in fines and legal fees), and Shah emerged with a complete victory.

With his new-found freedom, and his new-found national prominence, Shah went on to launch a radically different national newspaper in 1986. *Today* was a middle-market daily that used computer photo-setting, allowing journalists to type their copy directly in, and that sent its pages – complete with colour photographs (of an admittedly rudimentary nature) – by satellite to printing plants around the country. He also negotiated a single-union, no-strike agreement with the paper's production staff, who were members not of any established print union but of the EETPU, the electricians' union led by Eric Hammond. This was to be the model for the future, but by the time of the first issue, media and political attention had moved onwards from Warrington to Wapping in east London, where, inspired by Shah, Murdoch was staging his own showdown with the unions.

Wapping was the location of a site bought by News International in 1979, and in 1985 the company opened discussions with the unions about starting production there. There was no great urgency to the negotiations and no obvious prospect of success, for the gap between the employers' proposals (no closed shops, new technology, no right to strike) and those of the unions (jobs for life on existing terms) never looked likely to be bridged. Nor was there any desire so to do; the News International management was intent on moving its four titles into the plant and had no wish to take the printers with them, while an official from the SOGAT union made clear their position on Wapping: 'When will you get it through your thick heads, we will never let you use it? You may as well put a match to it – or we'll do it for you.'

As with the recently ended miners' strike, the groundwork and the strategic planning had been on one side only, for even while negotiations were dragging on in a desultory way, preparations were being made for the production and distribution of all the papers at Wapping. As the *Financial Times* put it, Murdoch had calculated his moves 'coldly and cynically, secretly and deviously, anticipating successfully the other actors in the drama'. In conditions of great secrecy, the building was being fitted out (the story was put about that it was to produce a new 24-hour paper, the *London Post*, which was nominally the subject of the negotiations), a deal was being struck with the EEPTU for a new workforce, and a contract was being signed with the haulage company TNT to distribute the copies by road, thus avoiding the likelihood of rail unions refusing to transport them. All that was needed was an excuse to trigger the move, a single false step by the printers. 'He wants them to go on strike at a moment which will suit him,' noted Woodrow Wyatt in January 1986, after talking with his friend, Rupert Murdoch. 'If they did he can sack everyone and print with five hundred and twelve people he has lined up, who have already learned to work the presses at Tower Hamlets. That would be instead of the four to five thousand currently employed.' So bullish and aggressive did the News International attitude become during this protracted phoney war that even Andrew Neil, one of Murdoch's most supportive employees, worried about the new era: 'Sometimes I think we're becoming far too callous in our desire to clean this place out,' he noted.

Later that January the unions duly obliged by calling a strike over Murdoch's intransigence in protest at the hypothetical *London Post*, and all members were promptly served with redundancy notices. At the same time *The Times*, the *Sunday Times*, the *Sun* and the *News of the World* were relocated to the new plant and the Wapping dispute (it was not technically a strike, since the union members were no longer employed) began. It was to last as long as had the miners' strike two years earlier.

The move was made possible by the journalists on the four titles, the vast majority of whom had no forewarning of its happening, but accepted it nonetheless. The National Union of Journalists (NUJ) instructed its members not to go, insisting they remain in solidarity with the print-workers, but there was precious little solidarity to be found. As recently as 1984, journalists on the *Sun* had gone on strike but, in the absence of any support from the printers, had been unable to stop production of the paper; they had lost their case then and saw no reason now to extend a fraternal hand. Nor did the pay differentials engender any thoughts of standing shoulder-to-shoulder: the average salary for production workers in Fleet Street was at the time £18,000, while the basic journalist's salary on *The Times* was £15,000. In such circumstances it was perhaps predictable that nearly 95 per cent of the 700 or so journalists employed by News International were ultimately prepared to move to Wapping. At a meeting of the NUJ chapel at the *Sun*, the vote was one hundred in favour of making the move, with just eight against.

And, as was only to be expected, the union movement as a whole offered no serious support either; if it had been unwilling and unable to fall in behind the NUM, then it was not going to mobilize secondary action on behalf of the printers. There was also the bald fact that the papers were being produced by union members (albeit from the EEPTU, regarded as pariahs by much of the union bureaucracy) and distributed by lorries driven by members of the Transport and General Workers Union. More surprising was the lack of solidarity from within the print unions themselves; the *Sunday Times* colour supplement was produced in Watford by SOGAT members, who didn't stop work, while NGA members in Northampton continued to print the related titles, the *Times Literary Supplement* and the *Times Education Supplement*. And when, nearly a year into the dispute, the SOGAT executive proposed a fifty-eight pence a week levy on all its members to assist those who were still out of work and whose unemployment benefit was about to end, the membership voted against the measure.

Beyond the unions, the wider public too failed to respond to the printers' cause, despite SOGAT spending an estimated £400,000 on publicity. From a reader's point of view, Wapping was a step forward: the papers continued to appear and it soon became clear that there was a marked improvement — they were bigger, better printed, more reliable. And if they were being produced by a much smaller workforce, then that only seemed to confirm the widespread stories of absurd over-manning in Fleet Street. So while the printers did enjoy the support of some on the left, no network emerged equivalent to that which had sustained the miners; there simply wasn't the same sympathy for those seen as privileged, well-paid workers in London. The TUC and the Labour Party officially boycotted all News International titles, so that their journalists were barred from Neil Kinnock's press conferences, while various local authorities withdrew advertising support, and in some cases stopped buying the papers for their public libraries (a move that was subsequently ruled unlawful), but it is doubtful that Murdoch lost much sleep over such tactics.

Those who did support the sacked printers, however, were whole-hearted in their commitment and, for the year that the dispute lasted, the streets of Wapping became the venue for a mass rally every Saturday evening, as thousands of pickets attempted to prevent the lorries laden with copies of the *News of the World* and the *Sunday Times* from leaving the plant. They were unsuccessful on every occasion – not a single day's production was lost – but the result was, more often than not, a series of violent running battles with the police, reminiscent of the miners' strike. 'It was horrific,' wrote Tony Benn in his diary after seeing the police charge the lines of demonstrators one Saturday night in May 1986. 'I couldn't believe it – the absolute horror of standing in the middle of the night in the middle of London, seeing the police flailing about with their truncheons at people who a moment earlier had been standing talking and knowing that it was authorized, planned. Everyone was involved, from people in their sixties to young children.' For those inside what became known as Fortress Wapping, those Saturday nights were no less traumatic. Shielded by lines of police and security guards, behind barbed-wire-clad walls and rolls of razor wire, the staff were always aware of the emergency tunnels that connected the buildings to provide an escape route if the demonstrators broke into the plant. Nor was the daily experience of going to work through ranks of pickets screaming abuse any more welcome than it had been for the working miners during the NUM strike.

The first anniversary of the dispute, in January 1987, saw the biggest demonstration of all, with 13,000 pickets involved in a confrontation that left 168 police officers injured and one picket, Michael Delaney, dead after being run over by a TNT lorry. (The inquest jury found that he had been unlawfully killed, though this verdict was overturned on appeal.) It was the last such protest. The unions called off the dispute in the face of dwindling funds – SOGAT had used up half its reserves during the dispute, and still had fines to come – and of the hopelessness of the cause, for it was surely inconceivable that Murdoch was going to back down.

The consequences of the Wapping dispute were far-reaching. This was the last great struggle of the old industrial unions; the miners, the Praetorian Guard of organized labour, had already been defeated, now so too were the printers, the most cosseted and strike-prone workforce in private industry. Thereafter the centre of balance of the union movement shifted away from industry and towards the state service sector. Again the government had sided solidly with the employers, providing vocal support and allowing a sympathetic attitude by the police and the legal system; Thatcher had given Murdoch a personal assurance, according to Andrew Neil, 'that enough police would be available to allow us to go about our lawful business'.

Such a supportive stance was entirely appropriate for a government that had long deplored the mob rule of mass-pickets and insisted upon the rule of law, but there was also an element of reciprocation for the unswerving loyalty displayed by Fleet Street to the Conservative cause. The gratitude didn't stop there, for a notable feature of the Thatcher years was the heaping of honours upon practising journalists of the right persuasion: knighthoods for editors Larry Lamb (of the *Sun*), John Junor (*Sunday Express*), David English (*Daily Mail*) and Nicholas Lloyd (*Daily Express*), as well as for favoured television interviewers Robin Day and Alastair Burnet, and a peerage for *News of the World* columnist Woodrow Wyatt. These honours were occasionally mocked by commentators, were sometimes even the subject of fierce criticism, but they were accepted with due reverence by their recipients. 'I would remind you,' Lloyd was reported to have snapped disdainfully at a colleague, 'that I was knighted by Margaret Thatcher for my services to journalism.' Notable exceptions to the ranks of those who felt the touch of the queen's sword on their shoulders were Rupert Murdoch, an avowed republican, and Kelvin MacKenzie, relentless in his pursuit of royal stories, neither of whom were much concerned with receiving honours (though Murdoch was later to accept a knighthood from the Pope).

In the wake of Warrington and Wapping, rival newspaper proprietors, shocked into action at seeing the power of the print unions finally broken, hurriedly began their own process of modernization. An entire layer of the newspaper workforce disappeared as hot metal yielded to computers, and the good times began in earnest for the industry. This was the era of the Lawson boom, and greater affluence, combined with the increased capacity provided by the new technology, sent sales soaring upwards. There was a further boost when a European Commission ruling ended the duopoly of television listings that had previously been enjoyed by the *Radio Times* (which provided a week's worth of BBC schedules) and the *TV Times* (which did the same for ITV and Channel 4); all other publications had been prevented from listing more than 24 hours of television programmes, or 48 hours at the weekend. Once that restriction had been swept aside at the end of the decade, the way was open for newspapers to produce weekly supplements covering all channels and for other magazines to enter the field, including *What's on TV* and *TV Quick*.

The latter was a German-owned concern, an indication of another trend in the late 1980s: the arrival of foreign publishers in the magazine market, particularly with women's magazines. Starting in 1986 with *Prima* (published by the Bertelsmann Group, the biggest media empire in the world), this saw the debuts over the next two years of *Best*, *More*, *Hello!*, *Marie Claire*, *New Woman*, *Riva* and *Bella*, though their appearance did not necessarily mean the end of the traditional titles, for *Woman*, *Woman's Own*, *Ideal Home* and *Good Housekeeping* all put on sales in the same period. New newspapers were also forthcoming, though the most intriguing possibility never materialized; during the course of the Wapping dispute, Murdoch offered the unions, in exchange for a settlement, the printing plant that had formerly produced *The Times* and the *Sunday Times*, together with the building in which it was housed, suggesting that they set up their own newspaper, to employ the printers that had been sacked – the offer was rejected. Meanwhile the existing titles grew in size, particularly at weekends, when first Sunday and then Saturday papers sprouted new sections on an almost weekly basis.

Others too were affected by Wapping. The NUJ was hit almost as hard as were the print unions, losing recognition at many of the national titles; all newspaper distribution was moved from rail to road; and the convivial drinking culture of the old Fleet Street began to recede into mythology, as other publishers also withdrew from the area. The biggest beneficiary, though, was News International itself: the job cuts and the increased production at the new plant saved the company a reported £65 million a year, making possible an expansion into television in Britain and America.

This move into other media had long been an ambition of Rupert Murdoch. Some years earlier Bruce Matthews, one of the most senior figures in News International, had asked Jeremy Isaacs about satellite television. When Isaacs replied that he didn't know anything about it, but 'surely you have expert analysts who can forecast the viability of that sort of massive business venture,' Matthews revealed the secret of Murdoch's success: 'It's not like that here. When Rupert says "go", we go.' It was to be some time before that particular jump was made, but British television was already seeing a major transformation with the launch in 1982 of Channel 4, under the stewardship of Isaacs himself.

The idea of a fourth television channel had been around since the Pilkington Committee on Broadcasting had reported in 1962, and been broadly accepted by both major parties during the 1970s, though its form was still in dispute right up to the Act that brought it into being in 1982. Intended as a public service broadcaster to supplement the work of the BBC, Channel 4 was placed in the novel position of commissioning but not making programmes, and was charged by the government with appealing 'to tastes and interests not generally catered for', while being 'experimental and innovative'. Financially too it was in a strange place, given arms-length funding by the ITV companies, who then sold the advertising on the new channel as a way of recouping its investment. Unfortunately, a dispute with the actors' union Equity over repeat fees meant that at the beginning there weren't enough adverts to fill the breaks, since only those commercials with no actors in them could be broadcast. The result was a series of what looked like home movies, starring cheerful, awkward businessmen who were spectacularly ill-suited to the small screen: characters such as Joe Williams, boss of OTV in Hackney, who told us what wonderful value his ex-rental television sets were, somewhat in the tradition of Bernard Matthews, the Norfolk farmer who had begun his long-running claims to produce 'bootiful' turkey products the previous year. There was a certain pleasure to be derived from the lowest budget, least subtle adverts ever screened appearing on what was supposed to be the sophisticated, intelligent new medium of Channel 4, but even so these emergency plugs weren't sufficient and it became common to see a minute or two of the station logo accompanied by the promise 'Next programme follows shortly . . .'

The programmes that did appear soon revealed a conflict of cultures in the establishment. Isaacs, as an ex-BBC man and a member of the north London media elite, came with an awareness of a pluralist, multi-cultural Britain, self-evidently at odds with the values of the Conservative government that had brought the channel into being. 'Should black Britons, should the young, should feminists, should homosexuals see themselves, canvass their ideas, on television?' asked Isaacs rhetorically in 1983. 'I see no reason why not. They are of this society, not outside it.' But, as Norman Tebbit pointed out to him: 'You've got it all wrong, you know, doing all those programmes for homosexuals and such. Parliament never meant that sort of thing. The different interests you are supposed to cater for are not like that at all. Golf and sailing and fishing. Hobbies. That's what we intended.' Even before the station was launched, *The Times* was reporting that 'the channel is just the sort of thing to inflame that school of opinion, so strong in the upper echelons of the Conservative Party, which believes that the left is in control of the nation's television'. In fact, much like the BBC, the new station was more liberal than it was hard left: there was no one from the labour movement on the board of Channel 4, though there were some Conservatives, while the SDP was over-represented in the senior management with founding chairman Edmund Dell, deputy chairman Richard Attenborough and board member Anne Sofer. (George Thomson, the chair of the IBA, was also an SDP member.)

Similarly, the programming was by no means as radical as Channel 4's opponents liked to claim; both the BBC and ITV had gay magazine programmes (*Coming Out* and *Gay Life* respectively) a decade before Channel 4 started *Out on Tuesday* in 1990. It did, however, have *Years Ahead*, a magazine series for the over-50s presented by former newsreader Robert Dougall, and *Broadside*, a current affairs show made by women, as well as two of the best talk-shows ever seen on British television: *Opinions*, which allowed a single figure to deliver a half-hour, straight-to-camera talk, and *After Dark*, a discussion programme that started at midnight and lasted until the participants were too exhausted to continue. The latter included a post-election show in June 1987 titled 'Is Britain Working?', on which the Conservative MP Teresa Gorman told the leftist pop singer Billy Bragg: 'You and your kind are finished. We are the future now.' She then stormed off the set, leaving Bragg to express the hope that 'Now we'll have a civilized discussion.' In its own way, it was a perfect encapsulation of the Tory mood of the time: triumphalism that refused to allow dissident opinion. The show was most celebrated, however, for a drunken appearance by the incident-prone Oliver Reed in 1991, in which he not only rambled incoherently during everyone else's contributions, but also at one point found himself lying on top of feminist writer Kate Millett; the show was taken off air for twenty minutes following an angry phone call claiming to be from the IBA, before it was ascertained that the call was a hoax and broadcasting was resumed, with Reed still drinking happily. The critic Victor Lewis-Smith later claimed to have been the perpetrator of the hoax.

The station also created, through Film on Four, some of the most memorable British movies of the decade (*The Draughtsman's Contract*, *Wish You Were Here*, *A Room with a View*), made on shoestring budgets and therefore often able to explore avenues that would otherwise have been inaccessible: 'You can't go to a big film company and say, "I want to make a film about a gay Pakistani who runs a launderette",' commented Hanif Kureishi, writer of *My Beautiful Launderette*. 'They'd tell you to get lost.' But despite these contributions, Channel 4 to a large extent made its reputation with repeats and imports, where its alchemical appeal to youth was capable of turning very base metal into viewing gold – a series like *The Gong Show*, an American parody of talent shows, would have struggled to get an airing, let alone a following, on any other British channel.

In all this, Channel 4 did bring a voice and a style that was quite distinct from the existing stations, which were increasingly reliant on game shows, one of the great successes of the decade, since they represented a cheap way of filling the ever-expanding schedules. Such programmes had been part of British television from the 1950s onwards, but it was the 1980s that turned out to be their moment in the sun. It was calculated that the budget of a game show worked out at just a third of the cost-per-minute of a sitcom, let alone a serious drama, and the prizes added little to the expense, thanks to IBA regulations: in 1988, for example, the IBA restricted the value of prizes on a series to £1,750 per show, averaged over four shows, so that if a small car (worth around £4,500) was given away in one episode, it was virtually certain that contestants on the next three weeks' programmes stood little chance of winning anything very much at all.

The game show boom began in 1980 with Bruce Forsyth's *Play Your Cards Right* and Bob Monkhouse's *Family Fortunes*. Thereafter the floodgates opened to include, amongst many others, *Blockbusters* with Bob Holness, *Bob's Full House* with Bob Monkhouse, *Bullseye* with Jim Bowen, *Catchphrase* with Roy Walker, *Fifteen to One* with William G. Stewart, *The Price is Right* with Leslie Crowther, *Strike It Lucky* with Michael Barrymore, *Telly Addicts* with Noel Edmonds, *3-2-1* with Ted Rogers, and *Wheel of Fortune* with Nicky Campbell. Then there were the hosts who specialized in the genre: Jimmy Tarbuck with *Winner Takes All* and *Tarby's Frame Game*, Paul Daniels with *Every Second Counts* and *Odd One Out*, Derek Hobson with *Jeopardy!* and *That's My Dog*, Tom O'Connor with *Gambit* and *Name That Tune*. Most of the hosts were established comedians, and so enthusiastic were schedulers about the concept that even Bernard Manning got a game show: *Under Manning* was based on the American hit *You Bet Your Life*, which had been hosted by Groucho Marx, and lasted for one series in the summer of 1981. Channel 4 also had game shows, of course, indeed its first ever programme (and its longest lived) was *Countdown*, but therein lay the difference; despite the inane puns of presenter Richard Whiteley, *Countdown* was at heart an intelligent word game. The channel's other great contribution was *Sticky Moments*, a comedy vehicle for Julian Clary in which he relentlessly mocked every aspect of the genre.

All of these drew their competitors from the general public, establishing an interim stage before the advent of reality television in the 1990s. Similarly the game shows that relied upon celebrities tended to feature the lower-budget end of minor stardom, just as reality television was later to do; *Blankety Blank* and *Punchlines* were both influenced by the earlier *Celebrity Squares*, pitching members of the public against each other with the help of a panel of so-called personalities, many of whom were more famous for appearing on these shows than for anything else they'd ever done. The nature of their stardom was summed up by journalist Tom Hibbert, who had made a career from exposing the vacuity and vanity of minor media figures, as he looked back on the era from the vantage point of the 1990s: 'In 1986 Britain was awash with celebrities like never before, under threat from the famous only famous for being famous, the famously awful, turning the soul of a once-brave country to mush.' Despite the best endeavours of Channel 4, the future for British television was not noticeably bright.

To no one's great surprise, when satellite television finally did arrive, with Rupert Murdoch's Sky in 1989 and British Satellite Broadcasting (BSB) the following year, it relied heavily on such cut-price celebrities. BSB signed up actor Christopher Biggins, journalist Nina Myskow and the former host of *Sale of the Century*, Nicholas Parsons, while Sky had Keith Chegwin from *Cheggers Plays Pop*, ex-*Daily Star* editor Derek Jameson and Frank Bough, last seen hosting the BBC's *Breakfast Time* (his colleague from that show, Selina Scott, was over on BSB). Little of this was very inspiring or even interesting, and the initial ratings demonstrated as much, though Andrew Neil, who had left the *Sunday Times* to become chairman of Sky, professed himself perfectly relaxed about the miniscule audiences, knowing how poor the programming was: 'There were some nights when I was perfectly happy that no one was watching,' he remarked.

Perhaps the only ones watching were the satirists. The BBC comedy series *KYTV* (1989) was based entirely on parodying a satellite broadcaster – 'the television of the future' – with promised programme highlights including *I Love Lucy*, *The Simon Dee Show* and episode one of *Crossroads*. *KYTV* also ridiculed satellite's sports coverage, but although it got the hyperbolic tone absolutely right (a nondescript boxing match is promoted under the slogan: 'Last time it was war, this time it's the Apocalypse'), its suggestions that coverage would include dominoes, the sack race and caravanning was to prove wide of the mark. In a move that presaged the future of football, BSB had already secured rights to screen FA Cup ties on Saturday evenings, to the great disquiet of fans, who didn't warm to the idea of matches being rescheduled to suit the convenience of broadcasters.

The start-up costs of these services were enormous, and well in excess of the revenue they were capable of generating in the early years. Sky was said to have cost £320 million to get up and running, and then proceeded to lose £2 million a week, but it was heavily subsidized by other parts of the Murdoch empire, particularly the *Sun*, which was making £1 million profit a week. BSB, on the other hand, had no such resources to fall back upon and could only hope to live long enough to reach its target of attracting three million subscribers by 1993, that being the level at which it would break even. In the event it didn't get anything like that amount of time, lasting little more than a year. Within a few weeks of BSB's launch, *Q* magazine was warning that the market was unlikely to sustain both it and Sky: 'It seems increasingly likely that the high seas of satellite TV may not prove wide enough for the two of them.' In November 1990 the two companies officially merged to become BSkyB, though no one was in any real doubt that it was effectively a takeover by Sky. 'It's smart to be square,' the BSB adverts had proclaimed, in reference to its distinctively shaped satellite dishes known as squarials, but few had been convinced.

What Sky was ultimately targeting was an audience of men in their forties in social groups C and D, hence its move into sport and particularly into football in the next decade. Absent from its schedules, therefore, was the greatest success story of all on television in the late 1980s: the soap opera. Soaps had been dominated by ITV for years – its first ever programme was *Round at the Redways*, starring real-life married couple Harry Greene and Marjie Lawrence – and had in recent times centred on the triumvirate of *Coronation Street*, *Crossroads* and *Emmerdale Farm*. Their appeal spread across social and age groups and had different emphases in different shows: *Emmerdale Farm*, for example, was aimed at a middle-aged female audience and thus celebrated its fifteenth birthday in 1987 with a book that included 'country recipes, knitting patterns, offers', while in the annual *NME* readers' poll the best TV show category was won in 1981 by *Coronation Street*, reflecting the younger cult appeal that helped boost that show's ratings (the winners on either side were *Not the Nine O'Clock News* and *The Young Ones*). The youth market, however, was shortly to transfer allegiance to Channel 4's *Brookside*, attracted by the younger cast and by its creator Phil Redmond, a familiar name to graduates of *Grange Hill*. For all its technical and storyline innovations, *Brookside*'s most radical departure in British soap history may well have been the failure to include a pub as a central focus, a development that might have been welcomed by those in the ranks of the nagocracy, had they not been so concerned by the amount of swearing going on. In the absence of a pub, there seemed to be a great many letters that required posting, in order to facilitate interaction between characters at the postbox.

Despite their undoubted popularity, however, soaps were considered somewhat tawdry affairs, beneath the notice of critics and a poor substitute for proper drama. That was until 1983. In that year a *Coronation Street* storyline saw Deirdre Barlow (Anne Kirkbride) having an affair with businessman Mike Baldwin (Johnny Briggs) and finding herself torn between him and her worthy, if dull husband, Ken (William Roache). In the context of the programme, it was a shock development, for Ken and Deirdre had been married to everyone's satisfaction just two years earlier – their wedding had conveniently coincided with that of Prince Charles and Diana Spencer – but even so, the level of media coverage was startling. For the first time a soap storyline became front-page news in its own right, and it wasn't only the tabloids who followed the twists and turns with eager enthusiasm; even *The Times* saw fit to announce in its news pages that

Deirdre had chosen to 'stay with Ken, her dependable husband, after all'. A line between fiction and reality had been crossed, setting the tone for the remainder of the century and beyond.

Because Ken and Deirdre were but the warm-up act. In 1985 the BBC launched *EastEnders*, its first serious attempt to challenge the pre-eminence of *Coronation Street* and the soap wars began in earnest. The debut episode was accompanied by sufficient hype to attract seventeen million curious viewers, but the early figures were not sustained and the audience fell as low as five million, before it started to climb back. Two factors contributed to its recovery: first, its transmission time was changed, to duck out of a head-to-head battle with *Emmerdale Farm* that it was regularly losing, and second, it developed sensationalist storylines that were a gift for the tabloids. Press interest had already been sparked with the revelation that Leslie Grantham, who played pub landlord 'Dirty' Den Watts, had earlier served a jail sentence for murder, but soon it was not only the actors but also the melodramatic plots that were turning up in the news pages.

Boosted by a Sunday afternoon omnibus programme (an idea taken from *Brookside*), *EastEnders* became the biggest show in the country: in a 39-month period from October 1985 it spent 167 weeks at No. 1 in the charts, interrupted on only two occasions, once by *Coronation Street* and once by *Bread*. This remarkable dominance of the nation's viewing culminated in the Christmas Day episodes of 1986, when Den served his wife Angie (Anita Dobson) with divorce papers, reaching a record audience of 30 million. It also created a new world in which soaps ruled the schedules and the ratings as never before: the last four years of the 1980s saw just two weeks when a soap didn't come out on top of the viewing charts (apart from *Bread* the other exception was a Christmas screening of Paul Hogan's film *Crocodile Dundee*); the comparable period a decade earlier had seen more than fifty non-soaps reach No. 1, including sitcoms, variety shows, football finals, movies, even *News at Ten*. The public appetite for soaps was such that *Coronation Street* added a third weekly episode in 1989, an example followed the next year by *Brookside*, while *EastEnders* was so big that even non-events were breathlessly reported by the media – EXCLUSIVE: DIRTY DEN TO STAY IN *EASTENDERS*, revealed a *Daily Mirror* front-page story.

There were many who disapproved of *EastEnders*, some regretting the absence of the humour that had long been the human heart of *Coronation Street*, others taking the high moral tone of Mary Whitehouse: 'Its verbal aggression and its atmosphere of physical violence, its homosexuality, its blackmailing pimp and its prostitute, its lies and deceit and its bad language, cannot go unchallenged,' she thundered. And indeed it was a much more aggressive and violent serial than its predecessors, even finding room for Nick Cotton, a heroin-addicted murderer and the first long-running character in a British soap who could be considered overtly, irredeemably evil. (The first episode opened with the dead body of one of his victims.) Or, alternatively, his viciousness was a symptom of the times. 'I feel sorry for him,' commented John Altman, the actor who played Cotton; 'he's a victim of Britain in the eighties. He looked for work, couldn't find it and turned to drugs and blackmail.' But crucially, despite the moral reservations of some, the *Sun* embraced the show with gusto, seeing it as a powerful weapon in their circulation battles, as the paper's chroniclers Peter Chippindale and Chris Horrie pointed out: 'The *Street*, with its ageing audience, had always been essentially the newspaper property of the *Mirror*. But *EastEnders* was young, southern and rough – just like the *Sun*.'

The supremacy of the soap opera as an art-form was such that it spread into advertising, which began to create its own mini-soaps for television. The first was a series of Renault adverts in 1984 starring Malcolm Stoddard as an executive named David, telling his wife Joanne (Rosalyn Landor) that he was going to start his own company. Others followed and in 1988 came the most successful of all, the Gold Blend series with Anthony Head and Sharon Maughan as next-door neighbours flirting through the metaphor of instant coffee. This saga was so long-running – and allegedly so popular – that a compilation video was released in 1993, along with a novelization, *Love Over Gold*, written by Susan Moody under the pseudonym Susannah James ('The untold story of TV's Greatest Romance,' promised the cover). It wasn't the first such book to come out of advertising. *You Got an Ology?* in 1990 was based on the British Telecom adverts starring Maureen Lipman as a Jewish mother named Beattie, fussing over her grown-up son Melvyn (Linal Haft), while in 1991 a book titled *Fly-Fishing* was published under the pseudonym J.R. Hartley, the name of the character portrayed by Norman Lumsden in a Yellow Pages advert dating back to 1983.

Meanwhile records by stars of soap operas, including Anita Dobson and Nick Berry of *EastEnders*, were becoming commonplace in the singles charts, while the appearance of the model Nick Kamen stripping down to his boxer shorts in a 1985 Levi's 501 advert was sufficient to launch him on a pop career. The same advert pushed Marvin Gaye's 'I Heard It Through the Grapevine' back into the top ten, just one example of a trend for retro-soundtracks on television commercials that also produced reissued hits for Nina Simone, Sam Cooke and Ben E. King amongst many others. In 1991 the Clash, having never previously reached the top ten singles chart in Britain (largely because of their refusal to appear on *Top of the Pops*) found themselves with a posthumous No. 1 in 'Should I Stay or Should I Go?' after it too featured on a Levi's advert.

By the end of the decade, the boundaries between the different branches of the media had blurred so much that it was hard to tell what was fact or fantasy. The word 'advertorial' was coined to denote newspaper pieces that were adverts semi-disguised as normal reporting, but the real confusion came in the news pages, where the story of the Gold Blend couple jostled for space with PR froth about the alleged antics of actors in *EastEnders* and with entirely speculative stories about the royal family, these normally requiring the publication of yet another photograph of Princess Diana, a soap fan who was herself fast coming to resemble a character in a soap opera. By contrast, the decline of the unions meant that industrial reporting dwindled while, in the absence of serious parliamentary opposition to the government, politics itself seemed at times to take on the nature of a soap. Amongst the recurring Westminster plotlines was the question of who was Margaret Thatcher's chosen favourite as her younger leading man, the chosen successor should she ever leave Downing Street; the fluctuations in fortunes of Cecil Parkinson, Norman Tebbit, John Moore, Kenneth Baker and others were followed in much the same manner as the ups and downs of 'Dirty' Den's fictional love-life. The tabloids led the way, but the middle-market papers tended to veer in the same direction, and even the broadsheets were not far behind, though the *Independent* did constitute an honourable exception – on its launch in 1986 it announced that it would not be making space available for 'news' of the royal family and admirably stuck with its decision.

To some degree, any confusions that did arise were a reflection of the multi-media ambitions of newspaper proprietors, as seen in News International's case with the number of plugs for Sky Television that appeared in its newspapers, though it was far from alone. The consortium behind BSB had similarly had issues of cross-ownership, including not only the Granada and Anglia television companies, but also Virgin, Amstrad and Pearson, owner of the *Financial Times*. In the media, as elsewhere, the buzzword of the time was 'synergy', the belief that operating in several different fields made a company more productive. Or as an advert for Charterhouse Bank put it: $2 + 2 = 5$.

The commercial advantages of having multiple divisions were seen when, for example, Virgin realized that the budget for its film of *1984* was soaring over budget and decided, against the wishes of the director Michael Radford, to remove the soundtrack that had been written by, as Richard Branson put it in his autobiography, 'an unknown composer called

Dominic Muldownie [*sic*]', in an attempt 'to recoup some of the disastrous overspend'. In fact, Muldowny was a respected and highly regarded young composer in his field, but his name carried little weight in the marketplace compared to that of the Eurythmics, the band whose music appeared in his place and whose soundtrack album was modestly successful, with the single 'Sexcrime' reaching the top five; the movie might not have benefited from the change but it was a financially sound decision. Similarly there was a logic when Andrew Lloyd-Webber's Really Useful Group branched out in 1983 from producing his musicals to buying West End theatres, in which those shows could be staged, though a subsequent venture into publishing – it bought, and later sold, Aurum, the publishers of this book – was less obvious.

Even some of the longest established names in retail saw a need to expand the range of goods they stocked in the name of diversification, so that Boots the Chemist and W.H. Smith's departed from their core market to become almost general stores; 'one no longer knows what sort of a shop they are,' despaired commentator Christopher Booker. Smith's drew attention to this development with the slogan 'Smith's for books and a whole lot more', while the Victoria and Albert Museum advertised itself as 'an ace caff with quite a nice museum attached', a campaign that attracted charges of crass commercialism, though it had echoes of the original appeal of the institution: in the nineteenth century the front part of the museum had been a café, intended to attract those coming after work.

There were examples too within the broadcast media of branching into new areas, as when Radio 1 decided to venture into comedy with the employment of Victor Lewis-Smith and with *The Mary Whitehouse Experience*. The intention was evidently to reclaim a youthful audience for a station that was looking cosily middle-aged – as mocked by Harry Enfield and Paul Whitehouse's superannuated DJs Smashie and Nicey – though it was not until the following decade, with the arrival of Matthew Bannister as controller of Radio 1, that this ambition was fully pursued, with rigorous across-the-board reforms. In the late 1980s, however, Bannister was busily engaged in reinventing Radio London, the local BBC station for the capital, to become GLR (Greater London Radio), 'a hip new station for sophisticated Londoners in the 25-45 demographic', in the words of its lunchtime presenter, Johnnie Walker. Launched in 1988, GLR only lasted for twelve years, but it proved highly influential, giving a career boost to a range of talent including Danny Baker, Chris Morris and Chris Evans, and setting out an alternative to the pop stations then in existence. Its targeting of very specific audiences was also to become the model for radio at a time of expansion in the industry, a trend that became ever more apparent after the 1990 launch of the independent station Jazz FM. (It was, claimed John Prescott, the only company in which he ever held shares.)

While there were always some who deplored the expansions of business into unrelated areas, real concern was reserved for the concentration of media power in the hands of individual companies, particularly when they were based outside the country. In 1985 Rupert Murdoch took on American nationality, since only US citizens were legally able to buy television stations there, and the following year Neil Kinnock expressed a desire to introduce equivalent legislation in Britain: 'I must say that it is time for us to think seriously about establishing similar citizenship conditions, not only because of the nationality-swapping history of Mr Murdoch, but also because of the new reality and the increasing probability of other non-British ownerships of important media of news and opinion.' But no such controls were forthcoming, and News International continued to expand and to branch into new areas: in 1987 it bought the *Today* paper founded by Eddie Shah. It also acquired the publishing firms of William Collins & Sons in Britain and Harper & Row in America, bringing them together to form HarperCollins in 1990.

Such moves did little to assuage the fear that the apparent proliferation of media options concealed a diminishing number of companies, exercising control behind the scenes. Such apprehensions, however, made little headway against the repeated insistence that more outlets meant more choice. It was an argument caricatured in a 1990 sketch on the BBC series *A Bit of Fry & Laurie*, in which a government minister responsible for a recent Broadcasting Bill is served by a restaurant waiter played by Stephen Fry. The waiter professes great admiration for the politician, even quoting one of his speeches: 'We must strive to offer the consumer a far greater range of choice. For too long broadcasting has been in the grip of a small elite. We must expand and offer more choice.' He then notices, to his apparent horror, that the place-setting includes silver cutlery and snatches it away, taking it off into the kitchen and returning with a bag containing thousands of identical, white plastic coffee-stirrers, which he proceeds to heap upon the table. 'At least you've got the choice now, haven't you?' he snarls. 'They may be complete crap, but you've got the choice. And that's so important.'

13
Establishment
'I will be your preacher teacher'

SIR HUMPHREY: It could well be argued that the Sermon on
the Mount, had it been a government report, should
certainly not have been published. A most irresponsible
document. All that stuff about the meek inheriting the
Earth! Could do irreparable damage to the defence
budget.
Jonathan Lynn & Antony Jay, *Yes Minister* (1981)

Instead of seeking like good Tories, as Disraeli adjured, 'to
maintain the institutions of the country', Thatcherites
were indifferent or hostile to them. They behaved, indeed,
like some unscrupulous property developer bulldozing
listed buildings that stood in the way of a quick profit.
Ian Gilmour, *Dancing with Dogma* (1992)

SCULLION: I don't want a new life; I want my old one.
Malcolm Bradbury, *Porterhouse Blue* (1987)

While others were busy sprouting new heads, the single most
important media institution in Britain spent the decade under attack
from politicians of all sides, but particularly from the government. The
BBC had been created in the 1920s by a Conservative government,
becoming the first nationalized industry, but in later years the Tories grew
wary of its monopoly position, and introduced first commercial television
and then commercial radio in an attempt to provide competition. It was
not apparently sufficient, for the deep distrust remained and grew to a level
almost of paranoia during the latter part of the Thatcher era. 'She disliked
the BBC,' was the terse summary of Douglas Hurd, who as home secretary
was responsible for broadcasting at the time, while Norman Tebbit was
characteristically more colourful, insisting that the corporation was 'a
sunset home for the insufferable, smug, sanctimonious, naïve, guilt-
ridden, weak and pink'.

Perhaps more accurate was Tony Benn's remark that the BBC was 'an agency of the SDP', an institution that was deeply distrustful of dogma, whether of left or right, and that hoped thereby to avoid too much controversy. In this aspiration, of course, it was almost entirely unsuccessful, instead finding itself embroiled in political quarrels on a regular basis, though the source of the criticism did noticeably shift during the decade.

In 1981 the BBC invited the socialist historian and anti-nuclear campaigner E.P. Thompson to deliver the prestigious Richard Dimbleby Lecture, with a projected theme of the Cold War. But as the date for the talk approached, despite widespread support within the corporation (even within the Dimbleby family), the choice of Thompson was vetoed by Sir Ian Trethowan, director general of the BBC, and the tenth annual lecture was instead cancelled. Undoubtedly the talk would have been politically partisan – Thompson was never less than ideologically committed – but scarcely more so than, say, Roy Jenkins' use of the same platform two years earlier as a political broadcast for the party he wished to launch, and many suspected that the BBC had been leant upon by a pro-nuclear government. The belief that the corporation was susceptible to establishment pressure seemed confirmed the same year with the eventual broadcast – a year later than scheduled – of *Blood Money*, a six-part thriller series written by Arden Winch. The delay was the result of an intervention by Buckingham Palace, who objected to the storyline (reflected in the original title, *Blood Royal*) of a schoolboy earl, 17th in line to the throne, being kidnapped and held for ransom; this, it was argued, by those who supposed modern terrorists to be devoid of inspiration, might spark the imaginations of bad men. Sensitivities in the royal family were obviously running high, following the murder of Lord Mountbatten in 1979 by the IRA, and in the version that was eventually screened, the boy had become instead the son of a United Nations official, leaving the impression that UN diplomats were assumed already to be on the agenda of extremists everywhere, or perhaps that the international community had more difficulty in obtaining the ear of the BBC than did the throne.

A change in government attitude came with the Falklands War and the BBC's refusal to accept without question the official propaganda line, an attitude that, depending on one's position, was either an honourable attempt to retain a sense of perspective or the most unforgivable treachery. Issues over the treatment of the war were to resurface periodically through the decade, with a particularly heated debate accompanying *Tumbledown*, a drama written by Charles Wood and broadcast in 1988, that told the story of Lieutenant Robert Lawrence MC of the Scots Guards, who had been severely wounded in the conflict. Advance publicity focused on the play's criticism of the standard of care accorded to injured servicemen, and on Lawrence's reflection that the war had not been worth the sacrifice, themes that had been perennial complaints in the services since at least the Napoleonic Wars. Nonetheless, even before it was screened, George Younger, the defence secretary, was still moved to say that it would cause 'great offence' and that he was 'deeply unhappy' about it all.

In fact when it did appear, it turned out that the piece was more traditional than might have been expected. Although the climactic – and most disturbing – scene was explicitly about the dehumanizing effects of war, showing Lawrence repeatedly bayoneting an Argentine soldier despite his pleas for mercy, much of the drama concerned Lawrence's extraordinary recovery from a gunshot wound to the head, and could almost have been mistaken as an orthodox hospital drama about, say, the victim of a drunken driver. And in one way at least, the play supported the official position on the war by scotching the idea that the Argentine army had been comprised simply of 17-year-old conscripts and that the victory had therefore been a walkover. But by breaking the silence that had surrounded the human consequences of the war, *Tumbledown* did threaten to drag reality into an increasingly mythical conflict, especially when other former soldiers from the Scots Guards lined up behind the drama: 'Mr Lawrence is telling the truth,' insisted one such, Chris Murley. 'The aftercare was non-existent.' And another, John Clark, agreed: 'We feel we were just used and discarded. I'm chuffed that at last the horrors of the war and the way we have been treated are coming out.'

While most critics applauded the dramatic strengths of the play, and Colin Firth's magnificent performance as the unlikeable, if charismatic, Lawrence, many also expressed reservations about the political dimensions, though Christopher Dunkley, writing in the *Financial Times* saw it as a necessary counterbalance: 'In a period when the government is so unassailably strong and most of the national press joins in proselytising its views it is, surely, particularly important that broadcasters – and especially the BBC – should do everything they can to maintain a diversity of opinion.' Equally, it might be added, a government that demanded only approval for its actions ran the risk of appearing deeply insecure. And the idea that a single drama, albeit a BAFTA-winner, could counterbalance the almost daily supply of pro-war movies screened on British television was patently absurd.

The BBC's position was not helped by the fact that it also commissioned dramatist Ian Curteis to write *The Falklands Play* and then decided not to film his work, allegedly for being jingoistic. Again, when it finally did appear – in a truncated form in 2002 – it proved to be not quite the piece that had been trailed. Centred on the Westminster side of the conflict, it showed Margaret Thatcher as a woman who knew the right course of action, but who was not always as resolute in private as she appeared in public. There was humour, particularly in Thatcher's contemptuous treatment of Francis Pym, and there were even suggestions that the differences between Argentina and Britain were more quantitative than qualitative: 'Public sector spending frozen totally, personal taxation up by 90 per cent – the whole country's going up in smoke,' reflects Lord Carrington on the situation in Argentina. 'There's a leader in *La Prensa* which says that the only thing that can hold this government together now is a war.' Ultimately, however, the play hinged on whether Britain still had the resolve to fight its corner, an angle that would certainly have found favour in Downing Street. 'Do we still believe what we certainly believed in in 1940, or is that now just the romance of history?' asks Thatcher of her cabinet colleagues. 'Nothing to do with the cold realities of Britain in 1982? Part of a nation that has actually, quietly died?'

The cancellation of *The Falklands Play* inevitably led to charges of left-wing bias from the right, but the allegation of pusillanimous capitulation from the other side was also still being heard. In 1987 the *New Statesman* journalist Duncan Campbell made a series titled *Secret Society*, one episode of which covered the intelligence-gathering satellite codenamed Zircon and the way that the project had avoided the scrutiny of the Public Affairs Committee. The government demanded that the programme not be broadcast, on grounds of national security, and the BBC somewhat cravenly complied. When Campbell then published an account of the story in the *New Statesman*, he found the police searching his flat, the offices of the magazine and the BBC offices in Scotland, in a move clearly intended to intimidate investigative journalists for the future. The government was condemned by Roy Jenkins for looking 'as though they were running a second-rate police state, infused equally with illiberalism and incompetence,' and the Labour frontbencher Robin Cook arranged for the programme to be shown in the Houses of Parliament under privilege laws, but Neil Kinnock, keen to be seen on the side of patriotic resolution, was less supportive, demanding in the Commons: 'Why did the government delay until yesterday seeking to take action against Mr Campbell? Why did they fail to secure the prevention of the publication in a magazine?' It was not his finest hour.

Similar pressure was applied in 1988 when the Thames TV current affairs series *This Week* announced it was screening 'Death on the Rock', an investigation into the shooting dead of three IRA members by the SAS in Gibraltar, though the IBA proved itself made of sterner stuff than the BBC and refused to block the programme. The official version of the incident was that the three terrorists, who were in Gibraltar intending to bomb a military band parade, had been shot as a last resort, when the SAS men feared that they were about to detonate the bomb. *This Week* uncovered an eye-witness named Carmen Proetta, who insisted that no warnings had been given and that the shootings were little more than cold-blooded executions, a conclusion also reached by the *Independent*: 'the three terrorists were, in effect, executed'. Less impressively, other sections of the print media not only went along with the government's account, downplaying the fact that the bomb components had not yet been assembled and were still in Spain, but also tried to smear Proetta. The *Sun* lead the ad hominem attacks with a front-page article, headlined THE TART, that claimed: 'she's an ex-prostitute, runs an escort agency, and is married to a sleazy drug peddler.' The claims were hardly germane to her testimony, nor did they prove to be true, and Proetta successfully sued five British papers for libel. It was an unsavoury episode and a mostly pointless one, since, as with the sinking of the *General Belgrano*, the truth was that the public was not much concerned with the niceties of the rules of engagement; three IRA terrorists had been killed and that was a desirable result as far as most were concerned.

The same could not have been said when, later the same year, the government announced that they were banning the representatives of eleven organizations in Northern Ireland from speaking on television and radio, in a move aimed primarily at Sinn Fein. The intention was to remove what was generally described as 'the oxygen of publicity' from the political wing of the IRA, but the effect was to make the government a laughing stock; footage of Sinn Fein leaders like Gerry Adams and Martin McGuiness continued to appear, but with the sound of their voices removed and with the film overdubbed by actors, speaking exactly the same words, frequently with an approximation of the original voice.

It was thus issues of war and security that attracted the greatest controversy in broadcasting. Another BBC play, *Airbase* (1988) by Malcolm McKay, didn't face attempts to prevent it being broadcast, but was greeted by much hostility for its portrayal of American servicemen in Britain as being prone to alcohol and drug abuse. The manufacturer of Gannex raincoats, Lord Kagan, recently emerged from his jail sentence for theft, was apoplectic, letting it be known that 'Not since the days of Goebbels had he seen such a vicious and tendentious misrepresentation of a group of people', while Mary Whitehouse felt moved to write personally to President Ronald Reagan to apologize on behalf of the nation. And it wasn't merely modern conflicts that were capable of stirring up such strong emotions. Alan Bleasdale's 1986 series *The Monocled Mutineer* was set during World War One, and depicted a mutiny amongst British army recruits. It was a 'tissue of lies,' stormed the *Daily Mail*, which wouldn't normally be much of a denunciation of a drama series, except that in this instance the BBC had erroneously claimed that it was a true story, thus handing ammunition to its enemies.

The brief media storm about *The Monocled Mutineer* reflected a wider battle about the nature of British history that ran through the decade. Early on, Thatcher had given her views on the country's imperialist past, talking about 'a British empire that took both freedom and the rule of law to countries that would never have known it otherwise', and the education secretary, Keith Joseph, had argued for schools to foster 'through the teaching of history a sense of pride in one's country and its achievements'. In reality, as he knew, many schools were now doing precisely the opposite; the trend was towards an anti-imperialist and anti-racist approach to history, and there was a move away from the doings and dates of princes and politicians in favour of an empathetic approach centred on the experiences of more humble sectors of society.

In the 1988 Education Reform Act, Joseph's successor at the department of education, Kenneth Baker, finally realized a long-held Tory hope for a centralized national curriculum, to which all state schools in England and Wales would be expected to teach, though the results were not all that had been hoped. When it came to history, Baker was said to have been disturbed by finding that more children could tell the difference between a bronto-saurus and a tyrannosaurus than could distinguish Charles I and Oliver Cromwell, while Thatcher, a former education secretary who involved herself fully in the debate, was adamant that British history should be at the centre of 'the initially tedious but ultimately rewarding business of memorizing what actually happened'. But the guidelines that emerged never met their expectations, and Thatcher became 'thoroughly exas-perated with the way in which the national curriculum proposals were being diverted from their original purpose'. Meanwhile complaints were voiced by the Joint Association of Classical Teachers, rightly fearful that Greek and Latin were going to be squeezed out of the curriculum, and by those who vainly hoped to see the teaching of English grammar included – a petition to this effect was presented to Baker by the comedy writer Frank Muir and the actor Michael Hordern.

Credit for frustrating the government's wishes lay with the educational establishment, which had been developing on independent lines for the last two decades, drifting ever further from the wishes of most politicians. It was the one major area in which egalitarian principles, so long out of fashion in the political world, continued to thrive happily, and most educational theorists were determined to fight their corner, even in this new post-1988 world with its grant-maintained schools and city technology colleges, outside the control of local authorities (polytechnics were also made independent of councils). Despite all attempts at reform, the influence of what the tabloids liked to call 'trendy teachers', advocating, for example, non-competitive sport, seemed to continue unabated; the awareness of such trends spread beyond Britain's shores, so that by 1990 it was being reported that Parisian schools staged novelty races known as the Course à l'Anglaise, in which the slowest runner was declared the winner. Coincidentally, 1988 also saw an impressive rise in 'A' Level examination results, which could have been the result of the Education Reform Act. Or it could have been a change in the way that exams were marked. Under the previous system for 'A' Levels, grades were awarded in proportion to pupils, so that the top 10 per cent in any one year would receive an A grade, the next 15 per cent a B, and so on. In 1988 this was changed to a system based instead on marks, which would, it was claimed, allow for a more objective measure, though critics argued that it actually allowed for greater subjectivity and for the manipulation of results. Over the following decade the proportion of pupils receiving an A or B grade at 'A' Level rose by 30 per cent.

Whether this improvement in results signalled the arrival in universities and workplaces of better educated students was to remain a subject of fierce debate for years to come. But for those who had been born too early to benefit from Baker's reforms, Thatcher's renewed rhetoric about British history prompted the opening of a new front in the right's war against liberalism, then at a peak with the passing of Section 28 of the Local Government Act. Earlier in the decade there had been a spate of big-budget television series and films set in the days of empire – *Brideshead Revisited* (1981), *Chariots of Fire* (1981), *The Jewel in the Crown* (1984), *The Far Pavilions* (1984) – which, some worried, ran the risk of sanitizing the imperial past, though others saw different causes for concern; Kelvin MacKenzie, editor of the *Sun*, was reported to have said of the film *Gandhi* that he wasn't interested in going to see 'a lot of fucking bollocks about an emaciated coon' (thankfully that was before Gandhi's SDP affiliations were revealed, or the phrasing might have been less temperate). At varying points over the next couple of years the *Sun* gave its views on Britain's colonization of Australia — 'The Aboriginals were treacherous and brutal. They had acquired none of the skills or the arts of civilization' — and of India: 'It was Britain which civilized the entire sub-continent. Built her railways. Gave her, for the first time in her history, an efficient administration and honest judges.' The paper was also amused to find copies of the novel *Biggles and the Dark Intruder* selling well in airports in India, and chortled: 'Clearly the Indians are missing the great days of the Raj. Bring back the Empire?' This latter report confirmed the suspicions of those who had concluded that the *Sun* was never knowingly informed; since the novel was written, and set, in 1967 and concerned prisoners escaping from Dartmoor gaol, its relevance to the Raj was perhaps a little overstated.

The subtext of such articles was of a piece with the media's broad support for the England cricket captain, Mike Gatting, on a 1987 tour of Pakistan, when he became involved in an unseemly row with the umpire, Shakoor Rana, that sparked a minor diplomatic incident (Gatting called him a 'shit-awful umpire,' Rana responded that he was a 'fucking cheating cunt'). 'Whack the Pakistanis out of sight,' urged the *Sun*, when the match was resumed after a day's suspension. And the tabloids had further sport when in 1990 Norman Tebbit suggested that 'A large proportion of Britain's Asian population fail to pass the cricket test. Which side do they cheer for? It's an interesting test. Are you still harking back to where you came from or where you are?' Tebbit's cricket test was widely attacked by the left as being deliberately offensive, though in fact he was (unwittingly) echoing comments made by the unimpeachably anti-racist Bishop Trevor Huddleston some twenty years earlier: 'I know West Indian families who regard themselves as wholly and absolutely English; the children will support, so to speak, the English test team against the West Indian one, because they are so English.'

The *Sun* was perhaps the most extreme in its defence of the legacy of empire, but others too were prepared to voice regrets over its passing. The first major foreign policy success of the Thatcher government had been the deal struck at the Lancaster House conference on the future of Rhodesia, allowing racially inclusive elections for the first time, and producing the modern state of Zimbabwe. To the surprise of most observers, those 1981 elections did not result in the anticipated arrival of a moderate coalition government run by Joshua Nkomo and Bishop Abel Musorewa, but in the elevation of Robert Mugabe to the position as prime minister, and there were some tears shed at the loss of another former colony, albeit one that had unilaterally declared itself independent some sixteen years earlier. 'We of the white tribe,' said a *Daily Mail* editorial, 'cannot but be moved by an undertow of melancholy.' Others, however, were jubilant at Mugabe's success; the Catholic newspaper the *Tablet* announced that 'an exemplary government has emerged', and Tony Benn wrote in his diary: 'It is a fantastic victory and I can't remember anything that has given me so much pleasure for a long time.' Given subsequent events in Zimbabwe, some may have later concluded that the *Mail*'s romantic nostalgia was as valid a note to strike as were the celebrations.

The fact that it was a Catholic publication so enthusiastically welcoming Mugabe was something of a surprise, for a gulf was opening up between the two major Christian churches in Britain when it came to politics, and the Catholic establishment was far less inclined to take up such left-leaning positions than was the Church of England. Bruce Kent, general secretary of CND and perhaps the most famous Catholic priest in the country, repeatedly found himself frustrated by a church that was 'conservative, top-down and middle-aged', and that never got further than mealy-mouthed equivocation when it came to what he saw as the moral horror of nuclear weapons: 'The contrast between these statements and the specific comments made by the bishops on a complex subject like embryo research could not have been more striking,' he despaired. In 1987 he finally left the priesthood, unable to take the conflict of loyalties any longer; he subsequently married and emerged as a Labour parliamentary candidate.

The Church of England, on the other hand, nurtured a much broader strand of dissent, so that members of the group Clergy Against Nuclear Arms included such senior figures as Edward Carpenter and Alan Webster, the Deans of Westminster Abbey and St Paul's Cathedral respectively. Carpenter in particular, a pacifist who once refused to read a prayer at a memorial service for wartime RAF chief Sir Arthur 'Bomber' Harris, could generally be relied upon to rock any boat in which he found himself: he took up the cause of Chinese-occupied Tibet at a time when it was receiving little attention, and was vocal in support of the campaign against factory farming. On this latter issue he was joined by Hugh Montefiore, the Bishop of Birmingham, who had earlier distressed some traditionalists by suggesting that Jesus might have been homosexual. And then there was David Sheppard, the former England cricketer who became Bishop of Liverpool and who, according to Paul Johnson in 1980 was soon 'providing his colleague Hugh Montefiore with hot competition for the title of Britain's silliest bishop'; the following year, Sheppard was in the forefront of those seeking an understanding of the root causes of the riots in his adopted city. These turbulent priests were somewhat in the media mould of John

Robinson, Bishop of Woolwich, whose 1963 book of liberal theology, *Honest to God*, had spurred Mary Whitehouse on to launch her crusade against filth and communism, and they aroused similar indignation.

All of them were put in the shade, however, by the appointment in 1984 of David Jenkins as Bishop of Durham, a man whose very existence was seen as an affront to the right. On the occasion of his enthronement, his address expressed support for the miners in their strike and criticized the government for appearing not to care about the human cost of their policies: 'Such a government cannot promote community or give hope in the very difficult days we are faced with,' he said. 'There must be no victory because the miners must not be defeated.' The usual cast of rent-a-quote Conservative MPs lined up to tell him, in the words of Nicholas Fairbairn, that: 'His duty is to save souls and not to preach socialism. If he wishes to worship earthly gods like Arthur Scargill, let him forsake the post to which he has just been wrongly appointed.'

By that stage Jenkins was already a figure of great controversy, having had the temerity to doubt the historical accuracy of traditional Christian myths such as the virgin birth of Jesus and His physical resurrection after death; these were not exactly radical views amongst theologians (a poll of thirty-one bishops found that ten agreed with him on the virgin birth), but they did constitute an attack on precisely that cultural form of Christianity about which even the most materialist media commentators could feel sentimental when warmed by a few Christmas drinks. Those who enjoyed being outraged duly professed their indignation in newspaper columns and television studios. Jenkins' consecration was staged at York Minster, where the service was twice interrupted by protesters, and when, three days later, the Minster was seriously damaged by fire, theories abounded that it could have been a case of arson committed by those who disapproved of his appointment; even better, the fire turned out to have been the result of a lightning strike, which some then attributed to 'divine intervention'.

The Archbishop of Canterbury, Robert Runcie, joined Jenkins in commenting on the miners' strike, suggesting that, although he supported Thatcher's declared aims of economic growth, 'if the human consequences of such aims mean unemployment on an unprecedented scale, poverty, bureaucracy, despair about the future of our communities, inequitable sharing of the sacrifice called for, then the objectives must be called in question'. This was by way of being a warning shot across the government's bows, prior to the arrival of a report into the Church's role in the inner cities, which had been commissioned by Runcie and was published in 1985

under the title *Faith in the City*. Inevitably, all the recommendations relating
to the Church itself were ignored by commentators, and attention focused
instead on its analysis of the causes of social decay: unemployment,
inequality and poor standards in healthcare, education and housing. Above
all, it argued for the fostering of a greater sense of community and, in so
doing, it called down upon its authors, and upon the Archbishop himself,
the wrath of those in the Conservative Party who regarded religion as a
purely personal issue of individual salvation, with no contribution to make
to social policy. 'The Church of England seems now to be run by a load of
communist clerics,' exploded Conservative MP John Carlisle, while
Norman Tebbit dismissed the report as 'a political plea to return to the
Butskellite policies which had created the desolate council estates.'

There was some truth in Tebbit's assertion, for few churchmen had a
great deal new to say in the political arena, simply restating what had been
orthodoxy a few years earlier, just as there was little new in anything that
the likes of Mary Whitehouse and James Anderton had to say on questions
of public morality. In 1981 Clifford Longley, the religious correspondent of
The Times, had written that 'The political face of British Christianity has
for at least half a generation been "social democratic" and is still tending
that way.' Some of the changes experienced by the Church of England
in the 1980s merely confirmed that opinion, suggesting a vain pursuit of
modernity and contemporary relevance at the expense of almost everything else.

It was the decade that saw the rise in influence of the evangelical wing of
the Church, resulting in what novelist Margaret Yorke described as 'family
services, where children ran freely about the aisles and played in the
chancel, and strange, jolly hymns were sung'. William Whitelaw, on
visiting St Aldates Church in Oxford, found himself in the midst of just
such a service, as recounted by Alan Clark: 'To his great alarm he
found that the church was filled to bursting and the atmosphere
evangelical in the highest degree. He described how the entire congregation
mimed the words of each hymn, raising both hands to heaven at such words
as "arise" etc.'

Clark himself reserved his fiercest displeasure for the Alternative Service
Book that was introduced in 1980. 'I am completely certain that this
degradation of the ancient form and language is a calculated act, a
deliberate subversion by a hard core whose secret purpose is to distort the
beliefs and practices of the Church of England,' he exploded, before
indulging himself in the violent imagery of the video nasties: 'All too well
do I understand the rage of the *Inquisitadores*. I would gladly burn them,

those trendy clerics, at the stake. What fun to hear them pinkly squealing. Or perhaps, as the faggots kindled, they would "come out", and call on the Devil to succour them.' Many others shared his opinion, with journalist Edward Pearce commenting that the language in the new services resembled a 'departmental memo to God'. And indeed it was hard to find any clear-cut reason for replacing the majestic beauty of the Book of Common Prayer ('We do earnestly repent, and are heartily sorry for these our misdoings. The remembrance of them is grievous unto us, the burden of them is intolerable. Have mercy upon us, have mercy upon us, most merciful Father') with the flat banality of the new liturgy: 'We are truly sorry, and repent of all our sins.' Or, as in *Not the Nine O'Clock News'* parody of the Apostles' Creed: 'I believe in God, the Father Almighty; or at least it stands to reason there has to be some sort of greater power; you know, like electricity sort of thing . . .' In the Book of Common Prayer, its defenders pointed out, 'the words themselves are worth their weight in glory'; the same could hardly be said of the Alternative Service Book.

There were those who objected on liturgical grounds, that the theology underpinning the new services was ill-considered and betrayed the Anglican traditions of Archbishop Cranmer, but for most churchgoers it was above all a linguistic issue, and writers in particular were not slow to voice their displeasure. Amongst them was the novelist Beryl Bainbridge: 'A belief in God requires an act of faith, and the sustaining of such an implausible proposition requires that the language and ritual of prayer, of baptism and burial and communion, should be both mystical and difficult.' Marghanita Laski argued that the greatest threat was not to the main body of believers, whose faith did not necessarily require poetry to be part of worship, but to those who regarded the Church of England as being a key component in the public life of the nation, and who would find that the rituals to which they had become accustomed were now being jettisoned. If the new forms came to dominate, she warned, 'then the Church of England will have opened a new cultural schism in our already over-divided society. We shall lose our common historical language of religious reference. And there will be no need or reason any more for the outsider to go to church.'

In P.D. James' novel *A Taste for Death*, she described a right-wing Conservative cabinet minister as someone who 'wasn't even particularly religious. He usually went to church on Sundays and on the major feast days because he enjoyed the liturgy – he wouldn't attend if they used the new Bible or Prayer Book.' That was certainly the position of many High Tories, but Margaret Thatcher's own attitude towards religion, coming from a Methodist background, was more low church and tended rather towards the practical than the spiritual or aesthetic. In her first major television interview after her election, she had explained the meaning of Jesus' most familiar parable: 'No one would remember the good Samaritan if he'd only had good intentions; he had money as well.' And in 1988 she addressed the General Assembly of the Church of Scotland, quoting from St Paul's second epistle to the Thessalonians: 'If a man will not work he shall not eat'. Though, as Ian Gilmour pointed out, she didn't proceed to the next verse condemning busybodies: 'For we hear that there are some which walk amongst you disorderly, but are busybodies.'

Thatcher ended that speech by citing 'I Vow to Thee, My Country' ('that beautiful hymn,' as she called it, though a poem that addresses itself to a nation is scarcely a hymn), and there was, unsurprisingly, conflict between her government and the Church when it came to what she perceived to be simple questions of patriotism. In particular the service of thanksgiving for the Falklands War at St Paul's Cathedral caused some tension when Runcie asked the congregation to share the grief of those on both sides who had been bereaved. She was said to have been furious, though Denis Thatcher's response was somewhat milder; he snorted that Runcie's sermon was 'better than expected', which was 'more than can be said for the rest of the bloody service'. In fact it could have been far worse, with reports that Alan Webster, the Dean of the Cathedral, had wanted the Lord's Prayer to be said in Spanish.

Runcie himself, as a veteran of the Second World War, in which he had won the Military Cross, had been supportive of the enterprise from the beginning, arguing that 'within the complexities of an imperfect world, self-defence and the use of armed force in defence of clear principles can sometimes be justified'. His expressed concern over the loss of life in the South Atlantic, however, led some of Thatcher's more fervent supporters to suggest that he was somehow being disloyal to his country. Just as the Falklands had led to a split between the government and the BBC, so too did it set the scene for later conflicts with the Church, with every speech by the Bishop of Durham, every mention of *Faith in the City*, serving to fuel the fire further. Even so, it appeared to be of little significance to Thatcher, who found no room in her memoirs for any of this, or even for a mention of Runcie. When approached by Humphrey Carpenter, who was writing a biography of the now retired Archbishop in the mid-1990s, she was at a loss to know why she was being asked to comment: 'there were no great church things during my time.' She was wrong; there was plenty of controversy to be found in religious affairs, but from her perspective it paled into insignificance when compared to her great crusade against entrenched interests and restrictive practices.

This had, in the first half of her premiership, primarily been directed against the trade unions and the nationalized industries, but with the defeat of the miners and the printers, and with the privatization programme well underway, attention could be diverted to other areas. The problem was that there was much less of a definable target when it came to, say, the civil service. The government was pledged to reduce public spending but the Whitehall mentality expressed in the first episode of *Yes, Minister* (in which Sir Humphrey Appleby says of the newly appointed minister of administrative affairs, Jim Hacker: 'We'll have him housetrained in no time') proved almost impossible to shift. When Alan Clark was an employment minister, he rejoiced at learning that the department's projected spending was below its budget, only to be corrected by an under secretary: 'It's important to get as close as possible to last year's provision in order to have a firm base from which to argue for increases this year.' Clark fumed to himself – 'This was crazy. Nightmare. Kafka' – but the block remained. Like the education industry, the civil service had developed its own mechanisms for dealing with what Robin Day famously called heretoday, gone-tomorrow politicians, and was adept at delaying real reform with endless inquiries and committees. The concept of the Royal Commission may have disappeared (Thatcher appointed not a single one during her time in Downing Street, to the great discomfort of the great and the good accustomed to sitting on such bodies), but the spirit of putting reform on the backburner lived on.

In fact much of the existing establishment, beyond the fields of politics and business, proved remarkably resilient to the attacks launched upon it, and equally resilient in its opposition to government, even in those rare cases where it proved to be the beneficiary of public policy. There were, for example, few quite so splenetic in their denunciations of Thatcher as the writers. 'Of all the elements combined in the complex of signs labelled Margaret Thatcher,' claimed the novelist Angela Carter, 'it is her voice that sums up the ambiguity of the entire construct. She coos like a dove, hisses like a serpent, bays like a hound.' Alan Bennett declared that she was a philistine 'typical of the people who go to the Chichester Festival'. And the television dramatist Dennis Potter could barely contain himself: 'Mrs Thatcher is the most obviously repellent manifestation of the most obviously arrogant, divisive and dangerous British government since the war. All that really counts is to get these yobs and louts away from the swill bucket.' Such hostility was hardly assuaged when Thatcher was reported to have replied to a question about her favourite books that she was currently re-reading Frederick Forsyth's thriller *The Fourth Protocol*, a novel in which she herself featured. 'The prime minister must be the only person in Britain who has read a whodunit, knows who has done it and then has to read it again to make sure,' mocked Norman Buchan, the former Labour Party arts spokesperson.

And yet of all the arts, it was literature – normally the poor relative when it came to state money – that did best out of the Thatcher government, seeing at last the introduction, after decades of lobbying, of the Public Lending Rights scheme, which rewarded writers when their books were borrowed from public libraries. Approval was also given for the building of a new British Library, next to St Pancras railway station in north London. The fact that the construction period for this project ran way over schedule and that the resulting building was desperately inadequate to its task – wasting vast amounts of space on an atrium, exhibition rooms and a shop, rather than on its primary function of housing books – was unfortunate, but not directly attributable to the government of the late 1980s.

Other state initiatives tended to concentrate on encouraging private sponsorship to replace public money, and occasionally even to introduce new areas of funding, as in the Per Cent for Art scheme initiated by the Arts Council in 1988, which sought to persuade property developers to spend 1 per cent of their contract budget on public art. It never really caught on as widely as had been hoped and, when implemented, often amounted to little more than a sculpture at the bus stop servicing a Tesco superstore in Slough, but it was in the spirit of the times. For the visual arts, above all other areas of artistic creativity, embraced the 1980s ethos of the free market with some enthusiasm. In May 1980, J.M.W. Turner's *Juliet and Her Nurse* set a world record for a painting when it sold for $6.4 million; exactly a decade later, a new benchmark was set by Vincent Van Gogh's *Portrait of Dr Gachet* at $82.5 million. As Gordon Gecko says in *Wall Street*: 'This painting here. I bought it ten years ago for sixty thousand dollars. I could sell it today for six hundred. The illusion has become real.' By the end of the decade, the Australian critic Robert Hughes, whose 1980 television series *The Shock of the New* had done much to make twentieth-century art accessible to a wider public, was gloomy about the future of both society and art: 'The year 1900 seemed to promise a renewed world, but there can be few who watch the approach of the year 2000 with anything but scepticism and dread. Our ancestors saw expanding cultural horizons, we see shrinking ones.'

The new mood, assiduously fostered by Thatcher, of a young country that owed no deference to established institutions tended to be seen most clearly in peripheral areas of culture. The lack of respect was evident, for example, in the *Sun*'s long-running battles with the royal family, which saw the paper break the traditional embargo on the honours list by running an advance story that two of those who had shown extraordinary courage at Zeebrugge were to receive the George Medal. It committed an even greater breach of protocol when it printed the Queen's Christmas card in October 1988, though a threat by the Palace to sue for infringement of copyright produced a swift apology and the payment of £100,000 to charity. But the decline of etiquette and the reduction of the royals to the status of soap stars did little during the decade to dent public support for royalty; the enormous success of *Hello!* magazine, with its uncritical, almost hagiographical, celebrations of the upper classes alongside showbiz celebrities revealed an unabated appetite for reading about minor royalty and the aristocracy. Indeed more damage was probably done to the image of the upper classes themselves in their attempt to find a role in this new world and, particularly, on television.

At its most entertaining, this produced a 1981 edition of the television game show *Family Fortunes*, hosted by Bob Monkhouse, showing a contest between the Bath family of Longleat and the Montague family of Beaulieu. It wasn't an entirely successful exercise, for none of the assembled aristocrats seemed to have fully comprehended the programme's format, in which contestants had to guess the most popular answers given by the public to various questions. The trick therefore was to think oneself into the persona of an ordinary person, and give the answer that he or she would in the circumstances, so that if asked to name a food with an edible skin, one should ideally reply 'apple'; Lady Sylvie Thynne, on the other hand, responded, 'haggis'. Asked to name a high-street store, Lord Bath answered 'Harrods', and when asked to name a kind of bird seen in an English garden, Lord Montague replied 'peacocks'. None were amongst the answers given by the general public.

Nor was the royal family much better at handling television. *The Grand Knockout Tournament* in 1987 was essentially a celebrity version of the old slapstick game show *It's a Knockout*, but with the added attraction of the presence of Princess Anne, Prince Andrew, Prince Edward and the Duchess of York, appearing as team leaders. It was successful in terms of gaining an audience and of raising money for charity, but the excruciating embarrassment of it all did the institution of the monarchy no good whatsoever. Slightly better, in that they were simply dull, were two documentaries the same year about the Queen Mother's love of racehorses (*Royal Champion*) and about the Duke of Edinburgh's Award scheme (*The Duke's Award*). But the only 1987 programme that enhanced the public perception of the royals was the panel show *A Question of Sport*, hosted by David Coleman, in an episode of which one of the team captains, the former Liverpool footballer, Emlyn Hughes, was shown a photograph of a mud-spattered Princess Anne taken at the Badminton Horse Trials and incorrectly identified her as the jockey John Reid, to his great discomfiture. The following week, which happened to be the 200th edition of the show, Anne appeared as a contestant on Hughes' team and won over most of the record audience of nineteen million viewers; they tuned in to watch him being humiliated all over again, and came away concluding that she was more fun than her public persona had previously suggested.

While these frivolities occupied the minor members of the royal family, the two most significant members of the younger generation of royals were each in their own way trying to find new roles for themselves. Princess Diana used her status as the most famous woman in the world to highlight causes that had previously been less than fashionable − leprosy, homelessness, the elderly − and became particularly associated with AIDS around the same time as the government's information initiative; her involvement in AIDS charities did as much as anything in the short term to help turn around public opinion about the condition, and her televized meetings with patients helped destroy myths about the syndrome being spread by normal social contact, though she was not the first public figure to be filmed shaking hands with a sufferer − that distinction belonged to health minister John Patten in 1985 (a man nicknamed 'the minister for gays' by his colleague, Kenneth Clarke).

Diana's then husband, Prince Charles, also pursued various campaigns, with a common thread running through them to the effect that the modern world had lost its way in some vague, ill-defined way. 'Much of British management doesn't seem to understand the importance of the human factor,' he explained in 1979, but he didn't linger long in the world of business, concentrating instead on environmental themes, on inner-city youth, through his Prince's Trust charity, and on architecture.

It was the latter interest that provoked greatest comment when he used the occasion of a speech at the 150th anniversary banquet of the Royal Institute of British Architects to attack a proposed new wing to the National Gallery, describing it as being 'like a monstrous carbuncle on the face of a much-loved and elegant friend'. The timing was poor − 'It was an outrageous speech to make at a celebration,' wrote sometime director general of the RIBA, Bill Rodgers − but the content struck home. The *Daily Express* welcomed Charles' denunciation of the 'shoddy, thoughtless, trendy, incompetent work' of architects, and added, with a curious sense of priorities: 'No body of men deserves censure more.' In the ensuing arguments (mostly conducted by those who were, like the Prince, blessed with elegant friends), the proposal was withdrawn and a new design commissioned, this time by the post-modernist American architect, Robert Venturi. In the circumstances, it caused no great surprise that when Charles' much-touted scheme for the development of Poundbury, on the outskirts of Dorchester, was unveiled, it was roundly ridiculed in architectural circles as being little more than pastiche. Nonetheless, he had something of a case when he said he wanted to get beyond experts to address 'the feelings and wishes of the mass of ordinary people in this country', and some of his other contributions were more welcome, particularly his endorsement of the kind of community architecture propounded by Rod Hackney and others, seeking to put human beings back at the centre of design.

Charles' distaste for modernist architecture was echoed by Margaret Thatcher, one of the few areas in which they appeared to agree, for more generally he appeared to represent everything she stood against – he was, after all, the most vocal representative of the ultimate monopoly, the most exclusive closed shop of all. But when there was a need for the renovation of some of the interior at 10 Downing Street, she called on the neo-classicist Quinlan Terry, the great hero of traditionalist architecture. And when she and her husband bought a house in Dulwich, it was a new-build mock-Georgian affair that caused even her devotee Woodrow Wyatt to admit: 'She has no taste. Nor does Denis.' Like Charles, Thatcher shared the general mood of public dissatisfaction with what architecture had wrought. There had been a time in living memory when architects were celebrated as heroic figures, building a new world for a new age (the town-planning visionary played by David Farrar in the 1960 British film *Beat Girl* was entirely typical); now it was almost as though they were being collectively charged with crimes against humanity, blamed for forcing people into the despised high-rise blocks that blighted the inner cities, while they themselves were more likely to be found 'in a Georgian rectory with a walled garden'. Social engineering, which had been part of their post-war brief, had become an accusation to be flung in their face, even if they argued that the central issue was not their designs but the lack of money available – after all, the Barbican estate in central London was every bit as brutal as Broadwater Farm, but suffered from none of the same social problems since it was not council housing. The stock of the architect was therefore already falling fast by the time Prince Charles joined the debate, but he undoubtedly hastened its decline.

Other professions also felt under attack, if not from the public, then from politicians. Universities that had once prided themselves on independent thought and academic research now felt undervalued and mistreated by a government apparently more interested in the skills required by business than in knowledge for its own sake. In the early 1980s major funding cuts were made to the higher education budget and thousands of jobs were lost; the results were satirized in Malcolm Bradbury's 1987 novella *Cuts*, in which a vice-chancellor tries to reform his university by getting sponsorship for lecturers and by introducing degrees in Snooker Studies. In 1984 the governing executive of Oxford University, where Thatcher had studied, proposed to award her an honorary doctorate and provoked a noisy rebellion by those seeking some form of retribution for her policies; the dons rejected the idea by a majority of two to one, though, remaining aloof from the fray, she merely issued a statement saying: 'If they do not wish to confer the honour, I am the last person who would wish to receive it.' To many commentators on the right, the campaign to refuse her the honour was the epitome of petty-minded spite, but the reality was that this was one of the few ways in which academics could make their displeasure clear. As a character in David Lodge's novel *Nice Work* explains when he's invited to join a one-day walkout by lecturers, the more traditional forms of industrial action simply weren't applicable: 'Who will notice? It's not as if we're like bus drivers or air traffic controllers. I fear the general public will find they can get along quite well without universities for a day.'

That novel also had great fun lampooning the growing academic obsession with theoretical constructs. In 1981 structuralism, a theory that had usurped existentialism in the hearts and minds of French intellectuals, suddenly became newsworthy when a dispute broke out in the English literature department at Cambridge University. Colin MacCabe, an assistant lecturer with a penchant for the new approach to literature, was denied a permanent position, despite the recommendation of an appointments board, and the entire faculty seemed to degenerate into a civil war that left most of the country simply baffled. In the fall-out, the casualties included one of Britain's best-known literary critics: 'Things have happened in the faculty that have sickened me,' commented Frank Kermode, as he announced his premature retirement from the King Edward VII Chair of English Literature, 'and that is putting it fairly mildly.' To anyone looking in from the outside, this obsession with structuralism, post-structuralism, deconstruction and other delights appeared to be little more than a pleasantly distracting, if dull, intellectual exercise, slightly more rarefied than watching *Countdown* on Channel Four, but very much of the same nature. (Not that there were very many people looking in from the outside, for Richard Whiteley ultimately proved a bigger draw, in Britain at any rate, than Jacques Derrida.) The art establishment was similarly taken over by theorists, at the expense of the art, so that in 1988, as Robert Hughes noted, 'when the British Council tried to find a New York venue for its Lucian Freud exhibition, no museum there would take it: the work of this great realist was not "modern", still less "post-modern", and did not fit their aesthetic ideology.'

Even as the cuts were being felt, the student body was finding itself equally antagonized by government policy, especially when Keith Joseph proposed in 1984 that, in order to fund an expansion of scientific research in universities, the then mandatory grants to students should be cut for those with well-off parents, and tuition fees introduced. The suggestion went down very badly with middle-class Tory voters, who saw student grants as one of the few returns they got from taxation – 'The middle classes are the meanest, most griping people,' as one cabinet minister put it – and a meeting of backbench MPs forced Joseph to back down. 'It will not be lost on the rest of the House,' pointed out David Steel in the Commons, 'that a Conservative backbench rebellion has for the first time been half successful where the interests of the better-off constituents are involved.' The idea returned, however, and by the end of the decade plans were underway for student loans, intended first to supplement, and then to replace, grants.

Even the legal profession, so heavily represented in the ranks of professional politicians, was finding the 1980s a somewhat bracing experience. In Frances Fyfield's novel *Shadows on the Mirror*, an old-fashioned solicitor has built a large and successful practice, employing forty-five other solicitors, by relying 'on common sense, pats on shoulders, a large handkerchief, tea, sympathy and stiff drinks', but now finds that 'he doesn't really belong anymore in a big commercial partnership full of whiz-kid lawyers'. The era of the avuncular lawyer, grown rotund with high-living, appeared to be passing in the face of a new generation who 'haven't even got time for lunch'. Even the chambers of the most famous representative of the type, Rumpole of the Bailey, became infected by a young barrister named Hearthstroke, who immediately set about trying to modernize the practice: 'he was one of those persons who took the view, one fashionable with our masters in government, that we were all set in this world to make money,' grumbled Rumpole. 'He might have made an excellent accountant or merchant banker; he wasn't, in my view, cut out for work at the criminal bar.' In 1989 the government brought in proposals for the reform of the legal profession, allowing, for example, solicitors to appear in higher courts, and encountered almost total hostility, including that of many who were naturally Conservatives. 'It cannot be right to annoy all one's friends at once,' worried Tory MP Winston Churchill.

But by her third term, Thatcher had managed to accumulate a more considerable body of establishment foes before her than any previous Conservative prime minister: the BBC, educationalists, the Church of England, the arts institutions, the professions and – many believed, though the evidence was never conclusive – the royal family. The blame for 'the government's clash with large sections of the middle classes', insisted the *Daily Mail*'s Andrew Alexander, lay squarely with those professionals who were opposed to 'the enterprise ethic', a verdict with which Rupert Murdoch would have agreed, for he had predicted such a conflict back at the start of the decade: 'It is the very simple fact that politicians, bureaucrats, the gentlemanly professionals at the top of the civil service, churchmen, professional men, publicists, Oxbridge and the whole establishment just don't like commerce.' Now that commerce had its own party in power, the dislike was being amply reciprocated, and many on the establishment right found their sympathies drifting, increasingly horrified by the rise of what Peregrine Worsthorne, editor of the *Sunday Telegraph*, identified as 'bourgeois triumphalism'.

In the heady days after Thatcher's 1983 landslide election, Worsthorne had identified himself firmly with the new order: 'Old fashioned Tories say there isn't any class war. New Tories make no bones about it: we are class warriors and we expect to be victorious.' But now that those professing themselves his allies were camped out on his lawn, he took fright, appalled at the lack of dignity and manners on display: 'The yuppies feel confident enough to shed all inhibitions about enjoying the spoils of the class war which they think Mrs Thatcher has fought on their behalf.' That was in 1987, and he was not alone in his sense of distaste. 'The Tory Party runs the real risk of sleek, complacent, self-applauding, grand apathy,' warned the *Daily Express*, while the *Daily Mail* was keen to move the agenda on: 'It is time for free-market capitalists to prove that this is not just a flint-hearted creed of greed and grab.' The *Daily Telegraph* was similarly worried: 'The lack of any evident moral underpinning for Mrs Thatcher's rule persists. Public opinion about the supposed materialism and selfishness of Thatcherism will grow if it is not addressed.'

These were sentiments previously voiced by the wets, but now heard from Conservatives who had been initially supportive of Thatcher. And their concerns were matched by some of her cabinet colleagues. 'The fruits of economic success could turn sour unless we can bring back greater social cohesion,' warned Douglas Hurd in 1988. Even her cheerleaders were expressing doubts. 'Like the extension of affluence, the weakening of paternalist bonds and the old social restraints has exacerbated many problems,' admitted Tebbit the same year. 'The development of responsibility, which should go with the enjoyment of what was once privilege, has lagged and anti-social behaviour has been on the increase.' Increasingly, it seemed, the suspicion was growing right across the establishment that Auberon Waugh might have had a point when he wrote in 1984: 'Everybody agrees that the Tories' public image is a national disaster. Personally I feel that it is probably quite an accurate public image and they are genuinely rather horrible people.'

14
Globalization

The *Sun*, as regular readers will know, has never liked
the French.
The *Sun* (1988)

Of late, certain politicians have been attempting to play
the green card in their grubby scramble for public
support. Believe me, such tokenism is entirely cynical.
The situation can never be reversed whilst market forces
remain superior to political will.
Ben Elton, *Stark* (1989)

Workers of the world forgive me.
Poster of Karl Marx in East Berlin (1990)

Except in times of war, foreign affairs have generally made little impact
on the British public in the modern era. The 1980s were an exception.
The speed with which the empire had fallen after the Second World War
produced a mood of introspection and a lowering of national self-esteem,
but by the peak of the Thatcher years, that shock had receded sufficiently
for the question to be addressed of how Britain fitted into an increasingly
interdependent world. It was a process aided by the arrival on the global
stage of two major figures whose impact transformed international politics:
first, the election in 1980 of Ronald Reagan as American president with an
agenda that revived the bitterest hostilities of the Cold War, and then in
1985 the emergence of Mikhail Gorbachev as the general secretary of the
Communist Party of the Soviet Union.

The first Soviet leader to have been born after the revolution, and
considerably younger than his immediate predecessors, Gorbachev
appeared to offer a new direction forward for Russia: more open, less rigidly
centralized. It was a fact that had already been noted on his visit to Britain
the previous year as a senior member of the Politburo: 'I like Mr

Gorbachev,' Margaret Thatcher had declared on that occasion; 'we can do business together.' She was right, though even she wasn't farsighted enough to see just how much business might be done, and she added a warning against 'starry-eyed thinking that one day communism will collapse like a pack of cards, because it will not.' Her reciprocal visit to the Soviet Union, in 1987, was one of the great foreign policy triumphs of any post-war British politician, with huge crowds turning out to greet her as a hero, despite, or more likely because of her uncompromising stance against communism and collectivism. The fact that at the same time Neil Kinnock was also making a much less acclaimed trip into the heart of ideologically hostile territory – in his case to Washington, where he was fobbed off with a perfunctory half-hour meeting with Reagan – made her success all the sweeter. She was in her element, and as she proceeded around a Moscow supermarket, buying some bread and pilchards and surrounded by hundreds of well-wishers, a British diplomat in attendance was heard to mutter: 'Loaves and little fishes – surely not?'

Quite what any of this meant in terms of the future of the world was as yet unclear, but by the time of Thatcher's visit to the Soviet Union, it was no longer possible to see that country as remote and isolated from Western Europe. In April 1986 an explosion at the Chernobyl nuclear power plant in Ukraine released a vast cloud of radioactive fallout, the worst nuclear power disaster yet experienced in the world. For two days the story went unreported until the fallout was detected in Sweden. The worst effects were felt in Belarus, just ten miles from the station, but the impact was considerably wider: in some parts of Britain, primarily Cumbria and North Wales, the slaughter of sheep was banned for over a year in response to the contamination of the grass on which they fed. In the words of novelist Fay Weldon, Chernobyl made 'a large world into a small one, by reason of our common fear of radiation'. In a different way, it also brought the nuclear energy industry closer together internationally; a disaster for one was seen as a public relations failure for all, and in 1989 the World Association of Nuclear Operators was founded, representing power industries in more than thirty countries.

And Chernobyl indirectly transformed the image of Gorbachev himself. The absence of any Soviet coverage was much noted abroad once the story had broken, but it was far from unusual in Eastern Europe for the press in the communist bloc had never shared the Western media's relish for reporting disaster, instead regarding discretion as the better part of journalism until such time as the central authorities decreed it was useful for the citizenry to know. The result was a banally bureaucratic attitude, as seen in the case of a Polish seaport which, having been battered by severe weather, had to wait to be told by the local press what had happened: 'The Polish Press Agency informs us from Warsaw that the day before yesterday a heavy storm raged on our coast'. The lack of investigative journalism was, some argued, balanced by the reluctance to spread panic, but such arguments cut little ice in the British media, where a leader column in *The Times* commented that the silence of the Soviet media concerning Chernobyl 'demonstrated the strict limits on the drive for more glasnost (openness) previously demanded by Mr Mikhail Gorbachev, the Kremlin leader'. Nonetheless it was revealing that this was the first-ever mention of the word glasnost in the newspaper. Far from being bound by the restrictions he had inherited, Gorbachev, as Ken Livingstone later noted, 'seized on the tragedy to increase the pace of change, and within months the terms glasnost and perestroika [restructuring] were in use around the world'.

The main effect of Chernobyl in Britain, however, was to reinforce a prejudice against nuclear power that had been growing with the rise of environmentalism. There had been a surge of interest in ecological issues in the early 1970s, which had faded somewhat as the economy steadily worsened, but a revival of concern a decade later added a new urgency to the debate. In 1983 the environmental protection agency in America warned for the first time in an official report that the pumping of carbon dioxide, methane and other gases into the atmosphere would result in an increase in global temperatures, up by 1 degree Fahrenheit in the next twenty years, 3.6 degrees by 2040 and up to 9 degrees by 2100, unless action was rapidly taken. The phrases 'greenhouse effect' and 'global warming' began to enter public consciousness, while concern was also raised over the depletion of the ozone layer in the atmosphere by the use of chloro-fluorocarbons (CFCs), found in aerosol cans, dry-cleaning products and refrigeration. Previous environmental arguments about the reduction of rainforests and the alarming rise in the extinction of animal and plant species suddenly took on a new apocalyptic immediacy, with the realization that human activity might actually be in danger of threatening the future of humanity itself. As a character on the television comedy show *KYTV* put it: 'We're talking about the melting of the icecaps, flood, famine and the end of all human life on Earth.'

In 1988 Prince Charles announced that he'd banned aerosols at his Highgrove home, and in September that year Margaret Thatcher became one of the first politicians in the world to admit the scale of the disaster that might result. In a speech to the Royal Society, she identified the dangers of greenhouse gases and called for action on the ozone layer: 'it is possible,' she argued, 'that we have begun a massive experiment with the system of this planet itself.' Thatcher had previously exhibited little interest in environmental questions ('When you've spent half your political life dealing with humdrum issues like the environment, it's exciting to have a real crisis on your hands,' she commented during the Falklands War), but, unusually for a politician let alone a prime minister, she had a background in science; having studied chemistry at Oxford and subsequently worked as a research chemist, she was one of the few MPs with the training to read and assess the evidence that scientists were starting to accumulate.

Unfortunately the most obvious way of dealing with climate change – a move away from generating energy by burning fossil fuels and towards nuclear power – was rendered politically difficult by the experience of Chernobyl; that disaster might have been, in the words of nuclear advocates Martyn Turner and Brian O'Connell, the result of a 'poorly designed reactor that lacked even the most basic safety technology' and might have been 'about as bad as any nuclear incident could get', but its spectre haunted the public imagination and shaped attitudes for a decade and more. The challenge was made yet greater, according to the then secretary of state for the environment, Nicholas Ridley, by the way that the most pressing concerns were diluted by a host of other issues, many of which he considered deeply irrelevant: 'water quality, sewage at sea, litter, chemical wastes, toxic fumes, lead in petrol, waste disposal, car fumes, lorry and aircraft noise, transistor radios, the rooting out of hedges and shelter belts, intensive farming and the protection of badgers.' The result was mocked in a 1990 episode of the comedy *Drop the Dead Donkey* in response to a white paper from the new environment secretary: 'Basically Chris Patten's going to save the planet by introducing strict controls on people playing their records too loud.'

From a green perspective, this was a single agenda; like freedom, ecology was indivisible. Some three million Britons were now estimated to be members of organizations like Greenpeace, CND and Friends of the Earth and, although their voices were not unified politically, there was a growing cultural groundswell that was, by the end of the decade, hard to ignore. David Attenborough's epic television series, *Life on Earth* (1979), *The Living Planet* (1984) and *Trials of Life* (1990), with their combination of spectacular aerial photography and detailed close-ups, were revealing the beauty of the natural world in a way previously unseen by British audiences, and their huge popularity perhaps helped environmentalism move during the decade from alternative fringe to the mainstream. Companies such as

Ecover and ARK appeared, selling environmentally-friendly household products such as washing powders, while a growing concern for animal welfare produced changes in behaviour: supermarkets began to stock free-range eggs, Beauty Without Cruelty led the campaign for cosmetics that hadn't been tested on animals, and vegetarianism spread from leftist students to schoolchildren (the Smiths' 1985 album *Meat is Murder* helped popularize the trend, and by 1989, according to one survey, 20 per cent of young people were vegetarian). The most celebrated manifestation of these high-street trends was the Body Shop, a cosmetics manufacturer and retailer founded by Anita Roddick that rejected animal testing and sought to source its materials with an awareness of human rights and environmental sustainability. 'The business of business should not just be about money,' insisted Roddick. 'It should be about public good, not private greed.' Her company continued to expand, with some 366 branches by 1989.

There was still a sense in some quarters that this was primarily a metropolitan preoccupation; when a couple in David Nobbs' comedy series, *A Bit of a Do* (1989), open a vegetarian restaurant, Ted Simcock (David Jason) rounds on them: 'You're lunatic fringe, animal rights, trendy health-food, freaky nut-nuts,' he explodes. 'You'll be bankrupt by Christmas. I've told you before: this is Yorkshire, not Shangri-sodding-La!' But the message was spreading and there was confirmation of the cultural acceptance of environmentalism in 'Survival', the last storyline of the original *Doctor Who* before the series was cancelled in 1989. Sylvester McCoy's Doctor finds himself on the dying planet of the Cheetah People and being given a lecture that was surely inspired by James Lovelock's Gaia theory. 'This planet's alive,' explains the Master (Anthony Ainley). 'The animals are part of the planet. When they fight each other, they trigger explosions, they hasten the planet's destruction.' 'How much longer before it blows up?' asks the Doctor, and the Master replies: 'Not long. They've been fighting a long time.'

The same message formed the core of Ben Elton's first novel, the million-selling *Stark*, also published in 1989. A group of billionaires, the most successful and powerful businessmen in the world, realize their activities have produced an imminent environmental catastrophe and that we are fast approaching 'the moment at which the world will cease to be able to sustain balanced life'. Able to hire the best available scientists to evaluate the state of the environment, they have come to this realization quicker than any government can. 'There are virtually no forests left. There are no longer any effective atmospheric barriers. Soon there will be no polar icecaps,' one of their number reflects. 'Without the forests, deserts will very soon take over the majority of land remaining above sea-level. Which will not be much because once the ice has melted all low-lying land will be submerged under a filthy sea.' And so the industrialists execute a longstanding plan to escape the Earth altogether, fleeing in a fleet of rockets to colonize the Moon. The novel made explicit reference to the Biblical myth of Noah's Ark, but where, in the book of Genesis, God decides to destroy all life because 'the wickedness of man was great in the earth', in the modern world the greed and rapacity of capitalism are sufficient to do the job on their own. Thus were the visions of nuclear holocaust that had peppered the early 1980s transformed into a new nightmare of environmental apocalypse.

Some of this was slowly to edge its way into the mainstream, but as Thatcher pointed out in her memoirs, the level of media interest in the subject of climate change could be gauged by the fact that no television cameras were present for her 1988 Royal Society speech. Far more to the taste of commentators had been her speech a week earlier to the College of Europe in Bruges, in which she had explicitly rejected the drift towards federalism: 'Europe will be stronger precisely because it has France as France, Spain as Spain, Britain as Britain, each with its own customs, traditions and identity. It would be folly to try to fit them into some sort of identikit European personality.' This was sensational stuff by the standards of the time, coming just two years after the Single European Act had been signed, aimed at creating a genuinely common market right across the European Community by 1992. Many wished to see that single market in trade followed by monetary and political union, a dream particularly identified with Jacques Delors, the French politician who had been appointed president of the European Commission and who was, in Thatcher's eyes, hell bent on centralization and the imposition of a Brussels bureaucracy on sovereign nations. Now she was setting out the limits beyond which she would not go, in a speech that, according to her husband, Denis Thatcher, would 'change the course of history'. It also seemed to mark a shift in political positions in Britain, a repudiation of the pro-European legacy bequeathed to the Conservative Party by Edward Heath.

The reality was that Thatcher had never truly shared the rampant Europhilia of Heath. 'She is an agnostic,' noted the former ambassador to France, Lord Soames, of her attitude to Europe. 'She won't become an atheist, but on the other hand she certainly won't become a true believer.' Others were not quite so confident: 'Mrs Thatcher hated Europe,' a senior Conservative told his parliamentary colleague Emma Nicholson. 'In 1979, in a private conversation, she said she loathed it. It was astonishing how well she hid it.' It was indeed. That same year she had explained her official position during the election campaign: 'You are going to get nowhere if you join a club and you spend all your time carping and criticizing it.' But she had gone on to do little but carp and criticize, almost paralyzing the European Community by using every summit meeting as a venue to demand a reduction in Britain's financial contribution, a battle that she finally, and rightly, won, though it was a victory that she accepted with extraordinarily bad grace. She was, in any event, temperamentally unsuited to the kind of horse-trading that necessarily accompanied the business of Europe; unable to build alliances within her own party except on her own unyielding terms, she was never going to find much common ground with European politicians who, elected by proportional representation, had grown up with the concept of coalition government.

But Britain's membership of the Community was by now a fait accompli, and for the right it had one major selling point: it was seen as a bulwark against socialism both strategically, by forming a solid bloc right up to the border of the Soviet sphere of influence, and domestically, where it tied the country into a capitalist union. But by the late 1980s these conditions were changing: under Gorbachev, the Soviet Union was looking less threatening even to Cold Warriors, and the Labour Party was turning its back on anything that smacked of socialism. Indeed the Labour leadership was itself re-evaluating its stance on Europe, partly because, as Bryan Gould wrote, of 'a feeling that we could not afford to antagonize our friends in Europe at the same time as we were taking on the Americans over nuclear weapons', and partly because sights had been lowered, and there seemed to be a possibility of achieving a slightly better deal for workers by cooperating with leftist governments abroad. By 1985, Tony Benn, the leading opponent of Britain in the EEC, noted that the left-wing journal *Tribune* was changing its position: 'There is this new ingredient – let's do it all through Europe if we can't do it at home.' In September 1988, the same month that Thatcher was delivering her Bruges speech, Jacques Delors appeared as a guest speaker at the TUC conference, where he was warmly received, in a symbolic acknowledgement of how far the Labour movement had travelled since its pledge five years earlier to withdraw from Europe. The Scottish National Party and Plaid Cymru too were adjusting their policies, from outright hostility – both had campaigned for withdrawal in the 1975 referendum – to advocating a form of semi-independence as autonomous regions in Europe: if the options were direct rule by Brussels, or indirect rule by Brussels via Westminster, why not cut out the middleman?

By the end of the decade therefore, the polarity in British politics in regard to Europe had been switched, to the dismay of traditionalists on both sides: 'During the long years of Labour hostility to the EC,' wrote Geoffrey Howe in his memoirs, 'it was our party which had kept the flame burning in Britain. Were we now to see those roles reversed?' It seemed that we were. Freed from the need to fight the encroachments of socialism, much of the Conservative Party had reverted to a more characteristic nationalism, while Labour had adopted for the first time an unequivocally positive stance. Euroscepticism, which had once been confined to the fringes of politics − Enoch Powell and Tony Benn in parliament, the National Front, the Communist Party of Great Britain and Sinn Fein outside − was now an almost respectable position.

In all this there were elements of class and age to be discerned. Those on the middle-class liberal left who were becoming increasingly dominant in the Labour Party, and who had formed the basis of the SDP, were enthusiastic in their endorsement of European culture, by which was normally meant a summer in Tuscany or, in the case of former advertising man Peter Mayle, *A Year in Provence* (1989), rather than any understanding of, say, Northern Germany. Meanwhile the prosperous *Sun*-reading sections of the working classes, whose cause was championed by Norman Tebbit, tended to have little sense of identity at all with Europe, save for an annual holiday in Anglicized resorts on the Costa del Sol. And even that was too much for the proprietor of the *Sun*: 'He dislikes Europe,' wrote Andrew Neil of Rupert Murdoch, 'and barely even visits as a tourist.' It was perhaps no accident that one of the most consistently popular sitcoms of the second half of the 1980s was *'Allo 'Allo*, a series set in a small French village during the Nazi occupation that gleefully perpetuated every national stereotype it could find: bumbling into a world populated by humourless Germans, by the sex- and food-obsessed French, and by the cowardly Italians, the English characters were out of their depth, unable to communicate with anyone who spoke another language.

There was still amongst much of the population a suspicion of non-English-speaking foreigners and their politics that was shared by Thatcher. In her newly liberated mood, she gave full vent to her feelings in an interview with the French paper *Le Monde* on the occasion of the bicentenary of the French Revolution in 1989; she insisted that Britain's own Glorious Revolution of 1688 had been of greater historical significance and that, far from being positive, the Reign of Terror in France had been the blueprint for modern totalitarianism. In her memoirs she restated this interpretation of history: 'The French Revolution was a Utopian attempt to overthrow a traditional order – one with many imperfections, certainly – in the name of abstract ideas, formulated by vain intellectuals, which lapsed, not by chance but through weakness and wickedness, into purges, mass murder and war.' Such attitudes were regularly denounced as being 'Little Englander', a term misappropriated from anti-imperialists during the Boer War, but they were balanced by a new mood of cultural internationalism that was evident in the country.

At a trivial level, there was, for example, a rapid rise in the British consumption of wine, up nearly 450 per cent in the quarter-century to 1995, and while this was primarily concentrated in the middle classes ('I don't like wine,' complained Wolfie in the television sitcom *Citizen Smith*. 'It's not an Englishman's drink, is it?'), there was also a concomitant shift in pubs from bitter to lager. What had once been seen in working-class male culture as a somewhat effete, even effeminate, drink became the preferred option of young men, largely thanks to the relentless advertising that popularized such brands as Hofmeister ('For great lager, follow the bear,' urged the slogan, as a man dressed as a bear swaggered around in a pork-pie hat, yellow jacket and shades), Carling Black Label ('I bet he drinks . . .') and, most oddly, Oranjeboom, the commercial for which informed us that it was 'a lager not a tune'. The change was tracked in soap opera: in the early 1970s the only *Coronation Street* regular who indulged was Elsie Tanner, who was occasionally seen drinking a lager-and-lime; by the time of *EastEnders*, lager was the favoured drink of the younger characters – Ian Beale, Simon 'Wicksie' Wicks, George 'Lofty' Holloway – as well as being the default option at the yuppie bar, the Dagmar. In the real world, the development was accompanied by increasing concerns about public drunkenness, encapsulated in the expression 'lager louts', but the business success was unarguable: by the end of the 1980s the UK was the third largest lager market in the world, behind the USA and Germany. In the rise of both wine and lager there could be detected a sense of an abandonment of British tradition, a loss of national self-confidence, a reaching-out for alternatives. And in both cases, there were hints of what would prove to be a major development in British culture: the embrace of Australia.

It started in 1982 with the arrival of draught Foster's lager in the pubs of London and the south-east, advertised on television by the hitherto unknown Paul Hogan. Rapidly establishing itself as a fashionable youth drink, sales were further boosted by the screening of Hogan's hit Australian comedy series on Channel 4 (it formed part of the first night's broadcast for the new channel) and by his subsequent film stardom with *Crocodile Dundee*. In 1988 the Football Association gave serious consideration to a £20 million offer to rename the FA Cup as the Foster's Cup, though the vestiges of tradition eventually triumphed, and the proposal was politely declined.

Brewed in Britain by the same company that made Carlsberg, and tasting very little different, Foster's sold on its classless image, its lack of cultural baggage in Britain. The appeal was largely that articulated by David Owen, who visited Australia for the first time in 1982 and was inspired by what he found: 'It made me realize how much Australian society unleashes people's energy, how vibrant, cocky and classless it had become and how depressed and defeatist Britain was by comparison. The mother country had a lot to learn from its offspring.' By 1986 Del Trotter in *Only Fools and Horses* was sufficiently tempted by a business opportunity that he was prepared to leave Peckham behind him to pursue his dream of being a millionaire in Sydney; it was only Rodney's conviction for possession of cannabis that prevented the move. The Trotters were not alone in staying at home: the exodus to Australia and Canada had reached a peak in 1980, when 42,000 people left Britain for those countries; a decade later, the figures had fallen to 2,800 and the cultural trend was in the other direction.

Meantime the daytime television schedules were beginning to fill up with a plethora of Australian soaps, including *The Flying Doctors*, *The Young Doctors*, *A Country Practice*, *Sons and Daughters* and *Richmond Hill*, while late at night *Prisoner – Cell Block H* was becoming a cult hit. In autumn 1986 the BBC bought yet another daytime soap, *Neighbours*, screened daily at lunchtimes and repeated the following morning, with no expectations of it save to fill airtime. The following year, however, its simple, youthful charm suddenly became enormously popular amongst school children during the summer holidays, who were then distraught when the new term started and they were deprived of their daily fix. Amongst those who mourned its loss was the 16-year-old daughter of Michael Grade, the controller of BBC1. At her request, he moved the repeat to a teatime slot and its future was secured: by 1988 it was attracting 18 million viewers, while its biggest stars, Kylie Minogue and Jason Donovan, workers at the Hit Factory of Stock Aitken and Waterman, were scoring hit singles both individually ('I Should Be So Lucky', 'Nothing Can Divide Us') and together ('Especially For You'). This last was in the top three at the same time as 'Suddenly' by Angry Anderson, the song chosen to accompany the screen wedding of Scott and Charlene, the characters portrayed by Donovan and Minogue.

The influence of *Neighbours* was felt in two directions. In terms of soap operas, it inspired an abrupt move downwards in terms of target demographics, such that *EastEnders* and *Coronation Street* began to place a new focus on their young characters. And in terms of culture more generally, it made Australia unexpectedly influential: ITV bought a rival soap, *Home and Away*, that was even more youth-orientated, barbecues (rebranded as barbies) became commonplace, Foster's was joined by Castlemaine XXXX, sales of Australian wines overtook those of the French, a rising inflexion at the end of sentences was imported into British speech patterns, and Bjorn Again – who played songs by, and dressed like, the 1970s Swedish group Abba – instigated a fashion for tribute bands that proved surprisingly popular. Within a few years movies like *Muriel's Wedding* and *Priscilla, Queen of the Desert* were acquiring huge cult followings.

There had been a strong Australian presence in British culture in previous years, of course, but, even allowing for the exception of Rolf Harris, the likes of Germaine Greer, Barry Humphries, Clive James and Nick Cave had for the most part purveyed a cool, intellectual iconoclasm, whereas this new wave offered instead a bleach-blond, naïve enthusiasm that was completely devoid of irony. And, for a nation used to watching the overweight, unhealthy figures of Stan Ogden, Eddie Yates and Fred Gee propping up the bar of the Rover's Return in *Coronation Street*, the scrubbed wholesomeness of Kylie Minogue and Jason Donovan was considerably easier on the eye. Even Australian band INXS, who belatedly broke big in Britain at the same time as *Neighbours*, seemed part of the same trend, looking and sounding like a sanitized, unthreatening rehash of rock history (though the death of singer Michael Hutchence in 1997, seemingly from autoerotic asphyxiation, gave them a retrospective aura of danger). It was no coincidence that the innocence and sheer fun of young Australia became successful in Britain just as the wheels came off the Thatcherite bandwagon: it supplied bouncy, uncomplicated escapism at a time of belt-tightening, and a large section of the population bought into it as light relief from the cynicism that had prevailed for two decades.

The same sense of a nation grown weary of conflict and seeking instead simple fun could also be detected in a Channel 4 series which debuted in December 1988. *Kazuko's Karaoke Klub* was billed as a chat show with a difference, on which the guests would be expected to sing a song to a backing tape (the first week featured Labour MP Paul Boateng singing 'As Time Goes By' and comedian Ruby Wax singing 'New York, New York'). An established part of Japanese social life for some years, karaoke was new to Britain and was initially regarded as being somewhere between appalling and exotic, a perception that was aided by the 1989 single 'Do the Karaoke' from the Anglo-Japanese art-rock band, the Frank Chickens. No one predicted that two decades later the idea of amateurs singing to backing tapes would be the mainstay of ITV's Saturday night schedules in the form of *The X Factor* and *Britain's Got Talent*, but the practice was embraced with an unexpected enthusiasm, and karaoke nights soon became a staple part of pub entertainment across the nation. Early attempts to use them to promote Japanese beer, however, proved no threat to the now-ubiquitous Australian lagers.

Coincidentally it was also Australia that demonstrated the limitations of the power of national governments in an increasingly international marketplace, when the former MI5 officer Peter Wright decided to publish an account of his discreditable and distasteful days in the service in a book titled *Spycatcher*. Publication in Britain was not an option since Wright was still confined by the Official Secrets Act, but in his retirement he had gone to live in Australia and there the Act did not operate. That, however, did not stop the British government attempting to gain an injunction in an Australian court in 1987 to stop the book. The man who drew the short straw, and was obliged to travel halfway around the world to pursue this doomed case, was the cabinet secretary, Sir Robert Armstrong. En route, he allegedly hit a press photographer at Heathrow Airport and proceeded to stake his place in books of quotations when he explained in court that it was sometimes necessary to be 'economical with the truth'. It was a perfectly respectable argument – no more or less than the attitude adopted by every government in the world that has some scruples about telling overt lies – but airing it in public did nothing to enhance the image of the British government. In any event, the case was lost, as everyone had always known it would be: the days when an Australian court might be expected to kowtow to a representative of the former colonial power were long gone.

For months afterwards, travellers returning from abroad would routinely bring a copy of the book back into the country, while Tony Benn tested the principles of freedom of speech by reading passages at Speakers' Corner, thus ensuring that Wright's confessions and fantasies were more widely disseminated than they would have been had the government not intervened. Finally, in October 1988 the Law Lords conceded that it was a nonsense for the law, in the words of Lord Griffiths, to 'seek to deny to our own citizens the right to be informed of matters which are freely available throughout the rest of the world'. The same exasperated impatience with the government was evident even in newspapers that had supported the attempted ban. 'Peter Wright is a bitter, treacherous and obsessive old man,' editorialized the *Daily Mirror*. 'The government was right to try to stop publication. It failed. But it wouldn't accept the defeat. Mrs Thatcher became as obsessive as Mr Wright. She pursued him through courts across the world. She censored in Britain what is freely available from Moscow to Washington.'

This was now a global society, in which national borders were proving permeable to information and culture. Channel 4, which had given Paul Hogan such a vital platform, performed a similar service for a host of other imports from the sublime heights of American television – *Cheers, The Golden Girls, The Cosby Show, St Elsewhere, Hill Street Blues* – to the cheerful absurdity of the Brazilian soap *Isaura, the Slave Girl*. Interspersed amongst these was a commitment to screening foreign sports that had previously not been available in Britain: Gaelic football from Croke Park in Dublin, the Tour de France, Australian rules football and even Sumo wrestling. Most influential of all was the broadcasting of American football, attracting a sizeable minority audience that peaked with the 1986 Super Bowl, when four million watched the Chicago Bears beat the New England Patriots. The same year there were 237 gridiron teams registered in the UK and it was attracting a substantial youth following amongst those disillusioned with soccer; when Oz in *Auf Wiedersehen, Pet* returns from a trip to America and gives his son, Rod, a Miami Dolphins jacket, he's surprised to find the boy complaining that it's not from his favourite team, the Pittsburgh Steelers, who he follows on television: 'Channel 4, every weekend, favourite sport.'

Again there was a sense of turning away from a parochial interest in British culture towards a new internationalism, principally amongst the young. And while politicians fretted about the role of Britain in Europe, the rise of house music was breaking down European national barriers in a way that had not been seen before in pop history. Originally imported from the gay clubs of Chicago, and influenced by the electronic pop of British bands earlier in the decade, house broke through in Britain with the No. 1 single 'Jack Your Body' by Steve 'Silk' Hurley in 1986. The reductionist take on disco was enthusiastically adopted in British clubs and by British musicians, particularly with the subsequent development in 1988 of acid house (much the same rhythms, but stripped down still further and enhanced with squelchy bass lines generated by the Roland TB-303 bass machine, a decidedly retro piece of equipment that suddenly became highly desirable). A series of home-grown No. 1 singles followed – 'Pump Up the Volume' by M/A/R/R/S, 'Theme From S'Express' by S'Express, 'The Only Way Is Up' by Yazz and the Plastic Population – as well as hits by the likes of Coldcut, Bomb The Bass and D Mob, all of which were equally popular on the Continent.

With its single-minded focus on electronic beats, requiring minimal lyrics, no conventional musicianship and no requirement to look cool, this was a truly transnational music; British DJs and clubbers travelled to Holland, Germany, France, Sweden and Spain, instigating a cultural exchange programme that spawned a myriad of sub-genres, fuelled by a democratic spirit hitherto alien to British pop. Because, like the fad for Australian popular culture, house came without cynicism. It was 'a complete break with all that had gone before,' wrote style journalist Robert Elms; 'inclusive, easy-going, all-embracing, it had none of that exclusive Soho elitism, that restless, agitated creativity and narcissism, that tribal competitiveness or stylistic urgency.' Even Boy George, the most celebrated poseur to emerge from the new romantic clubs earlier in the decade, took to dressing down when going out: 'There was no point going to clubs like Shoom in a crisp outfit when you were going to drop an E and do acid aerobics.' Oona King, a future Labour MP, was just one of those who felt that a new age of Aquarius was dawning: 'For many of those taking part it was a rejection of 1980s individualism. For some it was just about pill-popping. For most of us it felt like a triumph of collectivism, and it spawned the belief that we could take care of each other, although many commentators dismissed it as young people's hedonism.'

The use of drugs in this new world of clubbing inevitably attracted media attention. With acid house came rave parties and ecstasy, a drug that was new to Britain, though it had been fashionable for a few years in America, and the seeds of a moral panic were sown. But ecstasy, properly known as MDMA, struck a very different note in the culture, perhaps reflecting a departure from the depression that had dominated earlier in the decade. For where solvents, heroin and crack (a cheap smokable form of cocaine that had recently replaced heroin as a source of official concern, though it never made a major impact on Britain) were essentially private drugs of withdrawal, ecstasy was above all else public and social; it produced a sense of euphoric well-being and enhanced tactile sensation, and was thus seen as being eminently suitable for dancing and for sex. The difference could be seen in the terminology: where one got stoned on cannabis or blocked on amphetamines, with ecstasy the relevant expression was 'loved up', not a phrase that had ever been associated with, say, teenage glue-sniffers. The fact that it seemed to have few negative side-effects, facilitated staying up all night and replaced the egotism of cocaine with a sense of being connected, part of a group, made it very popular very quickly. The result was what was billed as the second summer of love in 1988, echoing the enthusiasm for LSD two decades earlier, though even in that year, when acid seemed to rule the roost, there was a final throwback to the explicitly political rock of the early 1980s.

In June 1988, Wembley Stadium, where Live Aid had been such a huge success three years earlier, staged a second one-day event. This time it was not for charity, but for the overtly political cause of supporting Nelson Mandela, the leader of the African National Congress, who had been in jail in South Africa since 1962 and had, through extensive campaigning, become the best-known African politician in Britain (the tower-block where the Trotters lived in *Only Fools and Horses* was named Nelson Mandela House). The ostensible justification for the event was the celebration of Mandela's seventieth birthday rather than the anti-apartheid campaign, but there was little doubt that this was a politically charged occasion, for while few in Britain were prepared to stand up and say that they supported the racial policies of the white South African government, Mandela and the ANC didn't enjoy whole-hearted support. He had been given a life sentence on charges of sabotage and of planning armed action aimed at overthrowing the government, and there were many, including Thatcher herself, who had no hesitation about seeing him as a convicted terrorist and the ANC as 'endorsing the Marxist revolution'. The minister for consumer affairs, Eric Forth, was on record as regretting that Mandela hadn't been hanged, and even in liberal circles, Mandela's espousal of armed resistance caused some concern, so that the campaigning organization Amnesty International did not include him on their list of political prisoners. The *Sun* was more forthright, insisting that 'The ANC is a criminal conspiracy publicly committed to terrorism in South Africa'. The same paper also had a tendency to query the popular understanding of apartheid by the judicious use of inverted commas, as in a 1988 article about Neil Kinnock 'condemning "racist" South Africa'.

The decision by the BBC to screen the entire event was therefore bound to attract criticism, and John Carlisle, the right-wing Conservative MP for Luton North and an indefatigable supporter of the South African government (he was nicknamed 'the member for Johannesburg North' by opposition MPs), attacked the corporation for 'providing oxygen to a terrorist organization'. The fact that it went ahead anyway was an indication of how the popular mood had been sufficiently affected by the anti-racism campaign of the last ten years that apartheid was now largely seen in moral terms. And so a diverse bill that included Simple Minds and the Eurythmics alongside Stevie Wonder and Whitney Houston took up ten hours of broadcast time, including three of the best political songs of the decade: 'Free Nelson Mandela' by Jerry Dammers, formerly of the Specials, 'Biko' by Peter Gabriel and '(Ain't Gonna Play) Sun City' by Steven van Zandt. The latter was part of the campaign to persuade musicians that performing in the holiday resort of Sun City, located in the supposedly independent bantustan of Bophuthatswana, was tantamount to breaking the United Nations cultural boycott of South Africa: British acts who had thus transgressed included Queen, Rod Stewart, Shakin' Stevens and Kim Wilde.

While the issue of Sun City was relatively straightforward, the cultural boycott threw up a series of anomalies, so that, for example, Paul Simon's album *Graceland* (1986) was criticized by many for having been partially recorded in South Africa, even though it brought black music from the country to a worldwide audience. Thus it was that demonstrations greeted Simon's concert at the Royal Albert Hall, at which he was supported by exiled South Africans Hugh Masekela and Miriam Makeba, both of whom also appeared at the Wembley event. Similarly there had been a demonstration at the 30th annual staging of the Paralympics in 1982 against the inclusion of disabled sportsmen and women from South Africa, even though there were black athletes amongst them.

The most protracted and controversial such issue surrounded the white South African runner Zola Budd. In January 1984, at the age of just seventeen and running in bare feet, she announced herself in world athletics by setting a new best for the 5,000 metres, taking six-and-a-half seconds off the previous world record of the American Mary Decker (though it should be noted that the distance was not then much run by women and was not an Olympic event). Her time, however, was not recognized as a record since it had been run in South Africa, which was beyond the pale of world sport, and the country's exclusion from international competition meant that she had little prospect of a sporting career. Then the *Daily Mail* discovered that her grandfather had been British and that she was thus entitled to British citizenship; with the paper's support, she was granted a passport in April, just two weeks after her application and in plenty of time to stake a claim to inclusion in the Los Angeles Olympics that year. Many were outraged at the fast-tracking of her claim – the average wait for citizenship was then four years – and were far from reassured by the bland comment from immigration minister David Waddington that 'She is an exceptional girl'. Amongst those complaining about the 'indecent haste' was Labour frontbencher Denis Howell, perhaps forgetting that, as minister of sport in the mid 1960s, he had performed a similar service for the black South African weightlifter Precious McKenzie, enabling him to compete for Britain in the 1966 Commonwealth Games.

Budd's subsequent career as a British athlete was mixed. The big event was supposed to be her showdown with Decker in the 3,000 metres at the Olympics, but it ended disastrously for both women. Just past the halfway point of the race, Decker, running behind Budd in second place, tripped over her leg and crashed out; Budd trailed in seventh amidst a storm of booing from the partisan American crowd and the British competitor Wendy Sly-Smith, who won silver, failed to receive the attention she deserved. Budd did go on to break the world records at 2,000 metres and again at 5,000 metres, and to win the world cross country championship twice, but her athletic achievements were always seen as being secondary to her status as a symbol of white South Africa. Wherever she appeared in Britain she was met by anti-apartheid protesters, unmoved by those who argued that a teenage athlete with no interest in politics could hardly be held responsible for the activities of her former government. Peter Pitt, chair of the GLC arts and recreation committee, threatened to withdraw funding from Crystal Palace athletics stadium if she ran there without having denounced the South African government. Her refusal to do so infuriated her opponents – she 'never publicly detached herself from apartheid, despite a number of opportunities,' seethed the anti-racist campaigner Chris Searle – though it was difficult to see that her silence on the subject was sufficient justification for the verbal and physical assaults she suffered. By the end of the decade she had returned to South Africa and retired from athletics, though she came back to represent her homeland in the 1992 Barcelona Olympics.

Her appearance at those Games was a symbol of the new South Africa being built following the eventual release of Mandela from jail in 1990 ('after all the years of pressure,' as Thatcher wrote, 'not least from me') to a hero's welcome and a book deal for his autobiography that was said to be the biggest advance ever offered by a publisher. But even this momentous event faded in the wake of the upheavals in the communist bloc the previous year.

The collapse of the Soviet domination of Eastern Europe had been prefaced by the creation in the early 1980s of the independent Polish trades union, Solidarity, which had been popular enough for the government to impose martial law in an attempt to crush it. The emergence of an alternative power base to the Polish state was not uniformly welcomed on the British left. Solidarity, declared Arthur Scargill, was 'an anti-socialist organization which desires the overthrow of a socialist state', while Tony Benn was similarly worried about its ideology: 'Some of its leaders really believe in market forces, the IMF, privatization, international capital, a free market economy and industrial discipline. There is no question whatever that the Labour Party and the TUC, in supporting Solidarity, are actually supporting Polish Thatcherism.'

The implication – that even martial law was preferable to Thatcherism – was not one calculated to win support. The same lack of proportionality could perhaps be detected in the adoption of the language of East European dissidents by British groups, including the journal *Samizdat*, founded by the historian Ben Pimlott, and the name the constitutional reform campaign Charter 88. The latter echoed the Czechoslovak group Charter 77, which circulated its founding statement underground before it appeared in Western newspapers, and which saw several leading figures, including the writer Václav Havel, being tried and imprisoned. Charter 88, on the other hand, was launched in the pages of the *New Statesman*, the *Guardian* and the *Independent*, and one didn't have to share Neil Kinnock's reported opinion of its signatories ('whiners, whingers and wankers') to conclude that opposing Thatcherism was not quite in the same category as opposing communism.

In any event, Solidarity proved too powerful a dream to be defeated by the state and, following semi-free Polish elections in June 1989, it came to power in a coalition government. The forces unleashed by Gorbachev's reforms in the Soviet Union were now flexing their muscles. In August that year two million people formed a human chain across the Baltic states of Estonia, Latvia and Lithuania in protest at the continuing Soviet occupation of their countries, and it was reported from East Germany that 'some Soviet magazines have even been banned in a vain attempt to prevent the spread of the glasnost virus'. The following month Hungary relaxed control over its border with Austria and tens of thousands left East Germany for the West, taking advantage of this newly-open escape route; when that exit was closed, Czechoslovakia took its place, another country experiencing a major liberalization that would shortly result in Havel being elected president.

'I keep telling the Soviet leaders when I meet them that their language about development and liberation will lack any credibility until they pull down the Berlin Wall,' remarked Kinnock in 1986. 'The wall must come down in the next twenty-five years.' He was being unnecessarily pessimistic. The pressure from below for change was becoming irresistible in East Germany, with protest rallies attracting up to a million people, and in November 1989 crossing points were opened in the Wall. Such was the demand – an estimated two million East Germans visited the West on the first weekend – that the official exits proved insufficient and people started to dismantle the Wall themselves, taking pickaxes and sledgehammers to destroy the greatest symbol of a divided post-war Europe. The Cold War was now officially over, declared to be at an end by the masses in whose name it had been waged.

After decades of communist rule, the totalitarian regimes of Eastern Europe collapsed with a rapidity that none had predicted. As recently as 1988, the bookmakers William Hill had offered odds of 200-1 that the Berlin Wall would fall before the end of the century, and found no takers. As the contagion spread through Eastern Europe, the Soviet Union, which had always underwritten its client dictatorships, stood helplessly on the side-lines, itself so wracked by internal division and so firmly on the path to reform that Rupert Murdoch was soon looking at the possibility of buying the state newspaper *Pravda*. Mostly this spate of revolutions was accomplished without violence, though it required force in Romania to remove and execute its dictator, Nicolae Ceaușescu, and an extraordinary nine months was capped by East German elections in March 1990 that saw the communists defeated and the victory of a coalition calling for the reunification of their country. In October, Germany once again became a single nation.

The peaceful way in which Eastern Europe was transformed came in marked contrast to the experience in China earlier in 1989 when protesters, who had spent seven weeks occupying Tiananmen Square in Beijing calling for change, were removed by the army in an operation that cost the lives of an unknown number, variously estimated as being between 300 and 3,000 demonstrators. The televized scenes of tanks rolling into the square to attack unarmed crowds were so horrific that even Tony Benn was moved to break the habit of a lifetime: 'I was asked to speak at a Chinese solidarity rally in Soho in London,' he noted in his diary. 'It was the first time I had ever spoken in public against a communist government.' Paddy Ashdown, meanwhile, could go one better: invited to speak at a demonstration outside the Chinese Embassy in London, he proceeded to deliver his speech in fluent Mandarin.

The fact that Benn was provoked to demonstrate publicly against a communist regime was an indication of the benefits that seemed to be available to the British left. Whether justly or not, socialists in Britain had long been damned in many people's eyes by association with the Soviet Union and Eastern Europe. Now that system was breaking down, perhaps new possibilities might be opening up, albeit in sometimes unlikely and hopeful directions. A full-page appeal in *International Socialism*, the journal of the Socialist Workers Party, in 1990 read like a parody of a disaster charity advert: 'A political earthquake is shaking the Eastern Bloc,' it began. 'Popular risings have brought down Stalinist bureaucracies which had seemed immovable.' But, of course, there had been real deprivation behind the Iron Curtain and there was now a desperate need for money so that the

SWP could pursue missionary work: 'The workers in the East need access to revolutionary ideas to transform the current struggles into real workers' revolutions. Please help us provide them.'

More realistically there were those who, after a decade of seeing battles being fought and lost, took heart from the example of Poland and East Germany. Ian Brown, singer with the year's most celebrated new group, the Stone Roses, articulated the feelings of many: 'Anything is possible. If Eastern Europe can change so quickly, so can England. It's strength of numbers. People coming together can always change things.' Mark Steel too saw connections as he looked back on the period: 'As dictatorships in Europe faced meltdown, the fallout sprinkled through Britain. The idea settled in the backs of millions of minds, so mildly that most weren't aware of its presence, that apparently unassailable leaders were due their comeuppance.' The enthusiasm was, however, only brief, for it rapidly became clear that the collapse of what had been termed actually existing socialism was to be the occasion of a socialist retreat in the West. The Cold War had been won on the terms of the free-marketers, and the traditional British left was irreparably damaged; even the influential journal *Marxism Today*, amongst the most forward-looking centres of leftist thought, couldn't survive in the new climate and folded in 1991, after limping to a close (by 1989, its monthly circulation had fallen to 13,000, being outsold more than four to one by the likes of *Flower Arranger* magazine).

The break-up of the communist bloc also left open the issue of what could replace it in the demonology of the West. 'St George and the Dragon is a poor show without a real dragon, the bigger and scarier the better, ideally with flames coming out of its mouth,' Enoch Powell had commented in 1983. 'The misunderstanding of Soviet Russia has become indispensable to the self-esteem of the American nation.' With that dragon having now been slain, there were some who hoped that the much talked-about peace dividend might turn out not to be merely financial (after a decade that had seen British defence spending rise by 20 per cent, even allowing for inflation), but also philosophical; that the environment would take the place of anti-communism as the big issue, that international cooperation would now focus on the greatest of all threats to humanity, and that global warming might be addressed as the most serious priority. And, briefly, there was genuine hope when 190 nations came together to sign the Montreal Protocol in 1989, phasing out the use of CFCs in a successful attempt to halt and then reverse the damage done to the ozone layer.

In Britain too there was some encouragement to be found in the elections to the European Parliament that were held in June that year, when the Green Party achieved an entirely unexpected 15 per cent of the vote, up from the 1 per cent its predecessor, the Ecology Party, had managed the last time out. Virtually all of this was at the expense of the Social and Liberal Democrats, who were still in disarray, but it was sufficient to suggest that there might be a mood swing in the nation; even the *Sun* briefly took on an environmental correspondent in response to the vote. Quite what this meant politically was uncertain, though there were some on the left, most notably Robin Cook and Peter Tatchell, who saw the possibility of developing a new philosophy and who were already exploring ways of building bridges between socialism and ecology. But many others remained sceptical: 'there can be no synthesis of ecological ideas and socialism,' insisted the SWP with some finality, though it was unlikely that the Greens lost much sleep over their stance. In fact, it was not in the political but the cultural sphere that environmentalism remained at its strongest; the Green vote turned out to be little more than a blip of a kind that would become common in Euro-elections, and environmental issues slipped back down the political agenda again, eclipsed by another ideological enemy that had now been identified to keep Western politicians occupied.

Amongst those adversely affected by Gorbachev's reforms were writers of espionage thrillers, who really did need a dragon with whom their St Georges could do battle. In *Stark*, Ben Elton argued that the KGB's post-war infiltration of the British security services had achieved little in strategic terms ('They have not invaded Britain or blown up any of Her Majesty's shipyards'), though it had 'sold an awful lot of novels'. Perhaps, he suggested mischievously, they were focusing on the wrong target: 'If the Soviets had thought to penetrate the West's publishing houses at the same time that they were penetrating its espionage organization, they might today have all the hard currency that they so desperately need.' But it was easy for him to mock; his livelihood did not depend on such work. For an author such as Anthony Price, the new conditions presented a real challenge. In his 1989 novel *The Memory Trap*, the nineteenth and last of his Dr David Audley books, he depicts his hero lamenting that 'the days of Audley, when everything had been so black and white, were passing – if not already past'. It is a sensation also being felt on the other side where a KGB general, a veteran of the failed Soviet campaign in Afghanistan, is becoming depressed at the effects of glasnost, the way it is destroying everything to which he has dedicated his life. 'Defeat,' observes a British agent, 'does strange things to heroes. Especially humiliating defeat.' And so, in one last act of defiance, and in an attempt to destabilize the West, the general reveals the location of a secret stash of chemical weapons, stored long ago on the Welsh border in anticipation of a Soviet invasion. And symbolically he chooses to pass on the location to a group of Islamic terrorists.

It was a prescient choice, for Islam was rapidly emerging as the favourite to take over the dragon's role formerly performed by the Soviet Union. The threat of Arab terrorism had been around for many years, of course, centred on the Palestinian struggle to regain their lands from Israeli occupation, but a new note of militant, political Islam had been sounded with the Iranian revolution in 1979, and through the ensuing decade the Ayatollah Khomeini in that country and Colonel Gaddafi in Libya had become bogeymen figures, particularly in America, whose government launched a bombing raid against Libya in 1986 from bases in Britain. That incident had aroused great public disquiet, since it was not generally seen as being Britain's quarrel, but the Islamic resurgence came much closer to home in 1989 with the issuing of a fatwa by Khomeini against Salman Rushdie, calling on Muslims to murder the writer and his publishers in revenge for alleged blasphemies in his novel *The Satanic Verses* (which, in the time-honoured tradition of self-appointed censors, Khomeini had not read).

There had been complaints before about what was seen as blasphemy in Jamil Dehlavi's film *The Blood of Hussain*, screened by Channel 4 in 1983, and even, going back to 1974, in ITV's *Father Brown* series, starring Kenneth More as G.K. Chesterton's fictional detective: an episode in which Muhammad was referred to as a 'dirty old humbug' provoked a protest march by 2,000 Muslims in Bradford. The fatwa against Rushdie, however, was in a different league altogether. Rushdie went into hiding, provided with permanent police protection, while copies of his book were burnt in the streets in several British cities and towns and Iran broke off diplomatic relations with Britain (leaving some to wonder why it had not been the other way around). It was the domestic reaction that was most immediately concerning: the very real anger expressed by thousands of British citizens, the way in which events abroad could make an impact at home, the conflict that it revealed at the heart of multicultural diversity about how tolerant society could afford to be to the intolerant.

For most it was a simple question of freedom of speech as opposed to religious fundamentalism: 'Whatever their political views,' wrote Kingsley Amis, 'all writers and all who wish literature well must see in the threat to Salman Rushdie an attack on freedom of expression.' But there was some confusion too about how to respond to the man at the centre of the controversy, who had been one of Thatcher's most unrelenting critics. In an unappealing act of equivocation, Geoffrey Howe, the foreign secretary,

professed himself equally displeased by the novel – 'The British government, the British people, don't have any affection for the book, which is
extremely rude about us' – though he had not read it either; indeed, in his
memoirs, he admits to being uncertain 'even if I had heard of him
[Rushdie]' at the time of the fatwa.

The *Sun* found itself torn between conflicting prejudices, calling initially
for a bellicose response: 'Tell the Mad Mullah: Touch Rushdie and face our
bombers'. It went on to warn that British Muslims must obey the law,
adding that 'If they don't like it, they should clear out', but it also found
space to reflect on Rushdie himself: 'Perhaps he wishes he had never left
Bombay. Would he be surprised to learn that a good number of people in
Britain also devoutly wish he had stayed there?' And, although Michael
Foot, as chair of the Booker Prize judges, had unsuccessfully argued the
case for the book to be named best novel of 1988, there were others in the
Labour Party less supportive. Bernie Grant had no sympathy for Rushdie's
position, suggesting that censorship should be tightened and the blasphemy laws extended to cover religions other than Christianity, while Roy
Hattersley gave his opinion that the writer should offer not to go into
paperback with the novel, a curious halfway position that succeeded in
infuriating liberals but did little to assuage the hurt felt by the twenty
thousand Muslims who lived in his constituency. The *Financial Times*
worried that the affair would 'increase anti-Muslim prejudice amongst the
non-Muslim British population,' which it certainly did, but it also had
some of its desired effect, as Hanif Kureishi reflected twenty years on:
'Nobody would have the balls today to write *The Satanic Verses*, let alone
publish it. Writing is now timid because writers are now terrified.'

15
Fall
'There she goes'

> The Chamber places Members in face to face
> confrontations with their antagonists in opposition
> parties, separated only by the distance of one sword's
> length, lulling the unwary into complacency and into
> forgetting that the greatest danger is always but a dagger's
> length away, on the benches behind.
> Michael Dobbs, *House of Cards* (1989)

> When the history of the 1980s is written, the name
> Margaret Thatcher will appear on every page.
> The *Sun* (1990)

> On her political gravestone will be the words: 'She Went
> Too Far'.
> Peter Jenkins in the *Independent* (1990)

Margaret Thatcher's achievement in 1987 of being the first party leader of the twentieth century to win three consecutive general elections, and her subsequent record as the longest serving prime minister of modern times, took her into uncharted territory. She had become so firmly entrenched in Downing Street that it was hard for many to envisage a time when she would not be there. Unfortunately, she herself appeared to be amongst that number, and her third term was marked by a series of comments that suggested she had no intention of leaving.

As early as April 1986 she was telling her friend Woodrow Wyatt that: 'As I go on in this job I sometimes think I can't go because who on earth is there to succeed me.' She made the same point publicly two years later in an interview with the *Sunday Times*: 'I shall hang on until I believe there are people who can take the banner forward with the same commitment, belief, vision, strength and singleness of purpose.' In November 1989 she hinted there was a limit even to her ambitions, when she told the *Sunday Correspondent* that it was unlikely she would fight a fifth general election, if she won the next one, but she swiftly retracted and insisted that she was: 'Quite prepared to carry on, yes. But let us get the fourth one over first.' She added, 'I have said I am quite prepared to go on, by popular acclaim.' In 1990 she went still further in a note of congratulations to the *Sun*, then celebrating the twenty-first anniversary of its ownership by Rupert Murdoch: 'Your 21st anniversary offers tremendous encouragement to a prime minister eleven and a half years into office. The *Sun* has become a great British institution. If it can come up fresh and bubbling and vital every day for 21 years, then so can I. And I shall do so.' As Norman Tebbit remarked: 'What would she do if she weren't prime minister? One doesn't see her retiring to gardening or making marmalade.' (There were echoes here of Audrey Fforbes-Hamilton in *To the Manor Born*, who dismissed her solicitor's attempts to make her realize that she would have to sell the manor house: 'Can you see me eking out my days listening to *The Archers* and waiting for the mobile library?')

Amongst the rank and file of the Conservative Party, such single-minded determination was greeted with great enthusiasm, as the chants of 'ten more years!' at the 1989 conference demonstrated. Amongst her senior colleagues, however, every such pronouncement merely increased the misery and bitterness felt by those who had their own aspirations. Most of those who might reasonably have expected to be contenders for the succession – Geoffrey Howe, Nigel Lawson, Norman Tebbit, Michael Heseltine, Douglas Hurd – were now in their late-fifties or early-sixties and perfectly capable of making the necessary calculations: even if she retired midway through a fourth term, it would probably be too late for them. By 1988 there was already media talk of the next leader coming from a younger generation represented by the health secretary Kenneth Clarke, by the Scottish secretary Malcolm Rifkind and by John Major, the chief secretary to the treasury. Nor was Thatcher's dismissive attitude to her cabinet much appreciated: 'Some time there will come along a person who can do it better than I can,' she conceded. 'And I'm always on the lookout. But I expect myself to do it for the fourth term.'

The length of her tenure was also causing disquiet on the backbenches. 'That's the trouble with governments which have been in a long time,' noted Wyatt. 'There are so many people who lose their jobs as ministers or think they ought to have been given jobs and haven't been.' That was perfectly true, but there was an additional, more personal element to Thatcher's predicament.

She had always prided herself on being different from other politicians, trusting her instincts to be in tune with the section of the electorate that she represented, even if they were diametrically opposed to the prevailing political wisdom. She would make up policy and take up positions on the hoof, so that when, for example, as leader of the opposition, she had commented on *Weekend World* that mass immigration meant 'People are really rather afraid that this country might be swamped by people with a different culture', she had no concrete proposals to put forward on immigration, just a gut feeling that she was speaking for those whose votes she needed. But the longer she was in office, the less reliable those instincts became and the further she drifted from the everyday world of her core constituency. By 1989 the privatization programme had reached the selling off of the water and sewerage companies and, though the share issue was again oversubscribed, there was a suspicion that things might now have gone too far; there were reported to be twenty-five different brands of bottled water on sale in an average branch of Tesco (the top brands costing more per litre than petrol), but still it felt wrong that the water coming out of the kitchen tap should be owned by a private company. So unpopular was water privatization that even the newly moderate Labour Party had a policy against it, albeit phrased in the vague terms of promising to bring the industry back under 'some form of public ownership'.

1989 was also the year in which the issue of identity cards for football supporters came to a head. Encouraged by the initiative of Luton Town's chairman, the Conservative MP David Evans, who had introduced a members-only policy at the club, the idea had been floating around for some time and the government had brought forward legislation to make the carrying of an identity card compulsory for anyone attending a match in England or Wales. In the wake of the Hillsborough disaster, the Football Supporters Bill received renewed attention in the highest quarters: 'It must be the end of terraces,' commented Thatcher in the aftermath of the tragedy. 'We must have seats and tickets only.' The debate raged all year over whether such a proposal was either feasible or just, alienating many of those young men in the South-East who, like their fictional representative, Harry Enfield's character Loadsamoney, might otherwise be found in the Thatcherite camp. Nor did the eventual abandonment of the Bill, when the Taylor Report on Hillsborough came down firmly against the idea, do anything to reassure suburban Conservatives.

But the prime minister's problem was an issue of perception as much as it was of policy, a feeling that – like Edna Everage, who had started as a Melbourne housewife and become the grandest of all dames – Thatcher had lost contact with everyday reality. Or, to take another figure from popular culture, it was revealing that when in 1988 Alexis Colby, the character played by Joan Collins, ran for public office in *Dynasty*, her point of reference was Margaret Thatcher: the Queen Bitch of American soap should have had little in common with the grocer's daughter from Grantham, but the comparison was no longer as implausible as it once might have been. As part of her preparation for the general elections in 1983 and 1987, Thatcher had packed her bags ready to leave office, a personal reminder not to take anything for granted; now she was seriously talking about what she would do when she won the election after next. The erection of gates to prevent access by the public to Downing Street, while a perfectly sensible security measure, somehow symbolized the distant status of a prime minister removed from the people. And when she announced in March 1989, on the birth of a child to her son, Mark, that 'We have become a grandmother', the use of the royal 'we' did little to reassure those of her supporters who worried that she was becoming hopelessly out of touch.

But then, as Alan Clark pointed out, it was hard to remain in touch after 'a decade of motorcades, in every capital city in the world'. She 'had become a remote figure,' complained the equally loyal Teresa Gorman; 'she had lost contact with her street-fighters on the back benches.' By late 1989 even Brian Walden, one of her stoutest supporters in the media, was asking her in a television interview about rumours that she was 'slightly off her trolley', and Thatcher, when confronted with opinion polls that showed she might be respected but was nonetheless disliked, simply couldn't understand why the nation still hadn't warmed to her: 'I don't know why they don't like me,' she complained.

None of this, of course, would have amounted to very much if things were going well elsewhere, if the economy had been sound. But it wasn't. The Lawson boom was fast running out of steam, inflation, unemployment and interest rates were on the rise again, and the Labour Party was opening up a 12-point lead in the opinion polls. The economy was going into recession and the tax receipts from North Sea oil, which had done so much to ease the government's position at the start of the 1980s and to fund the tax cuts in the middle of the decade, had already peaked and were now falling fast. Even Thatcher's most ardent fans were starting to lose faith; when the right-wing trio of Alan Clark, Ian Gow and Jonathan Aitken talked in the spring of 1990, the mood was one of gloom: 'We were stuck with the same inflation rate as when we came into power in 1979. Ten, eleven years of endeavour,' recorded Clark, 'and nothing to show for it but the passage of time and the intrusions of age.' Norman Lamont, who had followed Major as chief secretary to the treasury, was admitting privately that inflation wouldn't be brought down below 5 per cent in time for the next election and that he thought the Conservatives would lose. 'The PM and the government are in deep trouble,' wrote Edwina Currie in her diary in November 1989; 'our confidence seems to have gone.'

And behind the economy lurked two issues that were to have devastating consequences for Thatcher: the poll tax and Europe. Of these, it was the poll tax that played most strongly in the country, and the attitude towards Europe that fixated her senior colleagues.

If the 1983 Labour manifesto was the longest suicide note in history, then one of the shortest – at least in political terms – was surely to be found in the 1987 Conservative manifesto: 'We will legislate in the first session of the new parliament to abolish the unfair domestic rating system and replace rates with a fairer Community Charge. This will be a fixed rate charge for local services paid by those over the age of eighteen, except the mentally ill and elderly people living in homes and hospitals.'

The system of the domestic rates, a local property tax that raised revenue for councils, was deeply disliked, partly at least because of its perceived injustices: a pensioner couple whose children had left home could pay more, because they lived in a bigger house, than a childless couple who were both in work and living in a flat down the road. Under Edward Heath a system of rates rebates for the poor had been introduced, but that too created its own difficulties; by the mid-1980s less than half the population were paying rates at all, with the figures disproportionately skewed across the country, some inner-city areas having just a fifth of people paying the full amount. From a Conservative perspective, this was simply unfair, creating a system of representation without taxation, so that the residents of an upmarket area such as Hampstead were obliged to subsidize the poorer parts of the London Borough of Camden while knowing that they would always be outvoted by those who lived on the council estates of Gospel Oak and Somers Town. This was no way, it was argued, to build any sense of civic pride and responsibility, rather this was the undemocratic rule of those who contributed nothing. 'My father always said that everybody should pay something even if it's only sixpence,' insisted Thatcher.

There was also a coherent intellectual case to be made that the idea underpinning the rates was outdated. Created in the late nineteenth century, when local government was principally concerned with infrastructure improvements that were of greatest benefit to householders, a property tax had then been appropriate; now local services tended towards individuals and a change of taxation structure was therefore needed. But the root of the issue was simpler than this. Rates were, for most people, the only taxes that had to be paid directly – income tax was deducted at source, while VAT and other sales taxes were incorporated into retail prices, obscuring their scale – and as such they were resented in a way that no others were. This was largely why the Conservative government had introduced the concept of rate-capping earlier in the decade, but its own actions helped to exacerbate the problem; in 1979, central government had contributed 61 per cent of the budgets of local authorities, by 1990 that figure had fallen to 39 per cent, and local tax-payers had been alienated at every step of the way, still making monthly contributions and yet seeing services cut.

As early as 1979 Tom King, the then minister for local government, was suggesting that the rates might be replaced by a poll tax, a flat-rate charge made not on property but on people and, although it took some time to emerge, this was the system that was eventually adopted for that 1987 manifesto. Conscious that the term 'poll tax' was politically loaded (the last time such a levy had been imposed was in 1377 and had helped provoke the Peasants' Revolt) other language was employed, first the residents' charge, then the services charge, before the community charge was settled upon, though few took any notice and it became universally known as the poll tax. The Labour Party was opposed from the outset, with Jack Straw insisting in 1986 that it was the party's job to 'wake up the nation to its full, ugly implications very soon', but that was easier said than done. The issue simply didn't feature in the election campaign the following year, no matter how hard Labour pushed: 'we tried three times, with three separate press conferences, to get the story launched,' remembered Bryan Gould, 'but the press would not touch it.'

The first to benefit from the new tax was Scotland in 1989, where there was a legal requirement to have a revaluation of properties for the rates. Fearful of the negative political fallout that would result from such a process (revaluations were never popular), Scottish Conservatives pressed instead for an early introduction of the poll tax; as clear a political example of the old adage about frying pans and fires as one could wish to find. A storm of protest ensued, and something more than protest, for in this instance there was a simple direct action that individuals could take: a refusal to pay. Opponents claimed that Scotland was being used as a guinea pig and, though this suggested a touching faith in the government's willingness to change course if its policies proved unpopular, the resultant anger helped build a massive campaign aimed at non-registration and non-payment. It was led not by the Labour Party, which had decided not to resist too strongly – 'It was clearly much more sensible to keep the pressure on the Tories by allowing popular anger to find its own expression,' explained

Gould — but by the much reviled Militant, making its last and greatest contribution to British politics. So successful was the movement, at both national and grassroots levels, that by the end of the first year it was being reported that half a million people in Scotland faced legal action for non-payment and that 'sheriff officers who go to value goods for sale to cover debts are often met with large demonstrations'.

While it remained in Scotland, however, the poll tax was unable to harm the Conservatives too seriously, even if this was simply because most of the damage had already been done. Having been the largest party in Scotland within living memory, the Tories in the region had been hit hard during the Thatcher years, losing another eleven parliamentary seats in 1987 and being reduced to a rump of just ten MPs, compared to Labour's fifty and only just in front of the SDP/Liberal Alliance on nine. But the tax was due to turn up in England and Wales just a year later in April 1990 and there was much nervousness on the Conservative benches. The more politically astute figures at the top of the party were already aware that problems were looming, even if they could do little about it. Alan Clark reported that early in the parliament William Whitelaw had been asked by a colleague what he thought about the poll tax: 'The great man stopped in his tracks, and glared. His shoulders heaved, went into *rigor*, his face became empurpled and sweat poured down his forehead, cheeks and the end of his nose. He wrestled with some deep impediment of speech; finally burst, spluttering out the single word — "TROUBLE". Then he turned on his heel.' Chris Patten, who was appointed environment secretary in July 1989 and was thus responsible for the implementation of the tax, commented simply to one of his junior ministers: 'It's not going to work, is it?'

Both Whitelaw and Patten could ultimately be counted upon to remain loyal, but a total of fifty-three Tory MPs, including Michael Heseltine as well as many veterans of local government, voted against their own government at one stage or more of the poll tax legislation as it passed through the Commons. In another place, a rebellion in the Lords was defeated only by a mighty effort on the whips' part in dragging to the chamber hereditary peers who had seldom, if ever, seen the red benches; one debate produced the second largest number of votes that had ever been cast in the Lords, and there was a certain irony in the way that a measure intended to make a tier of government more accountable and democratic was forced through by the most unaccountable and undemocratic members of the entire political establishment.

The objections were numerous. First, there was the unfairness of an unavoidable tax that had no relation to the ability to pay; unlike, say, the

BBC licence fee, which was similarly levied at a flat rate but which could be ignored if one chose not to own a television set, this could not legally be escaped, and every member of a local community was liable to the same bill (though there were discounts available to the very poorest). Obviously this meant that the wealthiest in society would face a substantial reduction in their liability and, coming immediately after the 1988 budget that had reduced the top rate of income tax from 60 to 40 per cent, it certainly gave the impression that the government was looking after the rich at the expense of everyone else: 'The combination of the two was unfortunate, to say the least,' admitted Nicholas Ridley, one of the few ardent enthusiasts for the new tax in cabinet. Second, there was a fear that the widespread rebellion in Scotland would spread south of the border: 'The Rating and Valuation Association estimated there would be five million summonses a year for non-payment,' noted Ian Gilmour. Third, there were democratic considerations that weighed heavy on some, including a suspicion that many people would fail to put their names on the electoral register in the hope of avoiding payment, though as Woodrow Wyatt pointed out, this wasn't necessarily a major concern to the government: 'As they will be those people most likely to vote Labour, it could be a benefit.'

Less noted at the time was the computer database that would be established. Emma Nicholson, then a Tory MP, was one of the few members with any experience in computing (she had been working in the industry as far back as the 1960s), and she worried about the way 'knowledge about tax and savings, income and expenditure' would be kept together on local authority computer systems that 'had virtually no protection of any sort'. It wasn't a concern that many of her colleagues appreciated, leaving her feeling that 'we were demolishing a long-held bulwark against state power without either understanding what we were doing or even having a debate on it in parliament'. The state's incompetence in the field of data protection was to become of ever greater concern in later years.

But above all these objections was one overriding complaint: most people would see a hefty increase in the amount they were asked to pay. 'I am now inundated with letters about the new tax from horrified constituents who would have to pay five or six times as much as their rates,' recorded Edwina Currie. 'They are livid. For the first time, I'm beginning to wonder whether we will hold South Derbyshire.' Far from benefiting the middle classes, who had always been portrayed as losers under the old rating system, the poll tax hit them disproportionately hard, a situation made worse by the fact that rebates were only available to those without any savings, and by the way that non-working married women were charged the full amount, effectively taxing a husband twice on a single income. The Conservative heartlands were likely to suffer.

And the introduction of this charge could hardly have come at a worse time. High interest rates were pushing up the cost of mortgages, and the large number of people who had bought their own homes for the first time during the Thatcher years, and might therefore be assumed to be favourably inclined towards the Tories, were amongst those most affected. Simultaneously, the relentless rise in house prices, on which the feelgood factor of the last few years had been based, slipped into reverse; the term 'negative equity', to describe a property worth less than the mortgage held on it, began to be heard for the first time. Amongst those hit was Thatcherism's greatest cheerleader Kelvin MacKenzie, whose flat in Docklands had been bought at the height of the property market, and was now sold at a considerable loss.

Similarly personal debt, excluding mortgages, had doubled since 1981 as a function of the credit boom, leaving many families vulnerable to interest rate rises. During the consumer credit boom of the previous couple of years, wages had risen by 3 per cent per annum in real terms, while consumer debt was growing by 12.5 per cent. 'Had the community charge been introduced during a period of modest and stable mortgage rates,' wrote Bernard Ingham in his memoirs, 'it would have been accepted.' Whether he was right or not, the cumulative effect of this combination of factors was devastating on an already-fragile economy. Household spending was cut as hatches were battened down, and wage demands rose, fuelling the inflationary pressures already evident.

For the Labour Party the poll tax was, in the short term, a godsend. Its lead over the Conservatives stretched to 20 per cent, and the Mid-Staffordshire by-election, just ten days before the charge came into force in England and Wales, became effectively a single-issue referendum: Labour's candidate Sylvia Heal overturned a huge Tory majority with a 20 per cent swing, the biggest movement of votes from Conservative to Labour for fifty years. Much less to the party's taste was the spate of demonstrations through March 1990 at various town halls that frequently turned to violence. At an anti-poll tax meeting in Hackney, Paddy Ashdown found himself in the midst of a four-thousand-strong crowd engaged in a battle with the police: 'No doubt about who was organizing this,' he recorded. 'Militant much in evidence, but a lot of anarchists as well. And the extreme unpleasantness and brutality on their faces was rather shocking.' Other disturbances were reported not only in Lambeth and Haringey, but also in the most unlikely of towns, including Colchester, Taunton and Tunbridge

Wells. This was emphatically not the image of the new responsible Labour Party that Neil Kinnock was anxious to project, and he was quick in his denunciation of 'Toytown revolutionaries who pretend that the tax can be stopped and the government toppled by non-payment'.

The demonstrations culminated in a mass rally in Trafalgar Square on the eve of the tax's introduction, attended by between two and three hundred thousand people (or forty thousand if the police were to be believed, for police figures had been straying further and further from reality all decade). And predictably it too turned to violence: riot police were in attendance, demonstrators threw placards and other missiles, mounted charges were made into the crowds, over three hundred were arrested, hundreds more injured, and small groups spent several happy hours rampaging through the West End and looting shops before things finally quietened down. Some Labour MPs turned up for the event, but they had mostly been the usual suspects from the left like Tony Benn, Jeremy Corbyn and George Galloway – all of them amongst the thirty members who had said they would join the non-payment campaign. The party leadership, on the other hand, merely joined in the traditional chorus of condemnation of violent protest, though it was still unable to offer any suggestions for alternative ways to challenge government policy, or even an alternative to the poll tax itself.

Probably the truth was that leaders of all the Westminster parties were genuinely taken aback by the scale of the anti-poll tax movement. After all the defeats of the previous ten years, it was largely assumed that resistance to Thatcherism was futile, but perhaps the difference this time was that the government had – whether through negligence, arrogance or stupidity – dreamt up a single policy that was capable of uniting the vast majority of the country. For the poll tax was deeply unpopular with almost everyone and, although most would not have expressed their objections by rioting, there was greater sympathy with the Trafalgar Square demonstrators than many commentators had expected. The complacency of the past few years was coming home to roost. As Mark Steel put it: 'Thatcher, her minions, her press and her police were like a boxer who's become too used to winning and doesn't notice the hunger and speed of his next opponent, or the flab accumulating on his own stomach.'

Benn reported receiving just one hostile communication in the wake of the riots, an anonymous answerphone message saying: 'You fucking cunt! Now you've lost the next election for us.' Assuming that the man responsible was a Labour supporter, his analysis was probably wrong: Labour's refusal to take any decisive role in the campaign was far more damaging to its prospects than were the actions of a handful of maverick MPs articulating the views of the electorate. The task of providing opposition to the government seemed to have slipped off the party's agenda, and the lack of a clear lead was hardly inspiring; Kinnock had now spent longer in opposition than any of those who preceded him as Labour leader and he, like Thatcher, was looking as though he had run out of steam. The local elections that followed in May seemed to suggest opinions were hardening – in Scotland the Conservatives actually increased their share of the vote, but they were overtaken by the Scottish National Party, which supported the tactic of non-payment – and over the summer the Labour lead in the opinion polls began to fall.

While the streets were thus providing the setting for mass displays of anti-Thatcherite sentiments, the prime minister was suffering a series of blows in Westminster as well, all of them related in one way or another to the issue of Britain's role in Europe. At its heart was the exchange rate mechanism (ERM) of the European Monetary System, a measure that was intended to stabilize the exchange rates of the participating currencies by tying them loosely to the value of the Deutschmark, with the intention that over time the ties might be tightened and a single currency would ultimately be introduced.

The ERM was launched in 1979 and, although the United Kingdom (suspicious as ever of all such initiatives, from the European Community itself through to the Eurovision Song Contest) declined the offer to be a founding member, it enjoyed establishment support from the beginning. Now is 'a good time for Britain to join' advised *The Times* as early as 1981 and by the middle of the decade, the chancellor Nigel Lawson too was an advocate. Even the Labour Party, as part of its repositioning, came round to supporting British membership, with its new economic team of John Smith and Gordon Brown hoping that, in the event of a Labour government ever coming to power in the future, it might thereby avoid the currency crises that had so regularly plagued its predecessors. But Thatcher remained adamantly opposed, seeing the ERM – quite correctly – as part of the federalist project that would see yet more power siphoned off from British institutions to a centralized Europe. Lawson responded by unofficially linking the value of the pound to the deutschmark, which seemed to be getting the worst of both worlds, tailoring Britain's economic policy to the fluctuating exchange rate of a foreign currency, while having no reciprocal influence on the Bundesbank. Amongst the results were the unpredictable movements in interest rates that seldom reflected the needs of the British economy.

The deep division between prime minister and chancellor over such a major decision was damaging to the stability of the government, and in early 1988 Thatcher made it publicly clear that she didn't approve of Lawson's shadowing of the deutschmark. She went on to announce that Alan Walters, who had been her chief economic adviser in the early days, would be returning the following year to the same post after an absence of five years lecturing at Johns Hopkins University. This was generally understood to be an attempt by Thatcher to shore up her position in the dispute with Lawson, since Walters shared her opinion of the ERM (it was 'half-baked,' he commented), and was bound to end in tears, one way or another. 'Walters is often right but is unbelievably tactless, and that all makes it harder for Nigel to back down,' reflected Edwina Currie, as the splits became ever more open. Even Walters' supporters were bound to admit that his dogmatic manner was not calculated to smooth ruffled feathers. 'He was no politician,' conceded Nicholas Ridley, himself not noticeably gifted in diplomacy; 'indeed, he was a person who despised politics.'

By June 1989, as John Smith taunted Thatcher and Lawson in the Commons, singing the theme song from *Neighbours* ('Neighbours should be there for another') while they sat stony-faced opposite him, the situation had become politically untenable. The occasion was a debate on the European summit that month in Madrid, where – though this was not on public record at the time – both Lawson and Howe, now the foreign secretary, had threatened to resign unless Thatcher agreed a definite date for Britain's entry into the ERM. She called their bluff and her private response was scorn personified: 'My foreign secretary said if I didn't commit myself to a date, he'd resign. Well, I didn't commit myself, and he hasn't resigned. What sort of foreign secretary have I got?' she sneered. Instead she reshuffled her cabinet the following month, keeping Lawson but moving Howe to become leader of the House and giving him the meaningless title of deputy prime minister. In his place came John Major, the latest of her long line of favourites.

But still the problem persisted and, with the return of Walters now imminent, Lawson issued a 'him or me' ultimatum, which left Thatcher decidedly unimpressed. 'I told him not to be ridiculous,' she remembered. 'He was demeaning himself even by talking in such terms.' But Lawson was serious and, as Ridley pointed out, 'she couldn't have met his request without making herself look humiliated and impotent'. And so, at the end of October 1989, Lawson resigned. Shortly afterwards, Walters also resigned and, just as Thatcher had managed to lose both Michael Heseltine and Leon

Brittan over the Westlands fiasco, so now she was deprived of both chancellor and economic adviser. Another reshuffle followed and Major, after all of three months as foreign secretary, moved to another of the great offices of state as chancellor of the exchequer.

Thatcher could not help but be damaged by the resignation, but it was hardly terminal, since the issue of the ERM was not one to excite great public interest at a time when a descent into recession seemed more likely than not. Nor was the situation entirely unprecedented: Harold Macmillan had suffered the resignation of his entire treasury team in 1958 and yet had remained in power for another five years. Certainly she gave no indication that she might moderate her abrasive style, even though it was now considered a liability by almost everyone. 'After she had lost Nigel Lawson,' wrote Tory MP Julian Critchley, 'the pundits claimed that the one-time Iron Lady was suffering from metal fatigue, a condition which in no way diminished the intensity of her opinion or the rapidity of her tongue.' Even when the unthinkable happened and she was challenged for the leadership, for the first time since she had been elected by the party nearly fifteen years earlier, she continued to imply that she had no intention of ever relinquishing it.

The system then operating to choose the leadership of the Conservative Party was one of the most subtle and sophisticated that had ever been devised. Its creator was Humphrey Berkley, a Conservative MP in the mid-1960s (though he later joined the Labour Party, before defecting to the SDP and then rejoining Labour), and it allowed for an annual election at the start of each parliament. Any MP was entitled to stand, provided they had a proposer and seconder, whose names need not be made public, and only MPs were entitled to vote. In order to win the first ballot a candidate needed to obtain not merely a clear majority of the votes cast but also a margin of 15 per cent over the second-placed candidate; if this condition was not met, then a second ballot would be held in which a simple majority would be sufficient to win. But crucially the rules allowed for candidates to enter the contest in the second round. The intention was to allow a so-called stalking-horse candidate to be run against an incumbent leader, that is an MP who stood no chance of winning, but whose job it was to establish in the first round whether the leader enjoyed a sufficiently overwhelming body of support. Other, more weighty candidates could thereby keep their hands clean lest the challenge prove unsuccessful and they be accused of disloyalty; but if the challenge did prove that the leader was vulnerable, they could happily join in for the second ballot, insisting that they were standing for the good of the party rather than from any vaulting ambition on their own behalf.

This was precisely the system that had brought Margaret Thatcher to the leadership. She had challenged Edward Heath in 1975 when no one else was prepared so to do, and in some quarters she was regarded as being a stalking-horse. When she secured more votes than Heath in the first round, his position was revealed as being so weak that he had no choice but to step down, allowing what were supposed to be the serious candidates – led by William Whitelaw – to enter the fray. Except that she had built up such momentum that she won through. Theoretically she had been re-elected to the post in the autumn of every year since, though no challenger had ever dared make himself known. Now, in the wake of Lawson's resignation, a champion entered the lists on behalf of all those who felt she had reigned too long.

As a chivalric hero, however, Sir Anthony Meyer was not quite as impressive as one might have hoped. An hereditary baronet and a long-serving MP on the outermost liberal fringe of the party, he was five years older than Thatcher and virtually unheard of by the public, though he had been amongst those voting against the cancellation of the GLC elections. The term 'stalking-horse' was considered too grandiose for the occasion and Meyer was instead dubbed the stalking-donkey by the press. Mock as they might, he seemed content with his role and told anyone who would listen that his quarrel with the prime minister was about style as well as content: 'She seems to be convinced that she is invincible as well as infallible,' he said, and he persuaded enough others that he secured the votes of 33 MPs with 24 others spoiling their papers. Thatcher, of course, won easily (she got 314 votes), but the fact that she had been challenged at all, let alone that there was a decent-sized minority refusing to support her, was worrying. 'Although we all went round saying it was a great victory, it did give her prestige a knock,' wrote Currie in her diary, and Ian Gow, an ardent Thatcherite, admitted that 'he had a hard time persuading many colleagues to vote for the PM'. But she sailed on regardless. 'I think that is good enough for me to carry on,' she remarked breezily, paying no heed to Tory MP Tristan Garel-Jones when he warned: 'There are a hundred assassins lurking in the bushes, prime minister. Those people will come back and kill you.'

For the first half of 1990 the government's main task was to ride out the storm over the poll tax, but that was a purely negative stance, offering little in the way of encouraging the demoralized troops in Westminster or in the country. *Spitting Image* depicted politicians from all parties singing a version of the Moody Blues' hit 'Go Now' to Thatcher (now portrayed as a straitjacketed madwoman), while the journalist Ronald Butt, who had long been a staunch defender in *The Times*, was worrying that the Labour Party 'is increasingly seen as the responsible, moderate and socially responsive party. It is the Tories who are now disliked as doctrinaire, extreme and socially hard-faced.' And so the atmosphere of gloom, depression and defeatism continued.

At almost any other time, the unexpectedly impressive performance of the England football team – which reached the semi-finals of the World Cup that summer, prevented only by a penalty shoot-out from meeting Argentina in a final that would surely have avenged the 1986 defeat – would have played in the government's favour with the mood of positive optimism that descended on the country. The sense of hopefulness, after years of under-achievement, was reinforced by the fact that the team included some of the most creative players in the world with John Barnes, Peter Beardsley and Chris Waddle, and by the emergence of Paul 'Gazza' Gascoigne, arguably the most talented and inspiring footballer England had yet produced. Almost single-handedly, with his charismatic ability on the pitch, and his engaging public persona that verged on the idiot savant off it, Gascoigne dragged football out from its post-Heysel doghouse; when he was shown a yellow card in the semi-final and tears welled up in his eyes as he realized he would miss the final should England get through, his place in popular mythology was assured and the cult of Gazza-mania was born. Even when the team was subsequently taken to Downing Street to receive the congratulations of the prime minister and Gascoigne turned out to be one of the few people outside the Conservative Party to have something good to say about Thatcher ('I gave her a hug – it wasn't bad, she was nice and cuddly like'), it did him no harm.

On the other hand, it did her no good. And nor did the World Cup adventure itself, for she had already made clear that she viewed all football fans as potential hooligans, and the thwarted identity card scheme had made her into a hate figure on the terraces, even amongst those with little interest in politics. To compound the issue, the previous season had been soundtracked by chants of 'We're not paying the poll tax' ringing out from grounds around the country. Not even the readmission of English clubs into European competition, following their enforced exile, could remove the feeling that fans weren't seen by this government as decent members of society. More subtly, there was the fact that the new national hero was far removed from previous icons; a media-literate footballer who showed his emotions to the extent of crying during a match was a long way from the traditional hardman image of the game, and hinted at a cultural shift away from the world inhabited by Thatcher.

None of this, of course, registered much in Westminster where the issue of Europe was still lurking beneath the troubled waters. In the summer of 1990, three weeks after that semi-final defeat to West Germany, it surfaced in an entirely unexpected way. Nicholas Ridley, the last true believer in the cabinet, was then the trade and industry secretary and had even been Thatcher's preferred choice to replace Lawson as chancellor before she realized what a hostage to fortune the appointment of such a blunt politician would be. Her judgement was vindicated when he gave an interview to the *Spectator* magazine in July 1990, in which he shared his candid thoughts on European integration, calling the European Monetary System 'a German racket designed to take over Europe' and stating flatly: 'I'm not against giving up sovereignty in principle, but not to this lot. You might just as well give it to Adolf Hitler, frankly.' In case he wasn't being sufficiently controversial, he threw in a reference to Auschwitz and described France as being Germany's poodle. 'We appreciate frankness,' flinched Karl von Hase, a former German ambassador to Britain, 'but this is brutality.'

The fact that his interviewer, and the magazine's editor, was Dominic Lawson, son of the former chancellor, led some to suspect that Ridley had been tricked into making such incriminating and decidedly indiscreet remarks – he noted drily that the younger Lawson 'turned out not to be helpful' – but he wasn't the only one using such imagery. Thatcher's own hostility to the unification of Germany was well known, and she was said to speak 'far too emotionally in private about a Fourth Reich'. Furthermore, an opinion poll earlier in the year had shown that over half the British population were concerned about the possible return of fascism in a reunified Germany, and another poll taken after Ridley's interview revealed broad support. Nonetheless it was difficult to see how a man seen to make such offensive remarks about the two leading nations in Europe could continue to serve in the British government, and within the week his resignation had been proffered and accepted.

Ridley had never exactly kept his opinions a secret in Westminster, but the *Spectator* interview gave the public a much starker image than had previously been available of where the right wing of the Conservative Party now stood. It reinforced the opinion of those supportive of Europe that the inner circles of Thatcherism were irreconcilably hostile to the country's partners, while those who were themselves of a sceptical persuasion were hardly cheered that anyone venturing a dissident comment could be so easily forced out of his job. His departure left Thatcher even more isolated in her cabinet, for although his replacement, Peter Lilley, was another Thatcherite, he was hardly one of the same weight and calibre as Ridley.

Meanwhile, John Major found himself in a position of considerable and growing strength, for despite his youth and relative lack of experience, and despite the fact that his career had been entirely dependent on Thatcher's patronage, it was politically impossible for her to dismiss him after Nigel Lawson's departure. Clearly unassailable for the moment, he achieved what his two predecessors had failed to do: in October 1990 he announced Britain's entry into the ERM. Displaying unexpected political flair, he made the announcement on the last day of the Labour Party's conference, stealing all their headlines, and, to complete the boldness of the move, he cut interest rates by 1 percentage point at the same time. Most political and financial commentators applauded the move, including Lawson ('I warmly welcome this historic decision which I have long advocated'), though there were doubts expressed about the timing: the British level of inflation at nearly 11 per cent was almost twice that of the European average, and there was a threat of a new world recession, following the Iraqi invasion of Kuwait that had seen a sharp rise in oil prices. At the Conservative conference the following week, Ridley spoke to a fringe meeting and correctly predicted that the pound and the deutschmark 'will never have a stable relationship'.

The good headlines were but fleeting. The week after the conference, a by-election was held in Eastbourne, following the murder of Ian Gow by the IRA, and a safe Tory seat that had previously been held with a seventeen thousand majority fell to the Liberal Democrats on a swing of 20 per cent. The mood of misery that had temporarily lifted from the Conservatives settled again: under heavy media and political pressure, the government had done what was asked of it and joined the ERM, and still nothing was going right. Worse yet, Thatcher continued unrepentantly to use anti-European rhetoric, despite the change in policy. On 30 October she reported back to the Commons on another summit meeting, this time in Rome, where she had found herself in a minority of one on the question of the single currency, and she was unequivocal in her denunciation of Jacques Delors: 'He wanted the European parliament to be the democratic body of the Community,' she told the Commons. 'He wanted the commission to be the executive and he wanted the council of ministers to be the senate. No! No! No!' The intransigence implied by that triple negative was all the more powerful since it was televised, the House having recently agreed, against her wishes, to allow cameras into the chamber.

Eurosceptics were much heartened by her position – the *Sun* addressed the issue of monetary union with one of its most famous headlines: UP

YOURS DELORS! – but for many it was profoundly disheartening, and for one man in particular this was the last straw. On 1 November Geoffrey Howe resigned from the government in protest at her continued inflexibility. 'Well, now I'm *really* fucking depressed,' despaired Edwina Currie. That night Edward Heath was on the BBC programme *Question Time*, exhibiting what might be termed cautious jubilation, hinting that Howe might now challenge for the leadership – the annual election was due within weeks – and replying when asked if this was the beginning of the end for Thatcher: 'Well, there is always the beginning of an end for every prime minister. It remains to be seen.' Two days earlier the first contact had been made by the two teams digging the Channel Tunnel, a symbolic joining of Britain to the Continent for the first time since the last Ice Age, and there were many who saw it as a fitting moment for the European issue that was tearing away at the soul of the party to be resolved once and for all.

A resigning minister is entitled to make a statement to the House, traditionally heard in silence and without interruptions, and there was some, though not very feverish, anticipation about what Howe would say. But the Commons was in recess and silence descended for a fortnight, during which time two more by-elections were held in Bootle and in Bradford North; both were Labour seats, but the Conservative performance was again poor, particularly in the marginal constituency of Bradford North which saw a swing from Tory to Labour of 16 per cent and the Conservative candidate pushed into third place by the Liberal Democrats.

The depression deepened on Tory benches, with even the good and faithful servant Bernard Ingham reporting an MP had told him 'that for the first time his constituents were blaming Mrs Thatcher herself for the circumstances in which they found themselves.' The Northern Ireland minister Richard Needham, in a conversation on his car phone, gave his opinion that 'I wish the old cow would resign', only to find that the call had been intercepted by a terrorist group and leaked to the press. 'I don't think she realizes what a jam she's in,' wrote Alan Clark, reaching for his customary stock of wartime metaphors. 'It's the Bunker syndrome. Everyone round you is clicking their heels. The saluting sentries have highly polished boots and beautifully creased uniforms. But out there at the Front it's all disintegrating.' There was much speculation over the possibility of a leadership challenge, though few were prepared to speak out publicly; one of those who did was Anthony Meyer, making clear that things had moved out of his league by now: 'If Conservatives think, as they mostly do, that we cannot win with Margaret Thatcher, then they must stand up and be counted against her. With the right leader, and in my view that right leader is Michael Heseltine, the Tory Party can win a historic fourth term.' Nearly five years after he walked out of the cabinet, it seemed as though Heseltine's day of destiny was finally about to dawn.

Most importantly, those two weeks saw Howe become increasingly infuriated, both by Thatcher's attitude to his resignation, which he considered 'patronizing and self-righteous', and by a speech she gave at the Guildhall in London to the Lord Mayor's Banquet, in which she used a cricketing image to emphasize her continued self-belief while all around were doubting her: 'I am still at the crease, though the bowling has been pretty hostile of late. And, in case anyone doubted it, I can assure you there will be no ducking the bouncers, no stonewalling, no playing for time. The bowling's going to get hit all round the ground. That's my style.' It was, as journalist Alan Watkins pointed out, a messy metaphor – apart from anything else, 'ducking was precisely what one did with bouncers' – but the meaning was clear enough: not even Howe's resignation was sufficient to prompt any change in direction. And so he worked quietly on his speech.

Howe was in a unique position within the party. He had stood as a candidate against Thatcher in the leadership election of 1975 and, though he had picked up just nineteen votes, he proved remarkably resilient. By 1988 he was the only one of her rivals from that contest to remain in government – William Whitelaw and James Prior having departed, and Hugh Fraser, Edward Heath and John Peyton having never served under her. In fact, he was the last surviving member of the original Thatcher cabinet from 1979 and, in the words of Chris Patten, he 'was almost a permanent part of the British constitution'. He was popular with the parliamentary party, though there was no equivalent feeling amongst the electorate, where he was regarded as the man who brought the country the first Thatcherite recession and who had then proved to be, at best, an anonymous foreign secretary. Even amongst Conservative supporters, he was not exactly popular, regularly trailing Tebbit and Heseltine as their choice for the succession. If he had an image, it was as one of the dullest senior politicians of recent times, 'an unbelievably boring speaker,' noted Teresa Gorman. Nicknamed Mogadon Man for his low-key delivery, he had once literally sent David Owen to sleep during a live television pro-gramme on which they were both appearing, and was best known as the target of one of Denis Healey's better jokes – being criticized by Howe, Healey had said, was like being savaged by a dead sheep. That was intended, of course, as a putdown, even if the visual image it conjured up was not entirely reassuring: zombie sheep on the rampage sounded like something dreamt up by Sam Raimi, director of *The Evil Dead*, though it was not until his resignation statement that Howe lived up to such a billing. And even on the day of that speech, Alan Clark still felt that it couldn't make any difference: 'Who gives a toss for the old dormouse?' he asked his diary, rhetorically.

But there was life in the dormouse yet. With Lawson sitting supportively by his side, Howe candidly explained to the Commons why he felt it was impossible for him to continue to serve in Thatcher's government. He ridiculed 'the nightmare image' she conjured up of 'a continent that is positively teeming with ill-intentioned people, scheming, in her words, to extinguish democracy, to dissolve our national identities, to lead us through the back door into a federal Europe'. It was a tragedy for the country, he said, 'that the prime minister's perceived attitude towards Europe is running increasingly serious risks for the future of our nation.' He even picked up her cricketing imagery and somehow ended up still more confused than she had been: 'It's rather like sending your opening batsmen to the crease only for them to find the moment the first balls are bowled that their bats have been broken before the game by the team captain,' he declared, which made no sense at all. But again, one could see the point towards which he was fumbling, and in any event the really shocking fact was that a former chancellor and foreign secretary was prepared publicly to attack the prime minister who had appointed him, accusing her of undermining her senior colleagues. And in perhaps the most powerful passage of his speech, he seemed to assault the patriotic foundations of her philosophy, arguing both he and Lawson had spent years trying to persuade Thatcher not to let Britain 'retreat into a ghetto of sentimentality about our past and so diminish our own control over our destiny in the future'. He followed that with positive references back to Harold Macmillan and Winston Churchill, clearly seeking to place Thatcher outside the Conservative mainstream, as though she were being excommunicated.

The bitterness revealed by such comments was, it was assumed, an explosion of the accumulated, pent-up frustrations of being patronized, bullied and ridiculed by Thatcher (they had shared 'seven hundred meetings of cabinet or shadow cabinet over the last eighteen years,' he pointed out). But there was also the anger felt by many in the political establishment, both in Britain and in Europe more widely, that Thatcher was reneging on the nation's commitment to what was then still known as the European Economic Community, though it would soon be renamed the European Union. The debate between those who feared, like Thatcher, that democracy and national independence were being sold out, and those who subscribed to the federalist dream of a fully integrated Europe, was to dominate the Conservative Party for the whole of the next decade, but in the immediate moment there was the raw political thrill of hearing such a senior figure launch a coup. 'The conflict of loyalty, of loyalty to my right honourable friend the prime minister,' he said in his peroration, 'and of loyalty to what I perceive to be the true interests of the nation, has become all too great.' And he ended with a direct incitement to revolution: 'The time has come for others to consider their own response to the tragic conflict of loyalties with which I have myself wrestled for perhaps too long.'

The verdict was almost unanimous: nothing in Howe's political career became him like the leaving it. 'This was the most stunning speech I have ever heard in the House,' reported Paddy Ashdown. 'It rocked the government on its heels. Thatcher sat white-faced and, from time to time, bit her lip as if to stem the pain.' Peter Jenkins, writing in the *Independent*, went further: 'It was more than a resignation speech; it was a bill of impeachment.' And Tony Benn had little doubt: 'It has certainly transformed everything. We have really come to the end of the Thatcher era, I think.' After so many false dawns, this time he was right. Heseltine, who had been wavering about whether to strike, responded instantly to the challenge of Howe's last sentence and announced that he would be standing against Thatcher for the leadership of the party. Ever the populist, he signalled to the wider public that he was motivated by more than the European issues so beloved of the political elite: 'A significant consequence of my election as a leader would be an immediate and fundamental review of the poll tax, which I believe to be important for the revival of government fortunes.'

The date for the vote had already been fixed for the following Tuesday, which left the Thatcher camp very little time to rally their disaffected troops, but in any case it was far from certain that they understood how serious the situation was. When Emma Nicholson asked Brian Griffiths, head of the policy unit at Downing Street, to pass on a message that she wouldn't be voting for Thatcher, his surprised response – 'Are you telling me that this election actually matters?' – revealed how lightly the challenge was being taken. Thatcher herself was sufficiently blasé that she was due to be out of the country, at a conference with other European leaders in Paris, on the day of the ballot. But there was a mood in the country for change, and there were enough Conservative MPs who felt the same that the leadership should have been worried. 'She failed to see change in British society under her nose, or prepare for it,' was Edwina Currie's verdict; 'she slew the old dragons, but continued to wear the same bloodstained armour. Meanwhile a nicer, gentler, kinder Britain is waking up. She wanted to handbag it.' A spate of polls in the Sunday newspapers revealed that with Heseltine as leader, the Tories would benefit from a swing of between 6 and 10 percentage points and would overtake Labour.

On the evening of that same Sunday, BBC1 began transmission of a new drama series, Andrew Davies' adaptation of the novel *House of Cards*, written by the Conservative Party's former chief of staff, Michael Dobbs, and inspired by William Whitelaw's perceptive comment to him during the 1987 election: 'There is a woman who will never fight another election campaign.' In one of the most fortuitous pieces of scheduling in television history, the series concerned a leadership struggle in the Conservative Party and, though it was set in a post-Thatcherite near-future, it opened with her image; Ian Richardson, playing the Tory chief whip Francis Urquhart, was seen at his desk, picking up a picture of Thatcher and turning to the camera to address the audience directly: 'Nothing lasts for ever. Even the longest, the most glittering reign must come to an end some day.' The previously unthinkable was being acted out on national television.

When the results were announced Thatcher had a clear majority – 204 votes to Heseltine's 152 – but not quite the margin of 15 per cent of the total electorate needed for outright victory. There would have to be a second ballot, and Thatcher immediately announced from Paris that she would be standing again. She returned to the Commons to report on the conference ('She was announcing to the House the official end of the Cold War – perhaps the most important event of the whole decade,' noted Ridley ruefully), but the real action was behind the scenes. Later that night, members of the cabinet and others went in to see her individually; virtually all told her that she had no hope of winning and that, rather than end her premiership in ignominious defeat, she should step down for the sake of the party. It was also brought home that this was the only way to beat Heseltine, since it would release other members of the cabinet to stand against him. She was reportedly shocked by such open disloyalty – 'They sold me down the river,' she exclaimed – but was left with little option. And so, on Thursday, 22 November 1990 Margaret Thatcher, who had been in office longer than any other prime minister in the memory of anyone then living, announced that she would not be putting her name forward for the second ballot, that she would resign as leader of the party and as prime minister once a successor had been chosen.

In the country there was a mixture of shock, disbelief and release. Paddy Ashdown reported that he had heard the news announced at Glasgow airport 'and that everyone had burst into spontaneous clapping and cheering. I gather the same thing happened at King's Cross and Victoria.'

The future Labour MP Oona King was working as a temp in Vauxhall and immediately took an early lunch-break so she could go to Downing Street to celebrate: 'I grabbed a thick ink marker, a piece of cardboard and ran for the lift. In the foyer I drew up my impromptu placard: "I'm 23 years old and I've waited *exactly* half my life for today: bye-bye Maggie."' And on the BBC London radio station, GLR, Johnnie Walker told his listeners he was raising a pint of Guinness to toast Thatcher's demise: 'Can you imagine life without Maggie Thatcher? Some people have never known another prime minister. There're going to be street parties all over the country.' He was promptly sacked by the station controller, Matthew Bannister.

Her final appearance in the Commons as prime minister was in a vote of no confidence that had been pointlessly and incompetently called by Labour. She was at the very top of her form, reminding the House what a formidable politician she could be – 'Why did they sack you?' called out the Militant-supporting MP Dave Nellist – while Kinnock was correspondingly dreadful, which augured ill for the immediate future of his party. Labour had set such great store on her personal unpopularity that it was far from clear whether it would be able to respond positively to her departure. She was an 'evil woman,' snapped Jack Straw, seemingly furious that the bogeywoman, on the fear of whom so much rested, had been slain by her own side.

In her absence two other challengers stepped into the ring to fight it out with Heseltine: Douglas Hurd, the foreign secretary, and John Major. Thatcher made no bones about who she would be supporting: 'It may be inverted snobbishness but I don't want old style, old Etonian Tories of the old school to succeed me and go back to the old complacent, consensus ways,' she remarked in private. 'John Major is someone who has fought his way up from the bottom and is far more in tune with the skilled and ambitious and worthwhile working classes than Douglas Hurd is.' Perhaps in recognition of the way that Thatcher's anti-elitism had – at least for now – reshaped British political life, this turned into one of the few talking points of the campaign leading up to the second ballot. Hurd's father and grandfather had both been Conservative MPs and his privileged, patrician background (Eton, Cambridge, diplomatic service) would in earlier generations have been seen as constituting an impeccable c.v., but in this post-Thatcher world he was immediately put on the defensive, forced to argue that he only went to Eton because he had won a scholarship: 'That is what social mobility is all about, I understand.' In retrospect Hurd was to claim that had Thatcher known then that Major had had an affair with Edwina Currie, she would 'probably not have backed him', and his own chances would thereby have been enhanced, but his more serious problem was that opinion polls showed he had no chance of beating Labour, while Heseltine and Major were both said to be capable of so doing.

The support for Major in the country was a surprise to many, but it reflected the truth of Currie's analysis some months earlier: 'When she goes, the new PM, whether Tory successor or Labour, will be pro-Europe and gentler on social and economic issues, more interventionist, more helpful to minorities, treading more gently in the international scene.' Michael Dobbs had made the same point in *House of Cards*, as one of his characters reflected on the mood of Tory MPs: 'They wanted a new fashion. Something less abrasive, less domineering; they'd had enough of trial by ordeal and being shown up by a woman.' Even Alan Clark, dismissing the prospects of Heseltine, could see the need for change: 'people are sick of passion, they want reassurance.'

So they did, and Major seemed to be the best option for providing it. Above all, his courteous affability meant he had made no enemies and he carried no obvious ideological baggage. He was assumed to be a Thatcherite, not least by Thatcher herself, but there was precious little evidence for such a belief save for his non-establishment background; rather he was a cipher on whom all sectors of the party projected their own attitudes, and there was a suspicion that, like the Peter Sellers' character Chauncey Gardiner in the film *Being There* (1979), Major benefited from people hearing what they wanted to hear. Even on the question of Europe, there was some doubt quite where he stood; as Teresa Gorman pointed out, both the pro- and anti-European factions 'thought he was "their man"'. Outside Westminster, he might be little known to the public, mocked by *Spitting Image* as the grey man of politics whose greatest enthusiasm was for peas, but he seemed down-to-earth, decent and reliable, the kind of man you could count on to water your plants while you were away on holiday and at least his love of cricket might mean an end to mangled metaphors.

On the second ballot Major scored just under 50 per cent of the vote, technically not enough to win outright, but Heseltine, who had seen his own vote fall, could read the writing on the wall; he immediately withdrew from the contest, followed by Hurd, and Major was promptly elected unopposed as leader of the Conservative Party and therefore as prime minister, the youngest person to hold the post so far in the twentieth century. It was less than four weeks since Howe's resignation, and less than two since his Commons statement, an extraordinarily rapid regicide compared, say, to the six months it took Tony Benn to fail to secure the deputy leadership of a party that was in opposition. Major's unexpected victory was the culmination to one of the most sensational episodes in modern politics, though not everyone noticed, for despite the fervour at Westminster, in the rest of the country everyday life continued as normal. On the day of the second ballot, the television personality Gyles Brandreth, who would later become a Tory MP, was in Shepperton Studios, making an advert for frozen potato waffles and found that he was the only person present who seemed to care about the result: 'In the world of Birdseye Waffles, no one seems the least bit interested in who our next prime minister is going to be.'

The removal of Thatcher and her replacement by Major brought an immediate dividend for the Conservatives. Heseltine returned to the cabinet as environment secretary, charged with finding a replacement to the poll tax, Major found himself with a higher poll rating than Thatcher had ever achieved, and the country appeared to have concluded that it now had the change of government it had been seeking. Within the party itself there was said to be deep anger at the manner of Thatcher's despatch, and certainly there were strains reminiscent of those between Labour and the SDP in the early 1980s; Howe found Keith Joseph physically turning his back on him, with the words: 'I'm sorry, Geoffrey: we're not friends anymore.' But it was notable that none of those who voted for Heseltine on the first ballot were deselected as MPs by their local parties (save for Anthony Meyer, but he was being punished for the stalking-donkey episode), and it was to take another couple of years for the full bitterness to become truly apparent and for Europe to reveal itself as still being the single most divisive issue for Tories.

For the moment, they too shared in the national sense of relief. The last few months of Thatcher's premiership had been uncomfortable ones for the faithful, seeming to reprise so many of the uglier features from the dark days of 1980-81 that it was reasonable to ask whether ultimately it had all been worth it. Interest rates and inflation were back into double figures, there were riots on the streets, and the government was caught up in pay disputes with the public sector, led by ambulance workers, causing journalists to recall the winter of discontent under James Callaghan. Even on a personal level, the end carried echoes of the beginning: Thatcher's victory in 1979 had been overshadowed by the murder of her close political ally Airey Neave by terrorists; this year it had been another friend, Ian Gow. Britain was undeniably a different country to the one she had inherited, but it was far from certain that even she believed the changes that had been made were the ones she intended, or – if they were – whether they were secure enough to survive. Her continued refusal to accept that there was anyone with sufficient resolve to carry the struggle forward suggested a certain lack of confidence in her legacy. Perhaps most telling of all, Larry Lamb, the editor who had first brought the *Sun* out in full support of her leadership, the man who had written the front-page editorial in 1979 urging his readers to vote for the radical change she offered, had by the end of the decade 'lost his faith in Mrs Thatcher after seeing what her tenure of office had done to the country.' In moments of deep reflection, he said he had 'created a Frankenstein's monster.'

Back in 1982 with the first success in the Falklands War, Thatcher had urged the nation to 'rejoice, just rejoice', and it had duly done so. There was not much rejoicing at her departure, once the immediate moment had passed. The sheer weight of time meant that many of those in the country who had been hit hardest by her policies were simply demoralized by now. Mark Steel was performing at a benefit for a trades council in Nottingham on the night of her departure and was greeted by a Labour activist with the words: 'I don't know why you're so pleased about Thatcher going. They'll only put someone else in her place.' Opposition politicians who, like Labour's future deputy leader John Prescott, regarded her as 'the devil incarnate' were left with the reality that while the faces might have changed, the Tories were still in power, and might yet reinvent themselves under John Major, as they had in the wake of their 1945 election defeat. 'He is a new type of Thatcherite really,' reflected Tony Benn; 'not strident, probably slightly less ideological, more sympathetic to Europe, a hard man in terms of financial policy, but confident.' Even in intellectual and artistic circles, there was such distrust of the lower-middle-class ordinariness of the new prime minister that there was a reluctance to be too jubilant.

And so, despite Johnnie Walker's suggestion, there were no street parties, no wild festivities. Perhaps the only place where there was genuine rejoicing was on the wet wing of the Conservative Party. Certainly in the eyes of Ian Gilmour there was much to celebrate in the end of doctrinaire determination and the return to a more consensual form of politics, and he saw in her removal a happy resonance of the collapse of communism. 'Margaret Thatcher's overthrow brought to many in the Conservative parliamentary party a feeling of liberation,' he wrote: 'the occupation had at last ended, and after being for so long, as it were, part of Eastern Europe we had rejoined the West.'

OUTRO
Aftermath
'You're history'

't's a funny old world.' Margaret Thatcher's words to her cabinet on the morning of 22 November 1990, shortly before she went to Buckingham Palace to inform the Queen of her resignation, were perhaps a little lacking in gravitas, a little more banal than one might have hoped for on such an historic occasion. But she did have a point. She had won 57 per cent of the votes cast in the first leadership ballot and yet she had been forced out of the contest, while her challenger lived to fight again. The union of woman and office that the British electorate had joined together had been put asunder by her own colleagues. It was not unreasonable to reflect that British politics is indeed a funny old world. It is also a ruthless one, particularly within the Conservative Party. Much was made in later years of the unenviable position of Michael Heseltine: evidence, it was said, that he who wields the knife never wears the crown, though of course he was just following her example. It was she who had fatally stabbed Edward Heath and then succeeded to the throne. Perhaps the real moral was that she who lives by the sword dies by the sword.

Her consolation should have been that her work over the previous ten and a half years had created a legacy that would be unassailable, or would at the very least outlive her. The signs, however, were not immediately encouraging, as the second Thatcherite recession began to see even her favourites struggle. Saatchi & Saatchi, who had made their name as her advertising agency of choice, found themselves making a loss of nearly £60 million in 1989. Rupert Murdoch's News Corporation, weighed down by the expansion into Sky Television and the Fox network in America and teetering on the brink of financial collapse in 1990, only just succeeded in rescheduling its debts in time to ensure its survival. And in 1992 the company that owned One Canary Wharf in London's Docklands, seen by many as the physical symbol of the Thatcherite economic miracle, filed for bankruptcy.

Certain achievements were undeniable. It was unlikely the trade unions would ever regain the same influence over political decision-making that they had enjoyed in the 1970s; the move away from state-ownership of industry, save in certain narrowly defined areas, would probably not be seriously challenged; the sale of council housing had affected the lives of millions and transformed the property market; the battle to change the emphasis from income tax to indirect taxation had been comprehensively won; local councils lost many of their powers, and few dared hope central government might offer to return them. Even in these areas, however, there was a suspicion that Thatcherism hadn't been quite so radical as it might have been in pursuit of its dream of a property-owning, share-owning democracy. Had council housing been given away to those tenants who had paid twenty years of rent, had shares in the privatized state industries been distributed free to all adults in the country, had the democratic principles enforced on trade unions been equally applied to industry – all ideas that were floated on the right during the 1980s – then perhaps Thatcherism might not have been so divisive, might not have bequeathed a Britain in which a whole stratum of society was effectively written off.

Internationally, her proudest boasts were that she had been the first Western leader to embrace Mikhail Gorbachev, thereby helping to facilitate the rapprochement between America and the Soviet Union, and had been the first major politician anywhere to identify the dangers of climate change. She had also brought into being the Anglo-Irish Agreement of 1985, which seemed for a while as though it were a major step towards peace in Northern Ireland, though it was already proving to be of little lasting significance. The semi-detached attitude towards the European Community was similarly fragile, though her insistence in her Bruges speech that Europe did not end at the borders of Germany was influential. Nor did her successors always adhere to the principle of self-determination that she espoused in the wake of the 1983 American invasion of the Caribbean island of Grenada: 'Many people in many countries would love to be free of communism, but that doesn't mean to say we can just walk into them and say now you are free.'

Somewhat more nebulously, the Thatcherite attacks on the establishment – which sometimes appeared to be more concerned with the breaking of eggs than with the making of omelettes – helped produce a national culture that would go on to change the public's perceptions of those in power, even of politicians themselves. A layer of privilege, of expectation by birth, was removed in pursuit of a meritocracy. In the 1960s Britain congratulated itself on creating a new showbusiness aristocracy of pop stars and photographers, designers and hairdressers; in the 1980s, the same social mobility spread to business and industry, if not so noticeably to the professions.

And then there was the recapturing of the Falkland Islands, a war that was charged for many with great symbolic significance. In her final Commons appearance as prime minister, Thatcher talked about how it had reaffirmed 'a sense of this country's destiny, the centuries of history and experience which ensure that when principles have to be defended, when good has to be upheld, when evil has to be overcome, then Britain will take up arms'. This revival of one of Britain's most cherished myths was already, by the time of her departure, starting to wane, but its impact at the time was considerable. Thatcher made what most considered was the right judgement in response to the invasion of British territory, and the armed forces proved that here was at least one national institution that could be counted on in a crisis. The political significance of the war could be, and often was, overstated – the 1983 election was not won simply on the Falklands factor – but the victory in the South Atlantic did have a psychological impact on much of the country.

By any conventional evaluation, her term in office had been far from impressive. Unemployment was much higher when she left than when she arrived, inflation never stabilized and was now increasing, and GDP had grown by an average of just 1.8 per cent per annum, little of that in the area of manufacturing (in the dark days of the 1970s, the average rise had been 2.4 per cent). Wealth inequality had increased substantially, with a fall in the income of the poorest 10 per cent of society, and there were 60 per cent more people dependent on the state for their income than in 1979. Even taxation, as a share of GDP, had increased. 'I sometimes have considerable anxieties about Thatcherism,' wrote Larry Lamb, ten years after urging *Sun* readers to vote Conservative, and he cited not only the economic factors but also the way in which 'the quality of life, especially in our inner cities, is diminished.' But the Thatcherite agenda had never really sought to be judged by such mundane measures. 'What great cause would have been fought and won under the banner "I stand for consensus"?' she had demanded rhetorically in the early days of her premiership, spurning those who lacked the force of her convictions. She saw her work as a vocation, not hesitating to compare it to the greatest of all callings: 'Do you think you would ever have heard of Christianity if the apostles had gone out and said, "I believe in consensus"?'

Her crusade had aimed at the eradication of socialism in Britain, and here she and her supporters were quick to claim victory. In 1988 Woodrow

Wyatt celebrated her creation of a political landscape in which 'the two political parties, if they are to alternate, have to be much more like the Republican Party and the Democrats in America'. Nicholas Ridley agreed: 'She forced the political debate in Britain onto the ground of who can best run a market economy in Britain; it is no longer about whether we have a market economy or a socialist one.' And perhaps this was indeed her most significant achievement; whoever were the winners in the 1980s, the outright losers were clearly the old left in all its forms, whether the parliamentary socialism of Tony Benn, the union militancy of Arthur Scargill or the town-hall Trotskyism of Derek Hatton.

How much of this was her doing, however, was more questionable. Had the Labour Party in 1981 chosen as its leader Denis Healey rather than Michael Foot, and the SDP not therefore been formed, the probability is that she would have served only one term, replaced by a centre-left government that would have reached an accommodation with the unions and never embarked upon the privatization of state industries. Much of the damage done to socialism might actually be seen as the work of the Labour left, suffering from the loss of a sense of priorities. Or perhaps it could be seen as the result of the SDP splitting the anti-Thatcher vote.

And it could be argued that the SDP were the real victors of the ideological struggles of the 1980s. The party contested its last general election in 1987, but twenty years later, as the two ex-public schoolboys Tony Blair and David Cameron faced each other over the despatch boxes at prime minister's questions, it was hard not to be reminded of the final scene in George Orwell's *Animal Farm*, with both parties now looking like nothing so much as the gang of four reborn. Much of the Limehouse Declaration that had launched the SDP back in 1981 could quite easily have been written by either of these leaders, in terms of both its philosophy and its vagueness:

> We want to create an open, classless and more equal society, one which rejects ugly prejudices based upon sex, race or religion . . . We want more, not less, radical change in our society, but with a greater stability of direction . . . We want Britain to play a full and constructive role within the framework of the European Community, NATO, the United Nations and the Commonwealth.

Such sentiments became almost universal at Westminster in the later years of Thatcher's life, but it was hard to see her ever choosing to utter them. 'Our epitaph might be that we had saved the Labour Party,' noted David Owen as early as 1982, adding there were worse fates than that. The former members of the SDP could make a reasonable claim not only to have achieved that objective, but also to have shaped the immediate future of British politics.

Some of that influence was already apparent by the time of Thatcher's fall. It became unmistakable after the 1992 general election in which John Major confounded the opinion polls and led the Conservative Party to a shock victory, recording the largest number of votes ever given to a British party in a single election. When Thatcher came to publish her memoirs in 1993, she could talk about James Callaghan's administration as 'the last Labour government and perhaps the last ever', without it seeming too absurd a comment. For if Labour couldn't win in the depths of a recession that could hardly be blamed on anyone but the incumbent government, would it ever be able to win again? Neil Kinnock responded to the disappointment by stepping down as leader, having achieved in his eight and a half years everything but power. As a Labour leader, he had been more effective than many of his predecessors; he had, above all, genuinely led the party, persuading it to go down the path he had chosen, despite its initial reluctance, and had ensured its survival by neutralizing the threat of the third party. But he had never convinced the electorate that he was capable of taking the final step into Downing Street.

The effect of the 1992 defeat was debilitating to a generation of the left. 'I had always known it was impossible for one person to change the world on their own,' wrote John O'Farrell in his best-selling memoir of Labour's opposition years, *Things Can Only Get Better*. 'But I felt so bitter about the outcome of the 1992 election that I stopped particularly trying.' He was thirty years old and he retreated from activism, concentrating on his family and revelling in his first taste of bacon after ten years of political vegetarianism. (In *Fever Pitch*, the model for all such memoirs of the era, Nick Hornby, some five years older, had recorded an analogous rite of passage as he reached his thirties, in his case the purchase of a season-ticket for the seated part of Arsenal's Highbury stadium, leaving behind his days on the terraces.) O'Farrell's experience, while not entirely typical – for comparatively few were, or ever had been, political activists – did represent the broad trajectory of many who had benefited from what looked in retrospect like the golden age of being a student. More numerous than ever before, thanks to the demographic boom at the turn of the 1960s and to the expansion of tertiary education, students in the early years of Thatcherism were also more comfortable than their counterparts have been since, benefiting from the student grant scheme that was soon to disappear.

That generation had passed through early adulthood under Thatcher's premiership and its members were now emerging as the coming men and women in politics, business, the media, the arts and education. This was where the influence of Thatcherism needed to be felt if her legacy was to be secured. And certain elements were indeed in evidence: home ownership had become the norm, trade union membership was unusual in the private sector, few now defined themselves as socialist – these things had become accepted as part of the order of things. The phrase 'a planned economy' had all but disappeared from the language.

Just as noticeable, however, was the acceptance of the new left morality that had been championed by the likes of the GLC, the single-issue campaigners and the alternative comedians. Sexism, racism and what was now known as homophobia (but had for a while been termed hetero-sexism) were seen as taboos, while lip-service at least was essential on environmental matters. In 1989 Austin Mitchell wrote that Labour had become: 'A mass party without members, an ideological crusade without an agreed ideology, a people's party cut off from the people.' Recognizing the void where its heart had been, it adopted the new left agenda with enthusiasm and relief, and became increasingly confident in its espousal of what had been identity politics, albeit now in a much less strident and confrontational form than before.

And it was not merely the Labour Party. In 1994 Edwina Currie tabled an amendment to the Criminal Justice Bill seeking the equalization of the heterosexual and homosexual ages of consent; the amendment was defeated, but an interim compromise reached and the age for sex between gay men was reduced from twenty-one to eighteen. Many of the issues that had been so derided when floated by the new left became mainstream within a couple of decades, with, for example, the Disability Discrimination Act of 1995, the Civil Partnership Act of 2004, the introduction of more social hours for Commons sittings in an attempt to entice more women into parliament. Even the question of language was resolved on the left's terms, a development symbolized in 2009 when Carol Thatcher, daughter of the former prime minister, was removed from working on the BBC programme *The One Show* because she had compared a black tennis-player's hairstyle to that of a golliwog in a backstage conversation. Cultural norms had changed. The onward march of liberalism turned out to have suffered only temporary set-backs in the middle of the decade and was now firmly back on course; despite extreme hostility from the prime minister, the permissive 1960s virtues of sex and drugs and general tolerance had survived to infect a new generation.

Paradoxically, it was in the popular arts, an area where the government had come under constant attack through the 1980s, that this combination of tolerance and Thatcherism was most visible. It was here that liberal values had been defended most effectively – whether in alternative comedy, pop music, detective fiction or television – but here too that business ethics were becoming increasingly visible. The Thatcher-approved concept of self-employment could be seen, for example, in the way that the smarter comedians launched their own production companies, starting with Talkback Productions, founded by Mel Smith and Griff Rhys Jones in 1981, and Hat Trick, founded by Rory McGrath and Jimmy Mulville in 1986. Entrepreneurialism, with a slight nod to the do-it-yourself ethos of punk, was now seen as standard in the creative industries. The same phenomenon could be found in what had previously been considered the more elite world of the visual arts: the end of the decade saw the first stirrings of what would become known as the Young British Artists, as the likes of Damien Hirst and Sarah Lucas emerged as self-promoting populist stars; by 1991, when Channel 4 began its sponsorship of the Turner Prize, exhibitions had become newsworthy events even for the tabloids.

There was, in this context, a certain symbolism in the fact that the most influential pop act of the last years of the Thatcherite era was the band Soul II Soul, another project that had benefited from the Enterprise Allowance Scheme introduced by Norman Tebbit. Led by the producer Jazzie B, Soul II Soul started out as a sound system, DJing at parties and then starting to run clubs, before diversifying into making clothes and jewellery and opening their own retail outlets. The idea of creating their own music, actually launching a band, was something of a late addition to an already flourishing north London empire, but it was rapidly successful, with hits like 'Keep on Moving' and 'Back to Life (However Do You Want Me)' reinventing soul just when it seemed destined to decline into mechanical R&B. The latter single spent four weeks at No. 1 in 1989 at a time when the charts were not noticeably adventurous – it was preceded and succeeded at No. 1 by records from Jason Donovan and Sonia, both Stock Aitken and Waterman productions – and even made the top five in America.

But unlike, say, Jerry Dammers who had displayed similar entrepreneurial abilities in building the 2 Tone label at the start of the decade, Jazzie B was much more prepared to acknowledge that what he had achieved was part of the Thatcherite agenda. 'For me, Margaret Thatcher was quite important, because she helped to legitimize exactly what we were doing,' he recalled in a 2009 interview. 'Her whole ethos was about you being more enterprizing and getting on with it.' And, he reflected: 'The whole of

Britain was going through change. We needed a new direction, so coming through the '80s with Maggie in front, as it were, wasn't a bad thing for us. Some of us prospered.' He was unusual only in his honesty.

Depending on one's taste and perspective, then, one could look at the battleground of the 1980s and conclude that the spoils belonged to Margaret Thatcher or David Owen, Norman Tebbit or Ken Livingstone. No ideology had triumphed, and it could even be argued that ideology itself was amongst the fatalities: 'As I grow older,' reflected Tony Benn in 2009, 'I have reached the conclusion that issues unite people, whereas ideologies divide them.' It had been a big decade, a time when rival philosophies fought for the soul of the nation, seeking to provide the solution to the crises of the 1970s. And yet, out of the most dogmatic and doctrinaire period in modern British history had come a characteristically British muddle, in which many could point to successes, but none could claim outright victory. That, of course, was far from the wishes of most of those involved, and particularly of Thatcher herself, who abhorred muddle and compromise above all else.

It was, however, ultimately her decade. She stamped her image upon it in a way that few other politicians have ever achieved. The immediate associations conjured up by the mention of any other post-war decade do not centre on political figures, but the 1980s remain the Thatcher decade, for those who idolized her as the greatest leader since Winston Churchill, for those in whom she inspired an undying hatred, and for the millions who saw her as either a mixed blessing or a necessary evil. 'I suppose,' reflected her husband Denis gloomily in January 1991, 'they will be regarded as the disastrous Thatcher years.'

References

page five
So as you raise – *News of the World* 31
December 1979
I pointed – Blacker, *Fixx* p. 281
So who are they electing – Curtis,
Atkinson, Elton & Lloyd, *Blackadder* p. 237

Intro: Eighties
p. x I was eighteen – Steel, *Reasons to be
Cheerful* p. 205; **almost a fact** – Godfrey, *A
Decade of i-Deas* p. 215
p. xii always good for – Branson, *Losing My
Virginity* p.387; **it has been** – Burton, *Parallel
Lives* p.52; **admires Sir Keith** – Alvarado &
Stewart, *Made for Television* p. 94
p. xiii Economics are the method –
Hewison, *Culture and Consensus* p. 212; **The
economy had gone wrong** – Thatcher, *The
Path to Power* pp. 305–6; **Britic** – Jennings, *The
Paul Jennings Reader* p. 264; **Today has put** –
Osmond, *The Divided Kingdom* p. 25
p. xv acquisitive individualism – Young,
One of Us p. 526; **the crowd** – *The Times* 12
March 1982
p. xvi a liar – Engel & Morrison, *The
Sportspages Almanac 1991* p. 8; **In my
experience** – Hornby, *Fever Pitch* p.141; **this
is a vicious era** – Elms, *The Way We Wore*
p.240
p. xvii in the pursuit – *Private Eye, The Book of
Wimmin* p.74; **views polarized** – Hatton,
Inside Left p. 106; **there is virtually** –
Rentoul, *Tony Blair* p. 166; **private interests**
– Jacobs & Worcester, *We British* p. 31
p. xviii an icon – *Time* 13 November 1989
p. xix undermining the concept – Wyatt,
Journals Volume 1 p. 227
p. xx the economic and social structure –
Writers' Monthly magazine, March 1987; **Why
do we need** – Tebbit, *Upwardly Mobile*

pp.165–6; Production of movies – *The Times*
16 June 1990
p. xxi I don't think – Walker, *Icons in the Fire*
pp.119–20

**Part One: Putting out Fire with Gasoline:
1979–83**
p. 1 I see no chance – The Beat, 'Stand
Down Margaret' (1980); **I blame** – Clement
& La Frenais, 'If I Were a Carpenter', *Auf
Wiedersehen, Pet* (1983); **The stews** – Robert
Holmes, 'The Caves of Androzani', *Doctor
Who* (1984)

1: The First Thatcher Government
p. 3 It has always seemed – Banks, *The Wasp
Factory* p. 62; **Margaret Thatcher** –
Longford, *Diary of a Year* p. 27
p. 4 The absence – *The Times* 13 November
1979; **How did she** – *Sun* 13 October 1981
p. 5 she does like – *Sunday Express* 9 August
1976; **One has to remember** – Carpenter,
Robert Runcie p. 258
p. 6 we in Britain – Longford op. cit. p. 10;
she is *so* beautiful – Clark, *Into Politics* p.
147; **Cette femme Thatcher** – Young, *One of
Us* p. 383; **a psychotic killer** – Townsend,
Adrian Mole From Minor to Major p. 163; **grimly
visaged** – Dexter, *The Wench is Dead* p. 19;
Joyce Grenfell – Kingsley & Tibballs, *Box of
Delights* p. 194
p. 7 we've got a corporal – Owen, *Time to
Declare* p. 574; **sulk made flesh** – Pearce, *The
Senate of Lilliput* p. 146; **military loyalty** –
Ridley, *My Style of Government* p. 24;
p. 8 When I married – Watkins, *A
Conservative Coup* p. 113
p. 9 homilies of housekeeping – Young
op. cit. p. 147; **a counter-revolution** –
Mitchell, *Four Years in the Death of the Labour Party*

p. 15; **an uncongenial blend** – Critchley, *Westminster Blues* p. 99; **used to think** – Callaghan, *Time and Chance* p. 426; **been misused** – ibid. p. 427;

p.10 **at last** – *Daily Mail* 2 October 1979

p. 11 **Company profits** – Gilmour, *Dancing with Dogma* p. 25; **We did not promise** – McFadyean & Renn, *Thatcher's Reign* p. 27; **The baby boom** – *Daily Mirror* 2 January 1981; **I could have wept** – *The Times* 14 October 1980

p. 12 **government action** – Tebbit, *Upwardly Mobile* p. 114

p. 13 **whom she regarded** – Gilmour op. cit. p. 175; **socialism was still** – Thatcher, *The Downing Street Years* p. 306; **council tenants** – Campbell, *Wigan Pier Revisited* p. 32

p. 14 **There are no fences** – ibid. p. 45; **because of its starkness** – Young op. cit. p. 200; **a *Clockwork Orange* society** – Gilmour op. cit. p. 31; **People are realizing** – *Sun* 6 November 1980; **ardent Heath-haters** – Clark op. cit. p. 280–1

p.15 **articulate, but ineffectual** – Cole, *As It Seemed To Me* p. 209; **She's had it** – Amis, *Letters* p. 883; **a brilliant exponent** – Thatcher op. cit.p. p. 26; **We are not so stubborn** – *Daily Mail* 17 September 1980; **a very much better position** – *Daily Mirror* 2 January 1981

p.16 **the most delightful** – Patrick Cosgrave in the *Oxford Dictionary of National Biography*, retrieved 7 November 2009; **Bringing down the rate** – Keys, *Thatcher's Britain* p. 2; **spending too much** – *Daily Mail* 15 September 1980; **Mr Heath started** – *Daily Mirror* 18 July 1979; **waiting with bated breath** – Thatcher op. cit.p. p. 122

p. 17 **You know, Alan** – Young op. cit. p. 215; **Present policies** – *The Times* 30 March 1981; **I can do no better** – www.margaretthatcher.org retrieved 15/1/2008; **It is staggering** – *Sun* 1 May 1981; **clear favourite** – *Daily Mirror* 16 January 1981

p. 18 **Democracy cannot function** – Chapple, *Sparks Fly!* p. 167; **not dissatisfied** – *The Times* 15 May 1980

p. 19 **Benn is absolutely** – Clark op. cit. p. 202; **all those lovely** – *The Times* 5 May 1983; **I dare say** – *Daily Mirror* 12 September 1981

p. 20 **This country of ours** – Bennett, *Writing Home* p. 110

p. 21 **We knocked** – Gittins, *Top of the Pops*

p. 78; **I cannot remember** – *Daily Mirror* 10 September 1981; **We are the best** – Edworthy, *The Second Most Important Job in the Country* p. 159

p. 22 **What a wonderful change** – *Daily Mail* 2 April 1981

p. 23 **Was this not** – Clark op. cit. p. 247; **Willie Whitelaw** – *Sun* 14 October 1981

p. 24 **influence Margaret** – Goodman, *From Bevan To Blair* p. 245; **a great prime minister** – Selbourne, *Left Behind* p. 33; **I argued** – *Daily Mirror* 28 January 1981; **She was ruthless** – Dobbs, *House of Cards* p. 137; **huffy** – Thatcher op. cit. p. 151

p. 25 **It was a childhood** – *Sun* 9 October 1981; **There was a time** – *The Times* 12 September 1986

2: Comrades

p. 26 **Our type** – Pinner, *There'll Always Be an England* p. 49; **My father said** – Townsend, *Adrian Mole From Minor to Major* p. 209; **I have forgotten** – Mortimer, *Rumpole's Last Case* p. 116; **It was not** – Callaghan, *Time and Chance* p. 565

p. 27 **Serves us bloody right** – Mullin, *A Very British Coup* p. 66; **consensus politicians** – Gilmour, *Dancing with Dogma* p. 5

p. 28 **Your representative** – Edmund Burke, speech to the Electors of Bristol, 3 November 1774; **I suppose like** – Benn, *The End of an Era* p. 13; **The big event** – interview on DVD release of *A Very British Coup*; **Having lost** – *Daily Mirror* 6 July 1979

p. 29 **will split in two** – ibid. 27 July 1979; **planted a time-bomb** – *Daily Mail* 6 October 1979; **I feel like** – Pearce, *Denis Healey* p. 529; **I come not to praise** – Morgan, *Michael Foot* p. 373; **why was there** – Mitchell, *Four Years in the Death of the Labour Party* p. 40; **There is no guarantee** – Kogan & Kogan, *The Battle for the Labour Party* p. 69; **It is easy** – Morgan op. cit. p. 374; **I hope next year** – *Daily Mail* 4 October 1979

p. 30 **We'll come back** – Benn, *Conflicts of Interest* p. 543; **635 vacancies** – ibid. p. 545; **To the weak-hearted** – Pearce op. cit. p. 532; **There are some** – Radice op.cit. p. 287

p. 31 **He is always trying** – Strong, *Diaries* p. 404; **The good fairies** – Owen, *Time to Declare* p. 624; **I am fed up** – Benn, *The End of an Era* p. 17; **a shadow** – *Daily Mail* 4 February

1980; **in the vain hope** – Callaghan op. cit. p. 565; **take the shine** – Healey, *The Time of My Life* p. 466; **took the shine** – Radice, *Friends & Rivals* p. 280

p. 32 **I was glad** – Healey op. cit. p. 466; **those exhilarating years** – Livingstone, *If Voting Changed Anything, They'd Abolish It* p. 92; **a competent** – Benn op. cit. p. 30

p. 33 **cloud cuckoo land** – Owen op. cit. p. 450; **He tells them** – Longford, *Diary of a Year* p. 182; **Personality clashes** – Livingstone op. cit. p. 113; **Politics is about** – Benn op. cit. p. 171; **sweet reason** – *Daily Express* 10/6/1980; **frequently unrepresentative** – Davies, *To Build a New Jerusalem* p. 263

p. 34 **We must not be afraid** – Radice op. cit. p. 287; **Some of us** – *Sun* 2 October 1981; **We used to have** – Bradley, *Breaking the Mould?* p. 115; **It almost seemed** – Ashton, *Red Rose Blues* p. 211; **power without responsibility** – Mitchell op. cit. p. 63; **active not passive** – Benn op. cit. p. 68

p. 35 **elderly Byron enthusiast** – Lawson, *Bloody Margaret* p. 31

p. 36 **experimental plane** – Campbell, *Roy Jenkins* p. 206; **much loved** – Stewart, *The History of The Times* p. 79; **born old** – *Sun* 1 May 1981;

p. 37 **something rather engaging** – *Sun* 11 November 1980; **an inspiring figure** – ibid. 6 November 1980; **The flavour** – Longford op. cit.p. p. 24; **to allow the block vote** – Owen op. cit. p. 479

p. 38 **calamitous outcome** – Stephenson, *Claret and Chips* pp.185–6; **a better yesterday** – Owen op. cit. p. 536; **needs to be said** – *Daily Mirror* 22 January 1981

p. 39 **I could tolerate** – Neil, *Full Disclosure* p. 33; **somewhat indecisive** – *The Times* 10 February 1981

p. 40 **It lists** – Wharton, *The Best of Peter Simple* p. 20; **they're all *worthy*** – Williams, *Diaries* p. 631; **Our policy** – Owen op. cit. p. 536; **the sadness** – Mitchell op. cit. p. 78; **Pandora's parents** – Townsend, *Adrian Mole From Minor to Major* p. 157; **It is a sad day** – ibid. p. 163; **the SDP remains** – *Sun* 7 October 1981

p.41 **The Llandudno air** – Owen op. cit. p. 526

p. 42 **communism only gains** – Pinner op. cit. p. 122; **up to six** – *Sun* 14 October 1981; **Another loser** – *Daily Mirror* 26 January 1981

p. 43 **a pitcherfull** – Pearce, *Denis Healey* p. 548; **orgy of intolerance** – *Daily Mirror* 22 September 1981; **planned hooliganism** – ibid. 24 September 1981; **If he wins** – *Sun* 28 May 1981; **A cross on the ballot** – Chippindale & Horrie, *Stick It Up Your Punter!* p. 130; MR BENN – *Sun* 22 May 1981

p. 44 **Yes, I think** – Hollingsworth, *The Press and Political Dissent* p. 56; **People's Democracy** – ibid. p. 60; **The Labour Party** – O'Farrell, *Things Can Only Get Better* p. 67; **those figures** – Steel, *Reasons to be Cheerful* p. 119; **The fact is** – *Daily Mirror* 19 September 1981

p. 45 **traitors** – Seyd, *The Rise and Fall of the Labour Left* p. 136; **a hell of a year** – Drower, *Neil Kinnock* p. 91; **It was a victory** – *The Times* 28 September 1981; **we are concerned** – Benn op. cit. p. 185

p. 46 **You're not going** – Steel, *Against Goliath* p. 228; **a smart sensible coat** – Morgan op. cit. p. 391; **I sat next to him** – Mitchell op. cit. p. 53

p. 47 **We must look** – *The Times* 4 December 1981

p. 48 **an electoral disaster** – Morgan op. cit. p. 422; **a rather exotic** – Doig, *Westminster Babylon* p. 104; **male model's flair** – Hollingsworth op. cit. p. 141

p. 49 **He's created** – Radice op. cit. p. 303

p. 50 **If Healey** – Tebbit, *Upwardly Mobile* p. 203; **on an interim basis** – Heffer, *Never a Yes Man* p. 176; **What fools we were** – Healey, *Part of the Pattern* p. 216; **If I woke up** – Livingstone op. cit. p. 179; **so terrified** – Longford op. cit.p. p. 28

3: Alternatives

p. 51 **years of stagnation** – Mayall, Mayer, Elton, *The Young Ones*; **Make the most** – George Michael & Andrew Ridgeley, 'Wham Rap!' (Sony Music Entertainment, 1982); **Even our protests** – Jarman, *The Last of England*

p. 54 **sad and cynical** – *The Times*, 10 December 1980; **Good evening** – Carpenter, *That Was Satire that Was* p. 229

p. 55 **Heard about** – *Daily Mirror* 14 July 1979; **a 1988 survey** – Kingsley & Tibballs, *Box of Delights* p. 23; **strange survivor** – *The Times* 17 October 1980

p. 56 **its roots** – Britton & Butterworth,

Savoy Dreams p. 66; **Jewish stories** – Margolis, *Bernard Manning* p. xii; **like a preacher** – ibid. p. 128

p. 57 It was crowd control – *The Times* 26 October 1981; **Alternative comedy** – Harris, *The Mother-in-Law Joke* p. 3; **What was said** – Skinner, *Frank Skinner* p. 219; **To these performers** – Dawson, *No Tears for the Clown* p. 92

p. 58 For now their appeal – *The Times* 26 October 1981; **In her hunger** – Carpenter op. cit. p. 325

p. 60 best, brightest – *The Times* 11 May 1984; **youngsters divide** – Everett, *You'll Never Be 16 Again* p. 147; SEVEN TRIBES – *Sun* 2/10/1981

p. 62 simply the first – Chippindale & Horrie, *Stick It Up Your Punter!* p. 145

p. 63 They want a reason – Rimmer, *Like Punk Never Happened* p. 50; **A year ago** – *Daily Mail* 12 October 1979; **The music scene** – George, *Take It Like a Man* p. 212

p. 64 physically sick – Staple, *Original Rude Boy* p. 210; **Something nasty** – Andy Hill/Pete Sinfield, 'Land of Make Believe' (RCA Music Ltd/Paper Music Ltd)

p. 65 Which part of it – *Sunday Times* 18 May 2008; **Their complete control** – Rimbaud, *Shibboleth* p. 303

p. 66 Russian troops – Julian MacQueen, 'Domino Theory' (Melodia, 1981); **James Dean** – Mark Jones, 'Too Fast to Live, Too Young to Work' published in *Hard Lines: New Poetry and Prose, No.2* (Faber & Faber, 1985)

p. 67 in the end – *Liverpool Echo*, 1 October 1985; **The basic principle** – Gaunt, *Undaunted* p. 122; **The Tories** – Willgress, *Stand Down Margaret*; **If the future** – *New Statesman*, 22 November 2004

p. 68 It was slightly ironic – ibid.; **In the long run** – Strong, *Diaries* p. 248

p. 69 survey in 1989 – *Sunday Times* 29 October 1989; **bad news** – Longford, *Diary of a Year* pp.9–10; **an English degree** – Smith, *Lost in Music* pp.171–2; **I can't see** – Mortimer, *Titmuss Regained* p. 39

p. 70 Gulliver had gone – Murdoch, *The Book and the Brotherhood* p. 142; **first-class honours graduate** – Levin, *Speaking Up* p. 240; **the implication** – *The Times* 20 September 1987; **life's misfits** – Bellamy, *The Secret Lemonade Drinker* p. 120

p. 71 thought that he – Croft, *You Have Been Watching* p. 210; **after experiencing** – Lewisohn, *Radio Times Guide to TV Comedy* p. 605; **If you are one** – Tilbury & Bostock-Smith, *Shelley* p. 10; **What sort of work** – ibid. p. 46; **Being on the dole** – Walker, *The Autobiography* p. 276; **You start asking** – Barnard, *A City of Strangers* p. 189

p. 72 You and I – Lodge, *Nice Work* p. 311; **I've got no** – Smith, *Don't Leave Me This Way*, p. 134; **I don't believe** – Drabble, *The Radiant Way* p. 360; **too publicly committed** – James, *Innocent Blood* p. 28; **increasingly petty** – ibid. p. 27; **with a sense** – Mortimer, *Summer's Lease*, p. 31

p. 73 Learned people – Murdoch op. cit. p. 247; **his name had been** – Mortimer, *Paradise Postponed* p. 17; **Bloody good** – Amis, *Letters* p. 870; **I would not like** – Wyatt, *Journals Volume 1* p. 578; **she is not a conservative** – ibid. p. 585; **not a Tory newspaper** – *Sun* 3 May 1979

p. 74 Less government – Gilmour, *Dancing with Dogma* p. 119; **the same words** – Young, *One of Us* p. 391; **I notice now** – Benn, *The End of an Era* p. 257; **There was little interest** – Steel, *Reasons to be Cheerful* pp.88–9

p. 75 There's not too – Fenton, *Scorched Earth* p. 96

4: Resistance

p. 76 soon the red blood – Brown, Campbell, Campbell, Hassan, Travers, Falconer, Virtue, 'Little by Little' (Graduate, 1980); **I come from** – Ray Jenkins, 'Lies and Liars', *Juliet Bravo* (1981); **Thatcher has been** – Selbourne, *Left Behind* p. 51

p. 77 arranged marriage – Carpenter, *Robert Runcie* p. 223; **it's my son** – Morgan, *Michael Foot* p. 334

p. 78 common to cry – Pearse & Matheson, *Ken Livingstone* p. 20; **common problems of newlyweds** – Macintyre, *Mandelson* p. 58; **His victory** – *Sun* 9 May 1981; **my analysis** – Carvel, *Citizen Ken* p. 14; **If Labour** – Livingstone, *If Voting Changed Anything, They'd Abolish It* p. 128; **If London again** – *The Times* 9 May 1981

p. 79 old white men – Seyd, *The Rise and Fall of the Labour Left* p. 138; **This little Kremlin** – *Daily Mail* 17 September 1980; **Who would**

say – *The Times* 9 December 1981; **You can predict** – Wharton, *The Best of Peter Simple* p. 98; **the next best thing** – Pearse & Matheson op. cit.p. p. 93

p. 80 **poor man's Benn** – *Sun* 18 May 1981; **John the Baptist** – Pearse & Matheson op. cit.p. 69; **he was buggered** – Livingstone op. cit. p. 163; **Fucking newts** – Chippindale & Horrie, *Stick It Up Your Punter!* p. 131; **slugs and woodlice** – Stewart, *The History of The Times* p. 80

p. 81 **just criminals** – Livingstone op. cit. p. 167; **the conscience** – Carvel op. cit. pp.96–7

p. 82 **The point I was** – *The Times* 14 October 1981; **I have consistently** – Carvel op. cit. p. 88; **what I would say** – ibid.p. p. 94

p. 83 **only die once** – *The Times* 20 August 1980; **the biggest victory** – *The Times* 18 September 1980; **This channel** – Whitelaw, *The Whitelaw Memoirs* p. 221; **wholly false** – Thatcher, *The Downing Street Years* p. 390; **terrorist prisoners** – ibid. p. 391

p. 84 **Crime is crime** – *Daily Mail* 22 April 1981; **He chose** – Young, *One of Us* p. 467; **made up his mind** – Longford, *Diary of a Year* p. 99

p. 85 **For the media** – Steel, *Reasons to be Cheerful* p. 112; **Sefton has so far** – Bennett, *Writing Home* p. 124; **The IRA-loving** – Hollingsworth, *The Press and Political Dissent* p. 76

p. 86 **When those** – Keys, *Thatcher's Britain* p. 8; **such widespread abuse** – Tebbit, *Upwardly Mobile* p. 192; **Unemployment in Britain** – *Sun* 12 November 1980; **Everyone I know** – Millar, *Milk, Sulphate & Alby Starvation* p. 25

p. 87 **What have we got left** – *The Times* 28 August 1981; **nowhere to go** – Everett, *You'll Never Be 16 Again* p. 152; **I'm just living** – Golding, *Plangent Visions*, 1980

p. 88 **an alarming incidence** – Rendell, *Put on by Cunning* p. 47

p. 89 **Desperate businessmen** – *Daily Mirror* 18 July 1979; **We were warned** – Currie, *Life Lines* p. 104; **trio of young constables** – Hill, *Exit Lines* p. 8; **it's better** – ibid. p. 251; **What did I do** – Sampson, *Sus* p. 26

p. 90 **People were taken** – Scraton, *The State of the Police* pp.119–20; **The police are** – Pearse & Matheson op. cit.p. p. 34; **When you canvas** – ibid. p. 34

p. 91 **This is the start** – *Sun* 3 April 1980;

unacceptable – Whitelaw op. cit. p. 185; **the causes, then** – *Sun* 5 April 1980; **having in the past** – Scarman, *The Scarman Report* p. 75; **a shameful episode** – Whitelaw op. cit. p. 192; **Sorry about the colour** – Steel op. cit. p. 99

p. 92 **Black bastards** – ibid. p. 99; **his camera** – Kettle & Hodges, *Uprising!* p. 116; **Fuck monetarism** – Vasili, *Colouring over the White Line*, p. 183; **There is police violence** – *Sun* 3 October 1981; **The *casus belli*** – Cole, *As It Seemed to Me* p. 258; **Lambeth is now** – McSmith, *Faces of Labour* p. 254; **same apparatus** – Macintyre op.cit. p. 60; **An alternative view** – Pearse & Matheson op. cit. p. 35

p. 93 **Black people** – *Daily Mail* 7 April 1981; **we must develop** – Whitelaw op. cit. p. 193; **The thing** – Benn, *The End of an Era* p. 299; **racial prejudice** – Scarman op. cit. p. 198

p. 94 **the character** – Scraton op. cit. p. 95; **public opinion** – Hollingsworth op. cit. p. 117; **the majority** – Whitelaw op. cit. p. 188; **I grew up** – *The Times* 16 October 1981; **despite the three million** – Tebbit, *Upwardly Mobile* p. 199

p. 95 **No job to be found** – Jerry Dammers, 'Ghost Town' (Plangent Visions Music, 1981); **the most effective** – O'Farrell, *Things Can Only Get Better* p. 48; **Oh dear** – Gittins, *Top of the Pops* p. 90

5: War

p. 96 **The definition** – Rendell, *The Veiled One* p. 52; **Calling generals** – Colin Moulding, 'Generals and Majors' (Virgin Records, 1980); **When British territory** – *The Times* 4 April 1982

p. 97 **I should think** – Benn, *The End of an Era* p. 162

p. 99 **It wasn't a very good** – Meyer, *The View from the Bridge* p. 152; **seductive banality** – ibid. p. 143; **I hope people** – *The Times* 30 November 1983; **an unbalanced portrayal** – *The Times* 7 December 1983; **immature minds** – Kingsley & Tibballs, *Box of Delights* p. 214

p. 100 **too horrifying** – Ferris, *Sir Huge* p. 184

p. 101 **paranoid times** – production notes on 2003 DVD of *Edge of Darkness*; **paranoid talk** – interview on 2003 DVD of *A Very British Coup*; **one of the few MPs** – Lyall, *The Secret*

Servant p. 61

p. 102 **poets must be allowed** – Longford, *Diary of a Year* p. 81; **Whatever the horrors** – Heseltine, *Life in the Jungle* p. 247

p. 103 **British houses** – Stuart, *Douglas Hurd* p. 130; **Wartime Broadcasting Service** – *Daily Telegraph* 3 October 2008; IMPROVE YOUR GOLF – Donald (ed.), *Viz Comic* p. 114

p. 104 **the steady drip** – Kent, *Undiscovered Ends* p. 182; **It is the teaching** – *The Times* 4 May 1982; **Pupils in the schools** – *The Times* 27 September 1986

p. 105 **mice voting for cats** – Drower, *Neil Kinnock* p. 75; **Children's worries** – *Daily Mirror* 20 June 1984; **nightmares about the bomb** – Townsend, *Adrian Mole From Minor to Major* p. 156; **Britain needs** – Osmond, *The Divided Kingdom* p. 177

p. 106 **I beg you** – Drower op. cit. p. 95

p. 107 **a military irrelevance** – Thatcher, *The Downing Street Years* p. 177; **The news was** – Williams, *Diaries* p. 651; **Believe me** – Young, *One of Us* p. 264; **It's all over** – Clark, *Into Politics* pp.310–1; **1800 British settlers** – Benn op. cit. p. 202

p. 108 **The people of** – Thatcher. op. cit. p. 183; **the longer-term interest** – Morgan, *Michael Foot* p. 412; **leader of the opposition** – Weight, *Patriots* p. 615; **it was important** – Clark op. cit. p. 315; **We should not tie** – Benn op. cit. p. 207; **British Vietnam** – Woolf & Wilson, *Authors Take Sides on the Falklands* p. 30; **I know a fascist** – Morgan op. cit. p. 412; **within an ace** – Clark op. cit. p. 317

p. 109 **I estimated** – Cole, *As It Seemed To Me* p. 264; **In a strange way** – Whitelaw, *The Whitelaw Memoirs* p. 205; **When I did return** – Parris, *Chance Witness* p. 305; **You'll have to watch** – Chippindale & Horrie, *Stick It Up Your Punter!* p. 111

p. 110 **young people** – Everett, *You'll Never Be 16 Again* p. 156; **After the newsflash** – Davidson, *Close to the Edge* p. 126; **lunatic nationalistic pride** – Gilmour, *Dancing with Dogma* p. 305; **amusing morale booster** – Owen, *Time to Declare* p. 550; **elaborate even-handedness** – Tebbit, *Upwardly Mobile* p. 196

p. 111 **If the Falkland Islanders** – *Sunday Telegraph* 23 May 1982; **A lot of my job** – Young op. cit. p. 274

p. 112 **speak-your-weight** – Eddy &

Linklater, *The Falklands War* p. 210

p. 113 **a short cut** – Stewart, *The History of The Times* p. 128; **thirty-seven years** – Livingstone, *Livingstone's Labour* p. 2; **Arsenal beating Brentford** – Ashton, *Red Rose Blues* p. 223

p. 114 **We fought to show** – Young, *One of Us* pp. 280–1

p. 115 **split activists** – O'Farrell, *Things Can Only Get Better* pp. 76–7; **the left will have** – Burchill, *Love It or Shove It* p. 107; **what does it matter** – Clark, *Diaries* p. 5; **Now they are singing** – Bennett, *Writing Home* p. 123; **Victorian nursery** – Woolf & Wilson op. cit. p. 96

p. 116 IT'S WAR SENOR! – Searle, *Your Daily Dose* p. 20; **I would want** – *Daily Mail* 7 March 1984; **what about the war?** – Hollinghurst, *The Swimming Pool Library* pp.273–5

p. 118 **standard of living** – Mitchell, *Four Years in the Death of the Labour Party* p. 107; **a floppy toy** – Hollingsworth, *The Press and Political Dissent* p. 238; **The party's leftwing** – Chippindale & Horrie op. cit. p. 140

p. 119 **no more intention** – Drower op. cit. p. 111; **glories in slaughter** – ibid. pp. 115–6; **toughened by Tebbitry** – McSmith, *Faces of Labour* p. 8; **It will be seen** – *The Times* 6 June 1983

p. 120 **my biggest mistake** – Hibbert, *Best of Q Who the Hell . . .?* p. 34; **Mr Everett** – *Daily Mirror* 7 June 1983; **They were just cheering** – *The Times* 8 June 1983

p. 121 **one post-war election** – Gould, *Goodbye to All That* p. 148; **The Alliance is beginning** – Benn op. cit. p. 290; **the cost of stamps** – ibid. p. 298; **an absolutely amazing** – ibid. p. 324; **for the first time** – *Guardian* 23 June 1983

p. 122 **rescuing disaster** – Mitchell op. cit. p. 5; **a government majority** – Clark, *Diaries* p. 36

Part Two: When the Wind Blows
p. 123 **It was a quiet** – Barnard, *Political Suicide* p. 7; **What I do** – Brenton & Hare, *Pravda* p. 27

6: The Second Thatcher Government
p. 125 **Authoritative** – *Daily Mail* 5 March 1984; **Who will be** – *Daily Mirror* 9 April 1984;

British industry – Benn, *The End of an Era* p. 368; **seemed interminable** – Morgan, *Michael Foot* p. 429; **Unilateralism** – Leapman, *Kinnock* p. 33

p. **126 in the same league** – Crick, *Militant* p. 183; **meaningless promises** – Benn op. cit.p. p. 286; **why not lose it** – Hattersley, *Who Goes Home?* p. 238; **Prominent trade union** – Heffer, *Labour's Future* p. 42

p. **127 TV'S CRUELLEST SHOW** – Lewisohn, *Radio Times Guide to TV Comedy* p. 629

p. **129 He was widely regarded** – Gould, *Goodbye to All That* p. 167; **FUNNYMAN KINNOCK** – Chippindale & Horrie, *Stick It Up Your Punter!* p. 142; **a few drinks** – Gould op. cit. p. 163; **It's all right** – Hattersley op. cit. p. 286; **working-class background** – McSmith, *Faces of Labour* p. 31; **we can only defend** – Drower, *Neil Kinnock* p. 140

p. **130 a person who gives** – *Sunday Times* 3 December 1989

p. **131 political crush** – Macintyre, *Mandelson* p. 42; **more time with my family** – *Financial Times* 20 October 1983; **certain "buzz" words** – Benn op. cit. p. 359; **what a misery** – ibid. p. 424; **triumph of image** – Macintyre op. cit. p. 110; **The people's flag** – *The Times* 2 October 1986; **The people's rose** – Benn op. cit. p. 474

p. **132 Better to light a candle** – Leapman op. cit. p. 189; **a petty bourgeois** – Knight, *Parliamentary Sauce* p. 62; **a red-haired, smiling man** – Barnard, *Political Suicide* p. 116

p. **133 There isn't any anger** – *Daily Mirror* 27 March 1984; **one of the first** – Campbell, *Wigan Pier Revisited* p. 65; **You don't need** – ibid. p. 66

p. **134 Perhaps the sharpest** – Parris, *Chance Witness* p. 283; **Gravely I listened** – Clark, *Diaries* p. 72; **Give us jobs** – Heseltine, *Life in the Jungle* p. 227

p. **135 There used to be** – *Independent* 3 April 2003; **What use** – Holden, *Of Presidents, Prime Ministers and Princes* pp. 205–6; **Heysel was** – Edworthy, *The Second Most Important Job in the Country* p. 172

p. **136 The season following** – Hornby, *Fever Pitch* p.157; **For a laugh** – Gittins, *Top of the Pops* p. 145

p. **138 Davis's work** – Burn, *Pocket Money* p. 11; **We've got different views** – ibid. pp.13–14

p. **139 I think a lot** – ibid. p. 15; **charm, politeness** – *Daily Mail* 21 April 1981; **with a twenty-four hour** – Davies, *The Last Election* p. 37; **We are fucking back** – Borrows, *The Hurricane* p. 214

p. **140 a walking time bomb** – Donald, *Viz Comic* p. 18

p. **141 Order, method, discipline** – Burn op. cit. p. 65; **I was well known** – Whitelaw, *The Whitelaw Memoirs* p. 163; **confused and widely** – Hurd, *Memoirs* p. 319

p. **142 The trade unions** – Benn op. cit. p. 445; **What is more Victorian** – Young, *One of Us* p. 343

p. **143 He is big already** – Pearce, *The Senate of Lilliput* p. 125; **quite unwilling** – *Sunday Times* 29 December 1985; **We can take** – Wyatt, *Journals Volume 1* pp.216–7; **Why should we** – Doig, *Westminster Babylon* p. 288; **Your vision of her** – *The Times* 24 July 1987

p. **144 Bongo Bongo Land** – *Financial Times* 7 February 1985; **tended to be workshy** – *Daily Mail* 5 March 1984; **It is enough for her** – Lodge, *Nice Work* p. 47

p. **145 Union Jack buffs** – Clark, *Diaries* p. 65; **He can tell a good joke** – *Sun* 16 October 1981; **bought his own furniture** – *Independent* 19 May 2009; **combs his hair in public** – Sergeant, *Maggie* p. 45; **He's about seven foot tall** – Hoggart, *House of Cards* p. 71; **to Heseltine** – ibid. p. 56; **His hair is too long** – Clark, *Diaries: Into Politics* p. 361; **Then I must leave** – Heseltine, *Life in the Jungle* p. 310; **not a proper way** – Young op. cit. p. 447

p. **146 long-winded** – Thatcher, *The Downing Street Years* p. 435; **unbelievably incompetent** – Steel, *Against Goliath* p. 262; **For a few seconds** – Clark, *Diaries* p. 135; **a better issue** – Sergeant op. cit. p. 51; **so many people think** – Wyatt op. cit. p. 386

p. **147 gone up in the world** – Critchley, *Hung Parliament* p. 29; **more Estonians** – Clark, *The Tories* p. 485; **a brilliant tyrant** – Critchley, *Westminster Blues* p. 103; **neutered zombies** – Radio 3 news bulletin, 1984; **People always talk** – Barnard op. cit. p. 136; **the present cabinet** – *Daily Mail* 17 March 1984; **I have seen the future** – Watkins, *A Conservative Coup* p. 61; **It lacked subtlety** – *Independent* 15 May 1996

p. 148 our opponents – Tebbit, *Upwardly Mobile* p. 246; if he was to have – Rendell, *The Veiled One* pp.255–6
p. 149 It is a rather – *The Times* 3 November 1986; I do not believe – *The Times* 2 November 1986; having struck – Rimbaud, *Shibboleth* p. 320
p. 150 some of the most brutal – www.batrewick.co.uk retrieved 24 June 2009; If only they would return – Bennett, *Writing Home* p. 147; boys and girls – Keys, *Thatcher's Britain* p. 76
p. 151 The police are viewed – *A Different Reality* p. 63; the violent charge – Scraton, *The State of the Police* p. 15; factor of racialism – Dunhill, *The Boys in Blue* p. 126; white, bearded men – Hollingsworth, *The Press and Political Dissent* p. 129; Street-fighting experts – ibid. pp.129–30
p. 152 Always tell them – *Guardian* 21 January 2004; I condemn the police – *The Times* 8 October 1985; The police were to blame – ibid. 9 October 1985; Had it not been – *Financial Times* 12 October 1985; very hard – Macintyre op. cit. p. 90; Kinnock today – Benn op. cit. p. 426.

7: Identities
p. 153 There may be minorities – Wharton, *The Best of Peter Simple* p. 162; The penis these days – teleplay by Malcolm Bradbury from novel by Tom Sharpe; Sack all council workers – *Sun* 17 November 1986; Red Ron Probert – Mortimer, *Rumpole's Last Case* pp.28–9
p. 154 popular worries – *Guardian* 22 February 1974; the loony left – *The Times* 17 June 1975; Political interference – *The Times* 30 December 1980
p. 155 Anne Batt – *Daily Mail* 8 September 1977; distorting our policies – Livingstone, *If Voting Changed Anything, They'd Abolish It* p. 238; Most of the stories – O'Farrell, *Things Can Only Get Better* p. 125; You'd have to be mad – Owen, *Time to Declare* p. 580; We were set – King, *House Music* pp.27–8
p. 156 We recognized – Livingstone op. cit. p. 245; I would no more expect – McSmith, *Faces of Labour* p. 157; You're not really – Livingstone, *Livingstone's Labour* p. 90; the London boroughs – Hatton, *Inside Left* p. 89;

middle-class – ibid. p. 91
p. 157 It was as if – Steel, *Reasons to be Cheerful* p. 164; Any loony cause – Ashton, *Red Rose Blues* p. 219; terrorist groupies – *The Times* 9 September 1983; a bunch of dafties – *The Times* 25 April 1986; Women's Lib – Stewart, *Protest or Power* p. 100; no socialist analysis – Benn, *The End of an Era* p. 244
p. 158 normal functioning – http://byronik.com/claagnotes.pdf retrieved 6 July 2009; It really gives – Hollingsworth, *The Press and Political Dissent* p. 172
p. 159 Whatever idealism – ibid. p. 180; ragtag and bobtail – ibid. p. 185; At first, women – Dunhill, *The Boys in Blue* pp.175–6; When peace is so beautiful – Rendell, *The Veiled One* p. 170; Several members – Lodge, *Nice Work* p. 57
p. 160 slogans, sisterhood – Danks, *Better Off Dead* p. 19; I wondered – *Independent* 6 November 1998
p. 161 I thrilled to the knowledge – Hamer & Budge, *The Good, the Bad and the Gorgeous* p. 74; Many of today's – *Daily Star* 21 May 1981; had to have a bodyguard – *Daily Telegraph* 6 May 1981; That's ridiculous! – *Sun* 6 May 1981; MARTINA TURNS GIRLS – *Sun* 12 July 1990; a member of – Croft, *You Have Been Watching* p. 231; When a man – O'Farrell, *Things Can Only Get Better* p. 62
p. 162 Dungarees are quite sexy – Collins, *Heaven Knows I'm Miserable Now* p. 24; took the discussion – Kent, *Undiscovered Ends* p. 186; honorary man – Fenton, *Scorched Earth* p. 145; straightforward provincial – Sampson, *The Changing Anatomy of Britain* p. 41
p. 163 someone young – Clark, *Diaries* p. 37; Mr Gummer is 43 – Hoggart, *House of Cards* p. 98; She talks to me – *Daily Mirror* 9 January 1981
p. 164 There are lots – *Sun* 9 April 1980; What will your husband – Gorman, *No, Prime Minister!* p. 117; a workplace full – ibid. p. 168; It is doubtful – Leapman, *Kinnock* p. 180; what they call – Currie, *Diaries* p. 195
p.165 had known a sergeant – Robinson, *A Dedicated Man* p. 225; When he first – Hill, *Exit Lines* pp.298–9; Just because – ibid. p. 347
p.166 prancing poofter – Kingsley & Tibballs, *Box of Delights* p. 256

p. 167 **was more or less** – Skinner, *Frank Skinner* p. 225; **Ben Elton speaks** – Collins op. cit. pp.241–2; **hugely popular** – Steel op. cit. p. 168; **We're so looking** – Steel, *It's Not a Runner Bean* p. 45; **There is so little** – Harris, *The Mother-in-Law Joke* p. 91

p. 168 **He lacks a sense** – *Financial Times* 4 December 1987; **You can reduce** – *Sunday Times* 23 September 1990; **They are entertaining** – Dunant, *Exterminating Angels* p. 30; **Either we deromanticize** – ibid. p. 74; **It is the threat** – Thompson, *Peter Cook* pp.124–5; **The Tories had won** – Harris op. cit. p. 130

p. 169 **average, unpolitical** – Macintyre, *Mandelson* p. 155; **It would create** – Leapman op. cit. p. 74; **I consider** – *The Times* 14 June 1985

p. 170 **The Labour Party** – Leapman op. cit. p. 74; **the first stage** – *The Times* 5 August 1985; **really a vehicle** – Hattersley, *Who Goes Home?* p. 278; **I don't give a damn** – McSmith, *Faces of Labour* p. 215; **Our candidate** – Gould, *Goodbye to All That* p. 182

p. 171 **The gays and lesbians** – Macintyre op. cit. 118; **Labour-dominated** – Gilmour, *Dancing with Dogma* p. 265; **a huge gulf** – Livingstone, *If Voting Changed Anything, They'd Abolish It* p. 251

p. 172 **The 1985 elections** – ibid. p. 272; **If you want** – *Daily Mirror* 11 April 1984; **When it comes** – Hollingsworth op. cit. p. 103; **Marxism?** – Pearse & Matheson, *Ken Livingstone* p. 89; **personal was political** – Livingstone op. cit. p. 93; **The party** – Livingstone, *Livingstone's Labour* p. 8

p. 173 **There is no doubt** – Benn op. cit. p. 578

8: Enemies
p. 174 **We agreed** – Clark, *Diaries: Into Politics* p. 286; **Both the right** – Campbell, *Wigan Pier Revisited* p. 113; **We refuse** – Leapman, *Kinnock* p. 111

p. 175 **you don't care** – Osmond, *The Divided Kingdom* p. 44

p. 176 **If necessary** – Tebbit, *Upwardly Mobile* p. 182; **will save** – Beynon, *Digging Deeper* p. 92; **to fix responsibility** – Hain, *Political Strikes* p. 128; **No strike shall** – *The Times* 15 June 1926

p. 177 **What has happened** – *The Times* 31

March 1983; **the eventual battle** – Beynon op. cit. p. 35; **a list of** – Ridley, *My Style of Government* p. 67

p. 178 **I do not deny** – Young, *One of Us* p. 226; **come into politics** – Beynon op. cit. p. 36; **there has been** – Bennett, *Writing Home* pp.123–4; **We had to fight** – Young op. cit. p. 371; **Those who prate** – Leapman op. cit. pp.26–7

p. 179 **traditional enemy** – Clark, *The Tories* p. 476; **Labour's brigade** – Heffer, *Never a Yes Man* p. 204; **it cannot be right** – Beynon op. cit. p. 13; **The issue** – Benn, *The End of an Era* p. 341

p. 180 **Arthur Scargill's duty** – Hattersley, *Who Goes Home?* p. 271; **the bully boys** – MacGregor, *The Enemies Within* p. 180; **They were animals** – Scraton, *The State of the Police* p. 4

p. 181 **rosy-cheeked** – Selbourne, *Left Behind* pp.122–3; **They brought a lot** – Hill, *Under World* p. 319; **He was handy** – Robinson, *A Necessary End* p. 113

p. 182 **Without equivocation** – Hollingsworth, *The Press and Political Dissent* p. 266; **Hitler used his thugs** – ibid. p. 275; **Members of all** – Chippindale & Horrie, *Stick It Up Your Punter!* p. 176; **Napoleon of Barnsley** – *Daily Express* 22 June 1984; **she felt** – Stewart, *The History of The Times* p. 209; **Scargill's cannon fodder** – Hollingsworth op. cit. p. 273

p. 183 **Personally, I didn't like** – Prescott, *Docks to Downing Street* p. 148; **A kind of civil war** – Benn op. cit. p. 361; **bungled by both sides** – Williams, *Diaries* p. 699; **If the pickets** – *Daily Mail* 19 June 1984; **For the first time** – Scraton op. cit. p. 6

p. 184 **In Barnsley market** – Ashton, *Red Rose Blues* p. 247; **a field hospital** – Benn op. cit. p. 352; **Because the poor** – Hain, *Political Strikes* p. 142; **the biggest and most** – Beynon op. cit. p. 99; **it energized** – Collins, *Still Suitable for Miners* p. 147

p. 185 **gay or lesbian** – Burchill, *Love It or Shove It* p. 11; **Welsh valleys** – Denselow, *When the Music's Over* p. 213; **I hope thee's** – Steel, *It's Not a Runner Bean* p. 37; **Mrs Thatcher has** – *Daily Mirror* 29 March 1984

p. 186 **What would be** – Beynon op. cit.; **What's the strategy** – Leapman op. cit. p.

45; **They had not used** – Chapple, *Sparks Fly!* p. 225; **I am not here** – *Daily Mirror* 31 March 1984; **It was as if** – Steel, *Reasons to be Cheerful* p. 104

p. 187 MINERS START – Hollingsworth op. cit. p. 249; **Take away the coal** – Ashton op. cit. p. 229; **It was essential** – Brown, *Fighting Talk* p. 137; **Margaret Thatcher's** – Tebbit op. cit. p. 238

p. 188 **the fact that** – Thatcher, *The Downing Street Years* p. 382; **If they had just** – Clark op. cit. p. 99; **If the IRA** – Bennett, *Writing Home* p. 137; **Today we were unlucky** – *The Times* 13 October 1984

p. 189 **Our concessions** – Thatcher op. cit. p. 415

p. 190 **I am the leader** – Selbourne op. cit. p. 155; **Yes, they were** – Hatton, *Inside Left* pp.117–19; **Being martyrs** – McSmith, *Faces of Labour* p. 166

p. 191 **Councils like** – Hatton op. cit. p. 90; **hammer home** – ibid. p. 99; **We had badly** – ibid. p. 99

p. 192 **It was too much** – Heffer op. cit. p. 213; **I can't understand** – Benn op. cit. p. 424; **Neil's speech** – Leapman op. cit. pp.105-6; **the most moving** – Macintyre, *Mandelson* p. 84; **I'm not too old** – Leapman op. cit. p. 115

p. 193 **We did make** – Benn op. cit. p. 456; **we created** – Hatton op. cit. p. 108

9: Moralities

p. 195 **She had** – James, *A Taste for Death* p. 229; **It is increasingly** – *The Times* 28 December 1985; **He wasn't suitable** – Raymond, *He Died with His Eyes Open* p. 6; **more self-reliant** – www.margaretthatcher. org retrieved 20 July 2009

p. 196 **hard work** – Ridley, *My Style of Government* p. 18; **To spread alarm** – *The Times* 11 May 1982; **she ignores** – *Daily Mirror* 5 January 1981; **thirty minutes** – *The Times* 11 September 1985

p. 197 **as she is urging** – Wyatt, *Journals Volume 1* p. 567

p. 199 **We believed** – Kochan, *Ann Widdecombe* p. 117; **The film itself** – *Daily Mirror* 14 September 1981

p. 200 **Recently, one picture** – Whittaker, *Blue Period* p. 28; **Girls on horseback** –

Harris, *The Mother-in-Law Joke* p. 119; **He likes to feel** – *Daily Mirror* 4 July 1979; **Modelling has become** – Donald, *Viz Comic* p. 18

p. 201 **She looked** – Kavanagh, *Going to the Dogs* p. 26; **Girls of sixteen** – ibid. p. 145; **younger and younger** – Lamb, *Sunrise* p. 110; **display of pictures** – McSmith, *Faces of Labour* p. 199; **Men must learn** – *Daily Mail* 9 November 1987

p. 203 **We have removed** – *The Times* 12 November 1981; **a gross intrusion** – *Daily Express* 21 June 1984; **The nanny state** – The *Times* 4 October 1978; **Interference from** – *Financial Times* 21 November 1984

p. 204 **the basic structure** – *The Times* 26 September 1983; **The strange thing** – Ridley op. cit. p. 263; **After the triumphs** – Wharton, *The Best of Peter Simple* p. 78; **the established** – *The Times* 12 April 1986; **improve understanding** – Currie, *Life Lines* p. 65; **Drunken violence** – *Daily Mirror* 20 June 1988

p .205 **the desire to mutilate** – Lodge, *Nice Work* p. 220; **My interest** – ibid. p. 5; **all part** – ibid. p. 245; **She has something** – *Daily Mail* 3 March 1984; **renowned as a** – Gorman, *No, Prime Minister!* p. 186; **the nagocracy** – Elliott and Atkinson, *The Gods that Failed* p. 154

p. 206 **I believe** – Livingstone, *If Voting Changed Anything, They'd Abolish It* p. 55

p. 207 **I bitterly regret** – Barker, *The Video Nasties* p. 19

p. 208 **There is no more** – *The Times* 13 December 1983; **Britain fought** – *Daily Mail* 30 June 1983; **an indication** – Barker op. cit. p. 61

p. 209 **It is theoretically** – Ingrams, *You Might As Well Be Dead* pp.73-4; **No one has the right** – Barker op. cit. p.29; **Many British people** – *The Times* 17 December 1983

p. 210 **He praises** – Murdoch, *The Book and the Brotherhood* p. 229; **Pornography represented** – *The Times* 11 November 1983; **anything goes** – Savage, *Time Travel* p. 282; **I sense** – Scraton, *The State of the Police* p. 85; **armed police** – ibid. p. 41; **carrying out** – *Times Educational Supplement* 16 July 1982

p. 211 **audio nasties** – Rimbaud, *Shibboleth* p. 255; **It is our opinion** – ibid. p. 256; **He has recently** – Morgan, *The New Statesman* p. 12

p. 212 **So many** – *Q* issue 22, July 1988; **a conspiracy** – *Daily Mail* 22 February 1980; **Their job** – *Daily Mirror* 11 April 1984; **the pressures** – *The Times* 23 April 1981; **I fear** – Clark, *Diaries* p. 320

p. 213 **This is not** – *The Times* 2 February 1982; **was guilty of** – *The Times* 6 January 1982; **the trauma suffered** – *The Times* 4 February 1987

p. 214 **A declining market** – Symons, *Bloody Murder* p. 253

p. 215 **Another Depression** – ibid. p. 255; **bully-worship** – Orwell, *Decline of the English Murder* p. 75; **its crooks** – Rankin, *Knots & Crosses* p. 81

p. 216 **in the interest** – Rendell, *The Veiled One* p. 203; **he had many objections** – Robinson, *A Dedicated Man* p. 174; **A man's got to be mad** – Hill, *Child's Play* p. 299; **It was what** – Raymond, *The Devil's Home on Leave* p. 32

p. 217 **There is a racial problem** – *Daily Mirror* 13 January 1981; **indulged in an orgy** – *The Times* 4 October 1984

p. 218 **I think that** – 'Stonewall', *The Reunion* (Whistledown Productions, Radio 4, broadcast 20 September 2009); **to disabuse children** – *The Times* 11 November 1986; **We did it** – *Daily Mirror* 3 February 1988;

p. 219 **The tabloids were screaming** – *Guardian* 12 December 2003; **the subject of** – Williams, *Diaries* pp.774–775; **a punishment** – *The Times* 3 November 1988

p. 220 **we must endure** – Garfield, *The End of Innocence* p.30; **There is no** – Currie op. cit. p. 71; **California and New York** – Garfield op. cit. p.42; **All homosexuals** – Chippindale & Horrie, *Stick It Up Your Punter!* p. 181; STRAIGHT SEX – ibid. p. 325

p. 221 **active homosexuals** – Garfield op. cit. p.182; TORIES' MP – Doig, *Westminster Babylon* p. 124; **His parents** – *Independent* 25 November 1988; **in view of** – *The Times* 11 August 1986; **As the years go by** – Currie op. cit. p. 95

p. 222 **It is for people** – *The Times* 13 December 1986; **Some people** – *Daily Mail* 24 January 1987; **I think it is fairly safe** – *Sunday Times* 14 December 1986; **Say plainly** – Garfield op. cit. p.121; **people would associate** – *Daily Mirror* 2 February 1988

p. 223 **Oral sex** – Garfield op. cit. p.118; **I remember her** – Currie, *Diaries* p. 9; **a new depth** – *Daily Mail* 12 November 1987 ; "**Sex**" **means** – *The Times* 10 July 1986; **You won't stop** – O'Farrell, *Things Can Only Get Better* p. 162; **If you must** – *Sunday Times* 14 December 1986

p. 224 **Once you went** – Lawson, *Bloody Margaret* p. 207; **The problems** – Currie, *Life Lines* p. 111; **No metropolitan** – Walker, *Icons in the Fire* p. 109

10: Boom

p. 225 **It is no longer** – Lawson, *Bloody Margaret* p. 188

p. 226 **I am sure** – Ridley, *My Style of Government* p. 257; **I exercise** – Owen, *Time to Declare* p. 701; **It's like teeth** – Lawson op. cit. p. 176

p. 227 **If we were** – Keys, *Thatcher's Britain* p. 3; **We Conservatives** – *The Times* 11 October 1986

p. 228 **Mickey Mouse phones** – *Daily Mail* 4 October 1979; **How much more** – *Sunday Times* 13 July 1986; **First of all** – Faith, *A Very Different Country* p. 239; **selling the furniture** – *Daily Mail* 12 March 1984; **He has this future** – Colin Moulding, 'Making Plans For Nigel' (Virgin Records, 1979)

p. 229 **We had lots** – Tony Capstick, 'Capstick Comes Home' (Dingles Records, 1981)

p. 230 **A pair of** – Hillier, *The Style of the Century* p. 232

p. 231 **an acceptable management** – *The Times* 30 September 1986

p. 233 **one of the most** – *The Times* 24 July 1985; **we're living** – Frankie Goes to Hollywood, 'Two Tribes' (ZTT Records, 1984); **a new generation** – *The Times* 21 March 1984; **In the beginning** – Cartwright, *Look at It this Way* p. 133

p. 234 **Lynn had many** – Barnard, *A City of Strangers* pp.20–1; **it has been considered** – Knight, *Parliamentary Sauce* pp.45–6; **Making money** – Lewisohn, *Radio Times Guide to TV Comedy* p. 486

p. 235 **destructive to the** – *Sunday Times* 20 September 1987; **This oily member** – *The Times* 25 September 1986; **You know what** – Mortimer, *Paradise Postponed* p. 299; **what it** must be like – ibid. p. 183; **that deeply misunderstood** – Blacker, *Fixx* p. 145; **This strike** – ibid.p. p. p. p.311; **I see our** – ibid.p. 312

p. 236 **Charles had always** – Drabble, *The Radiant Way* p. 143; **Previously he had** – Barnard op. cit. p. 21; **I am, and have always** – Macdonell, *The Autobiography of a Cad* p. 197; **The redundant churches** – ibid. p. 208

p. 238 **wide open** – Currie, *Diaries* p. 22; **Those staring eyes** – ibid. p. 37

p. 239 **This isn't business** – Lodge, *Nice Work* p. 219; **I regard myself** – ibid. p. 313; **Here are a group** – *Independent* 8 December 1986

p. 240 **reported it missing** – *The Times* 19 September 1985

p. 241 **pop tycoon** – *Daily Mail* 1 March 1984; **pop millionaire** – *Daily Mirror* 9 April 1984; **setting myself** – Branson, *Losing My Virginity* p. 219; **I began to lose** – ibid. p. 263

p. 243 **the Barringdean Centre** – Rendell, *The Veiled One* p. 1; **we built cathedrals** – Pinner, *There'll Always Be an England* pp. 158–9; **With their sanitized** – Godfrey, *A Decade of i-Deas* p. 195; **Your future dream** – Cook, Jones, Matlock, Rotten, 'Anarchy in the UK' (EMI, 1976); **one of the legitimate** – Hewison, *Culture and Consensus* p. 272; **could lay a** – Stewart, *The History of The Times* p. 223

p. 245 **Edinburgh's Slightly** – *Daily Telegraph* 8 August 2009; **City of Culture** – Banks, *Espedair Street* p. 37; **Liverpool is at the present** – Melly, *Revolt Into Style* p. 214; **Liverpool, once the pride** – Walker, *Icons in the Fire* p. 20

p. 246 **one of the really remarkable** – Isaacs, *Storm Over 4* p. 77

p. 247 **the famous Liverpool** – *The Times* 9 May 1986; **they told me** – Campbell, *Wigan Pier Revisited* p. 15; **People in other** – Selbourne, *Left Behind* p. 152; **that sentimental** – Bennett, *Writing Home* p. 182; **It hardly matters** – *Daily Mirror* 29 March 1984

p. 248 **to knock Liverpool** – *Observer* 16 December 2007; **He's only a spokesman** – *Q* issue 22 July 1988; **One can have** – Kureishi & Savage, *The Faber Book of Pop* p. 598

p. 249 **This is not just** – Geldof, *Is That It?* p. 289; **In a period** – Denselow, *When the Music's Over* p. 246; **A generation** – Osborne,

Damn You, England p. 51; **a shambles** – *Press Gazette* 8 July 2005; **self-interested** – *Independent* 22 November 2001; **young upwardly** – Baez, *And a Voice to Sing With* p. 357

p. 250 **All of us had built** – Ure, *If I Was* p. 165; **We had an invasion** – *The Times* 22 June 1990; **I saw the Secret** – Wikipedia, retrieved 16 November 2009

p. 251 **I've got a** – Cryer, *You Won't Believe This But* p. 198; **I have never been** – Williams, *Diaries* p. 782; **Agents and directors** – Steel, *It's Not a Runner Bean* p. 90; **They were all** – *Sunday Times* 18 May 2008; **we're doing the party** – Collins, *Still Suitable for Miners* p. 167

p. 252 **The way I felt** – *Q* issue 26, November 1988; **LABOUR USES** – Chippindale & Horrie, *Stick It Up Your Punter!* p. 220

p. 253 **I think he's** – *The Times* 25 April 1988; **Thatcherism's shameless** – Green, *New Words* p. 154

p. 254 **we believe** – Chippindale & Horrie op. cit. p. 240

Part Three: Under the God

p. 255 **This is the** – Davies, *A Very Peculiar Practice: The New Frontier* p. 245; **Survival of the** – Rona Munro, 'Survival', *Doctor Who* (1989); **The question is** – Fry & Laurie, *A Bit of Fry and Laurie* p. 126

11: The Third Thatcher Government

p. 257 **How Thatcherite** – Macintyre, *Mandelson* p. 152; **You don't have to be** – *Daily Mail* 2 November 1987; **That's what makes** – Barnard, *A City of Strangers* p. 191; **This is the most** – Benn, *The End of an Era* p. 511

p. 258 **that wonderful** – Clark, *Diaries: Into Politics* p. 254; **packaging which** – Owen, *Time to Declare* p. 691; **It was a film** – Rodgers, *Fourth Among Equals* p. 257

p. 259 **to repeat the film** – Tebbit, *Upwardly Mobile* p. 263; **you don't think** – Macintyre op. cit. p. 123; **The increase** – *Permanent Revolution: Issue 9* (summer/autumn 1991) p. 9

p. 260 **in a welter** – Hurst, *Charles Kennedy* p. 62; **I feel ashamed** – Rodgers op. cit. p. 259

p. 261 **that the Liberals** – Clark op. cit. p. 221; **an ego fat** – Leapman, *Kinnock* p. 197

p. 262 **Your husband** – Owen, *Time to Declare*

p. 779; **battle of the mice** – ibid. p. 757; **he said that** – Brandreth, *Breaking the Code* p. 10
p. 263 the situation we inherit – McSmith, *Faces of Labour* p. 86; **The distance** – ibid. p. 78; **there was a** – Gould, *Goodbye to All That* p. 214; **Nye Bevan** – McSmith op. cit. p. 85; **how demoralized** – Ashdown, *The Ashdown Diaries* p. 24
p. 264 He believes – ibid. p. 81; **I think the** – Benn op. cit. p. 568; **To get into** – Knight, *Parliamentary Sauce* p. 172
p. 265 I like that – Wyatt, *Journals Volume 1* p. 242; **YUP! IT'S JUST** – Chippindale & Horrie, *Stick It Up Your Punter!* p. 238; **Mr Lawson** – *Daily Mail* 4 November 1987; **Stock market** – Williams, *Diaries* p. 765; **the unthinkable** – *The Times* 20 October 1987
p. 266 there has been – *Daily Mail* 2 November 1987; **Does he think** – Routledge, *Gordon Brown* p. 148
p. 267 Dazed from many – *The Times* 28 December 1988; **drowned for a pound** – Chippindale & Horrie op. cit. p. 215; **the usual hotch-potch** – George, *Take It Like a Man* p. 509; **barbaric** – *Daily Mail* 9 November 1987
p. 268 Mr MacKenzie – Chippindale & Horrie op. cit. p. 291; **For complacency** – Hornby, *Fever Pitch* p. 224
p. 269 Most of the egg – Currie, *Lifelines* p. 260; **At the time** – Ingham, *Kill the Messenger* p. 211
p. 270 the sort of people – *Independent* 7 June 1995; **At the beginning** – Gilmour, *Dancing with Dogma* p. 141; **they were everywhere** – Cartwright, *Look at It this Way* p. 262; **I didn't know** – *The Times* 14 April 1988
p. 271 A high and rising – Halcrow, *Keith Joseph* p. 83; **The working class** – Parsons, *Dispatches from the Front Line of Popular Culture* pp.227–8; **It's a guide** – *Sunday Times* 15 December 1985
p. 272 he has brought – *The Times* 4 December 1980; **In the arcade** – Amis, *Money* pp.24–5
p. 273 Your day's gone – Sykes, *If I Don't Write It, Nobody Else Will* p. 453; **I was still** – Dawson, *No Tears for the Clown* pp. 99–100
p. 274 Political correctness – Davidson, *Close to the Edge* pp.170–1; **It was just** – Tough, *The Krankies* p. 191; **the British public** –

Gittins, *Top of the Pops* p. 53; **upper-class** – Tough op. cit. p. 120
p. 276 if you care for – *Sunday Times* 22 October 1989; **I began to feel** – Dawson op. cit. p. 114; **The recession** – Williams, *Diaries* p. 647; **It's been a** – Dawson op. cit. p. 178

12: Media

p. 277 British newspapers – Leapman, *Kinnock* p. 182; **There is a new** – Townsend, *Adrian Mole From Minor to Major* p. 283; **We are accustomed** – *Daily Mail* 11 November 1987
p. 278 Fleet Street – Cameron, *Express Newspapers* p. 43; **No newspaper** – Chippindale & Horrie, *Stick It Up Your Punter!* p. 70; **factory-gate reader** – Wintour, *The Rise and Fall of Fleet Street* p. 162; **SORRY MICHAEL** – Hollingsworth, *The Press and Political Dissent* p. 235
p. 279 the most vulgar – Wintour op. cit. p. 262; **Tabloid readers** – Jameson, *Last of the Hot Metal Men* p. 75
p. 280 Who the hell – ibid. p. 77; **Bloody hell** – *Q* issue 17, February 1988; **The odds were** – Cameron op. cit. pp.143–4
p. 281 I was in the company – Goodman, *From Bevan To Blair* p. 261; **One: the papers** – Hollingsworth, *The Press and Political Dissent* p. 243; **He really is** – Benn, *Out of the Wilderness* p. 294; **rather melodramatic** – Geldof, *Is That It?* p. 280
p. 282 PULPIT POOFS – *The Times* 16 November 1987; **He is so hideously** – Chippindale & Horrie op. cit. p. 167
p. 283 the men read – Benn, *The End of an Era* p. 253; **Did Britain's** – Carrott, *Carrott Roots* p. 17; **stringently examined** – *Daily Mirror* 23 January 1981
p. 284 About one in four – Wintour op. cit. p. 241; **Over and again** – Deedes, *Dear Bill* pp.297–8
p. 285 The mob's on the rampage – Neil, *Full Disclosure* p. 88; **I condemn** – Leapman, *Kinnock* p. 37; **When will you** – Stewart, *The History of The Times* p. 226
p. 286 coldly and cynically – *Financial Times* 27 January 1986; **He wants them** – Wyatt, *Journals Volume 1* p. 54; **Sometimes I think** – Neil op. cit. p. 135
p. 288 It was horrific – Benn op. cit. p. 450; **that enough police** – Neil op. cit. p. 169

p. 289 **I would remind you** — Cameron op. cit. p. 156

p. 290 **surely you have** — Isaacs, *Storm Over 4* p. 68; **to tastes and interests** — Whitelaw, *The Whitelaw Memoirs* p. 220

p. 291 **Should black Britons** — Isaacs op. cit. p. 76; **You've got it** — ibid. p. 65; **the channel is** — *The Times* 26 October 1982

p. 292 **You and your kind** — Collins, *Still Suitable for Miners* p. 184; **Now we'll have** — *Independent* 15 June 1987; **You can't go** — *Sunday Times* 10 November 1985

p. 293 **In 1986 Britain** — Hibbert, *Best of Q Who the Hell . . .? p.* xiv

p. 294 **There were some nights** — Kingsley & Tibballs, *Box of Delights* p. 255; **It seems increasingly** — *Q issue 45, June 1990*

p. 295 **country recipes** — *Daily Mail* 2 November 1987

p. 296 **stay with Ken** — *The Times* 24 February 1983; **EXCLUSIVE** — *Daily Mirror* 11 February 1988; **Its verbal aggression** — Kingsley & Tibballs op. cit. p. 228

p. 297 **I feel sorry** — Kingsley, *Soap Box* p.267; **The *Street*** — Chippindale & Horrie op. cit. p. 151

p. 298 **2 + 2** — *The Times* 10 April 1970; **an unknown composer** — Branson, *Losing My Virginity* p. 213

p. 299 **one no longer** — *Daily Mail* 13 March 1984; **a hip new station** — Walker, *The Autobiography* p. 306

p. 300 **I must say** — Leapman, *Kinnock* p. 140

13: Establishment

p. 301 **Instead of seeking** — Gilmour, *Dancing with Dogma* p. 274; **I don't want** — teleplay by Malcolm Bradbury from novel by Tom Sharpe; **She disliked** — Hurd, *Memoirs* p. 332; **a sunset home** — Gilmour op. cit.*Dancing with Dogma* p. 252

p. 302 **an agency** — Stewart, *The History of The Times* p. 78

p. 303 **great offence** — *The Times* 30 May 1988; **Mr Lawrence** — *Daily Mirror* 1 June 1988

p. 304 **as though they** — Gilmour op. cit. p. 255; **Why did the government** — Watkins, *A Conservative Coup* p. 90

p. 305 **the three terrorists** — *Independent* 23 May 1989; **she's an ex-prostitute** — *Sun* 30 April 1988; **Not since the days** — *The Times* 28

April 1988

p. 306 **tissue of lies** — Kingsley & Tibballs, *Box of Delights* p. 236; **a British empire** — Keys, *Thatcher's Britain* p. 3; **through the teaching** — *The Times* 24 August 1984; **the initially tedious** — Thatcher, *The Downing Street Years* p. 595; **thoroughly exasperated** — ibid. p. 596

p. 307 **a lot of fucking bollocks** — Chippindale & Horrie, *Stick It Up Your Punter!* p. 180

p. 308 **the Aboriginals** — *Sun* 20 January 1988; **It was Britain** — *Sun* 6 September 1988; **Clearly the Indians** — *Sun* 6 February 1989; **fucking cheating** — *Guardian* 19 December 2005; **Whack the Pakistanis** — *Sun* 12 December 1987; **A large proportion** — *Guardian* 8 January 2004; **I know West Indian families** — Powell, *No Easy Answers* p. 109

p. 309 **We of the white tribe** — Kettle & Hodges, *Uprising!* p. 62; **an exemplary government** — Wharton, *The Best of Peter Simple* p. 51; **It is a fantastic victory** — Benn, *Conflicts of Interest* p. 584; **conservative, top-down** — Kent, *Undiscovered Ends* p. 198; **The contrast** — ibid. p. 199; **providing his colleague** — *Daily Mail* 5 September 1980

p. 310 **Such a government** — *The Times* 22 September 1984; **divine intervention** — *The Times* 10 July 1984; **if the human** — Carpenter, *Robert Runcie* p. 273

p. 311 **The Church of England** — Faith, *A Very Different Country* p. 242; **a political plea** — Tebbit, *Upwardly Mobile* p. 245; **The political face** — Bradley, *Breaking the Mould?* p. 110; **family services** — Yorke, *Find Me a Villain* p. 119; **To his great alarm** — Clark, *Diaries: Into Politics* p. 300; **I am completely certain** — Clark, *Diaries* p. 90; **All too well** — ibid. p. 91

p. 312 **departmental memo** — Pearce, *The Senate of Lilliput* p. 115; **the words themselves** — Martin & Mullen, *No Alternative*, p. ix; **A belief in God** — *Sunday Telegraph* 16 November 1980; **then the Church** — *The Times* 20 November 1980; **wasn't even particularly** — James, *A Taste for Death* p. 295

p. 313 **better than expected** — Young, *One of Us* p. 282; **within the complexities** — *The Times* 3 May 1982; **there were no** — Carpenter, *Robert Runcie* p. 259

p. 314 **It's important to get** — Clark op. cit. p. 40; **Of all the elements** — Young op. cit. p.

411; **typical of the people** – Davies, *To Build a New Jerusalem* p. 259; **Mrs Thatcher is the most** – *Independent* 12 June 1987;
p. 315 **The prime minister** – *Hansard* 15 February 1989; **The year 1900** – Hughes, *The Shock of the New* p. 425
p. 317 **the minister for gays** – Garfield, *The End of Innocence* p.107; **Much of British management** – *Daily Mail* 22 February 1979; **It was an outrageous** – Rodgers, *Fourth Among Equals* p. 269; **shoddy, thoughtless** – *Daily Express* 1 June 1984
p. 318 **the feelings and** – Rodgers op. cit. p. 270; **in a Georgian rectory** – Mortimer, *Titmuss Regained* p. 250; **she has no taste** – Wyatt, *Journals Volume 1* p. 186
p. 319 **If they do not wish** – Young op. cit. p. 402; **Who will notice?** – Lodge, *Nice Work* p. 62; **Things have happened** – *The Times* 28 July 1981
p. 320 **when the British Council** – Hughes op. cit. p. 372; **It will not be lost** – *The Times* 6 December 1984; **on common sense** – Fyfield, *Shadows on the Mirror* p. 27; **he doesn't really belong** – ibid. p. 110; **The middle classes** – Halcrow, *Keith Joseph* pp.182–3; **he was one of** – Mortimer, *Rumpole's Last Case* p. 124
p. 321 **It cannot be right** – Wyatt, *Journals Volume 2* p. 67; **the government's clash** – *Daily Mail* 1 March 1990; **It is the very simple fact** – Stewart op. cit. p. 49; **bourgeois triumphalism** – Young op. cit. p. 536; **Old fashioned Tories** – *Observer* 5 June 1983; **The Tory Party** – this and next two quotes reported in *Sunday Times* 11 October 1987
p. 322 **The fruits of** – Stuart, *Douglas Hurd* p. 162; **Like the extension** – Tebbit, *Upwardly Mobile* p. 267; **Everybody agrees** – *Daily Mail* 28 June 1984

14: Globalization
p. 323 **The *Sun*** – *Sun* 10 December 1986; **Of late** – Elton, *Stark* p. 360; **Workers of the world** – Davies, *To Build a New Jerusalem* p. 1
p. 324 **I like Mr Gorbachev** – Young, *One of Us* p. 393; **Loaves and little fishes** – Stewart, *The History of The Times* p. 318; **a large world** – Weldon, *The Cloning of Joanna May* p. 20
p. 325 **The Polish Press Agency** –

Whitaker, *News Limited* p. 44; **demonstrated the strict** – *The Times* 1 May 1986; **seized on the tragedy** – Livingstone, *Livingstone's Labour* p. 203
p. 326 **it is possible** – Thatcher, *The Downing Street Years* pp.640–1; **When you've spent** – Young op. cit. p. 273; **poorly designed** – Turner & O'Connell, *The Whole World's Watching* p. 93; **about as bad** – ibid. p. 94; **water quality** – Ridley, *My Style of Government* p. 105
p. 327 **The business of business** – Roddick, *Business as Unusual* p. 24; **the moment at which** – Elton op. cit. p. 162; **There are virtually** – ibid. pp. 337–8
p. 328 **Europe will be stronger** – Thatcher op. cit. p. 745; **change the course** – Cole, *As It Seemed To Me* p. 345; **She is an agnostic** – Young, *One of Us* p. 185; **Mrs Thatcher hated** – Nicholson, *Secret Society* p. 84
p. 329 **You are going to get** – Sergeant, *Maggie* p. 32; **a feeling that we** – Gould, *Goodbye to All That* p. 158; **There is this new ingredient** – Benn, *The End of an Era* p. 421
p. 330 **During the long years** – Howe, *Conflict of Loyalty* p. 661; **He dislikes Europe** – Neil, *Full Disclosure* p. 215; **The French Revolution** – Thatcher op. cit. p. 753
p. 334 **seek to deny** – Gilmour, *Dancing with Dogma* p. 249; **Peter Wright is a bitter** – *Daily Mirror* 3 June 1988; **a complete break** – Elms, *The Way We Wore* p. 263; **There was no point** – George, *Take It Like a Man* p. 533; **For many of those** – King, *House Music* p. 45
p. 337 **endorsing the Marxist** – Thatcher op. cit. p. 532; **The ANC is a criminal** – Searle, *Your Daily Dose* p. 35; **condemning "racist" South Africa** – *Sun* 14 July 1988; **the member for** – Knight, *Parliamentary Sauce* p. 210; **providing oxygen** – *The Times* 8 April 1988
p. 338 **She is an exceptional girl** – *Daily Mirror* 10 April 1984; **indecent haste** – *Daily Mirror* 9 August 1984
p. 339 **never publicly detached** – Searle op. cit. p. 56; **after all the years** – Thatcher op. cit. p. 531; **an anti-socialist organization** – Chapple, *Sparks Fly!* p. 199; **Some of its leaders** – Benn op. cit. p. 461
p. 340 **whiners, whingers** – Livingstone op. cit. p. 71

p. 341 **I was asked to speak** – Benn op. cit.
p. 569; **A political earthquake** – *International Socialism No. 47* (summer 1990) p. 2

p. 342 **Anything is possible** – Savage, *Time Travel* p. 267; **As dictatorships in Europe** – Steel, *Reasons to be Cheerful* p. 193; **St George and the Dragon** – Burchill, *Love It or Shove It* p. 118

p. 343 **there can be no synthesis** – *International Socialism 2:37*, Winter 1988; **They have not** – Elton op. cit. p. 245; **the days of Audley** – Price, *The Memory Trap* pp.229–30; **Defeat does strange things** – ibid. p. 144

p. 344 **Whatever their political views** – Amis, *Letters* p. 1110

p. 345 **The British government** – *Financial Times* 9 March 1989; **even if I had heard** – Howe op. cit. p. 512; **Tell the Mad Mullah** – *Sun* 18 February 1989; **If they don't like it** – *Sun* 25 February 1989; **Perhaps he wishes** – *Sun* 27 February 1989; **increase anti-Muslim** – *Financial Times* 16 February 1989; **Nobody would have** – *Sunday Times* 5 April 2009

15: Fall

p. 346 **The Chamber places** – Dobbs, *House of Cards* p. 77; **When the history** – Chippindale & Horrie, *Stick It Up Your Punter!* p. 359; **On her political gravestone** – *Independent* 14 November 1990; **As I go on** – Wyatt, *Journals Volume 1* p. 124; **I shall hang on** – *Sunday Times* 8 May 1988

p. 347 **Quite prepared** – *The Times* 24 November 1989; **Your 21st anniversary** – Chippindale & Horrie op. cit. p. 358; **What would she do** – *The Times* 22 June 1987; **Some time there will** – *The Times* 26 October 1988; **That's the trouble** – Wyatt, *Journals Volume 2* p. 377

p. 348 **some form of** – Gould, *Goodbye to All That* p. 203; **It must be** – Wyatt op. cit. p. 71

p. 349 **A decade of motorcades** – Clark, *The Tories* p. 494; **had become a remote figure** – Gorman, *No, Prime Minister!* pp.232–3; **I don't know why** – Wyatt op. cit. pp.76–7; **We were stuck** – Clark, *Diaries* p. 296

p. 350 **The PM and the government** – Currie, *Diaries* p. 158; **My father always said** – Wyatt, *Journals Volume 1* p. 467

p. 351 **wake up the nation** – Watkins, *A Conservative Coup* p. 63; **we tried three times** –

Gould, *Goodbye to All That* p. 189; **It was clearly much more** – ibid. p. 227

p. 352 **sheriff officers** – *Financial Times* 31 Mach 1990; **The great man stopped** – Clark op. cit. p. 195; **It's not going to work** – Watkins op. cit. p. 70

p. 353 **The combination of the two** – Ridley, *My Style of Government* p. 133; **The Rating and Valuation** – Gilmour, *Dancing with Dogma* p. 269; **As they will be** – Wyatt op. cit. p. 449; **knowledge about tax** – Nicholson, *Secret Society* p. 135; **I am now inundated** – Currie, *Diaries* p. 177

p. 354 **had the community charge** – Ingham, *Kill the Messenger* p. 244; **No doubt about who** – Ashdown, *The Ashdown Diaries* p. 79

p. 355 **Toytown revolutionaries** – *The Times* 10 March 1990; **Thatcher, her minions** – Steel, *Reasons to be Cheerful* p. 201; **You fucking cunt** – Benn, *End of an Era* p. 589

p. 356 **a good time** – *The Times* 6 October 1981

p. 357 **half-baked** – *Financial Times* 18 October 1989; **Walters is often** – Currie op. cit. p. 137; **He was no politician** – Ridley op. cit. p. 5; **My foreign secretary** – Cole, *As It Seemed To Me* p. 327; **I told him** – Thatcher, *The Downing Street Years* p. 716

p. 358 **she couldn't have** – Ridley op. cit. p. 216; **After she had lost** – Critchley, *Hung Parliament* p. 8

p. 359 **She seems to be** – Young, *One of Us* p. 560; **Although we all** – Currie op. cit. p. 164; **he had a hard time** – Clark op. cit. p. 280; **I think that is** – Ridley op. cit. p. 236; **There are a hundred** – Watkins op. cit. p. 11

p. 360 **is increasingly seen** – *The Times* 18 June 1990; **I gave her a hug** – *Football Trivia* (Paul Lamond Games, 2005)

p. 361 **a German racket** – *The Times* 13 July 1990; **I'm not against** – Watkins op. cit. p. 133; **We appreciate** – Knight, *Parliamentary Sauce* p. 113; **turned out not to be** – Ridley op. cit. p. 224; **far too emotionally** – Owen, *Time to Declare* p. 768

p. 362 **I warmly welcome** – Brandreth, *Breaking the Code* p. 16; **will never have** – Sergeant, *Maggie* p. 104

p. 363 **Well, there is always** – *The Times* 2 November 1990; **that for the first time** –

Ingham, *Kill the Messenger* p. 389; **I wish the old cow** – Wyatt, *Journals Volume 2* p. 384; **I don't think she realizes** – Clark op. cit. p. 343
p. 364 patronizing and self-righteous – Howe, *Conflict of Loyalty* p. 659; **If Conservatives think** – *Financial Times* 9 November 1990; **I am still at the crease** – Howe op. cit. pp.666–7; **ducking was precisely** – Watkins op. cit. p. 151; **was almost a permanent part** – ibid. p. 147; **an unbelievably boring** – Gorman op. cit. p. 233
p. 365 Who gives a toss – Clark op. cit. p. 346
p. 366 This was the most stunning – Ashdown op. cit. p. 96; **It has certainly** – Benn op. cit. p. 610; **It was more than** – *Independent* 14 November 1990; **A significant consequence** – Watkins op. cit. p. 154; **Are you telling me** – Nicholson op. cit. p. 148; **She failed to see** – Currie, *Diaries* p. 214
p. 367 There is a woman – quoted on *Politics Between the Covers* (BBC Radio 4) broadcast 21 November 2009; **She was announcing** – Ridley op. cit. pp.246–7; **They sold me** – Wyatt op. cit. p. 401; **and that everyone** – Ashdown op. cit. p. 99
p. 368 I grabbed a thick ink marker – King, *House Music* p. 38; **Can you imagine** – Walker, *The Autobiography* p. 310; **Why did they sack you** – Stewart, *The History of The Times* p. 384; **evil woman** – *The Times* 23 November 1990; **It may be inverted snobbishness** – Wyatt op. cit. pp.401–2
p. 369 That is what social mobility – Watkins op. cit. p. 198; **probably not have backed him** – Sergeant op. cit. p. 171; **When she goes** – Currie op. cit. p. 179; **They wanted a new fashion** – Dobbs op. cit. p. 21; **people are sick** – Clark op. cit. p. 363; **thought he was** – Gorman op. cit. p. 241
p. 370 In the world of – Brandreth op. cit. p. 23; **I'm sorry, Geoffrey** – Howe op. cit. p. 676
p. 371 lost his faith – Chippindale & Horrie, *Stick It Up Your Punter!* pp.335–6; **I don't know why** – Steel, *It's Not a Runner Bean* p. 108; **the devil incarnate** – Prescott, *Docks to Downing Street* p. 139; **He is a new type** – Benn op. cit. p. 618; **Margaret Thatcher's overthrow** – Gilmour, *Dancing with Dogma* p. 217

Outro: Aftermath
p. 373 Many people – Young, *One of Us* p. 348
p. 374 a sense of – *The Times* 23 November 1990; **the quality of life** – Lamb, *Sunrise* p.166; **What great cause** – Thatcher, *Downing Street Years*, p. 167; **Do you think** – Knight, *Parliamentary Sauce* p. 59
p. 375 the two political parties – Wyatt, *Journals Volume 1* p. 591; **She forced** – Ridley, *My Style of Government* p. 255; **Our epitaph** – Owen, *Time to Declare* p. 562
p. 376 the last Labour government – Thatcher op. cit. p. 4; **I had always known** – O'Farrell, *Things Can Only Get Better* p. 276
p. 377 A mass party – Rentoul, *Tony Blair* p. 90
p. 378 For me, Margaret Thatcher – Willgress, *Stand Down Margaret*
p. 379 As I grow – *Sunday Times* 8 November 2009; **I suppose** – Wyatt, *Journals Volume 2* p. 442

Bibliography

Much of the material included in this book, as will be apparent from the references, is drawn from the newspapers and magazines of the time.

A) NON-FICTION

Note: Where a paperback or revised edition is shown, it indicates that any page references in the text are to that edition.

Andrew Adonis & Stephen Pollard, *A Class Act: The Myth of Britain's Classless Society* (Hamish Hamilton, London, 1997 – pbk edn: Penguin, London, 1998)

Manuel Alvarado & John Stewart, *Made For Television: Euston Films Limited* (BFI, London, 1985)

Kingsley Amis (ed. Zachary Leader), *The Letters of Kingsley Amis* (HarperCollins, London, 2000)

Paddy Ashdown, *The Ashdown Diaries, Volume 1: 1988–1997* (Allen, London, 2000 – pbk edn: Penguin, London, 2000)

Joe Ashton, *Red Rose Blues: The Story of a Good Labour Man* (Macmillan, London, 2000)

Joan Baez, *And a Voice to Sing With* (Century Hutchinson, London, 1988)

Martin Barker (ed.), *The Video Nasties: Freedom and Censorship in the Media* (Pluto, London, 1984)

Robert Beckman, *The Downwave: Surviving the Second Great Depression* (Milestone, Portsmouth, 1983)

Tony Benn, ed. Ruth Winstone, *Out of the Wilderness: Diaries 1963–67* (Hutchinson, London, 1987 – pbk edn: Arrow, London, 1988)

Tony Benn, ed. Ruth Winstone, *Conflicts of Interest: Diaries 1977–80* (Hutchinson, London, 1990 – pbk edn: Arrow, London, 1991)

Tony Benn, ed. Ruth Winstone, *The End of an Era: Diaries 1980–90* (Hutchinson, London, 1992 – pbk edn: Arrow, London, 1994)

Alan Bennett, *Writing Home* (Faber & Faber, London, 1994 – pbk edn: 1995)

The Best of Sunday Sport (Sphere, London, 1989)

Huw Beynon (ed.), *Digging Deeper: Issues in the Miners' Strike* (Verso, London, 1985)

Christopher Booker, *The Neophiliacs: A Study of the Revolution in English Life in the Fifties and Sixties* (Collins, London, 1969 – pbk edn: Fontana, London, 1970)

Betty Boothroyd, *The Autobiography* (Century, London, 2001)

Bill Borrows, *The Hurricane: The Turbulent Life and Times of Alex Higgins* (Atlantic, London, 2002 – rev pbk edn: 2003)

Ian Bradley, *Breaking the Mould? The Birth and Prospects of the Social Democratic Party* (Martin Robertson, Oxford, 1981)

Gyles Brandreth, *Breaking the Code: Westminster Diaries* (Weidenfeld & Nicolson, London, 1999 – pbk edn: Phoenix, London, 2000)

Richard Branson, *Losing My Virginity: The Autobiography* (Virgin, London, 1998 – rev pbk edn: 2002)

David Britton & Michael Butterworth (ed.), *Savoy Dreams* (Savoy, Manchester, 1984)

Colin Brown, *Fighting Talk: The Biography of John Prescott* (Simon & Schuster, London, 1997)

Julie Burchill, *Love It or Shove It* (Century, London, 1985)

Gordon Burn, *Pocket Money: Bad-Boys, Business-Heads and Boom-Time Snooker* (Heinemann, London, 1986)

Peter Burton, *Parallel Lives* (GMP, London, 1985)

James Callaghan, *Time and Chance* (William Collins, London, 1987)

Andrew Cameron, *Express Newspapers: The Inside Story of a Turbulent Decade* (London House, London, 2000)

Beatrix Campbell, *Wigan Pier Revisited: Poverty and Politics in the 80s* (Virago, London, 1984)

John Campbell, *Roy Jenkins: A Biography* (Weidenfeld & Nicolson, London, 1983)

Humphrey Carpenter, *Robert Runcie: The Reluctant Archbishop* (Hodder & Stoughton, London, 1996 – pbk edn: Sceptre, London, 1997)

Humphrey Carpenter, *That Was Satire that Was: Beyond the Fringe, the Establishment Club, Private Eye and That Was the Week That Was* (Victor Gollancz, London, 2000)

John Carvel, *Citizen Ken* (Chatto & Windus, London, 1984)

Frank Chapple, *Sparks Fly! A Trade Union Life* (Michael Joseph, London, 1984)

Peter Chippindale & Chris Horrie, *Stick It Up Your Punter! The Rise and Fall of the Sun* (William Heinemann, London, 1990 – pbk edn: Mandarin, London, 1992)

Alan Clark, *Diaries* (Weidenfeld & Nicolson, London, 1993 – pbk edn: Orion, London, 1994)

Alan Clark, *The Tories: Conservatives and the Nation State 1922–1997* (Weidenfeld & Nicolson, London, 1998 – pbk edn: Phoenix, London, 1999)

Alan Clark, *Diaries: Into Politics 1972–1982* (Weidenfeld & Nicolson, London, 2000 – pbk edn: Orion, London, 2001)

John Cole, *As It Seemed to Me: Political Memoirs* (Weidenfeld & Nicolson, London, 1995 – revised pbk edn: Phoenix, London, 1996)

Andrew Collins, *Still Suitable for Miners – Billy Bragg: The Official Biography* (Virgin, London, 1998 – pbk edn: 2002)

Andrew Collins, *Heaven Knows I'm Miserable Now: My Difficult 80s* (Ebury Press, London, 2004 – pbk edn: 2005)

Michael Crick, *Militant* (Faber & Faber, London, 1984)

Roger Crimlis & Alwyn W. Turner, *Cult Rock Posters 1972–1982: From Boys in Drag to Buffalo Gals* (Aurum, London, 2006)

Julian Critchley, *Westminster Blues* (Elm Tree, London, 1985 – pbk edn: Futura, London, 1986)

David Croft, *You Have Been Watching . . . The Autobiography* (BBC Books, London, 2004)

Barry Cryer, *You Won't Believe This But: An Autobiography of Sorts* (Virgin, London, 1996)

Edwina Currie, *Life Lines: Politics and Health 1986–1988* (Sidgwick & Jackson, London, 1989)

Edwina Currie, *Diaries 1987–1992* (Little Brown, London, 2002 – pbk edn: Time Warner, London, 2003)

Iain Dale, *The Unofficial Book of Political Lists* (Robson Books, London, 1997)

Jim Davidson with Alec Lom, *Close to the Edge: My Autobiography* (Ebury, London, 2001)

A.J. Davies, *To Build a New Jerusalem: The Labour Movement from the 1880s to the 1990s* (Michael Joseph, London 1992)

Les Dawson, *No Tears for the Clown: An Autobiography* (Robson, London, 1992)

W.F. Deedes, *Dear Bill: WF Deedes Reports* (Macmillan, London, 1997)

A Different Reality: An Account of Black People's Experiences and Their Grievances Before and After the Handsworth Rebellion of September 1985 (West Midlands County Council, Birmingham, 1986)

Alan Doig, *Westminster Babylon: Sex, Money and Scandal in British Politics* (Allison & Busby, London, 1990)

G.M.F. Drower, *Neil Kinnock: The Path to Leadership* (Weidenfeld & Nicholson, London, 1984)

Christina Dunhill (ed.), *The Boys in Blue: Women's Challenge to the Police* (Virago, London, 1989)

Paul Eddy & Magnus Linklater (ed.), *The Falklands War: The Full Story by the Sunday Times Insight Team* (Sphere, London, 1982)

Niall Edworthy, *The Second Most Important Job in the Country* (Virgin, London, 1999 – pbk edn: 2000)

Larry Elliott & Dan Atkinson, *The Age of Insecurity* (Verso, London, 1998)

Larry Elliott & Dan Atkinson, *The Gods that Failed: How Blind Faith in Markets Has Cost Us Our Future* (Bodley Head, London, 2008)

Matthew Engel & Ian Morrison, *The Sportspages Almanac 1991: The Complete Sporting Factbook* (Simon & Schuster, London, 1990)

Peter Everett, *You'll Never Be 16 Again: An Illustrated History of the British Teenager* (BBC, London, 1986)

Nicholas Faith, *A Very Different Country: A Typically English Revolution* (Sinclair-Stevenson, London, 2002)

Ivan Fallon, *The Brothers: The Rise and Rise of Saatchi & Saatchi* (Hutchinson, London, 1988)

Paul Ferris, *Sir Huge: The Life of Huw Wheldon* (Michael Joseph, London, 1990)

Paul Ferris, *Sex and the British: A Twentieth Century History* (Michael Joseph, London, 1993)

Paul Gambaccini & Rod Taylor, *Television's Greatest Hits: Every Hit Television Programme since 1960* (Network, London, 1993)

Simon Garfield, *The End of Innocence: Britain in the Time of AIDS* (Faber & Faber, London, 1994)

Jon Gaunt, *Undaunted* (Virgin Books, London, 2007 – pbk edn: 2008)

Bob Geldof, *Is That It?* (Sidgwick & Jackson, London, 1986 – pbk edn: Penguin, London 1986)

Boy George with Spencer Bright, *Take It Like a Man: The Autobiography of Boy George* (Sidgwick & Jackson, London, 1995 – pbk edn: Pan, London, 1995)

Denis Gifford, *The Golden Age of Radio* (BT Batsford, London, 1985)

Ian Gilmour, *Dancing with Dogma: Britain under Thatcherism* (Simon & Schuster, London, 1992 – pbk edn: Pocket Books, London, 1993)

Ian Gittins, *Top of the Pops: Mishaps, Miming and Music – True Adventures of TV's No. 1 Pop Show* (BBC, London, 2007)

John Godfrey (ed.), *A Decade of i-Deas: the Encyclopaedia of the '80s* (Penguin, London, 1990)

Geoffrey Goodman, *From Bevan To Blair: Fifty Years' Reporting from the Political Front Line* (Pluto, London, 2003)

Teresa Gorman, *No, Prime Minister!* (John Blake, London, 2001)

Bryan Gould, *Goodbye to All That* (Macmillan, London, 1995)

Jonathon Green, *New Words: A Dictionary of Neologisms since 1960* (Bloomsbury, London, 1992 as *Neologisms* – pbk edn: 1992)

Jonathon Green, *Days in the Life: Voices from the English Underground 1961–1971* (William Heinemann, London, 1988 – pbk edn: Pimlico, London, 1998)

Peter Hain, *Political Strikes: The State and Trade Unionism in Britain* (Viking, London, 1986 – pbk edn: Penguin, Harmondsworth, 1986)

Luke Haines, *Bad Vibes: Britpop and My Part in Its Downfall* (William Heinemann, London, 2009)

Morrison Halcrow, *Keith Joseph: A Single Mind* (Macmillan, London, 1989)

Diane Hamer & Belinda Budge (ed.), *The Good, the Bad and the Gorgeous: Popular Culture's Romance with Lesbianism* (Pandora, London, 1994)

Brian Hanrahan & Robert Fox, *'I Counted Them All Out and I Counted Them All Back': The Battle for the Falklands* (BBC, London, 1982)

Dave Haslam, *Manchester, England: The Story of the Pop Cult City* (Fourth Estate, London, 1999)

Roy Hattersley, *Who Goes Home? Scenes from a Political Life* (Little Brown, London, 1995)

Derek Hatton, *Inside Left: The Story So Far . . .* (Bloomsbury, London, 1988)

Denis Healey, *The Time Of My Life* (Michael Joseph, London, 1989 – pbk edn: Penguin, London, 1990)

Edna Healey, *Part of the Pattern: Memoirs of a Wife at Westminster* (Headline Review, London, 2006 – pbk edn: 2007)

Eric Heffer, *Labour's Future: Socialist or SDP Mark 2?* (Verso, London, 1986)

Eric Heffer, *Never a Yes Man: The Life and Politics of an Adopted Liverpudlian* (Verso, London, 1991)

Michael Heseltine, *Life in the Jungle: My Autobiography* (Hodder & Stoughton, London, 2000)

Robert Hewison, *Culture and Consensus: England, Art and Politics since 1940* (Methuen, London, 1995 – rev pbk edn: 1997)

Tom Hibbert, *Best of Q Who the Hell . . . ?* (Virgin, London, 1994)

Bevis Hillier, *The Style of the Century* (Herbert Press, London, 1983 – rev. edn with new chapter by Kate McIntyre: 1998)

Simon Hoggart (ed.), *House of Cards: A Selection of Modern Political Humour* (Elm Tree, London, 1988)

Anthony Holden, *Of Presidents, Prime Ministers and Princes: A Decade in Fleet Street* (Weidenfeld & Nicolson, London, 1984)

Mark Hollingsworth, *The Press and Political Dissent* (Pluto, London, 1986)

Nick Hornby, *Fever Pitch* (Victor Gollancz, London, 1992 – pbk edn: 1993)

David J. Howe, Mark Stammers & Stephen James Walker, *Doctor Who: The Eighties* (Doctor Who Books, London, 1996)

Robert Hughes, *The Shock of the New: Art and the Century of Change* (updated & enlarged edn: Thames & Hudson, London, 1991 – orig. pub. 1980)

Seb Hunter, *Hell Bent for Leather: Confessions of a Heavy Metal Addict* (Fourth Estate, London, 2004 – pbk edn: Harper Perennial, London, 2005)

Douglas Hurd, *Memoirs* (Little, Brown, London, 2003)

Greg Hurst, *Charles Kennedy: A Tragic Flaw* (Politico's, London, 2006)

Bernard Ingham, *Kill the Messenger* (HarperCollins, London, 1991 – pbk ed: Fontana, London, 1991)

Richard Ingrams, *You Might As Well Be Dead* (Quartet, London, 1988)

Jeremy Isaacs, *Storm Over 4: A Personal Account* (Weidenfeld & Nicolson, London, 1989)

Eric Jacobs and Robert Worcester, *We British: Britain under the MORIscope* (Weidenfeld & Nicolson, London, 1990)

Derek Jameson, *Last of the Hot Metal Men: From Fleet Street to Showbiz* (Ebury Press, London, 1990)

Paul Jennings, *The Paul Jennings Reader: Collected Pieces 1943–89* (Bloomsbury, London, 1990)

Kevin Jefferys, *Anthony Crosland* (Richard Cohen, London, 1999)

William Kay, *Tycoons: Where They Came from and How They Made It* (Judy Piatkus, London, 1985 – pbk edn: Pan, London, 1986)

William Keegan, *Mr Lawson's Gamble* (Hodder & Stoughton, London, 1989)

Bruce Kent, *Undiscovered Ends: An Autobiography* (HarperCollins, London, 1992)

Martin Kettle & Lucy Hodges, *Uprising! The Police, the People and the Riots in Britain's Cities* (Pan, London, 1982)

David Keys, *Thatcher's Britain: A Guide to the Ruins* (Pluto Press/New Socialist, London, 1983)

Oona King, *House Music: The Oona King Diaries* (Bloomsbury, London, 2007)

Hilary Kingsley, *Soap Box: The Papermac Guide to Soap Opera* (Papermac, London, 1988)

Hilary Kingsley & Geoff Tibballs, *Box of Delights: The Golden Years of Television* (MacMillan, London, 1989)

Greg Knight (ed.), *Parliamentary Sauce: More Helpings of Political Invective* (Robson, London, 1993 – pbk edn: Arrow, London, 1994)

Nicholas Kochan, *Ann Widdecombe: Right from the Beginning* (Politico's, London, 2000)

David Kogan & Maurice Kogan, *The Battle for the Labour Party* (Kogan Page, London, 1982 – pbk edn: Fontana, London, 1983)

Hanif Kureishi & Jon Savage (ed.), *The Faber Book of Pop* (Faber & Faber, London, 1995)

Larry Lamb, *Sunrise: The Remarkable Rise and Rise of the Best-Selling Soaraway Sun* (Papermac, London, 1989)

Michael Leapman, *Kinnock* (Unwin Hyman, London, 1987)

Bernard Levin, *Speaking Up: More of the Best of His Journalism* (Jonathan Cape, London, 1982)

Mark Lewisohn, *Radio Times Guide to TV Comedy* (BBC Worldwide, London, 1998)

Ken Livingstone, *If Voting Changed Anything, They'd Abolish It* (William Collins, London, 1987 – pbk edn: Fontana, London, 1988)

Ken Livingstone, *Livingstone's Labour: A Programme for the Nineties* (Unwin Hyman, London, 1989)

Lord Longford, *Diary of a Year* (Weidenfeld & Nicolson, London, 1982)

Melanie McFadyean & Margaret Renn, *Thatcher's Reign: A Bad Case of the Blues* (Chatto & Windus, London, 1984)

Ian MacGregor, *The Enemies Within: The Story of the Miners' Strike 1984–5* (William Collins, London, 1986)

John McIlroy, 'Trade Unions and the Closed Shop' (Workers' Educational Association, London, 1981)

Donald Macintyre, *Mandelson: The Biography* (HarperCollins, London, 1999)

Andy McSmith, *Faces of Labour: The Inside Story* (Verso, London, 1996)

Jonathan Margolis, *Bernard Manning: A Biography* (Orion, London, 1996)

David Martin & Peter Mullen (ed.), *No Alternative: The Prayer Book Controversy* (Basil Blackwell, Oxford, 1981)

George Melly, *Revolt Into Style: The Pop Arts in Britain* (Allen Lane, London, 1970)

Nicholas Meyer, *The View from the Bridge: Memories of* Star Trek *and a Life in Hollywood* (Viking, New York, 2009)

Austin Mitchell, *Four Years in the Death of the Labour Party* (Methuen, London, 1983)

Bob Monkhouse, *Crying With Laughter: My Life Story* (Random House, London, 1993)

Kenneth O. Morgan, *Michael Foot: A Life* (HarperCollins, London, 2007)

Andrew Neil, *Full Disclosure* (Macmillan, London, 1996 – rev pbk edn: Pan, London, 1997)

Emma Nicholson, *Secret Society: Inside – and Outside – the Conservative Party* (Indigo, London, 1996)

Brendan O'Brien, *A Pocket History of the IRA* (O'Brien Press, Dublin, 1997)

Lucy O'Brien, *Annie Lennox: Sweet Dreams Are Made of This* (Sidgwick & Jackson, London, 1991 – pbk edn: St Martin's Press, New York, 1993)

John O'Farrell, *Things Can Only Get Better: Eighteen Miserable Years in the Life of a Labour Supporter* (Doubleday, London, 1998 – pbk edn: Black Swan, London, 1999)

George Orwell, *Decline of the English Murder and Other Essays* (Penguin, Harmondsworth, 1965)

John Osborne, *Damn You, England* (Faber & Faber, London, 1994 – pbk edn: 1999)

John Osmond, *The Divided Kingdom* (Constable, London, 1988)

David Owen, *Time to Declare* (Michael Joseph, London, 1991 – pbk edn: Penguin, London, 1992)

Matthew Parris, *Chance Witness: An Outsider's Life in Politics* (Viking, London, 2002 – pbk edn: Penguin, London, 2003)

Tony Parsons, *Dispatches from the Front Line of Popular Culture* (Virgin, London, 1994 – pbk edn: 1995)

Edward Pearce, *The Senate of Lilliput* (Faber & Faber, London, 1983)

Edward Pearce, *Denis Healey: A Life in Our Times* (Little, Brown, London, 2002)

Peter Gerard Pearse & Nigel Matheson, *Ken Livingstone, or The End of Civilization as We Know It: A Selection of Quotes, Quips and Quirks* (Proteus Books, London, 1982)

Henry Porter, *Lies, Damned Lies and Some Exclusives: Fleet Street Exposed* (Chatto & Windus, London, 1984)

Enoch Powell, *No Easy Answers* (Sheldon, London, 1973)

William Prendergast, *Z-Car Detective* (John Long, 1964 – pbk edn: Arrow, London, 1966)

John Prescott, *Prezza: My Story* (Headline Review, London, 2008 – pbk edn: *Docks to Downing Street: My Story*, 2009)

Private Eye, The Book of Wimmin: An Anthology of Contemporary Feminism (Private Eye, London, 1986)

Giles Radice, *Friends & Rivals: Crosland, Jenkins and Healey* (Little Brown, London, 2002 – pbk edn Abacus, London, 2003)

Steve Redhead, *Sing When You're Winning: The Last Football Book* (Pluto, London, 1987)

Dave Renton, *When We Touched the Sky: The Anti-Nazi League 1977–1981* (New Clarion Press, Cheltenham, 2006)

Nicholas Ridley, *'My Style of Government': The Thatcher Years* (Hutchinson, London, 1991 – pbk edn: Fontana, London, 1992)

Penny Rimbaud (aka JJ Ratter), *Shibboleth: My Revolting Life* (AK Press, Edinburgh, 1998)

Dave Rimmer, *Like Punk Never Happened: Culture Club and the New Pop* (Faber & Faber, London, 1985)

Anita Roddick, *Business as Unusual* (Thorsons, London, 2000)

Bill Rodgers, *Fourth Among Equals* (Politico's, London, 2000)

Paul Routledge, *Gordon Brown: The Biography* (Simon & Schuster, London, 1998)

Anthony Sampson, *The Changing Anatomy of Britain* (Hodder & Stoughton, London, 1982)

Jon Savage, *Time Travel – From the Sex Pistols to Nirvana: Pop, Media and Sexuality, 1977–96* (Chatto & Windus, London, 1996 – pbk edn: Vintage, London, 1997)

Lord Scarman, *The Scarman Report: The Brixton Disorders 10–12 April 1981* (HMSO, London, 1981 – pbk edn: Pelican, Harmondsworth, 1982)

Phil Scraton, *The State of the Police* (Pluto, London, 1985)

Chris Searle, *Your Daily Dose: Racism and the Sun* (Campaign for Press and Broadcasting Freedom, London, 1989)

David Selbourne, *Left Behind: Journeys into British Politics* (Jonathan Cape, London, 1987)

Anthony Seldon (ed.), *How Tory Governments Fall: The Tory Party in Power since 1783* (Fontana, London, 1996)

John Sergeant, *Maggie: Her Fatal Legacy* (Macmillan, London, 2005 – rev pbk edn: Pan, London, 2005)

Patrick Seyd, *The Rise and Fall of the Labour Left* (Macmillan Education, Basingstoke, 1987)

Peter Shore, *Leading the Left* (Weidenfeld & Nicolson, London, 1993)

Frank Skinner, *Frank Skinner* (Century, London, 2001)

Giles Smith, *Lost in Music: A Pop Odyssey* (Picador, London, 1995)

Neville Staple with Tony McMahon, *Original Rude Boy: From Borstal to the Specials – A Life of Crime and Music* (Aurum, London, 2009)

David Steel, *Against Goliath: David Steel's Story* (Weidenfeld & Nicolson, London, 1989)

Mark Steel, *It's Not a Runner Bean: Dispatches from a Slightly Successful Comedian* (Do-Not Press, London, 1996)

Mark Steel, *Reasons to be Cheerful: From Punk to New Labour through the Eyes of a Dedicated Troublemaker* (Scribner, London, 2001 – pbk edn: 2002)

Philip Stephens, *Tony Blair: The Price of Leadership* (Penguin, USA, 2004 – pbk edn: Politico's, London, 2004)

Graham Stewart, *The History of The Times, Volume VII 1981–2002: The Murdoch Years* (HarperCollins, London, 2005)

Margaret Stewart, *Protest or Power? A Study of the Labour Party* (George Allen & Unwin, London, 1974)

Roy Strong, *The Roy Strong Diaries 1967–1987* (Weidenfeld & Nicholson, London, 1997)

Mark Stuart, *Douglas Hurd: The Public Servant* (Mainstream, Edinburgh, 1998)

Eric Sykes, *If I Don't Write It, Nobody Else Will* (Fourth Estate, London, 2005 – pbk edn: Harper Perennial, London, 2006)

Julian Symons, *Bloody Murder: From the Detective Story to the Crime Novel – a History* (Faber & Faber, London, 1972 – rev pbk edn: Penguin, Harmondsworth, 1974)

Norman Tebbit, *Upwardly Mobile* (Weidenfeld & Nicolson, London, 1988)

Margaret Thatcher, *The Downing Street Years* (HarperCollins, London, 1993)

Margaret Thatcher, *The Path to Power* (HarperCollins, London, 1995)

Harry Thompson, *Peter Cook: A Biography* (Hodder & Stoughton, London, 1997 – pbk edn: 1998)

Ian and Janette Tough, *The Krankies – Fan Dabi Dozi: Our Amazing True Story* (John Blake, London, 2004)

Martyn Turner & Brian O'Connell, *The Whole World's Watching: Decarbonizing the Economy and Saving the World* (John Wiley & Sons, Chichester, 2001)

Midge Ure, *If I Was . . . The Autobiography* (Virgin, London, 2004)

Phil Vasili, *Colouring Over the White Line: The History of Black Footballers in Britain* (Mainstream, Edinburgh, 2000)

Alexander Walker, *Icons in the Fire: The Rise and Fall of Practically Everyone in the British Film Industry 1984–2000* (Orion, London, 2004 – pbk edn: 2005)

Johnnie Walker, *The Autobiography* (Michael Joseph, London, 2007 – pbk edn: Penguin, London, 2008)

Alan Watkins, *A Conservative Coup: The Fall of Margaret Thatcher* (Gerald Duckworth, London, 1991 – rev pbk edn: 1992)

Colin Watson, *Snobbery with Violence: English Crime Stories and Their Audience* (Eyre & Spottiswoode, London, 1971 – rev edn: Eyre Methuen, London, 1979)

Auberon Waugh, *Another Voice: An Alternative Anatomy of Britain* (Sidgwick & Jackson, London, 1986 – pbk edn: Fontana, London,1986)

Richard Weight, *Patriots: National Identity in Britain 1940–2000* (Macmillan, London, 2002 – pbk edn: Pan, London, 2003)

Michael Wharton, *The Best of Peter Simple 1980–1984* (Telegraph Publications, London, 1984)

Brian Whitaker, *News Limited: Why You Can't Read All About It* (Minority Press Group, London, 1981)

William Whitelaw, *The Whitelaw Memoirs* (Aurum, London, 1989)

Nicholas Whittaker, *Blue Period: Notes from a Life in the Titillation Trade* (Victor Gollancz, London, 1997)

David Widgery, *Beating Time: Riot 'n' Race 'n' Rock 'n' Roll* (Chatto & Windus, London, 1986)

Kenneth Williams, ed. Russell Davies, *The Kenneth Williams Diaries* (HarperCollins, London, 1993)

Charles Wintour, *The Rise and Fall of Fleet Street* (Hutchinson, London, 1989)

Cecil Woolf & Jean Moorcroft Wilson (ed.), *Authors Take Sides on the Falklands* (Cecil Woolf, London, 1982)

Woodrow Wyatt, ed. Sarah Curtis, *The Journals of Woodrow Wyatt Volume One* (Macmillan, London, 1998 – pbk edn: Pan, London, 1999)

Woodrow Wyatt, ed. Sarah Curtis, *The Journals of Woodrow Wyatt Volume Two* (Macmillan, London, 1999)

Hugo Young, *One of Us: A Biography of Margaret Thatcher* (Macmillan, London, 1989 – rev pbk edn: Pan, London, 1990)

B) FICTION

Note: Where a paperback edition is shown, it indicates that any page references in the text are to that edition.

Martin Amis, *Money* (Jonathan Cape, London, 1984 – pbk edn: Penguin, Harmondsworth, 1985)

Iain Banks, *The Wasp Factory* (Macmillan, London, 1984 – pbk edn: Abacus, London 1990)

Iain Banks, *Espedair Street* (Macmillan, London, 1987 – pbk edn: Futura, London, 1988)

Robert Barnard, *Political Suicide* (William Collins, London, 1986 – pbk edn: Corgi, London, 1988)

Robert Barnard, *A City of Strangers* (Bantam, London, 1990 – pbk edn: Corgi, London, 1991)

Guy Bellamy, *The Secret Lemonade Drinker* (Martin Secker & Warburg, London, 1977 – pbk edn: Penguin, London, 1988)

Terence Blacker, *Fixx* (Bloomsbury, London, 1989 – pbk edn: Corgi, London, 1990)

Howard Brenton & David Hare, *Pravda* (Methuen, London, 1995)

Jasper Carrott, *Carrott Roots and Other Myths* (Arrow, London, 1986)

Justin Cartwright, *Look at It this Way* (Macmillan, London, 1990 – pbk edn: Picador, London, 1991)

Julian Critchley, *Hung Parliament: An Entertainment* (Hutchinson, London, 1991 – pbk edn: 1992)

Richard Curtis, Rowan Atkinson, Ben Elton & John Lloyd, *Blackadder: The Whole Damn Dynasty 1485–1917* (Michael Joseph, London, 1998 – pbk edn: Penguin, London, 1999)

Denise Danks, *The Pizza House Crash* (Futura, London, 1989 – pbk edn: Orion, London, 2001)

Denise Danks, *Better Off Dead* (Macdonald & Co, London, 1991 – pbk edn: Futura, London, 1992)

Andrew Davies, *A Very Peculiar Practice: The New Frontier* (Methuen, London, 1988)

Pete Davies, *The Last Election* (André Deutsch, London 1986 – pbk edn: Pengin, Harmondsworth, 1987)

Colin Dexter, *The Secret of Annexe 3* (Macmillan, London, 1986 – pbk edn: Pan, London, 1987)

Colin Dexter, *The Wench is Dead* (Macmillan, London, 1989 – pbk edn: Pan, London, 1990)

Michael Dobbs, *House of Cards* (Collins, London, 1989 – pbk edn: HarperCollins, London, 1993)

Chris Donald (ed.), *Viz Comic: The Big Hard Number Two* (John Brown, London, 1986)

Margaret Drabble, *The Radiant Way* (Weidenfeld & Nicolson, London, 1987 – pbk edn: Penguin, London, 1988)

Peter Dunant, *Exterminating Angels* (André Deutsch, London, 1983 – pbk edn: Pluto, London, 1986)

Jack Osborne Easton, *Defence of the Realm* (Futura, London, 1985)

Ben Elton, *Stark* (Sphere, London, 1989)

Edward Fenton, *Scorched Earth* (Star, London, 1985)

Stephen Fry & Hugh Laurie, *A Bit of Fry and Laurie* (Mandarin, London, 1990)

Frances Fyfield, *Shadows on the Mirror* (William Heinemann, London, 1989 – pbk edn: Mandarin, London, 1990)

Paula Gosling, *The Woman in Red* (Macmillan, London, 1983 – pbk edn: Pan, London, 1984)

Sean Hardie & John Lloyd (ed.), *Not! The Nine O'Clock News* (BBC, London, 1980)

Martyn Harris, *The Mother-in-Law Joke* (Viking, London, 1992 – pbk edn: Penguin, London, 1992)

Reginald Hill, *Ruling Passion* (William Collins, London, 1973 – pbk edn: Grafton, London, 1987)

Reginald Hill, *Exit Lines* (William Collins, London, 1984 – pbk edn: Grafton, London, 1987)

Reginald Hill, *Child's Play* (William Collins, London, 1987 – pbk edn: Grafton, London, 1988)

Reginald Hill, *Under World* (HarperCollins, London, 1988 – pbk edn: Grafton, London, 1989)

Alan Hollinghurst, *The Swimming Pool Library* (Chatto & Windus, London, 1988 – pbk edn: Penguin, London, 1989)

Fred & Geoffrey Hoyle, *The Westminster Disaster* (William Heinemann, London, 1978 – pbk edn: Penguin, Harmondsworth, 1980)

P.D. James, *Innocent Blood* (Faber & Faber, London, 1980 – pbk edn: Sphere, London 1981)

P.D. James, *A Taste for Death* (Faber & Faber, London, 1986 – pbk edn: Penguin, London 1989)

P.D. James, *Devices and Desires* (Faber & Faber, London, 1989 – pbk edn: Penguin, London 1990)

Dan Kavanagh, *Going to the Dogs* (Viking, London, 1987 – pbk edn: Penguin, London, 1988)

Mark Lawson, *Bloody Margaret: Three Political Fantasies* (Pan Macmillan, London, 1991 – pbk edn: Picador, London, 1992)

David Lodge, *Nice Work* (Secker & Warburg, London, 1988 – Penguin, London, 1989)

Gavin Lyall, *The Secret Servant* (Hodder & Stoughton, London, 1980 – pbk edn: Pan, London, 1982)

A.G. Macdonell, *The Autobiography of a Cad* (Macmillan, London, 1938 – new edn: Prion, London, 2001)

Martin Millar, *Milk, Sulphate & Alby Starvation* (Fourth Estate, London, 1987)

Anna Morgan, *The New Statesman* (Javelin, London, 1987)

John Mortimer, *Paradise Postponed* (Viking, London, 1985 – pbk edn: Penguin, Harmondsworth, 1986)

John Mortimer, *Rumpole's Last Case* (Penguin, Harmondsworth, 1987)

John Mortimer, *Summer's Lease* (Penguin, London, 1988)

John Mortimer, *Titmuss Regained* (Penguin, London, 1990)

Chris Mullin, *A Very British Coup* (Hodder & Stoughton, London, 1982 – pbk edn: Coronet, London, 1983)

Iris Murdoch, *The Book and the Brotherhood* (Chatto & Windus, London, 1987 – pbk edn: Penguin, Harmondsworth, 1989)

David Pinner, *There'll Always Be an England* (Anthony Blond, London, 1984)

Anthony Price, *The Memory Trap* (Victor Gollancz, London, 1989 – Grafton, London, 1990)

Sheila Radley, *A Talent for Destruction* (Constable, London, 1982 – pbk edn: Penguin, Harmondsworth, 1984)

Sheila Radley, *Blood on the Happy Highway* (Constable, London, 1983 – pbk edn: Penguin, Harmondsworth, 1984)

Ian Rankin, *The Flood* (Polygon, Edinburgh, 1986 – pbk edn: Orion, London, 2006)

Ian Rankin, *Knots & Crosses* (Bodley Head, London, 1987 – new edn: BCA, London, 2007)

Derek Raymond, *He Died with His Eyes Open* (Martin Secker & Warburg, London, 1984 – pbk edn: Serpents Tail, London, 2007)

Derek Raymond, *The Devil's Home on Leave* (Martin Secker & Warburg, London, 1985 – pbk edn: Abacus, London, 1985)

Ruth Rendell, *Put on by Cunning* (Hutchinson, London, 1981 – pbk edn: Arrow, London, 1982)

Ruth Rendell, *An Unkindness of Ravens* (Hutchinson, London, 1985 – pbk edn: Arrow, London, 1994)

Ruth Rendell, *Live Flesh* (Century Hutchinson, London, 1986 – pbk edn: Arrow, London, 1986)

Ruth Rendell, *The Veiled One* (Hutchinson, London, 1988 – pbk edn: Arrow, London, 1989)

Peter Robinson, *Gallows View* (Viking, Toronto, 1987 – pbk edn: Pan, London, 2002)

Peter Robinson, *A Dedicated Man* (Viking, Toronto, 1988 – pbk edn: Pan, London, 2002)

Peter Robinson, *A Necessary End* (Viking, Toronto, 1988 – pbk edn: Pan, London, 2002)

Peter Robinson, *The Hanging Valley* (Viking, Toronto, 1989 – pbk edn: Pan, London, 2007)

Fay Sampson, *Sus* (Dobson Books, Durham, 1982)

Joan Smith, *Don't Leave Me This Way* (Faber & Faber, London, 1990 – pbk edn: 1991)

Peter Tilbury & Colin Bostock-Smith, *Shelley* (NEL, London, 1980)

Sue Townsend, *Adrian Mole From Minor to Major – The Mole Diaries: The First Ten Years* (Methuen, London, 1991 – pbk edn: Mandarin, London, 1992)

Fay Weldon, *The Cloning of Joanna May* (Collins, London, 1989 – pbk edn: Flamingo, London, 1993)

Margaret Yorke, *Find Me a Villain* (Hutchinson, London, 1983 – pbk edn: Arrow, London, 1984)

C) FILMS AND TELEVISION PROGRAMMES

Note: Films are listed by director. TV programmes are credited to their creators, though other writers may also have been involved in the series.

Chris Bernard, *Letter to Brezhnev* (Channel 4 Films, 1985)

Les Blair, *Number One* (Stageforum, 1985)

Alan Bleasdale, *The Black Stuff* (BBC TV, 1980)

Alan Bleasdale, *Boys from the Blackstuff* (BBC TV, 1982)

Jeremy Brock & Paul Unwin, *Casualty* (BBC TV, 1986–)

Tom Bussmann, *Whoops Apocalypse* (ITC, 1986)

Glenn Chandler, *Taggart* (STV, 1983–)

John Cleese & Connie Booth, *Fawlty Towers* (BBC TV, 1979)

Dick Clement, Ian La Frenais & Franc Roddam, *Auf Wiedersehen, Pet* (Witzend/Central TV, 1983–86)

Ian Curteis, *The Falklands Play* (BBC TV, 2002)

Richard Curtis, Rowan Atkinson & Ben Elton, *Blackadder* (BBC TV, 1983–89)

Harry Bromley Davenport, *Xtro* (New Line Cinema, 1982)

Angus Deayton & Geoffrey Perkins, *KYTV* (BBC TV, 1989–93)

David Drury, *Defence of the Realm* (Rank Organization, 1985)

Brian Eastman, *Porterhouse Blue* (Channel 4, 1987)

Ben Elton, *Filthy, Rich and Catflap* (BBC TV, 1987)

Bill Forsyth, *Gregory's Girl* (Lake Films, 1981)

Bill Forsyth, *Local Hero* (Goldcrest Films, 1983)

Stephen Frears, *My Beautiful Laundrette* (Channel 4 Films, 1985)

Stephen Fry & Hugh Laurie, *A Bit of Fry & Laurie* (BBC TV, 1986–95)

Andy Hamilton & Guy Jenkin, *Drop the Dead Donkey* (Channel 4, 1990–98)

Ken Hannam, *The Day of the Triffids* (BBC TV, 1981)

Ron Hutchinson, *Bird of Prey* (BBC TV, 1982–84)

Mick Jackson, *Threads* (BBC TV/9 Network, 1984)

Paul Jackson, *Saturday Live/Friday Night Live* (Channel 4, 1985–88)

Derek Jarman, *The Last of England* (Anglo International Films/Channel 4 Films, 1987)

Terry Jones, *Monty Python's Life of Brian* (Handmade Films, 1979)
Neil Jordan, *Mona Lisa* (Handmade Films, 1986)
Ian La Frenais & John Grant, *Lovejoy* (BBC TV, 1986–94)
Carla Lane, *Bread* (BBC TV, 1986–91)
John le Carré, *Smiley's People* (BBC TV, 1982)
Mike Leigh, *Meantime* (Central TV, 1984)
Mike Leigh, *High Hopes* (Channel 4 Films, 1988)
David Leland, *Tales Out of School* (Central TV, 1982)
Douglas Livingstone, *We'll Support You Evermore* (BBC TV, 1985)
John Lloyd & Sean Hardie, *Not the Nine O'Clock News* (BBC TV, 1979–82)
Jonathan Lynn & Antony Jay, *Yes, Minister* (BBC TV, 1980–84)
Jonathan Lynn & Antony Jay, *Yes, Prime Minister* (BBC TV, 1986–88)
Geoff McQueen, *Big Deal* (BBC TV, 1984–86)
Laurence Marks & Maurice Gran, *The New Statesman* (Alomo Productions, 1987–94)
Laurence Marks & Maurice Gran, *Birds of a Feather* (BBC TV, 1990–98)
Ian Kennedy Martin, *Juliet Bravo* (BBC TV, 1980–85)
Ian Kennedy Martin, *The Chinese Detective* (BBC TV, 1981–82)
Troy Kennedy Martin, *Edge of Darkness* (BBC TV, 1985)
Rik Mayall, Lise Mayer and Ben Elton, *The Young Ones* (BBC TV, 1982–84)
Nicholas Meyer, *The Day After* (ABC, 1983)
Chris Mullin, *A Very British Coup* (Skreba Films/Parallax Pictures/Channel 4, 1988)
Jimmy T. Murakami, *When the Wind Blows* (Meltdown Productions, 1986)
Sydney Newman, *Doctor Who* (BBC TV, 1963–89)
David Nobbs, *A Bit of a Do* (Yorkshire TV, 1989)
Richard Ommanney, *Three Up, Two Down* (BBC TV, 1985–89)
Jimmy Perry & David Croft, *Hi-de-Hi!* (BBC, 1980–87)
Michael Radford, *Nineteen Eighty-Four* (Virgin Films, 1984)
Phil Redmond, *Grange Hill* (BBC TV, 1978–2008)
Ken Riddington, *House of Cards* (BBC TV, 1990)
Vic Reeves & Bob Mortimer, *Vic Reeves Big Night Out* (Channel X, Channel 4, 1990–91)
Franco Rosso, *Babylon* (Chrysalis Group, 1980)
Philip Saville, *The Life and Loves of a She-Devil* (BBC TV, 1986)
Alexei Sayle, *Alexei Sayle's Stuff* (BBC TV, 1988–91)
Ian Sharp, *Who Dares Wins* (MGM, 1982)
Johnny Speight, *In Sickness and in Health* (BBC TV, 1985–92)
Peter Spence, *To the Manor Born* (BBC TV, 1979–81)
John Stevenson & Julian Roach, *Brass* (Granada TV, 1983–84)
Robert Banks Stewart, *Bergerac* (BBC/The Seven Network, 1981–91)
John Sullivan, *Only Fools and Horses* (BBC TV, 1981–2003)
Peter Tilbury, *Shelley* (Thames TV, 1979–83)
Kathryn Willgress, *Stand Down Margaret* (Somethin' Else Productions for BBC Radio 2, 2008)
Charles Wood, *Tumbledown* (BBC TV, 1988)
Victoria Wood, *Victoria Wood – As Seen On TV* (BBC TV, 1985–86)

D) INTERNET SITES
Internet Movie Database (imdb.com)
Margaret Thatcher Foundation (margaretthatcher.org)
News Bank Inc (infoweb.newsbank.com)
Oxford Dictionary of National Biography (oxforddnb.com)
UK Party Election Manifestos (psr.keele.ac.uk/area/uk/man.htm)
The Prince of Wales (princeofwales.gov.uk)

The Times Digital Archive 1785–1985 (infotrac.galegroup.com)
Trash Fiction (trashfiction.co.uk)
UK Game Shows (ukgameshows.com)
Urban 75 (urban75.net)
Wikipedia (en.wikipedia.org)

Credits

Chapter titles are taken from the following songs: Specials, '(Dawning of a) New Era'; John Lennon, '(Just Like) Starting Over'; Adam and the Ants, 'Dog Eat Dog'; Soft Cell, 'Bedsitter'; Barracudas, 'We're Living in Violent Times'; Culture Club, 'The War Song'; Wham!, 'The Edge of Heaven'; Eurythmics and Aretha Franklin, 'Sisters Are Doin' It for Themselves'; Frankie Goes To Hollywood, 'Two Tribes'; Kirsty MacColl, 'A New England'; Pet Shop Boys, 'Opportunities (Let's Make Lots of Money)'; Yazz and the Plastic Population, 'The Only Way Is Up'; Bros, 'When Will I Be Famous?'; George Michael, 'Father Figure'; Style Council, 'Walls Come Tumbling Down!'; Las, 'There She Goes'; Shakespears Sister, 'You're History'.

The titles of the three main sections are taken from songs by David Bowie: 'Catpeople (Putting out Fire)', 'When the Wind Blows' and 'Under the God'.

Acknowledgements

I'd like to express my gratitude to the following people, who spoke to me and provided assistance in various ways: Adam Ant, Adenike Deane-Pratt, Alan Edwards, Annajoy David, Brian Freeborn, Dan Atkinson, Donald Smith, Edwina Currie, Fritz Caitlin, Geoff Barlow, Geoffrey Marsh, Harry Greene, Ian Krankie, John Flaxman, John Jones, Joyce McLennan, Kathryn Willgress, Martyn Hall, Martyn Turner, Michael Burgess, Michael Butterworth, Michelle Coomber, Mike Herbage, Norman Tebbit, P.D. James, Richard Pain, Roger Crimlis, Sarah Bedford, Steve Thomas and York Membrey.

Obviously none of the above should be considered to condone the contents of this book. And my apologies to everyone whose work I've quoted in such a cavalier fashion, probably missing all the important points.

I'm grateful for the continuing faith and encouragement shown by Aurum Press. In particular, my editor Graham Coster has been invaluable in his involvement on this project, and I'd also like to mention my appreciation of additional comments from Sam Harrison, supportive words from Bill McCreadie, and the contributions of Graham Eames, Barbara Phelan and Liz Somers. Thanks too to copy-editor Stephen Watson and cover designer Clare Stacey.

And I'd like to take this opportunity of thanking some of those who gave me a break when I needed one: Gordon Turner, Ian Morley, Jamie Wilson, Matt Harvey and Mark Eastment.

This book is dedicated to Thamasin Marsh, who lived through every twist and turn.

Index